GREENBERG'S
GUIDE TO
LIONEL® TRAINS: 1970-1988

By Roland LaVoie

With the assistance of **T. Antonowicz,
Lou Caponi, Norman Fuhrmann,
Joe Grzyboski, Glenn Halverson,
Clark O'Dell, Chris Rohlfing, Tom Rollo,
Joe Sadorf, Jim Sattler, Richard Shanfeld,
I. D. Smith,** and **Jim Tomczyk.**

Trains from the collections of
**Al Rudman, Lou Caponi,
Francis Stem** and **Roland LaVoie,**
photographed by **Maury Feinstein.**

Additional trains from the collections of
Glenn and **Dave Halverson**
and **Auggie Conto**
photographed by **George Stern**.

Copyright © 1989

Greenberg Publishing Company, Inc.
7566 Main Street
Sykesville, MD 21784
(301) 795-7447

Second Edition

Manufactured in the United States of America

Greenberg Publishing Company offers the world's largest selection of Lionel, American Flyer, LGB, Ives, and other toy train publications as well as a selection of books on model and prototype railroading, dollhouse miniatures, and toys. For a copy of our current catalogue, send a stamped, self-addressed envelope to Greenberg Publishing Company, Inc. at the above address.

Greenberg Shows, Inc. sponsors the world's largest public model railroad, dollhouse, and toy shows. The shows feature extravagant operating model railroads for N, HO, O, Standard, and 1 Gauges as well as a huge marketplace for buying and selling nearly all model railroad equipment. The shows also feature a large selection of dollhouses and dollhouse furnishings. Shows are currently offered in metropolitan Baltimore, Boston, Ft. Lauderdale, Cherry Hill in New Jersey, Long Island in New York, Norfolk, Philadelphia, Pittsburgh, and Tampa. To receive our current show listing, please send a self-addressed stamped envelope marked *Train Show Schedule* to the address above.

ISBN 0-89778-117-1

Library of Congress Cataloging-in-Publication Data

Greenberg, Bruce C.
    Greenberg's Guide to Lionel Trains, 1970-1988

    Includes index.
    1. Railroads — Models. 2. Lionel Corporation.
I. LaVoie, Roland, 1943-   . II. Antonowicz, T.
III. Title. IV. Title: Guide to Lionel Trains, 1970-1988

TF197.G667 1989 625.1'9 88-35797
ISBN 0-89778-117-1

Table of Contents

Introduction

Locomotives

Rolling Stock

Other Items

FOREWORD

Greenberg's Guide for Lionel Trains, 1970-1988, is our most comprehensive report on the modern era (1970-1988) train marketplace. The contents of this book were previously published as *Greenberg's Guide to Lionel-Fundimensions Trains: 1970-1985*. This edition records a very uneven pattern of price changes. At the present time, however, in early 1989, prices are relatively stable.

PURPOSE

The purpose of this book is to provide a comprehensive listing with current prices for Lionel modern era locomotives, rolling stock, and accessories, in O and O27 Gauges, produced from 1970 through 1988. We include those variations which have been authenticated. In a few cases we ask our readers for further information where information is missing or doubtful. Values are reported for each item where there have been reported sales.

DETERMINING VALUES

Toy train values vary for a number of reasons. First, consider the **relative knowledge** of the buyer and seller. A seller may be unaware that he has a rare variation and sell it for the price of a common piece. Another source of price variation is **short-term fluctuation** which depends on what is being offered at a given train meet on a given day. If four 8100s are for sale at a small meet, we would expect that supply would outpace demand and lead to a reduction in price. A related source of variation is the **season** of the year. The train market is slower in the summer and sellers may at this time be more inclined to reduce prices if they really want to move an item. Another important source of price variation is the relative strength of the seller's **desire to sell** and the buyer's **eagerness to buy.** Clearly a seller in economic distress will be more eager to strike a bargain. A final source of variation is **the personalities** of the seller and buyer. Some sellers like to quickly turn over items and, therefore, price their items to move; others seek a higher price and will bring an item to meet after meet until they find a willing buyer.

Train values in this book are based on *obtained* prices, rather than asking prices. The prices represent a "ready sale," that is, prices most likely to effect a quick sale at most large train meets. They may sometimes appear lower than those seen on trains at meets for two reasons. First, items that sell often sell in the first hour of a train meet and, therefore, are no longer visible. (We have observed that a good portion of the action at most meets occurs in the first hour.) The items that do not sell in the first hour have a higher price tag and this price, although not representing the sales price, is the price observed. A related source of discrepancy is the willingness of some sellers to bargain over price.

Another factor which may affect prices is reconditioning done by the dealer. Some dealers take great pains to clean and service their pieces so that they look their best and operate properly. Others sell the items just as they have received them, dust and all. Naturally, the more effort the dealer expends in preparing his pieces for sale, the more he can expect to charge for them. This factor may account for significant price differences among dealers selling the same equipment.

From our studies of train prices, it appears that mail order prices for used trains are generally higher than those obtained at eastern train meets. This is appropriate considering the costs and efforts of producing and distributing a price list and packing and shipping items. Mail order items do sell at prices above those listed in this book. A final source of difference between observed prices and reported prices is region. Prices are clearly higher in the South and West where trains are less plentiful than along the East Coast.

On some items, we have indicated **No Reported Sales (NRS)** in the value column. This does not necessarily indicate that an item is particularly rare. It simply indicates that inadequate information is available for pricing these items.

CONDITION

For each item, we provide four categories: **Good, Very Good, Excellent,** and **Mint.** The Train Collectors Association (T C A) defines conditions as:

GOOD — Scratches, small dents, dirty

VERY GOOD — Few scratches, exceptionally clean, no dents or rust.

EXCELLENT — Minute scratches or nicks, no dents or rust

MINT — Brand new, absolutely unmarred, all original and unused, in original box

In the toy train field there is a great deal of concern with exterior appearance and less concern with operation. If operation is important to you, then ask the seller whether the train runs. If the seller indicates that he does not know whether the equipment operates, you should test it. Most train meets have test tracks provided for that purpose.

We include mint in this edition because of the important trade in post-1970 mint items. However there is substantial confusion in the minds of both sellers and buyers as to what constitutes "mint" condition. How do we define mint? Among very experienced train enthusiasts, a mint piece means that it is brand new, in its original box, never run, and extremely bright and clean (and the box is, too). An item may have been removed from the box and replaced in it, but it should show no evidence of handling. A piece is not mint if it shows any scratches, fingerprints, or evidence of discoloration. It is the nature of a market for the seller to see his item in a very positive light and to seek to obtain a mint price for an excellent piece. In contrast, a buyer will see the same item in a less favorable light and will attempt to buy a mint piece for the price of one in excellent condition. It is our responsibility to point out this difference in perspective **and** the difference in value implicit in each perspective, and to then let the buyer and seller settle or negotiate their different perspectives.

We do not show values for Fair or Restored. **Fair** items are valued substantially below Good. We have not included **Restored** because such items are not a significant portion of the market for postwar trains.

As we indicated, prices in this book were derived from large train meets or shows. If you have trains to sell and you sell them to a person planning to resell them, you will not obtain the prices reported in this book. Rather, you should expect to achieve about fifty percent of these prices. Basically, for your items to be of interest to a buyer who plans to resell them, he must purchase them for considerably less than the prices listed here.

We receive many inquiries as to whether or not a particular piece is a "good value." This book will help answer that question; but, there is NO substitute for experience in the marketplace. *We strongly recommend that novices do not make major purchases without the assistance of friends who have experience in buying and selling trains.* If you are buying a train and do not know whom to ask about its value, look for the people running the meet or show and discuss with them your need for assistance. Usually they can refer you to an experienced collector who will be willing to examine the piece and offer his opinion.

ACKNOWLEDGMENTS

I've said it before, and I'll say it again: No book of this kind is the product of any one person. This, the second edition describing Lionel trains of the modern era, 1970-1988, is instead the product of the contributions of well over a hundred people. I sometimes marvel at the generosity of the toy train collecting community; people who are extremely busy take time out to write to us and contribute articles, corrections and additions all the time. Other train collectors send us whole articles, assist with photographs, or show us their little prizes in person. Not many hobby pursuits can boast of such a cooperative population.

The first group of contributors include **article writers.** For this edition **Norman Fuhrmann** sent us the story of the 1973 T C A Convention Cars, and **Ed Barbret** updated Mr. Fuhrmann's data. We have included data from a letter by **Lee Jones**, which gives precise quantities for some of the earliest Fundimensions production. It was published in 1971 in the **Train Collectors' Quarterly**, but many collectors have never seen it, and we are glad to be able to bring you this information. **Jim Tomczyk** sent us an important note discussing the Julian box dating system used by Lionel, and **Tom Rollo**, a frequent contributor to these pages, explained its significance to me. **John Kouba** sent us an impressive rundown of the Santa Fe Service Station Special Set produced in 1986; two more of his articles will appear later in *Model Railroading With Lionel Trains.* **I. D. Smith**, an old friend of ours with an astonishing eye for detail, has given us a note on modern era Lionel's use of conversion couplers. **Mike Moore**, the owner of Town House Appliances of Niles, Illinois, has told us the complete story of the Town House and Tappan sets of recent years. **Ron Steffani** has found a fascinating Ford Motor Company salesman's display piece, and his essay is found in the steam engine chapter. Also included are essays on the 2-4-2 Columbia steamers and the six scarcest accessories of the modern era.

Our **Introduction** for this edition describes a day I spent with Bruce and Linda Greenberg in Mount Clemens and Detroit with Lionel's management. The story of our factory tour and interviews with **Dan Johns** and **Richard Kughn** make interesting reading. We would like to thank Mr. Kughn and Mr. Johns for their gracious hospitality to us, as well as **Lenny Dean** and **Michael Braga**, our tour guides through the Lionel factory, for giving us such insight into the manufacturing and marketing of these trains.

When it comes time to cite train buffs who make substantial contributions to our efforts, we just round up the usual suspects. **Glenn Halverson** has continued the fine research tradition he began with our first edition, listing more accessory and factory error entries and enlisting the help of his own resources from his upstate New York area. Glenn's sources include some highly knowledgeable collectors, including **Bernie Puralewski, Jeff Wilson,** and **Ron Niedhammer. Joe Sadorf** and **Richard Shanfeld**, two fine Philadelphia area collectors, are resources which I tapped frequently; their assistance was very valuable. **Jim Sattler**, one of the very best train collectors I know, has written an extremely valuable set of definitions for Factory Errors, Prototypes, Color Samples and Salesman's Samples; these definitions are reprinted from Volume II of our postwar guide because of their great value to modern era collectors. To update the introduction to this chapter to include modern era examples, **Clark O'Dell** spent considerable time and thought to produce a text that would be most useful to collectors. Speaking of factory errors, **David Fleming**, who wrote a fine article on the postwar milk cars earlier, has sent us a comprehensive listing of his factory error collection, and so has **Michael Sabatelle.** Also contributing some important additions to this chapter was **Joe Grzyboski**, a well-known Western Pennsylvania dealer. These three gentlemen tripled the size of our listings!

The editor of our current prewar volume, **Chris Rohlfing**, cross-checked absolutely everything from our last edition and sent many color and descriptive changes to us. He also made some important observations within the uncatalogued set listings. This book is a much more accurate document beacause of his efforts. **Al Rudman**, the proprietor of Trackside Hobbies, lent us many of Lionel's newest offerings for photography; he also gave us some good pricing advice. **Louis Caponi** of

Train 99 reviewed all our prices and made many excellent corrections and observations. If anybody knows the marketing of these trains, it's Lou. He and I have also had some extremely productive conversations at the Greenberg Train Shows, and he always seems to find time to have a chat with me. Good pricing advice has also come from **Joe Grzyboski** and **T. Antonowicz.**

Howard Holden assisted with paper goods and many of the Special Production and department store special products. We would also like to thank the owner of the **Triple T Collection,** who wishes to remain anonymous. This owner sent us great photographs and descriptions of many unusual items. Finally, we would like to thank **Mr. J. A. Fisher,** who sent us a complete rundown on the special James P. MacFarland Commemorative Set described in the Special Production chapter.

We would also like to thank our many manuscript readers, who take the time to review my preliminary editing and cover up some of my errors or misapprehensions. These people make me look better than I really am! They include **Chris Rohlfing, Cliff Lang, Clark O'Dell, Tom Rollo, Mike Sabatelle, Richard Sigurdson, I. D. Smith, Glenn Halverson,** and **Mike Foster.**

Other contributions have been made by the following interested and interesting train collectors and enthusiasts: **D. Anderson, R. Archer, H. Argue, N. Banis, R. Bartelt, E. Beckner, W. Berresford, A. Betts, L. Bohn, W. Botefuhr, J. Breslin, A. Broderdorf, R. P. Bryan, R. M. Caplan, D. L. Clad, F. Cieri, G. Cole, D. Coletta, R. Conrad, P. Costa,** and **W. Cunningham.**

Also: **D. Daugherty, M. Denuty, H. Edmunds, V. Galbo, Jr., J. R. Glockley, S. Goodman, C. J. Grass, R. Harbina, R. A. Hicks, D. Holland, D. Holst, G. Humbert, J. R. Hunt, N. Hussey, S. Hutchings, R. Jackson, J. Kovach, M. Kowalski,** and **R. Kuehnemund.**

Also: **T. Ladny, C. Lang, S. Lindsey, Jr., R. Lord, R. Loveless, R. MacDonald, J. Malcovsky, N. F. Marks, E. F. Monck, G. Mueller, R. E. Nelson, W. Nielsen, G. Orffeo, A. Passman, M. Paunovich, J. Porter, G. A. Rogers,** and **G. Romich.**

Also: **R. Sage, F. Salvatore, M. Samseli, J. M. Sawruk, M. Schoenberg, R. Shanfeld, G. Shewmake, R. Sigurdson, I. D. Smith, Pastor P. Smith, L. Stever, Jr., C. M. Switzer, Jr., T. Taylor, C. Theis,** and **C. Wallace.**

If you think the work for this book stopped when I punched the last key of my word processor, you're sadly mistaken. Much work goes on at the Greenberg offices; 7566 Main Street is a very busy place! I'm particularly indebted to **Cindy Floyd,** who has bailed me out of one computer jam after another with unfailing good humor; she can even decipher my writing — no small feat! Cindy helped to organize the text and coordinated communications with all of the many readers and assistants. Many others assisted in the preparation of layout and paste-up work as well as the index. **Donna Price** thoroughly proofread the material to insure consistency. Donna also helped to insure that all of the cross-referenced material showed up at both ends of each reference! **Maureen Crum** lent her talents to the thoughtful placement of photographs in the text and page layout. **Dallas Mallerich** coordinated photographs and captions and oversaw many of the last-minute production concerns.

Of course, I am indebted to **Bruce** and **Linda Greenberg** for their encouragement and tolerance of all my efforts. They have just moved their company to its third address in five years, each larger than the ones before them. I can't think of anyone who deserves their success more. Working with the Greenbergs is rewarding and fun!

Finally, I must add the observation that just as Sherlock Holmes had his Baker Street Irregulars, I have my friends, the Friday Night Irregulars at the **Toy Train Station** in Feasterville, Pennsylvania. These people, about a dozen in number, are great friends and conversationalists, and they have a rich knowledge of Lionel which they have shared constantly with me. In addition, **Joe Gordon and Joe Bratspis,** the proprietors and major-domos of that fine institution, have allowed me to poke through their stocks and repair room, upset boxes, put trains on lay-away for myself "just for a few weeks" and, in general, create mayhem within their store. I could not have done this book without their assistance and tolerance. To Joe and Joe, and the Friday Night Irregulars, I dedicate this edition with affection.

One closing note: Although I've heard many pessimists predict the doom of Lionel train production, I feel very confident about the future of these trains. In our books and movies, we find many examples of the affection Americans hold for Lionel trains: In his book *The Glory and the Dream*, William Manchester views fifty years of American culture through the contents of a big storage closet. One of the items in that closet is a Lionel transformer from the 1930s. In the 1981 movie *Arthur*, drunken playboy Dudley Moore is awakened one morning by the clatter of the Fundimensions Blue Comet on a layout behind his bed on a big shelf. In the 1983 film *Risky Business*, Tom Cruise soothes his nerves, shattered by a wild party, by retreating to his basement and running an 8551 Pennsylvania Electric around a layout. Lionel trains have achieved rare success — they are part of American culture. As we approach the year 2000 (the centennial of Lionel trains), these handsome toys remind us of the cherished world of our innocent past and promise us many years of enjoyment for ourselves and our children.

Roland E. LaVoie
Cherry Hill, New Jersey

INTRODUCTION

VISITING THE LION(EL) IN ITS DEN: A DAY WITH LIONEL, INC.

By Roland E. LaVoie

Every collector of Lionel Trains has a dream of one day taking a grand tour of the fabled Lionel factory. Early in its history, Lionel realized this, and advertising copy published in the early 1920s by Joshua Lionel Cowen himself took advantage of this desire in language such as: "Come on, boys! Tour through the Lionel Factory and see why Lionel Trains are the best!" The brochures of the time and the first pages of the catalogues showed inside pictures of the manufacturing process in exquisite detail. A real factory tour? That was something really special for the privileged few who took it!

Several people have written about such tours. In fact, many articles about the factory have appeared in train publications recently. However, there really is no substitute for an on-site, in-person tour. That is why I waited about two tenths of a millisecond to say "Yes!" when Bruce Greenberg called me one day and asked me to accompany him and his wife, Linda, on such a trip. To add to the significance of the day, an interview had been arranged for us with Mr. Richard Kughn, Lionel, Incorporated's new Chairman and driving force. As it turned out, the human side of the tour was far more important than the factory itself.

In this essay, I am going to try to assess not only the factory, but also the personalities and philosophies behind today's Lionel trains. As all train enthusiasts know, Lionel stands at a crossroads today. The unfortunate move to Mexico is now a thing of the past rather than a concern of the present. Lionel's competition within the rapidly expanding toy train hobby is getting more and more intense. The key question to answer is: Where is Lionel going in its efforts, and what are the strengths and obstacles which influence those efforts? The conclusions in this article are the opinions of this writer. However, to save some suspense, let me say that I am more optimistic about Lionel's future now than I was before I visited Mount Clemens.

Our day began with a short drive from the Detroit airport to the main offices of Lionel Trains, Inc. on Twenty-Three Mile Road in Mount Clemens. On the way, Bruce, Linda, and I discussed the kinds of questions we should ask Lionel's personnel. It was evident to me that each of us brought a unique perspective to the questioning process. No one is more aware of the history of Lionel than Bruce; he brings a keen appreciation of the motivations, political and otherwise, behind business decisions. Linda has an extremely astute appreciation of salesmanship and business efficiency — especially that all-important "bottom line." Supposedly, I represented the "average collector," the fellow who wants to know why certain products are made and why the availability of products varies so much.

Like all collectors, I wanted a line on the "hot prospects" for future appreciation in value. Between the three of us, a rather comprehensive set of questions could be asked.

After arriving at the main offices of Lionel Trains, Inc. and waiting to meet Dan Johns, we found ourselves staring at a large display board along one wall which showed the 360-plus parts which had gone into the manufacture of Lionel's 8406 Hudson Steam Locomotive. It occurred to us that many of these parts had to be subcontracted; gone are the days when Lionel did everything for itself. The conclusion we drew was that if just one of those parts — the driver wheels, for example — were to be delayed in production, the entire locomotive would fail to be issued on time. That is obviously one explanation for the delays in the more complex pieces, a subject which came up later on.

We were introduced to Dan Johns, Director of Product Integrity and Customer Services for Lionel, Inc. Mr. Johns is a friendly, affable man who is a 20-year veteran of Lionel. His office is a happy clutter of train memorabilia and books, many of them Greenberg Guides to Lionel. Much of our conversation with Mr. Johns went into the history of the earliest days in Mount Clemens, when Lionel, under MPC and Fundimensions management, was struggling to rebuild a market for Lionel Trains. A few of Mr. Johns' comments are related in an article about accessories elsewhere in this edition, but the summary of his comments was that despite learning "on the job" and doing some "scrambling," as he called it, the new Lionel management in those years was making the most efficient use of the parts it had on hand — eminently a sound business practice. "The 6560 Crane Car of 1971 is a good example of what we were trying to do at the time," he said. "We had box after box of complete parts for that car and where we needed particular parts to complete the piece we would have parts molded for them. I'm really amazed that you can detect the differences between the leftover and new parts the way you do. The reason you have different types of cranes in those boxes is that the numbers just didn't balance — we never had, say, 52 long crank wheels and 52 complete booms to match them. The parts bins were just flying around in those days. So there really is no way to tell just how many of a certain crane comes with certain parts. Our idea was to get the complete car out."

We then asked Mr. Johns about the Canadian sales operations, especially those of the earliest years. "We felt that there was a good market for Lionel Trains in Canada, especially if we could make them with railroad markings particular to that region. That's why you see the separate Canadian catalogues with a lot of cars with Canadian railway markings. After 1973, we saw that our regular line would sell just as well, so we discontinued the separate catalogues. You have to remember that we made all those specials for the Canadian sales distribution through Parker Brothers; they never produced anything them-

Each locomotive is tested prior to packaging. Long term Lionel employee Lenny Dean and Marketing Manager Mike Braga review the test track facility.

Automatic paint-spraying machine. A conveyor carries cars, one at a time, into the machine where they are automatically sprayed under and over. At the time of the photograph, the machine was painting Lionel Large Scale gondolas.

selves. We sent our own stuff north and brought in HO parts direct from overseas."

Questions about specific manufacturing techniques and their problems followed that discussion. In response to a question about methods of decorating cars, particularly the wood-sided reefers, Mr. Johns, whose job it is to monitor the quality standards of Lionel, told us, "Each decorating technique has its own advantages and disadvantages. We used decals on some of the cars because the printing process for heat transfer was too difficult or involved relative to the decorative effect we wanted. On the other hand, some of the reefers had deco schemes which were so complex that only heat transfers would do the job — the Favorite Spirits reefers are a good case in point, and those sold very well, as you know. We are simply trying to maintain the best quality control possible while trying to offer the most attractive products we can."

We asked about the painting and masking process, which we later saw for ourselves. Mr. Johns said, "The painting process can be one of the most painstaking things we do. We make every effort to produce Lionel without variation from the first piece off the line to the last. That's a difficult job, because a difference in tolerance of just .001 or .002 on a locomotive cab shell can make the difference between a line that is crisp and one that is ragged. Every engine uses at least two paint masks — many use more than that. Every five or six body shells we paint, we have to take those paint masks off and wash and lubricate them, or else we will get smeared lines."

"It's also very hard to make absolutely identical plastic body shells, so the masks do not always fit perfectly. That means the paint operator must take great care to maintain even consistency. Even the weather can have an effect on the paint jobs. In the summer we use different techniques from those we use in cold weather months."

During a discussion of sales and marketing techniques with Lionel Marketing Product Manager, Michael Braga, we asked how many catalogues were printed in a given year. "This year we printed about 175,000 catalogues, and I understand that they've become an instant sell-out with our collector consumers. Perhaps that's because we've included a full catalogue in every set for the first time in several years, but maybe it's

because our 1987 catalogue is the most exciting one yet. We think that if we can continue to make the right products, we can build a terrific market out there. We boosted our 1986 sales solidly over the previous year, and this year should be even better."

We asked about Lionel's employees and their relationship with the current leadership of Lionel. "We take pride in working to make our employees feel like they're part of a Lionel family," said Mr. Braga. "In the old days, Lionel had a great house magazine which stressed the idea that every employee had value and was important. We're going to try to do that again with our folksy newsletter, featuring contributions and news items from employee reporters. One recent issue even featured varieties of pet rocks! Safety issues are a big concern in the newsletter, too. As you can see, these people are very good at their jobs. We know that if we recognize that publicly, management-employee relations will just keep getting better. It's very important to all of us to receive recognition, and that's what keeping track at Lionel does for us."

All through the interview with Mr. Braga, we had been admiring a gondola sitting on his desk. The conversation turned to it, and he explained that this was a prototype of the gondola for the new Lionel Large Scale trains introduced in the fall of 1987. We saw that it was a high quality piece; it had nickel-plated "fishbelly" railings, a finely detailed paint job, and a very realistic look. Later on, we were to see the flatcar bases for the car as they went through the paint-spraying booths at the factory. One of us noted that the plastic used for the flatcar body was already black, but it was being painted black anyway to give it a desirable flat color finish. "We're very pleased with the way this new line is turning out," Mr. Braga said. "We think the Large Scale trains will do very well."

It was then time for our tour through the factory, which is located in another building some distance from the executive offices, with Mr. Braga and Lenny Dean, who is a legend at Lionel and who has been with Lionel for almost half a century. Mr. Dean is the last link to the great postwar years. We could not help but notice the universal enthusiasm and esteem with which Mr. Dean is greeted by Lionel's employees wherever he goes. He remains today just as much a train enthusiast as he has ever been. I had met him previously at a large train meet, where he took the time to show me the prototype for the new Rock Island 4-8-4 Northern steam engine which was produced in the fall of 1987.

Just outside of the factory we were greeted by the strident thumping sound of some very heavy equipment. We later learned that these were the track-making machines, which were turning out batches of O27 and Large Scale track. In a small anteroom, we were issued Lionel visitors' badges — and I can not say I was not tempted to hold onto mine when the tour was through! Stepping into the factory proper, we observed one of several test tracks in action. This track, described in other articles about the factory, features a hill climb which must be made within a certain time at a fixed voltage by any locomotive to be tested. A ring of a bell signifies a death knell for the engine if it can not get up the grade within a specified time. If it is rejected, it goes to a team of rework operators for inspection and repair.

Following our guides, we moved to our right into the paint-spraying area. Here, we saw some of the firm's decorating processes in action. At this writing, the plastic body shells are now being molded "in house" instead of being sent out by Lionel. The plastic injection-molding machines are in place and in full operation. Once the shells, called "shots," are molded in the heat of the factory, they go to the painting area for the decorating process needed to finish them. The first operation which greeted us was the flatcar bodies for the Large Scale gondola moving slowly through the automatic paint-spraying booth. These shots were clipped onto special holders as they went through the booth; we noted that the unpainted body was molded black and then painted a flat black. These were then set on racks to dry before going out to the production floor to have the wood-grained sides, trucks, and couplers added.

Moving along the long, narrow painting room, we saw the shells for the new top-of-the-line traditional train set, the Black Diamond Lehigh Valley GP-9, getting their spraying and masking treatment. The shells are gray plastic, and before they are

set into paint masks, every one of them is hand-sprayed the proper Lehigh Valley brick red. Then they require two different maskings for the safety striping in front. The first mask allows a white background to be put onto the front nose piece; then a second mask allows the black striping to be applied over the white area. This is an absolutely painstaking process and, as Dan Johns had told us, after every few applications the mask has to be removed, washed, and lubricated, and then remounted. The masks are washed in huge hot liquid baths which take up the entire middle section of the room. We saw a similar process in action for the yellow and silver SP-type caboose to be included in this set. The American Flyer S Gauge Southern Pacific gray and orange diesel was getting its own masking treatment.

Another decorating process at work in this room was the springboard process, which is used to apply striping to cab shells. The shell to be striped is placed flat along a large metal plate with a long, narrow slot shaped to the area which needs painting. At the press of a foot lever, a spray gun is activated to stripe the area with paint. At the time of our visit, some die-cast black-painted 4-4-2 locomotive boiler castings from the Nickel Plate Special train set were getting a yellow stripe along the running board and below the cab window in this way. A large rack of finished castings stood off to one side. For some reason, I noticed one which seemed different from the others. Upon closer examination, I saw that the particular locomotive had a number visible below the yellow stripe, while the others did not. I asked the employee operating the springboard machine how this could have happened. "Once in a while we get a casting from somewhere and don't notice that it has already been worked on," he said. "If we notice it, we pull it and re-do it." He then removed the casting from the rack for re-striping. I asked him if there was a chance this locomotive could have slipped into a set box undetected. "Yes, there is an outside chance," he said, "Although we do try to catch them, once in a while a piece gets by us." There, in a nutshell, is the genesis of a factory error!

The plastic bodies for the little tank locomotive included in the Rail Blazer sets were getting their silver smokebox and front treatments in the masking area as well, but with a slight

Lionel uses very elaborate metal masks to produce its intricate paint schemes. In this photograph, a red GP-9 diesel shell has been painted red and placed in position for painting a stripe. The mask is partially covering the locomotive.

In this photograph, the mask completely covers the locomotive and the worker is spraying the yellow side stripe.

The red-painted diesel next receives a white-painted front end. The shell has been inserted in the mask. The masks have been cleaned after every three or four pieces to remove paint build-up.

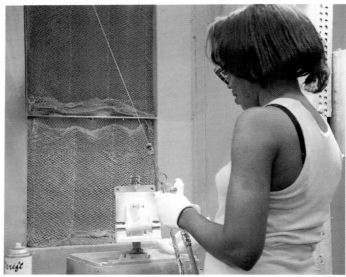

The red-painted diesel front end is painted white. It has now become the 18800 Lehigh Valley GP-9 for the Black Diamond Set of 1987.

difference. In this case a white plastic smokestack extension was being inserted into the shells, which had already been red-painted. Then the whole smokebox assembly was put into a mask and silver-painted by spray gun.

We moved on into the main factory room, where the assembly lines and the heat-stamping and Tampo machines are located. I had often wondered why some cars had come out of the factory stamped only on one side. The explanation is quite simple. Two heat-stamping or Tampo machines are often needed to decorate a car; one decorates one side of the car, which is then sent to a second machine, where the car gets treated on the other side. Among the thousands and thousands of engines and rolling stock that go through this decorating process, it is inevitable that a car will go through one machine but somehow miss going through the second one. If it gets as far as the final pack-out assembly line and is packed decorated side up, it could escape detection.

I was singularly impressed by Lionel's factory employees, especially their level of skill in assembling these products. They are extremely skilled at their tasks. Every move shows the practiced hand of one with great experience at a particular operation. They really do inspect each car before they send it on to the next step. I wonder that any factory errors get out of the factory at all; in fact, in recent years the number of factory errors found by collectors is minimal. Then I realized why the Fundimensions move to Mexico was unsuccessful. General Mills wanted Fundimensions to expand its production and cut its costs, both praiseworthy goals in themselves. However, the parent company failed to take into account the skill level needed to produce these trains, let alone the training difficulties it would encounter due to such considerations as language. These are toys, to be sure, but they are complex toys with little room for error. The employees at Lionel Trains, Inc. were working under very hot conditions when we were present (the

temperature read 93 degrees outside). Fortunately the large fans kept the air moving, but they were exercising great care as a matter of routine. The quality control, as we saw it, was very impressive.

When we moved into yet another work area, we observed two other operations of interest. I believe one of these has a great deal of significance. We watched the gold lettering being applied by the Tampo process to the new Pennsylvania 2400-type passenger cars. Lionel had received some complaints earlier that the gold lettering on the tuscan trailers and flatcar of the Pennsylvania TOFC car was too dull. Evidently Lionel did not want that mistake to occur again. I watched as a worker fastened the car into the machine and stamped each side of the car three times to make sure the lettering was bright enough — a total of six operations per car! These cars were then transferred to the truck fastening area, where the trucks were placed into position, the car put into a riveting machine, and a foot pedal operated the rivets which fastened the trucks to the car. The labor-intensiveness of this particular operation led us to some conclusions we discussed over lunch later on.

The other operation was the assembly of the Rail Blazer sets for shipment to distributors. At one end of a long assembly line, boxes for the set were assembled. Then, one by one, workers inserted the set components into the boxes as the sets came by. At the other end of the line, the set boxes were closed, shrink-wrapped, and placed into shipping cartons. Before the boxes were closed, I noticed a worker rubber-stamping the Julian dating code for the sets onto the set boxes. After the shipping carton was closed, the Julian number was stamped on the shipping carton itself. (See our article on this system in Chapter 14.) This system assists quality control by identifying any set boxes with defective components as to the exact date of assembly. In this way, the factory personnel can inspect a day's boxes for any further defects if there is a defective or missing component. Of course, this code can help collectors date their pieces and keep track of variations as well.

Our last observation was the track-making machines located just off the set assembly line. These huge machines are very old, but also very good at making track in huge quantities. Great ribbons of tin-plated metal on spools fed into one of the machines, which then crimped, shaped, and cut precise rails of curved O27 track. Another machine was turning out brass rails for the new Large Scale trains. Nearby, motor coil winding machines of ancient vintage were busily spider-webbing coils of wire for motors and transformers.

We then moved to a particularly interesting place, the parts and repair division, located next door to the main plant. We were greeted by Mr. Gary Svehar, the Supervisor of Technical Services. Bruce chatted with him about the new Greenberg Service Manual for Lionel Trains, Inc., which was nearly completed, and Mr. Svehar then showed us row after row of carefully labeled bins of parts of all types and descriptions. These bins, which resemble plastic milk crates, hold a fascinating cornucopia of Lionel train parts, some of which date back a long way. I asked Mr. Svehar what he thought was the oldest part in the place. "I really don't know," he said, "but it's possible that some parts go back to the prewar era." Sure enough, in looking around I spied a bin full of driver wheels for the 1664 Columbia Steam Locomotive, a prewar locomotive. Those parts could well have been half a century old. Mr. Svehar showed us a well-equipped workbench and testing area, perhaps the ultimate train tinkerer's work area! This concluded our tour of the Lionel facilities. We were also shown a mammoth storage room full of parts for trains which had been subcontracted. This room, which also contained overflow from the fabled archives, resembled nothing so much as a furniture warehouse! Some boxes of parts could only be acquired by extended fork lift trucks.

We thanked Mike Braga and Lenny Dean for their time and patience in answering our many questions. Over lunch, we discussed the significance of what we had just witnessed. I made a comment about the hellish temperature of the place and how tough it must be on the workers. Linda then made the comment, "You know, I feel as if I just saw a factory as it was in the Forties. That's a rather old-fashioned factory for such a modern effort, isn't it?"

Lionel has a semi-automatic machine that winds coils and armatures. Different kinds of wire are used for different coils.

This prescient comment led to a discussion about the labor-intense nature of that factory. It appears to us that the factory in its present state is perhaps Lionel's biggest obstacle. Most of the operations in the plant are time-consuming, labor-intensive efforts which almost beg for more modern operation. I mentioned the triple-stamping of the Pennsylvania passenger cars and wondered aloud how much time it must take for the thousands of cars to be stamped in such a way. We realized that we had a real insight into Lionel's production. We believe that the capacity of the factory to turn out trains is quite limited, by modern standards. We saw at once why Lionel cannot do a second run of a particular piece; production schedules are so tight that this cannot be done. If Lionel is successful in increasing the volume of trains it sells, the firm will face quite a decision in the next two years or so. What happens if the demand for those trains outruns the ability of that factory to produce them? Lionel may have to spend huge amounts of capital to modernize its plant, or even build a new factory — both of which would be extremely costly. As we had mentioned, the Lionel factory employees are very, very good at their jobs. However, we believe that the labor-intensive nature of the manufacturing process for these trains will face Lionel with a serious decision or two in the very near future.

Another factor to consider is the current rate of spoilage. In any factory operation, it is inevitable that somewhere along the way, pieces will be spoiled by improper painting, truck mounting, or other factors. Assume, for example, that the factory intends to produce 10,000 Pennsylvania observation cars. Even at a spoilage rate of five percent, which is very low, 500 of these shells will not be suitable for shipment — and dealers' orders will have to be scaled back in proportion by that amount. Like any respectable operation (which Lionel certainly is), Lionel wants to put its best product on dealer shelves. If anything, Lionel's craftsmen would be less tolerant than usual about products which were even a little bit off target for quality control, which we observed was very high. The fewer the shells

Lettering is usually applied by a hot-stamp machine. This machine has a plate which is inked for each impression. In this photograph a yellow SP type caboose is being lettered.

which make it to the final product, the fewer can be sent off for sale. That may account for some of the cutbacks in shipments noted by dealers. That is especially true in the case of the more complicated collector pieces. For example, we were told that there had been a delay in the production of the Rock Island 4-8-4 Northern because of delays in securing subcontracted parts for it. Other sources tell us that the first shipments of boiler castings for this engine showed the same roughness as the prototype and the casting mold had to be reworked. Whatever the case, it appears that Lionel pays a price in quantity for its insistence upon strict quality.

Our afternoon visit was to the headquarters of the new owner and Chairman of Lionel Trains, Inc., Richard Kughn, for an interview. We drove into Detroit, where we arrived at a large nondescript dark brown-painted, one-story building with no markings of any kind on the outside. This, the home of Mr. Kughn's Carail, Inc., was a converted bowling alley. We were not prepared for the sight which greeted us as we came through an unremarkable side door. There we were face to face with a 1907 Renault Landaulet Town Car in absolutely pristine condition — the sort of car which featured a chauffeur sitting open to the weather and someone like Marlene Dietrich sitting in the closed cab. Mr. Kughn is also a collector of antique automobiles and real railroad cars; within this facility is an antique auto lover's dream of a collection, complete with a service garage and mechanics! My eyes popped as I saw the headlights of two Duesenberg SJs staring at me with haughty grandeur.

We were shown into Mr. Kughn's office, if one wants to call it that. In reality, it is a spacious room which looks more like an elegant nightclub. Around two walls curves a great walnut bar, and the rest of the room is filled with large round tables. Mr. Kughn made his fortune as a national real estate developer. His cordless phone is never very far from his side, and he can move easily about his "kingdom" as he speaks to his business associates. Behind this room was a huge area where Mr. Kughn's awesome train collection is stored on rack after rack, and off to our right was what once was the space occupied by the bowling alley's lanes which now serves as a vast display area for Mr. Kughn's antique automobiles.

Mr. Kughn, a tall, slim man with boundless energy and enthusiasm, greeted us and took us through his train room. I

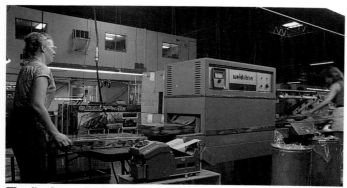

The final step in the set manufacturing process is the application of plastic shrink wrap to the set box. At the far end of the machine a worker wraps the set in plastic. The plastic shrinks to a tight fit as it passes through the oven. A worker at the other end inspects each box as she removes them from the conveyor.

have seen major collections before, but never anything like this one. Racks of locomotives and rolling stock stretched along the walls from floor to ceiling. Inside racks held a bewildering array of Lionel accessories and trains, many dating back to the very beginning of Lionel. Four pristine power stations from the mid-1930s stood side by side. Old Varney HO kits in original boxes lined one fascinating shelf. There were fine brass scale engines, Marx equipment, and privately remarked cars, including a replica of the UPS Operating Boxcar prototype which was never put into production (the real prototype is safe in the Lionel archives). There were numerous examples of 381 and 408 Electrics as well as 400E Standard Gauge Steamers in like-new condition. No dollar value can ever approximate the real value of such a collection to a train collector!

Our interview began with an unusual question I hoped would set a good tone. I asked Mr. Kughn to comment about any similarities or differences he saw between himself since he took over Lionel and Joshua Lionel Cowen himself. He laughed and said, "That's a question I'm not usually asked! Come to think of it, I guess we would have a few things in common. Both of us got into toy trains by accident, and we both liked the same things — tinkering and working with our hands. But the days when you could act paternalistically are long gone, of course. After all, he was the master of them all, making Lionel what it is. Nobody could market and sell trains like Cowen. In his prime, he made Lionel synonymous with apple pie and ice cream for Americans."

"I got into this hobby when I was seven years old, about 1935," he continued. "Believe it or not, I found my first set of trains in a trash barrel! I picked them up, fixed them, and in the course of time I realized that there was something magical about toy trains. I soon found some friends who had the same interests, and I've been an avid collector and fan of toy trains ever since."

Linda asked him what his chief motive in buying the company was. "There are many reasons, I think," he said. "I think Lionel trains offer a great learning experience for people. Recently, the country has put a new stress on traditional family values, and these trains fit right into those values. Toy trains offer a great opportunity for people to bring things together. The future may be different from the great Lionel era of the Fifties, but we still have the same needs and the same desires. I, for one, think that the American public is tired of toys which are fads lasting only a little while. Other kinds of toys disappear — look at the video game craze, for example — but Lionel Trains, almost alone among toys, have a rich history and real permanence. They will really endure as a shared family activity, and as both entertainment and educational devices, I believe that the time is right for their resurgence."

Mr. Kughn continued, "I see myself as perhaps serving a special function with Lionel Trains in the years ahead. During the last twenty years or so, many decisions have been made about Lionel Trains by committees and corporate people who did not necessarily know these trains as cultural phenomena. I'd like to change that by taking Lionel in a definite direction over the next few years and by giving the firm as much leadership and vision as I can muster. If you look at the 1987 catalogue, you'll see something about the direction I mean. I think Lionel can once again be a household word among the American people.

The famous and scarce Standard O freight cars from Lionel's 1986 direct mail offer. Top shelf: 6231 Railgon gondola with coal load, 6233 Canadian Pacific flatcar. Second shelf: 6232 Illinois Central boxcar, 6230 Erie-Lackawanna refrigerator car. Third shelf: Two very desirable two-bay ACF center-flow hoppers, the 6135 North Western and the 6134 Burlington Northern. Bottom shelf: The "hottest" cars of this set, two fine low-cupola woodsided cabooses. Left: 6920 Boston & Albany, made to match the 8606 B & A Scale Hudson steamer, and the 6907 New York Central, made to match the first scale Hudson, the 8406.

So we've been expanding the Traditional Series while keeping a fine Collector Series alive as well. We'll continue to do that."

When we asked for specifics, Mr. Kughn showed that he was not about to let secrets out too early. "I know what we are planning for next year," he said. "I can't get into specific details right now, but I can tell you that you should think of both old things and entirely new things. I can also guarantee you that when you see the Lionel line for 1988, you are going to absolutely love what you're going to see!" He had the Cheshire Cat grin of a man who can't wait for next year's Toy Fair to arrive! Since our visit, Lionel has unveiled Lionel Classics, a big expansion of Large Scale, and the sensational Rail Scope. Obviously, Mr. Kughn wasn't misleading us!

Linda asked him how he had heard that Lionel was to be for sale. "A couple of my friends know what a great train fan I am," he said, "and they told me that there were rumors afoot that Kenner-Parker wanted to sell the Lionel part of their operations. They joked with me and said that if I liked collecting trains so much, why didn't I buy the company for myself so I could have the world's biggest toy? I investigated the rumors

and found them to be true — Lionel was really up for sale. The more I thought about it, the more sense it made, not only as the fulfillment of a dream, but also as a profitable business venture. One thing led to another, and the rest you know. I officially took over as Lionel's owner on April 25, 1986. Even though I bought Lionel almost by accident, I saw it as a great opportunity. Kenner-Parker shouldn't be knocked for its short management period; they just weren't entrepreneurial about these trains in the sense they should be. After all, we're talking about going from a company that is part of a large corporation to one that is privately held. Remember that for most of its history, Lionel was a privately held company."

After a discussion about Lionel's relationship with its dealers, Bruce asked Mr. Kughn how he expected to make Lionel's new Large Scale trains competitive in the face of ferocious competition from established makers such as LGB and Kalamazoo Trains. In particular, Bruce mentioned a current magazine ad which seemed to attack Lionel's efforts directly. "That doesn't worry me in the slightest," Mr. Kughn replied. "That's good, old-fashioned competition, and we mean to be competitive in that market. We're convinced that the Large Scale trains will succeed for several reasons. First of all, they are Lionel, and that name still commands respect in the toy train world. Secondly, they are quality products. Note that our main competitor's lowest-priced engine has four drive wheels. Ours have six, and we've made extensive studies as to the best drive systems and so forth. Thirdly, they are an American-made product, and we think that the term "Made in America" has real meaning in today's marketplace. Finally, we will be price competitive against any other product. We have priced our beginner Large Scale train set very well, and we think we can establish a very respectable share of that market for ourselves."

Richard Kughn, President of Lionel Trains, Inc., at his personal museum, Carail. Mr Kughn, who has collected Lionel trains for many years, purchased Lionel from Kenner-Parker in April, 1986. He also owns several examples of the real thing, including Henry Ford's private Pullman, and an extensive antique car collection.

Several questions about marketing led to some revealing comments from Mr. Kughn about his goals. "It's wrong that little kids are not taught about toy trains because they have great educational value. And they're fun. Your shows do a real service in that regard. We think we have a good slogan going: "Because no childhood should be without a train." You may have noticed our boxes, too; the new ones have the legend: "Trains to grow up with, not out of." That should tell you a lot about our approach. We plan to use print media with ads to make parents and grandparents remember all the fun they used to have with toy trains and want to share that fun once again. We think that for our purposes, television is too expensive relative to its efficiency."

"We can't go back to the days when Lionel was sold by every little Mom and Pop store in town," he continued. "American business has gone beyond that from small to large retailers and from service-oriented stores to regional shopping centers. Our challenge is to use that system to market an old set of values, and I'm convinced we can do it!"

One question concerned the direct mail order strategy of mid-1986. We asked whether this was a way to bypass troublesome distributors or as a simple experiment in marketing. "That decision was made by the management under Kenner-Parker," he explained. "In one sense, it was the right thing to try because it represented exploring all the alternatives. However, you're right — it did create antagonism among our distributor network, and it put us in the position where, with mail order, we were in effect dealing with thousands of separate accounts. That caused quite a bit of trouble to us. We do not plan to use the direct mail order strategy again."

When the interview was concluded, we sprung one little surprise upon Mr. Kughn we had been saving. We presented him with a train set from the very late prewar era, No. 8011, which had not been previously described in any literature of those years. This set was remarkable in that it also contained the original sales slip; we had been able to identify the original owner and the exact date the set was purchased, November 17, 1942! Mr. Kughn was delighted. He said, "This set doesn't stay here, it goes home with me. I grew up only a short distance from North Olmstead, Ohio, and I'll try to track down the relatives of the original owner, and I'll report back to you." We had succeeded in making Mr. Kughn one of our Greenberg train sleuths, it seems!

It was impossible to walk away from our interview with Richard Kughn without being singularly impressed by this friendly, enthusiastic man. We all felt that Lionel was finally granted a real leader who could take the firm in a positive direction. We knew that we had interviewed a man of undisputed business and marketing ability — with the determination to carry out his decisions. For all the nostalgia and enthusiasm Mr. Kughn evidenced, he could not have gotten to the pinnacle of the business world he has reached because he is made of sugar candy!

On the plane trip home, I reflected upon this hectic, tumultuous, but rewarding day. I believe Lionel will endure. The firm has been through some troubled times in its history and survived and prospered because it is so much a part of American culture and so much of our treasured past we want so badly to resurrect. To be sure, some momentous decisions await the management at Lionel Trains, Inc. The firm, I think, must look towards modernization of its manufacturing processes as it expands, and it must do some fence-mending among its distributor network. Lionel and its dealers need each other to keep Lionel's share of the toy train marketplace against some stiffening competition. We may yet see the days return when Lionel fought tooth and nail against Marx and American Flyer. The names of the competitors have changed, but the marketplace challenge is still there.

I thought of the thesis for all of our Greenberg Guides to Lionel Trains: Lionel was, and is, a well-organized company which makes toy trains in a systematic way which can be observed and described by scholarship.

That is still as true as it ever was, for the maker and the collector alike. The Lionel name will survive because it is a part of us ourselves. "Not just a toy — a tradition." True words, indeed!

Chapter I
DIESELS, ELECTRICS, AND MOTORIZED UNITS

The production of these "Geeps" spans eleven years. Top shelf: 8665 Bangor & Aroostook "Jeremiah O'Brien" GP-9, sold with matching porthole caboose in same box as Bicentennial Commemorative in 1976, 8559 Norfolk and Western GP-9 Bicentennial Commemorative from catalogued "Spirit of America" Set of 1975. The example shown is a factory error; it is missing a silver circle of stars on the blue nose area. Middle shelf: The first Lionel Geep diesels. Left: 8030 Illinois Central GP-9, early; note heavy Type I railings. Right: 8031 Canadian National GP-9 with later Type II railings. Bottom shelf: 8064 Florida East Coast GP-9, 8158 Duluth, Missabe & Iron Range GP-35. A. Rudman, F. Stem, L. Caponi, and R. LaVoie Collections.

Nostalgia is a wonderful and powerful force which attracts many people to toy trains. Rare is the individual who does not cherish a memory of the prototype for a Lionel steam or diesel engine. In the case of the steamers, the "over 40" generation may well have seen the real-life original to the Jersey Central's Blue Comet and recalled a pleasant memory as the Fundimensions Blue Comet Hudson flashed by on a layout.

The only trouble with nostalgia as a motivating force is that it is pleasant for consumers, but not necessarily for producers of toy trains. As Fundimensions took over production of trains from the Lionel Corporation in 1970, its managers realized that a whole new generation awaited the production and rediscovery of these trains. The firm realized that this new generation did not necessarily share the nostalgia of their elders. Therefore, Fundimensions decided to market its locomotives not just to those with actual memories of steam locomotives, but also to those who would look for imitations of the contemporary world around them. That meant diesel engines, not steamers. The rapid proliferation of diesel engines made

economic sense in the early years of Fundimensions, even if it might have been at the expense of the steamers, because a new market for toy trains had to be developed.

There was another highly significant economic advantage to the rapid marketing of many types of diesels. Fundimensions could take advantage of new decorating processes much more easily on the flat plastic surfaces of the diesel cabs than it could on the rounded boilers of the steam locomotives. The postwar decorating techniques were limited to decals, heat stamping, and rubber stamping. Fundimensions, as a subsidiary of General Mills, had access to people knowledgeable in the new and versatile decorating tactics known as electrocal and tampo. Thus, colorful contemporary railroad paint schemes could be applied to Fundimensions' diesels — and color sells trains to the public.

Right from the start Fundimensions made their policy apparent. In the 1970 catalogue only a couple of 2-4-2 Columbia steamers actually saw production. However, the catalogue fea-

From top to bottom: 8353 GT, 8357 Pennsylvania, 8375 Chicago and Northwestern, 8454 Rio Grande, 8550 Jersey Central. A. Rudman, F. Stem, L. Caponi, and R. LaVoie Collections.

tured an exceptionally colorful orange and white Illinois Central GP-9, a bright blue Santa Fe NW-2 switcher, and an Alco AA pair of Santa Fe locomotives in the famous "war bonnet" paint scheme. The GP-9 was particularly attractive; at first, it had huge handrails made from old log car stakes which looked ungainly, but this handrail soon gave way to a more realistic — and fragile — plastic and wire handrail.

As the years went by, Fundimensions issued many different styles of diesels; it is perhaps best to discuss them by type rather than by year produced. Most of these styles have continued under Kenner-Parker and Lionel, Inc. management.

THE GP-7 AND GP-9 ROAD SWITCHERS

The only difference between Fundimensions' GP-7 and GP-9 models was the presence of a snap-on fan shroud atop the roof of the GP-9 model. The real GP-9 locomotives, it should be noted, came both ways. These diesels were very good models, even if they lacked the separate motor and power trucks of the

Lionel originals. They also lacked the horns and did not have Magnetraction. The first models off the assembly lines used hollow pickup rollers which proved an embarrassment for the company. These rollers would not bridge the switches, so Fundimensions dug up a stock of good leftover pickup assemblies and supplied them for the engines until the firm perfected solid roller snap-in assemblies for the power trucks, which performed reliably. We now understand that Service Stations were to provide the additional pickup assemblies and be reimbursed for the jobs by Lionel.

One of the GP-7 locomotives became a landmark for Fundimensions because it proved that there was a sizable collector's market for Lionel trains. In 1973 Fundimensions issued a special model of the locomotive which commemorated the 50th anniversary of the Electromotive Division of General Motors, the makers of the prototypes. This engine was done in gold with dark blue Chessie and General Motors markings, and it was sold out very rapidly. From that point on, Lionel has capitalized upon a collector's market which eagerly awaits each limited production item.

Over the years Lionel has issued many GP-7 and GP-9 diesels. Some of them have been entirely original in design, while others have been direct re-issues of famous GP-7 and GP-9 locomotives issued by the Lionel Corporation in the 1950s. Most of these engines are common and available at good prices for the beginning collector. On the whole, they are reliable runners which pull a medium-sized train well and give little trouble. A few of these engines made in the mid-1970s used a fiber worm gear instead of a brass or nylon one; these fiber gears strip easily under a heavy load. The rubber traction tires used on these locomotives do not slip if the operator cements them in place with rubber cement. With normal use and maintenance, they endure operations quite well.

Recently the GP series has seen two Lionel innovations. One is the use of an AC/DC can motor mounted right into the power truck. This arrangement is very close to the one found on the prototype. The first locomotive with this motor, the 8263 Santa Fe GP-7 of 1982, was not entirely successful. The engine is too light, and it has cheaper sliding contact shoes instead of the good roller pickups. For those reasons, it has not met with great success. Fundimensions did a much better job with the next locomotive built in this way, the 8375 Chicago & Northwestern GP-7 included in the Northern Freight Flyer of 1983. This locomotive is weighted and has two can motors, one on each power truck. It also has a fully electronic reversing switch and runs on very low voltage. This twin-motored engine has excellent hauling capacity; it is also easier to maintain because the motor never needs lubrication (though the gears do). The better roller pickups are a part of this engine as well. The twin-motored engine is far better than the single-motored locomotive. A dark blue Baltimore & Ohio GP-7 has also been produced, and a green and gold Southern GP-7 will haul the Southern Freight Runner Service Station Special Set for 1987. As part of the 1987 Traditional Series, Lionel will also produce a Lehigh Valley GP-9 in the Black Diamond Set with traditional Lehigh Valley red and yellow markings with black and white safety striping on the ends.

The other innovation in the "Geep" series was released in late 1984. It is a handsome New York Central GP-9 with extra

Some very popular Lionel GP-9 models. Top shelf: 8357 Pennsylvania, 8477 New York Central. Middle shelf: 8587 Wabash, numbered after its prototype and sold as a J. C. Penney Special, 8654 Boston & Maine. Bottom shelf: 8757 Conrail (which also came with white-painted frame) and 8759 Erie-Lackawanna. A. Rudman, F. Stem, L. Caponi, and R. LaVoie Collections.

detailing such as hand-inserted grab-irons on the front and rear. The motor in this engine is the preferable separate motor and power truck, as compared with the integral unit found in most Geeps. It also has twin-axle Magnetraction, lighted numberboards, and an electronic horn. The locomotive is painted in very realistic black, gray, and white New York Central colors which should be met with collector enthusiasm. It already shows signs of being a highly desirable collector's locomotive. A J. C. Penney Special in Wabash colors using this construction has been produced since the production of the New York Central, and in 1987 a handsome Milwaukee GP-9 was scheduled to be part of Fallen Flags Series No. 2.

THE GP-20 ROAD SWITCHER

In 1973 one of the mold and die experts at Fundimensions came up with a clever die insert for the GP-7 and GP-9 molds. By placing this insert into the die, Fundimensions came up with a new model, the GP-20, which had Union Pacific prototypes with fan shrouds and New York Central prototypes without the fan shrouds. This locomotive has not been issued in the quantities used for the GP-7 and GP-9, but it is the locomotive responsible for the introduction of a Fundimensions innovation — the electronic diesel horn.

Unfortunately for Fundimensions, the horn used the same troublesome controller issued with the steam engine whistles. This controller had a tendency to get stuck in the closed position and burn out the diode which changed part of the AC transformer current into DC for the horn. Therefore, it was made in very limited quantities, and any GP-20 dummy unit which has the electronic horn is quite scarce. It is a shame that the con-

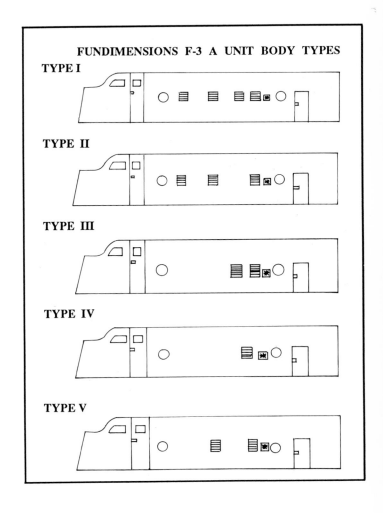

FUNDIMENSIONS F-3 A UNIT BODY TYPES

TYPE I

TYPE II

TYPE III

TYPE IV

TYPE V

troller did not work properly, because the horn sound itself was excellent. Some operators actually prefer it to the new electronic horns because it has a muffled sound like a real diesel heard from a distance. Some horns were used in the Union Pacific U36B dummy locomotive, and the rest were split up between the Santa Fe, Long Island, and Missouri Pacific GP-20 locomotives produced in 1973 and 1974. The electronic horn was revived successfully in 1981 in the 8157 Santa Fe Fairbanks-Morse Locomotive.

In 1983 an 8369 Erie-Lackawanna GP-20 with twin can motors was offered for separate sale. Like its GP-7 partners, it runs extremely well compared to its single-motored stablemates. My own example of this locomotive nearly tore the bumper off my test track when I ran it for the first time because I did not expect it to run so efficiently at such low voltage! It will pull a train at eight volts, giving the transformers an easy job to handle. A very pretty Northern Pacific GP-20 with twin can motor construction joined the Erie-Lackawanna model in 1986.

F-3 COVERED WAGON DIESELS

In the late 1930s the Electro-Motive Division of General Motors startled the real train world with its FT diesel demonstrator engines. These streamlined locomotives piled up mile after maintenance-free mile, and they routinely pulled trains of six thousand tons when the biggest steam engines could only handle half that much. Following the Second World War, these freight diesels and their sister passenger units, the E Series, rapidly replaced steam engines all over the country.

In 1947 General Motors introduced the F-3 Series, the first truly successful freight diesels. (This story is eloquently told in Robert Carper's book, *American Railroads In Transition: The Passing of the Steam Engines.*)

Despite some personal doubts on the part of Joshua Lionel Cowen, a die-hard steam fan, the Lionel Corporation was quick to take notice of these streamlined beauties. In 1948, just one year after the real locomotives emerged, Lionel produced its Santa Fe and New York Central F-3 locomotives. The Santa Fe model became the best-selling locomotive in Lionel's history because of its dependable twin-motor performance and its spectacular Santa Fe "war bonnet" paint scheme of red, silver, yellow, and black.

Fundimensions did not wait very long to recall this legend of the tinplate rails. In 1973 a special brochure announced the return of the F-3 diesel in Baltimore and Ohio markings. By 1978 Fundimensions had reissued many of the scarcest Lionel models; indeed, some of them, like the Canadian Pacific and Southern F-3 diesels, would become just as scarce as their forebears. In 1976 Fundimensions even reissued the Santa Fe model, expecting slow sales because of the presence of so many of the older locomotives within collections. However, Fundimensions did so good a job with the paint scheme that the firm could not make the Santa Fe locomotives fast enough, and today it is harder to find than any of its predecessors!

All of the F-3 models produced until 1978 were single-motor locomotives without Magnetraction, horns, and some of the intricate trim of the Lionel pieces. The F-3 disappeared from the catalogue in 1978, but not for long. Another special bulletin an-

Some General Motors GP (General Purpose) road switcher diesels. Top: 8662 Baltimore & Ohio GP-7 with Lionel's new twin can-motor drive system, 8666 Northern Pacific GP-9 from Northern Pacific Service Station Set of 1976. Middle: 8763 Norfolk & Western GP-9, 8775 Lehigh Valley GP-9. Bottom: 8854 CP Rail GP-9 from Great Plains Express Set of 1978, 8866 Minneapolis & St. Louis GP-9 from Service Station Special Set of 1978.

Some "chop-nosed" GP-20 diesels adapted from the Lionel GP mold. **Top shelf: 8066 Toledo, Peoria & Western** from Cross Country Express catalogued set of 1980-81, **8160 Burger King** from Favorite Food Set of 1981. **Middle shelf: 8352 Santa Fe**, one of the first GP-20s, **8369 Erie-Lackawanna** of 1983 with twin can motor drive system. **Bottom shelf: Limited edition 8463 Chessie** of 1974, **8679 Northern Pacific** twin can motor model of 1986. A. Rudman, F. Stem, L. Caponi, and R. LaVoie Collections.

nounced a twin-motor F-3 in New Haven markings for late 1978. It was followed the next year by a Brunswick green Pennsylvania twin-motored pair, and on this pair the deluxe trim was at last restored to the F-3. Collector pressure made Lionel issue a pair of Pennsylvania locomotives in tuscan as well, in order that the F-3 pair would match the Congressional Limited passenger cars of that year. Since that time, all F-3 locomotives have been twin-motored pairs, and several new models have appeared, such as the Southern Pacific, Union Pacific, and

Illinois Central pairs. A Burlington "Texas Zephyr" has been issued in chromed plastic, and the New York Central F-3 has been revived. "B" units have been available for nearly all of the F-3 locomotives produced.

The Fundimensions F-3 diesels are excellent runners either as single-motored or double-motored units, thanks to Fundimensions' use of a separate motor and power truck instead of the integral motor and power truck used on the GP series. They are usually brisk sellers which command a good

A spectacular chromed F-3 ABA set. **Top shelf: 8054 and 8055 C & S Burlington AA units. Bottom shelf: Matching 8062 B Unit.** The chromed plastic on this set is difficult to maintain in unblemished condition. A. Rudman Collection.

Another F-3 AA pair and some of the B units. Top shelf: 8970-8971 Pennsylvania. These were made when collectors complained that the 8952-53 green pair did not match the Congressional passenger cars. Second shelf: 8059 (Brunswick green, no horn) and 8060 tuscan B units. Third shelf: 8164 Pennsylvania Brunswick green unit (with horn), 8261 Southern Pacific B unit -- both extremely hard to find. Bottom shelf: 8371 New York Central and 8468 Baltimore & Ohio B units.

price premium. Strangely enough, the older Lionel F-3 locomotives have also increased in value, even though they have been reproduced. The probable reason for this is the strong appeal of this locomotive both as an operating unit and a historic locomotive.

THE ALCO UNITS

One of the first diesel locomotives revived by Fundimensions was the little Alco streamlined diesel. The first of these locomotives was a Santa Fe "A-A" pair in 1970; a "B" unit was soon available. The prototype of this locomotive is considered by diesel enthusiasts to be one of the most beautiful diesels ever made, especially in its PA passenger configuration. Unfortunately, Lionel's model is not to true scale and is not nearly as impressive as the F-3 diesel. Still, the least expensive sets of the early Fundimensions era were headed by many an Alco; most of the early ones had two-position reversing units and were somewhat cheaply made.

In 1975 and 1976 Fundimensions tested the waters to see what reception a deluxe version of the Alco might engender. The firm issued a triple Alco AA set in one box in Southern Pacific Daylight colors. Unlike their stablemates, these Alcos had die-cast trucks and three-position reversing units. In 1976

Fundimensions issued three Canadian National units, this time for separate sale. These locomotives came in the brilliant orange, black, and white zebra stripes of the prototype. Sales of these triple units were disappointing, so Fundimensions proceeded no further along these marketing lines. Since that time, the Alco has been limited to the lower end of the market; the most recent use of the Alco has been a Texas and Pacific pair for the Quicksilver Express Passenger Set. For 1988 Amtrak and Pennsylvania Alcos with twin can motors have been introduced.

The Fundimensions Alco is a great piece for a beginning locomotive collector to explore. Most of the Alcos are very low priced and readily available. Exceptions are the deluxe Alcos mentioned above and an 8022 AA pair made especially for J. C. Penney in 1970. A reasonably complete assembly of Fundimensions Alcos can be acquired in a short time without exorbitant expense.

THE U36B AND U36C "U-BOATS"

The first diesel locomotive which was a new Fundimensions model not patterned after any postwar product was the U36B, issued in 1974. Except for its non-scale length, Fundimensions' "U-boat" was a very good model of the rugged General Electric prototype. The first models were the aptly-numbered 1776 Seaboard Bicentennial Locomotive and the 8470 Chessie System at the head of Fundimensions' "Grand National" top-of-the-line freight set. Both these locomotives became very popular, and in rapid succession Fundimensions issued Union Pacific, Great Northern, Frisco, Burlington Northern, Southern, and Northern Pacific models.

One U36B deserves particular mention because it is one of the most valuable of all Fundimensions products. In 1977 Fundimensions began its Walt Disney series of hi-cube boxcars, and the 8773 Mickey Mouse U36B was chosen to head it. Because collectors of Disneyana compete with train collectors for it, this locomotive increased in value explosively by 1980. Another U36B is somewhat difficult to find, but it has not attracted collector attention yet. This is the Lionel 75th Anniversary locomotive, which headed a string of freight cars with historic Lionel logos. Many collectors shy away from this set because they feel it is unattractive, but the silver and red colors of the locomotive itself have admirers. This U36B is an excellent "sleeper" candidate; it is not very common, but is still reasonably priced.

In 1979 the U36 locomotive was issued with Fundimensions' new six-wheel locomotive trucks, which were first seen on the 1978 Milwaukee SD-18. Thus, the U36 became a U36C; since that time, most U-boats have been issued with these six-wheel trucks. The exception is 1979's 8962 Reading U36B.

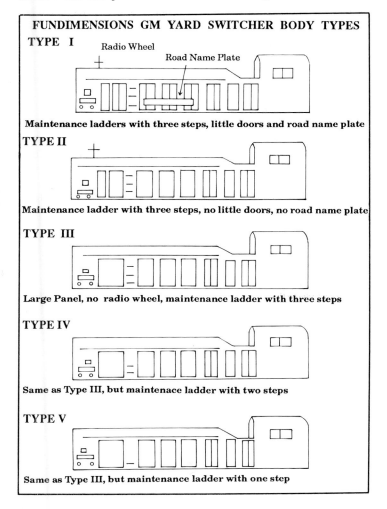

FUNDIMENSIONS GM YARD SWITCHER BODY TYPES

TYPE I

Radio Wheel

Road Name Plate

Maintenance ladders with three steps, little doors and road name plate

TYPE II

Maintenance ladder with three steps, no little doors, no road name plate

TYPE III

Large Panel, no radio wheel, maintenance ladder with three steps

TYPE IV

Same as Type III, but maintenace ladder with two steps

TYPE V

Same as Type III, but maintenance ladder with one step

As a class, the U-boats offer more detailing than their GP counterparts and are slightly higher priced. Dummy units are available for many of these locomotives, including one very scarce Union Pacific with an electronic horn. Their massive appearance has made them favorites of some Fundimensions collectors. In 1987 a new Santa Fe U36B was produced for the Traditional Series with a twin can-motor configuration. It appears that all future Traditional diesels will use the twin can-motor powering system, while the Collector Series locomotives will use the older motors and truck frames, which are more expensive to produce. This makes economic sense for Lionel, since its best interest is to keep the cost of the Traditional Series down while maintaining quality.

THE NW-2 SWITCHERS

From Day One, Lionel has called its switchers SW-1 models instead of the NW-2 diesels they really are. The firm is perpetuating a Lionel mistake in nomenclature which dates back to 1950! Whatever they are called, Fundimensions' switcher engines have never really been popular with collectors, even though some of them have become quite scarce and collectable. This series began in 1970 with the 8010 Santa Fe Switcher in blue and yellow colors; most of the early switchers followed the line of the cheaper Lionel models. In 1973 Fundimensions revived the black Erie switcher with its 8354; this locomotive had better features such as a three-position reversing switch. Subsequent issues included Pennsylvania, Chessie, C P Rail, Grand Trunk, and Burlington models.

Fundimensions has limited its use of NW-2 switchers to the bottom of the line sets in recent years, and only a few of these locomotives are truly scarce. These include the Erie, Chessie, Coca-Cola, and Pennsylvania models, and a special promotional switcher for Nibco Faucet Products in 1981. Operationally, the switchers have a tendency to jump the track when they encounter a turnout next to a curved track, unless they are run cab end first. Recently, the NW-2 has used the new Fundimensions AC/DC can motor in Burlington Northern and U. S. Marines markings. Like the Alcos, the NW-2 switchers are relatively easy to acquire at good prices and are a great specialization area for the beginning collector.

SOME SIX-WHEELED DIESELS

Typically, when Fundimensions introduces a new feature, it uses the feature over a wide range of its line to help amortize the cost of the tooling. That is certainly true of the handsome six-wheeled trucks in current use on many of its diesels. In 1978 Fundimensions placed the six-wheel trucks under a Milwaukee GP-20 cab, added a fan shroud, and changed the model to the SD-18. Santa Fe and Ontario Northland models were quick to follow, this time in both powered and dummy units. With a change in the cab roof from a rounded roof to a flat roof, the model became a "chop-nosed" SD-28. This version was produced in Burlington and Lionel Lines colors.

Nor were the high-nosed GP-7 and GP-9 models neglected in the use of the new six-wheel trucks. In 1980 Fundimensions produced a round-roofed Seaboard SD-9 to head its Mid-Atlantic Limited Collector Set; the next year, a high-nosed Geep with a flat roof, the SD-24, was made in attractive Canadian Pacific

More of Lionel's F-3 AA pairs. Top shelf: 8260 and 8262 Southern Pacific "Daylight." Second shelf: 8363 and 8364 Baltimore and Ohio, the first Modern Era F-3 units. Third shelf: 8365 and 8367 Canadian Pacific, available only as part of 1973 Service Station Special Set and now very scarce. Bottom shelf: 8370 and 8372 New York Central. A. Rudman, F. Stem, L. Caponi, and R. LaVoie Collections.

markings for the Maple Leaf Limited. This particular locomotive had an electronic horn, as did a Norfolk and Western SD-24 at the head end of the Continental Limited Set.

The early models of the six-wheeled diesels had a peculiar operating problem. The blind center wheels of these locomotives were made a little too large, causing the drive wheels to skid under heavy loads. The problem was soon corrected, and the usual answer to the early problem is to file down the blind wheels carefully. The later six-wheelers have traction tires on the blind wheels as well, effectively curing the trouble. Although these locomotives will run on O27 track, they are far better runners on the wider-radius O Gauge trackage, where their long wheelbase shows to better advantage.

THE FAIRBANKS-MORSE TRAINMASTERS

It is not easy to reproduce a legendary locomotive, so when news came in 1979 that Fundimensions was about to revive the scale-length Fairbanks-Morse Trainmaster, collectors were anxious to see if Fundimensions would do the locomotive justice. Indeed, the firm did — the Fundimensions Fairbanks-Morse is an exact duplicate of the Lionel model, right down to the die-cast trucks, air tanks, and battery box. The first models of this magnificent twin-motored diesel were a revival of the Virginian blue-striped and yellow-striped locomotive and a

stunning Southern Pacific "black widow" locomotive which had only existed as a Lionel prototype. Both locomotives sold extremely well and are still in great demand, especially the Southern Pacific.

Three more Fairbanks-Morse locomotives followed in quick succession. A Chicago and Northwestern green and yellow locomotive in 1980 met with only a lukewarm reception, possibly because the paint scheme resembled the Virginian in style a little too much. This model's markings were not accurate. The legend about the "Route of the 400 Streamliners" was omitted, possibly because it was done in reverse color schemes on the prototype which may have been difficult for Fundimensions to duplicate. The next year, Fundimensions produced a beautiful Santa Fe in blue and yellow freight colors, and the firm added the icing on the cake — the electronic diesel horn. Finally, Fundimensions issued a special production for J. C. Penney in 1983 which has become nearly impossible to obtain. This was the Wabash Fairbanks-Morse in gray and blue "bluebird" colors. The new Lionel management commemorated the centennial of the Statue of Liberty by issuing a Jersey Central "Miss Liberty" Fairbanks-Morse in 1986 with a matching boxcar and extended vision caboose. For 1988 a Southern model will be made with a matching scale high-cupola caboose.

Some nice splashes of color in these F-3 AA pairs. **Top shelf: 8464 and 8465 Rio Grande**, available only as part of 1974 Service Station Special Set. **Second shelf: 8480 and 8482 Union Pacific.** Some of these pairs had yellow paint which did not quite match. **Third shelf: 8555 and 8557 Milwaukee Road**, available only as part of 1975 Service Station Special set. **Bottom shelf: 8566 and 8567 Southern "Crescent Limited."** A. Rudman, F. Stem, L. Caponi, and R. LaVoie Collections.

All of the Fundimensions Fairbanks-Morse locomotives are desirable pieces. Operationally, they can only be outpulled by the die-cast GG-1 electrics. The Wabash and Southern Pacific locomotives are very hard to find. The Virginian, Jersey Central, and Santa Fe locomotives rank a notch below these in scarcity, and the Chicago and Northwestern seems to be the easiest piece to acquire. It should be noted that locomotives without horns can be retro-fitted with the electronic horn, and many Fairbanks-Morse owners have indeed done just that.

THE BUDD CARS

In 1977 Fundimensions introduced a Service Station Special Set which was really different from its predecessors. The firm revived the handsome Budd diesel railcars in Baltimore and Ohio markings. The set had a powered baggage car and two dummy passenger coaches. Soon afterward, Fundimensions issued a powered passenger coach and a dummy baggage car. In 1978 another set was issued, this time in colorful Amtrak markings.

The Budd railcars are very attractive, and they run well because of the separate motor and power truck. The silver paint on the Fundimensions cars is brighter than that of the Lionel originals, and it should have better wear characteristics. The silver color on these and the Santa Fe F-3 looks more "grainy" than the postwar color.

THE SD-40 DIESELS

In 1982 Fundimensions introduced a spectacular new modern diesel, a model of the brutish but attractive SD-40 so popular with railroads today. Fundimensions' model of this locomotive is scale length and has been considered one of the finest diesel models ever produced in tinplate. Scale O Gauge model railroaders have even purchased the body shell and trucks to adapt to their own operational requirements. It was first produced in bright Santa Fe blue and yellow freight colors; since then, each year has seen this locomotive issued in a new paint scheme. In 1983 a yellow, red, and green Union Pacific was made. Both of these locomotives were produced in single-motor configuration; many collectors found this hard to understand, since the locomotive was so large it would easily accommodate the extra motor.

The SD-40 produced in 1984 corrected the oversight. This time the locomotive was a beautiful gray, maroon, and yellow Erie-Lackawanna, and it had twin motors. Like the Union Pacific, it headed a limited production collector set. An SD-40 in Burlington Northern Cascade green and black colors was produced as part of the Burlington Northern Limited, a unit train of five matching Burlington Northern Standard O boxcars and an extended vision caboose. A sixth boxcar was later produced as part of a 1986 year-end package. A big blue Conrail SD-40 headed up another limited edition set for 1987; this model was slightly improved by the addition of reinforcers for the screw holes where the body fastens to the frame; cracks had developed in earlier models. The latest model of this engine is a Chessie System model with the bright yellow, blue, and vermilion Chessie paint scheme.

The SD-40 has been greeted with considerable acclaim by collectors because of its massive size and attractive design. It is a little too soon to tell which of these locomotives will become scarcer than others, but the twin-motor units should command a premium. The Burlington Northern has become difficult to find recently, and the new Conrail SD-40 has been a very hot seller for Lionel.

THE ELECTRICS

Fundimensions took quite some time to reissue the famous electric locomotives of the postwar era; but when they did, they produced some good locomotives indeed. The first of the electrics to emerge from the miniature erecting shops of Fundimensions was the EP-5 rectifier electric in 1975. Fundimen-

sions has always called this engine a "Little Joe," but that is an error; the real "Little Joe" was a quite different locomotive purchased by the Milwaukee Road and the Chicago, South Shore and South Bend Railroad. The name came about because these South Shore locomotives were originally intended for Russian export during World War II; hence the name "Little Joe" after Joseph Stalin. The EP-5 was an electric made for the New Haven by General Electric; it was famous for its rapid acceleration and thus earned the nickname "The Jet." Except for its length and its four-wheel trucks instead of the six-wheel types used on the real thing, Fundimensions' model of the EP-5 was very good. The pantographs on the Fundimensions models were an improvement over those of the postwar era. They used a strip of spring steel to create upward pressure instead of the fragile coil springs of the postwar models. As a result, these engines run much better on overhead catenary wires. In fact, postwar engines have been refitted with Fundimensions pantographs for this reason.

The first EP-5 was issued in Pennsylvania tuscan with gold striping and lettering. The next year it was followed by a Milwaukee locomotive in orange and black; in 1977 an attractive Great Northern EP-5 was made in dark green and orange. Finally, a special locomotive was made for J. C. Penney in 1982. This EP-5 had Pennsylvania markings like its 8551 predeces-

More B Units for extending your F-3 AA pairs. Top shelf: 8469 Canadian Pacific, 8474 Rio Grande. Second shelf: 8481 Union Pacific (some were a different shade of yellow from their AA counterparts), 8575 Milwaukee Road. Third shelf: 8581 Illinois Central, 8661 Southern. Bottom shelf: 8777 Santa Fe, 8864 New Haven. A. Rudman, F. Stem, L. Caponi, and R. LaVoie Collections.

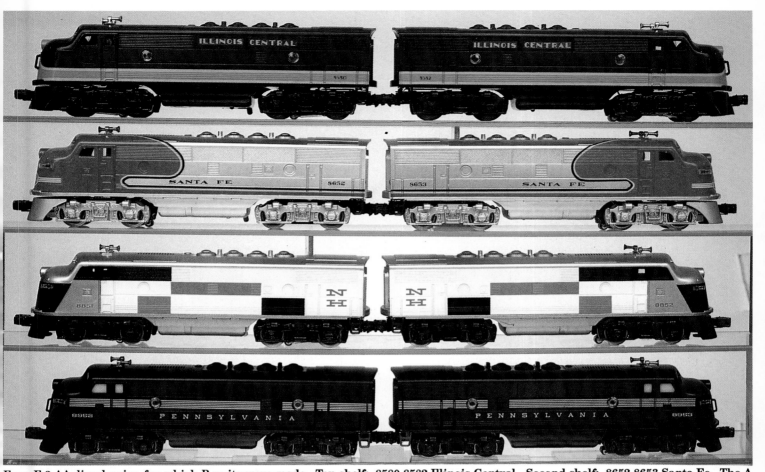

Four F-3 AA diesel pairs, for which B units were made. Top shelf: 8580-8582 Illinois Central. Second shelf: 8652-8653 Santa Fe. The A dummy is extremely hard to find. Third shelf: 8851-8852 New Haven. This engine, from 1978, was the first twin-motored F-3 produced in the modern era. Bottom: 8952-8953 Pennsylvania. Note the frosted window inserts -- an ordering mistake. There were two B units made for this pair, one with and one without a horn. A. Rudman, F. Stem, L. Caponi, and R. LaVoie Collections.

sor, but the nose and sides of the locomotive were in bright gold with tuscan lettering.

The EP-5 is a fine runner which looks good with either freight or passenger consists. The first two EP-5s issued are the most common, with the Great Northern somewhat harder to find and the Penney locomotive the hardest of all to acquire due to its limited production. Another Great Northern EP-5 is scheduled for 1988 production.

In 1976 Fundimensions resurrected the ungainly and brutish Virginian rectifier of postwar fame. Despite its boxy look, the locomotive was welcomed by collectors because its glossy blue and yellow colors looked good. It was followed by a New Haven model in 1977; this locomotive was done in bright orange with white striping, a black roof and frame, and the famous McGinnis "NH" logo. Finally in 1978 a blue and white Conrail rectifier was produced. No other locomotives of this type have been made since. These locomotives, still reasonably priced, are excellent runners worth attention.

Despite these good electrics, collectors were really waiting for the "creme de la creme" of all the electrics, the famous Pennsylvania GG-1. The prototype, an amazing locomotive, had a service life of nearly 50 years, and even today its

Raymond Loewy-designed lines look fresh and contemporary. Three of these locomotives, including the original No. 4800, are preserved at the Railroad Museum of Pennsylvania in Strasburg, Pennsylvania. (For the full story of this locomotive, see Karl Zimmerman's book, *The Remarkable GG-1*.)

Finally, in 1977, patience had its reward. Fundimensions put out a tuscan 8753 GG-1 which had the original die-cast body, two motors, and, for the first time in a Fundimensions locomotive, Magnetraction. The job was good overall, but a few minor flaws needed correcting. Collectors claimed that the nylon gearing did not hold up very well in this locomotive, and the body casting was rougher than it should have been. In 1978 Fundimensions issued an all-black GG-1 in Penn Central markings. This locomotive was an operational and cosmetic improvement over its predecessor, but collectors did not like its paint scheme and the locomotive was a slow seller. In 1981 another GG-1 was produced, this time in gloss Brunswick green with gold striping. This time the quality was right; the striping was the best ever applied to a GG-1 and the finish was very attractive. For 1987 Lionel, Inc. produced a GG-1 in a new bronze color with bluish-black striping and a matching N5C caboose to power the mint cars previously produced and form a unique "money train." Like all the GG-1 locomotives except the Penn Central, this GG-1 has been a hot seller, despite the fact that its odd color scheme has produced howls of dismay from some traditionalists.

The 1977 and 1981 GG-1 locomotives produced by Fundimensions are highly prized and sought by collectors and operators alike. These locomotives will outpull any other locomotive (except perhaps the Fairbanks-Morse Trainmaster) because all twelve wheels are drivers. Even the Penn Central GG-1 is beginning to attract attention, though it is not as highly valued as the other two. In fact, a case could be made that the Penn Central locomotive is a good bargain, as GG-1s go.

THE ALCO RS-3s

Lionel, Inc. has scheduled an entirely new diesel locomotive for 1989 production within the traditional series. This is an excellent model of the highly popular Alco RS-3 diesel switcher. The real RS-3 locomotives saw extensive service on many American railroads. Lionel's model copies the prototype faithfully; it will feature Santa Fe and Soo Line markings and a twin can-motor chassis. Preliminary reaction to this engine has been very enthusiastic.

THE MOTORIZED UNITS

One of the most attractive areas of production in the postwar era was the little specialty units which buzzed around layouts of the mid-1950s. These motorized units were delightful to

watch in action, and they are eagerly sought after by collectors. It was only natural that collectors would get curious about any possible reissues of these items.

Perhaps because of the complicated gearing in some of these units, Fundimensions did not begin to revive them until 1982, when the company issued an attractive snowplow locomotive in Canadian National maroon and gray markings. Since then, each year has seen the emergence of more of these little locomotives. In 1983 a Vulcan 0-4-0 switcher engine was produced in blue and yellow Alaska markings. In 1984 the rotary snowplow came out in black and yellow Rio Grande markings. (This time, the "a" in "Rio Grande" was stamped correctly! Most of the postwar Rio Grande snowplows had the "a" backwards!) In the same year a Pennsylvania "fire car" was also produced, complete with its hose reels and rotating fireman, just like the original. A New York Central ballast tamper unit in yellow and black was produced in 1985. This interesting unit works by track trips; when it encounters one, it slows down, and miniature pile drivers "tamp" stone ballast between the rails and ties.

Then, in 1986, came the modern incarnation of Lionel's famous little Birney trolley of the mid-1950s in the form of a bright orange and blue 8690. Delayed in production for almost two years, this little trolley represented significant advances in operation over its ancestor. It used spur-gear drive instead of the old crosscut-gear system, so it ran much more quietly and efficiently. The new trolley's body casting was more detailed, with headlight lenses and open stepwork. Opaque celluloid figures filled all the windows, including a conductor figure at

Some of the more attractive Alco units. **Top shelf: 8268** and **8269** Texas & Pacific "Quicksilver Express," which came with three matching 2400- type passenger cars in 1982. **Middle shelf: 8552** and **8553** Southern Pacific AA units, sold as a set with matching B unit below. **Bottom shelf: 8563** Rock Island, from 1975 uncatalogued Sears set, **8554** Southern Pacific B unit.

Six U36B engines. Top shelf: 8470 Chessie from 1974 Grand National Set, the first U36B, 8564 Union Pacific. Middle shelf: 8571 Frisco, 8650 Burlington Northern. Bottom shelf: 8669 Illinois Central Gulf, available only in Illinois Central Gulf catalogued set in 1976, 8755 Santa Fe. Dummy units were made for all of these but the 8669 Illinois Central Gulf. The 8573 Union Pacific dummy unit had a horn and is extremely scarce.

Some U36B and U36C locomotives, early and late. Top shelf: Two 1776 Seaboard Bicentennial Specials. Left: Regular production as part of Bicentennial Spirit of '76 Set. Right: Special production for TCA as part of Bicentennial passenger set. Note frame lettering and TCA emblem on red diagonal stripe. Middle shelf: 7500 Lionel 75th Anniversary Special of 1975, 8050 Delaware & Hudson U36C of 1980. Bottom shelf: 8061 Chessie U36C from Royal Limited Set of 1980, 8155 Monon of 1981. (Note design change on this engine's nose; double headlight of previous models is eliminated.) A. Rudman, F. Stem, L. Caponi, and R. LaVoie Collections

More attractive "U-Boats." Top shelf: 8771 Great Northern U36B from Rocky Mountain Special catalogued set of 1977, 8773 Mickey Mouse U36B, which has become highly prized by Disney collectors as well as train collectors. Middle shelf: 18801 Santa Fe U36B with twin can motor drive system, 8857 Northern Pacific U36B. Bottom shelf: 8955 Southern U36B, 8960 Southern Pacific U36C, available with dummy unit only in Southern Pacific Limited Set of 1979, a set which sold out even before it was distributed. A. Rudman, F. Stem, L. Caponi, and R. LaVoie Collections.

the end windows. It runs so efficiently that sometimes the reversing slide rebounds too far and the trolley freezes in neutral when it hits a bumper. If it is allowed to run slowly at low voltage, this problem does not occur. Lionel did a fine job of improving the original design of the trolley, and it has sold very well. A two-tone green San Francisco version has been made since the Lionelville version.

A Santa Fe rotary snowplow in red oxide and yellow was scheduled for 1987 by Lionel, Inc., and another exciting revival is in the works — the Lionel handcar. The original Lionel handcar of the mid-1960s burned out very easily, but Lionel has redesigned the drive system for it this time around. Significantly, it is listed as part of the Traditional Series and it has a very reasonable price, so it should be a good seller if the design is right. A Santa Claus version is scheduled for 1988 production.

The diesels, electrics, and motorized units have been produced in great numbers and variety by Lionel. Most are easily affordable, colorful, and certainly varied enough to appeal to anyone's preferences. As on the real railroads, these locomotives are the mainstays of the Lionel line, no matter how attractive the steamers may have become.

This introduction analyzes the following diesel bodies: GM Yard Switcher, F-3 Unit, Alco, GP-7 and GP-9, U36B, and GP-20. It also discusses GP and U36B motors and diesel railing types.

DIESEL BODY TYPES

GP-7 and GP-9 Body Types

The difference between a Lionel GP-7 and a GP-9 is the addition of a snap-on plastic dynamic brake casting. The GP-7 and GP-9 bodies show a progression not unlike those of the F-3s, Alcos, and Yard Switchers. Fundimensions made changes in body design to solve decorating problems or to coordinate body design with other production changes. We have identified five basic bodies:

Body Type I: 8030, 8031
1. One piece inserted in the body to form two headlight lenses, two marker light lenses, and two numberboards with actual numbers.
2. Hinges on side door panels beneath the road name.
3. Builder's plate carries the LIONEL and MPC logo.
4. No indentations for stamped-steel handrails since wire handrails used.
5. Louvers on hatch panels beneath the numerals "8030".
6. Two steps from the cab to the frame.

Body Type II: 8250 Santa Fe, same as Type I, but:
1. No numbers on numberboards.
2. No hinges on side door panels near the road name.

Body Type III: Early 1976, 8576 Penn Central, same as II, but:
1. Builder's plate carries only the LIONEL name.
2. Indentations in the cab side (addition of Type IV railings), since stamped-steel handrails are added.

Body Type IV: Early 1978, 8866 Minneapolis and St. Louis, same as III, but:
1. No louvers (but numbers) on the hatch panel on the cab below the window.
2. One step only from the cab to the frame.

Body Type V: Later 1978, 8854 C. P. Rail, same as IV, but:
1. No indentations in the cab because Type IV railing used.

GP-20 Body Types

Type I: No indentations for handrails.
Type II: Indentations for handrails.

Alco Body Types

Type I
1. Open slot on front pilot for coupler.
2. Closed slot numberboard.
3. "LIONEL MPC" builder's plate at lower rear.

Type II
1. Open slot on front pilot for coupler.
2. Open slot numberboard.
3. "LIONEL MPC" builder's plate behind cab door.

Type III
1. Open slot on front pilot for coupler.
2. Closed slot numberboard.
3. No builder's plate.

Type IV
1. Closed slot on front pilot, no coupler.
2. Open slot numberboard.
3. "LIONEL MPC" builder's plate behind cab door.

Type V
1. Open slot on front pilot, no strut.
2. Open slot numberboard.
3. "LIONEL" only on builder's plate behind cab door.

Type VI
1. Closed slot on front pilot.
2. Open slot numberboard.
3. "LIONEL" only on builder's plate behind door.

U36B Body Types

Type I: No indentations for handrails.
Type II: Indentations for handrails.

GP and U36B Motor Types

Type I: 8010-127 has two circular pickups as found on the old-style Scout. The pickups did not bridge the switches so Fundimensions added a pickup to the dummy truck on its later production. This pickup was similar to the old Lionel GP-style pickup.

Type II: 8250-125 has two roller pickups which are similar to those found on MPC tenders and passenger cars. The rollers are attached to a shoe that slides under a brass spring plate on

Lionel keeps calling these switchers SW-1 models, but their correct designation is NW-2. **Top shelf:** 8057 Burlington in red colors, 8374 Burlington Northern with green colors and new drive system. **Middle shelf:** Scarce 8471 Pennsylvania, 8473 Coca-Cola (note early use of "Catch The Wave" color scheme) from uncatalogued Coke Set of 1974. **Bottom shelf:** 8485 U. S. Marines in camouflage colors, very scarce 8556 Chessie System. A. Rudman, F. Stem, L. Caponi, and R. LaVoie Collections.

8660 CP Rail and 8761 Grand Trunk NW-2 switchers. A. Rudman, F. Stem, L. Caponi, and R. LaVoie Collections.

the truck. Fundimensions also added a pickup to the dummy trucks on its initial motor run. All GPs and U36Bs have two operating couplers, stamped metal frames and plastic steps attached to both trucks, and powered units have three-position E-units. All GP-20s have LIONEL builder's plates, U36Bs do not have any. Early MPC, GP-7, and GP-9 production included a Lionel MPC builder's plate. On later production the MPC part of the logo was dropped.

Diesel Railing Types

Type I Stamped Metal Post: Made apparently from Lionel flatcar stakes with a handrail passing through the stakes, railing end holes in north and south cab sides, oversized but sturdy.

Type II Plastic Posts-Handrail Combination: Better scaled but fragile, railing end holes in north and south cab sides.

Type III Stamped Metal Railing: Riveted to frame, with large rivets for end railings, railing is turned into cab with indentations on east and west cab sides.

Type IV Metal Railing: Railing spot-welded to frame, but not connected to cab, indentations in cab filled in and railing simply lies along cab side. The change from Type III to IV apparently occurred in mid-1978 because the 8866 is a Type IV. End railings are an integral part of its frame and were formed with the frame and not separately as in Type III. (Note: Some copies of the 8866 were apparently made with Type III railings.)

Gd VG Exc Mt

484: See 8587.

530: See 8378.

634 SANTA FE: Circa 1970, NW-2 yard switcher, rerun of 1965-66 unit, chrome-plated plastic bell and radio antenna. These are leftover postwar cabs which were given Fundimensions trim pieces. Thus, this piece can be faked by

Some impressive six-drivered diesels. Top shelf: 8063 Seaboard SD-9 from 1980 Mid-Atlantic Set, 8071 Virginian SD-18. Middle shelf: 8151 Burlington SD-28 from Burlington Set of 1981, 8152 Canadian Pacific SD-24 from 1981 Maple Leaf Limited set. Bottom shelf: 8162 Ontario Northland SD-18 (sold with matching dummy unit with horn), 8266 Norfolk & Western SD-24 from Continental Limited Set of 1982. Differences in cab configurations determine the type numbers of these locomotives. A. Rudman, F. Stem, L. Caponi, and R. LaVoie Collections.

More of Lionel's newer diesels. Top shelf: 8380 Lionel Lines SD-28, for which many matching cars have since been issued, 8855 Milwaukee Road SD-18, Lionel's first six-drivered diesel from the 1978 Milwaukee Limited Set. Note difference in orange color of these engines. Middle shelf: 8872 Santa Fe SD-18, which was sold with matching dummy. Bottom shelf: 8962 Reading U36-B from Quaker City Limited Set of 1979. A. Rudman, F. Stem, L. Caponi, and R. LaVoie Collections.

adding trim pieces to a postwar 634 cab and mounting it on an early Fundimensions chassis. R. LaVoie comment.

	30	40	55	65

1203: See Special Production chapter.

1776 NORFOLK & WESTERN: 1976, powered GP-9, Type II plastic railings, painted red; white and blue body with flat gold lettering, white circle of thirteen stars on nose; black underframe, lights, nose decal, Type II motor, no pickup on dummy truck, no MPC logo. This is actually catalogued as 8559 but is listed here for your convenience.

(A) Glossy red paint. -- -- 100 125
(B) Flat red paint. -- -- 100 125

See also Factory Errors and Prototypes.

1776 SEABOARD COAST LINE: 1976, powered G. E. U36B, stamped metal railings, red, white, and blue body with blue lettering; black underframe, lights, nose decal, Type II motor, no pickup on dummy truck, no MPC logo. This locomotive was part of the Spirit of '76 Set, which included thirteen boxcars representing each of the original Thirteen Colonies and a 7600 Frisco N5C Caboose. Fundimensions had more ambitious plans to make boxcars for the remaining 37 states, but this was never carried out. The 7610 Virginia and the 7611 New York are the scarcest cars in the set. C. Lang and R. LaVoie comments.

(A) No lettering on frame. -- -- 85 100
(B) White "SEABOARD COAST LINE" on frame. -- -- 90 125
(C) Same as 1776 (B), but with medium white "SEABOARD COAST LINE" on frame. -- -- 85 125

1776 BANGOR AND AROOSTOOK: 1976, catalogued as 8665, powered GP-9, "Jeremiah O'Brien", Type III railing; red, white, and blue with red, white, and blue lettering, catalogued and sold with a 9176 Caboose; "8665" not on engine, silver truck side frames, lights, nose decal, no MPC logo, "LIONEL" builder's plate, Type III body. -- -- 100 125

1976 SEABOARD COAST LINE: See Special Production chapter.

1983 NABISCO BRANDS: 1983, NW-2 switcher, teal blue-painted gray plastic cab, white panel with "1983" in red, "NABISCO / BRANDS / BISCUIT GROUP" in black, white square with black line and red triangle on side towards front, black frame and rails, lighted, two-position reverse, metal power truck frames and plastic dummy truck frames, sliding shoe contacts. Came as part of set with six cars as a promotional item used in-house by Nabisco. We also have a report that this set is not factory production, but was altered using standard production pieces. Reader comments invited. S. Lindsey Collection. **NRS**

4935 PENNSYLVANIA: See 8150.

7500 LIONEL 75th ANNIVERSARY: 1975-76, powered G. E. U36B diesel, part of Set 1505; red, silver, and black body, black frame, lights, "7500" on box. The 75th Anniversary set included 7501, 7505, and 7506 Boxcars, 7502, 7503, and 7507 Refrigerator Cars, a 7504 Covered Hopper, and a 7508 N5C Caboose. It was a slow seller at its issuance and is still available new at a relatively low price, which qualifies the set as a "sleeper" candidate for collectors. R. LaVoie comment.

-- -- 80 100

8010 A.T. & S.F.: 1970, NW-2 Yard Switcher, blue with yellow lettering.

-- -- 35 50

8020 SANTA FE: 1970-76, powered Alco FA-2 A unit, red and silver body, lights, comes with 8021 or 8020 Dummy.

(A) Powered 8020, Type I body. 20 30 40 95
(B) 1970-71, SANTA FE, dummy Alco FA-2 A unit, red and silver body. -- -- 30 75

8010 ATSF.

(C) Blue and silver body. Reportedly part of department store special and therefore scarcer than red version. Reader comments requested.

        -- -- **50 100**

8021 SANTA FE: 1971-72, 1974-76, dummy Alco FA-2 B unit; red and silver body, "SANTA FE" under vents.

        -- -- **40 55**

8022 SANTA FE: 1971, uncatalogued Alco FA-2, AA units; blue body shell with yellow striping and lettering; all except (D) below have frosted window inserts; Santa Fe nose decal in yellow; all examples have the "8" in the number "8022" stamped backwards. Made for J. C. Penney uncatalogued set with several different body types and chassis; headlight.

(A) Bright blue body, red numberboard inserts, no front coupler (end closed off), with nose decal. "Triple T" Collection.

        -- -- **70 95**

(B) Darker blue body, numberboard inserts closed off, die-cast dummy front coupler, without nose decal. "Triple T" Collection.

        -- **65 125 185**

(C) Powered and dummy A unit set, numbered "8022", only fifty sets, made for J. C. Penney's Ann Arbor, Michigan store. P. Catalano observation. Power unit has dark blue body, front coupler, red numberboards and nose decal. Dummy unit has gray plastic body painted blue, front coupler, red numberboards and nose decal. C. O'Dell Collection.

        -- **350 400**

(D) Same as (B), but black plastic cabs painted dark flat navy blue, no window or headlight inserts, no ornamental horns, no Santa Fe decal on nose. Samples observed came mounted on postwar Alco chassis with horn, headlight, and two-axle Magnetraction; the two chassis also have dummy metal couplers front and rear. The chassis may or may not have been original with these cabs; could be identical to (B) above. G. Halverson Collection.

        -- **65 125 185**

8023 CANADIAN NATIONAL: 1970, Alco A unit, green body, yellow lettering and stripes, two-position reverse, lighted. Made for Canadian distribution.

        20 30 35 40

Big "bruisers," the Fairbanks-Morse twin-motored giants. Top shelf: 8056 Chicago & North Western. Second shelf: 8157 Santa Fe, which introduced Lionel's new electronic diesel horn. Third shelf: 8687 Jersey Central "Miss Liberty" Statue of Liberty Centennial commemorative. Bottom shelf: The "Black Widow" -- 8951 Southern Pacific. Missing from this assemblage is the first Fairbanks-Morse, the 8950 Virginian of 1979. A. Rudman, F. Stem, L. Caponi, and R. LaVoie Collections.

Modern era Budd diesel railcars. Top shelf: 8766 Baltimore & Ohio powered baggage car, 8767 Baltimore & Ohio dummy passenger car. Middle shelf: 8768 Baltimore & Ohio dummy passenger car, 8868 Amtrak powered baggage car. Bottom shelf: 8869 and 8870 Amtrak dummy passenger cars. An 8764 B & O powered passenger car, an 8765 B & O dummy baggage car and an 8871 Amtrak dummy baggage car were also made to accompany these cars. A. Rudman, F. Stem, L. Caponi, and R. LaVoie Collections.

Top: 0000 Canadian National prototype. Bottom: 8025 Canadian National production model.

8025 CANADIAN NATIONAL: 1971, Alco FA-2 AA units, one powered, other dummy, black body, orange nose, white striping, both with same number, uncataloged, Parker Brothers distribution in Canada, imported by U. S. dealers. Price for both units. -- **80 125 150**

8030 ILLINOIS CENTRAL: 1970-71, powered GP-9, white and orange body with black lettering; one pickup on power truck, pickup on dummy truck, black frame, lights; Type I motor, "LIONEL / MPC" builder's plate, Type I body, loop pickup may or may not supplement pickup on dummy truck. Service Stations added leftover Hillside pickups to original hollow-roller pickups at Lionel's request. Upon completion of paperwork, Lionel replaced the pickup assembly and allowed the Service Station a $1.00 credit. The first few hundred examples produced with Type I railings were painted too lightly, allowing translucence on the locomotive ends which made them glow. C. Weber comments.

(A) Lighter orange, Type I motor, Type I railing, nose decal, loop.
 -- **35 55 65**

(B) Darker orange, Type II railing, no nose decal, Type II motor.
 -- **35 55 65**

(C) Same as (B), but with nose decal and extra set of pickups. C. Rohlfing Collection. -- **35 55 65**

(D) I T T Special Limited Edition Railway Set for Marine Expo 9 at Washington, D. C., Fall 1975, registered as "ISBN 0-912276-13-4" and "LC 74- 29700" with Library of Congress, "I T T Cable-Hydrospace" glossy black sticker with gold letters placed over "ILLINOIS CENTRAL" on locomotive side, no end decal. Twenty-five sets, each with an 8030 Engine, 8254 Dummy with the same sticker, three bright blue over-painted 9113 N&W Hoppers with clear central decals with white-lettered "cable I T T car", one hopper with an orange cover, 9160 Caboose with glossy black sticker with gold letters, two-engine four-car set. P. Catalano observation. May be post-factory production. -- -- -- **400**
See also Factory Errors and Prototypes.

8031 CANADIAN NATIONAL: 1970-71, powered GP-7; black and orange body, white lettering, lights, no nose decal, Type I motor, pickup on dummy, "Lionel / MPC" builder's plate, Type II body.

(A) Type I railing, Canadian edition. -- **50 65 125**

(B) Type II railing. -- **50 65 125**

(C) Same as (B), but slightly smaller and deeper-stamped "8031" on cab, metal railing ends behind cab. Instead of regular Type II railings, a one-piece black plastic insert is snapped into place along the cab side. The side railing is, therefore, black plastic instead of metal. Reader comments invited. Pictured with this railing in the 1971 Canadian catalogue. R. LaVoie observation.
 -- **50 65 125**

8050 DELAWARE & HUDSON: 1980, powered U36C, gray body, blue top, yellow striping and lettering, six-wheel trucks, matching 8051 Dummy available separately; 8050 only. -- -- **100 150**
See also Factory Errors and Prototypes.

8051 DELAWARE & HUDSON: 1980, dummy U36C, matches 8050.
 -- -- **50 75**

The first of Lionel's big, scale SD-40 diesels. Top shelf: 8265 Santa Fe. Middle shelf: 8376 Union Pacific. Both of these had single motors. Bottom shelf: The dual-motored 8458 Erie-Lackawanna. A. Rudman, F. Stem, L. Caponi, and R. LaVoie Collections.

Two more SD-40 diesels. Top shelf: 18200 Conrail, which came in the Conrail Limited Set with Standard O cars. Bottom shelf: 8585 Burlington Northern, which came with a unit train of Standard O boxcars. Both these engines have dual motors. A. Rudman, F. Stem, L. Caponi, and R. LaVoie Collections.

Three of the modern era's magnificent twin-motored GG-1 electrics. Top shelf: 18300 Pennsylvania from 1987 in bronze, made as a match for the mint car production. Middle shelf: 8753 Pennsylvania in tuscan from 1977, the first of the modern GG-1s. Bottom shelf: 8850 Penn Central model in black from 1978. A. Rudman, F. Stem, L. Caponi, and R. LaVoie Collections.

8054 C & S BURLINGTON: 1980, dual-motored F-3 A unit, metallic silver body with black and red markings, known as Texas Zephyr (C & S stands for Colorado and Southern, a group of railroads acquired by Burlington in 1908 and run as a division), matching dummy A unit (8055) and B unit (8062) available, priced with 8055 Dummy A unit.   -- -- 275 300

8055 C & S BURLINGTON: 1980, dummy F-3 A unit, illuminated; matches 8054. See previous entry for price.

8056 CHICAGO & NORTH WESTERN: 1980, dual-motored FM Trainmaster, Magnetraction; yellow and Brunswick green body, yellow safety striping, six-wheel trucks.   -- -- 275 300

8057 BURLINGTON: 1980, NW-2 yard switcher, red and gray, lettered "Way of the Zephyrs", three-position reverse unit, disc-operating couplers.
                      -- -- 65 150

8059 PENNSYLVANIA: 1980, F-3 B unit, dummy, Brunswick green, matches 8952 and 8953 F-3 A Units, clear plastic portholes. Unit comes with heat-stamped striping in Joe Grzyboski's Collection.   -- -- 200 295

8060 PENNSYLVANIA: 1980, F-3 B unit, dummy, tuscan; matches 8970 and 8971 F-3 A Units, clear plastic portholes.   -- -- 175 275

8061 WESTERN MARYLAND: 1980, powered U36C, yellow and orange body with blue roof; dark blue lettering, bright orange-painted frame; three-position reverse unit, silver-painted six-wheel trucks; from 1070 Royal Limited Set.
                      -- -- 100 125

8062 BURLINGTON: 1980, F-3 B unit, dummy; matches 8054 and 8055 F-3 A Units, clear plastic portholes.   -- -- -- 150

8063 SEABOARD: 1980, powered SD-9, very dark Brunswick green (almost black) body with yellow band with red trim and yellow frame, six-wheel trucks with blind center wheels and rubber tires on the three wheels on geared side, three-position reverse, disc-operating couplers with small tabs, heavy stamped-steel railing. Part of Mid-Atlantic Set of 1980.   -- -- 75 90

8064 FLORIDA EAST COAST: 1980, powered GP-9; red and yellow; catalogued with black trucks but made with silver trucks, three-position reverse unit.   -- -- 65 100

8065 FLORIDA EAST COAST: 1980, dummy GP-9; matches 8064.
                      -- -- 35 60

8066 TOLEDO, PEORIA & WESTERN: 1980, powered GP-20, orange and white body, white-painted frame and railings; three-position reverse unit,

The three ungainly but impressive EL-C rectifier electrics produced by Lionel to date. Top shelf: 8659 Virginian. Middle shelf: 8754 New Haven. Bottom shelf: 8859 Conrail. A. Rudman, F. Stem, L. Caponi, and R. LaVoie Collections.

catalogued with dynamic brake unit on roof, but made without brake unit; came with 1072 Cross Country Express Set. Catalogue shows red color, but not produced that way. C. Lang, H. Kaim, G. Halverson, and C. Rohlfing comments.
(A) Orange body with white lettering, regular production run.

-- -- 100 125

(B) Burnt orange with white lettering. G. Halverson Collection.

-- -- 125 150

See also Factory Errors and Prototypes.

8067 TEXAS AND PACIFIC: 1980, powered Alco FA-2 unit, two-position reverse unit, blue and white; illustrated as part of 1051 Texas & Pacific Diesel Set. **Not Manufactured**

8068 THE ROCK: 1980, GP-20, see Special Production chapter.

8071 VIRGINIAN: 1980, powered SD-18, blue and yellow; also see 8072, six-wheel trucks, silver truck sides. -- -- 100 150

8072 VIRGINIAN: 1980, dummy SD-18, matches 8071 Engine.

-- -- 60 75

8111 D T & I: 1971-74, NW-2 yard switcher, illuminated headlight, hand reverse. Orange with black lettering. Came with or without silver radio wheel. C. Rohlfing comment.

(A) Two green marker lights. -- 20 35 60
(B) Two red marker lights. -- 20 35 60

8150 PENNSYLVANIA: 1981, dual-powered GG-1 electric, green-painted die-cast body with five gold stripes; Magnetraction, three-position reverse unit.

-- 475 525 575

8111 DT&I.

Top shelf: Lenny Dean's pride and joy, the resurrected 8690 Lionelville Trolley with an improved drive system. Second shelf: Two more resurrected motorized units in bright colors, the 8264 Canadian Pacific Snowplow and the 8368 Alaska Switcher. Third shelf: The 8379 Pennsylvania Fire Car and the 18400 Santa Fe Rotary Snowplow. Bottom shelf: The 8459 Rio Grande Rotary Snowplow (this time with the *a* in "Grande" printed correctly!) and the 8578 New York Central Ballast Tamper, a really neat operating unit. A. Rudman, F. Stem, L. Caponi, and R. LaVoie Collections.

8151 BURLINGTON: 1981, powered SD-28, red with gray top, white nose stripes; white frame, numbers, and letters, six-wheel trucks; from 1160 Great Lakes Limited Set.   -- -- **115 150**

8152 CANADIAN PACIFIC: 1981, powered SD-24 flat top diesel, maroon and gray, with two yellow side stripes, three horizontal nose stripes; white frame, yellow numbers, maroon "Canadian Pacific" in script on gray background; horn, six-wheel trucks; from 1158 Maple Leaf Set.   -- -- **125 180**

8153 READING: 1981, powered NW-2 yard switcher, dark green front and top; black frame, yellow sides, dark green numbers and logo; two-position reverse; from 1154 Reading Yard King Set.   -- -- **40 90**

8154 ALASKA: 1981-82, powered, NW-2 yard switcher, dynamic air brake, same paint scheme as Lionel 614. Also offered by Montgomery Ward in 1982 with matching 6441 Bay Window Caboose in display case for $149.99.
                                             -- -- **100 125**

8155 MONON: 1981-82, powered U36B, gold sides and ends with dark blue roof and dark blue band running along cab bottom; also see 8156. Note that the nose piece of this and the more recent U36 locomotives has been modified to eliminate the headlights.   -- -- **60 75**

8156 MONON: 1981-82, dummy U36B, matches 8155.   -- -- **40 50**

8157 SANTA FE: 1981, dual-powered FM Trainmaster, blue with yellow trim, numbers, and letters, electronic horn.   -- -- **350 395**

8158 DULUTH MISSABE: 1981-82, powered GP-35, maroon with yellow middle side band, white numbers and letters; also see 8159.   -- -- **60 140**

8159 DULUTH MISSABE: 1981-82, dummy GP-35; matches 8158.
                                             -- -- **40 50**

8160 BURGER KING: 1981-82, powered GP-20, yellow body with red top, frame, numbers, and letters; from Favorite Foods Freight, available only as separate sale item.   -- -- **85 100**

8161 L. A. S. E. R.: 1981-82, gas turbine, bright chrome, blue lettering; part of 1150 L. A. S. E. R. Train Set, a return to a late 1950s-type Lionel space set, DC powered.   -- -- 15 50

8162 ONTARIO NORTHLAND: 1981, powered SD-18, part of the "Fall Release Items," blue with yellow trim and lettering; also see 8163.
-- -- 100 125

8163 ONTARIO NORTHLAND: 1981, dummy SD-18; also see 8162.
-- -- 60 75

8164 PENNSYLVANIA: 1981, F-3 B unit, green body, with horn. Distributors were required to purchase nearly $800 of goods to acquire one. Matches 8952-53 AA pair. Very difficult to find.   -- -- 275 325

8182 NIBCO: 1982, NW-2 switcher, part of special promotional Set 1264 made by Fundimensions for Nibco Plumbing Products; 2,000 made; offered as a premium for plumbers with purchase of faucet sets; set included regular production green 9033 Penn Central short Hopper and blue 9035 Conrail O27-type Boxcar; also had special unlighted 6482 NIBCO SP-type Caboose. There were also two custom billboards, a 50-watt transformer, O27 track, and a manumatic uncoupler with the set. The locomotive has a white body with blue-green "NIBCO" logo and number on the cab; green and blue ribbon runs the length of the cab; above it is blue lettering: "QUALITY PIPING PRODUCTS". Price for locomotive only.   -- -- 125 150

8200 CONRAIL: SD-40, see 18200.

8250 SANTA FE: 1972-75, powered GP-9, Type II railing, black and yellow body with yellow lettering; black underframe, nose decal, Type II motor, pickup on dummy truck, "LIONEL / MPC" builder's plate, Type II body.
-- 40 60 100

8252 DELAWARE & HUDSON: 1972, powered Alco FA-2 unit, dark blue and silver body, two-position E-unit, Type IV body, "D & H" decal on side and nose, blank numberboards, no front coupler.   -- -- 40 100
See also Factory Errors and Prototypes.

8253 DELAWARE & HUDSON: 1972, dummy Alco FA-2 A unit; matches 8252.
(A) Silver with side decal.   -- -- 20 40
(B) Silver without side decal.   -- -- 20 40
See also Factory Errors and Prototypes.

8254 ILLINOIS CENTRAL: 1972, dummy GP-9, Type II railings, black lettering, orange plastic body with white stripe; no lights, nose decal, LIONEL / MPC builder's plate, black frame.   -- -- 30 40

8255 SANTA FE: 1972, dummy GP-9; matches 8250, but not lighted.
-- -- 30 40

8258 CANADIAN NATIONAL: 1972, dummy GP-7, Type II railings, black and orange body with white lettering; no lights, no nose decal, LIONEL / MPC builder's plate.   -- -- 30 40

8260 SOUTHERN PACIFIC: 1982, dual-motored F-3 A unit in distinctive red, orange, white, and black "Daylight" paint scheme; three-position reverse unit, one-axle Magnetraction, one operating coupler on front, fixed coupler on rear, illuminated numberboards, portholes; part of Spring Collector Series as a limited edition, comes with matching dummy 8262. Price for both units.
-- -- 375 575
Six matching passenger cars available as separate sales only.

8261 SOUTHERN PACIFIC: 1982, dummy F-3 B unit; matches 8260. Very hard to obtain the B unit.   -- -- 400 900

8262: See 8260.

8263 SANTA FE: 1982, powered GP-7, blue and yellow; operating couplers, electronic reverse unit, split-field can motor mounted on power truck, electronic three-position reversing unit, sliding shoe pickups.   -- -- 35 100

8264 CANADIAN PACIFIC: 1982, Vulcan 2-4-2 switcher snowplow; gray body, maroon snowplow, frame, and trim; yellow lettering, non-operating headlight, gold ornamental bell; die-cast chassis, three-position reversing switch, operating die-cast coupler on rear. This unit often requires servicing before use because grease coagulates in the gear sump and the brushes arc. Remedy: flush out grease and sparingly lubricate with Lubriplate. Gears are noisy, as were original mid-1950s Lionel units. Body should be handled carefully because window struts are easily broken. R. Sigurdson comment.   -- -- 110 135

8265 SANTA FE: 1982, powered SD-40, new cab design, blue and yellow painted body; working headlight and lighted numberboards; operating couplers at both ends, Type C six-wheel trucks, single motor with single-wound motor field for mechanical E-unit, Magnetraction, electronic diesel horn; motor housing has integral locator tab; measured drawbar pull of 10 ounces. R. Sigurdson, D. Johns, and C. Rohlfing comments.   -- -- 275 395

8266 NORFOLK AND WESTERN: 1982, SD-24, maroon body with yellow trim; three-position reverse unit, die-cast six-wheel trucks, operating couplers, illuminated numberboards, electronic diesel horn; part of 1260 Continental Limited Set issued in Spring Collector Series.   -- -- 135 160

8268 TEXAS AND PACIFIC: 1982, Quicksilver Express Set, part of Set 1253 in 1983. Alco body, closed front end with red numberboards, dark blue with broad silver stripe and lettering, light blue eagle and blue and silver T & P logo on front; lighted, AC/DC can motor, solid state three-position reversing switch. To solve traction problems in the 1982 production, Lionel made available two iron weights with a piece of foam with double-sided adhesive for Service Station installation. The production of 1983 includes these weights. The set has sold exceptionally well. Price for powered A unit only.   -- -- 70 85

8269 TEXAS AND PACIFIC: 1982-83, dummy unit, matches 8268.
-- -- 30 40

8272 PENNSYLVANIA: 1982, EP-5 "double-end" electric, special edition made for J. C. Penney; tuscan body, gold-painted ends and heat dissipater box atop engine, broad gold striping across sides, tuscan lettering and numbering within side striping; single motor, no Magnetraction. Full price includes display board with (apparently) Gargraves piece of track and plastic display case. C. Darasko and G. Kline Collections.   -- -- 225 250

8300 PENNSYLVANIA: GG-1, see 18300.

8350 U. S. STEEL: 1974-75, gas turbine, 0-4-0, maroon plastic body with silver lettering; DC motor, forward and reverse by polarity, reverse on power packs, motor will burn out if run on AC.   -- -- 15 30

8351 SANTA FE: 1973-74, powered Alco, FA-2 A unit, blue and silver body; Sears set.   -- -- 35 75

8352 SANTA FE: 1973-75, powered GP-20, plastic railings, dark blue and yellow body with yellow lettering; black underframe, Santa Fe cross logo decal on nose (some pieces issued without it), Type II motor.   -- 40 60 100

8353 GRAND TRUNK: 1974-75, powered GP-7, Type II railings, gray plastic body painted blue and orange, white lettering; lights, Type II motor, LIONEL / MPC builder's plate, Type II body.   -- 40 60 100

8354 ERIE: 1973-75, NW-2 yard switcher, black plastic body, heat-stamped gold lettering, lights.
(A) Type III body.   -- -- 75 100
(B) Type IV body.   -- -- 75 100

8355 SANTA FE: 1973-75, dummy GP-20; matches 8352, pickup on one truck.
(A) With electronic diesel horn.   -- -- 60 80
(B) Without horn. Some come in boxes stating that the unit inside has the horn; buyers should check before purchase. Same comment applies to 8367 Long Island GP-20 Dummy Units.   -- -- 30 40

8356 GRAND TRUNK: 1974-75, dummy GP-7; matches 8353, no lights.
-- -- 30 40

8357 PENNSYLVANIA: 1973-75, powered GP-9; Type II railings, gray plastic body painted dark green, gold lettering; lights, no nose decal, Type II motor, black frame, LIONEL / MPC builder's plate, Type II body, 9,000 made.
-- -- 125 145

8350 U.S. Steel.

8358 PENNSYLVANIA: 1973-75, dummy GP-9, matches 8357, no lights, a few units are known to have been made with horns.
(A) No horn. -- -- **35 50**
(B) With factory-installed horn. -- -- **60 85**

8359 CHESSIE: 1973, powered GP-7, Type II railings, special gold paint for GM's 50th anniversary with blue lettering, reportedly 9,000 made. "8359" not on locomotive, lights, nose lettering, Type II motor, black frame, LIONEL/MPC builder's plate, Type II body; all-blue "B & O" and "GM 50" lettering, painted nose. W. Mitchell Collection. -- -- **100 150**
See also Factory Errors and Prototypes.

8360 LONG ISLAND: 1973-74, powered GP-20, Type II railings, charcoal gray-painted body with silver lettering; no nose decal, lights, LIONEL/MPC builder's plate, Type II body. Shown in advance catalogue as light gray with darker roof, but not made that way.
(A) Black frame. -- **35 60 75**
(B) Black frame with painted red stripe. Confirmation requested; may not have been produced this way. -- **45 75 90**

8361 WESTERN PACIFIC: 1973-74, powered Alco, FA-2, A unit, silver and orange body; see 8362 for matching B unit, lights. -- -- **40 75**

8362 WESTERN PACIFIC: 1973-74, dummy Alco, FA-2B unit; matches 8361. -- -- **25 50**

8363 BALTIMORE & OHIO: 1973-75, powered F-3 A unit, dark blue plastic body painted light blue with white and gray top, yellow lettering on black stripe; Type I body, lights. See next entry for matching dummy A unit. -- **100 140 250**

8364 BALTIMORE & OHIO: 1973-75, dummy F-3 A unit; matches 8363. -- **60 75 90**

8365 CANADIAN PACIFIC: 1973, powered F-3 A unit, Type I body, reportedly only 2,500 manufactured, uncatalogued, 1973 Service Station Special; for matching dummy A unit see 8366.
(A) Gray plastic body painted brown and gray. -- -- **250 300**
(B) Blue plastic body painted brown and gray. -- -- **250 300**

8366 CANADIAN PACIFIC: 1973, dummy A unit.
(A) Matches 8365(A). -- -- **125 150**
(B) Matches 8365(B). -- -- **125 150**

8367 LONG ISLAND: 1973, dummy GP-20; matches 8360, electronic diesel horn. Sound of this horn is extremely good; horn loudspeaker faces upwards in cab where motor usually goes, and the result is a realistic "muffled" diesel horn sound. No lights, but unit easy to convert to lighted dummy. R. LaVoie comments.
(A) Plain frame. -- -- **60 75**
(B) Red stripe on frame. Confirmation requested; may not have been made this way. -- -- **70 80**
(C) Same as (A), but no electronic diesel horn. Some came in boxes stating that the horn was included; purchasers should check before buying. -- -- **30 40**

8368 ALASKA RAILROAD: 1983, 2-4-2, motorized unit, yellow and blue with blue lettering "ALASKA RAILROAD 8368" and Eskimo logo; silver-finished bell, operating headlight, operating couplers, die-cast frame, three-position E unit; came in Type V orange and blue box. This unit often requires servicing before operation because grease coagulates in the gear sump and the brushes arc. Flush out grease and lubricate sparingly with Lubriplate. Gears are noisy, as were those on the motorized units of the 1950s. This unit intended to pull only two or three cars. The cab should be handled carefully because the window struts are easily broken. R. Sigurdson comment. -- -- **100 125**

8369 ERIE-LACKAWANNA: 1983, powered GP-20, dual DC motors, operates on AC or DC, operating headlight, electronic three-position reverse, one operating coupler, only offered for separate sale in Traditional Series catalogue; shown in catalogue as blue and tuscan engine, but made in gray and tuscan Erie-Lackawanna colors. Lionel also made a matching 6425 Caboose. Surprisingly good runner with a medium-sized train; the AC-DC can motors used on this unit operate on much lower voltage than older motor types. The twin-motored locomotives with this motor are better than their single-motored counterparts because good pickup rollers are used rather than sliding shoes. The interior of this locomotive has a large weight to help traction. Plastic truck frames and couplers. R. LaVoie Collection. -- -- **70 100**

8354 Erie.

8370 NEW YORK CENTRAL: 1983, powered F-3A unit, dual motors with two-axle Magnetraction, three-position reverse unit; headlight, illuminated numberboards, portholes, operating coupler at front end. Note matching 8371 and 8372 and passenger cars. In 1948-49 Lionel offered a N. Y. C. F-3 as 2333. -- -- **300 350**

8371 NEW YORK CENTRAL: 1983, dummy F-3B unit; matches 8370 and 8372. Electronic diesel horn, portholes, not illuminated, dummy couplers. -- -- **100 125**

8372 NEW YORK CENTRAL: 1983, dummy F-3A unit, headlight, illuminated numberboards, portholes, operating coupler at cab end; matches 8370 and 8372. -- -- **85 100**

8374 BURLINGTON NORTHERN: 1983, DC-powered NW-2 yard switcher, rectifier for AC or DC operation; green and black plastic body, white lettering and logo, black-enameled frame, two red indicator lights and operating headlight; two disc operating couplers, three-position electronic reversing unit; only offered for separate sale in Traditional Series Catalogue. Lionel also made a matching 6427 Transfer Caboose. -- -- **45 95**

8375 CHICAGO & NORTHWESTERN: 1983, DC-powered GP-7, dual motors with rectifier for AC or DC operation, headlight, operating couplers, electronic reverse unit; yellow and green body; part of 1354 Northern Freight Flyer Set. See 8369 entry for operating comments. -- **60 80 100**

8376 UNION PACIFIC: 1983, powered SD-40, Magnetraction, six-wheel die-cast metal trucks, headlight, electronic diesel horn, three-position reverse unit, operating couplers at both ends; yellow and gray body with red stripe, green hood top. Engine has a single motor with a double-wound field for the electronic E-unit. It has a drawbar pull of 10 ounces (this may vary between locomotives). The engine requires O Gauge track and will not pass through O27 Gauge switches. The motor body housing has a separate stamped metal locator tab mounted in it. Part of a special limited edition set, 1361 Gold Coast Limited, with 9290 Barrel Car, 9888 Reefer, 9468 Boxcar, 6114 Hopper, 6357 Tank, and 6904 Caboose. R. Sigurdson and D. Johns comments. Price for locomotive only. -- -- **325 375**

8377 U S: 1983, switcher, 0-4-0, olive drab, engine does not have applied lettering as shown in the Traditional Series Catalogue. Lionel supplied a decal sheet for the operator. This locomotive is part of the low price introductory 1355 Commando Assault Train Set with 6561 Flatcar with cruise missile, 6562 Flatcar with crates, 6564 Flatcar with tanks, 6435 Caboose, playmat, figures, and supply truck kit. Set price $50. -- -- **20 50**

8378 WABASH: 1983, Fairbanks-Morse Trainmaster, dual motors, Magnetraction. Special production for J. C. Penney Christmas special, not listed in Lionel catalogue. "8378" does not appear on body; "530" appears on body near cab. Deep blue body, gray and white striping, Wabash flag logo on cab below window. These "Bluebird" markings are quite similar to the 2337 and 2339 Geeps made by Lionel in the 1950s, except that the blue color is darker. The carton is marked "8378-203"; it contained the engine box and a boxed display case marked "GLASS". Despite this marking, the case is plastic; it has an oak base with a piece of Gargraves Phantom track fastened to it. Two plastic bumpers are also supplied. An instruction sheet marked "LIONEL WABASH BLUEBIRD, 09-8378-250" came with the box, and a second sheet found with regular production units, 70-8157-250, was also included. A short run of about 800 was made in Mount Clemens just before the factory moved to Mexico. Thereafter, reports about production conflict. Some say that there was no more production. Others say that Mexican production did occur and can be distinguished from Mount Clemens production by an aluminized paper sticker attached to the underside of the engine which has "CPG" and "Made In Mexico" information, whereas the pieces made in Mt. Clemens have "MADE IN U. S. A." on their plates. Reportedly, there are slight color differences in the Mexican locomotive. In addition, the Wabash flags are installed at an angle, and the finish is not as sharp. The Mount Clemens pieces were made from September to December 1983, and when it was discovered that there were substantial back orders, Mexican production began in April 1984. Back orders received the Mexican-made pieces. The total production run was supposed to be about 5,000, but it is likely that far fewer were actually made. D. Johns, P. Catalano, R. Shanfeld, and R. LaVoie comments; G. Kline, N. Banis, S. Goodman, and R. Darasko Collections.

(A) Mount Clemens production.   -- -- 750 850
(B) Mexican production.   -- -- 700 800

8379 PENNSYLVANIA: 1983, motorized fire-fighting car, tuscan body with black and white bumpers and black wheels, white fire hose with gold nozzle, gray hose, reel, and pump, black clad fireman with flesh-colored hands and face, yellow outriggers. Highly detailed body, gold plastic bell, illuminated red dome light atop cab which blinks after warm-up; bump reverse; gold "PENNSYLVANIA" PRR Keystone and "8379" on side of body; number is divided in center by Keystone. Originally shown with "6521" number in Fall Collector Center brochure. After some use, there is a tendency for the bumper frame to loosen and slide to the neutral position. This can be alleviated by increasing the reversing slide contact spring tension. The reversing slide adjustment can also be made by bending the two tabs on the slide outward to increase friction between the shoe assembly and the car frame. The operating instructions state that the unit should not be left in the neutral position for more than five minutes. The reason for this is that the contact spring may bridge the gap between the contact rivets, which can cause the two fields to buck each other and burn out. The earliest instruction sheets did not mention this potential problem. In some cases, this unit needed adjustment prior to initial operation. R. Sigurdson, C. Rohlfing, and D. Johns comments.   -- -- 110 135

8380 LIONEL LINES: 1983, powered SD-28, dark blue upper body, upper cab and nose top, black frame, red, white, and blue Lionel logo on cab side and nose; six-wheel trucks, Type IV handrails; blue number is below the logo on the cab, blue "LIONEL LINES" in modern sans-serif lettering below color division, lighted cab, chromed plastic five-horn unit atop cab, squared-off cab roof; from Fall Collector Center.

(A) Medium orange lower body and nose.   -- -- 125 250
(B) Darker orange lower body and nose. R. Lord comment. -- -- 125 250

8452 ERIE: 1974, powered Alco FA-2 A unit.
(A) Black plastic body painted green with yellow lettering, lights; see next entry for B unit.   -- 25 35 75
(B) Same as (A), but closed pilot, red numberboards and no front decal. G. Halverson Collection.   **NRS**

8453 ERIE: 1974, dummy Alco FA-2 B unit; matches 8452 A unit (in previous entry).   -- 20 25 50

8454 RIO GRANDE: 1974-75, powered GP-7, Type II railings, black body with orange lettering, dull yellow hash marks, black frame, lights, Type II motor, LIONEL / MPC builder's plate, Type II body.   -- 40 60 100

8455 RIO GRANDE: 1974-75, dummy GP-7; matches 8454, no lights.
                                                    -- -- 30 40

8456 NORFOLK SOUTHERN: 1974, GP-7, unpainted gray body, black frame, red and white "N S" logo, lights.   40 50 60 75

8458 ERIE-LACKAWANNA: 1984, SD-40, gray cab, maroon and yellow striping, yellow lettering, yellow-painted frame; two motors, electronic diesel horn, Magnetraction, lights at both ends, die-cast six-wheel trucks; part of Erie-Lackawanna Limited Collector Set.   -- -- 300 350

8459 RIO GRANDE: 1984, rotary snowplow, black cab, yellow cab sides with black "Rio Grande" script and number (this time the "a" in "Grande" has been inserted correctly, rather than backwards as in the Lionel unit of the 1950s). Yellow handrails and plow housing, black plow fan with yellow markings, 2-4-2 Vulcan with three-position reversing switch, one operating die-cast coupler on rear, no headlight but lens is present, gold ornamental bell. This unit runs well upon delivery, and its gears are quieter than the previous 8264, 8368, and 8379. The window struts are less likely to break because they are made with a double

section. This engine intended to pull only two or three cars. Packed in Type V collector box, Mt. Clemens production. R. Sigurdson and R. LaVoie comments.
                                                    -- -- 100 125

8460 M K T: 1973-75, NW-2 yard switcher, gray plastic body painted red, white lettering; manual forward and reverse, Type IV body, dummy coupler.
                                                    -- -- 35 75

See also Factory Errors and Prototypes.

8463 CHESSIE: 1974, powered GP-20, Type II railings, blue and yellow body with blue lettering and vermilion stripe; limited edition of 10,000, lights, black frame, nose decal, Type II motor, "LIONEL" logo.   -- -- 80 125

8464 RIO GRANDE: 1974, powered F-3 A unit, yellow body with black lettering, silver roof, solid portholes, lights; only 3,000 manufactured, uncatalogued 1974 Service Station Special, Type I body.   -- 75 100 150

8465 RIO GRANDE: 1974, dummy F-3 A unit; matches 8464; 3,000 manufactured, lights, Type I body.   -- 40 50 75

8466 AMTRAK: 1974-75, powered F-3 A unit, silver body and sides, black roof and nose hood, red and blue logo; sealed portholes, lights, Type III body.
                                                    -- 85 110 300

8467 AMTRAK: 1974-75, dummy F-3 A unit; matches 8466.
                                                    -- 40 50 100

8468 BALTIMORE & OHIO: 1974, dummy F-3 B unit, blue body with yellow lettering, sealed portholes; matches 8363 and 8364 A units.
(A) Top edge of sides not painted.   -- -- 65 100
(B) Top edge of sides painted.   -- -- 65 100

8469 CANADIAN PACIFIC: 1974, dummy F-3 B unit, sealed portholes; matches 8365, 8366, top edge of side not painted maroon. Hard to find.
                                                    -- 100 150 300

8470 CHESSIE: 1974, powered G. E. U36B, stamped metal railings, blue, orange, and yellow body with blue lettering; from Grand National Set, black frame, lights, nose decal, Type II motor, no MPC logo. Shown in 1974 catalogue with large emblem and lettering, but not produced that way.
                                                    -- 70 100 125

8471 PENNSYLVANIA: 1973-74, NW-2 yard switcher, dark green body with yellow lettering, red Keystone on cab sides. Somewhat hard to find.
                                                    -- -- 135 185

8473 Coca-Cola Switcher with three steps on the door behind "Coke".

8473 COCA COLA: 1975, NW-2 yard switcher, red body with white lettering; two-position reverse.
(A) "Three-step" variety, Type III body.   -- 35 50 125
(B) "Two-step" variety, Type IV body.   -- 30 50 100
(C) "One-step" variety, Type V body.   -- 30 50 100

8474 RIO GRANDE: 1975, dummy F-3 B unit, yellow and green body, silver roof, sealed portholes; matches 8464, 8465.   -- -- 65 100

8475 AMTRAK: 1975, dummy F-3 B unit, silver body and sides, black roof, red and blue logo, sealed portholes; matches 8466, 8467. -- -- 80 100

8477 NEW YORK CENTRAL: 1984, powered GP-9, black body, large gray stripe edged by smaller white stripes on side, small "NEW YORK CENTRAL" lettering above gray stripe, gray and white striping on cab ends with New York Central logo, separate molded plastic grab-irons on front and rear; AC motor operates on either AC or DC. The power truck is similar, but not identical, to the older Lionel power trucks of the Geeps produced in the 1950s. The magnets in this truck appear to be much larger, producing stronger Magnetraction. Electronic diesel horn, three-position E-type reverse unit, operating headlights, operating couplers, die-cast truck side frames, stamped-steel frame and handrails. Already in considerable demand by collectors and appreciating in price rapidly.   -- 175 200 235

8480 UNION PACIFIC: 1984, F-3A locomotive, yellow body, red and gray striping and lettering, dark gray roof and nose, dark gray frame and trucks, lighted numberboards, Union Pacific shield-and-wing decal on nose; two motors, Magnetraction. Collectors have complained that many examples do not match in color; the engine has been found in medium and darker yellow shades, and many boxes have to be examined to find matching colors. Price for powered A unit only.   -- -- 200 250

8481 UNION PACIFIC: F-3B dummy unit, electronic diesel horn; matches 8480.   -- -- 100 125

8482 UNION PACIFIC: F-3A dummy unit; matches 8480, lighted.   -- -- 90 100

8485 U. S. MARINES: 1984, NW-2 switcher, olive and black camouflage-painted cab, black frame and rails; lighted, three-position electronic reversing switch, AC/DC can motor; operating plastic couplers, plastic truck side frames, weighted, sliding shoe contacts.   -- -- 55 60

8500 MILWAUKEE: GP-9, see 18500.

8550 JERSEY CENTRAL: 1975, powered GP-9, Type II railings, red- and white-painted body with white lettering, black frame; lights, nose decal; Type II motor, no pickup on dummy truck; "LIONEL" builder's plate.   -- 60 80 95

8551 PENNSYLVANIA: 1975, powered, "Little Joe" G. E. EP-5 electric, tuscan body with gold stripes on body and lettering, lights; two pantographs, can be wired for overhead operation on catenary, separate motor and power truck.   -- 100 120 250

8552 SOUTHERN PACIFIC: 1975, powered Alco FA-2 A unit, light orange and dark orange body, black roof, silver ends, stripes, and lettering, lights; set of three with 8553, 8554. C. Rohlfing comment. Price for set. -- 150 175 300

8553 SOUTHERN PACIFIC: 1975, dummy Alco FA-2 B unit; matches 8552. (Only B unit dummy with operating couplers at both ends, wheelbase altered to accommodate trucks.) See 8552.

8554 SOUTHERN PACIFIC: 1975, dummy Alco FA-2 A unit; matches 8552. See 8552.

8555 MILWAUKEE ROAD: 1975, uncatalogued 1975 Service Station Special, powered F-3 A unit, gray and orange body, yellow lettering, sealed portholes, lights, Type II mold.   -- 125 150 175

8556 CHESSIE: 1975-76, NW-2 yard switcher, yellow and blue, lights, Type V body.   -- 110 150 195
See also Factory Errors and Prototypes.

8557 MILWAUKEE ROAD: 1975, dummy F-3 A unit, gray and orange body; matches 8555, Type II body.   -- 40 50 100

8558 MILWAUKEE ROAD: 1976, powered General Electric EP-5 electric, maroon, orange, and black body, lights; two silver pantographs, can be wired for catenary operation, separate motor and power truck. -- 85 110 175

8559 N & W 1776: 1975, see 1776(A), (B), and (C).

8569 Soo.

8560 CHESSIE: 1975, dummy G. E. U36B, matches 8470, some reports stress this is not quite an exact match for the 8470 because the vermilion stripe at the top of the cab is slightly wider than on the powered locomotive.
(A) No lights or light pickup. G. Halverson and T. Ladny comments.
                    -- -- 55 100
(B) Lighted unit with pickup on one truck. G. Halverson comment.
                    -- -- 55 100

8561 JERSEY CENTRAL: 1975-76, dummy GP-9; matches 8550, not lighted.
                    -- -- 50 60

8562 MISSOURI PACIFIC: 1975-76, powered GP-20, Type II railings, blue with white lettering, hash marks; black underframe, Type II motor.
                    -- 55 70 85

8563 ROCK ISLAND: 1975, uncatalogued, powered Alco FA-2 A unit, red body with white letters, yellow stripe, closed pilot, available only in Sears Set 1594.   -- -- 40 100

8564 UNION PACIFIC: 1975, powered G. E. U36B, Type III railing, gray and yellow body with red stripe; from North American Set, black frame, lights, nose decal, Type II motor.   -- 75 100 125

8565 MISSOURI PACIFIC: 1975-76, dummy GP-20; matches 8562, a few with horns are known to exist. Check before purchase; some units without horns are packaged in boxes marked for units equipped with horns.
(A) No horn.   -- -- 40 50
(B) With horn. Very hard to find.   -- -- 80 100

8566 SOUTHERN: 1975-77, powered F-3 A unit, green body with gray stripes; sealed portholes, lights, Type IV body, gold lettering. -- 125 175 300

8567 SOUTHERN: 1975-77, dummy F-3 A unit. -- 60 100 125

8568 PREAMBLE EXPRESS: 1975, powered F-3 A unit, red, white, and blue body, sealed portholes; Spirit of '76, East Coast Clearance Engine, lights, Type IV body. No dummy unit made, although some custom-made post-factory engines in this scheme have been found as well as cab shells placed on dummy chassis.
                    -- -- 65 100

8569 SOO: 1975-77, NW-2, yard switcher, red body with white lettering; lights, dummy couplers, two-position reverse. -- 30 40 100

8570 LIBERTY SPECIAL: 1975, powered Alco FA-2, blue top, white body, with red nose and stripe, lights. Came with three 9700-series boxcars and matching unlighted SP-type caboose in Liberty Special Set. -- 30 40 100

8558 Milwaukee Road "Little Joe" EP-5 Electric. A. Rudman Collection.

8571 FRISCO: 1975-76, powered G. E. U36B, Type III railing, white and red with red lettering, black frame; lights, no nose decal, Type II motor.

--	60	75	95

8572 FRISCO: 1975-76, dummy G. E. U36B, matches 8571, lights, pickup on one truck.

--	--	40	50

8573 UNION PACIFIC: 1975, dummy G. E. U36B, stamped metal railing; matches 8564, except no lights, pickup on one truck.
(A) With horn, reportedly only 1,200 made.   -- -- 150 250
(B) Without horn. Purchaser should check boxes before purchase.   -- -- 50 200

8575 MILWAUKEE ROAD: Dummy F-3B unit, matches 8555.

--	--	--	175

8576 PENN CENTRAL: 1975-76, powered GP-7, Type III railings, black body with white lettering.
(A) Door outline shows through "PENN CENTRAL" lettering, black frame, lights, nose decal, Type II motor, Lionel / MPC builder's plate.   -- 60 75 85
(B) Same as (A), but door outline painted solid, "LIONEL" builder's plate, Type III body.   -- 60 75 85

8578 NEW YORK CENTRAL: 1985, ballast tamper, yellow body, black frame and railings, black lettering, black tamper frame, silver tampers, silver headlight atop cab, silver battery box, brown central window, blue man inside cab, dummy rear coupler. Track trip activates tampers and reduces speed of unit.   -- -- 90 110

8580 ILLINOIS CENTRAL: 1985, F-3A powered diesel; separate sale item from City of New Orleans set, medium brown body (not dark brown as shown in catalogue), orange and yellow striping, yellow lettering, lighted cab and numberboards (which have engine numbers for the first time), clear portholes, black front grab-irons, two motors, Magnetraction, black frame and trucks. Price with matching 8582 Dummy F-3A unit.   -- -- 250 295

8581 ILLINOIS CENTRAL: 1985, F-3B dummy unit, electronic diesel horn, matches 8580 and 8582 but sold separately.   -- -- 100 125

8582 ILLINOIS CENTRAL: 1985, F-3A dummy unit, matches 8580 and 8581, sold as pair with 8580. See 8580.

8585 BURLINGTON NORTHERN: 1985, SD-40, Cascade green lower body, black upper body and roof, white number, "BN" logo, and safety stripes, green-painted handrails; two motors, Magnetraction, electronic diesel horn, black six-wheel die-cast trucks, lighted cab and numberboards. Part of Burlington Northern Limited Set.   -- -- 275 300

8587 WABASH: 1985, GP-9, made for J. C. Penney and priced at $269.95 in Christmas catalogue; note that this engine has been available far less expensively from train dealers. Same construction as 8477 New York Central: Magnetraction, separately molded ladders; blue and gray Wabash Bluebird paint scheme, white lettering and "484" on numberboards; came with display case. R. Sigurdson and N. Banis Collections.   -- -- 200 300

8650 BURLINGTON NORTHERN: 1976-77, powered G. E. U36B, Type III railing, black and green body with white lettering, hash marks; black frame, lights, Type II motor.   -- -- 85 110

8651 BURLINGTON NORTHERN: 1976-77, dummy G. E. U36B; matches 8650, lights, pickup on one truck.   -- -- 55 75

8652 SANTA FE: 1976-77, powered F-3 A unit, red and silver; lights, sealed portholes, Type V mold, sold separately.   -- 75 100 250

8653 SANTA FE: 1976-77, dummy F-3 A unit; matches 8562, Type V mold. Very difficult to find, sold separately.   -- 80 100 200

8654 BOSTON & MAINE: 1976, powered GP-9, Type III railings, blue, white, and black body, white and black lettering, white frame; lights, no nose decal, "LIONEL" builder's plate, Type III body.   -- 60 75 110

8655 BOSTON & MAINE: 1976, dummy GP-9; matches 8654, not lighted.   -- -- 30 50

8656 CANADIAN NATIONAL: 1976, powered Alco FA-2 A unit, orange, black, and white, lights, three-position reverse. Much harder to find than is generally realized.   -- 50 75 150

8657 CANADIAN NATIONAL: 1976, dummy Alco FA-2 B unit; matches 8656. Two dummy couplers, no tank/step underbody detail. R. Young comment.   -- -- 50 75

8658 CANADIAN NATIONAL: 1976, dummy Alco FA-2 A unit; matches 8656. Very hard to find.   -- 75 100 200

8659 VIRGINIAN: 1976-77, G. E. EL-C rectifier electric, blue body with yellow stripe and lettering, yellow frame; can be wired for catenary, separate motor and power truck.
(A) Thin, light-colored nose decal.   -- 100 125 145
(B) Same as (A), but with thick, light-colored nose decal.   -- 100 125 145
(C) Same as (A), but with regular dark yellow nose decal.   -- 100 125 145

8660 CP RAIL: 1976,77, NW-2 yard switcher, red body with white lettering, lights.   -- 50 60 95

8661 SOUTHERN: Dummy F-3B unit, matches 8566 and 8567 F3A units. Hard to find.   -- -- 60 100

8662 BALTIMORE & OHIO: 1986, GP-7, dark blue body, yellow stripe and lettering, two can motors mounted on trucks, electronic three-position reverse, headlight. Part of 1652 B & O Freight Set.   -- -- 70 85

8664 AMTRAK: 1976-77, powered Alco FA-2 A unit, light, fixed rear coupler, body has black roof and nose top, silver sides and nose skirt, red nose and blue lettering. Came as part of the Lake Shore Limited Set, which included 6403, 6404, 6405, and 6406 Amtrak short O27 passenger cars. A B-unit dummy engine was available separately, as were passenger cars 6410, 6411, and 6412.   -- -- 60 70

8665 BANGOR AND AROOSTOOK: See 1776.

8666 NORTHERN PACIFIC: 1976, uncatalogued, powered GP-9, stamped metal railings, black and gold body with red stripe, gold and red lettering; 1976 Service Station Special, gold frame, lights, no nose decal, Type II motor, no MPC logo.   -- -- 100 125

8667 AMTRAK: 1976-77, dummy Alco B unit, black roof and nose top, silver sides and nose skirt, red nose, blue lettering; matches 8664, difficult to find.   -- 30 50 75

8668 NORTHERN PACIFIC: 1976, dummy GP-9, matches 8666.   -- -- 60 70

8669 ILLINOIS CENTRAL: 1976, powered G. E. U36B, stamped metal railings, white and orange with black lettering, from Illinois Central Set, black frame, lights, Type II motor, nose decals.   -- -- 100 125

8670 Chessie.

8670 CHESSIE: 1976, Gas Turbine, 0-4-0, yellow body with blue trim; fixed couplers, DC motor, polarity reverse, runs only on DC, sliding shoe pickup, not lighted.   -- -- 15 35

8679 NORTHERN PACIFIC: 1986, GP-20, black and gold body, red stripe separates black from gold areas, red, black, and white NP Monad heralds on cab sides, front and rear, gold lettering and number, twin can motors mounted on trucks, electronic three-position reversing unit, headlight. R. LaVoie Collection.   -- -- 80 100

8687 JERSEY CENTRAL: 1986, Fairbanks-Morse, dark flat olive green body, cream striping, logos, and numbering, two AC motors, Magnetraction, lights at both ends, electronic horn (though catalogue makes no mention of this), three-position reverse. Issued with companion 7404 Boxcar and 6917 Caboose sold separately; commemorative of 100th anniversary of Statue of Liberty.

-- -- **300 375**

8690 LIONEL LINES: Released in January 1987; trolley; four-wheel Birney-style reissue of No. 60 of postwar years with improvements. Bright orange-painted gray body with new open steps and headlight openings, blue roof and large, outsized blue plastic sheathing over bumpers; silhouettes in all windows, ends and sides; "8490" in number slots and in styrofoam packing box, indicating delay in production; bump reverse which can rebound and stall trolley in neutral if unit is operated at too high a voltage; spur-gear drive motor replaces crosscut gear of older unit; this model runs much better at lower voltage; blue lettering, striping, and number. The 8490 part number also shows up on the window inserts. Reportedly, this was a project largely encouraged by Lenny Dean. The trolley has sold very well and is still readily available. R. Sigurdson, W. Berresford, and R. LaVoie comments.

-- -- **100 110**

8750 THE ROCK: 1977, powered GP-7, Type III railings, blue and white body with white and blue lettering, white frame; lights, nose decal, Type II motor, "LIONEL" builder's plate, Type III body.

-- -- **70 85**

8751 THE ROCK: 1977, dummy GP-7; matches 8750, no lights.

-- -- **30 40**

8753 PENNSYLVANIA: 1977, uncatalogued, powered GG-1 electric, wine red with gold stripes; two motors, Magnetraction; 6000 produced.

-- **375 425 550**

8754 NEW HAVEN: 1977-78, powered G. E. EL-C rectifier electric, lights, black roof, orange sides, white stripes, black lettering, black frame; can be wired for catenary, separate motor and power truck.

-- **85 120 175**

8755 SANTA FE: 1977-78, powered G. E. U36B, stamped metal railing, blue and yellow body with blue and yellow lettering, silver metal truck side frame, yellow frame; lights, nose decal, Type II motor.

-- -- **85 100**

8756 SANTA FE: 1977-78, dummy G. E. U36B; matches 8755, not lighted.

-- -- **50 70**

8757 CONRAIL: 1977-78, powered GP-9, Type III railing, gray plastic body painted blue, white lettering; lights, nose decal, Type II motor, no pickup on dummy truck, no MPC logo.
(A) Black underframe and railings. -- -- **75 90**
(B) White underframe and railings. -- -- **85 100**

8758 SOUTHERN: 1978, GP-7 dummy; matches 8774, green and white. This unit is unique in that it has a lower number than does its powered unit.

-- -- **40 60**

8759 ERIE LACKAWANNA: 1977-79, powered GP-9, Type III railing, gray plastic body painted gray, tuscan, and yellow, yellow lettering, yellow frame; lights, nose decal, Type II motor, no MPC logo. -- -- **80 110**

8760 ERIE LACKAWANNA: 1977-79, dummy GP-9; matches 8759.

-- -- **50 70**

8761 GRAND TRUNK: 1977-78, NW-2 yard switcher, blue, white, and orange paint; three-position E-unit, two disc-operating couplers, light.

-- -- **75 195**

8762 GREAT NORTHERN: 1977-78, powered G. E. EP-5 electric, gray plastic painted dark green and orange, yellow lettering and stripes, four red and white logos, two large decals on nose; two pantographs, can be wired for catenary, separate motor and power truck. -- **100 140 250**

8763 NORFOLK & WESTERN: 1977-78 powered GP-9, Type III railing, gray plastic painted black, white lettering, black frame; lights, nose decal, Type II motor, no MPC logo. -- -- **75 90**
See also Factory Errors and Prototypes.

8764 BALTIMORE & OHIO: 1977, powered Budd R D C passenger car, gray plastic body painted silver with blue lettering, metal frame, plastic battery box hangs from frame, three-position E-unit with lever on bottom, two disc-operating couplers, rubber tread on two wheels with gears, F-3-type power trucks with plastic two-step assembly. (The plastic assembly formerly appeared on the Lionel 44-ton dummy truck.) This is a remanufacture of the Lionel 1950s version and differs from it in the following ways: the reissues have different numbers, a plastic trim horn replaces a metal trim horn, rubber tire traction replaces Magnetraction, and highly shiny silver paint replaces flat silver-gray paint.

-- **80 100 125**

8765 BALTIMORE & OHIO: 1977, dummy Budd R D C baggage/mail, "US Mail Railway Post Office", "Budd R D C" in blue letters pierced by red line on small decal, lights, two disc-operating couplers, gray plastic painted silver with blue lettering.

-- -- **50 100**

8766 BALTIMORE & OHIO: 1977, powered Budd R D C baggage/mail, gray plastic painted shiny silver with blue lettering; lights; part of 1977 Service Station Special Set 1766, uncatalogued, with 8767 and 8768. Price for set.

-- **250 300 350**

8767 BALTIMORE & OHIO: 1977, dummy Budd R D C passenger car; matches 8766, part of set with 8766 and 8768. Price for set. -- **250 300 350**

8768 BALTIMORE & OHIO: 1977, dummy Budd R D C passenger car; matches 8766, part of set with 8766 and 8767. Price for set. -- **250 300 350**

8769 Republic Steel.

8769 REPUBLIC STEEL: 1977, DC-powered, gas turbine, blue with yellow trim; fixed couplers, sliding contact pickups, for use with DC current only.

-- -- **15 35**

8770 E. M. D.: 1977, NW-2 yard switcher, General Motors E. M. D. factory demonstrator paint scheme, blue and white body with white lettering, lights.
(A) Two disc-operating couplers, three-position E-unit. -- **50 60 95**
(B) Fixed couplers, two-position reverse unit. -- **30 40 80**

8771 GREAT NORTHERN: 1977, powered G. E. U36B, Type III railing, gray plastic painted black, white, and blue with white lettering; from Rocky Mountain Special Set, black frame, lights, Type II motor. -- **80 100 120**

8772 G M & O: 1977, powered GP-20, Type III railing, gray plastic body painted red and white; from Heartland Set, white frame, lights, nose decal, Type II motor, "LIONEL" logo. -- **55 70 85**

8773 MICKEY MOUSE: 1977-78, powered G. E. U36B, gray plastic body painted orange and white with Mickey, Pluto, and Donald. This item has shown greater appreciation than most modern era engines. -- **250 300 500**

8774 SOUTHERN: 1977-78, powered, GP-7, small pickup rollers mounted on power truck, gray plastic body painted green and white, gold stripe and gold lettering, Southern decal at front end; black frame, Type IV railing, Type III body, Type II motor. -- **65 80 100**

8775 LEHIGH VALLEY: 1977-78, powered GP-9, gray plastic body painted bright red, yellow heat-stamped lettering and stripe; Type III railing, Type III cab, three-position E-unit. -- **70 85 100**

8776 C & N W: 1977-78, powered GP-20, gray plastic body painted yellow and very dark green, green lettering, red, white, and black decal beneath cab window; numberboards do not have numbers, black frame, Type III railing.

-- **55 70 95**

8777 SANTA FE: 1977-78, dummy F-3 B unit; matches 8652, fixed couplers at both ends, Santa Fe decal on side, no portholes, no separate grate units.

-- **85 100 300**

8778 LEHIGH VALLEY: 1977-78, dummy GP-9; matches 8775, not lighted.

-- -- **60 75**

8779 C & N W: 1977-78, dummy GP-20; matches 8776, not lighted, two disc-operating couplers. -- -- **30 40**

8800 LEHIGH VALLEY GP-9: See 18800.

8801 SANTA FE U36B: See 18801.

8802 SOUTHERN GP-9: See 18802.

8850 PENN CENTRAL: 1978-79, powered GG-1 electric, black-painted die-cast body with white "PENN CENTRAL" and Penn Central logo on side; two Magnetraction motors, magnetic couplers, head lamps at both ends, operating pantographs with black insulators, shiny metal shoes on pantographs, E-unit lever goes through roof. This engine did not sell as well as the first GG-1 rerun. However, according to reliable sources, about the same number of black GG-1s were made as the 8753.   -- 300 325 450

8851 NEW HAVEN: 1978-79, powered A unit, Type VI body, three ridges run from the cab door to the rear of the side, gray plastic body painted silver-white, orange, and black. "NH" in white letters on nose, the "N" has no serifs on the bottom right side — this matches the original Lionel F-3 New Haven, but differs from the way "NH" is shown on the boxcars. Silver-painted frame, black truck side frames, disc-operating front coupler, two motors, rubber tires; came with 8852 as set. Price for set.   -- -- 225 250

8852 NEW HAVEN: 1978-79, dummy F-3 A unit, Type VI body; matches 8851, lights; came with 8851 as set. Price for set.   -- -- 225 250

8854 C P RAIL: 1978-79, GP-9, gray plastic body painted red, white, and black, white lettering, white and black C P design; black truck sides, two disc-operating couplers, two geared wheels with rubber tires, Type IV railing, came with Great Plains Express Set, "LIONEL" builder's plates, Type V body.
                -- 75 85 100

8855 MILWAUKEE ROAD: 1978, powered SD-18, the first in the SD-18 locomotive series, it is a combination of a U36B chassis with six-wheel trucks and a GP-20 cab unit with added dynamic brake and five-unit horn cluster. In real railroad parlance, a "cab" unit is a GM F diesel or an Alco FA diesel, and a "hood" unit is a GP, "U-Boat," or SD diesel. However, in tinplate terms, when we refer to the "cab," we are talking about the plastic shell of any tinplate diesel. Because of the increased truck size, the "battery box" was redesigned and now reads "LIONEL MT. CLEMENS MICHIGAN 28045". Two disc-operating couplers, three-position reverse unit, rubber tires on end geared wheels (center wheels are blind). (For better operation note that center blind drivers are often too high and cause the rubber tire drivers to lose traction, particularly under a heavy load. Solution: hold the running engine upright and gently place a fine file against the blind driver and reduce its diameter.) Gray plastic body painted dull orange and black, black and white lettering, red and white logo underneath cab window; light, two disc-operating couplers, three-position E-unit. Sold only as part of the specially boxed Milwaukee Road set and not available for separate sale. Most sets are believed to have been sold to collectors and not run, matching dummy not available, five-horn cluster and bell, Type IV frame, Type II motor.
                -- -- 100 135

8857 NORTHERN PACIFIC: 1978-80, powered G. E. U36B, gray plastic painted black with orange band along base, yellow cab end, yellow frame and rails, burnished truck side frames, Monad logo on cab decal; disc-operating couplers, five-unit plastic horn on hood roof, three-position E-unit, Type IV railing, Type II motor.   -- 60 75 95

8858 NORTHERN PACIFIC: 1978-80, dummy G. E. U36B; matches 8857, not lighted.   -- -- 30 40

8859 CONRAIL: 1978-80, 1982, powered G. E. EL-C rectifier electric, gray plastic body painted blue, white lettering and Conrail design, two disc-operating couplers, black truck side frames, one operating pantograph, shiny metal pantograph shoe, can be wired for catenary operation, separate motor and power truck. Though as many of this rectifier were produced as the Virginian and the New Haven examples, this version is not found quite as often. It was offered by Montgomery Ward in 1982 with a display case for $149.99. -- 90 120 145

8860 ROCK: 1978-79, powered NW-2 yard switcher, gray plastic body painted blue, black and white lettering and logo, white-enameled frame, white nose with two pronounced red indicator lights, blue paint around headlight; two disc-operating couplers, three-position E-unit, rubber tires on two geared wheels, plastic unit suspended from frame behind E-unit, Type II motor.   -- 50 75 95

8861 SANTA FE: 1978-79, powered Alco FA-2 A unit, red and silver paint; light, two-position reverse, Type II motor.   -- 25 35 90

8862 SANTA FE: 1978-79, dummy Alco FA-2; matches 8861.
                -- 20 25 40

8864 NEW HAVEN: 1978, dummy F-3 B unit; matches 8851 and 8852, not lighted.   -- -- 75 100

8866 MINNEAPOLIS & ST. LOUIS: 1978, GP-9 powered Service Station Special sold by Lionel to Service Stations for their exclusive sale as part of a special set. This is the only item not specifically available for separate sale in the 1978 Service Station Special Set, although in reality it was available separately when dealers broke up the sets. Gray plastic body painted red and white, blue cab roof, white and red lettering, red and white logo beneath cab windows and on hood front; two disc-operating couplers, three-position E-unit, rubber tires on two geared wheels, Type IV body, Type III railing with cab indentations. (Note that the matching 8867 Dummy unit has a Type IV railing. This fact supports the belief that the railing design change occurred in 1978.) Other components of the set are the 9408 Lionel "Circus" Stock Car, the 9138 Sunoco Three-dome Tank Car, the 9213 M. & St. L. Covered Hopper, the 9726 Erie-Lackawanna Boxcar, and the 9271 Minneapolis & St. Louis Bay Window Caboose. This set, still available at a relatively inexpensive price (about $225 at press time), is a good bet as a "sleeper" and could appreciate in value because it was the last of the Service Station Special Sets sold until the custom was revived in 1986 with the Santa Fe Work Train Set (see John Kouba's article elsewhere in this edition). The 8867 Dummy unit was sold separately. R. LaVoie comment.
(A) Type III body and railing (see illustration).   -- 80 100 125
(B) Type IV body and railing.   -- 80 100 125

8867 MINNEAPOLIS & ST. LOUIS: 1978, dummy GP-9; matches 8866, lighted (apparently the only GP-9 dummy with lights), Type IV railing, two disc-operating couplers.   -- -- 60 75

8868 AMTRAK: 1978, 1980, powered Budd R D C baggage/mail unit, gray plastic body painted silver, blue lettering, white band through windows with red and blue stripes; lights, three-position reverse unit, two disc-operating couplers. R. Pauli Collection.   -- 100 150 175

8869 AMTRAK: 1978, 1980, dummy Budd R D C passenger car, lighted, two disc-operating couplers; matches 8868.   -- -- 65 75

8870 AMTRAK: 1978, 1980, dummy Budd R D C passenger car, lighted; matches 8868.   -- -- 65 75

8871 AMTRAK: 1978, 1980, dummy Budd R D C baggage/mail; matches 8868, lighted, two disc-operating couplers.   -- -- 65 75

8872 SANTA FE: 1978-79, gray plastic body painted yellow and blue, blue and yellow lettering, Santa Fe decal on nose, yellow frame (see 8855 for SD-18 background); six-wheel trucks, two disc-operating couplers, Type IV handrails, one light, three-position reverse unit.   -- -- 100 125

8873 SANTA FE: 1978-79, dummy, lights; matches 8872.
                -- -- 60 75

8950 VIRGINIAN: 1978, dual-motored, Magnetraction, Fairbanks-Morse Trainmaster; rerun of postwar 2331 Locomotive with new number. This reissue was an exact copy of the original except for slightly brighter paint — right down to the tendency of the Fairbanks-Morse body shell to crack at the screw holes. Caution is advised when disassembling this and the earlier modern era Fairbanks-Morse locomotives. The 8687 Jersey Central has reinforced screw holes to prevent the problem. R. LaVoie comments.   -- 275 350 450

8951 SOUTHERN PACIFIC: 1979, dual-motored, Magnetraction, Fairbanks-Morse; rerun of prototype Trainmaster shown at 1954 Toy Fair with new number.   -- 425 495 550

8952 PENNSYLVANIA: 1979, F-3 A unit, Type VII body, powered; comes with matching Dummy A unit 8953, gray plastic body painted Brunswick green, five gold stripes, portholes with clear plastic lenses, nose grab-irons, frosted-white cab windows; two motors, each motor has two geared wheels with rubber tires and a single pickup roller, disc-operating coupler on front, fixed coupler on rear, steps on rear, red, black, and gold Keystone nose decal, five stripes merge on nose, decal, gold stripes and lettering are electrocals. (Note that the area in which the electrocal is applied has a flat finish readily visible when the train is held upon its side.) Has clear numberboards without numbers. The frosted cab windows were due to a parts ordering error by Lionel. Price includes 8953. -- 300 350 500

8953 PENNSYLVANIA: 1979, F-3 A unit, dummy; matches 8952. See 8952 for price.

8955 SOUTHERN: 1979, U36B, gray plastic body painted green and white with gold lettering, five-horn cluster on roof, brakewheel on hood near cab, gold stripe runs completely around cab, "SOUTHERN RAILROAD" decal on hood near cab; Type IV frame, two disc-operating couplers, geared motor wheels with rubber tires. -- 75 100 180

8956 SOUTHERN: 1979, U36B dummy; matches 8955. -- -- 45 55

8957 BURLINGTON NORTHERN: 1979, powered GP-20, black and green body, white lettering, no stripe. -- 70 80 110

8958 BURLINGTON NORTHERN: 1979, GP-20 dummy, matches 8957. -- -- 40 60

8960 SOUTHERN PACIFIC: 1979, G. E. U36C, powered, basically a U36B frame and cab with six-wheel trucks with added brakewheel on cab, two small marker lights near forward facing hood; Type IV frame, shortened battery box, two disc-operating couplers with tabs, bright red-orange and yellow "Daylight" colors, white lettering. Some units have been found with the railings spot-welded off center so that the frame looks as if it has been bent. -- 70 80 95

8961 SOUTHERN PACIFIC: 1979, G. E. U36C dummy; matches 8960. -- -- 35 45

8962 READING: 1979, U36B, powered, green and yellow body, "BEE LINE SERVICE", die-cast trucks, metal wheels and handrails, disc-operating couplers, one working headlight, illuminated numberplates without numbers, and three-position reverse unit. Part of Quaker City Limited Set. Miller observation. -- 80 90 110

8970 PENNSYLVANIA: 1979-80, dual-motored F-3 A unit, tuscan-painted body, five gold stripes, grab-bars, clear portholes. Price includes matching 8971 Dummy. -- 225 400 500

8971 PENNSYLVANIA: 1979-80, F-3 dummy; matches 8970. See 8970 for price.

18200 CONRAIL: 1987, SD-40 diesel, bright blue body with white Conrail wheel logo, striping, and lettering, blue side rails, white end rails, black frame, reinforcing rivets added where screws fasten body to frame, headlight, Magnetraction, electronic horn, two AC motors, three-position reverse, numbered "8200" on cab. Part of 11700 Conrail Limited Set. -- -- 250 275

18201 CHESSIE: 1988, SD-40 diesel, yellow, vermilion, and dark blue cab, vermilion-painted side and end rails, dark blue Chessie Cat lettering and logo, two motors, Magnetraction, six-wheel trucks, headlights, three-position reverse, electronic diesel horn. Part of 11705 Chessie System Unit Train. -- -- 250 275

18300 PENNSYLVANIA: 1987, GG-1 electric, bronze-painted die-cast body, purple-black striping and lettering, red Keystones on sides and ends, two AC motors, Magnetraction, lights at both ends. Offered with matching Pennsylvania N5C porthole caboose sold separately. Designed to pull train of various Lionel mint cars issued in previous years. Actually numbered "8300" on cab. -- -- 450 525

18301 SOUTHERN: Announced for 1988, Fairbanks-Morse diesel locomotive, green cab with white-painted lower sides and ends, white stripe at roof line, gold lettering and numbering, two motors, headlights, Magnetraction, die-cast six-wheel trucks, stamped metal frame and railings, electronic diesel horn. Expected to be a brisk seller; price is introductory and subject to market speculation. -- -- -- 375

18302 GREAT NORTHERN: Announced for 1988, EP-5 "Little Joe" rectifier electric, orange and dark green cab with yellow striping, numbering, and lettering, red, white, and green Great Northern "goat" logos on sides, headlights at both ends, operating pantographs, three-position reverse, horn. Part of Fallen Flags Series No. 3. Essentially similar to 8762 model of 1977, but differs in drive train and inclusion of horn. -- -- -- 225

18400 SANTA FE: 1987, 2-4-2 rotary snowplow, red oxide body, yellow snowplow fan with brown spiral stripe, yellow and brown Santa Fe cross logo, yellow number, black frame and railings, three-position reverse, operating coupler on one end. -- -- -- 120

18401 LIONEL: 1987, handcar, bright orange body (shown unmarked in catalogue), black push handles, two blue men with flesh-painted faces, shielded gears, no reverse, DC can motor with rectifier for AC operation, new spur drive motor. Pictured with exposed gearwork, but production model expected to have gears shielded. Advertised in catalogue with remote-control reverse.

(A) First run: dark orange body. M. Sabatelle comment. -- -- -- 60

(B) Second run: light orange body. M. Sabatelle observation. -- -- -- 50

18402 LIONEL LINES: Announced for 1988, operating burro crane, black die-cast frame, yellow cab, red lettering, light gray boom. Three control levers for switching from self-propulsion to rotating cab, raising or lowering the hook and reversing functions of first two levers. Essentially a revival of the 3360 unit of the mid-1950s, this has always been a cleverly-designed and interesting operating unit, although its complexity makes it susceptible to breakdown. -- -- -- 110

18403 SANTA: Scheduled for 1988, handcar, green handcar body, figures of Mr. and Mrs. Claus dressed in traditional attire pump handcar, no lettering on car. -- -- -- 50

18404 SAN FRANCISCO: 1988, Birney-style trolley; four-wheel green body, dark olive green roof, yellow lettering, black plastic bumper covers, "8404" on cab window insert; mechanically identical to 8690. R. Sigurdson comments. -- -- -- 95

18500 MILWAUKEE ROAD: 1987, GP-9, orange and black body shell (orange color continuous through cab as in rare postwar version), white "8500" number on black part of cab, black lettering on sides and ends, red and white Milwaukee logo on cab, Magnetraction, three-position reverse, headlight, black frame. Part of separate-sale Fallen Flags Set No. 2. -- -- -- 225

18800 LEHIGH VALLEY: 1987, GP-9, gray plastic body shell painted brick red, yellow "8800" number, lettering, and striping, black and white safety stripes on cab ends, black frame, twin can motors mounted in trucks, electronic three-position reversing unit, headlight. Part of 11702 Black Diamond Freight Set. -- -- -- 110

18801 SANTA FE: 1987, U36-B, blue and yellow Santa Fe freight color scheme, yellow "Santa Fe", blue number "8801" on cab, black frame, twin can motors mounted in trucks, electronic three-position reversing unit, headlight, separate-sale item. -- -- -- 85

18802 SOUTHERN: 1987, GP-9, green- and white-painted body, gold stripe separates green and white colors, gold lettering and "8802" number, black frame, headlight, twin can motors mounted in trucks, electronic three-position reversing unit. Part of 11704 Southern Freight Runner Service Station Set for 1987. -- -- -- 125

18803 SANTA FE: Scheduled for 1988, Alco RS-3 diesel switcher. This is a brand new model for Lionel which copies one of the most widely used switchers of all time. Dark blue cab with yellow-painted ends, yellow stripe along upper edge of cab, yellow Santa Fe emblem and cross logo, brakewheel directly mounted on cab front end, large crew cab with four windows on each end and two windows on sides, large exhaust stack atop cab, large simulated fan shroud at one cab end, stamped-steel frame and railings, apparently illuminated numberboards at top of cab ends, relatively small battery box below frame, two can motors mounted on trucks, plastic truck side frames and couplers, weight in cab, illuminated at front end only. -- -- -- 100

18804 SOO LINE: Scheduled for 1988, Alco RS-3 diesel switcher, general description same as 18803 entry above, but lacks illuminated numberboards shown on Santa Fe model in catalogue (production pieces are not likely to be illuminated in this way). This model has a black plastic cab, yellow-painted ends with black safety striping, yellow lettering and number "8804" on cab, stamped metal frame and railings, plastic truck side frames and couplers, twin can motors mounted on trucks, weight in cab, illuminated at front end. -- -- -- 100

18901 PENNSYLVANIA: Scheduled for 1988, Alco A unit, dark tuscan red-painted body shell, gold striping along cab sides and front, gold "PENNSYLVANIA" lettering and "8901" number, plastic truck side frames and couplers, stamped metal chassis, two can-type motors mounted on trucks, electronic three-position reverse, weight in cab, headlight. Separate sale item made as a match for 16000-series Pennsylvania Passenger Car introduced in 1987. Price includes 18902 dummy unit. -- -- -- 125

18902 PENNSYLVANIA: Scheduled for 1988, Alco dummy A unit, matches 18901 powered unit above, illuminated. Price for both units. -- -- -- 125

18903 AMTRAK: 1988, Alco A Unit, silver-painted body, black roof, red nose, blue number "8903", red and blue Amtrak arrow logo, blue Amtrak lettering, plastic truck side frames and couplers, stamped metal chassis, twin can motors mounted on trucks, weight in cab, electronic three-position reverse, headlight. Essentially an updated version of the 8664 Amtrak Alco produced in 1976 as part of the Lake Shore Limited Set. Part of 11707 Silver Spike Passenger Set. Price includes 18904 dummy unit.   -- -- -- **125**

18904 AMTRAK: 1988, dummy Alco A unit, matches 18903 powered unit above, illuminated. Price for both units.   -- -- -- **125**

33000 LIONEL LINES: Announced for 1988, Rail Scope GP-9, dark gray and black cab, white lettering and number "3300", red, white, and blue Lionel logo, twin can motors, headlight. This revolutionary locomotive has a miniature video transmitter inside the cab which projects an "engineer's-eye" view to a television set. The photo image is sent by electronic pulse through the rails, where it is sent through a converter to the antenna terminals of a television. The result is a sharp black and white picture of the operator's layout as if the operator were inside the locomotive. The operator can even videotape his layout from the TV image! Can be used with any television, although Lionel is marketing its own TV (see next entry). Large Scale and HO versions also available. Price for locomotive only.
                                                                              -- -- -- **275**

33002 LIONEL LINES RAIL SCOPE GP-9: Same as 33000 entry, except includes 4-1/2" black and white television set with red and black plastic case on swivel bracket.   -- -- -- **375**

Chapter II
STEAM ENGINES

Some General-style steamers and a tricky comparison. Top shelf: 8004 Rock Island & Peoria. Middle shelf: 8701 Western & Atlantic, the first General revival from 1977. Bottom shelf: 8630 Western & Atlantic, which appears identical to 8701 but has an entirely different drive system. Note small reversing switch projecting from back of cab. This model came as part of uncatalogued American Express General set in 1986. A. Rudman, F. Stem, L. Caponi, and R. LaVoie Collections.

During its years of existence, Lionel has been very creative with its steam engines in one sense and not so creative in another. That apparent contradiction is not easy to explain, but some knowledge of the manufacturing process might help in understanding the paradox.

The molds for steam engines tend to be more detailed and expensive than those for the diesel engines. In the first place, the boilers are rounded instead of square-sided, making for a more intricate mold-creating process. Additionally, the molds have to be made strong enough to withstand die-casting with metal, even though the same mold can be (and has been) used with plastic. Tooling costs can be enormous; for example, when Fundimensions issued its American Flyer passenger cars, the firm found that key pieces of the observation car molds were

missing. It cost Fundimensions well over $30,000 just to supply those pieces and change the molds.

Imagine, if you will, the enormous costs of creating a steam engine mold from scratch, and you will see why Lionel chose not to be creative, at least at first. Instead, Fundimensions nearly always used the steam engine molds it inherited from the original Lionel Corporation and modified them as needed. With one startling exception, Kenner-Parker and Lionel, Inc. have followed the same policy. (The exception is the all-new Rock Island Northern, a real breakthrough in steam locomotive design both in prototype and in tinplate.) Now, if you want to put out a product which at least seems to be new, what would you do? The most cost-effective strategy would be to modify currently existing molds and to issue new paint schemes, and

Top shelf: 8315 Baltimore and Ohio General steamer from B & O passenger set of 1983. Bottom shelf: 8410 Redwood Valley Express General locomotive. Note stack and headlight differences between the two.

in that sense, Lionel has been extremely creative with its steam engines.

Of course, there is a price to be paid — dies and molds eventually wear out with use. We may be coming to a time when Lionel will have to invest in retooling with entirely new steam engine dies or freshened versions of the old ones; either way, considerable expense will be involved. That is just what seems to be happening with the 1987 Rock Island Northern. As an example, consider that there are two basic molds for the Hudson 4-6-4 steam engine — the smaller Baldwin boiler and the larger Alco boiler. The last time the Baldwin mold was used (until recently) was in 1979 for the 8900 A T S F Hudson. Since then, every Hudson made by Fundimensions has used the larger Alco boiler. The probable reason is wear and tear on the Baldwin boiler mold. Compare an 8603 or 8900 Fundimensions Locomotive with an original 665 or 2065 Lionel Hudson from the 1950s and 1960s, and you will see the advance of fuzziness in detail as the die has worn. The Wabash Pacific issued in 1986 used the Baldwin mold once again, and it is evident that the die has indeed been cleaned and reworked, most likely by a new plating of chrome on the inside of the die surface. The foregoing explanation probably accounts for the slow variation in steam engines relative to the rapid expansion of the diesel engines. In 1970 Fundimensions began its production of steamers with simple 2-4-2 Columbia locomotives in plastic. A die-cast Great Northern Hudson was pictured in the catalogue, but never made. Only in 1972 did Fundimensions issue the 8206 Hudson Steamer, and it was the only large steamer made until 1976, when the 8600 and 8603 Hudsons appeared. After that, however, the story gets much more complicated, probably because Fundimensions had built its market to sufficient numbers to justify the issue of many new steamers.

The small steam engines issued by Fundimensions range from very inexpensive 0-4-0 switchers made almost entirely of plastic to die-cast 4-4-2 and plastic 2-6-4 locomotives. One of these small locomotives, the 8141 Pennsylvania 2-4-2 Columbia of 1971, was the recipient of a significant technical innovation of the firm — the Electronic Sound of Steam. (See the article on the Columbia 2-4-2 locomotives from these years later in this chapter.) An intermittent copper contact was attached to the locomotive smoke unit and geared so that the contact was made and broken with each revolution of the drive wheels. This contact led back through a wire to the rear of the locomotive, where it was clipped to a wire leading to the tender. The tender contained an electronic circuit board and a small loudspeaker which translated the contact into a realistic hissing sound simulating the chug of a steam engine. With a few refinements, this system is still in use. The real steamers chug twice per wheel revolution, while the Lionel sound system gives only one chug. Perhaps it is just as well; two chugs per wheel revolution would "blur" the sound at high speeds.

Two other smaller steamers, a die-cast 4-4-2 8204 and the 8206 Hudson, were the first recipients of a Fundimensions innovation which was not so successful — an electronic steam whistle. Though the whistle itself sounded very good, it tended to make the Sound of Steam muddy. The worst problem was contained in the controller Fundimensions issued with this whistle. The controller contained an electronic diode which rectified some of the transformer's current into a DC charge which activated the whistle. Unfortunately, the diode contacts tended to stick in the closed position, and this quickly burned out the diode. After dropping the whistle in 1973, Fundimensions revived it in 1980 with the two Berkshire locomotives of that year. This time they had solved the problem relating to the Sound of Steam, and they wisely let operators use the old

A tale told by three early Columbia steamers. Top: The 8041 New York Central version of 1970. Note the white number, the visible armature shaft end, and the plastic slide valve guides. Center: The mis-numbered 8041 Pennsylvania model of early 1971 with Sound of Steam. This example came from a Silver Star set and is very hard to find. Bottom: The regular-issue 8141 Pennsylvania model of later 1971. Does anyone have a white-numbered 8141 out there? R. LaVoie Collection.

Lionel transformers with DC rectifier discs to work the whistle. It is probably one of the best whistles ever put into a tinplate engine; it even has a "trill" (a falling tone when the control is released) like the real whistles had when blown by an expert engineer!

The 4-4-2 locomotives have been made mostly in die-cast versions, beginning with the 8142 C & O. These locomotives have used a modified version of the old Lionel 637/2037 boiler, last used on 2-6-4 locomotives in the 1960s. They are good pullers, but many collectors would favor them more had they been issued with a three-position reversing switch instead of the two-position unit they used. The two-position unit has no neutral position, thus limiting the operating use of these locomotives. One of the latest 4-4-2 locomotives, the 8402 Reading, has a boiler front which many collectors consider very ugly. Most of the 4-4-2 locomotives are fairly good looking, however. The latest one, a Pennsylvania die-cast 4-4-2 designed to pull a newly issued set of tuscan and black 2400-style passenger cars, resurrects a little and quaint square-back tender not seen since it came with one version of the 8040 Nickel Plate Road Locomotive all the way back in 1972.

One small 0-4-0 locomotive would have been very interesting, but it was pulled from production at the last minute. The 8901 was scheduled to be the locomotive for the Radio Control Express. It would have had a battery-powered DC motor and a radio control for starting, stopping, and reversing the locomotive. This arrangement reminded many collectors of the Electronic Control Sets of 1946-1950, which were well ahead of their time. However, the Radio Control Express was an expensive set which was judged by Fundimensions to be limited in appeal. In addition, battery consumption was judged to be excessive. It was never mass marketed.

One of the few original small locomotive designs was a strange looking 0-4-0 dockside switcher. Delicate but whimsical, this little locomotive headed a set with a small four-wheeled tender, but as marketed for separate sale it did not have a tender. The 8209 Docksider was catalogued for four years; recently, the docksider has been used in a 1985 Santa Fe work train, and it has pulled a few low-priced sets since then, most recently the Rail Blazer set of 1987.

Until 1985 Lionel had made just one deluxe switch engine modeled after the old Lionel 1600 models. This was a die-cast Pennsylvania switcher first issued in 1975. It had a slope-back tender with a working backup light (curiously, with a red lens instead of a clear one) and a three-position reverse. Lionel revived this model for 1985 in an 8516 New York Central guise as part of a Yard Chief work train set, which was a huge success. Lionel outfitted its new switcher with the new can motor geared to a set of spur gears; all the Traditional Series steam locomotives have used this arrangement since that year — rather successfully. The New York Central switcher was the first one ever with a smoke unit, and did it ever smoke! See

Two recent Hudsons and the first modern era model. Top: The 5484 TCA special production model (see Special Production chapter for photo of entire train). Middle shelf: The 8101 Chicago & Alton, which reintroduced the 2224W tender after an absence of over 40 years. Bottom: The first Hudson from 1972, the 8206 New York Central. Note the differences between the Alco-type boiler shells of the first two and the Baldwin-type boiler shell of the 8206. A. Rudman, F. Stem, L. Caponi, and R. LaVoie Collections.

John Kouba's article on its successor, the Santa Fe switcher in the 1986 Service Station Set, later in this chapter.

Except for the Scale Hudson with a 773 boiler, the Hudson locomotives issued by Fundimensions have come in only two boiler styles. The smaller of the two is the Baldwin boiler, which has horizontal shaded windows on its cab. The larger one is the Hudson with an Alco boiler, which has square windows on the cab which are cross-hatched into four smaller windows. Lately, the Alco boiler has been used more than the Baldwin boiler.

As mentioned before, the 4-6-4 Hudson locomotives did not show much variation until 1977; but beginning in that year many new ones were issued, culminating in the reissue in 1984 (actually released in 1985) of the magnificent scale 773-style New York Central Hudson, the 8406. By 1977 collectors had begun to ask for revivals of their favorite Lionel postwar steamers. Fundimensions responded well, but not quite as expected. The firm put out a beautiful 8702 Southern Crescent Hudson in Southern green and gold livery; they also made five matching passenger cars, all to be sold separately, not as a set. In practice, this usually meant that there were many more sets of cars than there were locomotives. So well received was this Hudson that the next year Fundimensions revived one of the most revered names in Lionel history, the Blue Comet. This locomotive was done in two shades of glossy blue with gold trim

and had a feedwater heater on its boiler front. It too had its own set of matching passenger cars in a rich two-tone blue color scheme with gold lettering and a broad cream stripe. Collectors snapped up this locomotive and its cars even more eagerly than they had the Southern Crescent, even though the plain 2046W Tender did not do the locomotive full justice. Recently, new diner cars were issued for both sets. After issuing the 8900 Santa Fe Hudson, the first in the Famous American Railroad Series, Fundimensions issued another Hudson-powered passenger set, the Chicago and Alton, in 1981. This time they had a real surprise for collectors. Instead of the plastic 2046W Tender, this locomotive came with a revived 2224W Tender not seen on a Lionel product since 1940! This tender was die-cast and magnificently detailed. It had new six-wheel trucks, a whistle, and the Sound of Steam. Many collectors like the maroon, red, and gold paint scheme of this set. The last regularly issued Hudson to date has been the 8210 Joshua Lionel Cowen Commemorative Locomotive in bronze, black, and gold. The same boiler has been used since then, but with different wheel arrangements. Mention must also be made of a very scarce Hudson, the Atlantic Coast Line, made for J. C. Penney as a special in 1980. This engine is almost impossible to acquire and has shown substantial appreciation in value.

In recent years Lionel has revived the postwar 736 2-8-4 Berkshire Locomotive with several models, including the 8002

Three attractive Hudsons, Lionel's steamers at their best. Top: 8702 Southern Crescent of 1977. Middle: 8801 Jersey Central Blue Comet of 1978. Bottom: 8900 Santa Fe from Famous American Railroads Set No. 1 of 1979. A. Rudman, F. Stem, L. Caponi, and R. La-Voie Collections.

Union Pacific in a two-tone gray with smoke deflectors, the 8003 Chessie Steam Special Locomotive with a bright paint scheme of blue, gray, yellow, and vermilion Chessie colors, and a nice 8215 Nickel Plate Road Locomotive in the traditional black. Only the Nickel Plate Locomotive has had the 2224W die-cast Tender; the other two have the plastic 2046W Tender. Another beautiful Berkshire came out in 1986 as a special issue for J. C. Penney; this was the 8615 Louisville and Nashville model of the L & N's "Big Emma" series. This boiler style was used for two offshoots, the 2-8-2 8309 Southern Mikado in green, tuscan, and gold Southern markings with the 224W Tender and the 3100 Great Northern 4-8-4 Locomotive in green and tuscan with the 2046W Tender. In 1981 Fundimensions revived the beautiful Norfolk and Western "J" class stream-lined 4-8-4 Locomotive, originally numbered 746 but numbered 611 after the prototype. This locomotive headed a matched set of maroon and black Powhatan Arrow aluminum passenger cars to form a train well over ten feet long! It had all the deluxe Lionel features, including smoke from the cylinders, a feature introduced by Marx a long time ago. (The maintenance crew at the Norfolk and Western shops in Roanoke, Virginia would have been greatly troubled by any sign of steam leaking from the cylinders because this would indicate a bad job of packing the seals!) The "J" boiler was used in 1983 for the 8307 Southern Pacific "Daylight" Locomotive, a fine model of the original which could also be used to pull matching aluminum passenger cars.

Lionel did not neglect another old favorite, the "General" old-time 4-4-0 Locomotive first made by Lionel in the late 1950s. In 1977 the Western & Atlantic No. 3 (8701) met with great success, especially after the old-time cars were issued for it. Since then, the "General" Locomotive has been used in chromed Rock Island, blue and black B & O, and other color schemes. One version of this locomotive became a special issue for J. C. Penney, another was part of a special American Express offer, and another will be part of the 1988 Service Station Set.

Finally, in 1985, Lionel revived one of the great favorites of all the Lionel steamers — the Pennsylvania 6-8-6 S-2 steam turbine. The original 671, 2020, 681, and 682 versions of this locomotive sold by the tens of thousands in the postwar era. Lionel has issued the locomotive in a handsome gray, Brunswick green, and black color scheme with its streamlined tender, whistle, Sound of Steam, smoke, and even the delicate oiler linkage from the old 682. This locomotive is bound to become a collector favorite very rapidly. It even has the legendary backup lights in the tender!

Development of the scale Hudsons has continued since the original 8406 (actually numbered 783) became such a big collector favorite. The trouble has been that these scale Hudsons have been rather difficult and expensive to acquire. In 1986 the 8606 Boston and Albany came out as part of a mail-order offer available only from Lionel itself, not the usual dealer network. This arrangement, as one may guess, did not sit with the dealers too well, so when Lionel, Inc. management took con-

Three big, desirable eight-drivered Lionel locomotives. Top: 3100 Great Northern 4-8-4 from Famous American Railroad Set No. 3 of 1981. Middle: 8002 Union Pacific Berkshire 2-8-4 from Famous American Railroad Set No. 2 of 1980. Bottom: 8003 Chessie Steam Special Berkshire of 1980. A. Rudman, F. Stem, L. Caponi, and R. LaVoie Collections.

trol of the trains, a declaration was made that this particular scheme would not occur again. Due to its limited distribution, the Boston and Albany Hudson has been very hard to acquire. It is somewhat dressier than its New York Central predecessor with its white-painted smokebox front and white-edged driver tires. A third scale Hudson has been released in late 1988, and it is one collectors have been eagerly awaiting. This is the 18002 New York Central (actually numbered 785) in gun-metal gray — and, amazingly, the spoked wheels which have not been seen since the prewar 763E of 1938-1942! This is a commemorative locomotive for the 50th anniversary of the New York Central's proud thoroughbred steamer.

Imagine, if you will, the real surprise for 1987 — an entirely new Rock Island 4-8-4 Northern steam locomotive in gun-metal gray with a die-cast tender and all the deluxe features of the Hudson! The 18001, actually numbered 5100, has an all-new boiler and tender design with the proper "chunky" look of the real Northerns. It rides on a tried and true chassis, that of the Norfolk and Western J Class model of six years ago. Collectors lined up for this engine, which was delayed in production due to delays in parts or trouble with the boiler castings — we are not sure which. When the engine came out, some examples had defective armatures which caused serious running problems. However, Lionel Inc. corrected the problem quickly, and the engine is an excellent runner. A Lackawanna version is scheduled for 1988 production.

If Lionel's options in tool and die-making have been somewhat limited until recently, the firm has certainly gotten the most mileage out of what has been available for its steamers. Lionel has succeeded in carrying on the great tradition of tinplate steamers with some of the nicest and best made products imaginable — even though the cost of these locomotives has been prohibitive for some collectors. The lesser Lionel steamers run reasonably well, are highly collectable, and, as a group, offer the chance for a fine collection. It took a while for the variety, but it was worth the wait.

Gd VG Exc Mt

3 UNION PACIFIC: 1981, see 8104.

3 W. & A. R.R.: 1977, see 8701; 1986, see 8630.

611: See 8100.

659: See 8101.

665E JOHNNY CASH BLUE TRAIN: See Special Production chapter.

672: See 8610.

779: See 8215.

783: See 8406.

784: See 8606.

785: See 18002.

1970: See 8615.

3100 GREAT NORTHERN: 1981, 4-8-4, Famous American Railroad Series No. 3; electronic whistle and Sound of Steam, Magnetraction, three-position E-unit; dark green boiler, silver boiler front and smokebox, "elephant ears," tuscan

Spectacular steamers, all three! Top shelf: 8404 Pennsylvania Steam Turbine, part of Famous American Railroad Set No. 5 and numbered 6200 after it prototype. Middle shelf: 8307 Southern Pacific "Daylight" 4-8-4, numbered 4449 after its prototype. This engine has become very hard to find. Bottom shelf: 8100 Norfolk & Western "J" Class 4-8-4, for which matching passenger cars were made for a "Powhatan Arrow" set.

cab roof, black sand and steam domes, white-edged running board; dark green streamlined tender with "GREAT NORTHERN" logo on side, superb "runner."

-- 350 400 475

4449: See 8307.

4501: See 8309.

5100: See 18001.

5484 T C A: 1985, see Special Production chapter.

8001 NICKEL PLATE: 1980, 2-6-4, plastic K-4 locomotive, remake of 2025 / 675 die-cast Steamer from late 1940s. This (with 8007) is the first Lionel six-wheel driver plastic locomotive. DC-powered engine; running on AC current will burn out the motor.

-- -- 40 50

8002 UNION PACIFIC: 1980, 2-8-4, Berkshire, second in Lionel's Famous American Railroad Series (FARR); two-tone gray boiler, yellow-edged running board; electronic whistle, electronic Sound of Steam, Magnetraction, smoke, three-position reverse unit; gray tender with dark gray center band, yellow-lettered "UNION PACIFIC", with FARR diamond logo. The UP prototype is actually a 4-8-4 Northern since the UP did not use a 2-8-4 Berkshire; it is the first Lionel locomotive with smoke deflectors astride the boiler. The gray paint on the boiler has a tendency to turn to an olive-gray shade when it is exposed to heat over a long period of time. Approximately 6,000 made. L. Bohn, M. Sabatelle, and R. LaVoie comments.

-- 350 375 450

8003 CHESSIE: 1980, 2-8-4; die-cast Berkshire. This locomotive marked an important development in Fundimensions' history, the rerun of the 2-8-4 Berkshire, Lionel's top-of-the-line postwar steam engine. Fundimensions also offered handsome matching passenger cars as separate sale items. In 1986 Lionel, Inc. added a diner car to the set. The Chessie Steam Special engine and cars were based on a prototype Chessie train which actually toured the United States to

celebrate the 150th Anniversary of American railroading. The model engine featured an electronic whistle, electronic Sound of Steam, smoke, Magnetraction, and a three-position reverse unit. The engine boiler is light gray (forward of the bell) and dark gray (behind the bell); it has a yellow-edged running board, yellow and red stripes beneath the cab window, and "8003" under cab window. Dark gray tender with six-wheel trucks and large yellow area topped by orange band, "Chessie System" lettering on side. The engine as delivered did not run well. After adjustments it ran better, and its sound, properly synchronized, is delightful. Miller observation. Apparently the difficulties only occurred with early production; other operators have stated that this locomotive has been an excellent, trouble-free runner right from the start. Approximately 4,500 made, and about 5,000 sets of cars produced. C. Lang and M. Sabatelle comments.

-- 400 450 500

8004 ROCK ISLAND & PEORIA: 1980, 1982, 4-4-0, General chassis but modeled after an engine built by the Rock Island and Peoria Railroad in the late 1800s for the World's Fair; engine has chrome boiler, tuscan cab and steam chest, black stack and boiler bands, smoke, and two-position reverse unit; tender has tuscan sides with mountain mural. About 4,000 made. M. Sabatelle comment.

-- -- 150 170

8005 A T S F: 1980, 1982, 4-4-0, General chassis, DC powered, very lightweight locomotive, red and maroon engine with gold trim; 8005T Tender with gold rectangle trim with "ATSF". Came as part of 1053 The James Gang Set with three cars, figures, and building. Observed with two frame types. Type I uses leftover AC frames from previous production with worm wheel on axle for AC motor. Type II frames lack this worm wheel on axle. M. Sabatelle comment. Price for engine and tender only. 50,000 made.

-- -- 30 40

8006 ATLANTIC COAST LINE: 1980, 4-6-4, gun-metal-painted die-cast boiler, one-piece boiler front with "LIONEL" cast beneath the headlight and num-

Two more Hudsons and an adapted Pacific. Top shelf: 8210 Joshua Lionel Cowen Commemorative. Middle shelf: 8600 New York Central, available only with the 1976 Empire State Express Set. Bottom shelf: 8210 Wabash, first in the Fallen Flags Series sets. A. Rudman, F. Stem, L. Caponi, and R. LaVoie Collections.

bered "2065-15" on inside, steam chest side is decorated in white with a rectangle; inside of the rectangle is another rectangle with rounded corners. The engine, known as "The Silver Shadow," has white tires and a high gloss black paint beneath the white-painted running board edge. The New York Central-style tender has a water scoop; two-thirds of the prototype tender was a coal bunker. The line of rivets that descends from the rear of the coal bunker indicates the demarcation between water and coal in the prototype. The model tender has die-cast six-wheel trucks. This model was made for J. C. Penney as a special item and was not catalogued by Lionel. It came with a display track, probably Gargraves Phantom track, mounted on a wooden base in a clear plastic case. Only 2,200 reportedly were manufactured and these were sold out very quickly. Degano, Lang, and White observations.   --   --   **500 700**
See also Factory Errors and Prototypes.

8007 NEW YORK, NEW HAVEN & HARTFORD: 1980, 2-6-4, plastic K-4 locomotive with silver boiler front, a remake of 2025 / 675 die-cast Steamer from later 1940s. This is the first time Lionel has ever made a six-driver plastic locomotive. Locomotive, with smoke, gold-striped running board edge; square-backed 8007T Tender with gold "NEW YORK, NEW HAVEN & HARTFORD" stripe and mechanical Sound of Steam. The K-4 prototype appeared only on the Pennsylvania Railroad, but Fundimensions' management reportedly liked the New Haven logo. Came as part of 1050 New Englander Set. DC-powered engine; running on AC will burn out the motor.   --   --   **40 50**

8008 CHESSIE: 1980, 4-4-2, dark blue-painted die-cast locomotive with yellow-painted running board edge, smoke, red firebox light (a feature not seen since the 226E Steamer was made in 1938); dark blue 8008T Tender with large yellow area topped with orange stripe, Chessie System logo, and mechanical Sound of Steam. Came as part of 1052 Chesapeake Flyer Set. DC-powered engine; running on AC will burn out the motor. One example has been found mounted on an 8800 Lionel Lines AC-drive chassis. 10,000 units made. M. Sabatelle Collection.   --   --   **50 60**

LEADERS OF THE LIONEL REVIVAL: THE 2-4-2 COLUMBIA STEAMERS, 1970-1976

Over the course of its long and illustrious history, Lionel has produced an astonishing variety of engines and rolling stock. Perhaps it is inevitable that collectors and operators emphasize certain types of production, since obviously some types possess more glamour and attraction than others. For example, among the earlier modern era locomotives, the Hudson steamers and the better diesels get most of the attention.

The trouble with this slanted attention is that some interesting items sometimes go begging for attention when they have their own interesting stories to tell. Again and again, in both the postwar and modern eras, the inexpensive items, produced in great quantities, tell us more about Lionel's manufacturing techniques and marketplace thinking than do the more expensive, scarcer items. One advantage for the train "archaeologist" is that the less expensive items tend to exist in greater quantities at less cost; therefore, they can be studied more readily.

(8406) Scale Hudson. B. Schilling Collection, G. Stern photograph.

One such category is Lionel's 2-4-2 Columbia Steam Locomotives produced between 1970 and 1976, the crucial first years of the Lionel revival. Unlike most inexpensive items, some of these Columbias are difficult to find now because in those years the toy train market was quite a bit smaller than it is now. Yet no other locomotive produced in these years can tell more about Lionel's attention to detail than these little steamers. They were sold separately and included in both catalogued and uncatalogued sets. When the Electronic Sound of Steam was introduced in 1971, Lionel chose a Columbia as the first engine to receive the system. The body shell was produced in die-cast and plastic versions, and these little engines pulled slope-back, square-back, and streamlined tenders in both oil and coal versions. The Columbia was a dependable runner, too, since Lionel wisely chose not to revive the old Scout motor of the postwar years which had proved so troublesome. Instead, the firm issued all its Columbias with a good spur-gear motor which could pull a light to medium train at low power consumption — an important consideration, since Lionel still cannot produce the powerful postwar transformers due to Federal safety regulations. No other locomotive, diesel or steamer, has been so versatile or has served Lionel so well for so long.

Yet the Columbia, because of its mundane and unimpressive appearance, has not raised much collector attention. Very little has been written about its manufacturing changes over the years, and some varieties of the modern era have never been described adequately. Just to cite one example: In 1973, a two-tone blue 8303 Jersey Central Columbia was included with the "Blue Streak" catalogued freight set. Later, this engine was made in black both for catalogued sets and for special Sears sets. At least four versions of this engine may exist in black Jersey Central colors, all with different numbers and features. The scarce 8604 black Jersey Central came with a two-position reversing switch, a headlight, smoke, and the Electronic Sound of Steam in one set. It also came with no light or smoke, manual reversing, and a mechanical sound of steam tender in another — all with the same boiler shell and number!

The ancestry of the Columbia steam locomotive goes back a long way, all the way back to the prewar 1684 and its siblings produced in the early 1940s. Scout sets using the Columbia wheel arrangement were produced in 1948 and afterward, and the 2034 and 1130 were mainstays of the lower-priced O27 sets in the early 1950s. A terrific number of Columbia locomotives were produced in the 200 Series beginning in the middle 1950s right up to the last years of the postwar era.

In 1970 and 1971 the new Lionel management under General Mills did what any efficiently run company would do — use up supplies of existing postwar parts left over from the earlier management. For that reason, it is important to know the critical variables on the postwar Columbias before we can show manufacturing changes on the early modern era locomotives.

On the postwar Columbias, the front truck plate held the front wheels by a rivet; this plate was chromed and was stamped in one of three ways. The earliest truck plates had a full "MADE IN U.S.A. THE LIONEL CORPORATION NEW YORK" stamping in three lines. Later plates had just "LIONEL" or they were blank. There was always a small oval slot in these plates at the point where the plate bent down to clear the motor housing.

The front drive wheels on the postwar Columbias always had an unused hole projecting outward from the wheel's surface. This is because the same wheels were used on the six-drivered engines such as the 2026 and 2037, where the hole was used to attach the extra drive rods. The first reduction gear on the spur-drive motors had a plastic plate which showed the end of the armature rod. The rear truck-holding drawbar could be either chromed or black. Some time in the middle 1950s, extra piping was added to the Columbia boiler shell, and in 1958 a flared smokestack replaced the straight stack of the earlier models to facilitate adding smoke fluid to the plastic smoke units used on the Columbias. Both these changes continued into all the Columbias of the modern era. The hex nut holding the single-drive rod onto the rear drive wheels of the postwar Columbias was always chromed; it is black on all modern era Columbias. The motor frame of all the postwar Columbias was blackened; these blackened motor frames were used on the 1970 production models, but thereafter all the motor frames were shiny unblackened metal.

The 1130T Tenders used on postwar Columbias had solid plastic coal piles, a metal tender frame with a four-line Lionel identification embossed into it, closed ports at the rear, no square holes in front or back of the coal pile, and no numbering on the rear identification plate.

The earliest modern era Columbias, the 8040 Nickel Plate Road and 8041 New York Central models of 1970, continued many postwar features but added some new ones. The front truck plate of these locomotives featured a new embossing: "BY LIONEL M.P.C. / MT. CLEMENS, MICH." This front truck plate retained the small oval of the postwar plates in 1970, but that oval disappeared in 1971. They had holes in the front

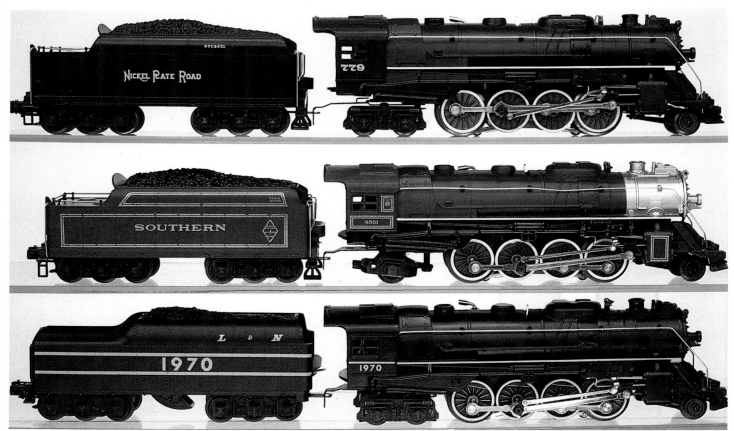

Three more eight-drivered steamers from Lionel's recent production. Top: 8215 Nickel Plate Road 2-8-4 Berkshire, numbered 779 after its prototype. Middle: 8309 Southern 2-8-2, numbered 4501 after its prototype and part of Famous American Railroad Set No. 4 of 1983. Bottom: 8615 Louisville & Nashville "Big Emma" Berkshire of 1986, sold through J. C. Penney. A. Rudman, F. Stem, L. Caponi, and R. LaVoie Collections.

drive wheels, the postwar open-axle gear plate, and no Sound of Steam wire hole in the back of the cab. The slide valves had new black plastic sliding pieces which proved too flimsy for use and were replaced after 1970. The tenders had new plastic detailed frames into which the tender cab simply snapped. In the case of the 8041's 1130T Tender, the coal pile remained solid, the ports at the rear remained closed, and there were no square escape holes at the front and rear of the coal pile. The earliest 1970 production models used leftover AAR trucks, but most had the far more common Symington-Wayne design. One feature differentiated the 1970 1130T Tender found with the 8041 from its postwar predecessors: the presence of "8060-T" stamped into the identification plate on the rear of the tender.

Some important changes in construction in 1971 allow the collector to differentiate 1970 and 1971 production in several locomotives made through 1972. The motor frame of all Columbias produced in 1971 and thereafter is shiny metal, not black as it had been. The slide valve guides became the older metal pieces once again in 1971 instead of the fragile plastic pieces. (Some of the plastic pieces must have been left over, however, because an 8042 from the author's collection has them; it is known to have come in a set produced in early 1972.) The holes in the front drive wheels remain in 1971 production; these were not changed until 1972, when the place on the wheel where the

hole was is blank. The cover atop the first reduction gear changes in 1971 from the open one of postwar years to a closed one in which the armature rod end is not visible. Most of the rear trucks have a black holding piece, but some produced in 1973 and later are chrome once again.

A hole appears in the cab end just below the firebox doors. (In one example from 1971, it is actually through the firebox doors.) For 1971 the hole is small; it is enlarged for 1972 and later production. This hole allows the wire for the Electronic Sound of Steam connection to pass through to the tender wire. In 1973 and later, some of the front truck holding plates are stamped "LIONEL" instead of the previous MPC stamping. Most likely this is because Lionel trains were separated from General Mills' MPC Division some time in late 1972 or early 1973, though these also could have been leftover postwar parts.

The metal frame for the 1130T Tenders returns after 1970 and the plastic frame is abandoned after just one year; this is because the Sound of Steam needed the metal frame for a ground. A new metal frame was introduced into the 1130T tenders beginning in 1971, and there are two types. One type has a large rectangular hole just below the Sound of Steam speaker and four large circular holes, one at each corner. The other is identical except for two circular holes where the rectangle is on the first variety. After 1971 the "8060-T" stamping in the identification plate disappears and the plate becomes blank.

The addition of the Sound of Steam feature necessitated some other changes to the 1130T Tender shells as well. In order for the sound to escape, the rear ports were opened and three square escape holes were added, two in front of the coal pile and one at its rear. The coal pile itself was made so thin that in places it was actually open to the interior of the tender. This "lattice work" coal pile was a clever way to keep the realism of a coal pile, yet allow the chug sound to escape. Its big disadvantage is, of course, its extreme fragility. Later on, beginning in 1973, the 1130T Tender shell was modified to add an oil-burning top piece to replace the coal pile and to add another new plastic bottom which contained the large rotating wheel for the mechanical sound of steam.

One other variation in manufacturing is of some note. On the Columbia locomotive, the rear drawbar passes through a retaining slot. The lower bar of this slot was a separate metal piece riveted to the chassis in 1970 and 1971 for both plastic and die-cast versions of the Columbia. In 1972 and thereafter this piece is retained on the die-cast Columbias, but it becomes an integral part of the boiler casting on the plastic models.

The Columbias of the early modern era came with several different types of tenders. Many were equipped with the short streamlined 1130T Tender, as we have discussed, but one Canadian Grand Trunk Locomotive of 1971 came with the 234T Santa Fe-type square-back Tender, several models came with the 1615T slope-back switcher Tender, and one version of the 8040 Nickel Plate Road came with a strange, stubby square-back tender in 1972 which was issued in 1987 with the 18602 Pennsylvania die-cast 4-4-2 steam Locomotive.

Aside from the models produced for Canadian customers in 1971 and 1972, which are very scarce, the development of the gray 8041 New York Central Columbia into the 1971 gray 8141 Pennsylvania produced perhaps the hardest Columbia of all to find. Aside from the changes described above, the 8041 number below the cab window of the New York Central model changed from white to red for the 8141 Pennsylvania. However, a number of locomotives marked 8041 in red have been found with the Sound of Steam and the Pennsylvania Tender. These engines are 1971 products; the author's example came in a 1971 catalogued set, the Silver Star. Other locomotives are identical except for an 8141 number in red; this is the correct number for the Pennsylvania version. Was the 8041 Pennsylvania a special model for uncatalogued sets? Was it one of a few trial pieces for the Sound of Steam mechanism? Our best conclusion is that the Columbia equipped with the Sound of Steam feature, a red number 8041, and the Pennsylvania Tender is a highly scarce factory error. Chances are that the earliest runs of this locomotive in 1971 went through the manufacturing process and into a few sets before the erroneous number was discovered and changed into the correct 8141 number. It is, of course, much harder to find than either its New York Central predecessor or its correctly-numbered 8141 Pennsylvania equivalent. One report states that the red-numbered 8141 was the version made for separate sale and a white-numbered 8141 was made for the sets. We have not been able to confirm the existence of a white-numbered 8141, and

we think that the red-numbered 8141 was made both for sets and for separate sale.

To add to the confusion regarding this piece, a further variation has just recently come to light. On one red-numbered 8141, the number below the cab windows was raised above the level of the plastic surface and then painted red. This meant that the number had to be an integral part of the mold rather than a later add-on by heat or rubber stamping. This is a most unusual practice for Lionel. This example also had the integral plastic rear drawbar crosspiece rather than the earlier metal piece riveted onto the casting. Perhaps other strange variations of this engine exist "out there!"

Other scarce Columbias include all those in uncatalogued sets, especially those with their own numbers and identities made for Sears and other department store special sets. The 8040 Canadian National with slope-back tender and the 8042 Grand Trunk Western with 234T square-back Tender are Canadian issues; the department store specials include the 8043 Nickel Plate, made for Sears, the 8308 and (unconfirmed) 8309 black Jersey Centrals, and both versions of the 8604 black Jersey Central.

The Columbia locomotives represent great collecting opportunities for the collector. Although some are very hard to find, none command outrageous prices, and nearly all can be acquired at very modest cost in excellent condition. The Columbias carried the corporate risk of Lionel in the early modern era far more than did the diesels or larger steamers. Had this little steamer not been a dependable runner, Lionel would have had a much tougher time reconstituting its position amid the world of toy trains. These locomotives deserve a great deal more attention than they have received to date, and so do some of the other small steamers of the early modern era, such as the 2-4-0 locomotives produced in great numbers and types. More studies are needed to show the true place of these little steamers in bringing about the revival of Lionel Trains in the 1970s.

Note: The 8040 has been made in several different railroad markings.
8040 NICKEL PLATE: 1970-72, 2-4-2, black plastic body, no light, manual-reverse switch atop boiler.
(A) Black motor sides, plastic cylinder slide valves, white flat lettering, "NICKEL PLATE / ROAD" on slope-back tender, came with Set 1081, lowest priced set in the line. R. LaVoie and G. Halverson comments.   -- 15 20 30
(B) Same as (A), but 1971-72 production: shiny metal motor sides, metal cylinder slide valves. R. LaVoie Collection.   -- 15 20 30
(C) 1972, same as (B), but white raised lettering, "NICKEL PLATE / ROAD" on short box tender, number unknown, came with Set 1081, the lowest priced set in the 1972 line. See photograph. This tender was not used again until 1987. G. Halverson comment.   -- 15 20 30
8040 CANADIAN NATIONAL: 1971, 2-4-2, black plastic body, headlight, flat numbering on locomotive, rubber tire on rear driver, two-position reverse, slope-back tender with white lettering "CANADIAN NATIONAL" on side in rectan-

8040 Nickel Plate with slope-back tender.

8040 Nickel Plate with box tender.

gular box, AAR trucks, dummy coupler. Came as part of Set T-1081 with maroon 9143 CN Gondola, 9020 UP Flatcar, and maroon 9065 CN Caboose. This set was listed in both the small and the large versions of the 1971 Canadian catalogue. K. Wills and D. Anderson Collections.   **-- 30 40 100**

8041 NEW YORK CENTRAL: 1970-71, 2-4-2, silver-gray plastic body, white lettering on tender, red stripe on locomotive, 8060T (1130T-style) tender with AAR trucks, dummy coupler, plastic base. C. Rohlfing comments.

(A) 1970, number on cab in white.   **-- 20 30 40**

(B) 1971, same as (A), but shows changes made to locomotive for 1971, has "PENNSYLVANIA" tender, Electronic Sound of Steam, and "8041" number on cab in red. This is actually a locomotive which should have been numbered 8141, but in production some examples were made before the number was changed. The sample examined came as part of an original 1971 Silver Star Set. Very hard to find. R. LaVoie Collection.   **-- 40 60 75**

8042 Grand Trunk Western.

8042 GRAND TRUNK WESTERN: 1970, 1972, 2-4-2, black die-cast metal body, headlight, smoke, white lettering.

(A) 1970, thin cab floor.   **-- 15 20 30**

(B) 1970, thick cab floor.   **-- 15 20 30**

(C) 1972, same as (B), but came as part of uncatalogued Set 1291 with 1130T Pennsylvania Tender painted flat black with white lettering, Symington-Wayne trucks and dummy coupler. R. LaVoie Collection.   **-- 25 30 40**

8043 NICKEL PLATE: 1970, 2-4-2, black plastic body with white lettering, slope-back tender, manufactured for Sears as part of Set 1091. Very hard to find.   **-- 35 45 60**

8062 GREAT NORTHERN: 4-6-4 Hudson, 1970, catalogued but not manufactured.   **Not Manufactured**

8100 NORFOLK & WESTERN: 1981, 4-8-4, J Class, streamlined engine, whistle, electronic Sound of Steam, three-position reverse unit, engine and tender paint match extruded aluminum Powhatan Arrow passenger cars. These cars were available only as separate sale items. This N & W was the first Lionel engine to simulate steam smoke actually issuing from its steam cylinders. (Marx introduced this feature many years before on its little 1666, and it works better!) Black die-cast boiler, black plastic "bullet" boiler front, broad maroon trim stripe edged in yellow, matching long-striped 2671W Tender with die-cast six-wheel trucks. "611" appears on the side of the engine; "8100" appears on box only.   **-- 750 800 1000**

8101 CHICAGO & ALTON: 1981, 4-6-4, maroon-painted die-cast boiler (color scheme based on "The Red Train," which actually was pulled by a 4-6-2 Pacific, not a 4-6-4 Hudson), silver smokebox and boiler front, gold striping with gold "C & A" inside rectangle under cab window, whistle, electronic Sound of Steam, three-position reverse unit, smoke; maroon die-cast 2224W Tender with red frame, fully detailed riveting, steps, and handrails, black coal pile, gold striping; six-wheel die-cast trucks and gold-numbered "659" on side; "8101" appears only on box. Matching passenger cars available for separate sale. Tender is a remake of Lionel 2224 Tender, not produced since it came with the 224 2-6-2 Engine beginning in 1938. R. LaVoie comment.   **-- 300 350 500**

8140 Southern 0-4-0.

8102 UNION PACIFIC: 1981-82, 4-4-2, dark gray-painted die-cast boiler with yellow-edged running board, yellow numbers and letters; electronic Sound of Steam, smoke, headlight, two-position reverse unit, traction tires and 8102T square-back Tender. Part of 1151 Union Pacific Thunder Freight and 1153 Union Pacific Thunder Freight Deluxe Sets made for J. C. Penney.   **-- 50 60 75**

8104 UNION PACIFIC: 1981, 4-4-0, General-type locomotive, green cab, pilot, lamp, wheel spokes, and bell, black stack, chrome-finished boiler, "3" appears on side of head lamp and under cab window, green plastic "General"-style tender with archbar trucks and simulated wood pile. This locomotive was sold by J. C. Penney as an uncatalogued special called "The Golden Arrow;" display case for locomotive with wooden base and plastic cover.   **-- -- 225 300**

See also Factory Errors and Prototypes.

8140 SOUTHERN: 1971, 2-4-0 or 0-4-0, mechanical Sound of Steam, green and black body with gold lettering on tender cab; reportedly available as part of Sears Set 1190 with all-black body.

(A) 2-4-2.   **-- 15 25 35**

(B) 0-4-0.   **-- 15 25 35**

8141 PENNSYLVANIA: 1971, 2-4-2, gray plastic body with red stripe; electronic Sound of Steam (the first locomotive to carry this feature), smoke, headlight. See the entry for 8040 for a misnumbered version of this engine.

(A) White number on cab, from Set 1183. Confirmation requested.   **-- 25 30 40**

(B) Same as (A), except heat-stamped red number on cab. This was the version sold separately, but it is also found with sets. Riley Collection.   **-- 25 30 40**

(C) Same as (B), but number raised in relief as part of locomotive's boiler casting and then painted red. This was a very unusual practice for Lionel. J. Bratspis Collection.   **-- 30 40 55**

8140 Southern 2-4-0.

THE FORD 8142 SALESMAN'S DISPLAY: THE STRANGE CASE OF THE TRAVELING ENGINE

By Ronald Steffani

In 1972 the Ford Motor Company's Parts and Service Division offered a Lionel train set as a premium to customers purchasing Motorcraft automobile parts. To demonstrate the set's locomotive to prospective parts customers, each Ford parts sales representative was given a Lionel 8142 Chesapeake &

Ohio 4-4-2 Locomotive and Tender with a 4050 50-watt Transformer mounted on a hardwood display board.

The locomotive was modified by Lionel to run as a static display model. The engine was built without its usual center-rail roller pickups (or else they were removed from regular production models). A mounting hole was drilled and tapped into the bottom front of the engine so that it could be bolted onto the display stand. A wire was soldered to the motor so that power could be run to the engine. Two pieces of O27 straight track had their center rails removed, and this track was fastened to the maple display board. The transformer was also mounted to the right side of the display board with screws. The engine, with its Sound of Steam tender attached, was mounted to the display board with bolts and brackets so that the drivers of the locomotive were just above the two-rail track sections. The wire from the locomotive was attached to one of the transformer posts, and the other post was supplied with a wire soldered to one of the outside rails to complete the circuit. A small tube of smoke fluid was supplied so that when the engine was run on the display stand it smoked and chuffed.

In addition to the static display, the sales representative was supplied with a carrying case for it. This case was a gray metal tool chest measuring 24" x 7" x 7-1/2". If the Ford sales representative was successful in persuading the customer to purchase the appropriate amount of auto parts, the customer received a train set with a regular production 8142 Locomotive and Tender, a 9012 T A & G Hopper, a 9141 Burlington Northern Gondola, a 9042 Autolite short Boxcar, and a 9064 C & O SP Caboose. Presumably, track and a transformer were also included.

I recently obtained a "traveling engine" display from a retired Ford sales representative, but the engine, transformer, and track had been removed from the display board. I have been able to determine part of the mounting scheme for the engine, tender, transformer, and track, but not all of the details. Very little information could be obtained through correspondence with both the Ford Motor Company and Lionel. Neither company seems to have any records concerning how the engine was mounted on the display board, how many display units were made, or how many premium train sets were distributed.

Both companies graciously responded to my inquiries for information about the display. Gary Svehar, Supervisor of Technical Services for Lionel, confirmed that Lionel did in fact make the display pieces, but no other records were available. J. C. Barney, Jr. of the Ford Parts and Service Division also stated that no records were available. Mr. Barney, however, did say that the promotional program had been a success and that it may be offered again some time in the future.

It appears that any further information about the "traveling engine" will have to come from train collectors or Ford parts sales representatives. If you have this item or know someone who has additional information regarding the "traveling engine" display, please contact us. We are certain that the complete history of this unique product can be pieced together with the right help. (Editor's Note: As long ago as 1935, Lionel had used operating static displays such as this one; in that case, the purpose of the display was to demonstrate Lionel's new remote-control steam engine whistle. There may be other cases of operating static displays which have not surfaced as yet.)

8142 Chesapeake & Ohio.

8142 CHESAPEAKE & OHIO: 1971, 4-4-2, black die-cast metal body, white lettering, smoke.

(A) Electronic Sound of Steam.	--	40	55	65
(B) Same as (A), but also has electronic whistle.	--	50	60	70

(C) Special model for Ford Motor Parts Division promotion, about 100 made: no center-rail pickup assembly, hole drilled and tapped into underside of pilot to mount engine to two-rail modified O27 track on maple display board. The board also had a transformer so that the engine could be used as a static display. R. Steffani Collection. **NRS**

8143 MILWAUKEE: 1971, 4-4-2, black die-cast body, smoke, headlight, Electronic Sound of Steam, two-position reverse, 1130T Tender with orange stripe and gold lettering.   **20 25 30 40**

8200 KICKAPOO DOCKSIDE: 1972, 0-4-0 switcher, black plastic body, gold lettering and trim. Part of Kickapoo Valley and Northern set.

    -- **20 25 30**

8203 Pennsylvania.

8203 PENNSYLVANIA: 1972, 2-4-2, Columbia-type, electronic Sound of Steam, smoke, charcoal black plastic body, red stripe and lettering.

(A) With 1130T oil-type Tender. G. Salamone Collection.	--	20	30	40
(B) With 1130T coal-type Tender. G. Salamone Collection.	--	20	30	40

8204 CHESAPEAKE & OHIO: 1972, 4-4-2, black die-cast metal body, Sound of Steam, whistle, smoke, headlight, two-position reverse.

    -- **45 60 70**

8206 NEW YORK CENTRAL: 1972-74, 4-6-4, metal die-cast body, Sound of Steam, smoke, whistle, headlight, white lettering. Many of these locomotives were assembled with off-center drive wheels which cause the locomotives to wobble from side to side as they run. Typically, the die casting is very fuzzy on the shiny black examples, and the whistles and Sound of Steam do not sound clear. Used examples should be tested before purchase. R. LaVoie comments.

8200 Kickapoo Dockside Switcher.

8209 Pioneer Dockside Switcher.

(A) Flat charcoal black body.	--	175	200	225
(B) Shiny black body.	--	175	200	225

8209 PIONEER DOCKSIDE SWITCHER: 1972, 0-4-0, same as 8200, except for number and four-wheel tender. This locomotive with its tender bears a very close resemblance to a logging engine once used by the Northern Pacific. Sold in 1972 as part of Pioneer Dockside Switcher Set with tender, but became separate sale item without tender in 1973. I. D. Smith comments.

(A) With tender.	--	30	40	50
(B) Without tender.	--	20	25	30

8210 COWEN: 1982, 4-6-4, Hudson, gold- and burgundy-painted die-cast engine, headlight, smoke, Magnetraction, die-cast tender with six-wheel trucks, electronic whistle, electronic Sound of Steam, simulated gold "Joshua Lionel Cowen" nameplate. Note: when boxes are opened many units are reported to have broken rear trucks. Deitrich observation. -- 325 350 400

8212 BLACK CAVE: 1982, 0-4-0, black plastic body, 1615T slope-back Tender, luminous side rods, stack, bell, and boiler front, with glow-in-the-dark decals, DC motor; part of 1254 Black Cave Flyer Set. J. Sawruk Collection. -- 15 20 25

8213 RIO GRANDE: 1982-83, 2-4-2, die-cast metal body; smoke, headlight, electronic reversing unit, split-field motor, tender with mechanical Sound of Steam; part of 1252 Heavy Iron Set. -- -- 60 70

8214 PENNSYLVANIA: 1982-83, 2-4-2, die-cast metal body, headlight, smoke, electronic reverse unit, split-field motor; tender with mechanical Sound of Steam. -- -- 60 75

8215 NICKEL PLATE ROAD: 1982, 2-8-4, die-cast black-painted boiler with white stripe on side, white-painted wheel rims, gold "779" on cab, Magnetraction, smoke, optical headlight lens on swing-out boiler front. Die-cast 2224W Tender in black with gold script lettering, six-wheel die-cast trucks, operating coupler, electronic whistle, and Sound of Steam. Pictured in 1982 Fall Collector Center. Excellent runner; hard to find recently. -- 475 550 625

8300 SANTA FE: 1973-75, 2-4-0, black plastic body, slope-back tender with gold "ATSF" lettering, Symington-Wayne trucks, and dummy coupler. C. Rohlfing comment. -- 15 20 25

8302 SOUTHERN: 1973-76, 2-4-0, mechanical Sound of Steam, black plastic body painted green, plastic silver bell on top, headlight, MPC logo on both sides; from Sears Set 6-1384, oil-type tender. -- 20 25 30

8303 JERSEY CENTRAL: 1973-74, 2-4-2, electronic Sound of Steam, smoke, blue plastic body, light blue and gold lettering, dark blue trim. Part of the 1385 Blue Streak Freight Set. -- 30 40 50

8303 Jersey Central.

8304 Rock Island.

Note: There are four different 8304 Locomotives, all with two-position reverse units.

8304 ROCK ISLAND: 1973-74, 4-4-2, black die-cast body, electronic Sound of Steam, white lettering. -- 40 55 65

8304 Baltimore & Ohio.

8304 BALTIMORE & OHIO: 1975, 4-4-2, black die-cast body, white lettering, electronic Sound of Steam. Came as part of Capitol Limited Passenger Set. -- 50 65 75

8304 Chesapeake & Ohio.

8304 CHESAPEAKE & OHIO: 1974-77, 4-4-2, black die-cast body, gold lettering, electronic Sound of Steam, smoke. -- 40 55 65

8304 Pennsylvania.

8304 PENNSYLVANIA: 1974, 4-4-2, black die-cast body, gold lettering, electronic Sound of Steam, smoke, headlight. Came as part of Broadway Limited Passenger Set. -- 50 65 75

8305 MILWAUKEE ROAD: 1973, 4-4-2, black die-cast body, red and gold stripes with gold lettering on tender, electronic Sound of Steam, electronic whistle, two-position reverse, dummy coupler, smoke, headlight. Came as part of Milwaukee Special Passenger Set. C. Rohlfing comments. -- 50 60 75

8306 PENNSYLVANIA: 1974, 4-4-2, black plastic body, smoke, Sound of Steam, two-position reverse. Confirmation requested. -- -- 30 40

8307 SOUTHERN PACIFIC: 1983, 4-8-4, "Southern Pacific Daylight," "4449" below cab window and on boiler front, vertical dual headlights, Magnetraction, smoke from stack and "simulated" steam (actually smoke from generator) from cylinders, three-position E-unit, electronic Sound of Steam and whistle. Orange, white, and black paint scheme, silver boiler front. Matching passenger cars were available for separate sale.

8305 Milwaukee Road.

Catalogue portrays a 2046W coal Tender, but production version has prototypical oil-burning tender and "99" unlighted numberboards halfway down the top of the boiler sides. Early reports indicate that this locomotive is an outstanding runner. However, in early production there was a problem with chipping paint on the boiler. Lionel corrected this problem quickly. Since its issuance, this locomotive has become one of the scarcest and most desirable of the modern era's steam engines. It is now very hard to obtain.   **-- 1300 1500 1900**

8308 JERSEY CENTRAL: 1973-74, 2-4-2, black plastic body, gold lettering, 1130T-type Tender; made for Sears Set 1392. Two types of 1130T Tender shells exist. One is a black plastic unpainted shell with gold lettering. The other is a blue plastic shell painted black with gold lettering, probably an 8303 leftover shell. M. Sabatelle Collection.   **-- 30 40 50**

8309 SOUTHERN: 1983, 2-8-2, gold, "4501" beneath locomotive cab window and "SOUTHERN" lettering and "FAMOUS AMERICAN RAILROAD SERIES" diamond logo on tender side. Die-cast locomotive is green with silver boiler front and tuscan cab roof. Freight cars with special "FARR 4" markings: 6104 Hopper, 6306 Tank, 9451 Boxcar, 9887 Reefer, and 6431 Caboose were available for separate sale.   **-- 350 400 450**

8309 JERSEY CENTRAL: 1974, uncatalogued, 2-4-2, further details requested.   **-- 30 40 50**

8310 Nickel Plate Road.

Note: The following five locomotives are similar except for their road names and paint schemes. They were modifications of 1600-series switcher boiler pieces with new long plastic pilot pieces to accommodate the front trucks.

8310 NICKEL PLATE: 1973, 2-4-0, black die-cast body, gold lettering, slope-back tender; part of Sears Set 1390.   **-- 20 30 40**

8310 JERSEY CENTRAL: 2-4-0, uncatalogued, black die-cast body, gold lettering, mechanical Sound of Steam; part of Sears Set 1492.   **-- 20 30 40**

8310 NICKEL PLATE ROAD: 1974-75, 2-4-0, black die-cast body, gold lettering, slope-back tender lettered "NICKEL PLATE ROAD".   **-- 20 30 40**

8310 JERSEY CENTRAL: 1974-75, uncatalogued, 2-4-0, black die-cast body, gold lettering, mechanical Sound of Steam.   **-- 20 30 40**

8310 A T S F: 1974-75, 2-4-0, black die-cast body, gold lettering, slope-back tender lettered "A T S F", made for Sears; pictured in 1974 Sears catalogue with 1130T oil Tender as part of Set 79N96185C; also available for separate sale through Sears as 79N 96462. W. Haffen and K. Wills Collections.
(A) With 1615T slope-back Tender.   **-- 20 30 40**
(B) With 1130T oil-type Tender.   **-- 20 30 40**

8311 SOUTHERN: 1973, 0-4-0, uncatalogued, black plastic body; made for J. C. Penney Set 1395.   **-- 20 30 40**

8313 SANTA FE: 1983, 0-4-0, black plastic locomotive body with gold boiler front, stack, and bell, gold number "8313" under cab window and gold Santa Fe logo and "A. T. & S. F." on slope-back tender. DC-powered, no headlight, fixed coupler on tender. This is the same locomotive model that appeared in the Black Cave Set and is noteworthy for how few pieces of metal are used in its construction. Part of Set 1352, Rocky Mountain Freight, shown in Traditional Series Catalogue. Set value: $50. Locomotive and tender price.   **-- -- 15 20**

8310 Jersey Central.

8314 SOUTHERN STREAK: 1983, 2-4-0, dark green plastic locomotive body with headlight, DC powered, white number "8314" under cab window and white lettering "SOUTHERN STREAK" on tender sides, square-back oil-type tender with hatch and mechanical Sound of Steam, fixed coupler on tender. Part of 1353 Southern Streak Set shown in Traditional Series Catalogue. Locomotive and tender price.   **-- -- 20 25**

8315 B & O: 1983, 4-4-0, "General"-style plastic locomotive with blue boiler and stack, black pilot, steam cylinders, and cab, and black tender. White lettering and numbering: "8315" beneath cab windows and "B & O" on tender sides. DC motor with rectifier for AC operation as well as DC operation, illustrated with non-illuminating headlight but made with operating headlight which takes a small screw-base bulb, fixed coupler on tender, electronic three-position reverse unit, part of Set 1351, Baltimore and Ohio, shown in Traditional Series Catalogue. Locomotive and tender price.   **-- 70 85 100**

8402 READING: 4-4-2, 1984-85: black die-cast body, silver number on cab, solid state reversing unit, can motor, 1130T oil-type Tender with mechanical Sound of Steam, silver lettering, and black and silver Reading logo.   **-- -- 60 75**

8403 CHESSIE SYSTEM: 4-4-2, 1984-85, part of Set 1402, die-cast blue-painted boiler, headlight, smoke, solid state reversing unit, can motor, 1130T oil-type Tender with mechanical Sound of Steam, yellow stripe, number, and logo.   **-- -- 60 75**

8404 PENNSYLVANIA: 1984-85, 6-8-6 S-2 turbine, Brunswick green-painted die-cast boiler, graphite gray smokebox and boiler front; white striping, trim, and "6200" on boiler cab, red and gold "6200" Keystone on boiler front, oiler linkage, white-edged drive wheels, Magnetraction, electronic Sound of Steam, electronic whistle, smoke; 2671W-type Tender with operating red backup lights, Brunswick green with white "PENNSYLVANIA" lettering high on sides, die-cast six-wheel passenger trucks, water scoop. There have been a few complaints about poorly operating reversing units and Sound of Steam units which do not work well in reverse, but direct observation has shown that this locomotive, essentially a dressed-up postwar 682, is an excellent runner and a strong puller which operates efficiently on as little as eight volts. R. LaVoie comment.
     -- 375 400 475

8406 NEW YORK CENTRAL: 1984, 4-6-4, 1/4" scale die-cast Hudson, 23" long, reissue of the 1964 version of the 773 without the cylinder slide valve casting but with the die-cast 2426W Tender. Locomotive has detailed Baker valve gear, die-cast smoke unit with simulated steam from the smoke chests (something the proud New York Central would have not allowed, since this would indicate leaky valve packing), Magnetraction, optical headlight, electronic Sound of Steam and whistle, 2426W-type Tender with six-wheel Fundimensions passenger trucks, "NEW YORK CENTRAL" in small white serif lettering ("783" is the number on the boiler cab). This engine's Magnetraction has been improved over its predecessor 773 because there are more magnets and they are larger. The steps on the boiler front are missing in catalogue photographs but are included in the production run. The locomotive has won praise for its sharp boiler detail. At the time of its issue, such was the demand for this locomotive that it was easily the most expensive single item ever produced by either the original Lionel Corporation or Fundimensions. There were persistent reports of hoarding of this locomotive; its initial purchase price for those who pre-ordered it was about $575, but the price nearly doubled in just a few months. Purchasers of the current model should beware of sharp fluctuations in supply and demand, especially at the time any new Hudson is produced. In fact, the price of this model has softened somewhat since the introduction of the 8606 Boston and Albany and the 18002 gunmetal New York Central Hudson. R. LaVoie comments.
     -- -- 850 1000

8410 REDWOOD VALLEY EXPRESS: 1984-85, 4-4-0, "General"-style locomotive with tuscan boiler, yellow cab, pilot, and drive wheels, cylindrical head-light, tall thin stack instead of usual balloon stack, gold trim; DC-only motor, tender with simulated woodpile, arch bar trucks with dummy coupler, brown "REDWOOD VALLEY EXPRESS" and logo on tender sides. Came as part of Red-wood Valley Express Set 1403. Price for locomotive and tender only.

-- -- 40 45

8500 Pennsylvania.

8500 PENNSYLVANIA: 1975, 2-4-0, black plastic body, gold lettering, mechanical Sound of Steam. -- 15 20 25

8502 A.T.S.F.

8502 SANTA FE: 1975, 2-4-0, black plastic body, gold lettering, slope-back tender. -- 15 20 25

8506 Pennsylvania.

8506 PENNSYLVANIA: 1976-77, 0-4-0, black die-cast body, 1600-series switcher, spur-drive motor, gold lettering, slope-back tender with red light which lights only when locomotive is in reverse. -- 80 100 150

8507 A. T. S. F.

8507 A T S F: 1975, 2-4-0, black plastic cab with gold heat-stamped number, detailed cab interior, "LIONEL" on firebox door (as on postwar 1060), molded win-dow shades, plated main rods only, manual reverse with curved reversing lever slot in boiler top behind Phillips screw, shiny ornamental bell, slope-back tender with simulated backup light, "A. T. S. F." in gold on tender sides, Symington-Wayne trucks, dummy coupler. Part of a set sold by K-Mart in 1975; reader com-ments needed concerning set details. Triezenberg Collection.

-- 20 25 30

8510 PENNSYLVANIA: 1975, not catalogued, 0-4-0, slope-back tender, made for Sears. -- 20 25 30

8512 SANTA FE: 1985, dockside switcher, 0-4-0, DC-only operation, part of Midland Freight Set in 1985 Traditional Catalogue. Dark blue plastic body, yel-low lettering and number, silver smokebox, stack, and steam chests, yellow Santa Fe logo, short coal box behind cab instead of tender, one dummy coupler on rear. Price for locomotive only: -- -- 20 30

8516 NEW YORK CENTRAL: 1985, 0-4-0 switcher, part of Yard Chief Set in Traditional Catalogue. Die-cast postwar 1600-series switcher body, headlight, smoke (a first for any Lionel switcher), three-position electronic reversing switch, front operating coupler, slope-back tender with operating coupler on rear, Symington-Wayne trucks; white "NEW YORK CENTRAL" lettering, operating backup light with white lens, four-prong connector plug from locomotive to tender. Despite its light tender, the engine is a superb runner on low voltage, thanks to its can motor connected to spur-drive gearing. It may very well be the best smok-ing engine Lionel has ever produced! For operating details, see John Kouba's ar-ticle on the Santa Fe Service Station Special in Chapter XVII. Price for locomotive and tender. -- -- 125 160

8600 NEW YORK CENTRAL: 1976, 4-6-4, black die-cast body, white letter-ing, electronic Sound of Steam, smoke, Magnetraction, silver boiler front, shown as 646 in 1976 catalogue; part of Empire State Express Set.

-- 200 225 300

8601 Rock Island.

8601 ROCK ISLAND: 1976-77, 0-4-0, black plastic body, large white numbers on cab, slope-back tender with red "ROCK ISLAND" logo. -- 15 20 25

8602 RIO GRANDE: 1976-78, 2-4-0, plastic body, white lettering; tender with mechanical Sound of Steam. -- 20 25 30

8602 PENNSYLVANIA: See 18602.

8603 CHESAPEAKE & OHIO: 1976-77, 4-6-4, black die-cast body, white lettering, silver boiler front, electronic Sound of Steam, headlight, smoke, rubber tires, tender lettered "CHESAPEAKE & OHIO", over 19-1/2 inches long. The ear-lier Baldwin disc drivers had polished steel rims, but when reports of corrosion arose, Fundimensions changed production to white-painted driver rims. The painted rims are probably more scarce. Typically, the details on the Baldwin disc drivers on these locomotives are not very sharp. As with the earlier 8206 New York Central Hudson, many examples were assembled with off-center drive wheels, causing the locomotive to wobble when it moves down the track. Used examples should be test-run. R. LaVoie comment.

(A) Polished-steel driver rims. R. LaVoie Collection. -- 150 175 275
(B) White-painted driver rims. Boehmer Collection. -- 150 200 300

8604 JERSEY CENTRAL: 1976, 2-4-2, black plastic body, gold number on cab, smoke, headlight, two-position or manual reversing unit.
(A) Part of Sears Set 1696, 1130T oil-type Tender, gold Jersey Central lettering and logo, mechanical Sound of Steam, Symington-Wayne trucks, dummy coupler. Came in set with 9020 Flatcar, 9044 Boxcar, 9011 Hopper Car, and 9069 Caboose. Set also included ten curved and four straight track and a pair of manual switches. D. Johns and P. Catalano comments, G. Halverson and L. Kositsky Collections.

-- 30 40 50

8602 Rio Grande.

8603 Chesapeake & Ohio.

(B) Same locomotive as (A), but slope-back tender with no lettering. G. Halverson Collection.   -- 30 40 50

(C) Same as (A), but locomotive has manual reverse and no headlight, no smoke unit, green plastic 1130T oil-type Tender painted gloss black. R. LaVoie Collection.   -- 30 40 50

8604 Jersey Central.

8604 WABASH: See 18604.

8606 BOSTON & ALBANY: 1986, 773-type Hudson, black boiler, white-painted boiler front, striping, and driver edges, white "784" on cab, 2426W-type die-cast Tender with coal pile, six-wheel die-cast passenger trucks, white lettering. Locomotive has smoke with emissions from cylinders, headlight, Magnetraction, solid drivers, electronic Sound of Steam, and whistle. This engine was offered as part of a late 1986 direct-mail campaign from Lionel; the firm's bypassing of its usual dealer network caused considerable friction between the company and its distributors. Some reports state that only a little more than 2,000 of these engines were made. The few train dealers who have these locomotives are asking double Lionel's original asking price. The Boston & Albany has become a very scarce, highly desirable locomotive.   -- -- 1200 1600

8610 WABASH: 1986-87, 4-6-2 Pacific steam locomotive, first of the new "Fallen Flags"-series locomotives. Santa Fe-type Baldwin Hudson boiler casting painted dark blue with graphite silver smokebox, gold "WABASH" on cab, smoke deflectors, white stripe along cab, 2046W-type Tender with gold stripes and gold "672," six-wheel die-cast passenger trucks, smoke, headlight, Magnetraction, electronic Sound of Steam, and whistle. The locomotive as produced is much more attractive than it appears to be in the 1986 Collector Catalogue; it is accurately depicted in the 1987 catalogue.   -- 350 500 600

8615 LOUISVILLE & NASHVILLE: 1986, 2-8-4 Berkshire steam locomotive, made as a special Christmas 1986 offering from J. C. Penney; came with display case, wood base with track, and plastic bumpers. This is a model patterned after the L & N steamer nicknamed "Big Emma." Gloss black-painted boiler, yellow stripe on running boards, yellow "1970" on cab, white-painted driver edges, Magnetraction, smoke, 2671W-type tender with electronic Sound of Steam and whistle, large yellow "1970" on tender between two yellow lengthwise stripes, six-wheel die-cast passenger trucks. According to 1986 J. C. Penney catalogue, this was a limited edition of 3,000. L. Bohn comments.   -- -- 650 800

8616 A. T. & S. F.: 1986, 4-4-2 steam locomotive, flat-nosed boiler front, white lettering on cab, die-cast boiler, headlight, smoke, electronic three-position reverse, spur-drive can motor, 1130T oil-type Tender with mechanical Sound of Steam, Symington-Wayne trucks, large white number on tender sides.   -- -- 65 75

8617 NICKEL PLATE ROAD: 1986, 2-4-2 steam locomotive, die-cast boiler with yellow running board stripe, NKP logo on steam chest, headlight, smoke, electronic three-position reverse, spur-drive can motor, 234T Santa Fe-type square-back Tender with mechanical Sound of Steam, Symington-Wayne trucks, yellow lettering and logo. Part of Set 1602, the Nickel Plate Special. This particular set has been used for many special promotions for the last few years. For example, it was one of the prizes offered in McDonald's Monopoly game promotion.   -- -- 65 75

8625 PENNSYLVANIA: 1986, 2-4-0 steam locomotive, black plastic 1060-type boiler, white stripe and number on cab, DC operation only, headlight, 1130T oil-

type Tender with mechanical Sound of Steam, Symington-Wayne trucks. Part of Set 1615, the Cannonball Express.   -- -- 25 35

8630 W & A: 1986, (Western & Atlantic) 4-4-0 "General"-type steam locomotive, no number on engine except "No. 3", identical to 8701 in color and lettering but powered by can motor-drive system instead of AC crosscut-geared motor of earlier version; offered as part of uncatalogued Set 1608 through American Express Travel-Related Services.   -- -- -- 135

8635 A. T. & S. F.: 1986, 0-4-0 steam switcher, black die-cast boiler with white number on cab, 1615T-type Tender with white lettering and cross logo, backup light, and Symington-Wayne trucks; locomotive has spur-drive can motor, electronic three-position reverse, headlight, and smoke unit. Identical in construction to 8516 New York Central produced the year before. This engine was part of the Santa Fe Work Train, the 1986 Service Station Special Set. For additional information see John Kouba's article in Chapter XVII.   -- -- 120 145

8700 ROCK ISLAND: See 18700.

8701 GENERAL: 1977-78, 4-4-0, cab numbered "No. 3", rerun of Lionel 1882 General, 1959-62, black plastic boiler and frame, red cab, gold boiler bands, dome, and bell, yellow lettering, headlight, smoke, two-position reverse, black plastic tender with yellow-lettered "Western & Atlantic".   -- 100 125 175

8702 CRESCENT LIMITED: 1977, 4-6-4, also known as Southern Crescent, green-painted die-cast boiler with silver-painted boiler front, gold crescent and border on steam chest, crescent emblem and "8702" in gold on cab; Magnetraction, white-outlined drivers, liquid smoke. This locomotive appears to have exactly the same castings as the 646. Originally the 8702 came in flat green; the second run was in shiny green. It appears that equal quantities were produced. The tender is painted green with a black coal pile, lettered "CRESCENT LIMITED" in gold with gold border, Symington-Wayne trucks, Sound of Steam, dummy coupler.   -- 225 300 400

8702 V & T: See 18702.

8703 WABASH: 1977, 2-4-2, black plastic body, white stripe on locomotive and tender; electronic Sound of Steam, smoke, headlight.   -- 20 25 35

8800 LIONEL LINES: 1978-81, 4-4-2, die-cast boiler, red marker lights, battery box on pilot, similar to Lionel 2037 with the following modifications: the marker lights, which protrude above the boiler on a 2037, were moved to a more protected location inside the boiler front; the "Made by Lionel" builder's plate was replaced with a Lionel / MPC logo; and the valve gear was given a moving control rod reminiscent of the 1666. The main rod is heavily sculptured with ridges; there is a side rod; liquid smoke unit, two-position reversing unit; a wire connects the tender and locomotive, with electronic Sound of Steam in the 8800T Tender and a fixed rear tender coupler. Tender base is marked "8141T-10" and has a large black "L" in white and black box and "LIONEL LINES" in sans-serif rounded letters across its side. (Same engine as Chesapeake Flyer with one rubber tire on locomotive.)   -- 60 75 125

8801 THE BLUE COMET: 1978-79, 4-6-4, dark blue upper boiler section, lighter blue lower boiler section, gold-outlined steam chest, "8801" in gold on cab, decal on locomotive feedwater tank reads "THE BLUE COMET"; "LIONEL" on small plate beneath headlight; drivers outlined in white, blind center drivers, plastic trailing trucks, side frames, and a modified 646 boiler. A major modification is its feedwater tank which has a 665 boiler front with marker lights on the boiler front door and a small nameplate beneath the headlight. The tender's paint design is similar to that of the locomotive, with a dark blue upper section, black coal pile, light blue lower section with gold circle, and gold-lettered "NEW JERSEY CENTRAL". The Blue Comet brings back memories of the top-of-the-line, classic Standard and O Gauge locomotives of the 1930s. The Blue Comet has met with great popularity. As with many of the limited sets, the passenger cars made to match this locomotive are still readily available, but the locomotive itself is very hard to find. This lends support to the belief that many more sets of cars were produced than were the locomotives needed to pull them as part of a matched set. R. LaVoie comment.   -- 300 350 400

8803 SANTA FE: 1979, 0-4-0, black plastic engine with silver boiler front and red plastic drivers, two-position reverse, 8803T square-back Tender with Santa Fe logo. Part of 1860 Timberline Set, 1862 Logging Empire Set, 1892 Penney Logging Empire, and 1893 Toys 'R Us Logging Empire.   -- -- 10 20

8900 A. T. S. F.: 1979, 4-6-4, black-painted die-cast boiler with silver-painted boiler front, green marker lights, tuscan-painted cab roof, Magnetraction, same boiler as 2065 without the feedwater tank; rear trailing truck has same side frames as 2065, side configuration same as 2065 but brighter, shinier plating; nylon gears substitute for metal gears. Tender has "8900" in very large white numerals and a small diamond-shaped block outlined in gold with gold-lettered "Famous American Railroad Series" with a spike (indicates it is first in a series); water scoop pickup, Sound of Steam inside tender (power pickup for Sound of Steam comes in part from tender trucks and in part from wire from locomotive); fixed coupler on rear of tender with rear number plate "2671W-6", gray wheels on tender. Our search indicates that most if not all pre-Fundimensions 2671-W Tenders did not carry a plate with such a number. The number has been carried on the tender plate since MPC began using this tender.   -- 300 350 400

8902 ATLANTIC COAST LINE: 1979-82, 1985-87, 2-4-0, black plastic engine, DC-powered, 8902T slope-back Tender with "ATLANTIC COAST LINE" logo; available as part of 1960 and 1993 Midnight Flyer Sets, 1990 Mystery Glow Midnight Flyer, and 1155 Cannonball Freight Set. Also resurrected many times since first issuance for low-priced department store special sets.

-- -- 15 20

8903 RIO GRANDE: 1979, 2-4-2, black plastic engine, DC-powered, 8602T Tender with mechanical Sound of Steam; white script "Rio Grande". Available as part of 1963 Black River Freight Set.   -- 15 20 25

8904 WABASH: 1979, 1981, 2-4-2 die-cast engine with white stripe along running board, smoke, working headlight, two-position reverse unit, AC-powered; 8904T oil-type Tender with or without mechanical Sound of Steam; dark-lettered "WABASH" on white stripe across tender side; from 1962 Wabash Cannonball Set or 1991 Wabash Deluxe Express.

(A) With mechanical Sound of Steam, 8906T.   -- 30 35 40

(B) Without mechanical Sound of Steam, 8904T.   -- 25 30 35

8905 SWITCHER: 1979, 0-4-0, plastic engine, no headlight, diamond-shaped stack, DC-powered, fixed coupler, no tender; part of Set 1965, the Smokey Mountain Line.   -- -- 10 20

18001 ROCK ISLAND: 1987, 4-8-4 Northern steam locomotive, completely new die-cast scale design using new boiler on Norfolk and Western J Class chassis. Dark gun-metal gray boiler, graphite-gray smokebox, headlight with number boards centered in boiler front (actually numbered 5100 after prototype), top-mounted metal bell on boiler front, eight-paneled cab windows, white "5100" number on cab, new die-cast square-back tender, gun-metal gray with white Rock Island logo, detailed coal load, six-wheel die-cast passenger trucks, electronic Sound of Steam, Magnetraction, electronic whistle, smoke with cylinder emissions, headlight, three-position reverse. The prototype casting for this locomotive was too rough for production, but it illustrated the proper "chunky" look of the real locomotive. This engine is unlike any steam locomotive ever produced by Lionel; despite initial castings and parts supply problems, the locomotive received considerable collector praise when it was finally issued. Early examples surfaced with defective armatures, but Lionel, Inc. was very attentive to the problem. It is an excellent runner. See entry for 18003 for an interesting story about the boiler casting. Its price stabilized when the Lackawanna version was announced.   -- -- 650 795

18002 NEW YORK CENTRAL: 1987-88, 773-type Hudson steam engine, gun-metal gray boiler, black pilot and lower frame, spoked drivers with chromed metal rims (the first appearance of these drivers since the 763E of 1938); locomotive will lack Magnetraction because of these wheels. White "785" number on cab, smoke with cylinder emissions, headlight, three-position reverse; 2426W-type die-cast gun-metal Tender with six-wheel die-cast passenger trucks, electronic Sound of Steam, and whistle. This locomotive was offered as part of the 1987 year-end package to commemorate the 50th anniversary of the introduction of the Lionel New York Central Hudson; it comes with a 5/8" x 3/8" commemorative metal plaque. It was released in 1988. The price has climbed quickly because this locomotive is modeled after the highly desirable 763E of prewar years. At one time, rumors were afoot that this locomotive would even be issued with the round Vanderbilt tender, but this proved untrue. This locomotive featured an improved motor design over its two predecessors. To prevent binding of the armature against the brushplate, a specially-slotted armature and an additional retaining clip (671M-22) were used. This design uses four thrust washers (671M-23), two thrust bearings (681-12), and two retaining clips (671M-22) in-

stead of the old design, which had a single-slotted armature shaft, two thrust washers (671M-23), and one thrust bearing (681-121). All armatures are interchangeable, but if an earlier type is used in a revised motor, it must be properly spaced. M. Sabatelle comments.   -- -- 950 1100

18003 LACKAWANNA: 1988, 4-8-4 Northern steam locomotive, semi-gloss black-painted boiler with graphite gray-painted smokebox, white "1501" prototype number below cab window and on sand dome, white stripe along boiler and white-striped drivers, number in white alongside and below headlight, silver-plated ornamental bell on boiler front, smoke from stack and steam chests, headlight, Magnetraction; large die-cast tender with coal load, highly detailed sides with white "Lackawanna" lettering, die-cast six-wheel passenger trucks, electronic Sound of Steam, electronic steam whistle. Special note: When the Rock Island predecessor to this engine came out in 1987 after delays in production, collectors noted that its boiler casting was made in Taiwan. In view of Lionel, Inc. being determined to make its products domestically, this bears explanation. Our sources tell us that the original domestically-produced castings for the Rock Island engine were extremely rough and unacceptable to Lionel. These were rejected and a hurried call to the Orient produced properly made castings. The Lackawanna casting is significantly improved over the Rock Island casting, however, we do not know if the casting on this version is being made domestically or abroad (reader comments invited). In addition to the casting problem, early versions of the Rock Island came through with defective armatures which quickly burned out motors. These have been repaired by Lionel, and when properly outfitted the Northern runs extremely well. Price given here is introductory and subject to market speculation, although the price of the Rock Island model has stabilized recently.   -- -- -- 650

18600 ATLANTIC COAST LINE: 1987, 4-4-2, die-cast boiler, slope-back tender with Symington-Wayne trucks, smoke, headlight, can motor, three-position electronic reverse, part of Timberline Freight Set sold through J. C. Penney. M. Sabatelle Collection.   -- -- -- 95

18601 GREAT NORTHERN: 1988, 2-4-2 steam locomotive, die-cast boiler painted dark green with silver-painted smokebox and front, white "8601" on cab, headlight, smoke unit, three-position electronic reverse and "can" motor, Santa Fe 234-type square-back tender painted dark green with black coal load, red, white, and green circular "goat" logo, Symington-Wayne trucks, operating coupler. Does not have mechanical Sound of Steam feature as on previous locomotives of its type; this feature, which has never worked very well, may have been abandoned for future production.   -- -- -- 95

18602 PENNSYLVANIA: 1987, 4-4-2 steam locomotive, flat-front die-cast boiler, white number on cab, short square-back tender not issued since an 8040 model of 1972 carried it; this engine's tender differs from the earlier model in that it has a railing added to the tender's back deck; also has small, compressed "PENNSYLVANIA" lettering in white, very true to prototype, and Symington-Wayne trucks. Locomotive has smoke, headlight, spur-drive can motor, and three-position electronic reverse. Advertised in catalogue as match for 16000-series Pennsylvania passenger cars, but sold separately in Type II box.

-- -- -- 90

18604 WABASH: 1988, 2-4-2 steam locomotive, die-cast boiler, headlight, smoke, can-style motor, electronic three-position reverse, wide white stripe along boiler, number "8604" on cab, 234 Santa Fe-style square-back Tender with Symington-Wayne trucks, "WABASH" lettering on white stripe, operating coupler. Essentially an updated version of the 8904 Wabash Steamer produced in 1979 with an 1130T Tender. Part of 11703 Iron Horse Freight Set.

-- -- -- 80

18700 ROCK ISLAND: 1987, 0-4-0 tank switcher, bright red body, silver-painted smokebox, stack, and steam chests, white number and Rock Island logo, part of Set 11701, the Rail Blazer.   -- -- -- 25

18702 V. & T. R. R.: 1988 (Virginia and Truckee Railroad), 4-4-0 General-type steam engine with dark maroon boiler and cab, gold trim, gold "8702" and "RENO", DC can motor with rectifier for AC operation, smoke, headlight, three-position electronic reverse, tender with maroon body, gold outlining and "V. & T R. R.", arch bar trucks, brown simulated wood pile and operating coupler. Part of "Dry Gulch Line" Service Station Set for 1988; price not available at press time, but set is expected to sell initially for $225 to $250.   **NRS**

Chapter III
AUTOMOBILE CARRIERS

The Fundimensions automobile carrier cars can be called the "odd men out" of the freight car lineup. They really do not fit easily into any freight car category but their own, and even though they are modeled to scale after real prototypes, they look very odd on tinplate layouts. None of these cars was ever equipped with automobiles, for the very good reason that only HO Gauge model cars similar to the Mattel "Hot Wheels," Lesney "Matchbox," or Corgi automobiles will fit into the automobile racks — and these are decidedly out of place on an O or O27 layout! Their long, narrow look is curious within a tinplate train.

The worst problem with these cars, however, is the way they operate on a layout. The Fundimensions automobile carrier has offset trucks so it can turn around the tight O27 curves — in fact, the Symington-Wayne truck with a large rounded back end with an extra hole was developed for these cars — but these trucks are usually secured to the body of the car with plastic rivets, which allow a great deal of play between the trucks and the body. As a result of this, and their high center of gravity, they have a nasty tendency to tip over as they round a curve. This is true even when the car is not loaded. The operator has to load relatively heavy metal cars on the bottom rack and extremely light plastic cars on the top rack; even then, the automobile carrier is very unsteady.

Perhaps the problems associated with these cars are the reason why so few of them, relatively speaking, have been produced. There have been no new examples of this car since the 9351 Pennsylvania Automobile Carrier of 1980, and in all only ten numbers have been made, some with considerable variation. The discontinuance of these cars, however, means that the collector has a great opportunity to pursue a neglected area of production. The history of Lionel trains is replete with poor sellers which later became very valuable, and Fundimensions production should be no exception.

The first of the Fundimensions automobile carriers was the yellow 9126 Chesapeake and Ohio, followed quickly by a blue 9123 of the same railroad and a two-tier 9125 Norfolk and Western. Of these, the 9123 has several extremely scarce variations. The collector should be aware that the supposedly scarce versions of this car with both tiers lettered with the C & O logo can be faked very easily. The tiers snap onto one another by means of plastic prongs. It is relatively easy to take apart two ordinary 9123 cars and simply switch the marked and the unmarked tier. This fake can be detected by the absence of the "Trailer-Train" lettering on the lower tier. However, one of the 9123 examples is yellow instead of blue, and this is a genuine rarity. The body of this car can be found in both black and blue, with the black version being harder to find.

The 9125 Norfolk and Western Automobile Carrier also came in both black and blue versions, but it has the distinction of being the only two-tiered car ever offered from the factory. It was part of sets and was never offered for separate sale. The black version of this car is very hard to find, and locating a blue version is no easy task, either. This is one of the more desirable of the carriers.

The only automobile carrier ever equipped with deluxe Standard O trucks was the 9216 Great Northern in blue, which was part of the 1978 Milwaukee Special Limited Edition Set. Other cars in the series carried Penn Central, Illinois Central Gulf, Santa Fe, and Pennsylvania markings, and a T C A 1973 Dearborn car was also issued.

It is a shame that the automobile carriers never met expectations as a class of cars, for they would have added a modern touch to Fundimensions' freight car lineup. With so many of Fundimensions' experiments being highly successful, it is perhaps inevitable that a few of them would not be so fruitful. Despite their flaws, these cars remain as an interesting area for the collector.

9123 Chesapeake & Ohio.

                                          Gd VG Exc Mt

1973 TCA: See Special Production chapter.

9123 CHESAPEAKE & OHIO: 1974, two- or three-tier body, either one or two boards lettered, Symington-Wayne trucks, operating couplers.

(A) Three-tier black body, yellow lettering, upper board on each side lettered "C & O". Johnson Collection.   10 20 25 35

(B) Three-tier blue body, yellow lettering, one board lettered.
                                          4 10 15 25

(C) Two-tier black plastic body, yellow lettering, "C & O FOR PROGRESS" on boards, "TRAILER TRAIN RTTX 9123" and "BLT 1-73" on frame, Symington-Wayne trucks, metal wheels, disc-operating couplers, not catalogued, came in factory sealed 1386 Rock Island Express Set in lieu of the blue 9125 two-tier N & W Automobile Carrier shown on the box and in the 1973-74 catalogues. Very Rare. Johnson Collection.   -- -- -- 600

See also Factory Errors and Prototypes.

9125 Norfolk & Western.

9126 Chesapeake & Ohio.

9125 N & W: 1974, two-tier blue or black body, white lettering, single-board lettered, Symington-Wayne trucks, operating couplers; sold only in sets.
(A) Blue body, lettered with road name, number, and built date, "TRAILER TRAIN".　　　　　　　　　　　　　**15　20　30　40**
(B) Black body. G. Wilson Collection.　　　**20　30　40　60**

9126 C AND O: 1973-74, three-tier body, either one or two boards lettered, Symington-Wayne trucks, operating couplers. Came in 1388 Golden State Arrow and 1460 Grand National Sets; Grand National Set also had blue 9123 C & O three-tiered Car instead of 9126. C. Lang comment.
(A) Yellow body, blue lettering, one board lettered.　**10　12　15　25**
(B) Light yellow body, light blue lettering, one board lettered.
　　　　　　　　　　　　　　　　　　　　10　12　15　25
(C) Light yellow-painted yellow plastic body, bright royal blue lettering. The painted body is unusual for this car. Reader comments requested. G. Halverson Collection.　　　　　　　　　　　　　　**NRS**
See also Factory Errors and Prototypes.

9129 Norfolk & Western.

9129 N & W: 1975, brown body, white lettering, single board stamped, Symington-Wayne trucks, two operating couplers.　**10　12　15　30**

9139 Penn Central.

9145 Illinois Central Gulf.

9139 PENN CENTRAL: 1977, green body, white lettering, single board stamped, Symington-Wayne trucks, two operating couplers; part of Illinois Central Gulf Freight Set. C. Lang comment.　**10　12　15　30**

9145 ILLINOIS CENTRAL GULF: 1977, orange body, black lettering, single board stamped, Symington-Wayne trucks, two operating couplers.
　　　　　　　　　　　　　　　　　　　10　15　20　30

9216 GREAT NORTHERN: 1978, blue plastic, white lettering, from Milwaukee Special Set, black car stops on each level, Standard O trucks. To date, this is the only Fundimensions automobile carrier issued with die-cast trucks.
　　　　　　　　　　　　　　　　　　　10　15　20　40

9281 A. T. S. F.: 1978-79, two-level carrier in red plastic, white lettering, white and red Santa Fe electrocal on upper boards on both sides, lower boards blank, "BLT 1-78", black vehicle stops on ends, Symington-Wayne trucks.
　　　　　　　　　　　　　　　　　　　8　12　20　30

9351 PENNSYLVANIA: 1980, three-tier tuscan body, gold lettering with old-style red and gold Keystone insignia on upper board, blank lower board.
　　　　　　　　　　　　　　　　　　　8　20　25　40

Chapter IV
BOXCARS AND STOCK CARS

With the assistance of Dr. Charles Weber

Ask a Fundimensions collector about his specialty, and the chances are he/she will tell you about some form or class of boxcar. That really is no surprise, for box, refrigerator, and stock cars are by far the most numerous and variable pieces of rolling stock issued by Lionel in the modern era. This was also true of postwar production, and it is easy to see why. In the first place, boxcars are fixed in the public mind as the "typical" rolling stock, aside from passenger cars, which have their own stories to tell. Look at any movie dealing with railroads, and chances are you will see many different boxcars. Read some of the great railroad fiction by such luminaries of the genre as Gilbert Lathrop and E. S. Dellinger, and you will probably read of some desperate struggle against the elements by courageous brakemen trying to control a runaway train by turning brakewheels — atop the boxcars. Another reason for the popularity of collecting boxcars is more specific to tinplate production. As we have seen many times, color and graphics sell toy trains, and what better place to put your most colorful

graphics than on the flat sides of a box or refrigerator car? The many types of box, refrigerator, and stock cars outsell all other types of tinplate rolling stock combined. These cars are truly crucial to the success of Lionel as a producer of toy trains.

The only real trouble in collecting these cars lies in their utterly astonishing variety and vast quantity. Type collectors will have a difficult time collecting all of a particular series because of the sheer weight of numbers. When you consider that there are 80 boxcars in the 9700 Series alone, not to mention the 70 or so 9800-series refrigerator cars, the 9200-series and 9400-series boxcars, the Wood-sided Reefers, the mint cars, the bunk cars, the Bicentennial Series, the Tobacco Road and Favorite Spirits Series, and the smaller box and stock cars, you would need quite a bit of shelf space for the whole production!

Variation collectors have even more problems than the type collectors, because many of these cars have seemingly endless variations in body styles and molds, frames, doors, colors, and so on. It is not unusual for many of these cars — the 9748 C P Rail Boxcar comes to mind — to exist in fifteen or more variations!

The bullion car is one of Lionel's most unusual boxcars. Top shelf: 7515 Denver Mint, 7517 Philadelphia Mint. Middle shelf: 7518 Carson City, 9349 San Francisco. Bottom shelf: 9319 T C A Anniversary, 9320 Fort Knox. G. and D. Halverson and A. Conto Collections.

9200 and 9700 Boxcar Variations

Type V Body

One partially complete rivet row
Blank end plates
Metal or plastic door guides at top and bottom

Type VI Body (previously '70 Body)

Absence of even partially complete rivet row
Blank end plates
Metal or plastic door guides at top and bottom

Type VII Body (previously '71 Body)

Absence of even partially complete rivet row
"9200" on one end plate, "LIONEL MPC" on other
Metal or plastic door guides at top and bottom

Type VIII Body

Absence of even partially complete rivet row
"9200" on one end plate, "LIONEL MPC" on other
One plastic door guide at top, hooks on bottom

Type IX Body (previously '72 Body)

Absence of even partially complete rivet row
"9700" on one end plate, "LIONEL MPC" on other
One plastic door guide at top, hooks on bottom.

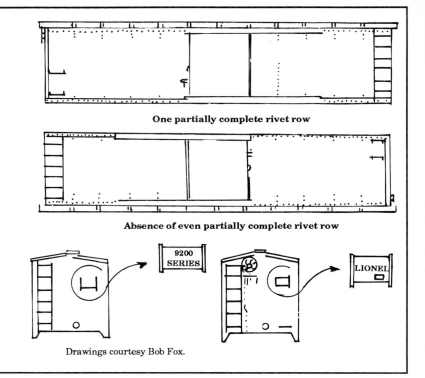

One partially complete rivet row

Absence of even partially complete rivet row

9200 SERIES

LIONEL

Drawings courtesy Bob Fox.

Therein lies considerable controversy. Why should a beginning collector bother with variations of the same car at all, if it is nearly hopeless to try to get them all? Some collectors believe that these variations should be neither stressed nor even mentioned in pricing and quantity studies. The answers to these questions revolve primarily around interest; you should have the opportunity to observe what you are interested in, and many collectors are very interested in the boxcar variations because they come from the same heritage as those found in the old and venerated postwar 6464 Series. One of the real pioneers in the study of boxcar variations, Dr. Charles Weber, stated the case recently in a reply to a collector who asked why these variations were important enough to report. His letter is highly significant and, with his permission, deserves quoting in full.

"In the 'early days' of collecting 6464 boxcars, we started noticing that similar cars when placed next to each other looked different. Why? Investigation showed that some were painted and some were not. Some came from different batches of paint. Then we noticed that even unpainted cars showed similar slight but recognizable differences."

"So, those of us who were nuts over these cars started to collect anything which looked different. It followed, then, that as we were studying these cars, we would also notice some differences which do not readily show — specifically, the colors of the plastic used to mold the cars. Therefore, we noted those differences for completeness."

"Very few of us seek out variations which can't be seen, such as these molds which have been painted over. But, if the price is right, we might even buy such a minor variation. In any event, whether one collects these minor variations or not, it is still interesting for many of us to learn about them. If a given

collector isn't interested, that's his business, but lots of us are interested. That's why they make chocolate and vanilla!"

Dr. Weber and his fellow collectors began their studies in the mid to late 1960s. The interested reader should also look up Bob Swanson's authoritative study of the 6454 Boxcars in the Tenth Anniversary Edition of *Greenberg's Guide to Lionel Trains, 1945-1969, Volume I*. The pioneering efforts of Dr. Weber and others have indeed carried over into Lionel's modern era production, which also has its interesting variations.

What is the best advice for the beginning collector? The best place to start collecting these cars is probably the 9800-series refrigerator cars. There are only a few cars in this series which are really hard to find, and the number of variations is not particularly large. In addition, these cars are rather handsome and attractively priced; some of the more common cars have recently been sold at "clearance" sales for as little as $10 - $15, brand new in the box! Collectors have not shown as much interest in these cars as they have in the 9200, 9700, and 9400 Boxcar series, so the field is wide open for the beginner. After experience with the toy train marketplace, the collector can turn to other box and refrigerator car series where the prices are more variable and the variations more complex. Just what are the critical variables in collecting variations of these cars? Perhaps a rundown of these variables would be helpful to the collector at this juncture.

THE 9200-, 9700-, AND 9400-SERIES BOXCARS: CRITICAL VARIABLES

1. Body Types: There are five basic body types found in these three series of boxcars; the last one, known as the Type IX body, is by far the most common and has been used since late in 1972. Types I to IV refer to postwar production and need not concern us here. (However, *Greenberg's Guide to Lionel Trains, 1945-1969, Volume I*, has a complete rundown on these types.) The first body type, V, features one partially complete rivet row vertically to the right of the door. The end plates are blank, and it is found with Type I or II door guides (see below). Type VI is identical, but the partially complete rivet row is absent. The Type VII body has Type I or II door guides, but this time the end plates are stamped "9200 / SERIES" at one end and "LIONEL" at the other end with the early MPC logo. The Type VIII body is the same as Type VII, but it has Type III door guides. Finally, the common Type IX body has Type III door guides and a "9700 / SERIES" end plate.

Curiously, when Fundimensions changed from the 9700 Series to the 9400 Series, the firm never changed the end plate; it still reads "9700 / SERIES". Even the latest varieties made by Lionel, Inc. in 1987 still carry this end plate — a curious carry-over!

2. Door Guides: There are three basic types of door guides used in the 9200, 9700, and 9400 Series. The first, Type I, is a repetition of postwar practice; upper and lower door guides are both metal and are fastened by rivets. The Type II door guide is somewhat less common; it represents a brief transition period. This arrangement has two plastic door guides which simply snap into the rivet holes. The common Type III door guide has a plastic top guide, but the lower end of the car door has two plastic hook extensions which slide back and forth on a sill molded into the car body.

3. Frame Types: Since these frames are easily switched, the frame type is not a major factor in determining the car's value. The Type I stamped metal frame has a concave "bubble" on the bottom center and two holes, no doubt once intended for an operating car's wiring. In the Type II frame, the "bubble" is no longer present, but the two holes are still there. The Type III frame retains the holes, but this time there is stamped lettering present: "LIONEL 00-6464-009". This is the original 6464 part number; the body and doors also carry 6464 part numbers, reflecting the heritage of these cars.

4. Body Mold Colors: The phrase "body mold" refers to the color of plastic used for the body, whether it is painted or not. In the first five years of its existence, Fundimensions used plastic which came in the form of solid pellets. Since it was hard to control the color of the plastic, some odd combinations sometimes resulted. For example, a car painted brown might have been molded in orange plastic in one case and brown plastic in another. To compound matters further, the door might have been molded of an entirely different color than the body. Some time in late 1975 or early 1976, Fundimensions switched to a liquid plastic compound which was much easier to color-control. As a result, boxcars made after 1975 show far fewer variations in body mold and paint. To determine the body mold color, open the car door and look inside the car; the inside surfaces are unpainted. Be mindful that in some cases, the body itself is unpainted plastic. Sometimes the body is found both ways! A typical entry might read: "Tuscan-painted orange body, tuscan-painted gray doors."

THE 9200-SERIES BOXCARS

The 9200-series boxcars were first out of the block when Fundimensions began its production of Lionel trains in 1970. They featured the same construction characteristics as their illustrious 6464 predecessors, along with Fundimensions improvements such as the Delrin plastic trucks and fast angle wheels. They were advertised as part of a "Famous Name Collector Series," so it seems evident that Fundimensions had an adult audience in mind for these cars, at least in part. These cars were produced until 1972, when they were superseded by the 9700 Series.

The type collector will have a comparatively easy time acquiring a representative sample of these cars, because strictly speaking there are only 15 cars in the series: numbers 9200 through 9211, 9214, 9215, and 9230. But oh, the variations in these cars! The 9200 Illinois Central, probably the most common of these cars, has at least a dozen variations, with more yet to be catalogued! The series makes use of all five body types (yes, there are 9200 Boxcars with 9700 end boards!), all three door attachment types, and all three frame types. Sometimes all the body types, and all the door types can be found on different samples of the same car number! To make matters worse, some cars, such as the 9210 B & O Automobile Doubledoor Boxcar, have had different colors of doors added outside the factory. These are not, of course, regarded as legitimate factory pieces, but some collectors are still interested in them.

Most of the 9200-series Boxcars come in Type I boxes, but a few of the later ones come in the earliest of the Type II red and white boxes. These are worth looking for, since they represent late production and often indicate a 9200 Boxcar with 9700 features. The 9200, 9206, 9209, 9214, and 9230 are known to come in Type II boxes, and no doubt many others do as well.

Only a few of the 9200 Boxcars are truly rare; specific examples are the 9202 Santa Fe in orange with black lettering and the pre-production 9207 Soo Line in 9700 white and black colors. The orange and black 9202 has a particularly fascinating story. The assembly line workers had to clear a small quantity of orange plastic from the molds before they began production of the red 9202. Enough plastic remained to make about 65 "shots," as these trial moldings are called. Normally, these "shots" are discarded, but this time some of the workers added detail to them. Eventually, these cars made their way into the collector mainstream, becoming the single most rare Fundimensions boxcar to date. (A letter from Lee Jones to Frank Hare tells the story of this car a little differently. According to Jones, the orange 9202 was deliberately made in its small quantity to supply gifts to executives and friends of the management of the time.) The same thing happened to the two dozen or so pre-production samples of the 9207 Soo Line cars. Especially in recent years, Lionel's management has been very careful not to let "odd" production slip past the assembly line for the most part, but now and then odd lots such as these will emerge.

Some of the 9200 Boxcars are harder to find than others, of course, but good stocks of new cars with their boxes can be found rather easily. As the first of the new Fundimensions line, these cars are eminently collectable.

THE 9700-SERIES BOXCARS

The 9700 Series of boxcars began with the production of the 9700 Southern Boxcar in 1972 and ended in 1978, with two "stragglers" made in 1979 and 1982. By the time the series yielded to the 9400 Series, 80 different numbers had been issued; every number from 9700 to 9789 was used except 9720-22, 9736, 9741, 9746, 9756, and 9765-66. The challenge for the collector, therefore, is one of both types and varieties. It is possible to build up a very good type collection because only a few examples of the 9700 Series are really hard to find. For the most part, these consist of special issues for Toy Fairs, Season's Greetings, and various collectors' clubs.

Beginning with the cars first produced in 1976, the number of variations drops off sharply. This occurs because Fundimensions re-designed its injection molders for liquid plastic instead of pelletized plastic. The color of the liquid plastic can be made to match the paint on the cars much more closely with liquid plastic. Between 1972 and 1975, or from numbers 9700 to about 9758, large numbers of variations abound; these have been well documented by collectors ever since the series was first produced. For instance, we have identified 19 variations of the 9748 C P Rail and 14 variations of the 9739 Rio Grande alone! A complete collection of variations would entail the acquisition of hundreds of boxcars, and more varieties turn up all the time!

It was with the 9700 Series that Fundimensions began to resurrect old favorites from the 6464 Series produced in postwar years. The first of these cars was the 9707 M K T Stock Car in its original red color with white lettering and yellow doors; its predecessor with white lettering and doors is the scarcest of all the postwar stock cars. The next car in the series was a duplication of the red, white, and blue Post Office car. Many others followed. Unfortunately for collectors, some of the cars were considerably more difficult to acquire than others, thanks to Fundimensions' practice of including some cars with year-end special dealer promotions. In these packages dealers were required to purchase specified amounts of merchandise as a package and a number of the special 9700 Boxcars were included free. The dealer could then charge whatever he wanted for the special car. This made some collector favorites like the 9757 Central of Georgia quite difficult to obtain, while regular-issue favorites like the 9754 New York Central Pacemaker were readily available.

Another marketing ploy by Fundimensions was rather novel and fairly successful in building interest in new lines. Special coupons were included in some of the first runs of the 9800-series refrigerator cars and some of the 9100-series covered hopper cars. Two of these coupons with five dollars enabled the customer to acquire a special 9700-series boxcar available nowhere else. The 9719 New Haven Double-door Boxcar and the 9742 Minneapolis and St. Louis Boxcar were marketed in this way. Both of these cars had been favorites in the postwar 6464 Series, so the demand for the limited supply was brisk. Strangely enough, both of these cars can be found at a reasonable cost on the open market today. Fundimensions also marketed a 9511 "Minneapolis" Passenger Car in this manner.

One of the 9700 Boxcars produced for the Lionel Collectors' Club of America was an anomaly which has not been repeated. The 9733 Airco Boxcar was really two cars in one. When the

collector took the boxcar body off the frame, he found a single-dome tank car included within the boxcar body! Many collectors have put the tank car body on its own frame and added trim pieces to form a second Airco car, which is numbered 97330. If you find this highly desirable car, make sure that both car bodies are included if the car's full price is demanded.

There are, more or less, three tiers of scarcity for the 9700-series boxcars. The most common cars are those which were catalogued as regular issues, though a few of the catalogued cars are somewhat harder to find than others. These cars, such as the 9781 Delaware and Hudson, the 9737 Central Vermont, and the 9768 Boston and Maine, are still readily available at this writing. The second tier includes some scarcer regularly catalogued cars such as the 9710 Rutland, some cars included only in sets such as the 9772 Great Northern, and some of the more common collector organization cars such as the 9728 L C C A Stock Car. The third and scarcest tier includes cars which are catalogued but very scarce, such as the 9703 C P Rail; cars which were not catalogued but part of the series, such as the 9778 Season's Greetings and the (9762) Toy Fair cars; and the scarcer collector organization cars such as the 9727 T. A. & G. You can expect the value of these cars to rise disproportionately as time passes.

The 9700-series boxcars are colorful, well made, and astonishingly diverse, thanks to Lionel's excellent use of both nostalgia and modern graphics. They are still widely available at good prices, and collectors are only now beginning to appreciate their collectability. Therefore, these cars offer excellent collecting opportunities for the beginner who is willing to research and look in odd corners of dealers' stocks.

THE 9400-SERIES BOXCARS

Perhaps it is fitting that Fundimensions began the 9400 Series in 1978 with a tuscan 9400 Conrail Boxcar, a car which existed only in blue on the real railroad. The 9400 Series is identical in construction techniques to its 9700 predecessors, even to the extent that all the 9400-series cars still have 9700-series end plates! However, there are two very important differences between the 9400 Series and the 9700 Series, one of which makes it very difficult to collect the whole series.

One major difference between the 9400s and the 9700s is the presence of many color schemes of short-line railroads, as opposed to the almost exclusive modeling of Class I railroads within the 9700 Series. In the 9400-series, the collector will find cars modeled after the Minneapolis, Northfield and Southern, the New Hope and Ivyland, the Chattahoochee Industrial Railroad, and the Napierville Junction Railroad — all of which are short line, localized railroads. This represents the real world rather well because of the increased number of these railroads in recent years. Many of the paint schemes are very colorful and attractive to operators as well.

The other difference is much more significant to collectors. Many more of the 9400-series boxcars are special issues which can only be found in collector sets or as special package issues produced in extremely limited quantities. For this reason, many of the 9400-series cars command high prices, and this makes the series less of a good bet for a beginning collector than the 9700 Series would be. It is also significant that far fewer variations of these cars have turned up; essentially, this means

Spirit of '76 cars. Top shelf: 1776 U36B. Second shelf: 7601 Delaware, 7602 Pennsylvania. Third shelf: 7603 New Jersey, 7604 Georgia. Bottom shelf: 7605 Connecticut, 7606 Massachusetts. G. and D. Halverson and A. Conto Collections.

that Lionel standardized its plastics and paints much more than in the early 9700 Boxcars. It also means that many of the 9400-series boxcars have had only one production run. A look at the catalogues tends to confirm this supposition. In the earlier Fundimensions years, a 9700 Boxcar might run through three years in the catalogues. The 9400 Boxcars, on the other hand, were only catalogued for one year — if they were catalogued at all. Therefore, we are seeing more variety with less production — almost a guarantee of future scarcity. With some of the cars, the future is now! It is not unusual for a 9400-series boxcar out of a collector set to double or even triple in value before it even hits the toy train marketplace! That makes collecting the 9400 Series a difficult proposition. Some marketing ploys between series have annoyed collectors quite a bit. For example, in 1978 Fundimensions produced its Great Plains Express with a 9729 C P Rail Boxcar available only in that set. Since it was not sold separately, the collector of 9700 Boxcars had to purchase the set to get the boxcar. In the next year, Fundimensions marketed the set again, but this time it had a 9417 C P Rail Boxcar identical to its 9729 predecessor except for the number and gold lettering! The collector who wanted complete numbers for both series had to buy the Great Plains Express

set all over again to get the 9417 Boxcar! Neither Fundimensions nor its successors have made this mistake since, but the severe restriction of some cars in the 9400 Series to limited sets has angered some collectors.

The 9400 Series was concluded in 1986 with the production of the 9492 Lionel Lines Boxcar, the highest in the series. A new series, this time with a five-digit number, the 19200 Series, was introduced in 1987. It is somewhat early to predict the relative scarcity of the whole series, but the extensive use of special issues would indicate that these will get collector attention at the expense of the regular issues.

THE BUNK AND TOOL CARS

In 1983 Lionel produced a surprise for collectors in the form of a totally new piece of rolling stock — the bunk car. In the real world of railroading, these cars were used to house overnight the track gangs working on long-term repair jobs out on the road. Usually, the bunk car was converted from a boxcar, and Lionel has followed the prototype extremely well.

The new Lionel bunk car uses the ends, roof, and trucks of the Wood-sided Reefer series, but the sides and bottom show

71

Lionel's continued ingenuity in combining parts from existing series. The side and bottom pieces are unmistakably 9800-series refrigerator car parts which have been heavily modified. The bottom retains the air tanks of the 9800 Series, and the wooden scribing on the sides is vertical instead of horizontal, as on the Wood-sided Reefers. Four windows per side have been added which are divided into four smaller panes. A new insert has been added to the door openings so that the sides are one piece with a much smaller entrance door instead of the plug door of the 9800s. Small square holes cut out of the sides accommodate white marker lamps next to the doors, while another hole in the roof is provided for a short smokestack. The result of these modifications is a car which is remarkably faithful to its prototype.

So far, quite a few bunk cars have been produced, some as part of limited end-of-year packages or special sets. The first five produced were the 5717 Santa Fe in gray, the 5724 Pennsylvania in yellow, the 5726 Southern in dark green, the 5727 U. S. Marines in olive-drab camouflage paint, and the 5735 New York Central in gray. All but the U. S. Marines and New York Central cars were lighted; the Marines car partially compensated for its unlighted status by including a sheet of decals

for owner "customizing." Each of the lighted cars has a small plastic envelope in its box which contains the detachable smokestack and two clear marker lights for the car sides. Canadian Pacific, Lionel Lines, and red oxide Santa Fe bunk cars have been produced in the last two years. A tuscan Jersey Central version (with matching tool car) is scheduled for 1988 production.

Of the first five bunk cars, the first one, the 5717 Santa Fe, seems to be the hardest to find because far fewer of them were produced than had been planned. These cars are very recent, so it is somewhat difficult to predict their order of scarcity. However, most collectors feel that the 5726 Southern will be a relatively scarce car, while the 5724 Pennsylvania will be fairly common. The 5727 U. S. Marines Car is probably the easiest to obtain. The 5735 New York Central Car is also desirable because it was part of a special freight set, the Yard Chief, which was very popular with collectors. Of the most recent three, the Canadian Pacific version is easily obtained, but the Lionel Lines and Santa Fe in red oxide are harder to acquire because they were limited-production items from (respectively) a year-end package and a special Service Station set.

More Spirit of '76 cars. Top shelf: 7607 Maryland, 7608 South Carolina. Second shelf: 7609 New Hampshire, 7610 Virginia. Third shelf: 7611 New York, 7612 North Carolina. Bottom shelf: 7613 Rhode Island, 7600 Caboose. G. and D. Halverson and A. Conto Collections.

For 1986 Lionel had another surprise in mind. In that year a B & O Freight Set was portrayed in the Traditional Catalogue. This set had a new and attractive variation of the bunk car, Lionel's new tool car. Elsewhere in this edition, John Kouba, in his article on the Santa Fe Service Station Special for 1986, has detailed the differences between the bunk and tool cars. Briefly stated, Lionel modified the sides of the bunk car by replacing the four square windows with two large rectangular ones. In addition, doors were molded into the car ends, and the marker lights and smokestack of the bunk car were eliminated. So far, the tool car has been issued in unlighted 5739 B & O and 5760 Santa Fe versions and a lighted gray 19651 Santa Fe version. No doubt many more will follow, because the tool car is an excellent variant of the bunk car which has met with an enthusiastic reception.

The bunk and tool cars are good additions to a beginner's set, if only because they represent a very creative approach to rolling stock on the part of Lionel. These unusual cars will probably show good appreciation in value.

THE MINT CARS

In 1979 Fundimensions included a revival of the postwar Fort Knox mint car in its Southern Pacific collector set. This fanciful car, rather silly in terms of any real railroad, always had a whimsical charm to it, and its inclusion was one of the reasons why this set sold out so quickly. The car uses the body first developed in the postwar years for the operating aquarium car. The sides of the boxcar each have two large clear plastic panels. These are "revealed" by imitation fold-up curtains molded into the car body atop the clear panels. Each pair of clear panels is separated by a door resembling a safe with a combination lock. Inside the car, a gold or silver plastic insert simulates stacks of bullion. The roof has a coin slot and the ends of the car have circular ventilation grates.

All of the Lionel mint cars produced in the modern era are equipped with Standard O trucks; and eight have been issued since 1979. Aside from the Fort Knox car and a special mint car issued for the Train Collectors Association, one car has been issued for each of the real mints of the United States, past and present: San Francisco, Denver, Philadelphia, Carson City, New Orleans, and Dahlonega (a Southern mint used during the Civil War). With the issue of the Dahlonega car, this series as such should end, unless Lionel, Inc. decides to issue cars named after famous banking houses. (The mind boggles a bit at the thought of a Chase-Manhattan mint car or a Crocker National Bank mint car!) Many collectors consider these cars a little silly, but they are so impossibly whimsical that they have an appeal of their own. By combining them with a postwar 3535 Security Car, a Marines searchlight car, and an appropriate locomotive, the Lionel operator could run one of the more unusual trains in his/her collection! The Carson City and New Orleans cars seem to be the easiest of these cars to find. The Philadelphia, San Francisco, Denver, and Dahlonega cars are a notch above these in scarcity, while the Fort Knox and the T C A Special are the hardest to find.

Perhaps Lionel, Inc. did have a special train in mind for these cars all along. In 1987 the firm issued a special bronze-painted GG-1 electric locomotive with a matching Pennsylvania N5C caboose. According to the catalogue description, this engine and caboose were meant to accompany the mint cars. If you really have dreamed of running a "money train," you were not too far removed from Lionel's thinking!

THE 9600 HI-CUBE BOXCARS

In 1976 Fundimensions added another completely new boxcar to its growing variety reflecting modern prototype practices. This was the all-plastic Hi-Cube boxcar, derived from a 40-foot boxcar which is built 12 to 18 inches higher than the norm. Like their prototypes, Fundimensions' Hi-Cubes had no catwalks on the roof; they also featured extensive riveting detail along the car sides, going against the trend towards eliminating rivet detailing. The Hi-Cubes featured large sliding doors fastened in place by hooks at both top and bottom. In addition, an all-new plastic frame was created for them.

Instantly, the Hi-Cubes diverged into two distinct series. One featured real railroad names. There were ten of these numbered from 9600 to 9609 and also a 9610 Frisco Hi-Cube which was only available as part of the 1977 Rocky Mountain Set. A 9611 T C A "Flying Yankee" Hi-Cube was made for that association's 1978 national convention in Boston. (See entry 1018-1979 for a good story about the conversion of this car to the T C A Mortgage Burning Ceremony Car.) The other was the Mickey Mouse Hi-Cube Series, a colorful issue of these cars with Disney logos and characters. These cars ran from numbers 9660 to 9672, with the last number issued as the extremely scarce Mickey Mouse 50th Birthday Car in 1978. After that year the cars were phased out, only to reappear in 1982 in numbers 9626-29 with slightly simplified paint schemes which repeated previous prototype road name issues. They were again deleted after 1984. One other Hi-Cube was produced for the Toy Train Operating Society's 1978 convention in Hollywood.

Most of the common issue Hi-Cubes are not in great demand; only the 9600 Chessie, the 9610 Frisco, and the special convention issues have aroused any real interest. Of the Disney cars, which are in considerably greater demand, the Pinocchio, Snow White, and Pluto cars are very hard to find, and the 50th Birthday Car is a true rarity.

Although the Hi-Cubes are colorful and contemporary, many operators complain that the rolling characteristics of these cars are poor. Because of their plastic frames and high center of gravity, they have a tendency to tip over unless they are weighted. Despite this problem, these cars show real effort by Lionel to add a contemporary flair to tinplate railroading. However, with the recent emphasis on the Standard O boxcars, it is not likely that any of these cars will again be produced in the foreseeable future.

THE OPERATING BOXCARS

In 1972, amid much fanfare, Fundimensions began the production of a car which has defied obsolescence; it did not vanish from the catalogues until 1985. This is the 9301 Operating Post Office Car, in which the press of a button opens the car door and activates a little man who tosses a mail sack out the door. This car had no company until as late as 1982, when the 9218 Monon Mail Delivery Car joined it in the Fundimensions line-up. Since that year, other operating boxcars modeled after the old postwar 3484-94 cars have been revived.

By this time, most of the old favorites in operating boxcars have been resurrected by Lionel. These cars include the horse transport car, in which two horses bob heads out of side ports in a small stock car; the operating giraffe car in three versions; the cop and hobo car; the icing station refrigerator car; and a few others.

Nor have the larger operating box and stock cars been neglected. In the last few years, Fundimensions has released the fanciful poultry dispatch car, known irreverently as the "chicken sweeper" car, in which the press of a button opens the car door and releases a man with a broom suspended on a hairspring; he appears to be sweeping feathers out of the car door. Even the non-operating version of this car was introduced in 1987. The deluxe Borden operating milk car, an old favorite, has been a brisk seller and the operating Churchill Downs horse car and corral will probably be another item in heavy demand. A second milk car, this time a Carnation car reminiscent of the highly desirable postwar Bosco car, has been added to the line, as well as a red Santa Fe operating boxcar and even a second icing station car in white and blue Reading colors. For 1988 a colorful N Y R B (New York Central) icing station car, a "Circle L Ranch" cattle car, and even a revival of the famous Bosco Milk Car have been produced.

The operating boxcars have been welcome additions to the Lionel train consist because they add animation to an operator's layout. Many of these cars are still priced very reasonably, and no collection is really complete without a few of them.

THE O27 SHORT BOXCARS

Like its postwar predecessors, Fundimensions and its successors have made shorter inexpensive boxcars for the Traditional sets and special department store promotional sets from the beginning. These little cars, sometimes erroneously referred to as "plug door" boxcars, are probably the most neglected of all the boxcars because they lack the glamour of their larger cousins. Yet some of these cars are extremely hard to find; they represent a real opportunity for the beginning collector to get a scarce car at a reasonable price. Although most of these cars came in sets an occasional straggler will be found for separate sale, usually in a Type II box.

By far, the scarcest of these cars are the special ones made up for department stores such as J. C. Penney, True Value Hardware, Toys 'R Us, and Kiddie City. There are, in fact, at least five different Toys 'R Us cars, each with variations!

The O27 boxcars are very much like their 6014 postwar predecessors, but they have a new molded plastic bottom piece in place of the metal frame used on the 6014 Series. Most have one operating and one dummy coupler. Some have railroad markings, such as the Conrail, Erie-Lackawanna, and Santa Fe cars, while others have corporate markings such as Wheaties, Ford Motorcraft, and Hershey's Chocolate.

Since very few collectors pay attention to these cars, the small O27 boxcars are a wide-open field for the beginning collector. They are even available as throw-ins in collections of assorted junk! These cars deserve far more attention than they have gotten to date.

SOME ODDS AND ENDS

Mention should be made of a few more series of boxcars which do not fit conveniently into any category. The 7600-series Bicentennial long boxcars were produced from 1974 to 1976; they feature colorful markings for each of the 13 original states, and many have variations. The Virginia and New York cars are highly prized in this set, but most of the rest are quite readily available in their Bicentennial boxes.

The 7800 Soda Pop Road Series should have been a very popular set when it was first introduced in 1977, but only six cars were produced overall. Of these cars, which use 9700-style bodies with colorful corporate logos, the Pepsi car is in a little more demand than the other five. Cars with Sprite, Tab, and Fanta logos were included as part of a Coca-Cola set, but they are part of the 9700 Series. The 7700 Tobacco Road Series was produced from 1976 to 1978. These long boxcars featured some of the biggest names in the tobacco industry and were obviously aimed at an adult audience. Nine of them were eventually produced, with the El Producto and Mail Pouch cars being a little harder to find than the rest of the series, which is very common and readily available. Finally, mention must be made of the strange little 9090 Mini-Max Boxcar. This odd little car was made in 1971 only. It had all-door sides which swung open to reveal a scribed floor and three little pallet containers which could be loaded and unloaded. This car is quite hard to find today, especially in a separate sale Type I box and in a light blue color. In the past two years, we have found that the production history of this little car is quite a bit more complex than we had thought, and we have written an update on it for this edition (see the 9090 listings).

If variety is the spice of tinplate life, Lionel has certainly added it with its incredibly well-varied and extensive line of box, refrigerator, and stock cars. It can truly be said that these cars range from the realistic to the whimsical and that there is a boxcar in the Lionel product line for everyone.

	Gd	VG	Exc	Mt

0512 See Special Production chapter.

0780 LIONEL RAILROADER CLUB BOXCAR: 1982, white-painted white body, red-painted white doors, red roof and ends, Type IX body, Symington-Wayne trucks; black electrocal of steam locomotive front end at right of door; red "1982" and black "SPECIAL EDITION THE INSIDE TRACK" to left of door; red "LIONEL" and "0780" and black "RAILROADER CLUB" to right of door. This car was only available to members of the Lionel Railroader Club, a Fundimensions-sponsored organization continued by Lionel, Inc. F. Stem Collection.

		--	--	50	65

1018-1979 T C A MORTGAGE BURNING CEREMONY CAR: 1979, light tan-painted gray plastic body, light yellow-painted white door, hi-cube boxcar; orange, black, and red rectangular mortgage burning logo at left, orange Toy Train Museum logo and black lettering at right. There is an intriguing story behind the making of this car. In 1978 the T C A held its convention in Boston. The 9611 "Flying Yankee" Hi-Cube Boxcar was produced for this convention in official Boston and Maine sky blue and black (see 9611-1978 entry). Large anticipated sales of the Flying Yankee Car never materialized, and at convention's end the T C A found itself in possession of a considerable backlog of unsold cars. In the next year, the organization was to finish paying the mortgage on its museum in Strasburg, Pennsylvania. Rather than order a special car, the T C A shipped its entire backlog of 9611 Flying Yankee Cars to the Pleasant Valley Process Company of Cogan Station, Pennsylvania. There, the Flying Yankee cars were repainted into the Mortgage Burning Ceremony car. Faint traces of the original black paint show through the light tan paint on the ends and roof. J. Bratspis observation.

		--	--	--	95

1984 RITZ: 1984, hi-cube boxcar, red body, yellow doors, yellow lettering "50th ANNIVERSARY / RITZ 1984", Ritz canister, Symington-Wayne trucks. This was part of a special promotional set issued by Nabisco Brands, some of which may have been done outside the factory. Reader comments invited. S. Lindsey, Jr. Collection. **NRS**

5717 A. T. S. F.: 1983, bunk car. Gray body with black lettering and number. This was the first in a series of cars original to the Fundimensions line. Basically, it features heavily modified 9800-series reefer sides and bottom combined with a 5700-series reefer roof and ends. The original door opening is made narrower and a smaller, non-opening door is made as part of the car side. Four square windows per side are present, each of them cross-hatched into four smaller sections. There are holes in the sides for clear plastic marker lights and a hole in the roof for a short black chimney stack; these pieces come in a little plastic packet included with the car. Opaque plastic window pieces are fitted into the windows from the inside in lighted versions of the car. The first production pieces of this car were found with parts missing, broken, or haphazardly assembled, but the problem was soon corrected. Fewer of the Santa Fe cars were produced than expected, making it somewhat scarce. R. LaVoie comment and Collection.

-- -- 40 45

5718: See 9849.

5724 PENNSYLVANIA: 1984, bunk car, see 5717 for construction details. Light yellow-painted gray body; black "PRR / 5724" and black and yellow Keystone logo, arch bar trucks, illuminated. R. LaVoie Collection.

-- -- 20 25

5726 SOUTHERN: 1983-84, bunk car, see 5717 for construction details. Dark green-painted gray body; white "S.S.R.R. / 5726" below left pair of windows, arch bar trucks, illuminated. R. LaVoie Collection. -- -- 30 40

5727 U. S. MARINES: 1984-85, bunk car, camouflage-painted olive and yellow-gray plastic body; white lettering, no window inserts, unlighted, arch bar trucks. Came with sheet of decals with U. S. Army and U. S. Marines markings to be applied to car by purchaser. -- -- 12 15

5728 CANADIAN NATIONAL: 1986, bunk car, maroon-painted body, white lettering and script logo, arch bar trucks, illuminated. -- -- 15 20

5733 LIONEL LINES: 1986, bunk car, bright orange sides, bright blue roof and ends, new Lionel, Inc. logo applied by decal on side, blue and black lettering, arch bar trucks, illuminated. Part of 1986 year-end "Stocking Stuffer" package and somewhat hard to find. -- -- 40 50

5735 NEW YORK CENTRAL: 1985, bunk car, light gray body, black lettering and NYC oval logo, unlighted, Symington Wayne trucks. Part of Yard Chief

Top shelf: 9035 and 9037 Conrail boxcars. Second shelf: 9040 Wheaties, 9041 Hershey's. Third shelf: 9041 Hershey's, 9042 Autolite. Bottom shelf: 9043 Erie Lackawanna, 9045 Toys "R" Us. G. and D. Halverson and A. Conto Collections.

Top shelf: 9046 True Value, 9048 Toys "R" Us. Second shelf: 9053 True Value, 9054 J C Penney. Third shelf: 9365 Toys "R" Us, 9376 Soo Line. Bottom shelf: 9388 Toys "R" Us, unlettered boxcar. G. and D. Halverson and A. Conto Collections.

Steam Switcher Set; catalogued as illuminated with arch bar trucks and number 6127, but not produced that way.   -- -- 35 45

5739 B & O: 1986, tool car, heavily modified wood-sided reefer body. Gray body, black lettering and logo, centered small doors on sides and ends, two tall eight-pane windows flanking doors on each side, 9800-series reefer bottom piece, Symington-Wayne trucks, not illuminated. Part of Set 1652, the B & O Freight.   -- -- 40 50

5745 A. T. & S. F.: 1986, bunk car, red oxide sides, silver-painted roof and ends, yellow lettering and cross logo, Standard O trucks, not illuminated. Part of Santa Fe Work Train Service Station Special.   -- -- 40 50

5760 A. T. & S. F.: 1986, tool car, red oxide sides, silver-painted roof and ends, red oxide doors in ends, yellow lettering and cross logo, Standard O trucks, not illuminated. Part of Santa Fe Work Train Service Station Special.   -- -- 40 50

6014-900 FRISCO: See Special Production chapter.

6127 NEW YORK CENTRAL: See 5735.

6232 ILLINOIS CENTRAL: 1986, Standard O boxcar, orange body, black and white IC logo, black lettering, Standard O trucks. Part of special direct-mail offer from Lionel.   -- -- 80 100

6234 BURLINGTON NORTHERN: 1985, Standard O boxcar, part of Burlington Northern Limited Set: Cascade green body and doors, white lettering and large BN logo, black roof and catwalk, Standard O trucks.   -- -- -- 40

6235 BURLINGTON NORTHERN: Standard O boxcar, matches 6234.
                    -- -- -- 40

6236 BURLINGTON NORTHERN: Standard O boxcar, matches 6234.
                    -- -- -- 40

6237 BURLINGTON NORTHERN: Standard O boxcar, matches 6234.
                    -- -- -- 40

6238 BURLINGTON NORTHERN: Standard O boxcar, matches 6234.
                    -- -- -- 40

6239 BURLINGTON NORTHERN: 1986, Standard O boxcar, matches 6234 through 6238; sold separately as part of year-end "Stocking Stuffer" package.
                    -- -- -- 40

6464-1 WESTERN PACIFIC: See Factory Errors and Prototypes.

6464-50 MINNEAPOLIS & ST. LOUIS: See Factory Errors and Prototypes.

6464-500 TIMKEN: 1970, Fundimensions product with postwar number; identifiable by "BLT. 1970 / BY LIONEL MPC" to right of doors; metal door guides.

9090 MINI-MAX Boxcars and pallets. G. and D. Halverson and A. Conto Collections.

(A) Type V body, yellow body and doors, black lettering, orange, black, and white Timken decal logo, postwar bar-end metal trucks. Rare; approximately 500 made. G. Halverson comment.　　　　　　　　　-- -- -- 250

(B) Same as (A), but light yellow body and door paint.　　　-- -- -- 200

(C) Type VI orange-painted body and doors, AAR trucks; approximately 1,300 made. G. Halverson comment.　　　　　　　-- -- 100 150

(D) Same as (C), but postwar bar-end metal trucks.　　-- -- 100 150

(E) Same as (C), but Type VII body with 9200 numberboard. Extremely rare; only about 50 produced. G. Halverson comment.　　　-- -- -- 450

6464-1970: See Special Production chapter.

6464-1971: See Special Production chapter.

7301 N & W: 1982, cattle car, brown and white lettering, Standard O trucks; from Continental Limited Set.　　　　　　-- -- 40 50

7302 T & P: 1983, short-body cattle car, brown with white lettering.　　　　　　　　　　　　　　-- -- -- 10

7303 ERIE: 1984-85, stock car, dull slate blue body, white lettering and Erie logo, Standard O trucks; from Erie-Lackawanna Limited Set.　-- -- 30 35

7304 SOUTHERN: 1983, stock car, dark green body, tuscan roof and ends, tuscan double-tier doors; white "SOUTHERN" and "7304" to right of doors, circular white Southern logo to left of doors, gold Famous American Railroads No. 4

Top shelf: 9200 Illinois Central, 9201 Penn Central. Second shelf: 9202 Santa Fe, 9203 Union Pacific. Third shelf: 9204 Northern Pacific, 9205 Norfolk and Western. Bottom shelf: 9206 Great Northern, 9207 Soo Line. G. and D. Halverson and A. Conto Collections.

diamond-shaped logo, Standard O trucks. Extra car meant to accompany Southern Set but offered in year-end package for separate sale; hard to find.

--	--	45	55

7309 SOUTHERN: 1986, short stock car, tuscan body, white lettering, Symington-Wayne trucks. -- -- 10 15

7312 W & A: 1986, (Western & Atlantic) short stock car, tuscan body, yellow lettering and shield, two operating couplers, arch bar trucks. Part of un-catalogued American Express Set 1608. T. Taylor Collection. -- -- -- 25

7401 CHESSIE SYSTEM: 1984-85, short stock car, red body; white lettering, Symington-Wayne trucks, one operating and one dummy coupler; part of 1402 Chessie System Set in Traditional catalogue. C. Lang comment.

-- -- -- 10

7403 L N A C: 1984, boxcar. See Special Production chapter.

7404 JERSEY CENTRAL: 1986, boxcar, dark green body, cream lettering and logo, Standard O trucks; same design as 9787 except for trucks and cream lettering instead of gold. Made to accompany Jersey Central "Miss Liberty" Fairbanks-Morse locomotive and extended vision caboose, but sold separately.

-- -- 30 35

7501 LIONEL 75th ANNIVERSARY: 1975, Cowen picture, blue body, silver roof and ends, 9700-type boxcar. -- 10 15 20

7502 LIONEL 75th ANNIVERSARY: See Refrigerator Cars chapter.

7503 LIONEL 75th ANNIVERSARY: See Refrigerator Cars chapter.

7505 LIONEL 75th ANNIVERSARY: 1975, 9700-series boxcar, accessories, silver body, red roof and ends. -- 10 15 20

7506 LIONEL 75th ANNIVERSARY: 1975, 9700-series boxcar, famous catalogues, green body, gold roof and ends. -- 10 15 20

7507 LIONEL 75th ANNIVERSARY: See Refrigerator Cars chapter.

7515 DENVER MINT: 1981, light gold paint on clear plastic, stack of silver ingots inside car, Standard O trucks. See introduction for construction details. Other mint cars produced: 7517, 7518, 7522, 7530, 9319, 9320, and 9349. C. Lang comment. -- -- 85 95

7517 PHILADELPHIA MINT: 1982, clear plastic body painted burnished bronze, coin slot, circular grates at each end, silver bullion inside, Standard O trucks, disc-operating couplers; from Spring '82 Collector Center.

-- -- 45 55

7518 CARSON CITY MINT: 1983, clear plastic body painted black, silver bullion inside car. Plastic appears to be thinner and less crisply cast than other mint cars. Standard O trucks. -- -- 35 40

7520 NIBCO: 1982, boxcar, special promotion for Nibco Plumbing Products offered as a premium to plumbers; reportedly only 500 made. 9700-type boxcar with Type IX body and Type III frame, white body, green doors; green and blue ribbon running across car on both sides of door, blue lettering, gold NIBCO emblem on upper left side, blue "NIBCO / EXPRESS" and "QUALITY PIPING PRODUCTS" to right of door. This car was offered independently of the NIBCO 1264 Train Set; see 8182 Diesel engine entry in Chapter I for set details. Very hard to find. -- -- -- 500

7522 NEW ORLEANS MINT: 1984-85, dark gloss blue body, clear plastic windows on sides, silver ingots stacked inside car, circular grates on each end, fake "safe" door between windows on both sides, Standard O trucks.

-- -- 25 35

7525 See Special Production chapter.

7530 DAHLONEGA: 1986, mint car, dark pink-orange-painted mint car body, silver lettering, silver bullion load, clear sides, Standard O trucks. Part of year-end "Stocking Stuffer" package. -- -- 65 75

SPIRIT OF '76 SERIES CARS

The Spirit of '76 Boxcars were numbered 7601 through 7613 for the first thirteen states admitted to the Union. Each state's car names the state capital and portrays its flag, admission date, state flower, bird, tree, and motto. At one time, Fundimensions may have had an ambitious plan to produce these colorful cars for the remaining 37 states, but this never happened. C. Lang comment.

TYPE I AND TYPE II BODIES

Type I: Black metal strip runs car length and is used to attach trucks. Underneath the strip at each end are square holes. Black metal strip is attached to the bottom of the car by one screw, the trucks then attach to the black strip.

Type II: No strip version with a round hole at each end on the bottom. Round hole is for the screw that holds the one-piece roof and ends to the car sides.

7601 DELAWARE: 1975-76.
(A) Type I light yellow body and door painted light yellow, blue roof painted blue; blue lettering, yellow-orange diamond in flag. C. Lang and C. Weber comments, D. Mitarotonda Collection. -- 10 15 20
(B) Type I cream-white body and door painted light yellow, blue roof painted blue; blue lettering. -- 10 15 20
(C) Type II light yellow body and door painted light yellow, blue roof painted blue; light gold diamond in flag; blue lettering. D. Mitarotonda Collection.
-- 10 15 20

7602 PENNSYLVANIA: 1975-76, light blue plastic body painted light blue, orange plastic roof painted orange; black or blue lettering.
(A) Type I body, light blue plastic door painted light blue; black lettering.
-- 10 20 25
(B) Type II body, cream-white plastic door painted light blue.
-- 10 20 25

7603 NEW JERSEY: 1975-76.
(A) Type I light green plastic body and door painted light green, gray roof painted gold; yellow-orange flag. C. Weber comments, D. Mitarotonda Collection.
-- 10 15 20
(B) Same as (A), but Type II body. -- 10 15 20
(C) Type II light green body and door painted light green, clear white roof painted gold; light gold flag. D. Mitarotonda Collection. -- 10 15 20

7604 GEORGIA: 1975-76, blue lettering.
(A) Type I light blue body painted light blue, clear white door painted light blue, clear-white roof painted red; red flag, yellow-gold bars and stripes border. D. Mitarotonda Collection. -- 10 20 30
(B) Type I cream-white plastic body and door painted light blue, red roof painted flat red. W. Eddins Collection. -- 10 20 30
(C) Type II light blue body and door painted light blue, red roof painted dark red; dark red flag, lighter gold bars and stripes border. D. Mitarotonda Collection.
-- 10 20 30
(D) Type II light blue plastic body and door painted light blue, glossy red roof painted glossy deep red. W. Eddins Collection. -- 10 20 30

7605 CONNECTICUT: 1975-76, black lettering.
(A) Type I body, cream-white plastic body and door painted medium pale blue, blue roof painted dark blue. C. Weber comment. -- 10 20 30
(B) Type II body, medium pale blue plastic body and door painted medium pale blue, dark blue roof painted dark blue. -- 10 20 30
(C) Same as (A), but white roof painted dark blue. D. Mitarotonda Collection.
-- 10 20 30

7606 MASSACHUSETTS: 1975-76, black lettering.
(A) Type I body, cream-white plastic body and door painted light yellow, cream-white roof painted white. Doors slightly more yellow-orange than sides. C. Weber comment. -- 10 15 20
(B) Type I body, cream-white plastic body and door painted medium yellow, cream-white roof painted white. Doors slightly more yellow-orange than sides. C. Weber comment. -- 10 15 20
(C) Type I body, shiny white plastic body and door painted dark yellow, cream-white roof painted white, flag is bordered in dark gold, purple crest, light purple shadowing. D. Mitarotonda Collection. -- 10 15 20
(D) Type I body, shiny white plastic body and door painted very dark yellow, cream white roof painted white, flag is bordered in yellow gold, dark blue crest, light blue shadowing. D. Mitarotonda Collection. -- 10 15 20

7607 MARYLAND: 1975-76, black lettering.
(A) Type I body, white plastic body and door painted light yellow, white roof painted black; checkered quadrants of the flag are alternating gold and black squares, gold flagstaff is topped by a dark gold eagle. D. Mitarotonda Collection.
-- 10 15 20

(B) Type II body, light yellow body and door painted light yellow; yellow and black checkered flag quadrants, light gold cross tops flagstaff, black roof painted black. D. Mitarotonda Collection. -- 10 15 20

(C) Type II body, cream-white plastic body and door painted mustard, cream-white roof painted black. -- 10 15 20

(D) Type I body, cream-white plastic body and door painted dark yellow, cream-white roof painted black. -- 10 15 20

(E) Type II light yellow body and door painted light yellow, black roof painted black; black and yellow alternating flag quadrant squares, white quadrants slightly shadowed, yellow-gold cross tops yellow-gold flagstaff. D. Mitarotonda Collection. -- 10 15 20

7608 SOUTH CAROLINA: 1975-76, black lettering.
(A) Type I body, dark yellow body and door painted mustard, brown roof painted chocolate brown. W. Mitchell and D. Mitarotonda Collections.
-- 10 15 25

(B) Same as (A), but white door painted darker mustard. D. Mitarotonda Collection. -- 10 15 25

(C) Type II body, dark mustard plastic body and medium mustard door painted dark mustard, mustard roof painted chocolate brown; medium blue flag.
-- 10 15 25

(D) Same as (A), but cream white door painted mustard, cream white roof and ends painted brown. C. Rohlfing Collection. -- 10 15 25

7609 NEW HAMPSHIRE: 1975-76, black lettering. Harder to find than most of the series.
(A) Type I body, dark yellow plastic body and door painted dark yellow, light green roof painted dark green. -- 30 35 45

(B) Type II body, dark yellow plastic body painted dark yellow, dark yellow door painted dark yellow, green roof painted dark green; dark blue flag bordered in light gold with light gold leaves and printing on the flag. D. Mitarotonda Collection. -- 30 35 45

(C) Same as (A), but Type II body and white border around right side of map, half moon on map by star. -- 30 35 45

(D) Type I body, dark yellow plastic body painted dark yellow, white door painted dark yellow, white roof painted dark green, purple flag bordered in gold, gold leaves and printing on flag. D. Mitarotonda Collection. -- 30 35 45

7610 VIRGINIA: 1975-76, black lettering. Rarest of the series, though nobody seems to know why fewer of these cars were produced. C. Lang comment. Some say cars were distributed to the State of Virginia for promotion. J. Grzyboski comment.
(A) Type I body, cream-white plastic body and door painted orange, cream-white roof painted dark blue. -- 100 150 195

(B) Type I body, orange plastic body and door painted orange, blue roof painted blue; no quarter moon on map. -- 100 150 195

(C) Same as (B), but Type II body. -- 100 150 195

(D) Type I body, cream-white body painted orange, orange door painted orange, dark blue roof painted dark blue. D. Mitarotonda Collection.
-- 100 150 195

7611 NEW YORK: 1975-76, black lettering. Harder to find than most other cars in the series.
(A) Type I cream-white plastic body and medium yellow door painted light yellow, dark blue roof painted dark blue. -- 40 60 75

(B) Type II cream plastic body and medium yellow door painted dark yellow; near perfect flag, dark blue roof painted dark blue. -- 40 60 75

Top shelf: 9208 C P Rail, 9209 Burlington Northern. **Second shelf:** 9210 Baltimore & Ohio, 9211 Penn Central. **Third shelf:** 9214 Northern Pacific, 9215 Norfolk and Western. **Bottom shelf:** 9217 Soo Line, 9218 Monon. G. and D. Halverson and A. Conto Collections.

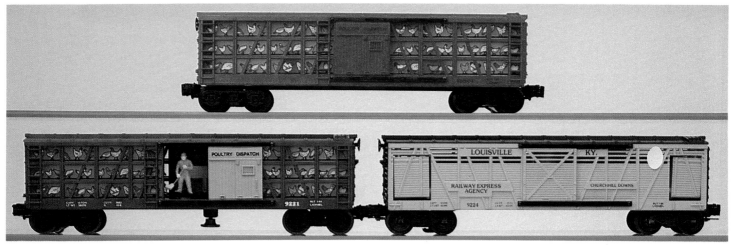

Top shelf: 19801 Non-operating Poultry Dispatch Car. Bottom shelf: 9221 Operating Poultry Dispatch Car (note "chicken sweeper" figure in door), 9224 R E A stock car. A. Rudman Collection.

(C) Type II cream plastic body and medium yellow door painted dark yellow; flag with red border, dark blue roof painted dark blue. -- **40 60 75**

(D) Type II dark cream plastic body and medium yellow door painted dark yellow; flag with red and white border, dark blue roof painted dark blue. -- **40 60 75**

(E) Type II cream plastic body and white door painted medium yellow; flag with white border, dark blue roof painted dark blue. -- **40 60 75**

(F) Type I pale yellow body and medium yellow door painted dark yellow (door darker than body), clear white roof painted dark blue. D. Mitarotonda Collection. -- **40 60 75**

(G) Type I medium yellow body and medium yellow doors painted dark yellow (doors darker than body), clear white roof painted dark blue. D. Mitarotonda Collection. -- **40 60 75**

7612 NORTH CAROLINA: 1975-76, black lettering.

(A) Type I cream plastic body painted dark mustard, yellow door painted medium mustard, slight contrast between door and darker body, cream-white roof painted black; flag heavily shadowed in blue tint, yellow letters and banners subsequently show green tint. D. Mitarotonda Collection. -- **12 20 45**

(B) Type I white plastic body and cream door painted light mustard, cream-white roof painted black. -- **12 20 45**

(C) Type II mustard body and door painted dark mustard, no contrast between door and body, black roof painted black; flag in light shadow, blue portion is dark blue. D. Mitarotonda Collection. -- **12 20 45**

(D) Type II dark yellow body painted light mustard, yellow door painted dark mustard, large contrast between darker door and body, black roof painted black; flag in medium shadow, red portion is light red. D. Mitarotonda Collection. -- **12 20 45**

(E) Same as (A), but doors darker than sides. C. Weber Collection. -- **12 20 45**

7613 RHODE ISLAND: 1975-76, black lettering.

(A) Type I body, aqua-blue plastic body and door painted green, gray roof painted gold. Very hard to find. J. Grzyboski Collection. -- **40 50 65**

(B) Type II body, green plastic body and door painted green, white roof painted gold. -- **20 25 30**

(C) Type I body, aqua-blue body painted dark green, dark green door painted dark green, green roof painted gold. D. Mitarotonda Collection. **NRS**

7700 UNCLE SAM: 1976, white-painted body and door, red-painted roof, plastic top door guides with molded hook on bottom, white and black lettering.

(A) Opaque white plastic body and door. **30 40 60 75**

(B) Translucent white plastic body. **30 40 60 75**

7701 CAMEL: 1976-77, brown, black, and silver lettering, plastic top door guides with molded hook on bottom, dark brown roof and ends.

(A) Opaque white plastic body and doors painted medium yellow. -- **10 12 14**

(B) Same as (A), but medium dark yellow body and light yellow doors. -- **10 12 14**

(C) Same as (A), but dark yellow body and doors. -- **10 12 14**

(D) Translucent white plastic body painted light yellow, dark yellow doors. -- **10 12 14**

7702 PRINCE ALBERT: 1976-77, red plastic body painted red and yellow, door painted yellow, black roof; yellow, black and white lettering, black and white oval electrocal to right of door, plastic top door guides with molded hook on bottom. C. Lang comment. -- **10 12 14**

7703 BEECH-NUT: 1976-77, opaque white plastic body painted white, red roof and ends, blue doors painted blue; blue and red lettering, plastic top door guides with molded hook on bottom, Beech-Nut electrocal to right of door. C. Lang comment. -- **10 12 14**

7704 TOY FAIR: 1985. See Special Production chapter.

7705 TOY FAIR: 1986. See Special Production chapter.

7706 SIR WALTER RALEIGH: 1977-78, opaque white plastic body painted orange, blue roof, translucent white door painted gold; white and gold lettering, black and gold electrocals on each side of door, plastic top on door guides with molded hook on bottom. C. Lang comment. -- **10 12 14**

7707 WHITE OWL: 1977-78, opaque white plastic body painted white, brown roof, translucent white door painted gold; brown lettering, brown and white square electrocal to right of door, plastic top door guides with molded bottom hook. C. Lang comment. -- **10 12 14**

7708 WINSTON: 1977-78, red plastic body painted red, gold roof, translucent white door painted gold; white and red lettering, red and white oblong electrocal to right of door, plastic top door guides with molded bottom hook. C. Lang comment. -- **10 12 14**

7709 SALEM: 1978, green-painted sides, gold roof, ends, and doors, electrocals on both sides of doors. C. Lang comment. -- **10 12 14**

7710 MAIL POUCH: 1978, white-painted sides, red roof and ends, tuscan doors, red and tuscan lettering, red, tuscan, and white Mail Pouch electrocal to left of door; green, yellow, black, gray, tuscan, and white barn electrocal to right of door, Symington-Wayne trucks. C. Rohlfing Collection. -- **10 15 20**

7711 EL PRODUCTO: 1978, white sides, yellow doors, red roof and ends, red and black lettering, Symington-Wayne trucks. C. Rohlfing Collection. -- **10 15 20**

7712 A T S F: 1979, yellow sides, silver roof; black "SHIP AND TRAVEL SANTA FE ALL THE WAY"; gold "FARR 1" diamond-shaped logo; part of Famous American Railroad Series No. 1, but sold separately. -- **25 35 45**

7800 PEPSI: 1977, white plastic body painted white, red roof and ends, blue doors painted blue; red and blue lettering, Type IX body, Type III door guides, Symington-Wayne trucks, Type III frame, "LIONEL" on right side. -- **15 20 30**

7801 A & W: 1977, white plastic body painted yellow, orange roof and ends; brown lettering, white doors painted brown, Type IX body, Type III door guides, Symington-Wayne trucks, Type III frame, "LIONEL" on right side.

-- **10 15 20**

7802 CANADA DRY: 1977, green plastic body painted green, gold roof and ends, cream door painted gold; white and gold lettering, Type IX body, Type III door guides, Symington-Wayne trucks, Type III frame, "LIONEL" on left side.

-- **10 20 25**

7803 TRAINS 'N TRUCKING: 1978, white body, gold-painted doors and roof; green and gold lettering. C. Rohlfing and R. LaVoie Collections.

10 15 20 40

7806 SEASONS GREETINGS: 1976.

(A) Silver-painted body, green door; white lettering, Type IX body. R. P. Bryan Collection. -- **100 125 150**

(B) Same as (A), but white-painted body, black doors, red lettering. Other variations may exist; reader comments and confirmation requested. R. P. Bryan comment. **NRS**

7807 TOY FAIR: 1977. See Special Production chapter.

7808 NORTHERN PACIFIC: 1978, stock car, brown with silver roof, black door; silver lettering, "The Pig Palace" electrocal on white plastic board glued to slats at right of doors. Part of 1764 Heartland Express. C. Lang comment.

20 25 35 45

7809 VERNORS: 1978, gloss dark green roof, ends and doors, yellow-painted sides, dark green lettering and logos. C. Rohlfing Collection.

-- **10 15 20**

7810 CRUSH: 1978, orange-painted sides, light green roof and ends, white doors and lettering, green, orange, and silver logos, Symington-Wayne trucks. C. Rohlfing Collection. -- **15 20 25**

7811 DR. PEPPER: 1978, dark orange-painted roof and ends, dark maroon body, white doors, white lettering. C. Rohlfing Collection. -- **10 15 20**

7812 T C A HOUSTON: 1977, stock car. See Special Production chapter.

7813 SEASONS GREETINGS FROM LIONEL: 1977, 9700-type boxcar, white body, gold roof and ends, unpainted red doors; red and dark green lettering to left of door, red and dark green toy logos to right of door. C. Lang comment. .

-- **100 125 150**

7814 SEASONS GREETINGS: 1978, 9700-style boxcar, white body, dark blue roof and ends, royal blue doors; red "1978 SEASON'S GREETINGS" to left of door, Fundimensions "F" logo in red and blue to right of door. C. Lang comment. -- **100 125 150**

7815 TOY FAIR: 1978. See Special Production chapter.

7816 TOY FAIR: 1979. See Special Production chapter.

7817 TOY FAIR: 1980. See Special Production chapter.

SMALL SHORT O27 BOXCARS:

The short O27 boxcars produced by Fundimensions had Symington-Wayne trucks and one operating and one dummy coupler, with few exceptions. C. Lang comment.

7900 OUTLAW CAR: 1982-83, orange stock car with outlaw and sheriff who move in and out of car windows as car moves, mechanism like Horse Transport Car. -- -- **11 14**

7901 LIONEL LINES: 1982-83, cop and hobo car, "HYDRAULIC PLATFORM MAINTENANCE CAR", red short boxcar body, Symington-Wayne trucks, one operating and one dummy coupler, one figure moves from car platform to overhead trestle while other figure moves from trestle to car platform. Somewhat hard to find recently. -- -- **30 35**

7902 A. T. S. F.: 1982-83, red plastic short boxcar body, white lettering; from 1353 Southern Streak Set (1983). -- -- **6 8**

7903 ROCK: 1983, blue plastic short boxcar body; white lettering, one fixed coupler, one disc-operating coupler, metal wheels, Type V body. L. Caponi and C. Rohlfing comments. -- -- **6 8**

7904 SAN DIEGO ZOO: 1983, dark red plastic car with all-yellow giraffe; white lettering "SAN DIEGO ZOO / BLT 1983 / LIONEL", Symington-Wayne

trucks, one operating and one dummy coupler, rerun of 3376 and 3386 from 1960s. With telltale and cam device. Catalogue shows car numbered "7903" in error. C. Rohlfing comment, R. LaVoie Collection. -- -- **30 40**

7908 TAPPAN: 1986, short boxcar, red short boxcar body, white diagonal lettering "Good Cooking Begins With A Great Range" and "Tappan Is Cooking!" Symington-Wayne trucks, one operating and one dummy coupler, "7908" horizontal in lower right corner. Came as part of uncatalogued Tappan promotional Set; also came with black and white insert for billboard frame lettered diagonally "TAPPAN IS COOKING!" S. Hutchings, M. Samseli, J. Sawruk, and "Triple T" Collections. -- -- -- **50**

7909 LOUISVILLE & NASHVILLE: 1983, blue plastic short O27 boxcar, yellow lettering, Symington-Wayne trucks, two dummy couplers, plastic trucks, part of 1352 Rocky Mountain Freight Set. -- -- -- **10**

7910 CHESSIE SYSTEM: Catalogued 1984-85, but produced in 1986; boxcar, mold resembles old 6454 mold but is different in many significant ways; see Robert Swanson's discussion in the 1987 *Greenberg's Guide to Lionel Trains, 1945-1969, Vol. I;* with dark blue body; yellow lettering, yellow Chessie cat logo, Symington-Wayne trucks, one operating and one dummy coupler, metal door guides with opening doors. The reintroduction of the 6454 mold marks the first time Lionel has used this boxcar style, which has not been produced since 1953. The rivet detail has been fully restored, and the boxcar's lettering has been rubber-stamped right over it. The body fastens to the frame with two Phillips screws instead of the single screw and slot system used on other boxcars. The frame is the same one used on the Sheriff and Outlaw and Horse Transport Cars produced by Lionel; the large hole where the swinging mechanism would be is closed by a plastic plug. Actually, the special 7912 Toys 'R Us "Geoffrey Car" was the first car to use this mold (see entry below). This is a highly significant development, since it means that Lionel, Inc. can produce a line of high-quality boxcars at a very reasonable price. R. LaVoie comment and Collection. -- -- -- **15**

7912 GEOFFREY CAR: 1982-83, operating giraffe car, special production for Toys 'R Us retail toy stores. White 6454-mold body, orange "TOYS 'R US" logo to left of door, yellow and black "STAR CAR" logo to right of door, sliding doors with metal guides, orange giraffe with brown spots. This giraffe figure is far more elaborate than the one used in regular production. It has a larger nose and a nape on its neck. Car has Symington-Wayne trucks, one operating and one dummy coupler. The instruction sheet for the car is labeled "GEOFFEY CAR" instead of "GIRAFFE CAR". This car came as part of a "Heavy Iron" special set with a die-cast 8213 Rio Grande 2-4-2 Steam Locomotive, a short yellow flatcar with stakes, a 9013 Nickel Plate Road Short Gondola with two gray canisters, and an orange Rio Grande unlighted SP-type caboose. Price for 7912 car only. R. Shanfeld Collection. -- -- **100 135**

7913 TURTLE BACK ZOO: 1985, operating giraffe car, green short stock car body, plain yellow giraffe and cam follower piece, white lettering and logo, Symington-Wayne trucks, one operating and one dummy coupler. Comes with cam, mounting plate, and black pole with white telltales. -- -- **20 25**

7914 GEOFFREY'S CARNIVAL CARRIER: 1985, operating giraffe car, part of uncatalogued Toys 'R Us Set 1549. Essentially similar to 7912 of 1982-83, but has Toys 'R Us logo to right of sliding door and "Geoffrey's Carnival Carrier" to left. T. Wagner and J. Sawruk Collections. -- -- **100 135**

7920 SEARS CENTENNIAL: 1985-86, short boxcar, white body, green and blue lettering, Symington-Wayne trucks. Sold as part of Sears equivalent to Lionel Set 1402 in 1985 and Sears equivalent to Lionel Set 1602 in 1986. Lettering "Sears New Century" to right of doors, "Centenial Celebration 1886-1986" to left of doors; note misspelling of word *Centenial* [sic], which apparently is found on all samples. Part of Sears Set 79N1562. V. Gallo, Jr., J. Sawruk, and "Triple T" Collections. -- -- -- **50**

7925 ERIE-LACKAWANNA: 1986, short boxcar, light gray body, maroon lettering, Symington-Wayne trucks. Part of Set 1615, the Cannonball Express. Appears identical to earlier 9043 except for number. -- -- **8 10**

7926 NICKEL PLATE ROAD: 1986-87, short boxcar, yellow body, black lettering, Symington-Wayne trucks. Part of Set 1602, the Nickel Plate Special.

-- -- **8 10**

7931 TOWN HOUSE TV & APPLIANCES: 1986, short boxcar, see article on Town House Sets in this edition for full background. Medium gray body, black Town House logo and number to left of door, six appliance brand names in black to right of door (brand names differ on each side). Symington-Wayne trucks, one operating and one dummy coupler. Part of uncatalogued Set 1658. R. LaVoie Collection. See Special Production chapter.   -- -- -- **50**

7932 KAY BEE TOYS: 1986, short boxcar, white body, "LIONEL" to left of door, "KAY BEE / TOY STORES" and soldier logo to right of door, Symington-Wayne trucks, one operating and one dummy coupler. J. Sawruk and T. Wagner Collections.   -- -- -- **50**

7979 TRUE VALUE: 1986, short boxcar, part of uncatalogued Set 1685; description of colors and logos needed.   -- -- -- **50**

9001 CONRAIL: 1986, short boxcar, blue body; identical to 9035 except for number and "C R 9001" on one line instead of two. Part of uncatalogued Set 1687.   -- -- **12 15**

9035 CONRAIL: 1978-82, blue Type V body, white lettering.   -- -- **4 7**

9037 CONRAIL: 1978-81, brown or blue Type V body, white lettering, plastic trucks and wheels.
(A) Brown.   -- -- **4 7**
(B) Blue.   -- -- **4 7**

9039 CHEERIOS: 1971-72, short O27 boxcar, yellow body, black lettering and logo, Symington-Wayne trucks, one operating and one dummy coupler.
   4 5 6 8

9040 WHEATIES: 1970, orange body, white and blue lettering, MPC logo. Some came as separate sale items in Type I boxes.
(A) Type V body, AAR trucks, one operating coupler, one fixed coupler, plastic wheels.   -- **5 7 10**
(B) Type IV body, Symington-Wayne trucks, one operating coupler, one fixed coupler, plastic wheels.   -- **5 7 10**
(C) Type V body, Symington-Wayne trucks, one operating coupler, one fixed coupler, plastic wheels.   -- **5 7 10**
(D) Type V body, Symington-Wayne trucks, one operating coupler, one manumatic coupler, metal wheels.   -- **5 7 10**

9041 HERSHEY'S: 1971, silver lettering, metal wheels, one operating coupler, one fixed coupler, MPC logo. Some came in Type II boxes for separate sale.
(A) Type IV chocolate body, AAR trucks, plastic wheels, silk-screened lettering. S. Askenas Collection.   -- **5 7 10**
(B) Type V dark chocolate body, Symington-Wayne trucks, plastic wheels.   -- **5 7 10**
(C) Type V maroon body, Symington-Wayne trucks, two fixed couplers.   -- **5 7 10**
(D) Same as (C), but one disc coupler, one fixed coupler. S. Askenas Collection.   -- **5 7 10**
(E) Type IV chocolate body, Symington-Wayne trucks. C. Rohlfing Collection.   -- **5 7 10**

9042 AUTOLITE: 1972, O27 short boxcar, Type V white body embossed with "Part 100-4-3" on the inside; black and orange lettering, Symington-Wayne trucks, one operating coupler, one fixed coupler, metal wheels, MPC logo on car end. Apparently, this car was only included in one set, the 1284 Allegheny, although it also came in a Type I box as a separate sale item. The catalogue illustration shows the car with a Ford logo on the upper right on page 7, but with the logo overprinted in black on the separate sale car on page 12. The example observed has the Ford logo. Reader comments are invited as to a possible tie-in sale with the Ford Motor Company, especially in view of the fact that the prototype for this car has been discovered. See entry MX-9145 in the Factory Errors and Prototype section. R. DuBeau comment. In 1971 speculators bought stocks of sets with Autolite boxcars with the expectation that this car would be a limited-production item, but the car was catalogued in the next year. This also happened with the supposedly scarce white Cracker Jack refrigerator car. C. Weber comment.   -- **5 8 12**

9043 ERIE LACKAWANNA: 1973-74, gray body, maroon lettering, Type V body, Symington-Wayne trucks, one operating coupler, one manumatic fixed coupler, plastic wheels, no MPC logo. Some versions packaged in Type II boxes for separate sale.   -- **4 8 10**

9044 D & R G W: 1975, 1979, orange body, black lettering, Type V body, Symington-Wayne trucks, one operating coupler, one manumatic fixed coupler, no MPC logo.   **3 4 6 8**

9045 TOYS 'R US: White short boxcar body, orange lettering, giraffe with hat to left of door, Toys 'R Us logo to right. On special order, Fundimensions and its successors have made O27 short boxcars for national retail stores such as Toys 'R Us, True Value Hardware, Sears, and J. C. Penney. These cars, like the regular issues, have Symington-Wayne trucks, one operating and one dummy coupler; white body, orange and black lettering; Type V body, plastic wheels, no MPC logo. C. Lang comment, H. Holden Collection.   **20 30 40 50**

9046 TRUE VALUE: 1976, white body, red and black lettering, paint can to left of door, True Value logo to right, Type V body, Symington-Wayne trucks, one operating coupler, one fixed coupler, no MPC logo. Part of special Set 1698 with 8601 Steam Locomotive, 9020 Flatcar, 9078 Caboose, four straight and eight curved O27 track pieces. D. Johns and G. Halverson comments, H. Holden Collection.   **20 30 40 50**

9047 TOYS 'R US: White body, orange lettering, giraffe with hobo sack to right of door, Toys 'R Us logo to left, Type V body, Symington-Wayne trucks, one operating coupler, one manumatic dummy coupler, plastic wheels, no MPC logo. H. Holden Collection.   -- **20 30 40**

9048 TOYS 'R US: White body, orange lettering, giraffe with lantern to right of door, Toys 'R Us logo to left, Symington-Wayne trucks, one operating coupler, one manumatic coupler, plastic wheels. H. Holden Collection.
   -- **20 30 40**

Top shelf: 9360 National Hockey League, 9359 National Basketball Association. Bottom shelf: 9362 Major League Baseball. G. and D. Halverson and A. Conto Collections.

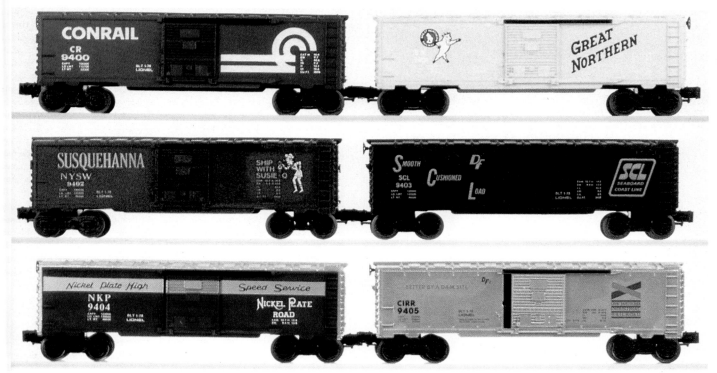

Top shelf: 9400 Conrail, 9401 Great Northern. **Middle shelf: 9402 Susquehanna, 9403 S C L. Bottom shelf: 9404 Nickel Plate, 9405 C I R R. G. and D. Halverson and A. Conto Collections.**

(9049) TOYS 'R US: 1979, white body, orange- and black-lettered "GEOF-FREY POWER", number does not appear on car; part of uncatalogued Set 1971. G. Halverson Collection.   -- -- 35 50

9052 TOYS 'R US: White body, orange and black lettering, Symington-Wayne trucks, one operating coupler, one manumatic coupler, plastic wheels.
                    -- 20 30 40

9053 TRUE VALUE: 1977, green short O27 boxcar with True Value yellow, black, and red decals on right, paint can on left, red number on car. Originally came in specially marked True Value bag within set; mint condition must include this bag. Came as part of special Set 1792, identical to Set 1698 except for special car (see 9046 for set contents). D. Johns comments, G. Halverson and H. Holden Collections.   -- -- 35 50

9054 J. C. PENNEY: Orange body, black lettering, "75th Anniversary" logo to left of door, J. C. Penney logo to right, Symington-Wayne trucks, one operating and one dummy coupler. H. HoldenCollection.   -- -- 35 50

THE 9090 MINI-MAX BOXCAR: AN UPDATE

In our first edition, William Meyer gave the history and basic construction of this intriguing little car made only in 1971. Since that time, much new information has surfaced about the car. The critical variables are still the roof and end piece color and the placement of the "G" logo into the fourth panel from the right or the left, but the presence or absence of struts can no longer be regarded as a critical variable.

Recently, we have discovered that a small sheet of paper with instructions was placed inside the car when it was made ready for shipment. This little sheet, which measures 3" x 4", reads as follows:

"MINI MAX CAR.........NO. 6-9090"

"When you open the door of your new Mini Max Car, you will note that there may be posts reaching from the roof to the floor. To make your Mini Max car authentic to the original, simply

cut these posts away. They have been left there for structural packing and shipping strength. Thank you and good railroad-ing."

In the end, Lionel did not give its customers very good advice. When the roof supports are removed, inevitably the car roof sags in the middle, sometimes to the point where the sides cannot be fully raised. This is probably why no further examples of this car were ever made, despite the presence of a "9090 Series" end plate which certainly indicated Lionel's desire to make more varieties of them.

We have also found some interesting variations in the little palletainers which were originally included with the cars but are missing many times when the car is found today. We do not know which are the scarcer palletainers, but they have now been observed in light yellow, lime green, and bright orange-red, always with black bases.

Variations in the packaging boxes and their end stampings have recently come to light as well. Curiously, a few cars have surfaced packaged in plain white boxes but with factory end stampings. These boxes could well be leftovers from the last stage of postwar Hillside production. Most of the cars are packaged in Type I boxes, but the end stampings differ. Earlier versions have the stamping "MINI MAX / 9090" in two lines; some of the plain white boxes have a red-penned "X" after the number. Later versions have "9090 / MINI MAX" stamped on the boxes; note the reversal of the lines. The stampings on the boxes can be either purple or black ink.

For this edition, we have restructured our listings into three main variations. We fully expect that there are several more variations of this car; in fact, we would like to confirm a few reputed factory errors with missing lettering. We ask our

Two special operating giraffe cars made for Toys 'R Us Stores. **Top shelf: 7914 Geoffrey's Carnival Carrier. Bottom: 7912 Geoffrey's Star Car. Note the construction differences between these and the regular-production giraffe cars. These are done with the new 7910 boxcar mold. Both are very hard to find. A. Rudman Collection.**

readers to comment on their cars so that we can have a full listing in our next edition.

9090 MINI MAX: 1971, blue roof and ends, white doors; dark blue lettering, four metal wheels. Separate sale cars came in Type I boxes. Light blue versions are harder to find. G. Halverson and R. LaVoie comments.
(A) Plain white box with "MINI MAX / 9090" stamped on both ends in purple with red-penned "X" after number, light blue roof and ends, "G" in fourth panel from left, three orange-red palletainers. R. LaVoie Collection.

20	25	50	75

(B) Type I box stamped "MINI MAX / 9090" in black on both ends, dark blue roof and ends, "G" in fourth panel from left, three lime green palletainers. R. LaVoie Collection.

10	15	50	75

(C) Type I box, "9090 / MINI MAX" stamped in purple on both ends (note reversal of B), dark blue roof and ends, "G" in fourth panel from right, three pale yellow palletainers. R. LaVoie Collection.

10	15	20	40

See also Factory Errors and Prototypes.

MX 9145 AUTOLITE: 1972. See Factory Errors and Prototypes.

9200-SERIES BOXCARS

9200 ILLINOIS CENTRAL: Several body types, black and white lettering. This is the only boxcar produced since 1970 with all five body types, all three door guide types, and all three frames! It also is found with all the truck and uncoupler armature varieties. We expect several more variations of this car to surface eventually.
(A) Orange-painted Type V orange body and doors, "IC" spread, deep heat-stamped lettering, metal door guides, open AAR trucks with bar inset into uncoupler discs, MPC logo to left of fourth bottom rivet. G. Halverson Collection.

10	15	20	25

(B) Same as (A), but Type VI body, "IC" close. G. Halverson Collection.

8	10	15	20

(C) Type VI body, metal door guides, flat orange-painted orange body and doors, AAR trucks, Type I frame, "IC" spread. 8 10 15 20
(D) Dull orange-painted Type VI body, orange-painted orange doors (brighter than body paint), "IC" spread, metal door guides, Symington-Wayne trucks, wheel axles blackened. G. Halverson Collection. 8 10 15 20
(E) Orange-painted orange plastic Type VI body and doors, "IC" spread, two plastic door guides, MPC logo atop fourth bottom rivet, Symington-Wayne trucks with black uncoupler discs. G. Halverson and R. LaVoie Collections.

10	15	20	25

(F) Type VII body, metal door guides, glossy orange-painted orange body and doors, AAR trucks, Type I frame, "IC" close. 8 10 15 20
(G) Same as (F), but plastic door guides. 8 10 15 20
(H) Same as (F), but plastic door guides, Symington-Wayne trucks, "IC" spread.

8	10	15	20

(I) Same as (F), but dull dark orange-painted orange body, "IC" spread.

10	12	15	20

(J) Type VIII body, flat orange-painted gray body and doors, Symington-Wayne trucks, Type II frame, "IC" spread. 8 10 12 15
(K) Same as (I), but Type IX body. 8 10 20 45
(L) Type IX body, glossy orange-painted orange body, flat orange-painted gray doors, Symington-Wayne trucks, Type II frame, "IC" spread. Came in Type II box and is also found with Type III frame. R. LaVoie Collection.

10	12	20	45

(M) Unpainted orange Type VII body, Type II door guides, postwar bar-end trucks with plastic knuckles, Type I box. Reader comments requested. J. Porter Collection. NRS
See also Factory Errors and Prototypes.

9201 PENN CENTRAL: Type VI body, metal door guides, white lettering, AAR trucks, Type I frame.
(A) Jade green-painted jade green plastic body and door. 12 15 20 30
(B) Dark green-painted dark green plastic body and door. 12 15 30 35

9202 SANTA FE: Type VI body, metal door guides, AAR trucks, Type I frame, all have red-painted red bodies and white lettering.
(A) Silver-painted gray door. 12 20 30 40
(B) Same as (A), but only two dots on left side of door. 20 30 40 75
(C) Gray-painted gray door. 20 30 40 55
See also Factory Errors and Prototypes.

9203 UNION PACIFIC: Type V body, metal door guides, yellow-painted yellow doors; blue lettering, red-, blue-, and white-striped UP shield to right of door, AAR trucks, Type I frame. C. Lang comment.
(A) Yellow-painted yellow body. 15 20 35 45
(B) Light yellow-painted light yellow body. 15 20 35 40

9204 NORTHERN PACIFIC: White and black-outlined letters, Type I frame, AAR trucks except as noted.
(A) Type VI body, dark green-painted dark green body and shiny green door, metal door guides, dark red logo insert, built date. 10 22 30 35
(B) Green-painted Type VI green body, bright lime green unpainted doors, metal door guides, open AAR trucks with bar in uncoupler discs. G. Halverson Collection.

10	22	30	35

(C) Same as (A), but light red logo insert. 10 22 30 35
(D) Type VII body, apple green-painted apple green body and door, no built date, metal door guides. 10 17 28 35
(E) Same as (D), but plastic door guides and Symington-Wayne trucks.

10	17	28	35

(F) Same as (C), but body is painted same green color as 9209 Burlington Northern Boxcar. C. Lang Collection. 10 22 30 35

9205 NORFOLK & WESTERN: Type VI body, metal door guides, white lettering, AAR trucks except as noted, Type I frame.
(A) Dark blue-painted dark blue body and navy blue door. 10 15 20 25
(B) Same as (A), but Symington-Wayne trucks. 10 15 20 25
(C) Medium blue-painted medium blue body and navy blue door.

10	15	20	25

(D) Royal (reddish) blue-painted royal blue body and door. G. Halverson and R. LaVoie Collections. 12 20 25 35
(E) Same as (A), but postwar bar-end trucks with plastic knuckles. Reader comments requested. J. Porter Collection. 10 15 20 25

Top shelf: 9406 D & R G W, 9411 Lackawanna. Second shelf: 9407 Union Pacific, 9408 Lionel Lines. Third shelf: 9412 R F & P, 9413 Napierville Junction. Bottom shelf: 9414 Cotton Belt, 9415 Providence & Worcester. G. and D. Halverson and A. Conto Collections.

9206 GREAT NORTHERN: White lettering, metal door guides, AAR trucks except as noted, Type I frame.
(A) Type VI body, light blue-painted body and door.   10   15   20   25
(B) Type VII body, paler blue-painted paler blue body and light blue door.
                                                        10   15   20   25
(C) Type VII body, palest blue-painted palest blue body and light blue door, Symington-Wayne trucks, Type II box.   10   15   20   25

9207 SOO: Type VII body, Type I frame.
(A) Red-painted red body and red door; white lettering, AAR trucks, metal door guides.   10   15   20   25
(B) Flat red-painted red body and door; white lettering, Symington-Wayne trucks, metal door guides.   10   15   20   25
(C) Shiny red-painted red body and door; white lettering, Symington-Wayne trucks, plastic door guides.   10   15   20   25
See also Factory Errors and Prototypes.

9208 C P RAIL: Type VII body, black lettering, Type I frame. One sample observed came in Type I box dated 2/71. T. Rollo comment.
(A) Medium yellow-painted medium yellow body and door; metal door guides, Symington-Wayne trucks.   10   15   20   25
(B) Light yellow-painted light yellow body and door, metal door guides, Symington-Wayne trucks.   10   15   20   25
(C) Light yellow-painted light yellow body, light yellow-painted medium yellow door, plastic door guides, AAR trucks.   10   15   20   25
(D) Dark yellow-painted dark yellow body, dark yellow-painted medium yellow door, AAR trucks, plastic door guide.   10   15   20   25

(E) Same as (D), but Symington-Wayne trucks, Type II frame. C. Rohlfing comment.   10   15   20   25

9209 BURLINGTON NORTHERN: Type I frame, white lettering.
(A) Type VII body, apple green-painted apple green body and dark green-painted dark green door, AAR trucks, metal door guides.   10   15   20   25
(B) Type VII body, dark green-painted dark green body and doors, metal door guides, Symington-Wayne trucks.   10   15   20   25
(C) Same as (B), but Type VIII body.   10   15   20   25
(D) Same as (B), but Type IX body and Type III door guides, Type II box.
                                       15   20   25   40
(E) Same as (B), but plastic door guides.   10   15   20   25
(F) Same as (A), but Type VII body and plastic door guides. Knopf Collection.
                                            10   15   20   25

9210 B & O: Double-door automobile car, 6468-type body, metal door guides, Type I frame; white lettering, all doors with different colors added outside the factory (only the black door is authentic factory production, but the other varieties are listed here because there is considerable collector interest in them), all Symington-Wayne trucks except (A).
(A) Black-painted black body and doors, AAR trucks.   10   12   20   30
(B) Same as (A), but dark 9771 N & W navy blue-painted blue doors. C. Lang Collection.   8   10   15   20
(C) Same as (A), but 9749 Penn Central jade green-painted green doors. C. Lang Collection.   8   10   15   20
(D) Same as (A), but 9200 IC orange-painted orange doors. C. Lang Collection.
                                                       8   10   15   20

(E) Same as (A), but 9703 C P Rail burnt-orange-painted orange doors. C. Lang Collection.

8	10	15	20

(F) Same as (A), but turquoise-painted turquoise doors.

8	10	15	20

(G) Unpainted black body and doors, Symington-Wayne Type IIA trucks, plastic wheels, Type I box. J. Porter Collection.

10	12	20	25

9211 PENN CENTRAL: Type VII body, except for (A), silver-painted gray doors, white lettering, Type I frame.

(A) Jade green-painted Type VI jade green body, AAR trucks, 1000 made, no end imprints, metal door guides.

15	20	30	35

(B) Jade green-painted jade green body, Symington-Wayne trucks, metal door guides.

12	15	20	25

(C) Pale green-painted pale green body, AAR trucks, metal door guides.

12	15	20	25

(D) Medium green-painted medium green body, AAR trucks, metal door guides.

12	15	20	25

(E) Same as (D), but plastic door guides.

12	15	20	25

(F) Same as (D), but Symington-Wayne trucks.

12	15	20	25

(G) Dark green-painted dark green body, Symington-Wayne trucks, plastic door guides.

12	15	20	25

(H) Same as (A), but postwar bar-end trucks with plastic knuckles, Type I box. Reader comments requested. J. Porter Collection.

12	15	20	25

9212: Assigned to Lionel Collector's Club of America, 1976 Flatcar. See Special Production chapter.

9213: Not assigned.

9214 NORTHERN PACIFIC: Type VII maroon plastic body except for (D), white- and black-outlined lettering, Type I frame, metal door guides, red oxide-painted maroon doors.

A) Flat red oxide-painted body, Symington-Wayne trucks.

10	12	20	25

(B) Red oxide-painted body, AAR trucks.

10	12	20	25

(C) Red oxide-painted Type VII body and doors, two plastic door guides, Symington-Wayne trucks, black uncoupler discs. G. Halverson Collection.

10	20	30	40

(D) Red oxide-painted Type IX tuscan body, tuscan-painted tuscan door, Symington-Wayne trucks, Type II frame, Type II box. R. LaVoie Collection.

10	20	30	40

9215 NORFOLK & WESTERN: Type VII body, silver-painted gray doors, white lettering, Type I frame.

(A) Royal blue-painted royal blue Type VI plastic body, plastic door guides, AAR trucks; 1000 manufactured.

15	20	30	35

(B) Dark blue-painted dark blue body, metal door guides, Symington-Wayne trucks.

10	15	20	25

(C) Same as (B), except plastic door guides.

10	15	20	25

Top shelf: 9416 M D &W, 9417 C P Rail. Second shelf: 9418 Famous Historic Railroads, 9419 Union Pacific. Third shelf: 9420 B & O, 9421 Maine Central. Bottom shelf: 9422 E J & E, 9423 New Haven. G. and D. Halverson and A. Conto Collections.

(D) Same as (B), except plastic door guides and AAR trucks.

                               10   15   20   25

(E) Same as (A), but postwar bar-end trucks with plastic knuckles, Type I box. Reader comments requested. J. Porter Collection.   **10   15   20   25**

9217 SOO: 1982, operating boxcar, plunger opens door, worker moves towards door, brownish-maroon-painted body, white lettering, Standard O trucks. C. Rohlfing comment.   **--   --   20   25**

9218 MONON: 1981-82, operating mail delivery boxcar, plunger opens door, worker tosses mail sack out of door. Tuscan body, white stripe across top of car with deep red lettering, white reporting marks, Standard O trucks. C. Rohlfing and C. Lang comments, R. LaVoie Collection.   **--   --   20   25**

9219 MISSOURI PACIFIC: 1983, operating boxcar with plunger mechanism, door opens, worker moves toward door, blue sides with gray stripe and gray ends and roof, Standard O trucks. Reissue of 3494-150 M.P. from 1956. Reader comments on the specific differences and similarities of these cars would be appreciated.   **--   --   30   35**

9221 POULTRY DISPATCH: 1983, sometimes known as the "Chicken Sweeper" car, reissue of 3434 from 1959-60. Dull brown-painted stock car body, white lettering, unpainted gray doors, Symington-Wayne trucks, three celluloid rows of chickens on way to market show through car slats, two bayonet-base light bulbs inside car provide illumination. When plunger is pulled down by remote track section, door opens and gray man with broom mounted on delicate hair-spring appears to be swinging back and forth, sweeping feathers out of car. T. Ladny and R. LaVoie Collections.   **--   --   25   35**

9223 READING: 1984-85, operating boxcar, tuscan-painted body and doors; white lettering, black and white diamond-shaped "READING LINES" logo, gray man appears when plunger opens car door, Standard O trucks.

                                --   --   25   30

9224 LOUISVILLE: 1984-85, operating horse car and corral, reissue of 3356 postwar accessory in new colors. Long stock car body with yellow sides and doors, tuscan roof, ends, and lettering; postwar bar-end metal trucks with one sliding shoe pickup for operation. Horse corral has white frame and fencing and dark green corral chute and watering trough. Nine light brown horses are included. When car is on remote-control track and button is pushed, car doors drop down to meet corral platform and horses move into and out of car by vibrator action in car and corral. The word "CHURCHILL" is misspelled as "CHURCHHILL" on all cars, though the catalogue shows the correct spelling. Price for complete accessory. T. Ladny and R. LaVoie Collections.   **--   --   75   90**

9228 CANADIAN PACIFIC: 1986, operating boxcar, silver-painted sides, black-painted roof and ends, gray man, red lettering and Canadian Pacific "beaver" logo, Standard O trucks.   **--   --   20   25**

9229 EXPRESS MAIL: 1984-85, operating boxcar, dark blue sides and doors, orange ends and roof; white lettering and Post Office logo, white and yellow-orange Express Mail logo, Symington-Wayne trucks, gray man tosses out mail sack when door opens by plunger action.   **--   --   20   25**

Top shelf: 9424 T P & W, 9425 British Columbia. **Second shelf:** 9426 C & O, 9427 Bay Line. **Third shelf:** 9428 T P & W, 9429 The Early Years. **Bottom shelf:** 9430 The Standard Gauge Years, 9431 The Prewar Years. G. and D. Halverson and A. Conto Collections.

Top shelf: 9432 The Postwar Years, 9433 The Golden Years. Second shelf: 9434 Joshua Lionel Cohen, 9435 Central of Georgia. Third shelf: 9436 Burlington, 9437 Northern Pacific. Bottom shelf: 9438 Ontario Northland, 9439 Ashley Drew & Northern. G. and D. Halverson and A. Conto Collections.

9230 MONON: Type VII body (A)-(D) and Type IX body (E)-(F), white lettering, Symington-Wayne trucks. One sample had box dated 2/70. T. Rollo comment.

(A) Tuscan-painted maroon body, red oxide-painted maroon doors, Type I frame, metal door guides. 8 10 12 15

(B) Same as (A), but red oxide-painted red oxide body. 10 12 15 20

(C) Same as (A), but Type VII postwar bar-end metal trucks which appear to be original with car. Probable early production. J. Aleshire Collection. NRS

(D) Flat red oxide-painted flat red oxide body, red oxide-painted maroon doors, Type I frame, plastic door guides. 10 12 15 20

(E) Tuscan-painted tuscan body, tuscan-painted tuscan doors, Type I frame. 10 12 15 20

(F) Same as (E), but Type II frame. Came in Type II box. 10 12 15 20

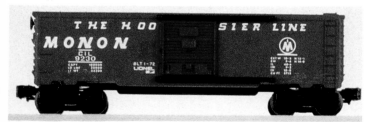

9230 Monon Boxcar.

9237 UNITED PARCEL SERVICE: 1984, operating boxcar, dark brown body; white UPS logo and lettering, plunger opens door and gray man advances to door opening. Pictured in 1984 Traditional catalogue, but never produced because at the last moment, after the prototypes had been made, United Parcel Service withdrew its permission to make the car. Two prototypes with decals, both painted flat medium brown, are in the collection of Richard Kughn.

Not Manufactured

9280 A T S F: 1978-80, horse transport car, short stock car body; white horses bob in and out, red with white lettering. 4 6 8 12

9301 U. S. MAIL: 1975-83, red-, white-, and blue-painted red plastic body and door; white and black lettering, 1972-type body mold, Symington-Wayne trucks, Type I frame, single door guides, "LIONEL" on left, man tosses mail sack when door is opened by plunger.

(A) Dark blue paint, MPC plate. 6 10 13 20

(B) Light blue paint with darker blue doors, MPC plate. 6 10 13 20

(C) Medium blue paint, no MPC plate. 6 10 13 20

(D) Light blue paint, no MPC plate. 6 10 13 20

See also Special Production chapter.

9305 SANTA FE: 1980, 1982, stock car with bobbing tan plastic sheriff and outlaw figures, mechanism identical to 9280. Dark green short stock car body, gold lettering, plastic wheels, arch bar trucks, one operating and one dummy coupler; from James Gang Set. C. Lang comment, J. Sawruk Collection.

-- -- 10 14

9308 AQUARIUM CAR: 1981-83, reissue of 3435 from 1959-62; green-painted clear plastic body; gold lettering, Symington-Wayne trucks, windows with fish tanks, two bayonet-base bulbs inside car for illumination, vibrator motor turns two spools with film attached which is painted with fish; turning action makes fish appear to swim through car. C. Lang and C. Rohlfing comments, T. Ladny Collection. -- -- 60 75
See also Factory Errors and Prototypes.

9319 T C A SILVER JUBILEE: 1979, mint car. See Special Production chapter.

9320 FORT KNOX GOLD RESERVE: 1979, clear plastic body painted silver, coin slot, circular grates at each end, "gold reserve" bullion stacks inside, Standard O trucks; from Southern Pacific Limited Set. Very hard to find.
-- 100 175 225

9339 GREAT NORTHERN: 1979-81, 1983, green plastic short O27 boxcar; white lettering, Symington-Wayne trucks; part of 1960 Midnight Flyer Set (1980-81) and 1252 Heavy Iron Set (1983). C. Lang comment.
(A) 1980-81, one operating and one dummy coupler. -- 2 4 6
(B) 1983, two operating couplers. -- 2 4 6

9349 SAN FRANCISCO MINT: 1980, dark maroon body, gold lettering, gold ingots stacked inside car, Standard "O" trucks. Type III box with ends marked "9349 Gold Bullion Car". -- 75 100 135

9359 NATIONAL BASKETBALL ASSN: 1980, short O27 boxcar, came in year-end special only, many labels provided with car so that the purchaser could decide which to place on car. White body, red roof and ends, red and black lettering when decorated, Symington-Wayne trucks. C. Rohlfing Collection.
-- -- 20 25

9360 NATIONAL HOCKEY LEAGUE: 1980, short O27 boxcar, came in year-end special, many labels provided so that car purchaser could decide which to place on car. White body, orange roof and ends, large silver Stanley Cup logo when decorated, Symington-Wayne trucks. C. Rohlfing Collection.
-- -- 20 25

9361 Not Used: 1980, this number was for the National Football League Car. At the last minute the League withdrew permission (perhaps they wanted a fee, which Lionel did not want to pay) and production was canceled.
Not Manufactured

9362 MAJOR LEAGUE BASEBALL: 1980, came in year-end special, many labels provided with car, each for a different team, purchaser to decide which to place on car. White body, dark blue roof and ends, Symington-Wayne trucks. C. Rohlfing Collection. -- -- 20 25

9365 TOYS 'R US: 1979, part of 1993 Toys 'R Us Midnight Flyer Set. White short boxcar body, orange "Toys 'R Us" logo to left of door, giraffe in engineer hat to right of door, Symington-Wayne trucks, one operating and one dummy coupler. G. Halverson Collection. -- -- 40 50

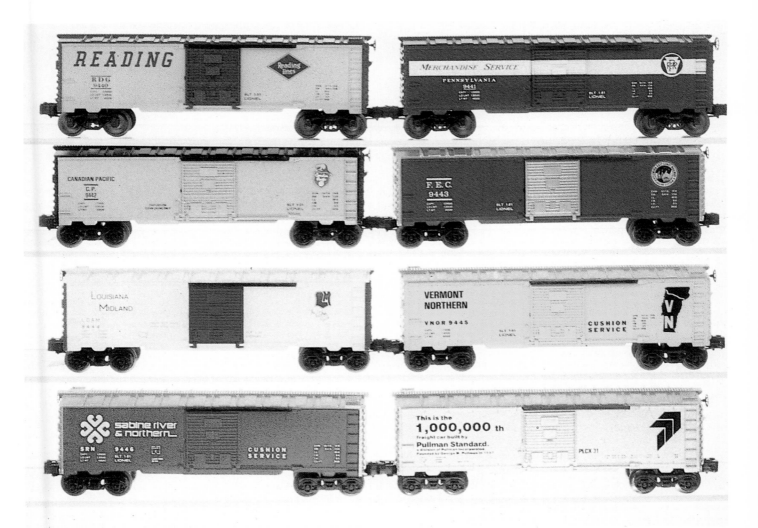

Top shelf: 9440 Reading, 9441 Pennsylvania. Second shelf: 9442 Canadian Pacific, 9443 F E C. Third shelf: 9444 Louisiana Midland, 9445 Vermont Northern. Bottom shelf: 9446 Sabine River & Northern, 9447 Pullman Standard. G. and D. Halverson and A. Conto Collections.

Top shelf: 9448 Santa Fe Stock Car, 9450 Great Northern from FARR Series 3. Second shelf: 9449 Great Northern from FARR Series 3, 9451 Southern from FARR Series 4. Third shelf: 9452 Western Pacific, 9453 Maryland and Pennsylvania. Bottom shelf: 9454 New Hope & Ivyland, 9455 Milwaukee Road. G. and D. Halverson, and A. Conto Collections.

9376 SOO: 1981, part of uncatalogued 1157 Wabash Cannonball Set. White short boxcar body, large black "SOO LINE" flanks doors, black lettering, Symington-Wayne trucks, one operating and one dummy coupler. G. Halverson Collection. -- -- 20 25

9388 TOYS 'R US: 1981, part of 1159 Toys 'R Us Midnight Flyer Set. White short boxcar body, giraffe with engineer hat, and crossing signal to left of door, orange "Toys 'R Us" logo to right of door, Symington-Wayne trucks, one operating and one dummy coupler. G. Halverson Collection. -- -- 40 50

9400 CONRAIL: 1978.
(A) Tuscan-painted tuscan plastic body and door; white lettering, Type IX body mold, Type III door guides, Symington-Wayne trucks, Type III frame, "LIONEL" on left. 5 7 12 15
(B) Same as (A), but brown-painted brown body and door. 5 7 12 15
See also Special Production chapter.

9401 GREAT NORTHERN: 1978, pale green-painted pale green plastic body and door; black and white lettering; red, white, and black goat logo, Type IX body mold, Type III door guides, Symington-Wayne trucks, Type III frame, "LIONEL" on left. C. Lang, C. Rohlfing, and G. Rogers comments. 6 8 10 12

9402 SUSQUEHANNA: 1978, green-painted green plastic body and door; gold lettering; red, gold, and gray "SUSIE-Q" logo to right of door, "LIONEL" and built date to left of door, Type IX body mold, Type III door guides, Symington-Wayne trucks, Type III frame. C. Lang comment. 10 15 25 30

9403 S C L: 1978, (Seaboard Coast Line); black-painted black plastic body and door, yellow lettering, Type IX body mold, Type III door guides, Symington-Wayne trucks, Type III frame, "LIONEL" on right.

(A) Yellow lettering. 8 10 12 15
(B) Extremely bold yellow lettering. 10 12 15 20
(C) Shiny white lettering, scarce. At least one observed sample has had its lettering chemically altered from yellow to white. We do not know if this caution applies to all such pieces. C. Weber comment. NRS

9404 NICKEL PLATE: 1978, maroon- and silver-painted maroon body and door; black and white lettering, Type IX body mold, Type III door guides, Symington-Wayne trucks, Type III frame, "LIONEL" on left. 10 12 15 20

9405 C I R R: 1978, (Chattahoochie Industrial Railroad), silver-painted gray plastic body and door; orange and black lettering, Type IX body mold, Type III door guides, Symington-Wayne trucks, Type III frame, "LIONEL" on left. 4 6 10 12

9406 D & R G W: 1978, "Rio Grande", white- and brown-painted white plastic body, brown-painted brown plastic door; black and red lettering, Type IX body

(Photograph, following page) Disney character train. Top shelf: 8773 U36B, 9183 caboose. Second shelf: 9660 Mickey Mouse, 9661 Goofy. Third shelf: 9662 Donald Duck, 9663 Dumbo. Fourth shelf: 9664 Cinderella, 9665 Peter Pan. Fifth shelf: 9666 Pinocchio, 9667 Snow White. Sixth shelf: 9668 Pluto, 9669 Bambi. Seventh shelf: 9670 Alice in Wonderland, 9671 Fantasia. Bottom shelf: 9672 Happy Birthday. G. and D. Halverson and A. Conto Collections.

Top shelf: 9460 Detroit & Toledo Shore Line, 9466 Wanamaker Railway Lines. Second shelf: 9467 World's Fair, 9468 Union Pacific. Third shelf: 9470 E. J. & E., 9471 Atlantic Coast Line. Bottom shelf: 9473 Lehigh Valley, 9472 Detroit & Mackinac. G. and D. Halverson and A. Conto Collections.

mold, Type III door guides, Symington-Wayne trucks, Type III frame, "LIONEL" on right, "Cookie Box".   3   5   10   12

9407 UNION PACIFIC: 1978, "LIVESTOCK DISPATCH", gray- and yellow-painted yellow plastic body, black-painted black doors; red lettering, Type I mold, three metal door guides, Symington-Wayne trucks, Type I frame, "LIONEL" on right.   10   12   15   20

9408 LIONEL LINES: 1978, "CIRCUS CAR", white- and red-painted white plastic body, white-painted white plastic door; red lettering, red-painted catwalk and hatches atop roof, Type I mold, three metal door guides, Standard O trucks, Type I frame, "LIONEL" on left; part of 1868 Minneapolis & St. Louis Service Station Set. Essentially a remake of the postwar 6376 model. R. Sigurdson comment.   15   20   30   40

9411 LACKAWANNA: 1978, tuscan-painted tuscan plastic body and door; white lettering, Type IX body mold, Type III door guides, Standard O trucks, Type III frame, "LIONEL" on right, "The Route of Phoebe Snow" script and built date to right of door; part of Milwaukee Special Set.   10   15   30   45

9412 RICHMOND, FREDERICKSBURG & POTOMAC: 1979, blue-painted body, silver-painted doors, white lettering and map logo. C. Rohlfing and G. Rogers Collections.   7   9   12   15

9413 NAPIERVILLE JUNCTION: 1979, yellow-painted sides, red-painted roof and ends, black lettering.
(A) Red leaf logo, same red as roof and ends. R. Vagner Collection.   4   6   8   10
(B) Light red leaf logo, different red from roof and ends. C. Rohlfing and R. Vagner Collections.   8   10   12   15

9414 COTTON BELT: 1980, tuscan body, white lettering, blue lightning streak logo.   4   6   8   10

9415 PROVIDENCE & WORCESTER: 1979, red-painted body, white and black lettering.   4   6   10   12
See also Special Production chapter.

9416 MINNESOTA, DAKOTA & WESTERN: 1979, white sides, green-painted roof and ends, green doors.   4   6   8   10

9417 C P RAIL: 1979, black, white, and red sides, gold letters; from 1860 Great Plains Express Set. This car was shown in the 1979 catalogue, but it did not become part of the set until 1980, when it replaced the 9729 car identical except for number and white lettering. C. Lang comment.   --   25   35   45

9418 FAMOUS AMERICAN RAILROAD SERIES: 1979, (FARR), railroad emblem car with markings of Southern, Santa Fe, Great Northern, Union Pacific, and Pennsylvania Railroads, emblem of FARR series reads #1. Gold-painted body, red roof and ends; orange, white, and black lettering. C. Rohlfing Collection.   --   60   75   100

9419 UNION PACIFIC: 1980, tuscan sides, black roof and ends, black doors, part of FARR Series 2 (Famous American Railroads), sold separately.   --   --   20   25

9420 B & O: 1980, Sentinel, dark blue and silver, same color scheme as 9801 Standard O-series boxcar, but decals on that car are done in electrocals on this car.   --   20   25   30
See also Special Production chapter.

9420 B & O Sentinel Boxcar.

9421 MAINE CENTRAL: 1980, yellow sides, dark green doors, dark green "MAINE CENTRAL" logo and lettering, Symington-Wayne trucks. C. Rohlfing and G. Rogers Collections. -- -- **12 15**

9422 ELGIN, JOLIET & EASTERN: 1980, light green and orange body, light green and orange contrasting lettering and logo, Symington-Wayne trucks. C. Rohlfing and G. Rogers Collections. -- -- **15 20**

9423 NEW YORK, NEW HAVEN & HARTFORD: 1980, tuscan-painted tuscan body and doors, black roof, white New Haven script logo, Symington-Wayne trucks. G. Rogers Collection. -- -- **15 20**
See also Special Production chapter.

9424 TOLEDO, PEORIA & WESTERN: 1980, orange sides, silver roof and ends; white lettering "TOLEDO PEORIA & WESTERN", Symington-Wayne trucks. C. Rohlfing comment. -- **10 15 20**

9425 BRITISH COLUMBIA: 1980, double-door boxcar, dark green sides and roof, one light green and one dark green door per side; white lettering, yellow and white logo. -- **15 20 25**

9426 CHESAPEAKE & OHIO: 1980, horizontally divided blue and yellow sides, silver roof and ends; yellow and blue contrasting lettering, Symington-Wayne trucks. -- **15 20 30**

9427 BAY LINE: 1980.
(A) Green body with yellow logo, green lettering, "THE BAY LINE" inside of broad yellow stripe; white number and technical data. -- -- **10 15**
(B) Similar to (A), but logo and stripe are white. See comments under 9403 by Charles Weber. **NRS**

9428 TOLEDO, PEORIA & WESTERN: 1980, distinctive light green and cream body, same colors used in lettering to contrast with sides, very different from 9424, Symington-Wayne trucks; available only with 1072 Cross Country Express Set. C. Lang and C. Rohlfing comments. -- **25 30 40**

9429 THE EARLY YEARS: 1980, "COMMEMORATING THE 100th BIRTHDAY OF JOSHUA LIONEL COWEN" (car came in a special limited edition box as did the 9430, 9431, 9432, 9433, and 9434). Light yellow sides, red roof and ends, Standard O trucks. C. Rohlfing comment. -- -- **25 30**

9430 THE STANDARD GAUGE YEARS: 1980, "100th BIRTHDAY", matches 9429, silver sides, maroon roof and ends, Standard O trucks. C. Rohlfing comment. -- -- **25 30**

9431 THE PREWAR YEARS: 1980, matches 9429, gray sides, black roof and ends, Standard O trucks. C. Rohlfing comment. -- -- **25 30**

9432 THE POSTWAR YEARS: 1980, matches 9429, available only with 1070 Royal Limited Set. Tan sides, green roof and ends, Standard O trucks. C. Rohlfing comment. -- -- **100 125**

9433 THE GOLDEN YEARS: 1980, matches 9429, available only with 1071 Mid-Atlantic Set. Gold sides, dark blue roof and ends, Standard O trucks. C. Rohlfing comment. -- -- **90 110**

9434 JOSHUA LIONEL COWEN — THE MAN: 1980, the last car in the series; series began with 9429. Yellow sides, brown roof and ends, Standard O trucks. C. Rohlfing comment. -- -- **70 100**

9435 CENTRAL OF GEORGIA: 1981, see Special Production chapter.

9436 BURLINGTON: 1981, red with white lettering, Standard O trucks, copy of postwar prototype which was never produced; came with 1160 Great Lakes Limited Set. -- -- **40 50**

9437 NORTHERN PACIFIC: 1981, stock car, dark green body, black doors; white lettering, Standard O trucks; from 1160 Great Lakes Limited Set. C. Lang and C. Rohlfing comments. -- -- **40 50**

9438 ONTARIO NORTHLAND: 1981, dark blue body, yellow ends; yellow lettering, "triple lightning" logo in yellow on side. Harding Collection, C. Rohlfing comment. -- -- **20 25**

9439 ASHLEY, DREW & NORTHERN: 1981, green with white doors and lettering; yellow, green, and white logo, Symington-Wayne trucks. -- -- **10 15**

9440 READING: 1981, yellow sides, green roof and ends, green doors, green lettering, Standard O trucks; from 1158 Maple Leaf Limited Set. C. Rohlfing and G. Rogers comments. -- -- **50 60**

9441 PENNSYLVANIA: 1981, tuscan with white stripe, white and red lettering; "MERCHANDISE SERVICE", Standard O trucks; from 1158 Maple Leaf Limited Set. -- -- **50 60**

9442 CANADIAN PACIFIC: 1981, silver-painted gray body, dark red lettering, black roof and ends, Symington-Wayne trucks. C. Lang and C. Rohlfing comments, G. Rogers Collection. -- -- **15 20**

9443 F E C: 1981, tuscan sides, silver roof and ends; white lettering, white striping on sides, "FLORIDA EAST COAST RAILWAY". C. Rohlfing, G. Rogers, and C. Lang comments. -- -- **10 15**

9444 LOUISIANA MIDLAND: 1981, white sides, blue ends and doors; red and blue lettering, Symington-Wayne trucks. C. Rohlfing comment. -- -- **10 15**

9445 VERMONT NORTHERN: 1981, yellow sides, silver roof and ends, black lettering, Symington-Wayne trucks. C. Lang, G. Rogers, and C. Rohlfing comments. -- -- **10 15**

9446 SABINE RIVER AND NORTHERN: 1981, red body and doors, silver roof and ends; white logo and lettering, Symington-Wayne trucks. C. Rohlfing comment, R. DuBeau and J. Vega Collections. -- -- **10 15**

9447 PULLMAN STANDARD: 1981, "This is the 1,000,000th", Symington-Wayne trucks.
(A) Silver body, black lettering. R. LaVoie Collection. -- -- **15 20**
(B) Gold body with black lettering. This and a similar silver-bodied car with gold lettering may have been faked by a chemical change. Reader comments requested. C. Lang and R. LaVoie comments. **NRS**

9448 A T S F: 1981, double-door stock car, brown with white lettering, black doors, Symington-Wayne trucks; from 1154 Reading Yard King Set. -- **25 30 40**

9449 GREAT NORTHERN: 1981, boxcar, dark green and orange body; "FARR 3" diamond logo in gold, black, and white lettering; GREAT NORTHERN goat logo, Famous American Railroads, Series 3; car sold separately. C. Lang and G. Rogers comments. -- -- **40 50**

9450 GREAT NORTHERN: 1981, stock car, FARR Series 3; red sides, black roof, doors, and ends; Symington-Wayne trucks. Like the others in this set, this car was sold separately. This particular car was part of a year-end special. R. Sigurdson and C. Rohlfing comments. -- -- **50 80**

9451 SOUTHERN: 1983, tuscan body, white lettering, FARR Series 4, Standard O trucks; car sold separately. C. Rohlfing comment. -- -- **30 40**

9452 WESTERN PACIFIC: 1982-83, tuscan-painted body, white lettering, Symington-Wayne trucks. -- -- **10 15**

9453 M P A: 1982-83, blue-painted body, yellow lettering, Symington-Wayne trucks. C. Rohlfing and G. Rogers comments. -- -- **10 15**

9454 NEW HOPE & IVYLAND: 1982-83, dark green-painted body, white lettering, Symington-Wayne trucks. Shown in catalogue with circular arrow logo, but not made that way; instead, "McHUGH / BROS. / LINES" is present in white. R. LaVoie comment. -- -- **10 15**

9455 MILWAUKEE ROAD: 1982-83, yellow-painted body, black lettering, black "AMERICA'S RESOURCEFUL RAILROAD" to left of door, Symington-Wayne trucks. C. Lang comment. -- -- **10 15**

9456 PENNSYLVANIA: 1984-85, double-door boxcar, tuscan-painted tuscan body and doors, metal door guides; white lettering, white and black PRR Keystone logo on black circle, gold diamond-shaped FARR 5 logo, Standard O trucks. -- **25 35 45**

9460 DETROIT, TOLEDO & SHORE LINE: 1982, see Special Production chapter.

9461 NORFOLK SOUTHERN: 1982, tuscan body, yellow doors, Standard O trucks; from Continental Limited Set. -- -- **45 60**

9462 SOUTHERN PACIFIC: 1983, silver-painted gray body, black-painted roof and ends, unpainted black doors, black lettering, circular black and white SP logo to right of doors. G. Rogers and R. LaVoie Collections, C. Rohlfing comment. -- **15 20 25**

9463 TEXAS & PACIFIC: 1983, yellow sides and roof, black lettering, yellow doors, black T & P logo, Symington-Wayne trucks. C. Lang and C. Rohlfing comments. -- -- **12 15**

9464 NASHVILLE, CHATTANOOGA & ST. LOUIS: 1983, light red body, yellow-orange stripe on side; white lettering, Symington-Wayne trucks. The Type III box ends are labeled "North Carolina & St. Louis", but this is an error. C. Lang and C. Rohlfing comments. -- -- **12 15**

9465 A T S F: 1983, dark green body, yellow lettering and logo, dark green doors, Symington-Wayne trucks. Pictured as blue in catalogue, but not produced that way. C. Lang and C. Rohlfing comments. -- -- **20 25**

9466 WANAMAKER RAILWAY LINES: 1982, wine-painted plastic body with gold-painted door and gold lettering. This car commemorated the Ives special Wanamaker cars of the early 1920s. At that time, Ives produced specially lettered cars for John Wanamaker, then and now the preeminent department store of Philadelphia. The moving force behind this new commemorative car was Nicholas Ladd, a long-time train enthusiast and senior Wanamaker store manager. The Eagle logo is original Wanamaker art adapted by Arthur Bink. The Wanamaker Railway Lines logo was copied from the original lettering on an authentic Ives Wanamaker car. Note that the Lionel artist intentionally made the "M" look like an "N" in the script. It is not a factory error. Lionel produced 2,500 of these cars. Interested Wanamaker employees bought 1,400 of them and another 1,000 were sold over the counter at a special train fair held at Wanamaker's Philadelphia store in conjunction with the car's release. The remaining 100 cars were retained by the store. Some examples were sold with a special red box which commands a $25 premium. C. O'Dell comment. -- -- **75 125**

9467 WORLD'S FAIR: 1982, see Special Production chapter.

9468 UNION PACIFIC: 1983, double-door boxcar, tuscan body, yellow lettering, Standard O trucks; available only in 1361 Gold Coast Limited Set. C. Rohlfing comment. -- -- **40 50**

9469 NEW YORK CENTRAL: 1985, Pacemaker Standard O boxcar, red and gray Pacemaker paint scheme; white lettering, Standard O trucks. Shown with black-painted catwalk in catalogue, but came with catwalk in same red color as roof. F. Cieri and C. Rohlfing Collections. -- -- **45 80**

9470 E. J. & E.: 1984-85, (Elgin, Joliet & Eastern), dark green body, yellow lettering and Great Lakes logo, Symington-Wayne trucks. C. Rohlfing and G. Rogers Collections. -- -- **12 20**

9471 ATLANTIC COAST LINE: 1984-85, tuscan body, white lettering, circular white Atlantic Coast Line logo, Symington-Wayne trucks. -- -- **12 20**

9472 DETROIT & MACKINAC: 1984-85, white roof and ends, white and red half-and-half sides and doors, white and red contrasting lettering, Symington-Wayne trucks. -- -- **15 20**

9473 LEHIGH VALLEY: 1984-85, light green body, silver-painted roof, light green doors, white lettering, Symington-Wayne trucks. C. Rohlfing comments.
(A) Red and blue LV flag press-on sticker attached to doors. D. Anderson Collection. -- -- **15 20**
(B) Same as (A), but flag on doors is missing. P. Costa Collection. -- -- **15 20**

9474 ERIE-LACKAWANNA: 1984-85, boxcar, tuscan-painted body and doors, white lettering and logo, Standard O trucks; from Erie-Lackawanna Limited Set. -- -- **35 40**

9475 DELAWARE & HUDSON "I LOVE NEW YORK": 1984-85, unusual blue and white paint scheme with colors on sides and doors separated diagonally from upper left to lower right; large black serif "I", red heart, and "N Y", white D & H shield logo and lettering, Standard O trucks. May be in demand by operators for unit trains. -- -- **25 35**

The first cars of a terrific boxcar series. Top shelf: 9700 Southern (note green dot added by dealer in the "O" of "Southern"), 9701 Baltimore and Ohio regular-issue. Middle shelf: Special all-black 9701 Baltimore & Ohio issued for 1972 TCA Convention, 9702 Soo Line. Bottom shelf: 9704 Norfolk & Western, 9703 C P Rail. A. Rudman, L. Caponi, F. Stem, and R. LaVoie Collections.

These 9700 boxcars date from 1972-73. Top shelf: 9705 Rio Grande, 9706 Chesapeake & Ohio. Contrast these with the later 9714 and 9715 models in different colors. Middle shelf: 9707 M K T Stock Car (note longer body), 9708 Post Office. Bottom shelf: 9709 State of Maine (Bangor & Aroostook), 9710 Rutland. The 9708, 9709, and 9710 models have many variations. A. Rudman, L. Caponi, F. Stem, and R. La-Voie Collections.

9476 PENNSYLVANIA: 1984-85, tuscan-painted body and doors, white lettering, white and black PRR Keystone logo, gold "FARR 5" diamond-shaped logo, Standard O trucks. -- -- 25 35

9480 MINNEAPOLIS, NORTHFIELD & SOUTHERN: 1985, dark gloss blue body and doors; white lettering, dark red MNS logo, tuscan and white diamond-shaped logo, Symington-Wayne trucks. -- -- 12 15

9481 SEABOARD SYSTEM: 1985, tuscan body and doors; white lettering, white interlocked "S" logo, Symington-Wayne trucks. -- -- 12 15

9482 NORFOLK SOUTHERN: 1985, gray body and doors; black lettering, black and red "NS" logo, orange rectangle, Symington-Wayne trucks. -- -- 15 20

9483 MANUFACTURERS RAILWAY COMPANY: 1985, white sides and doors, red lower side sills, black roof and ends; black lettering, black and yellow logo, Symington-Wayne trucks. -- -- 12 15

9484 LIONEL 85TH ANNIVERSARY: 1985, silver-gray body, black doors, black roof and ends; gold lettering; red, white, and blue circular Lionel logo; gold and black steam engine electrocal, Symington-Wayne trucks. C. Rohlfing, G. Rogers, and R. LaVoie Collections. -- -- 25 30

9486 I LOVE MICHIGAN: 1986, boxcar, white sides, violet-painted roof and ends, red, white, and black lettering, Symington-Wayne trucks. -- -- 15 20

See also Special Production chapter.

9491 LIONEL: 1986, Christmas boxcar, silver sides, red roof, ends, and doors; red, white, dark or light blue, and black new Lionel logo; green lettering, Symington-Wayne trucks. Part of 1986 year-end "Stocking Stuffer" package. R. LaVoie Collection. -- -- 35 40

9492 LIONEL LINES: 1986, boxcar, bright orange sides, bright blue roof and ends, blue doors; new red, white, black, and blue Lionel logo to left of door; "1986 / A NEW TRADITION" in blue lettering to right, Symington-Wayne trucks. -- -- 25 50

9600 CHESSIE: 1976, hi-cube, dark blue body; yellow lettering and door.
(A) Thin door stop. 7 9 20 25
(B) Thick door stop. 7 9 20 25

9601 ILLINOIS CENTRAL: 1976-77, hi-cube, orange body; black lettering and door. 10 15 20 25

9602 A T S F: 1977, hi-cube, red body; white lettering, two-inch high emblem, silver door. 10 15 20 25
See also Factory Errors and Prototypes.

9603 PENN CENTRAL: 1976-77, hi-cube, green body; white lettering, silver door. 10 15 20 25

9604 N W: 1976-77, hi-cube, black body; white lettering, silver door. 10 15 20 25

9605 N H: 1976-77, hi-cube, orange body; white lettering, black door. 10 15 20 25

9606 UNION PACIFIC: 1976-77, hi-cube, yellow body; blue lettering, yellow door.
(A) Lighter yellow. 10 15 20 25
(B) Darker yellow. 10 15 20 25

9607 S P: 1976-77, hi-cube, red body, gray stripe arrow, gray roof, white letters. 10 15 20 25

9608 BURLINGTON NORTHERN: 1977, hi-cube, green body; white lettering. 10 15 20 25

9610 FRISCO: 1977, hi-cube, yellow body; black lettering, available only in Rocky Mountain Set. 12 20 30 50

9611 TCA: 1978, see Special Production chapter.

9620 N H L WALES CONFERENCE: 1980, Type IX 9700 boxcar body, white car with different team symbols on each side, black roof and ends, Symington-Wayne trucks. -- -- 9 20

Patterns begin to repeat with these 9700s. Top shelf: 9711 Southern (compare with 9700), 9712 Baltimore & Ohio double-door (compare with 9701). Middle shelf: 9713 C P Rail (compare with 9703), 9714 Rio Grande (compare with 9705). Bottom shelf: 9715 C & O (compare with 9706), 9716 Penn Central, first version (compare with later 9749). A. Rudman, L. Caponi, F. Stem, and R. LaVoie Collections.

9621 N H L CAMPBELL CONFERENCE: 1980, Type IX 9700 boxcar body, white car with different team symbols on each side, orange roof and ends, Symington-Wayne trucks, opening doors. -- -- **9 20**

9622 N B A WESTERN CONFERENCE: 1980, Type IX 9700 boxcar body, white car with different team symbols on each side, silver roof and ends, Symington-Wayne trucks, opening doors. -- -- **9 20**

9623 N B A EASTERN CONFERENCE: 1980, Type IX 9700 boxcar body, white car with different team symbols on each side, dark blue roof and ends, Symington-Wayne trucks, opening doors. -- -- **9 20**

9624 NATIONAL LEAGUE: 1980, Type IX 9700 boxcar body, white car with different baseball team symbols on each side, red roof and ends, Symington-Wayne trucks, opening doors. -- -- **20 25**

9625 AMERICAN LEAGUE: 1980, Type IX 9700 boxcar body, white car with different baseball team symbols on each side, gold-painted roof and ends, Symington-Wayne trucks, opening doors. -- -- **15 20**

9626 A T S F: 1982-83, hi-cube, red with white lettering and door, Symington-Wayne trucks. This and the following entries differ from the earlier hi-cube boxcars mostly because they do not have the white-painted clearance warning on the car ends. -- -- **10 12**

9627 UNION PACIFIC: 1982-83, hi-cube, yellow with red lettering, white door, Symington-Wayne trucks. J. Breslin Collection. -- -- **10 12**

9628 BURLINGTON NORTHERN: 1982-83, hi-cube, green with white lettering and door, Symington-Wayne trucks. -- -- **10 12**

9629 CHESSIE 1983, hi-cube, dark blue with yellow lettering and logo, Symington-Wayne trucks. T. Ladny Collection. -- -- **10 12**

MICKEY MOUSE SET

Note: The Mickey Mouse Set consists of cars 9660-9672 plus an 8773 U36B Engine, 9183 Caboose, and the limited edition 9672 50th Anniversary Boxcar. Set price. -- -- **1200 1400**

9660 MICKEY MOUSE: 1977-78, hi-cube, white body, yellow roof and ends. **8 10 20 40**

9661 GOOFY: 1977-78, hi-cube, white body, red roof and ends. **8 10 20 40**

9662 DONALD DUCK: 1977-78, hi-cube, white body, green roof and ends. **8 10 20 40**

9663 DUMBO: 1978, hi-cube, white body, red roof and ends. **15 20 35 60**

9664 CINDERELLA: 1978, hi-cube, white body, lavender roof and ends. C. Rohlfing comment. **15 20 30 45**

9665 PETER PAN: 1978, hi-cube, white body, orange roof and ends. **10 12 20 40**

9666 PINOCCHIO: 1978, hi-cube, white body, blue roof and ends. **40 75 100 125**

9667 SNOW WHITE: 1978, hi-cube, white body, green roof and ends. By far the hardest car to find in the regularly issued series. **150 175 200 350**

9668 PLUTO: 1978, hi-cube, white body, brown roof and ends. **30 75 100 125**

9669 BAMBI: 1978, hi-cube, white body, lime green roof, ends, and doors. C. Rohlfing comment. **10 30 40 60**

9670 ALICE IN WONDERLAND: 1978, hi-cube, white body, jade green roof, ends, and doors. C. Rohlfing comment. **10 30 40 60**

9671 FANTASIA: 1978, hi-cube, white body, dark blue roof, ends, and doors. C. Rohlfing comment. **10 30 40 60**

9672 MICKEY MOUSE 50th ANNIVERSARY: 1978, hi-cube, white body, gold roof and ends, dull gold doors, limited edition. C. Rohlfing comment. -- **225 250 300**

9678 T T O S: 1978, see Special Production chapter.

9700-SERIES BOXCARS

9700 SOUTHERN: 1972-73, Type IX body except for (A), red-painted red door, white lettering, Symington-Wayne trucks, Type I frame.
(A) "SOO" red-painted Type VI "SOO" red plastic body, metal door guides. -- **75 125 175**

Some new patterns and great resurrections in this batch of 9700s. Top shelf: 9717 Union Pacific (compare with later 9755), 9718 Canadian National. Middle shelf: 9719 New Haven "coupon" car which retains the 1956 built date of its 6464 predecessor, 9723 Western Pacific. Bottom shelf: 9724 Missouri Pacific (compare with later 9219 operating version), 9725 M K T Stock Car (compare with earlier 9707). A. Rudman, L. Caponi, F. Stem, and R. LaVoie Collections.

(B) Shiny red-painted shiny red body .	6	8	20	25
(C) Dark red-painted dark red body, green dot added by dealer. The prototype had green paint within the "O" of "SOUTHERN" to symbolize the railroad's motto, "Southern Gives A Green Light To Innovations". To make the car more realistic, dealers received sheets of stick-on green dots to place into the "O" of "Southern". C. Lang comment, R. LaVoie Collection.	6	8	20	25
(D) Same as (C), but no green dot.	6	8	15	20

See also Factory Errors and Prototypes.

9700-1976: See Special Production chapter under entry 9779.

9701 BALTIMORE & OHIO: 1971-73, double-door automobile car with metal door guides, Symington-Wayne trucks. Different-colored doors were added outside the factory; only the black doors are authentic factory production. However, since there is substantial collector interest in the door variations, we include them in this listing.

(A) Shiny black-painted black body, flat black-painted black doors, white lettering,Type I frame; 900 made for 1971 TCA National Convention. Cars were serially numbered with silver rubber-stamped lettering on bottom of frame. Beware of fake stamping.	40	60	80	100
(B) Same as (A), but only one built date.	40	60	80	100
(C) Silver-painted gray plastic body, black-painted black doors, black lettering, Type II frame.	6	8	20	25
(D) Same as (C), but Type I frame.	6	8	20	25

NOTE: The following varieties have had doors installed outside the factory:

(E) Same as (C), but dark blue-painted dark blue doors.	6	8	11	30
(F) Same as (C), but medium blue-painted medium blue doors.	6	8	11	30
(G) Same as (C), but light blue-painted light blue doors, Type I frame.	6	8	11	30
(H) Same as (C), but green-painted 9209 Burlington Northern green doors, Type I frame. C. Lang Collection.	6	8	11	30
(I) Same as (C), but 9200 IC orange-painted orange doors. C. Lang Collection.	6	8	11	30

(J) Same as (C), but burnt orange-painted burnt orange doors.	6	8	11	30
(K) Same as (C), but silver-painted gray doors, Type I frame.	6	8	11	30
(L) Same as (C), but silver-painted gray doors.	6	8	11	30
(M) Same as (C), but dark navy blue 9205 NW doors. C. Lang Collection.	6	8	11	30
(N) Same as (C), but dark red 9207 Soo doors. C. Lang Collection.	6	8	11	15

See also Special Production and Factory Errors and Prototypes chapters.

9702 SOO: 1972-73, white sides, black roof painted on white body, red-painted red door, black lettering, Symington-Wayne trucks

(A) Type VIII body, Type I frame.	6	10	20	25
(B) Type IX body, Type II frame.	8	10	20	30

9703 C P RAIL: 1970-71, Type IX body, black lettering, Symington-Wayne trucks. Some collectors have reported that this car was specifically made for Canadian distribution; reader comments invited.

(A) Burnt orange-painted burnt-orange body, burnt orange-painted red doors, Type II frame.	30	40	55	65
(B) Light burnt orange-painted medium red body, medium red-painted red doors, Type I frame.	30	40	55	65

See also Factory Errors and Prototypes.

9704 NORFOLK & WESTERN: 1972, Type IX body except (A), white lettering except (C), Symington-Wayne trucks.

(A) Tuscan-painted Type VII maroon body, metal door guides, tuscan-painted maroon doors, Type I frame.	--	100	125	150
(B) Tuscan-painted tuscan body, tuscan-painted tuscan doors, Type II frame.	--	6	10	25
(C) Same as (B), but gray lettering.	--	6	10	25
(D) Same as (B), but Type I frame.	--	10	15	25
(E) Tuscan-painted gray body, tuscan-painted tuscan doors, Type I frame.	--	10	15	30

Some interesting history is behind these 9700 Boxcars. Top shelf: 9726 Erie Lackawanna from the Minneapolis & St. Louis Service Station Set, 9727 T. A. & G. for 1973 L C C A Convention, a rare car. Middle shelf: 9728 Union Pacific stock car for 1978 LCCA Convention, 9729 C P Rail from Great Plains Express of 1978; later replaced with 9417 model in the same set in 1980. Bottom shelf: Two versions of the 9730 C P Rail Boxcar. Left: Later black-lettered version. Right: Earlier white-lettered version. The black-lettered version is scarcer. A. Rudman, L. Caponi, F. Stem, and R. LaVoie Collections.

9705 DENVER & RIO GRANDE: 1972-73, silver-painted gray plastic doors, black lettering, Symington-Wayne trucks.
(A) Dark orange-painted Type VIII orange plastic body, Type I frame, deeply stamped lettering. -- 50 75 100
(B) Light orange-painted Type IX orange plastic body, Type I frame. -- 10 12 25
(C) Dark orange-painted orange plastic body, Type I frame. -- 10 12 25
(D) Dark orange unpainted orange body, silver-painted gray doors; very deeply stamped gloss black lettering, MPC logo, Symington-Wayne trucks, Type IX body, Type II frame, probably late production. R. LaVoie Collection.
-- 10 12 25
(E) Same as (C), but Type II frame. C. Rohlfing Collection. -- 10 12 15

9706 C & O: Yellow lettering, Symington-Wayne trucks.
(A) Blue-painted blue plastic body, yellow-painted yellow door, Type II frame, Type VIII body. -- 8 15 20
(B) Same as (A), but Type I frame and Type IX body. 6 8 15 20
(C) Same as (A), but blue-painted gray plastic body. 6 8 15 20
See also Factory Errors and Prototypes.

9707 M K T: 1972-74, stock car, metal door guides, red-painted translucent plastic except (D); white lettering, Symington-Wayne trucks, 6356-19 frame.
(A) Light yellow-painted light yellow door, electrocal decoration.
6 8 15 20
(B) Medium yellow-painted medium yellow door, rubber-stamped lettering.
6 8 15 20
(C) Same as (B), but heat-stamped lettering. 6 8 15 20
(D) Dark red-painted red plastic, medium yellow-painted medium yellow doors. Reader confirmation requested. NRS
(E) Flat red-painted red body, unpainted yellow doors, dull white rubber-stamped lettering. R. LaVoie Collection. 8 10 20 25

(F) Same as (E), but yellow-painted yellow doors. Came as part of 1388 Golden State Arrow Set. G. Halverson Collection. 8 10 20 25

9708 U S MAIL: 1972-74, Type IX body, painted red plastic body except (I); white and black lettering, Symington-Wayne trucks, Type II frame, MPC logo on (A)-(D), no MPC logo on (E)-(J), painted red plastic door.
(A) Dark red- and light blue-painted body, red-painted door.
5 10 15 25
(B) Same as (A), but red- and light blue-painted door. 5 10 15 25
(C) Dark red- and medium blue-painted body, red- and medium blue-painted door. 5 10 15 25
(D) Same as (C), but red- and dark blue-painted door. 5 10 15 25
(E) Light red- and dark blue-painted body, red- and dark blue-painted doors, no MPC logo. 5 10 15 25
(F) Dark red- and light blue-painted body, red- and medium blue-painted door.
5 10 15 25
(G) Dark red- and medium blue-painted body, red- and medium blue-painted door. 5 10 15 25
(H) Dark red- and medium blue-painted body, red- and dark blue-painted door.
5 10 15 25
(I) Medium blue- and dark red-painted gray body, red-painted door. Rare. Reader comments requested. -- -- -- 400
See also Special Production and Factory Errors and Prototypes chapters.

9709 B A R: 1973-74, Type VIII bodies: (A)-(C); Type IX bodies: (D)-(H); Symington-Wayne trucks, Type II frame.
(A) Blue- and dark red-painted gray body, white and black lettering, printed white and black on both sides. One observed example came in an original Type I box dated 1971 with a black-painted sticker on one end. R. LaVoie Collection.
15 20 30 40

(B) Blue- and dark red-painted gray body, red-painted red door, white and black lettering. Red doors added outside factory. R. Vagner comment.

15	20	30	40

(C) Dark blue- and medium red-painted blue body, blue- and red-painted blue doors; white and black lettering.

15	20	30	40

(D) Medium blue- and light red-painted medium blue body, dark blue- and red-painted red doors; white and black lettering.

15	20	30	40

(E) Blue- and light red-painted gray body, blue- and red-painted gray doors; white- and black-painted lettering.

20	35	40	50

(F) Blue- and red-painted blue body, dark blue- and dark red-painted dark blue doors, Type IX body, Type II frame. C. Rohlfing Collection.

20	35	40	50

See also Factory Errors and Prototypes.

9710 RUTLAND: 1973-74, Type VIII bodies: (A),(B), and (C); Type IX bodies: (D) to (G); yellow-painted yellow doors, green and yellow lettering, Type II frame.

(A) Medium yellow- and green-painted gray body; shifted shield.

12	20	30	40

(B) Light yellow- and green-painted gray body; shifted shield.

12	20	30	40

(C) Same as (B), but shield centered, "9710" not underscored.

25	30	40	50

(D) Dark yellow- and green-painted gray body; shifted shield.

25	30	40	50

(E) Medium yellow- and light green-painted green body; shifted shield, no "CAPY 100000".

20	25	40	50

(F) Light yellow- and light green-painted green body; shifted shield, "9200" on car end.

20	25	30	40

(G) Dark yellow- and green-painted gray body; shifted shield.

12	20	30	40

9711 SOUTHERN: 1974, Type IX body, white lettering, Symington-Wayne trucks, Type II frame, "LIONEL" to the right of door, except (C).

(A) Tuscan-painted tuscan body, tuscan-painted white doors.

10	12	20	25

(B) Same as (A), but tuscan-painted tuscan doors.

10	12	20	25

(C) Same as (A), but tuscan-painted tuscan doors, "LIONEL" to the left of door.

10	12	20	25

(D) Tuscan-painted translucent body, reported but not verified. NRS

9712 BALTIMORE & OHIO: 1973-74, double-door automobile car, metal door guides, blue-painted blue body, yellow-painted yellow door; yellow lettering, Symington-Wayne trucks, Type II frame.

9	12	25	35

9713 C P RAIL: 1973-74, Type IX body, green-painted green doors; black lettering, Symington-Wayne trucks, Type II frame.

(A) Green-painted green body.

8	10	20	25

(B) Light green-painted green body.

8	10	20	25

(C) Same as (A), but metallic gold overprinted, "SEASONS GREETINGS '74".

--	--	125	150

(D) Green-painted clear body, reported but not verified. NRS

9714 RIO GRANDE: 1973-74, Type IX body, silver-painted, Symington-Wayne trucks, Type II frame.

(A) Silver-painted gray body, red-painted red doors; red lettering.

10	15	20	25

(B) Same as (A), but silver-painted translucent white body.

10	15	20	25

(C) Same as (A), but orange-painted orange doors; orange lettering.

--	--	--	295

(D) Same as (A), but silver-painted translucent doors, dark orange lettering.

--	--	--	280

9715 CHESAPEAKE & OHIO: 1973-74, Type IX body, Symington-Wayne trucks, Type II frame. Many examples have washed-out yellow lettering; slight premium for bold, well-contrasted lettering.

(A) Black-painted black body, yellow-painted yellow door.

10	15	20	25

(B) Same as (A), but yellow-painted white door.

10	15	20	25

(C) Black-painted white body, light yellow-painted white door.

10	15	20	25

(D) Same as (C), but dark yellow-painted white door.

10	15	20	25

A few exotic 9700s in this batch. Top shelf: 9731 Milwaukee Road. Beware of faked silver-painted roofs; all but first 500 were plain red. 9732 Southern Pacific, available only in Southern Pacific Set of 1979. Middle shelf: 9733 Airco, a weird car with a tank car body inside the boxcar produced for the 1979 L C C A Convention, and 9734 Bangor & Aroostook from Quaker City set of 1978. Bottom shelf: 9735 Grand Trunk, 9737 Central Vermont. A. Rudman, L. Caponi, F. Stem, and R. LaVoie Collections.

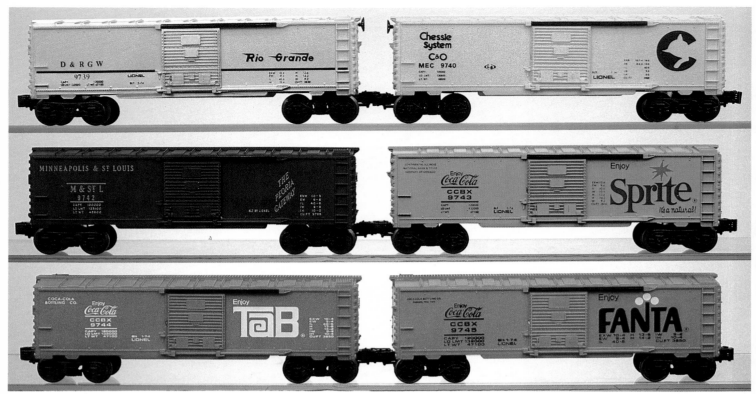

Some standard production and special 9700s. The 9738 Illinois Terminal Boxcar is missing from this sequence. Top shelf: 9739 Rio Grande (compare with 9705 and 9714 models), which has a rare variation missing the black stripe, 9740 Chessie System. Middle shelf: 9742 Minneapolis & St. Louis, available only as part of a coupon mail promotion, 9743 Sprite. Bottom shelf: 9744 Tab, 9745 Fanta. The 9743, 9744, and 9745 cars came as part of an uncatalogued Coca-Cola Set in 1974. A. Rudman, L. Caponi, F. Stem, and R. LaVoie Collections.

9716 PENN CENTRAL: 1973-74, Type IX body, green-painted green body and green door, Symington-Wayne trucks, Type II frame.   10   15   20   25

9717 UNION PACIFIC: 1973-74, Type IX body, black roof, yellow-painted yellow door; black lettering, Symington-Wayne trucks, Type II frame.
(A) Light yellow-painted yellow body.   10   15   20   30
(B) Medium yellow-painted yellow body.   10   12   15   20

9718 CANADIAN NATIONAL: 1973-74, Type IX body, white lettering, Symington-Wayne trucks, Type II frame.
(A) Tuscan-painted tuscan body, yellow-painted yellow door.
   10   15   20   25
(B) Tuscan-painted orange body, yellow-painted translucent door.
   12   15   25   35
(C) Same as (B), but yellow-painted yellow door.   12   15   25   35
(D) Tuscan red-painted tuscan red body, yellow-painted yellow door.   **NRS**
(E) Tuscan red-painted gray body, yellow-painted yellow door. J. Breslin and P. Catalano comments.   --   --   --   100

9719 NEW HAVEN: Double-door boxcar, orange-painted orange body, black-painted black door, Symington-Wayne trucks, Type II frame, coupon car available only through special mail offer. Has built date "BLT 3-56", the same built date as its 6468 postwar predecessor. G. Rogers comment.
(A) Black and white lettering.   12   15   25   35
(B) Black overprinted on white lettering.   --   --   --   75
(C) White overprinted on black lettering.   --   --   --   75

9720 ASSORTED CASE OF CARS: **NRS**

9721 ASSORTED CASE OF CARS: **NRS**

9722: Not used

9723 WESTERN PACIFIC: 1974, Type IX plastic body, black lettering, Symington-Wayne trucks, Type II frame.
(A) Unpainted orange plastic body and doors.   15   20   30   40
(B) Fanta orange-painted orange body and orange doors.   30   35   40   45

(C) Fanta orange-painted orange body and white doors. Doors added outside factory. R. Vagner comment.   30   35   40   45
(D) Fanta orange-painted orange body, orange-painted translucent doors, Type IX body, Type II frame. C. Rohlfing Collection.   30   35   40   45
(E) Same as (A), but gold overstamp "SEASON'S GREETINGS 1974". C. Lang Collection.   --   --   125   150
See also Special Production chapter.

9724 MISSOURI PACIFIC: 1974, Type IX plastic body, black and white lettering, Symington-Wayne trucks, Type II frame, silver-painted roof and side band.
(A) Medium blue-painted opaque-white body, yellow- and silver-painted yellow doors.   25   30   35   40
(B) Same as (A), but medium blue-painted gray body.   25   30   35   40
(C) Dark blue-painted gray body, yellow- and silver-painted yellow doors.
   25   35   40   45
(D) Dark blue-painted navy body, yellow-painted yellow doors.
   25   35   40   45

9725 M K T: 1974-75, double-door stock car, "The Katy SERVES THE SOUTHWEST", black-painted black door, Symington-Wayne trucks, Type I frame.
(A) Light yellow-painted yellow body.   10   12   15   20
(B) Medium yellow-painted yellow body.   10   12   15   20
(C) Medium dark yellow-painted yellow body.   10   12   15   20
(D) Dark yellow-painted yellow body.   10   12   15   20
See also Special Production chapter.

9726 ERIE LACKAWANNA: 1978, glossy blue-painted Type IX body, blue-painted blue doors; white lettering, Type III frame, Standard O trucks, part of 1868 Minneapolis & St. Louis Service Station Set.
(A) Shiny blue-painted blue body.   15   20   25   30
(B) Lighter shiny blue-painted blue body.   15   20   25   30
(C) Glossy Brunswick green-painted body and doors instead of blue. Reader comments requested concerning possibility of chemically-altered change in color. R. Vagner Collection.   **NRS**

Standard production 9700s. Top shelf: 9747 Chessie System Double-door, 9748 C P Rail, which has more variations than any other 9700 Boxcar. Middle shelf: 9749 Penn Central (compare with previous 9716), 9750 Detroit, Toledo & Ironton. Bottom shelf: 9751 Frisco, 9752 Louisville & Nashville. A. Rudman, L. Caponi, F. Stem, and R. LaVoie Collections.

Standard production and special-interest 9700s. Top shelf: 9753 Maine Central, 9754 New York Central "Pacemaker," which suddenly became popular for unit trains when a matching extended vision caboose was issued. Middle shelf: 9755 Union Pacific (compare with earlier 9717), 9757 Central of Georgia, part of dealer's end-of-year package. Bottom shelf: 9758 Alaska, 9759 Paul Revere, part of uncatalogued Liberty Special Set in 1975. A. Rudman, L. Caponi, F. Stem, and R. LaVoie Collections.

More 9700s, including a surprise entry in the series. **Top shelf: 9760** Liberty Bell and **9761** George Washington, both part of the Liberty Special uncatalogued set. **Middle shelf: 9762** Toy Fair Car of 1975, the surprise. Since the number is not on the car, many collectors are not aware that this car is part of the 9700 Series. Also: **9763** Rio Grande Stock Car. **Bottom shelf: 9764** Grand Trunk Double-door, **9767** Railbox. A. Rudman, L. Caponi, F. Stern, and R. LaVoie Collections.

9727 T. A. & G.: 1973. See Special Production chapter.

9728 UNION PACIFIC: 1978, stock car. See Special Production chapter.

9729 C P RAIL: Type IX body, Symington-Wayne trucks, black-, white- and red-painted black body, black-painted black door; white lettering, Type III frame, from Great Plains Set, some sets came with 9417 car identical except for number and gold lettering. C. Lang and C. Rohlfing comments. **10 20 30 40**

9730 C P RAIL: 1974-75, Type IX body, Symington-Wayne trucks, Type II frame, white-lettered (A) and (B), black-lettered (C) through (F).
White Lettering
(A) Silver-painted gray body, silver-painted gray door. **10 20 25 30**
(B) Same as (A), but silver-painted white body. **10 20 25 30**
Black Lettering
(C) Same as (A), but flat silver-painted white body. **10 20 30 35**
(D) Same as (A), but silver-painted opaque door. **10 20 30 35**
(E) Same as (A), but silver-painted white door. **10 20 30 35**
(F) Same as (A), but silver-painted yellow door. **10 20 30 35**

9731 MILWAUKEE ROAD: 1974-75, Type IX body, white lettering, red door, Symington-Wayne trucks, Type II frame.
(A) Light red-painted red body. **8 10 15 20**
(B) Medium red-painted red body. **8 10 15 20**
(C) Red-painted red body, silver-painted roof, as shown in 1974 catalogue. Reportedly, 100 examples were made this way. However, since the car can be easily faked by painting the roof, it is difficult to place a value on this variation. C. O'Dell, R. LaVoie, and C. Lang comments. **NRS**

9732 SOUTHERN PACIFIC: 1979, black roof and silver sides on gray plastic Type IX body, black-painted black door, black and orange lettering, Standard O trucks, Type III frame, from Southern Pacific Limited Set. Car has black-lettered "OVERNIGHTS" misused plural on all examples. C. Lang and T. Ladny comments. **-- -- 30 40**

9733 AIRCO: 1979, see Special Production chapter.

9734 BANGOR & AROOSTOOK: Type IX body, red body, red doors, white lettering, Standard O trucks; from Quaker City Limited Set of 1979. R. Vagner and T. Ladny comments. **15 25 30 35**

9735 GRAND TRUNK WESTERN: 1974-75, Type IX body, white lettering, Symington-Wayne trucks, Type II frame.
(A) Blue-painted blue body, blue-painted dark blue doors. **8 10 15 20**
(B) Same as (A), but blue-painted opaque body. **8 10 15 20**
(C) Blue-painted opaque body, blue-painted white doors. **8 10 15 20**

9736: Not used.

9737 CENTRAL VERMONT: 1974-75, Type IX body, white lettering, Symington-Wayne trucks, Type II frame.
(A) Tuscan-painted tuscan body and tuscan doors. **10 15 20 25**
(B) Tuscan-painted orange body and tuscan-painted white doors. Hard-to-find variation. **30 35 45 60**
(C) Same as (B), but tuscan-painted tuscan body. R. LaVoie Collection. **10 15 20 25**

9738 ILLINOIS TERMINAL: 1982, Type IX body, yellow-painted sides, light green roof and ends, light green- and red-outlined lettering, Standard O trucks; part of 1260 The Continental Limited Set. C. Rohlfing Collection. **-- -- 50 65**

9739 RIO GRANDE: 1975, Type IX body, black lettering, Symington-Wayne trucks, Type II frame. Regular issues with stripe were also part of 1974 Rio Grande Service Station Special Set. C. Lang comment.
(A) Dark yellow- and silver-painted yellow body, silver-painted yellow doors, no stripe. Rare. **100 140 160 200**
(B) Light yellow- and silver-painted transparent white body, silver-painted gray doors, no stripe. Rare. **100 140 160 200**
(C) Medium dark yellow- and silver-painted yellow body, same doors as (B), long stripe. **10 12 15 20**
(D) Dark yellow- and silver-painted yellow body, same doors as (B), long stripe. **10 12 15 20**

(E) Medium yellow- and silver-painted yellow body, same doors as (B), long stripe.

| | 10 | 12 | 15 | 20 |

(F) Light yellow- and light silver-painted yellow body, same doors as (B), long stripe.

| | 10 | 12 | 15 | 20 |

(G) Same as (F), but silver-painted yellow doors.

| | 10 | 12 | 15 | 20 |

(H) Dark yellow- and silver-painted yellow body, same doors as (B), short stripe.

| | 10 | 12 | 15 | 20 |

(I) Light yellow- and silver-painted opaque body, silver-painted opaque doors, short stripe.

| | 10 | 12 | 15 | 20 |

(J) Medium yellow- and silver-painted opaque body, silver-painted opaque doors, long stripe.

| | 10 | 12 | 15 | 20 |

(K) Same as (J), but silver-painted gray doors.

| | 10 | 12 | 15 | 20 |

(L) Light yellow- and light silver-painted opaque body, silver-painted opaque doors, long stripe.

| | 10 | 12 | 15 | 20 |

(M) Medium yellow- and silver-painted yellow body, silver-painted translucent doors, long stripe. R. LaVoie Collection.

| | 10 | 12 | 15 | 20 |

See also Special Production chapter.

9740 CHESSIE: 1974-75, Type IX body, yellow-painted yellow doors, except (D) and (E), blue lettering, Symington-Wayne trucks, Type II frame

(A) Dark yellow-painted yellow body.

| | 10 | 12 | 15 | 20 |

(B) Medium yellow-painted yellow body.

| | 10 | 12 | 15 | 20 |

(C) Light yellow-painted yellow body.

| | 10 | 12 | 15 | 20 |

(D) Light yellow-painted yellow body, yellow-painted white doors.

| | 10 | 12 | 15 | 20 |

(E) Light yellow-painted opaque body, same doors as (D).

| | 10 | 12 | 15 | 20 |

9741: Not used

9742 MINNEAPOLIS & ST LOUIS: Type IX body, metallic gold lettering, Symington-Wayne trucks, Type II frame, coupon car offered to purchasers of specially marked boxes of refrigerator or covered hopper cars. Two coupons and $5 would be sent to Lionel factory at Mt. Clemens. Other cars used for this marketing approach were the 9719 New Haven Double-door Boxcar and the 9511 Milwaukee "Minneapolis" Passenger Car. The cars originally could not be purchased from dealers. R. LaVoie comment.

(A) Green-painted green body and doors.

| | 10 | 15 | 25 | 35 |

(B) Light green-painted green body, green-painted gray doors, metallic red overstamped "Seasons Greetings 1973" in gold. C. Lang Collection.

| | 60 | 80 | 100 | 125 |

(C) Same as (B), but dark green-painted green body.

| | 60 | 80 | 100 | 125 |

(D) Green-painted white body, green-painted gray doors.

| | 10 | 15 | 25 | 35 |

(E) Same as (D), but green-painted white doors.

| | 10 | 15 | 25 | 35 |

(F) Same as (A), but green-painted gray doors, Type IX body, Type II frame. C. Rohlfing Collection.

| | 10 | 15 | 25 | 35 |

9743 SPRITE: Type IX body, Symington-Wayne trucks, Type II frame, dark green lettering. This car and the next two entries listed were part of an uncatalogued 1463 Coca-Cola Switcher Set in 1974. C. Lang comment.

(A) Light green-painted light green body, green-painted green door.

| | 7 | 9 | 15 | 25 |

(B) Medium green-painted dark green body, doors same as (A).

| | 7 | 9 | 15 | 25 |

(C) Light green-painted white body, green-painted white door.

| | 7 | 9 | 15 | 25 |

(D) Same as (C), but green-painted green doors.

| | 7 | 9 | 15 | 25 |

(E) Medium green-painted medium green body, medium-painted dark green doors.

| | 7 | 9 | 15 | 25 |

9744 TAB: Type IX body, white lettering, Symington-Wayne trucks, Type II frame.

(A) Medium magenta-painted light red body, magenta-painted red doors.

| | 7 | 9 | 15 | 25 |

(B) Dark magenta-painted dark red body, magenta-painted red doors.

| | 7 | 9 | 15 | 25 |

(C) Medium magenta-painted white body, magenta-painted white doors.

| | 7 | 9 | 15 | 25 |

(D) Light magenta-painted white body, magenta-painted red doors.

| | 7 | 9 | 15 | 25 |

(E) Same as (D), but pink body painted light magenta, magenta-painted red doors.

| | 7 | 9 | 15 | 25 |

Later production of the 9700 Series. Top shelf: 9768 Boston & Maine, 9769 Bessemer & Lake Erie. Middle shelf: 9770 Northern Pacific, 9771 Norfolk & Western. Bottom shelf: 9772 Great Northern, 9773 New York Central Stock Car. Both of these came in the Empire State Express Set of 1976. A. Rudman, L. Caponi, F. Stem, and R. LaVoie Collections.

9745 FANTA: Type IX body, black lettering, Symington-Wayne trucks, Type II frame.

(A) Light orange-painted orange body, orange-painted orange doors.

| | 7 | 9 | 15 | 25 |

(B) Flat medium orange-painted orange body, same doors as (A).

| | 7 | 9 | 15 | 25 |

(C) Shiny medium orange-painted orange body, same doors as (A).

| | 7 | 9 | 15 | 25 |

(D) Same body as (C), orange-painted white doors. 7 9 15 25

(E) Dark orange-painted orange body, same doors as (A). 7 9 15 25

(F) Light orange-painted white body, same doors as (A). 7 9 15 25

(G) Medium orange-painted white body, orange-painted white doors.

| | 7 | 9 | 15 | 25 |

9746: Not used.

9747 CHESSIE SYSTEM: 1975-76, double-door automobile boxcar, blue-painted blue doors; yellow lettering, Symington-Wayne trucks, Type II frame.

(A) Flat blue-painted blue body. 5 7 15 20

(B) Slightly darker, shiny blue-painted blue body. 5 7 15 20

9748 C P RAIL: 1975-76, Type IX body, white lettering, Symington-Wayne trucks, Type II frame, medium blue-painted medium blue doors: (A) through (G), medium blue-painted white doors: (H) through (N). There are more variations of this car than for any other 9700-series car.

A-G: Medium blue-painted medium blue doors.

(A) Dark blue-painted dark blue body. 8 10 15 20

(B) Medium blue-painted dark blue body. 8 10 15 20

(C) Medium light blue-painted dark blue body. 8 10 15 20

(D) Medium light blue-painted medium blue body. 8 10 15 20

(E) Dark light blue-painted medium blue body. 8 10 12 15

(F) Medium dark blue-painted medium blue body. 8 10 15 20

(G) Medium blue-painted medium blue body. 8 10 15 20

H-N: Medium blue-painted white doors.

(H) Flat medium dark blue-painted medium blue body. 8 10 15 20

(I) Medium dark blue-painted medium blue body. 8 10 15 20

(J) Medium light blue-painted medium blue body. 8 10 15 20

(K) Medium light blue-painted white body. 8 10 15 20

(L) Medium dark blue-painted white body. 8 10 15 20

(M) Lightest blue-painted white body. 8 10 15 20

(N) Royal sides but lighter royal top on royal body. 8 10 15 20

(O) Royal-painted royal body, royal-painted royal doors. 8 10 15 20

(P) Royal-painted medium blue body, royal-painted white doors.

| | 8 | 10 | 15 | 20 |

(Q) Royal-painted sides and medium blue top on medium blue body, light blue-painted white doors. 8 10 15 20

(R) Purple-painted medium blue body, purple-painted white doors .

| | 8 | 10 | 15 | 20 |

(S) Royal-painted light blue body, royal-painted royal doors. 8 10 15 20

9749 PENN CENTRAL: 1975-76, Type IX body, white and red lettering, Symington-Wayne trucks, Type II frame

(A) Green-painted green body, green-painted gray doors. 8 10 15 20

(B) Same as (A), but green-painted jade doors. 8 10 15 20

(C) Same as (A), but green-painted lime green doors. 8 10 15 20

(D) Slightly darker green-painted green body, green-painted gray doors.

| | 8 | 10 | 15 | 20 |

(E) Lightest green-painted white body, green-painted white doors.

| | 8 | 10 | 15 | 20 |

(F) Same as (A), but green-painted green doors. 8 10 15 20

9750 D T & I: 1975-76, Type IX body, yellow lettering, Symington-Wayne trucks, Type II frame, glossy green body except (E).

(A) Medium green-painted dark green body, medium green-painted dark green doors. 5 6 10 12

(B) Same as (A), but medium green-painted clear doors. 5 6 10 12

(C) Medium green-painted light green body, medium green-painted dark green doors. 5 6 10 12

(D) Medium green-painted white body, medium green-painted dark green doors.

| | 5 | 6 | 10 | 12 |

(E) Flat green-painted light green body, flat green-painted light green doors.

| | 5 | 6 | 10 | 12 |

(F) Light green-painted white body, medium green-painted dark green doors.

| | 5 | 6 | 10 | 12 |

(G) Same as (A), but large yellow square "RIDIN' THE RAILS" logo with picture of Johnny Cash to left of doors. The authenticity of this car has been questioned. F. Cordone Collection. **NRS**

9751 FRISCO: 1975-76, Type IX body, white lettering, Symington-Wayne trucks, Type II frame, red-painted red doors.

(A) Flat red-painted red body. 8 10 15 20

(B) Shiny red-painted red body. 8 10 15 20

9752 LOUISVILLE & NASHVILLE: 1975-76, Type IX body, yellow lettering, Symington-Wayne trucks, Type II frame.

(A) Light blue-painted royal blue body, medium blue-painted royal blue doors.

| | 8 | 10 | 15 | 20 |

(B) Medium blue-painted navy blue body, same doors as (A). 8 10 15 20

(C) Light blue-painted royal blue body, medium blue-painted white doors.

| | 8 | 10 | 15 | 20 |

(D) Medium blue-painted navy blue body, same doors as (C). 8 10 15 20

9753 MAINE CENTRAL: 1975-76, Type IX body, green lettering, Symington-Wayne trucks, Type II frame.

(A) Medium yellow-painted yellow body, dark yellow-painted yellow doors.

| | 8 | 10 | 15 | 20 |

(B) Light yellow-painted yellow body, light yellow-painted white doors.

| | 8 | 10 | 15 | 20 |

(C) Medium yellow-painted yellow body, same doors as (B). 8 10 15 20

(D) Darker yellow-painted yellow body, medium yellow-painted white doors.

| | 8 | 10 | 15 | 20 |

(E) Light yellow-painted white body, same doors as (D). 8 10 15 20

See also Special Production chapter.

9754 NEW YORK CENTRAL: 1976-77, "Pacemaker FREIGHT SERVICE", Type IX body, white lettering, Symington-Wayne trucks, Type II frame, red-painted red doors. Essentially similar to postwar 6464-125. C. Lang comment.

(A) Light flat red-painted red body. 10 15 20 30

(B) Medium red-painted red body. 10 15 20 30

(C) Dark red-painted red body. 10 15 20 30

(D) Same as (B), but Type III frame. R. LaVoie Collection. 10 15 20 30

(E) Same as (C), but Type III frame. C. Rohlfing Collection.

| | 10 | 15 | 20 | 30 |

See also Special Production chapter.

9755 UNION PACIFIC: 1975-76, Type IX body, white lettering, Symington-Wayne trucks, Type II frame.

(A) Tuscan-painted brown body, tuscan-painted brown doors.

| | 10 | 15 | 20 | 30 |

(B) Tuscan-painted white body, tuscan-painted white doors.

| | 10 | 15 | 20 | 30 |

(C) Tuscan-painted brown body, tuscan-painted white doors.

| | 10 | 15 | 20 | 30 |

9757 CENTRAL OF GEORGIA: 1974, Type IX body, red lettering, Symington-Wayne trucks, Type II frame, tuscan car with large silver oval on side. Uncatalogued; came as part of dealers' year-end special package. See introduction for details.

(A) Tuscan-painted brown body, silver-painted gray doors, lightly speckled oval.

| | 10 | 15 | 20 | 30 |

(B) Same as (A), but medium speckled oval. 10 15 20 30

(C) Same as (A), but shiny silver oval. 10 15 20 30

(D) Same as (A), but silver-painted clear doors, shiny silver oval.

| | 10 | 15 | 20 | 30 |

(E) Same as (A), but silver-painted yellow doors, shiny silver oval.

| | 10 | 15 | 20 | 30 |

(F) Tuscan-painted clear body, silver-painted yellow doors, shiny silver oval.

| | 10 | 15 | 20 | 30 |

See also Factory Errors and Prototypes.

9758 ALASKA: 1976-77, Type IX body, lettering usually yellow, Symington-Wayne trucks, Type II frame, blue car with yellow stripe. Reader comments requested on possibility of chemical alteration on versions with white lettering.

(A) Blue-painted dark blue body, blue-painted white doors.

| | 10 | 12 | 20 | 30 |

(B) Same as (A), but blue-painted blue doors. 12 10 20 30

More 9700s, including some specials. Top shelf: 9774 T C A "Southern Belle" made for 1975 T C A Convention, 9775 Minneapolis & St. Louis from Northern Pacific Service Station Set of 1976. Middle shelf: 9777 Virginian and the scarce 9778 Season's Greetings car of 1975. Bottom shelf: 9779 T C A Bicentennial Convention Car of 1976. "Philadelphia" on all the cars is missing the second "L". Also: 9780 Johnny Cash from dealer year-end special. The 9776 Southern Pacific "Overnight" car from the 1976 Northern Pacific Service Station Set is missing from this series of photos. A. Rudman, L. Caponi, F. Stem, and R. LaVoie Collections.

(C) Blue-painted medium blue body, blue-painted white doors.

| | | 10 | 12 | 20 | 30 |

(D) Blue-painted white body, blue-painted white doors. 10 12 20 30

(E) Same as (D), but white lettering, yellow stripe above lettering and logo. R. M. Caplan Collection. -- -- 325 350

(F) Blue-painted blue body, blue-painted blue doors, white lettering. -- -- -- 325

See also Factory Errors and Prototypes.

9759 PAUL REVERE: 1975-76, Type IX body, white sides, red-painted white plastic roof and ends, blue- or dark blue-painted white plastic door, blue lettering, Symington-Wayne trucks, Type II frame. This and the next two entries were part of the Liberty Special uncatalogued set made in 1975-76. C. Rohlfing and C. Lang comments. 10 12 15 25

9760 LIBERTY BELL: 1975-76, white Type IX body, dark blue-painted white roof and ends, red-painted red plastic door; blue lettering, Symington-Wayne trucks, Type II frame. C. Rohlfing comment. 10 12 15 25

9761 GEORGE WASHINGTON: 1975-76, white Type IX body, red-painted white roof and ends, dark blue-painted white plastic door; blue lettering, Symington-Wayne trucks, Type II frame. C. Rohlfing comment. 10 12 15 25

(9762) TOY FAIR: 1975. See Special Production chapter. Number does not appear on car.

9763 RIO GRANDE: 1976, stock car, orange-painted orange plastic body, black-painted black plastic door; black lettering, Symington-Wayne trucks, Type I frame, metal door guides.

(A) Bright orange paint. 10 15 20 25

(B) Dull orange paint. 10 15 20 25

9764 GRAND TRUNK WESTERN: 1976-77, double-door boxcar, blue-painted blue plastic body, blue-painted dark blue door; white lettering, Symington-Wayne trucks, Type II or III frame, all rivet detail missing.

10 15 20 25

9765: Not used

9766: Not used

9767 RAILBOX: 1976-77, Type IX body, yellow-painted yellow plastic body, black-painted black plastic door; black lettering, Symington-Wayne trucks.

(A) Light yellow paint, Type III frame. 10 15 20 25

(B) Medium yellow paint, Type II frame. 10 15 20 25

(C) Dark yellow paint, Type II frame. 10 15 20 25

9768 BOSTON AND MAINE: 1976-77, Type IX body, black and white lettering, Symington-Wayne trucks, black-painted black doors.

(A) Glossy blue-painted gray body, Type II frame. 8 10 15 20

(B) Flat blue-painted gray body, Type III frame. 8 10 15 20

(C) Same as (B), but Type III frame. R. LaVoie Collection. 8 10 15 20

9769 B. & L. E.: 1976-77, Type IX body, black and white lettering, Symington-Wayne trucks.

(A) Flat orange-painted orange body, orange-painted white doors, Type II frame. 8 10 15 20

(B) Shiny orange-painted orange body, orange-painted orange doors, Type III frame. 8 10 15 20

(C) Shiny orange-painted orange body, orange-painted white doors, Type III frame. 8 10 15 20

(D) Same as (C), but Type II frame. 8 10 15 20

9770 NORTHERN PACIFIC: 1976-77, Type IX body, orange-painted orange doors; white and black lettering, Symington-Wayne trucks.

(A) Glossy orange-painted orange body, Type II frame. 8 10 12 15

Some late 9700-series boxcars. Top shelf: 9781 Delaware & Hudson, 9782 Rock Island "The Rock". Middle shelf: 9783 Baltimore & Ohio "Time-Saver Service", 9784 Santa Fe. Bottom shelf: 9785 Conrail (dark blue; a lighter blue is very scarce), 9786 Chicago & North Western. A. Rudman, L. Caponi, F. Stem, and R. LaVoie Collections.

(B) Flat orange-painted orange body, Type III frame.   8   10   12   15

(C) Flat orange-painted opaque-white body, Type III frame.   8   10   12   15

9771 NORFOLK AND WESTERN: 1976-77, Type IX body, white lettering, Symington-Wayne trucks. This car was included as part of 1762 Wabash Cannonball Steam Engine Freight Set in 1977 as well as a separate sale item. C. Lang comment.

(A) Dark blue-painted blue body, dark blue-painted blue doors, Type III frame.   4   6   10   15

(B) Same as (A), but dark blue-painted gray body.   4   6   10   15

(C) Same as (A), but dark blue-painted white doors, Type II frame.   4   6   10   15

See also Special Production chapter.

9772 GREAT NORTHERN: 1975, Type IX body, green- and orange-painted green body, green- and orange-painted green door; yellow and black lettering, Symington-Wayne trucks, Type III frame; part of 1665 Empire State Express Set.   20   30   50   70

See also Factory Errors and Prototypes.

9773 N Y C: 1976, double-door stock car, black-painted black doors, black lettering, Symington-Wayne trucks, Type I frame; part of 1665 Empire State Express Set. C. Lang comment.

(A) Light yellow-painted yellow body.   12   15   25   35

(B) Dark yellow-painted yellow body.   12   15   25   35

9774 THE SOUTHERN BELLE: 1975, see Special Production chapter.

9775 MINNEAPOLIS & ST. LOUIS: 1975, Type IX body, uncatalogued, red-painted red doors; white lettering, Type II frame, Standard O trucks; from Service Station set.

(A) Light red-painted red body.   12   15   20   30

(B) Dark red-painted red body.   12   15   20   30

9776 SOUTHERN PACIFIC: 1976, uncatalogued, Type IX body, black-painted body, black-painted black doors; white and gold lettering, Standard O trucks, Type II frame, from Northern Pacific Service Station Set of 1976. C. Lang comment.

(A) Black-painted black body.   15   20   30   40

(B) Black-painted opaque white body.   NRS

See also Factory Errors and Prototypes.

9777 VIRGINIAN: 1976-77, Type IX body, yellow lettering, Symington-Wayne trucks.

(A) Blue-painted light blue body, dark blue-painted dark blue doors, Type II frame.   8   10   15   20

(B) Blue-painted light blue body, light blue-painted light blue doors, Type III frame.   8   10   15   20

(C) Blue-painted medium blue body, light blue-painted light blue doors, Type III frame.   8   10   15   20

(D) Blue-painted light blue body, blue-painted white doors, Type II frame.   8   10   15   20

9778 SEASONS GREETINGS 1975: Uncatalogued, Type IX body, blue-painted blue body, silver-painted gray doors; silver lettering, Symington-Wayne trucks, Type II frame.   --   100   150   200

9779 T C A: See Special Production chapter.

9780 JOHNNY CASH: Uncatalogued, Type IX body, black roof, silver sides painted on gray body, black-painted black doors; black lettering, Symington-Wayne trucks, Type III frame.   --   25   30   40

9781 DELAWARE & HUDSON: 1977-78, Type IX body, yellow-painted yellow door, Symington-Wayne trucks, Type III frame.

(A) Light yellow-painted yellow body, blue lettering.   6   8   15   20

(B) Medium yellow-painted yellow body, dark blue lettering.   6   8   15   20

9782 THE ROCK: 1977-78, Type IX body, white and black lettering, Symington-Wayne trucks, Type III frame.

(A) Blue-painted gray body, blue-painted gray doors.   10   15   20   25

(B) Blue-painted light blue body, blue-painted blue doors.   10   15   20   25

9783 BALTIMORE & OHIO: 1977-78, Type IX body, blue sides and ends, silver roof painted on blue body, blue-painted blue doors; white and blue letter-

The last of the 9700-series boxcars. Top shelf: 9787 Jersey Central, 9788 Lehigh Valley. Bottom shelf: 9789 Pickens, available only in the Rocky Mountain Special Set of 1978. A. Rudman, L. Caponi, F. Stem, and R. LaVoie Collections.

ing, Symington-Wayne trucks, Type III frame, "Time Saver Service". Similar to postwar 6464-400. C. Lang comment.
6 12 20 25

9784 A T S F: 1977-78, Type IX body, red-painted red body and red doors; white lettering, flat black-painted roof and ends, Symington-Wayne trucks, Type III frame. **10 15 20 25**
See also Factory Errors and Prototypes.

9785 CONRAIL: 1977-79, Type IX body, white lettering, Symington-Wayne trucks, Type III frame.
(A) Medium blue-painted blue body and doors. **10 15 20 25**
(B) Light blue-painted blue body and doors. This was not a normal paint variation, but an attempt by Fundimensions to correct the car's color. The sample paint chip sent by Conrail to Fundimensions was too dark to match the Conrail prototypes. This variety is much more scarce than the medium blue version. R. LaVoie comment. **-- -- 40 50**
See also Special Production chapter.

9786 CHICAGO AND NORTH WESTERN: 1977-79, Type IX body, tuscan-painted tuscan doors; white lettering, Symington-Wayne trucks, Type III frame, tuscan-painted gray body. **10 12 15 20**
See also Special Production chapter.

9787 CENTRAL OF NEW JERSEY: 1977-79, Type IX body, Brunswick green-painted green body and doors; metallic gold lettering, Symington-Wayne trucks, Type III frame. Recently issued 7404 is similar except for cream lettering and logo replacing the gold stamping on this version. **10 12 15 25**

9788 LEHIGH VALLEY: 1977-79, Type IX body, cream-painted cream body and doors; black lettering, Symington-Wayne trucks, Type III frame.
(A) Decal flag on door. **10 12 15 20**
(B) No decal flag on door. **10 12 15 20**

9789 PICKENS: 1977, Type IX body, blue-painted blue body and doors; white lettering, circular red, white, and blue arrow logo, Symington-Wayne trucks, Type III frame, from Rocky Mountain Special Set of 1977. **10 15 25 35**

9801 BALTIMORE & OHIO: 1975, Standard O boxcar, gray mold, silver body.
(A) Light blue stripe. **15 20 30 40**
(B) Dark blue stripe. **15 20 30 40**
See also Factory Errors and Prototypes.

9803 JOHNSON'S WAX: 1975, Standard O boxcar, red mold, black and white lettering.
(A) Painted red, white, and dark blue. **10 12 20 30**
(B) Painted red, white, and light blue. **10 12 20 30**

9806 ROCK ISLAND: 1975, Standard O boxcar, red mold, tuscan paint; white lettering. **30 40 60 80**

9808 UNION PACIFIC: 1975-76, Standard O boxcar.
(A) White mold painted dark yellow, yellow door mold painted light yellow.
60 70 80 100
(B) Light yellow mold painted dark yellow, yellow door mold painted light yellow. **60 70 80 100**

9826 P & L E: 1976-77, Standard O boxcar, white lettering.
(A) Flat green, first run, 500 manufactured. **40 60 80 125**
(B) Shiny green. **20 30 40 60**

16200 ROCK ISLAND: 1987, short boxcar, red body, white lettering and logo, arch bar trucks, part of Rail Blazer Set 11701. **-- -- -- 10**

16201 WABASH: 1988, short boxcar, dark blue body, white lettering and numbers, white Wabash flag emblem, Symington-Wayne trucks, operating couplers. Part of 11703 Iron Horse Freight Set. **-- -- -- 10**

16603 DETROIT ZOO: 1987, operating giraffe car, tuscan-painted short stock car body, white lettering and Lionel Lion logo, Symington-Wayne trucks, one operating and one dummy coupler, includes cam, track plate, pole, and telltale fringes. **-- -- -- 25**

16605 BRONX ZOO: 1988, operating giraffe car, blue short stock car body, white lettering and number, yellow giraffe with brown spots, Symington-Wayne trucks, operating couplers. Nearly a direct remake of the postwar 3376-3386 models. Includes telltale, track clip, and cam plate. **-- -- -- 28**

16701 SOUTHERN: 1987, tool car, green sides, black roof and ends, gold Southern lettering and circular logo, Standard O trucks, unlighted, but has translucent window inserts, part of Southern Freight Runner Service Station Special Set 11704. **-- -- -- 45**

16801 LIONEL RAILROADER CLUB: 1988, bunk car, see Special Production chapter.

17870: See Special Production chapter.

17201 CONRAIL: 1987, Standard O boxcar, tuscan body, white lettering and Conrail "wheel" logo, black catwalk, Standard O trucks, part of Conrail Limited Set 11700. **-- -- -- 40**

19200 TIDEWATER SOUTHERN: 1987, boxcar. This boxcar marks the beginning of the fourth major boxcar series of the modern era as a successor to the 9200, 9700, and 9400 Series. Tuscan body, yellow lettering, yellow-orange feather logo, Symington-Wayne trucks. **-- -- -- 15**

19201 LANCASTER & CHESTER: 1987, boxcar, blue lower sides and ends, light gray upper sides and roof, contrasting blue and white lettering and logo, Symington-Wayne trucks. **-- -- -- 15**

19202 PENNSYLVANIA: 1987, boxcar, flat dark Brunswick green body, white lettering, white and red banner, logo, and PRR Keystone, Symington-Wayne trucks. **-- -- -- 25**

Boxcars and reefers, a good mix. Top shelf: The first two of the new 19200-series boxcars, the 19200 Tidewater Southern and the 19201 Lancaster & Chester. Second shelf: The next two 19200s, the 19202 Pennsylvania (in considerable demand) and the 19203 Detroit & Toledo. Third shelf: The very nicely styled 19802 Carnation Operating Milk Car and the 19803 Reading Icing Station Car meant to accompany the Icing Station accessories. Bottom shelf: The spiffy 19805 Santa Fe Operating Boxcar and the 19504 Northern Pacific Wood-sided Reefer (nice colors, but beware of peeling red Monad decals). A. Rudman, L. Caponi, F. Stem, and R. LaVoie Collections.

19203 DETROIT & TOLEDO SHORELINE: 1987, boxcar, yellow body, red lettering and square logo, Symington-Wayne trucks. Same design as LCCA special boxcar of 1986 except for new colors. -- -- -- **15**

19204 MILWAUKEE ROAD: 1987, boxcar, brown body, broad yellow stripe runs length of car through doors, contrasting yellow and brown lettering, red and white rectangular Milwaukee logo, Standard O trucks, part of Milwaukee Fallen Flags Set No. 2. -- -- -- **25**

19205 GREAT NORTHERN: 1988, double-door boxcar, dark green roof and ends, orange sides and doors, dark green lettering, red and white circular "goat" logo, Standard O trucks. Part of Fallen Flags Set No. 3. -- -- -- **25**

19206 SEABOARD: 1988, boxcar, black body and doors, gold lettering, gold and red double-"S" logo, Symington-Wayne trucks. -- -- -- **20**

19207 C P RAIL: 1988, double-door boxcar, bright burnt orange body and doors, black lettering, black and white circle-triangle logo at right end of side, Symington-Wayne trucks. Because of its bright colors, this boxcar is expected to be in more demand than the other 1988 boxcars. -- -- -- **20**

19208 SOUTHERN: 1988, double-door boxcar, tuscan body and doors, white lettering and DF logo, Symington-Wayne trucks. -- -- -- **17**

19209 FLORIDA EAST COAST: 1988, boxcar, dark blue body and doors, yellow lettering and "Speedway" logo, Symington-Wayne trucks. -- -- -- **17**

19651 A. T. & S. F.: 1987, tool car, medium gray body, black lettering, translucent window and door inserts, arch bar trucks, illuminated. -- -- -- **25**

19652 JERSEY CENTRAL: 1988, bunk car, dark brown body; white lettering, number, and Jersey Central logo; Symington-Wayne trucks, operating couplers, illuminated. -- -- -- **27**

19653 JERSEY CENTRAL: 1988, tool car, dark brown body, white lettering, number, and Jersey Central logo, Symington-Wayne trucks, operating couplers, illuminated. -- -- -- **27**

19800 CIRCLE L RANCH: 1988, operating cattle car, tan slatted sides, light gray roof and ends, postwar-style bar-end trucks (necessary because sliding shoe is needed to operate car), comes with medium orange and white cattle corral, and eight brown cattle; postwar rubber fingers removed from cattle undersides and replaced with felt (an old American Flyer trick) for better operation. When button is pressed, ramps on car drop and cattle move by vibration out of car, around the corral, and back into car. Essentially similar to postwar 3356 model. Expected to be in great demand. M. Sabatelle and R. LaVoie comments. -- -- -- **100**

19801 POULTRY DISPATCH CAR: 1987, non-operating reissue of 6434 of postwar years. Flat red stock car body, red door, black lettering, two lights inside show celluloid strips of chickens on way to market, Symington-Wayne trucks. For operating version, see entry 9221. -- -- -- **25**

Top shelf: 9228 Canadian Pacific, 9486 I Love Michigan. Bottom shelf: 9491 Lionel's Christmas Car, 9492 Lionel Lines.

19805 SANTA FE: 1987, operating boxcar, red body, white Santa Fe lettering, red and white Santa Fe cross logo, gray man, Standard O trucks.

-- -- -- **32**

19809 ERIE-LACKAWANNA: 1988, operating boxcar, red-brown painted body; white lettering, number, and EL logo, gray unpainted man tosses mail sack out of door, Standard O trucks, operating couplers.   -- -- -- **35**

19900 TOY FAIR: 1987, see Special Production chapter.

19901 I LOVE VIRGINIA: 1987, boxcar, yellow sides, blue roof and ends, pink and blue lettering, Symington-Wayne trucks.   -- -- -- **20**

19902 TOY FAIR: 1988, see Special Production chapter.

19903 LIONEL: 1987, Christmas Car, white sides, green roof and ends, red doors; red, white, blue, and black Lionel logo; red and green lettering features "Merry Christmas" in five languages, Symington-Wayne trucks. Part of special year-end package for 1987, "Happy Lionel Holidays".   -- -- -- **30**

19904 LIONEL: 1988, Christmas car, white sides, red roof, doors, and ends, "Merry Christmas 1988", Symington-Wayne trucks.   -- -- -- **35**

19905 I LOVE CALIFORNIA: 1988, boxcar, medium blue sides, gold-painted roof and ends, yellow lettering and number, red heart logo, Symington-Wayne trucks, operating couplers.   -- -- -- **20**

NO NUMBER: 9040-type short boxcar, dark green body, luminous decals to be affixed by purchaser, "Acme Explosives Company", ignited round bomb and "Acme TNT Company". Came with 1984 Black Cave Flyer Set.   -- -- -- **5**

Chapter V
CABOOSES

It is ironic that Fundimensions is producing the best cabooses ever seen in tinplate just as these cars are being phased out on real railroads across the nation. The caboose is a car steeped in nostalgia. Who of us has not seen a picture of a train crew enjoying breakfast cooked over a coal stove in one of these waycars? For most of us, a freight train without a caboose is unthinkable. However, the caboose complicates switching assignments, and its need has been considerably lessened by detachable signal devices for the last car on the train and the commodious, air-conditioned cabs of the modern diesel locomotives. Real railroaders do not feel quite as romantically attached to the caboose; veterans of the rails would be quick to tell you that these cars were not all cozy little houses on rails. Unless the caboose was quite modern, it was drafty in winter despite the heat of the coal stove and, in summer, somewhere west of the Eternal Inferno. Thus, cabooses are becoming highly specialized or nonexistent in today's railroading.

This is not to deny that real railroading lacks the color and romance we ascribe to it — far from it. As an example of the unexpected influence of railroading in our lives, consider the streetcars of Brooklyn in the 1890s. The motormen who ran these cars had no idea of the potential power of electric traction since they had learned their trade with horse-drawn cars. As a result, they were extremely reckless drivers who endangered pedestrians every day.

The local baseball team's players had to cross the streetcar tracks to get to their ball field, and several team members had close shaves with these trolleys. As a result, their team eventually became known as the Brooklyn Dodgers! The name remains today, long after the cars have gone. (This and other transportation stories of interest can be found in George Gipe's *The Last Time When:* New York, World Almanac Publications, 1981.)

Tinplate railroading, however, demands cabooses for its trains, romantic or not, and in the modern era Lionel has responded with a fine variety of these cars. Some are modeled after their prewar predecessors, like the N5C porthole caboose, while others, such as the magnificent extended vision cabooses, are unique to the new breed of Lionel's trainmakers.

THE SOUTHERN PACIFIC
SQUARE-CUPOLA CABOOSES

The square-cupola Southern Pacific caboose has been produced from the first year of 1970; this is fitting, since this caboose was the mainstay of postwar production. The Fundimensions version of the SP caboose has a new plastic undercarriage which snaps onto the cab. Two separate molds have been used for these cabooses. The earliest versions feature tall cupola windows, while a later version has much shorter windows. Both molds have been used to the present day.

Most of the SP cabooses have been used for inexpensive sets and have been unlighted, but a few of these, such as the 9166

Rio Grande and the 9178 Illinois Central Gulf, are lighted and have translucent white plastic window inserts. These "deluxe" SP cabooses are mostly to be found in early collector sets from the mid-1970s. Some, like the 9172 Penn Central and the 9173 Jersey Central, were offered for separate sale. Recent production of these cabooses in traditional sets has featured "glow-in-the-dark" window inserts.

The most desirable of the SP cabooses are the ones from the sets, but no SP caboose produced by Fundimensions or its successors can be considered truly rare. Some of the earliest unlighted SP cabooses marketed for Canadian production are in fact very difficult to find, but collectors have not shown too much interest in them — yet.

THE N5C PORTHOLE CABOOSES

The N5C porthole caboose has been one of the mainstays of Lionel's modern era production, along with the bay window caboose. In real life, this caboose type was used only by the Pennsylvania Railroad, but that has not stopped Lionel from issuing this caboose in dozens of railroad names and colors. Since all these cabooses are lighted and the design is very attractive, it is no wonder that they are so plentiful. Production of the N5C has languished in recent years in favor of the bay window cabooses and the new extended vision cabooses, but in 1985 a new Pennsylvania porthole caboose was issued with the set of cars intended for the new 6-8-6 steam turbine locomotive, and for 1987 another one in a bronze paint scheme was issued to accompany a new bronze-finished GG-1. These particular examples are unique to the N5C line because they used O27 die-cast passenger trucks and, in the case of the bronze model, brand-new die-cast arch bar trucks instead of the usual Symington-Wayne plastic trucks. (Of course, the caboose would look better with Standard O trucks, but these trucks cannot be adapted for a light roller pickup.)

The first of the N5C cabooses was the 9160 Illinois Central of 1970. Early production used AAR trucks with old postwar wheel sets, but these quickly changed to Symington-Wayne trucks and fast-angle wheels. Canadian National, Pennsylvania, and Santa Fe models were quick to follow, and in subsequent years these cabooses were produced in a considerable variety of road names. Special issues accompanied the Bicentennial, 75th Anniversary, and Disney Sets, while others were made to match the available diesel locomotives in the new Lionel line.

In all, about 25 of these cabooses have been produced in one guise or another. Their availability is highly variable today. Even some of the regular issues have become hard to find, and the cabooses from the sets only turn up occasionally. The most difficult to find seems to be the red 9165 Canadian Pacific, which was only found in a Service Station Set. Many others, such as the 9161 CP Rail, are quite common. These little high-quality cabooses are bright additions to the beginning

Top shelf: 6401 Virginian, 6421 Joshua Lionel Cowen. Second shelf: 6422 Duluth Missabe, 6425 Erie Lackawanna. Third shelf: 6431 Southern, 6433 Canadian Pacific. Bottom shelf: 6438 Great Northern, 6441 Alaska Railroad.

collector's rolling stock. In recent years, they have fallen under the shadow of the bay window and extended vision cabooses, so they are usually available at good prices.

THE BAY WINDOW CABOOSES

Lionel's postwar model of the bay window caboose was issued in only two regular production varieties, Lionel Lines and Erie, but when Fundimensions revived this handsome car, the firm produced a considerable number and variety of them. The first Fundimensions bay window caboose came as part of the Empire State Express Set of 1976 in green New York Central markings. The original intent of Fundimensions was to limit this caboose to special sets, but the demand for the caboose became so acute that it soon entered regular cataloguing and production.

Two examples of the bay window cabooses illustrate collector insistence upon matching locomotives and cabooses, no matter what the practice on the prototype railroad. In 1976 Fundimensions issued the Northern Pacific Service Station

Special Set with a black and gold Northern Pacific GP-9 locomotive and a green, silver, and yellow Northern Pacific bay window caboose, true to the prototype. Collectors did not like the fact that the caboose was not a color match for the locomotive, so the company issued a black and gold Northern Pacific bay window caboose which did match the GP-9. Where the New York Central caboose had Symington-Wayne plastic trucks with long coupler extensions, both Northern Pacific cabooses had die-cast O27 passenger trucks. Since then, the bay window cabooses have come with both types of trucks.

Two years later, in 1978, history repeated itself. Fundimensions produced a magnificent Santa Fe SD-18 six-wheeled locomotive in blue and yellow freight colors. The bay window caboose meant to accompany this locomotive was made in red and black colors, just as the real railroad issued them. Once more, collectors howled that the caboose did not match the engines, so Fundimensions ceased making the 9274 red and black model in favor of a 9317 Santa Fe bay window Caboose in blue and yellow colors. This means, of course, that the red and black

Top shelf: 9174 New York Central, 9177 Northern Pacific. Second shelf: 9184 Erie, 9188 Great Northern. Third shelf: 9231 Reading, 9259 L. C. C. A. Bottom shelf: 9268 Northern Pacific, 9269 Milwaukee Road.

caboose has become a real collector's item; reportedly, fewer than 3,000 were made.

It was not long before the bay window caboose became the dominant caboose of the Fundimensions lineup. Beginning in the late 1970s and through the early 1980s, several new issues turned up in every catalogue and other new ones were used in limited edition sets. About 35 of these cabooses have been produced since their introduction in 1976 — an average of almost four new ones per year! In recent years, these cabooses have been sidetracked in favor of the new extended vision and wood-sided cabooses.

The reasons for the popularity of the bay window caboose are not hard to understand. The construction of this caboose is excellent. It retains the stamped-metal frame of the postwar cabooses, and its metal ladder trim adds an authentic touch. The lighting system is a little curious, but it is effective. Clear plastic rods reach from the light bulb to the little red marker lights on the rear of the caboose, providing a fiber-optic pathway for the illumination. Earlier versions used the postwar spring clip and a 57 bayonet-base bulb, whether the trucks were

plastic or die-cast. This practice continued until the 1978 Minneapolis and St. Louis model. The windows in the central bay are shaded by black paper so that the clear plastic windows on the caboose sides receive most of the light. The light bulb on 1978 and later versions of this caboose, and many other pieces of modern era Lionel rolling stock and locomotives, is a 12-volt plug-in clear lamp used in quite a few automotive applications. (Lamps designed for Chrysler Corporation side marker, instrument panel, and turn signal lights are exact duplicates of these light bulbs.) All versions of these cabooses have two operating couplers, whether the trucks are plastic or die-cast. The coupler shanks used for the plastic trucks tend to be somewhat fragile.

THE FUNDIMENSIONS EXTENDED VISION CABOOSES

In 1982 Fundimensions issued a fine collector train set in Norfolk and Western markings known as the Continental Limited. The handsome maroon SD-24 six-wheeled locomotive had an electronic horn, and the rolling stock was all of very high

Top shelf: 9271 Minneapolis & St. Louis, 9272 New Haven. Second shelf: 9273 Southern, 9274 Santa Fe. Third shelf: 9309 T P & W, 9316 Southern Pacific. Bottom shelf: 9317 A. T. S. F., 9323 A. T. S. F.

quality. However, the real surprise was reserved for the caboose, which was unlike anything ever seen in tinplate. The extended vision caboose is a large, scale-length square-cupola caboose which on the real railroad illustrates the state of the art in caboose construction. Many collectors regard this caboose as the finest tinplate caboose ever produced. The extended vision cabooses produced to date have all been limited edition items.

The Lionel extended vision caboose has a stamped metal frame with a black plastic battery box and brake cylinder piece attaching to the frame by means of a black plastic channel. All of these cabooses are equipped with O27 passenger-style diecast trucks with two operating couplers. The sides, ends, and roof are molded in one piece with a large hole in the roof. A separately molded cupola piece is snapped onto the roof atop this hole; it is secured by projections in the body shell on the sides. Sometimes this separate cupola piece can lead to problems. On the 6905 Nickel Plate Road Caboose, the lettering "Nickel Plate High Speed Service" goes across the top of the

sides in such a way that one of the words is on the cupola. If the cupola is snapped onto the body in reverse, the sides will read "Nickel Speed High Speed Service" and "Nickel Plate High Plate Service". This is not a factory error — just an incorrectly installed cupola.

The sides of the extended vision cabooses are absolutely smooth except for molded grab-rails near the platform, two large square windows per side, and molded signal lamps at both ends. Inside the car, four clear plastic rods lead to the signal lamps for brighter illumination, and all the windows on the sides and on the cupola are lighted as well. Plastic snap-in end railing pieces and a tall plastic chimney complete the decor of the caboose — or do they? Some of these cabooses have been produced with slots cut into the ends of the roofs so that metal trim ladders can be attached as they are on the bay window cabooses. However, the extended vision cabooses have no roof catwalks! The 6900 Norfolk and Western and the 6901 Ontario Northland Cabooses do not have these ladders, but the 6903 Santa Fe does. In some cases the caboose is pictured in the

113

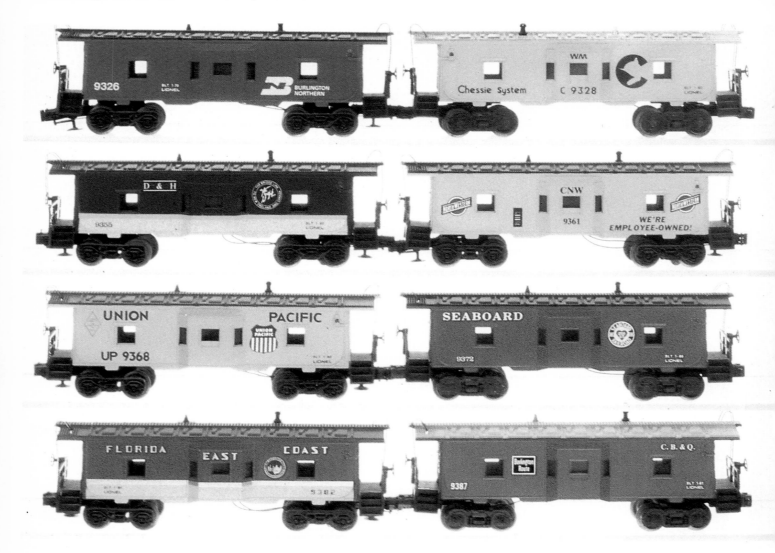

Top shelf: 9326 Burlington Northern, 9328 Chessie. Second shelf: 9355 D & H, 9361 Chicago & Northwestern. Third shelf: 9368 Union Pacific, 9372 Seaboard. Bottom shelf: 9382 Florida East Coast, 9387 Burlington.

catalogues without the ladders, but the production pieces have them. In other cases the reverse is true. These now-you-see-them, now-you-don't ladders could make for some interesting variations. (We would like to hear from our readers about whether their samples have the ladders or not. It is quite possible that some pieces were made both ways!)

Because of their handsome scale appearance and high demand, most of the extended vision cabooses command substantial price premiums. The one exception seems to be the 6901 Ontario Northland Caboose, which has not been in much demand. The 6910 New York Central Pacemaker Extended Vision Caboose might become the most scarce of these cabooses because of extreme demand from scale Hudson, New York Central F-3, and New York Central GP-9 owners. The 6903 Santa Fe is also appreciating very rapidly.

These cabooses are also magnificent matches for the new SD-40 scale diesels. Besides the Norfolk and Western, Ontario Northland, Nickel Plate, Santa Fe, and New York Central examples, extended vision cabooses in Union Pacific, Erie-Lack-awanna, and Burlington Northern colors have been made. A special "Miss Liberty" commemorative extended vision caboose was made in 1986 in Jersey Central colors.

THE WOOD-SIDED SCALE CABOOSES

All the way back in the late 1930s, Lionel introduced a beautifully-executed scale model wood-sided caboose to accompany its fine scale switchers of the period. Collectors have always regarded this caboose with awe and respect, for it is a fine scale model. They paid large sums of money for any surviving cabooses of this type because they did not have a modern version available to them — until late 1986. In that year, Lionel introduced two new reproductions of this fine wood-sided caboose as part of an extremely limited direct-mail offer. One was an extremely handsome New York Central model slightly dressed up over its antique predecessor. This caboose had fine dark brown coloring offset by black main and cupola roofs. The other caboose was plain brown, but it had the same lifelike detail and it was a direct match for the 8606 Boston and Albany Hudson with its crisp white B & A markings. To be sure, some

114

Top shelf: 6901 Ontario Northland, 6903 Santa Fe. Bottom shelf: 6905 Nickel Plate Road, 6904 Union Pacific.

of the fine detail work of the prewar version had to be sacrificed because its cost was just too prohibitive, but Lionel made up for that in another way — a new form of die-cast truck.

The new die-cast truck, unlike the excellent Standard O trucks, could be adapted for illumination rollers — and these two cabooses were indeed lighted. The sides and roofs were expertly wood-scribed, the metal ladders were present, and there were the same highly detailed square windows as the prewar piece. Collectors were very happy with this design, but the cabooses were in very short supply.

For the next year, the news was even better for Lionel fans. Another version of the wood-sided caboose, also in New York Central markings, was scheduled to be produced to match the new gun-metal gray New York Central Hudson; this one would have a lighter, plain brown color, and the front marker lights of the first two would be eliminated (making the two rear ones light better).

In addition, the first variation of this caboose has been produced for the Conrail Limited Set for 1987. This is a fine development for the wood-sided caboose; since Lionel uses a "plug-in" design for the cupola, all the firm had to do was to design a new high-window cupola, plug it onto the wood-sided caboose's roof, and — Presto! A new high-cupola wood-sided caboose was born! This one came in bright Conrail blue with white lettering, and it was a scale dead-ringer for the old Canadian National wooden cabooses of the early years of this century. Conrail actually gave some of these ancient cabooses a new paint job and used them in its early years. This one looks magnificent; it has drawn praise from collectors and is in hot demand at the moment. Rock Island and Southern versions of this caboose have since been made, and a Lackawanna version is scheduled for 1988. All these cabooses have been made as matches for Lionel's best locomotives. Expect Lionel to keep going with a winner and produce new models of this fine caboose in the next few years. One could not blame them!

SOME OTHER FUNDIMENSIONS CABOOSES

Besides those mentioned above, there are three other styles of modern era cabooses, two of them particular to the modern era alone. Several work cabooses have been issued for the Lionel traditional series ever since the first years of the company, beginning with the 9021 Santa Fe in 1970. This little caboose featured a "convertible" cab which could be taken off so that the car could be used as a simple flatcar. This example was followed by a similar D. T. & I. model in 1971 and a Soo Line work caboose in 1975. Other work cabooses have been made for the Trains and Trucking and Working on the Railroad Sets of 1977 and 1978, but by and large these cabooses have been supplanted by the newer center-cab maintenance caboose. One example, the 6916 New York Central, was produced in 1985 as part of the Yard Chief Steam Switcher Work Train; this piece was followed by a work caboose for the 1986 Santa Fe Work Train Service Station Special which even had Standard O trucks — perhaps a case of overkill! None of these cabooses attracts much attention, except for a few early varieties of the 9021 Santa Fe and that curio Santa Fe with the Standard O trucks.

The four-wheeled bobber caboose was first made for the Kickapoo Valley and Northern Set of 1972. It is an all-plastic car completely new with Fundimensions production. Although it looks small and it has been used only on lower-priced sets, it is surprisingly faithful to its prototype, some of which can be seen on the Strasburg Railroad in Strasburg, Pennsylvania. Along with the 9090 Mini-Max Boxcar, it is the only four-wheeled car in the modern Lionel repertoire. This caboose has been made in Chessie, Santa Fe, Rock Island, and Reading colors over the years; the Reading in green was even available for separate sale. A version with extra trim pieces was produced as part of a Santa Fe Dockside Switcher Set, the Midland Freight, in 1985. Another one in bright red forms the tail of the 1987 Rail Blazer Set. These whimsical, rather cute

S P Caboose Types

To the best of our knowledge, Fundimensions did not reuse Lionel molds I through IV and began its production with a new model (Type V).

Type V

1. Two rivets on side bottom corners.
2. No window frames on front and back cupola windows.
3. Plain plastic handrail stanchions on cupola roof.
4. Slightly larger doorknobs.
5. Plainer plastic handrail stanchions by front and rear doors.
6. Steps not built into car mold.
7. Horizontal window bars.
8. Missing short vertical row of rivets on body under cupola between cupola windows, no rivets on ledge over side windows.

Type VI

1. Two rivets on side bottom corners.
2. No window frames on front and back cupola windows.
3. Plain plastic handrail stanchions on cupola.
4. Slightly larger doorknobs.
5. Plainer handrail stanchions by front and rear doors.
6. Steps not built into car mold.
7. Horizontal window bars.
8. Missing short vertical row of rivets on body under cupola.
9. Wood-grained catwalk and hatches.

Type VII

1. Two and a half rivets on side bottom corners.
2. No window frames on front and back cupola windows. 3. Plain plastic handrail stanchions on cupola.
4. Small doorknobs. 5. Plainer handrail stanchions by front and rear doors.
6. Steps not built into car mold.
7. Horizontal window bars.
8. Missing short vertical row of rivets on body under cupola.
9. No wood-grained catwalk.

S P End Types

Type I: Smooth walkway surface.
Type II: Rough walkway surface.

N5C Caboose Types

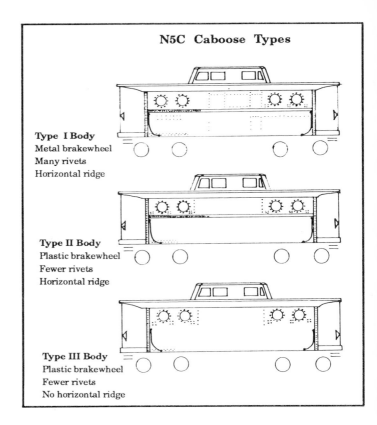

Type I Body
Metal brakewheel
Many rivets
Horizontal ridge

Type II Body
Plastic brakewheel
Fewer rivets
Horizontal ridge

Type III Body
Plastic brakewheel
Fewer rivets
No horizontal ridge

cabooses are good additions to a collection, although as part of the lower-priced lines they do not attract much collector attention.

Finally, in 1981, a new type of caboose emerged with the production of the Reading Yard King Set. This was the maintenance caboose, sometimes called the transfer caboose. Essentially, this caboose consists of a flatcar with pipe-style railings on both sides leading to a small square cab mounted at the center of the flatcar. Another version of the Reading caboose was produced for separate sale, with the green and yellow colors reversed from the one included with the Yard King Set. Several other cabooses of this design have emerged in recent years, among them Chicago and Northwestern, Burlington Northern, Erie-Lackawanna, and New York Central examples. Despite the fact that this caboose design is of relatively recent vintage, it has an old-time look about it which looks very good with a string of wood-sided reefers in a train. The separate-sale Reading and the Burlington Northern are the easiest ones to acquire, but the collector can expect several more examples of this caboose in the Traditional series in years to come.

With its cabooses, modern era Lionel has achieved a nice balance of the old-fashioned railroad and the contemporary scene. The new designs are very praiseworthy, especially the extended vision and wood-sided models, and the older designs have been carried into graphics and railroad lines far beyond anything produced in the postwar years. As with many other modern era Lionel lines of rolling stock, the variety is welcome.

	Gd	VG	Exc	Mt

1776 N & W: 1976, N5C Type II, white sides, red roof, gold lettering; from N & W Spirit of '76 Set.

	Gd	VG	Exc	Mt
(A) Flat red roof.	10	15	20	25
(B) Shiny, darker red roof.	9	12	15	20

6401 VIRGINIAN: 1981, bay window, yellow sides with broad blue stripe through center, including bay; yellow and blue safety striping along lower side, "V G N" logo with yellow letters inside circular blue field surrounded by yellow and blue rings; blue, heat-stamped, sans-serif lettering "BLT 1-81 / LIONEL" in two lines at one end and "6401" at other end, Symington-Wayne trucks with disc couplers. Brewer Collection. Catalogued on page 22 of the small 1981 catalogue. Matches 8950 Virginian Fairbanks-Morse. Also a good match for 8659 Virginian Rectifier Electric and Virginian SD-18 pair, 8071-72.   -- **15   20   25**

6420 READING: 1981-82, transfer caboose, dark yellow shanty on flatcar with dark green base; available only as part of Reading Yard King Freight Set 1154.
-- -- **15   20**

6421 COWEN: 1982, bay window, gold and dark tuscan with picture of Cowen; lettered "JOSHUA LIONEL COWEN" and "BLT 1-81 LIONEL", 027-style die-cast passenger trucks; issued as a limited edition in the "Spring Collector Series" and meant to match the Joshua Lionel Cowen commemorative Hudson and 9400-series commemorative boxcars.   -- -- **25   30**

6422 DULUTH MISSABE: 1981-82, bay window, tuscan body; yellow stripes, white lettering, Symington-Wayne trucks, illuminated. C. Rohlfing comment.
-- -- **20   25**

6425 ERIE-LACKAWANNA: 1983-84, bay window caboose, gray body; maroon striping edged with yellow stripes, yellow lettering, Symington-Wayne trucks. Matches 8369 GP-20 and 8759 GP-9 Diesels. C. Lang and R. LaVoie Collections.   -- -- **20   25**

Left column: 9057 CP Rail, 9058 Lionel Lines, 9060 Nickel Plate. Right column: 9061 Santa Fe, 9062 Penn Central, 9063 Grand Trunk.

6426 READING: 1982, maintenance caboose, yellow flatcar, green cab, yellow diamond; reverse color scheme from Yard King Set caboose, Symington-Wayne trucks. -- -- **10 12**

6427 BURLINGTON NORTHERN: 1984, transfer caboose, green flatcar body and cab, black roof and railings, white and green BN logo and lettering, Symington-Wayne trucks. -- -- **8 10**

6428 CHICAGO & NORTHWESTERN: 1984, maintenance/transfer caboose (both terms are used for this caboose), dark green wood-scribed flatcar body, dark green plastic pipe-style handrails, yellow center cab, white flatcar lettering, black cab lettering. Part of 1314 Northern Freight Flyer Set. C. Lang comment. -- -- **12 15**

6430 SANTA FE: 1983, red and gold, came from 1352 Rocky Mountain Freight Set. C. O'Dell comment. -- -- **6 8**

6431 SOUTHERN: 1983, bay window, dark red sides and roof, white lettering, gold FARR 4 logo on sides, die-cast O27 passenger trucks, illuminated, (shown in catalogue with green sides), part of FARR 4 series and available only as a separate sale item. L. Caponi and C. Rohlfing comments. -- -- **35 45**

6432 UNION PACIFIC: 1981, SP Type, part of 1151 U. P. Thunder Freight. Silver body, black roof, yellow lettering, red, white, and blue shield logo, Symington-Wayne trucks. M. Sabatelle comments. -- -- **10 12**

6433 CANADIAN PACIFIC: 1981, bay window, gray with maroon roof and lettering, O27-style die-cast passenger trucks, illuminated, part of 1158 Maple Leaf Limited Set. -- -- **35 50**

6435: 1983, unlettered, maintenance caboose, olive drab with two railings on one side of shanty and dual gun on other, Symington-Wayne trucks, one fixed coupler;

part of 1355 Commando Assault Set, came without lettering on car, decals furnished with set. -- -- -- **20**

6438 GREAT NORTHERN: 1981, bay window, dark orange and dark green body and ends, dark green roof; dark green stripe along bottom, black lettering, diamond-shaped FARR 3 logo in gold; yellow, black, and white mountain goat logo, illuminated, Symington-Wayne trucks, only sold separately. C. Rohlfing and T. Ladny comments. -- -- **35 45**

6439 READING: 1984-85, bay window caboose, green roof, yellow and green body; yellow lettering, illuminated, Symington-Wayne trucks. -- -- **20 30**

6441 ALASKA: 1982, bay window, dark blue-painted blue body and roof, yellow lettering and logo, Symington-Wayne trucks, illuminated. C. Lang and C. Rohlfing comments. -- -- **25 30**

6449 WENDY'S: 1981-82, N5C, red body, yellow, white and black lettering, yellow roof; part of Favorite Food Series, sold separately only. -- -- **40 45**

6482 NIBCO: 1982, SP Type, part of special promotional Set 1264; see entry 8182 in Diesel chapter for background. Unlighted, but with "glow-in-the-dark" windows. Red unpainted plastic body, black plastic railings; silver and black "NIBCO EXPRESS" script logo between third and fourth side windows, Symington-Wayne trucks. Very hard to find. Raber Collection. -- -- -- **100**

6483 NEW JERSEY CENTRAL: 1982, SP Type, see Special Production chapter.

Left column: 9064 C & O, 9065 Canadian National, 9066 Southern. Right column: 9069 Jersey Central, 9070 Rock Island, 9073 Coke.

6485 CHESSIE SYSTEM: 1984-85, SP Type caboose, yellow plastic body with black trim, blue lettering and logo, one operating coupler, Symington-Wayne trucks; part of Set 1402. -- -- -- 10

6486 SOUTHERN: 1985, green and white. C. O'Dell comment.
-- -- 8 12

6491 ERIE-LACKAWANNA: 1985, maintenance/transfer caboose, black flatcar body and handrail piping, dark red cab, black roof and stack, white lettering and logo, Symington-Wayne trucks. -- -- -- 12

6493 LANCASTER & CHESTER: 1986, bay window, medium blue body, gray-painted roof, white lettering and logo, illuminated, Symington-Wayne trucks. -- -- 20 25

6494 A T S F: 1985, bobber caboose, blue body, silver frame, end rails, and stack, dummy couplers. From 1985 Midland Freight Set. -- -- 8 10

6496 A T S F: 1986, work caboose, black plastic base with white lettering, red cab with yellow cross logo and number, red tool bin, short stack, ladder, Standard O trucks, from 1986 Santa Fe Work Train Service Station Special. J. Kouba Collection. -- -- -- 30

6506 L. A. S. E. R.: 1981-82, security car with gun, black base, chrome-finished cab, blue cab lettering; part of 1150 L. A. S. E. R. Train Set.
-- -- 15 30

6900 N & W: 1982, extended vision caboose, dark red body, black roof; white lettering, no ladders to roof on ends, die-cast O27-style passenger trucks; part of 1260 Continental Limited Set, shown as "7301" in 1982 catalogue illustration.
-- -- 75 95

6901 ONTARIO NORTHLAND: 1982, extended vision caboose, yellow and dark blue body, turquoise cupola roof; die-cast O27-style passenger trucks, dark blue "triple lightning" logo on sides. Separate sale item from 1982 Fall Collector Center. -- -- 30 50

6903 SANTA FE: 1983, extended vision, blue and yellow body, yellow main roof, blue cupola sides and roof, yellow lettering, ladders at ends, black smokestack, O27-style die-cast passenger trucks, illuminated. Separate sale item from 1983 Collector Preview brochure. C. Rohlfing and R. LaVoie Collections.
-- -- 75 95

6904 UNION PACIFIC: 1983, extended vision, yellow body, red and white lettering; red, white, and blue shield logo, red line along roof edge, silver main and cupola roofs, black smokestack, O27-style die-cast passenger trucks; part of 1361 Gold Coast Limited Set and only available as part of the set. C. Rohlfing comments. -- -- 85 100

6905 NICKEL PLATE ROAD: 1983-84, extended vision caboose, dark red body, black roof, white lettering on body side, gray stripe with black "NICKEL PLATE HIGH SPEED SERVICE" lettering, "NICKEL PLATE ROAD" in old fashioned white serif letters, below cupola, number in white below lettering. Some cars came with cupolas installed incorrectly; these are not factory errors in the usual sense, since reversing the cupola produces the correct lettering. O27-style die-cast passenger trucks. Designed to match 8215 Nickel Plate Road 2-8-4 Berkshire Locomotive. Separate sale item from 1983 Fall Collector Center. LaVoie comment. -- -- 50 60

See also Factory Errors and Prototypes.

118

Left column: 9068 Reading, 9071 A. T. & S. F. Right column: 9078 Rock Island, 9179 Chessie.

6906 ERIE-LACKAWANNA: 1984-85, extended vision caboose, gray, maroon, and yellow paint scheme, O27 die-cast passenger trucks; part of Erie-Lackawanna Limited Set. -- -- 65 85

6907 NEW YORK CENTRAL: 1986, scale wood-sided caboose, a new design for Lionel in the modern era and the first production of this caboose since prewar years. Tuscan body, black roof and cupola roof; ladders, tall stack, marker lights at all four corners, white lettering, black and white NYC oval logo, new die-cast arch bar trucks, illuminated. Available only as part of a direct mail-ordering package from Lionel. -- -- -- 175

6908 PENNSYLVANIA: 1984-85, N5C porthole caboose, deep maroon body, black main roof, yellow-painted cupola and cupola roof, white lettering, white and black PRR Keystone, diamond-shaped FARR 5 logo, illuminated, O27-style die-cast passenger trucks (the only N5C to be thus equipped to date).
-- -- 40 65

6910 NEW YORK CENTRAL: 1984-85, extended vision caboose, red upper sides and ends, gray lower sides ("Pacemaker" paint scheme), black roof; "NYC / 6910" in black on the gray area and New York Central oval in white on the red area, ladders to roof, O27-style die-cast passenger trucks. Separate sale item from 1984 Spring Collector Center. This caboose is in great demand because it matches the 8406 Hudson Steam Locomotive and the 8477 New York Central GP-9 — not to mention numerous other New York Central locomotives produced in the past. R. LaVoie comment and Collection. -- -- 85 95

6912 REDWOOD VALLEY EXPRESS: 1983-84, SP Type , tuscan body, yellow lettering and logo, one operating coupler, arch bar trucks, part of Redwood Valley Express Set 1403. -- -- -- 10

6913 BURLINGTON NORTHERN: 1985, extended vision caboose, Cascade green body, yellow ends, gray roof; white BN logo and lettering, O27-style die-cast passenger trucks; from Burlington Northern Limited Collector Set of 1985.
-- -- 45 55

6916 NEW YORK CENTRAL: 1985, work caboose, black flatcar base, gray cab and tool bin; black NYC oval logo, white lettering, Symington-Wayne trucks, one operating coupler; from Yard Chief Switcher Engine Set.
-- -- 12 15

6917 JERSEY CENTRAL: 1986, extended vision, dark flat green body, cream lettering, logo and "MISS LIBERTY 1986" within circle of stars, illuminated, cream-painted cupola roof and ends, ladders, die-cast O27 passenger trucks. Made to match Jersey Central Liberty Fairbanks-Morse and 7404 Boxcar, but sold separately. -- -- 40 50

6918 B & O: 1986, SP Type, dark blue body, yellow lettering and logo, Symington-Wayne trucks. Part of B & O Freight Set 1652.
-- -- -- 15

6919 NICKEL PLATE ROAD: 1986, SP Type, red body, white lettering, Symington-Wayne trucks, part of Nickel Plate Special Set 1602.
-- -- -- 10

6920 B & A: 1986, (Boston & Albany), scale wood-sided caboose, tuscan body, roof, and cupola roof; ladders, tall stack, marker lights at all four corners, white lettering, black and white NYC oval logo (the B & A was a subsidiary of the New York Central), die-cast arch bar trucks, illuminated. Available only as part of a direct mail-order offer from Lionel. -- -- 85 150

6921 PENNSYLVANIA: 1986, SP Type, red body, white lettering and large white PRR Keystone, Symington-Wayne trucks. Part of Cannonball Express Set 1615. -- -- -- 10

7508 LIONEL: 1975-76, N5C Type II, silver sides, 75th ANNIVERSARY SPECIAL, "BLT 1-75", illuminated, enclosed windows; broad red stripe runs halfway across body, circular 75th Anniversary logo, Symington-Wayne trucks.
7 11 20 25

7508 Lionel

Left column: 9075 Rock Island, 9076 We the People, 9077 Rio Grande. Right column: 9080 Wabash, 9166 Rio Grande, 9169 Milwaukee.

7600 FRISCO: 1975-76, N5C Type II, red, white, and blue sides, lights, enclosed windows, Spirit of '76 Series.

(A) Flat red roof.	6	8	20	30
(B) Shiny red roof.	6	8	20	30

See also Special Production chapter.

9021 SANTA FE: 1970-74, work caboose, black frame with yellow lettering, caboose converts into "wood" deck flatcar.

(A) Medium red cab, light red toolbox, "9021" on frame, AAR trucks, plastic wheels, one manumatic coupler, one fixed coupler. (Note: A "manumatic" coupler operates, but it does not have the thumb tack pressed into the armature shaft so

7600 Frisco.

that a remote track will pull it down. Obviously, any manumatic coupler can be quickly made into a remote-control coupler.) 3 5 7 10

(B) Same as (A), but light red cab, two manumatic couplers.

      3 5 7 10

(C) Dark shiny cab and toolbox, Symington-Wayne trucks, one operating coupler, one fixed coupler, "9021" not on frame. 3 5 7 10

(D) Same as (A), but orange cab. Came in early sets; somewhat difficult to find.

      12 15 20 30

(E) Same as (A), but "9022" on frame. C. Rohlfing Collection.

      7 10 12 15

9025 DETROIT, TOLEDO & IRONTON: 1971-74, work caboose, black frame with white lettering, orange cab with black lettering, orange toolbox, metal wheels, operating coupler in front, fixed rear coupler. 4 6 8 10

9027 SOO: 1975, work caboose, black frame with white lettering, red cab with white lettering, dark red toolbox, plastic wheels, one manumatic coupler in front, caboose converts into flatcar with stakes. 4 6 8 10

9057 C P RAIL: 1978-79, SP Type VII, yellow unpainted plastic body, black-painted trim on sides, black lettering, Type II ends, Symington-Wayne trucks, one manumatic coupler, one dummy; stack, from Great Plains Express Set.

      5 7 9 11

9058 LIONEL LINES: 1978-79, SP Type VII, orange unpainted plastic; black lettering, Type II ends, Symington-Wayne trucks, plastic wheels, manumatic couplers. 3 5 8 10

9021, 9025, 9027 Work Cabooses.

9060 NICKEL PLATE: 1970-71, SP Type VI or VII, three shades of brown bodies, white lettering, MPC logo, Type I ends, tuscan or black frame.
(A) Type VI, light brown body, tall-window cupola. "Triple T" Collection.

3	5	6	8

(B) Type VII light red-brown body, short-window cupola. R. LaVoie and "Triple T" Collections.

3	5	6	8

(C) Type VII medium brown body, short-window cupola. "Triple T" Collection.

3	5	6	8

9061 A T S F: 1970-71, 78, SP Type V or VII, red body, yellow lettering and cross logo.
(A) SP Type V light red body, tall-window cupola, MPC logo, AAR trucks, Type I end. "Triple T" Collection.

3	5	6	8

9160 Illinois Central.

(B) SP Type VII medium red body, short-window cupola, Symington-Wayne trucks, one manumatic coupler, Type II ends, metal wheels. "Triple T" Collection.

3	5	6	8

(C) Same as (B), but with Type I ends.

3	5	6	8

9062 PENN CENTRAL: 1970-71, SP Type V or VII, green body; white lettering, Type I ends.
(A) SP Type V, MPC logo, tall-window cupola, AAR trucks. 2 3 5 9
(B) SP Type VII body, short-window cupola, MPC logo. 2 3 5 9
(C) Same as (B), but no MPC logo. R. LaVoie Collection. 2 3 5 9

9063 GRAND TRUNK: 1970, SP Type V or VI, light orange or maroon body, white lettering, AAR trucks, MPC logo, Type I ends.
(A) SP Type V, orange body, tall-window cupola. "Triple T" Collection.

10	15	20	25

(B) Same as (A), but dark orange body. R. LaVoie Collection.

8	10	15	20

(C) SP Type VI maroon body, tall-window cupola, Canadian release. Somewhat hard to find. "Triple T" Collection. 15 20 25 30
(D) SP Type VI brown-red boyd, Type II ends, one AAR and one Symington-Wayne truck. C. Rohlfing Collection. 15 20 25 30

9064 C & O: 1971, Type VI or VII, yellow body, red stripe, blue lettering, Type I ends, MPC logo.
(A) SP Type VI, light yellow body, light red stripe, light blue lettering.

3	5	7	10

(B) SP Type VI, medium light yellow, red stripe, blue lettering.

3	5	7	10

(C) SP Type VI, medium yellow, red stripe, blue lettering. 3 5 7 10
(D) SP Type VII, medium light yellow, red stripe, blue lettering.

3	5	7	10

9065 CANADIAN NATIONAL: 1971-72, SP Type VI, maroon with white lettering, Type I ends, tall-window cupola, MPC logo, Canadian release. Somewhat hard to find. Mint condition for this and other Canadian production pieces must include original Type I Parker Brothers box. R. LaVoie Collection.

10	15	20	25

9066 SOUTHERN: SP Type VI, white lettering, Symington-Wayne trucks, Type III SP body, Type I end, no MPC logo.
(A) Red body. 5 6 8 10
(B) Very dark red body (almost maroon). C. Rohlfing Collection. -- -- -- 75

9067 KICKAPOO VALLEY & NORTHERN: 1972, bobber, black frame, four wheels, gold lettering. Came only in the Kickapoo Valley and Northern Set of 1972.
(A) Red body. 3 5 7 10
(B) Yellow body. 3 5 7 10
(C) Green body. 3 5 7 10

9068 READING: 1973-75, bobber, green body, yellow lettering, black frame. Came as separate sale item in Type II box. 3 5 6 8

9069 JERSEY CENTRAL: 1973-74, SP Type VII, brown body, white lettering, Type I ends. 3 5 6 8

9070 ROCK ISLAND: 1973-74, SP Type VII, gray with black and gray lettering, Type I ends. 6 8 12 15

9071 A T & S F: 1974-75, bobber, red body, white lettering, black frame, part of Sears Set 79C9715C (Sears catalogue number) and catalogued Set 1760 from 1977, the Steel Hauler. Also part of Set 1790, Lionel Leisure Steel Set, sold by Kiddie City stores. J. R. Hunt Collection. 5 6 8 10

9073 COKE: 1973, SP Type VII, red body, white lettering, Type I ends, no MPC logo. Came as part of Coca-Cola Switcher Set.
(A) Light red body. 3 5 10 15
(B) Medium red body. 3 5 10 15
(C) Dark flat red body. 3 5 10 15

9075 ROCK ISLAND: SP Type VII, red body, white lettering, Type I ends, no MPC logo. 6 10 12 15

9076 WE THE PEOPLE: SP Type VII, white and red sides, blue roof, white and blue lettering, American flag, Type I ends, no MPC logo. Came as part of Liberty Special Set. 8 12 15 20

Left column: 9171 Missouri Pacific, 9172 Penn Central.   Right column: 9173 Jersey Central, 9178 Illinois Central Gulf.

9077 RIO GRANDE: 1977-79, 1981, orange body, black lettering, Type II ends, no MPC logo.

(A) SP Type VI body. C. Rohlfing Collection.	3	4	6	8
(B) SP Type VII body.	3	4	6	8

9078 ROCK ISLAND: 1977, 1979, bobber, red body, white lettering, black frame.   3   5   6   8

9079 A T S F: Announced for 1979, but not manufactured.
                                              Not Manufactured

9080 WABASH: 1977, SP Type VII, red body, black roof, white lettering, Type II ends, no MPC logo. Part of Wabash Cannonball Steam Engine Set.
                                              5   7   10   15

9085 A T S F: 1980-81, work caboose, plastic trucks and wheels, one operating coupler, one fixed coupler.   3   4   5   6

9160 I C: 1971, N5C Type II except for (B).
(A) Darker flat orange sides and roof, black lettering, white "ic", Symington-Wayne trucks, one operating coupler.   15   20   25   35
(B) Flat light orange sides and roof, black lettering, white "ic", AAR trucks, pre-1970 wheels, two operating couplers, Type I body. Earliest production; hard to find.   15   20   25   35
(C) Darker flat orange sides and roof, black lettering, white "ic", black circle.
                                              15   20   25   35
(D) Darker flat orange sides and roof, yellow "ic".   15   20   25   35
(E) Orange and white sides, white roof, black lettering, white "ic", white areas added by Glen Uhl, an Ohio Lionel dealer.   --   --   --   150

(F) Flat light orange roof, orange sides, black lettering, white "ic", Symington-Wayne trucks, one disc coupler, one fixed coupler.   15   20   25   35
See also Special Production chapter.

9161 CANADIAN NATIONAL: 1971, N5C Type II, orange body, white lettering, black roof, illuminated, "BLT 1-72", Symington-Wayne trucks. Can have one or two operating couplers. Many examples have heavy blurred lettering, especially built date and MPC logo. Slight price premium (about $3) for crisp, clear lettering.   8   10   15   35

9162 PENNSYLVANIA: 1972-76, N5C Type II, tuscan, white lettering, Symington-Wayne trucks; includes green or red marker lights, illuminated. Somewhat difficult to find.   10   15   20   30

9163 A T S F: 1973-76, N5C Type II, red-painted gray body with white lettering, illuminated, blue Santa Fe herald, Symington-Wayne trucks. Part of 1388 Golden State Arrow Set of 1973; available as a separate sale item thereafter. C. Lang comment.   6   8   15   20

9165 CANADIAN PACIFIC: 1973, N5C Type II, red with white lettering, lights; came in C. P. Service Station Special. Difficult to find.
                                              15   20   35   45

9166 RIO GRANDE: 1974, SP Type VII, yellow body, silver roof and stripes, black lettering, no MPC logo, illuminated, stack, enclosed windows, Type I ends.
(A) Light yellow sides.   10   15   20   25
(B) Medium yellow sides.   10   15   20   25

9161 Canadian National.

9162 Pennsylvania.

9163 A T S F.

9165 Canadian Pacific.

9167 CHESSIE: 1974-76, N5C Type II, light yellow sides, silver roof, orange stripe, blue lettering. Part of Grand National Set of 1974; available as a separate sale item thereafter. 10 15 20 30

9167 Chessie.

9168 UNION PACIFIC: 1975-76, N5C Type II, yellow sides, red or green lettering, black roof, illuminated, enclosed windows.
(A) Red lettering. 10 12 15 25
(B) Green heat-stamped lettering; rare. Confirmation of authenticity requested. One of three known to exist. G. Halverson Collection. **NRS**
9169 MILWAUKEE ROAD: 1975, SP Type VII, brown sides, black roof, red lettering, illuminated, enclosed windows, Type I ends. Part of Milwaukee Ser-

9168 Union Pacific.

vice Station Set of 1975, but unlike previous year's 9166 Rio Grande, never offered for separate sale. 10 15 20 30
9170 N & W: 1976, listed under 1776.
9171 MISSOURI PACIFIC: 1975-77, SP Type, red sides and roof, white lettering, illuminated, stack, enclosed windows, Type I ends.
(A) SP Type VI. 6 8 15 20
(B) SP Type VII. 6 8 15 20
9172 P C: 1975-77, SP Type VII, black sides and roof, white lettering, illuminated, stack, enclosed windows, Type I ends. 8 10 15 25
9173 JERSEY CENTRAL: 1975-77, SP Type VI or VII, red sides and roof, white lettering, illuminated, stack, enclosed windows, Type I ends.
(A) SP Type VI. 8 10 15 20
(B) SP Type VII. 8 10 15 20
(C) Same as (A), but Type II ends. C. Rohlfing Collection. 8 10 15 20
9174 P & L E: 1976, (New York Central), bay window, green sides, black roof; white lettering, Symington-Wayne trucks; from Empire State Express Set of 1976. Difficult to find. 40 50 75 90

9175 Virginian.

9175 VIRGINIAN: 1975-77, N5C Type II, dark blue sides, yellow roof; yellow lettering, illuminated, Symington-Wayne trucks, enclosed windows.
(A) One operating coupler. 10 12 15 25
(B) Two operating couplers, factory production. R. LaVoie Collection.
10 12 15 25

9176 Bangor and Aroostook.

9176 BANGOR & AROOSTOOK: 1976, N5C Type II, red, white, and blue with red roof, illuminated, enclosed windows, 1976 Bicentennial Issue; came with 8665 Locomotive in one long box. Seldom sold separately from engine.
12 15 20 35
9177 NORTHERN PACIFIC: 1976, bay window, silver roof, green and dark or medium yellow sides; black lettering, red and white NP logo, O27-style die-cast passenger trucks, from Northern Pacific Service Station Special Set. This was the first bay window caboose to use die-cast trucks. C. Lang comment.
(A) Dark yellow sides. 9 15 25 35
(B) Medium yellow sides. 9 15 25 35
9178 ILLINOIS CENTRAL GULF: SP Type VII, light or dark orange, silver roof, black lettering, white "IC", Type II ends, part of 1976 Illinois Central Gulf Freight Set and never offered for separate sale.
(A) Light orange. 10 15 20 25

9180 The Rock.

9183 Mickey Mouse.

(B) Dark orange.   10   15   20   25

9179 CHESSIE: 1979, bobber, yellow body, blue lettering, black frame, four plastic wheels.   3   5   6   8

9180 ROCK: 1977-78, N5C, blue, black, and white sides, white roof, illuminted, enclosed windows, Symington-Wayne trucks.
(A) Type II body.   10   15   20   40
(B) Type III body. C. Rohlfing Collection.   10   15   20   40

9181 Boston & Maine.

9181 BOSTON & MAINE: 1977, N5C, blue, black, and white body, illuminated, enclosed windows, Symington-Wayne trucks.
(A) Type II body.   10   12   15   25
(B) Type III body. C. Rohlfing Collection.   10   12   15   25

9182 Norfolk & Western.

9182 NORFOLK & WESTERN: 1977-80, N5C, black body, white lettering, illuminated, enclosed windows, Symington-Wayne trucks.
(A) Type II body.   10   12   15   35
(B) Type III body. C. Rohlfing Collection.   10   12   15   35

9183 MICKEY MOUSE: 1977-78, N5C, white sides, red/orange roof, Type III body, Mickey and lettering decal in yellow, black, red, and blue; Symington-Wayne trucks, one operating coupler.   20   25   35   50

9184 ERIE: 1977-78, bay window, red body, white lettering, Symington-Wayne trucks, two operating couplers.   10   12   20   25

9185 G T: 1977, N5C, gray plastic painted blue, orange ends, white lettering, red marker lights, Symington-Wayne trucks, one tab coupler, illuminated.
(A) Type II body.   10   12   20   35
(B) Type III body. C. Rohlfing Collection.   10   12   20   35

9186 Conrail.

9186 CONRAIL: 1977-78, N5C, gray plastic painted blue, black roof, white lettering, red marker lights, Symington-Wayne trucks, one tab coupler, illuminated.
(A) Type II body.   15   20   25   30
(B) Type III body. C. Rohlfing Collection.   10   12   15   20

9187 Gulf Mobile & Ohio.

9187 GULF MOBILE & OHIO: 1977-78, SP Type, gray plastic painted red, black roof, white lettering, Type VII SP body, Type II ends, illuminated, metal wheels, Symington-Wayne trucks, one tab operating coupler. From Heartland Express Set; not offered for separate sale. C. Rohlfing Collection.   10   15   20   30

9188 GREAT NORTHERN: 1977, bay window, blue and white sides, black roof, white lettering, two operating couplers, illuminated; from Rocky Mountain Special Set.   13   15   25   35

9189 NORFOLK SOUTHERN: 1974, NC5, red body, black and white "NS" logo, Symington-Wayne trucks.   8   10   12   15

9231 READING: 1979, bay window, green and yellow sides, yellow lettering, green roof, Symington-Wayne trucks; part of Quaker City Limited Set.   15   20   25   30

9239 LIONEL LINES: 1983, N5C, bright orange sides, dark blue roof, red, white and blue "LIONEL" circular logo centered on car side, "LIONEL LINES" in blue modern sans-serif letters, over- and underscored by two blue stripes which run the length of the car, black railings, platforms and steps, number at lower right in blue, illuminated, Symington-Wayne trucks; matches 8380 engine. R. LaVoie comment.   --   --   35   75

9259X SOUTHERN: 1977, bay window, see Special Production Chapter.

9268 NORTHERN PACIFIC: 1976, bay window, black and gold sides; yellow hash marks, red lettering, gold ends and roofs, die-cast O27-style passenger trucks. Made in response to collector complaints that the 9177 Northern Pacific bay window Caboose did not match the locomotive in that year's Service Station Special Set. See 9274 entry for a similar situation.   --   30   40   45

9269 MILWAUKEE ROAD: 1978, bay window, dull orange and black, red logo, die-cast O27-style passenger trucks. Part of Milwaukee Special Freight Set of 1978.   --   35   45   55

9270 NORTHERN PACIFIC: Type III N5C orange-painted gray body, white letters. C. Rohlfing Collection.   10   12   15   20

9271 MINNEAPOLIS & ST. LOUIS: 1978-79, bay window, red sides with large white stripe, blue roof, white lettering, illuminated, two operating couplers, O27-style die-cast passenger trucks. Part of 1868 Minneapolis & St. Louis Service Station Set.   12   15   20   30

9272 NEW HAVEN: 1978-80, bay window, dark red body, white and black lettering, illuminated, two operating couplers, Symington-Wayne trucks.
     8   10   20   25

9273 SOUTHERN: 1978, bay window, green and white body, gold stripes.
     10   20   30   40

9274 SANTA FE: 1979, bay window, black roof, red sides, white letters, two operating couplers, Symington-Wayne trucks. Reportedly, only 3,000 made because collectors complained that it did not match the Santa Fe SD-18 diesels made the previous year. In response, Fundimensions stopped making this caboose in favor of the blue and yellow 9317.   40   50   60   75

9276 TEXAS & PACIFIC: 1980, SP Type, dark blue with white lettering; catalogued as part of freight set but not made.   **Not Manufactured**

9287 SOUTHERN: 1978, Type III N5C body, gray plastic painted red, red roof, white lettering, red markers, Symington-Wayne trucks, one tab coupler, illuminated. C. Rohlfing comment.   10   12   15   20

9288 LEHIGH VALLEY: 1978, 1980, Type III N5C body, gray plastic painted red, yellow roof; yellow lettering, red markers, Symington-Wayne trucks, one tab coupler, illuminated. C. Rohlfing comment.   10   12   15   20

9289 CHICAGO & NORTH WESTERN: 1978, 1980, Type III N5C gray plastic body painted yellow, Brunswick green roof; black lettering, red marker lights, Symington-Wayne trucks, illuminated. C. Rohlfing comment.
(A) One operating coupler.   10   15   20   30
(B) Same as (A), except two operating couplers, factory production. Dunn Collection.   10   15   20   30
See also Special Production chapter.

9309 TOLEDO, PEORIA & WESTERN: 1980-81, bay window, orange body with silver roof and white lettering, Symington-Wayne trucks, from 1072 Cross Country Express Set. Shown in red in catalogue, but not made for production that way, although we have reports of a red example which may be a prototype. C. Lang, C. Rohlfing, and I. D. Smith comments.
(A) Orange body, silver roof, and white lettering. G. Kline Collection.
     --   15   25   35

(B) Same as (A), but red body. Possible prototype. Reader comments requested. W. Eddins Collection.   **NRS**

9316 SOUTHERN PACIFIC: 1979, bay window, silver with black roof, illuminated, O27-style die-cast passenger trucks, from 1970 Southern Pacific Limited Set.   --   --   45   60

9317 A T S F: 1979, bay window, blue and yellow body, yellow ends; yellow lettering, Symington-Wayne trucks, illuminated; matches A T S F SD-18 Locomotive. See entry 9274 for story behind this caboose.   15   20   30   40

9323 A T S F: 1979, bay window, tuscan body, black roof, white lettering, black and white Santa Fe cross logo, gold diamond-shaped FARR 1 logo, Symington-Wayne trucks, illuminated, from FARR Series I; available as separate sale only.
     20   25   35   45

9326 BURLINGTON NORTHERN: 1979-80, bay window, green-painted body, black roof, white lettering, Symington-Wayne trucks, illuminated.
     12   15   20   25

9328 WM CHESSIE SYSTEM: 1980, bay window, yellow with silver roof; blue lettering and logo, O27-style die-cast passenger trucks; from 1070 Royal Limited Set.   --   --   40   50

9341 ATLANTIC COAST LINE: 1979-82, 1986-87, SP Type, red with white lettering, glow-in-the-dark windows (1979-80 only), Symington-Wayne trucks, from 1960 Midnight Flyer Set. This caboose and its 8902 Locomotive have been resurrected many times since the original production run for department store and other low-priced special sets. R. LaVoie comment.   --   --   6   8

9346 WABASH: 1979, SP Type, dark red sides, white lettering, black roof; from 1991 Wabash Deluxe Express. Young Collection.   --   --   10   12

9355 DELAWARE & HUDSON: 1980, 1982, bay window, dark blue and gray body, yellow stripe, Symington-Wayne trucks, illuminated; matches 8050-8051 D H U36C Diesels.   --   --   20   25
See also Special Production chapter for 1982 version.

9357 SMOKEY MOUNTAIN LINE: 1979, bobber, one-piece plastic cab and roof, one-piece black unpainted plastic frame, two black unpainted plastic end railing units, plastic wheels on metal axles, fixed plastic coupler fastened to frame by metal screw (for a total of three metal parts), body and frame highly detailed, frame underside lettered "LIONEL MPC 9067-10"; came with 1979 Smokey Mountain Line Set.
(A) Unpainted red plastic body, white lettering. G. Halverson collection.
     2   4   8   0
(B) Unpainted green plastic body, black heat-stamped lettering "SML", logo between windows.   2   4   8   10
(C) Unpainted yellow plastic body "SML" lettering. C. O'Dell Collection.
     5   10   15   20

9361 CHICAGO & NORTHWESTERN: 1980, bay window, yellow sides, Brunswick green roof, illuminated, Symington-Wayne trucks. Previous to the production of this caboose, several Midwestern train shops repainted other bay window cabooses into this color scheme. C. Rohlfing and R. LaVoie comments.
     --   15   20   30

9368 UNION PACIFIC: 1980, bay window, yellow with red roof and lettering, Symington-Wayne trucks; red, white, and blue UP shield logo, diamond-shaped FARR 2 logo, Famous American Railroad series number two, only sold separately.   --   15   20   30

9372 SEABOARD: 1980, bay window, dark red body, black roof, white lettering, red, white, and black circular Seaboard logo, die-cast O27-style passenger trucks, from 1071 Mid Atlantic Limited Set.   --   15   25   35

9380 NEW YORK, NEW HAVEN & HARTFORD: 1980, SP Type, silver-painted body, black roof and cupola, black New Haven script lettering, Symington-Wayne trucks, two operating couplers; came with 1050 New Englander Set. Zylstra Collection.   --   --   10   12

9381 CHESSIE: 1980, SP Type, yellow sides and end, silver roof, blue lettering; from 1052 Chesapeake Flyer Set.   --   --   8   10

9382 FLORIDA EAST COAST: 1980, bay window, red and yellow with silver stripe, illuminated, Symington-Wayne trucks; matches 8064 and 8065 GP-9 Diesels.   --   --   20   25

9387 BURLINGTON: 1981, bay window, red sides, white lettering, illuminated, O27-style die-cast passenger trucks; from 1160 Great Lakes Limited Set.   --   --   30   40

16500 ROCK ISLAND: 1987, bobber, bright red body, white lettering, gray frame, end rails and stack, part of Rail Blazer Set 11701.   --   --   --   7

16501 LEHIGH VALLEY: 1987, SP Type, yellow body, silver roof, black frame and end rails, black lettering, illuminated, Symington-Wayne trucks. Part of Black Diamond Set 11702.   --   --   15   20

16503 NEW YORK CENTRAL: 1987, transfer caboose, black flatcar body and railings, white lettering, medium gray cab with black number and black and white NYC oval logo, Symington-Wayne trucks.   --   --   --   12

16504 SOUTHERN: 1987, N5C, red sides, yellow ends and railings, black roof and cupola, yellow Southern lettering and circular logo, die-cast leaf-spring trucks, illuminated. Part of Southern Freight Runner Service Station Special Set 11704.   --   --   --   35

16505 WABASH: Scheduled for 1988, SP Type caboose, red body, white lettering, logo, and numbers, Symington-Wayne trucks, one operating coupler. Part of 11703 Iron Horse Freight Set. -- -- -- 8

16506 SANTA FE: Scheduled for 1988, bay window caboose, blue body, yellow end, yellow Santa Fe lettering and cross logo, Symington-Wayne trucks, operating couplers, illuminated. Appears to be identical to 9317 model made in 1979 except for number. -- -- -- 25

17600 NEW YORK CENTRAL: 1987, scale wood-sided caboose, light brown body, white lettering and number, black ladders, end rails, and cupola roof rails, pictured with marker lights only at rear instead of at all four corners, die-cast leaf-spring trucks, illuminated. Sold as a match for 18002 gun-metal New York Central Hudson in year-end "Happy Lionel Holidays!" package. -- -- 75 90

17601 SOUTHERN: 1988, high-cupola wood-sided caboose, red body, black main and cupola roofs, yellow lettering and SR circular logo, die-cast leaf-spring trucks. Made to match 18301 Southern Fairbanks-Morse Diesel. -- -- 70 85

17602 CONRAIL: 1987, high-cupola scale wood-sided caboose, bright blue body, white striping, lettering, and Conrail logo, black roof and cupola roof, low-window wood-sided cupola replaced by new high-window version, marker lights only at rear, illuminated, die-cast leaf-spring trucks. Part of Conrail Limited Set 11700. -- -- 70 85

17603 ROCK ISLAND: 1988, high-cupola wood-sided caboose, dark maroon body (shows as tuscan in catalogue), roof, and cupola, black trim pieces, die-cast leaf-spring trucks, white number and Rock Island logo. Matches Rock Island Northern. -- -- 60 75

17604 LACKAWANNA: Scheduled for 1988 as match for 18003 Lackawanna Northern Steam Locomotive. Low-cupola wood-sided caboose, dark brown body, black trim pieces, white lettering and logo, die-cast leaf-spring trucks. -- -- -- 60

19700 CHESSIE: 1988, extended vision, yellow sides, dark blue main and cupola roofs, dark blue lettering and logo, die-cast passenger-type trucks. Catalogued with large vermilion stripe on lower half of caboose sides, but production pieces lack this stripe and are solid yellow. -- -- -- 60

19701 MILWAUKEE ROAD: 1987, N5C, dull orange sides and ends, black roof and cupola, red and white rectangular Milwaukee logo, black number on side, die-cast leaf-spring trucks. Part of Fallen Flags Set 2. -- -- -- 45

19702 PENNSYLVANIA: 1987, N5C, bronze-painted body, purplish-black lettering and number, red, white, and black large PRR Keystone centered on sides, illuminated, die-cast leaf-spring trucks. Made as a match for 18300 Pennsylvania GG-1. -- -- -- 50

19703 GREAT NORTHERN: 1988, extended vision caboose, dark red body, black main and cupola roofs, white lettering; red, black, and white goat logo, die-cast passenger trucks. Part of Fallen Flags Set No. 3. -- -- -- 45

19807 PENNSYLVANIA: 1988, smoking extended vision caboose, tuscan body and roofs, black trim pieces, gold lettering and number, die-cast leaf-spring trucks. -- -- -- 65

BLACK CAVE: 1984, SP Type, red body, no window inserts, luminous Black Cave Flyer decals to be installed by purchaser. J. Sawruk Collection. -- -- 5 10

NABISCO: 1984, work caboose, yellow frame, medium red cab and tool bin, "Nabisco" logo on cab side, Symington-Wayne trucks, one operating coupler. Made as part of a special promotional set for Nabisco; part of this set may have been made outside the factory. Reader comments requested. S. Lindsey, Jr. Collection. **NRS**

Chapter VI
FLATCARS

In the postwar years, the Lionel Corporation made the flatcar its most versatile freight carrier. The long plastic flatcar was used to haul just about every load under the sun, from transformers to Christmas trees. If the load could not be put onto the flatcar directly, Lionel saw to it that the car was adapted to the purpose. For example, Lionel would fit a flatcar with bulkheads and put a liquified gas container between them.

In the modern era, Lionel has not come close to making the flatcar the all-around performer of the postwar years, but the company has made excellent use of the flatcar in many areas. Essentially, there have been three types of flatcars used by Fundimensions and its successors in their production.

One of the first cars to emerge was a new design for a short flatcar, typified by the 9020 Union Pacific. This car has a wood-scribed top and bottom, and as issued in sets the car came with little plastic stakes which fit into small holes around the perimeter of the car. These stakes are seldom found with the cars when they show up on dealers' tables at train shows. This little flatcar was issued in Santa Fe, Chesapeake & Ohio, M K T, and Republic Steel markings as well as Union Pacific logos. The scarcest of them is a black 9020 with AAR trucks, probably from the earliest stages of production. The car was also equipped with bulkheads and logs; since it was a car which was usually in inexpensive sets, it usually had one operating and one dummy coupler.

A second type of flatcar is the re-release of the Lionel 1877-type "General" flatcar. This is another short flatcar which was originally issued with plug-in fences and horses as part of the rolling stock meant to accompany the "General" locomotive of 1977. Since then, it has been used as a base for many different flatcars in inexpensive sets. None to date have been issued with the metal truss rods which were used on some of the postwar versions of the car. The latest version of this car was part of a special American Express uncatalogued set in 1986.

The third type of flatcar has been the full 11-inch flatcar which was so common in postwar production. Fundimensions has revived both of the basic molds for this car. The 6424-11 mold has been used most often for the T O F C flatcars with trailers, while the 6511-2 mold has shown up as the base for the Fundimensions searchlight cars and the derrick cars. This flatcar, in Chesapeake and Ohio markings, was the one used for the revival of the excellent Harnischfeger crane-carrying car in 1976; it was joined almost immediately by a Penn Central car carrying a big steam shovel. Both of these came in large boxes as kits to be assembled by the purchaser, just as the postwar versions did. A 9121 Louisville and Nashville car came with both a bulldozer and a scraper; this car was included in some deluxe sets beginning in 1974 and was available separately for several years. The dozer and scraper kits themselves, if in intact condition, are worth more than the car! However, in fairness, there is a bright maroon version of the 9121 which is much harder to find than the tuscan version.

The most frequent use of the long flatcar in the modern era has been with the T O F C flatcars with trailers. ("T O F C" is the railroad abbreviation for "Trailer On Flat Car".) Since its first years, the company has issued approximately twenty of these cars, and they are in keeping with Lionel's desire to use its graphic capabilities well. These flatcars would look better with a single longer trailer instead of two short trailers, but Lionel is merely repeating postwar practice by using the two small vans. The real T O F C cars can be used both ways.

The first of the T O F C cars was the 9120 Northern Pacific in 1970, one of the first cars issued by the new company. This car was green with white lettering, and it had two white vans with corrugated sides and no markings. The trailers were constructed a little differently from their postwar predecessors. The postwar trailers had a separate metal tongue riveted to the underside of the trailer which held the plastic prop wheels. This metal piece was riveted to the trailer. Fundimensions cast the trailer body in one plastic piece, including the tongue support. The flatcar has plug-in side slip barriers, just as did the postwar original, and the trailers are all single-axled and double-wheeled. It is not too unusual to find leftover postwar trailers on some of the earliest production; once again, that is efficient use of existing stock.

One of the scarcer T O F C flatcars was issued in early 1972. It was another Northern Pacific T O F C car with the same color scheme as the 9120, but with the number 9122 and a 1972 built date. This car came in a Type II box, where its predecessor had a Type I box. The plastic cover for the trailer axles on the 9120 was black; on the 9122, the axle was green. Very early in the production run, the colors of the 9122 were changed to a tuscan flatcar and gray trailers. As a result, the green 9122 is one of the scarcer T O F C cars.

By 1976 Fundimensions had made the decision to expand its line of T O F C cars to add a modern look to its rolling stock. To dress up the car, the firm made the trailers smooth-sided instead of corrugated; this allowed the use of bright modern railroad logos on the trailers. The first of these cars was the Cascade green 9133 Burlington Northern; it was quickly followed by cars in C P Rail, I C Gulf, Great Northern, Southern Pacific, Chicago and Northwestern, and Union Pacific markings, among several others. In recent years, there have been Louisville & Nashville, Delaware & Hudson, and Pennsylvania markings. With the 1987 production of the Pennsylvania T O F C, Lionel, Inc. learned a lesson. In the early production run, collectors complained that the gold lettering on the dark maroon vans was too dull. Lionel corrected that by triple-stamping every one of the trailers in the late part of the run, and the lettering is noticeably brighter. Curiously, all the flatcars themselves have dull gold lettering; they were probably run off before the change was made.

One of the more interesting T O F C flatcars is the one made in 1976 for the Lionel Collectors' Club of America convention in Atlanta, Georgia. This trailer car is not on a regular flatcar but

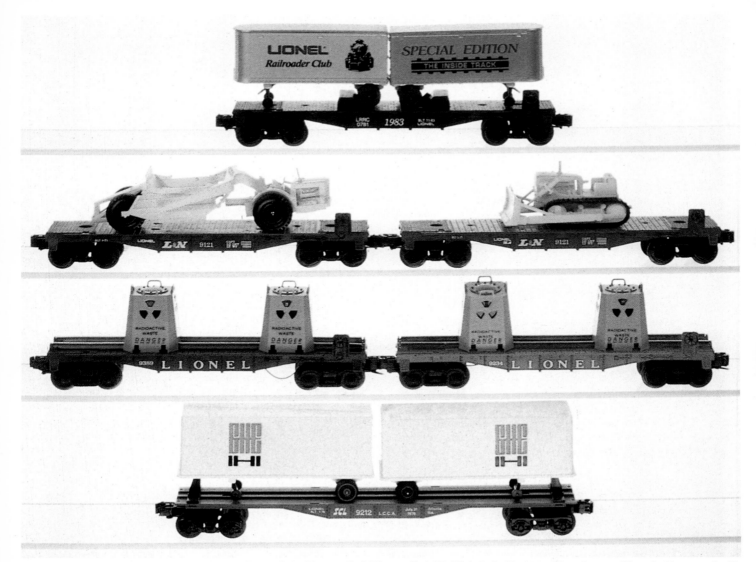

Top shelf: **0781 Lionel Railroader Club.** Second shelf: **9121 L & N, 9121 L & N.** Third shelf: **9389 Lionel, 9234 Lionel.** Bottom shelf: **9212 SCL.**

on a newer tri-level automobile car without the second and third racks. The trailers themselves are not Lionel and are much larger than the style Lionel uses. Fundimensions apparently sent the whole shipment to the L C C A with only one side of the flatcars stamped. The club offered to have members' cars restamped on demand, but on the whole the version with one side stamped is still more common.

A few other flatcar types have made random appearances at times. One was the Fundimensions revival of the Radioactive Waste car in two versions, one as part of a limited edition set and one for separate sale. On this flatcar, two rails are laid for the length of the car, and two lighted canisters are clipped onto the rails. As the car rides along, the canisters blink red warning lights — scarcely a romantic addition to a layout, but a definite curiosity! The big four-truck die-cast transformer car has also been revived for separate sale as part of the Mid-Atlantic Limited set of 1980. The set car was painted brown and had the old postwar bar-end metal trucks. A second four-truck flatcar was offered for separate sale in that year; it was gray-painted and had the die-cast O27 passenger trucks. It carried two maroon bridge girders instead of a transformer. For 1987, two old postwar favorites made a reappearance; these were the 16610 Track Maintenance Car and the 16301 Barrel Ramp Car.

Finally, one of the nicest flatcars ever made for tinplate was produced as part of the Standard O Series in 1976. This was the 9823 Santa Fe Flatcar, which was scale-length and came with a plastic crate load. Another version of this scale flatcar, this time in New York Central markings, was produced in 1985. A Canadian Pacific version of the Standard O flatcar was made in 1986 as part of a special direct-mail offer from Lionel, and for 1987 there is a Conrail version for the Conrail Limited set.

Lionel's use of the flatcar has been clearly different from the use made of the car in the postwar years. The flatcar has been used more to give a modern look to the modern era Lionel freight line than to serve as a "do-it-all" platform. Although very few of these cars are scarce, they can form an important part of the collector's freight consist, especially the rather nice T O F C cars and the Standard O versions.

	Gd	VG	Exc	Mt

0781 LIONEL RAILROADER CLUB: 1983, see Special Production chapter.

6233 CANADIAN PACIFIC: 1986, Standard O flatcar with stakes, black flatcar body, white lettering, 24 black plastic stakes, Standard O trucks. Available only as part of a direct-mail offer from Lionel. -- -- **75 100**

6500: See entry 9233, this chapter.

6504 L. A. S. E. R.: 1981-82, helicopter on black flatcar, similar to Lionel 3419; from 1150 L. A. S. E. R. Set. -- -- **12 30**

6505 L. A. S. E. R.: 1981-82, satellite tracking car, similar to Lionel 3540; black car, light blue housing, from 1150 L. A. S. E. R. Set. -- -- **12 30**

6506 L. A. S. E. R.: 1981-82, security car, see Chapter VI, Cabooses. -- -- **12 30**

6507 L. A. S. E. R.: 1981-82, A. L. C. M. cruise missile on black flatcar; from 1150 L. A. S. E. R. Set. C. Rohlfing comment. -- -- **12 30**

6509 LIONEL: 1981, depressed-center die-cast flatcar with four trucks, gray-painted die-cast body, two maroon bridge girders with white "LIONEL" attached to car by rubber bands, four sets die-cast O27-style passenger trucks, bottom of base reads "MACHINERY CAR / PART NO. / 6418- 4 / LIONEL / MT. CLEMENS, MICH. / 48045". This was the car sold as a separate sale item; it was one of the first cars to be packaged in a Type IV collector box. C. Lang comment, W. Barnes Collection. -- -- **35 45**

6515 UNION PACIFIC: 1986, short flatcar with stakes, identical to 9020 except for number; yellow body, blue lettering, black stakes, Symington-Wayne trucks, one operating and one dummy coupler. Part of uncatalogued Set 1687. J. Sawruk Collection. -- -- -- **10**

6521 NEW YORK CENTRAL: 1985, Standard O flatcar, tuscan body, scribed floor, white lettering and logo, Standard O trucks, 24 tall plastic stakes supplied with car to fit into holes around car perimeter, no load included. -- -- **35 50**

Top shelf: 9233 Lionel. Second shelf: 6509. Third shelf: 9282 Great Northern, 9333 Southern Pacific. Bottom shelf: 9383 Union Pacific, 9352 Chicago & Northwestern.

6531 EXPRESS MAIL: 1985, T O F C flatcar, blue 6424-11 flatcar body, white lettering, two blue vans with orange roofs, white lettering and orange and white Express Mail logo, Symington-Wayne trucks.   -- -- **20 25**

6561: 1983, unlettered, olive drab flatcar with cruise missile, fixed couplers; from 1355 Commando Assault Train, decals furnished with set. L. Caponi comment.   -- -- -- **10**

6562: 1983, unlettered, olive drab flatcar with crates and barrels, fixed couplers; from 1355 Commando Assault Train, decals furnished with set. L. Caponi comment.   -- -- -- **10**

6564: 1983, unlettered, olive drab flatcar with two tanks, fixed couplers; from 1355 Commando Assault Train, decals furnished with set. L. Caponi comment.   -- -- -- **10**

6573 REDWOOD VALLEY EXPRESS: 1984-85, flatcar with log dump bin, 1877-style tuscan flatcar body with yellow lettering, gray bolsters and log bin, three brown-stained logs, arch bar trucks; part of Set 1403.   -- -- -- **10**

6575 REDWOOD VALLEY EXPRESS: 1984-85, flatcar, 1877-style flatcar body with yellow lettering, yellow fence-style stakes around car perimeter, crate loads, arch bar trucks; part of Set 1403.   -- -- -- **10**

6585 PENNSYLVANIA: 1986, short flatcar with fences and logs, black short flatcar body, white lettering, yellow fencing, Symington-Wayne trucks. Part of Cannonball Express Set 1615.   -- -- -- **10**

6587 W & A: 1986, (Western & Atlantic) General-style flatcar with fences, tuscan body, yellow lettering and fencing, included one black and one white horse. Part of uncatalogued American Express Set No. 1608. T. Taylor Collection.   -- -- **20 30**

6670 DERRICK: See Operating Cars chapter.

9014 TRAILER TRAIN: 1978, yellow body, black lettering and stakes, plastic trucks and wheels, manumatic couplers; from 1864 Santa Fe Double Diesel Set. Confirmed as produced. C. O'Dell Collection.   -- -- **8 10**

9019 FLATCAR: 1978, a base that came with either a superstructure for a box or crane car, work caboose, or log loader; as part of 1862 Logging Empire or 1860 Timberline Set. This is actually a four-wheel car with eight-wheel trucks simulated on the sides of the base, similar to Marx practice of many years ago. J. Sawruk comment.   -- -- **1 2**

9020 Union Pacific.

9020 UNION PACIFIC: 1970-77, plastic wheels, one manumatic coupler, one fixed coupler.

(A) Medium yellow body, black lettering.	2	3	4	5
(B) Light yellow body, light blue lettering.	2	3	4	5
(C) Dark yellow body, dark blue lettering.	2	3	4	5
(D) Medium yellow body, blue lettering.	2	3	4	5
(E) Medium light yellow body, blue lettering.	2	3	4	5

(F) Medium yellow body, blue lettering, wood-grained floor.
                2 3 4 5

(G) Medium light yellow body, blue lettering, wood-grained floor.
                2 3 4 5

(H) 1970, early production, unpainted tuscan plastic, heat-stamped, yellow-lettered, "CAPY 100000 LD LMT 121800 LT WT 47200 UP 9020 UNION PACIFIC BLT 1-70", wood-grained floor, 16 stakes, AAR trucks, one fixed, one disc-operating coupler. Came as part of early set with 8041 New York Central 2-4-2 Steam Locomotive with red stripe but no whistle or smoke; green 9141 B N long Gondola with white lettering, three red canisters, and AAR trucks; 9010 GN Hopper Car and 9062 PC Caboose. C. Anderson, R. LaVoie, and Wolf Collections.
                -- -- **15 20**

(I) Same as (H), but dark red body, no wood-graining on floor. C. Rohlfing Collection.   -- -- **15 20**

(J) 1970, first production: black flatcar body with yellow lettering same as (H) and (I) above, small brakewheel flush with floor at one end, AAR trucks, ribbed, detailed wood-grained floor. Very hard to find. "Triple T" Collection.
                -- **20 30 45**

9022 A. T. & S. F.

9022 A. T. &S. F.: 1971, 1975, 1978, yellow lettering, metal wheels, one operating coupler, one fixed coupler, eight plastic stakes, bulkheads, four unstained dowel-cut logs; part of 1586 Chesapeake Flyer Freight Set. C. Lang comment.

(A) Red body, wood-grained floor.	3	4	8	10
(B) Red body, plain floor.	3	4	8	10
(C) Black body.	3	4	8	10

9023 MKT.

9023 M K T: 1973-74, 1978, black body, white lettering, metal wheels, one operating coupler, one fixed coupler, eight plastic stakes, bulkheads, four unstained dowel-cut logs; part of 1386 Rock Island Express Freight Set. C. Lang comment.   **4 6 8 12**

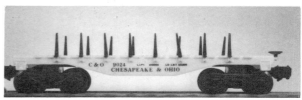

9024 Chesapeake & Ohio.

9024 CHESAPEAKE & OHIO: 1974, yellow body, blue lettering, plastic wheels, fixed couplers.   **1 2 4 5**

9026 REPUBLIC STEEL: 1975-77, 1980, blue body, white lettering, plastic wheels, one manumatic coupler, one fixed coupler, wood-grained floor.
                1 2 3 4

9120 NORTHERN PACIFIC: 1970-71, T O F C flatcar, green body, white lettering, white vans with corrugated sides and no lettering, two operating couplers, wheel stops.

(A) AAR trucks, MPC builder's plates, no side slip bars. Some examples have vans with postwar body shells and Fundimensions roofs. G. Halverson comment.
                6 10 15 20

(B) Same as (A), but later production; Symington-Wayne trucks, no MPC builder's plates, with side slip bars.   **6 8 12 15**

9120 Northern Pacific.

9121 L & N: 1971, 1974, 1976, 1978-79, some versions with yellow dozer and scraper kit, Symington-Wayne trucks, mold 6424-11, die three. Prices shown are for flatcars only; add $8 for both dozer and scraper kits in intact and complete condition and $15 if these kits are still sealed and unbuilt.

(A) 1971, brown body, white lettering as follows, "BLT 1-71 / LIONEL / (MPC logo) / L & N / CAPY 100000 / LD LMT 103800 / LT WT 65200". Came in Type I box with yellow dozer and scraper kits, AAR trucks; also offered in early sets. R. Loveless Collection. **8 10 15 20**

(B) Same as (A), but maroon flatcar body. This version somewhat hard to find. G. Halverson and R. LaVoie Collections. **15 20 35 45**

(C) Same as (A), but without "BLT 1-71" and MPC logo under "LIONEL". R. Loveless and K. Wills Collections. **6 10 15 20**

(D) Same as (A), but Symington-Wayne trucks. C. Rohlfing Collection. **8 10 15 20**

(E) Same as (C), but MPC logo is missing while built date is still present. R. Loveless Collection. **8 10 15 20**

(F) 1974-76, 1978-79, brown body, white lettering, came in special Type II box when offered for separate sale, included both kits. Also part of Grand National Set in 1974 and 1560 North American Set in 1975. Kaiser Collection. **6 10 15 20**

See also Factory Errors and Prototypes.

9122 Northern Pacific.

9122 NORTHERN PACIFIC: 1972-75, flatcar, Symington-Wayne trucks, 6424-11 body mold.

(A) Green body, white lettering and white unlettered vans with corrugated sides, black axle covers, Symington-Wayne trucks, identical to 9120 except for number and "2-72" built date, came in early Type II box. Somewhat hard to find. R. LaVoie Collection. **10 20 30 40**

(B) Same as (A), but vans are gray. R. LaVoie Collection. **10 15 20 25**

(C) Tuscan flatcar body with white lettering, unlettered gray vans with corrugated sides and green axle covers. **6 10 20 25**

(D) Same as (B), but vans are postwar leftover pieces. G. Halverson Collection. **6 10 20 25**

(E) Tuscan flatcar body, yellow grader kit (no dozer kit); part of 1560 North American Set. J. Breslin Collection. **10 15 20 25**

9124 PENN CENTRAL: Green unpainted plastic body, lettered "P C PENN CENTRAL BLT 1-73 CAPY 140000 LD LMT 136700 LT WT 63300", comes with three logs, two black plastic ribs, mold number "6424-11" on underside, arch bar trucks, one operating coupler with plastic semi-disc for manual operation (known as manumatic coupler), one fixed coupler.

(A) As described above. Cunningham and Ristau Collections. **-- 8 10 15**

(B) Same as (A), but dozer kit instead of logs, "Capy 140,000, LD. LMT. 156,700", Symington-Wayne trucks; came as part of 1866 Great Plains Express Set. C. Rohlfing Collection. **5 8 10 15**

(C) Same as (A), but two white vans. C. O'Dell Collection. **-- -- -- 50**

9133 Burlington Northern.

9133 BURLINGTON NORTHERN: 1976, 1980, green body, white lettering and logo, mold 6424-11, Die Three, Symington-Wayne trucks.

(A) No load. **8 10 12 15**

(B) 1980, two matching Burlington Northern vans with smooth sides and white BN logo. **10 15 20 45**

9149 C P Rail.

9149 CP RAIL: Red body, white lettering, silver, white, and black vans with white letters, Symington-Wayne trucks. **10 15 20 40**

9157 C & O.

9157 C & O: 1976-78, 1981, blue body, yellow lettering, P & H yellow crane kit, Symington-Wayne trucks. Hard to find with crane kit intact.
12 15 25 45

9158 PENN CENTRAL: 1976-77; 1980, green body, white lettering, steam shovel kit, Symington-Wayne trucks. Hard to find with steam shovel kit intact.

(A) Gray rubber treads on steam shovel cab. **12 15 25 50**

(B) Black rubber treads on steam shovel cab. **12 15 25 40**

9212 L C C A: T O F C, 1976, see Special Production chapter.

9222 L & N: 1983, T O F C flatcar, two "L & N" gray vans with black lettering.

(A) Tuscan flatcar with white lettering. C. Lang Collection.
-- -- 15 20

9158 Penn Central.

(B) Maroon flatcar with pale yellow lettering. C. Lang Collection.

-- -- 15 20

9226 DELAWARE & HUDSON: 1984, T O F C flatcar, bright blue flatcar body with yellow lettering and logo, gray vans, Symington-Wayne trucks.
(A) Black lettering and D & H logo on vans. -- -- 15 20
(B) Same as (A), but van sides have "PREMIUM / SALTINE CRACKERS" decal on van sides. Part of special promotional set for Nabisco; this car was most likely produced outside the factory. S. Lindsey, Jr. Collection. **NRS**

9232 ALLIS CHALMERS: 1980, gray atomic reactor load, orange base, blue lettering; rerun of 6519 from 1958-61; part of 1072 Cross Country Express Set. C. Lang comment. -- -- 20 30

9233 TRANSFORMER: 1980, tuscan-painted depressed-center die-cast flatcar with red transformer with white insulators, lettered "LIONEL TRANSFORMER CAR", four die-cast O27 passenger trucks; part of 1071 Mid Atlantic Limited Set. Originally scheduled for number 6500, but 9233 was the actual production number. T. Ladny Collection. -- -- 35 45

9234 RADIOACTIVE WASTE: 1980, red flatcar with white-lettered "LIONEL", two rails run car length, two removable energy containers with flashing red lights, die-cast O27 passenger trucks; part of 1070 Royal Limited Set. C. Lang comment, T. Ladny Collection. -- -- 30 40

9282 GREAT NORTHERN: 1978, 1981-82, T O F C flatcar.
(A) Flatcar mold 6424-11, Die Three, orange body, green lettering, black plastic brakewheel easily broken, green vans with elaborate G N orange and green decal, trailer undersides marked "LIONEL" with "M P C 1000" without letters "M P C", van with hole for tractor and tractor lift. 8 15 20 30
(B) Same as (A), but Die Four mold, vans marked "LIONEL 80 / MT. CLEMENS MICH / MADE IN U. S. A." H. Edmunds Collection. 8 15 20 30

9285 I C GULF: 1977, black body, mold 6424-11, Die Three, white lettering, silver vans with black lettering, I C orange and black "pig on wheels" logo on van sides, Symington-Wayne trucks; came as part of 1785 Rocky Mountain Special Set and never offered for separate sale. C. Lang comment, R. LaVoie Collection. 15 20 25 50

9306 A T S F: 1980, brown body and fence, gold lettering, two brown horses, arch bar trucks, plastic wheels; part of 1053 The James Gang Set. J. Sawruk Collection. -- -- 9 13

See also Factory Errors and Prototypes.

NOTE: 9325 is used on several different cars.

9325 N W: 1980-81, part of uncatalogued 1157 Wabash Cannonball Set and 9196 Rolling Stock Assortment. Black plastic body, 8-1/2" long, with heat-stamped white letters on side; "BLT 1-79 N & W 9325 NORFOLK AND WESTERN LIONEL". Simulated wood-grained floor, partial floor cut-out about 9/16" in diameter, plastic brakewheel, two-rung tan plastic fencing around floor perimeter, with three plastic pieces offset to clear brakewheel on end, Symington-Wayne trucks, plastic wheels, one operating and one dummy coupler. Bottom stamped "9325-T-5A LIONEL MT. CLEMENS MICH. 48045". Came in box with ends marked "LIONEL O27 GAUGE FLAT CAR WITH FENCES 6-9325". B. Smith and Runft Collections. See also 9324 and 9325 entries in Operating Car chapter. -- 3 5 8

9333 SOUTHERN PACIFIC T O F C: 1980, flatcar, tuscan body, Symington-Wayne trucks, white lettering, one brakewheel, two white vans with

black wheels and black "SOUTHERN PACIFIC" lettering on sides with red-outlined large "S" and "P". D. Griggs Collection. -- -- 20 45

9352 CHICAGO & NORTHWESTERN: 1980, Brunswick green flatcar with two yellow Chicago & Northwestern vans, lettered "FALCON SERVICE" with bird logo. C. Rohlfing comment. -- 20 35 60

9379 LIONEL: Catalogued in 1980 as part of Texas and Pacific Diesel Set, but never made, flatcar with derrick. **Not Manufactured**

9383 UNION PACIFIC: 1980, T O F C flatcar, dark gray flatcar with white lettering, light yellow vans with red lettering and stripe and red, white and blue U P shield logo, gold diamond-shaped FARR 2 logo. This was the extra freight car marketed separately to accompany the Union Pacific Famous American Railroads Set. C. Rohlfing and C. Lang comments, R. LaVoie Collection.
-- -- 20 25 35

9389 RADIOACTIVE WASTE: 1981, maroon body flatcar, white "LIONEL" lettering and number, two rails run car length, two removable tan energy containers with flashing red lights, O27-style die-cast passenger trucks. Separate sale item in Type III box identical to 9234 Set car except for number and flatcar color. R. LaVoie comment, W. Berresford Collection. -- -- 25 30

9553 WESTERN & ATLANTIC: 1978-79, brown base and fence, gold lettering, six horses, arch bar trucks, operating couplers, metal wheels, available separately; matches General locomotive and coaches.
(A) As described above. -- -- 15 20
(B) Same as (A), except yellow fencing; hard to find. G. Halverson Collection. -- -- 35 45

9823 A. T. & S. F.: 1976, Standard O flatcar, tuscan body, white lettering, Standard O trucks; two sets of tan plastic crates, 24 pointed black stakes supplied with car fit into holes around car perimeter. Very hard to find.
30 50 75 100

16300 ROCK ISLAND: 1987, short flatcar with fences and crates, red short flatcar body, white lettering, black fencing, gray crates, arch bar trucks. Part of Rail Blazer Set 11701. -- -- -- 6

16301 LIONEL: 1987, barrel ramp car, bright blue flatcar body, yellow lettering and number, white superstructure (same structure was used for ramp of postwar culvert loader and unloader accessories), eight small varnished wooden barrels, Symington-Wayne trucks, Type VI box. R. LaVoie Collection.
-- -- -- 15

16303 PENNSYLVANIA: 1987, T O F C flatcar, tuscan flatcar body, gold lettering and numbers, two tuscan vans with gold lettering and Keystone logo, Symington-Wayne trucks.
(A) Dull gold lettering on both flatcar and vans, early production run.
-- -- 20 25
(B) Same as (A), but flatcar has dull gold lettering and vans have much brighter gold lettering, later production run. R. LaVoie comment. -- -- 20 25

16306 SANTA FE: 1988, barrel ramp car, red flatcar body and barrel ramp, white lettering, eight stained barrels, Symington-Wayne trucks.
-- -- -- 16

16307 NICKEL PLATE ROAD: 1988, flatcar with trailers, bright blue flatcar body with white lettering, two silver-painted trailers with blue logo and lettering, Symington-Wayne trucks. The trailers are a new design; they have two axles each instead of one, and the front ends are squared off rather than rounded.
-- -- -- 20

16308 BURLINGTON NORTHERN: Scheduled for 1988, T O F C flatcar, green flatcar, white lettering and number, Symington-Wayne trucks, operating couplers, one larger trailer painted silver with green lettering and large green B N logo. This is apparently the same trailer design as the separate-sale 12725 Lionel Tractor and Trailer. Most collectors feel that it looks much more realistic than the two diminutive postwar carry-over trailers offered up to this time. Just before we went to press, we learned that the production of this car has been postponed. Apparently Lionel is having trouble making or acquiring the new trailers. The 12725 Tractor Trailer has also been postponed.
Not Manufactured

16610 LIONEL: 1987, track maintenance flatcar, gray flatcar body, black lettering and number, bright blue two-deck superstructure with white lettering, two yellow men, one on each deck, Symington-Wayne trucks. -- -- -- 18

17501 CONRAIL: 1987, standard O flatcar, brown flatcar body, white lettering and logo, 24 black plastic stakes, Standard O trucks. Part of Conrail Limited Set 11700. -- -- -- 35

Chapter VII
GONDOLAS

On real railroads, no piece of rolling stock takes as much steady abuse as the gondola car. Big loads of scrap steel, 55-gallon drums, machine parts, crushed automobiles, and other assorted refuse of our highly industrialized society are routinely dropped with a bang into these decidedly non-glamorous cars with nary a thought for the car's appearance or shape. One never sees gondolas in new condition, it would seem. Instead, they are observed in varying stages of abuse and decay; some have rusted sides, some are dented beyond belief, but somehow all of them keep rolling on the rails and doing their jobs.

In a way, the Lionel gondolas were subjected to their own kind of abuse in the postwar period. Innumerable New York Central gondolas were made in black, red, green, and blue versions, and because these cars were meant to be loaded and played with, they probably took more abuse at the hands of young railroaders than any other cars. Look through a tinplate junkpile at a train show, and chances are that most of the junk cars are gondolas. Not only that, but the cars were cheapened as the years went by. The postwar gondolas began with impressive metal frames and trucks and finished with absolutely bare undersides and cheap non-operating trucks and couplers.

In recent years, Lionel may have reversed that trend by bringing some style to the lowly gondola car. Several of the most recent gondola issues have been equipped with the magnificent Standard O trucks; some have even been offered as separate-sale limited production items, such as the 6208 B & O meant to complete the Royal Limited Set. New colors and rail markings have brightened the car considerably, and even the less expensive short gondolas have at least been made in brighter colors than their postwar predecessors.

Basically there have been three types of gondola bodies used by Fundimensions and its successors, one of a completely new design. The first one is the reissue of the short 6142 type of the postwar years. Typical of these direct reissues is the 9032 Southern Pacific Gondola of 1975. Like all the new Lionel versions of the gondola, this car has molded brakewheels on each side rather than the older practice of separately installed metal ones or no brakewheels at all.

The second gondola is also a short car, but it is a version which is new with modern era Lionel. This car is illustrated by the 9033 Penn Central of 1977. If you look closely, you can distinguish this car from the earlier carry-over model by the thick rim on the long sides of the car and the smaller molded brakewheel on the car sides. Like the other short gondola, this car has been used in inexpensive sets.

The third type of gondola is by far the most numerous and the most varied in type; it is the long 6462-type gondola. This car shows several construction variations from its later postwar predecessors. The modern Lionel car has molded brakewheels, where the older car either had metal ones or none at all. In the later postwar cars the bottom was absolutely smooth and devoid of all ornamentation. Fundimensions

added girder and rivet work to the bottom of its 6462-type gondolas, and they look much better as a result.

If you look closely at the bottom of the newer Lionel gondolas, you will see a circle with the numbers "6462-2" and either "1" or "2" under the part number. This marking was present on the postwar cars as well. The presence of "1" and "2" numbering does not mean that a separate mold was used. It refers to the side of the mold from which the car emerged after the plastic injection process. The mold for the 6462-type cars was made in such a way that two cars were made at a time. The "1" and "2" numbers merely tell you which mold side your particular car came from.

The first of the early long gondolas was the 9140 Burlington model of 1970. This car was made in at least three shades of green, none being particularly more scarce than another. However, there is one version of the 9141 Burlington Northern from 1971 which is genuinely rare. Most of the 9141 production was green, but a few were made in tuscan. This car is highly prized. So is the 9143 Canadian National Gondola made for Canadian sets distributed by Parker Brothers in 1971. This car is also very hard to find. Two Santa Fe gondolas of similar design can cause confusion as well. One of them, the 9284, was available in 1977 and 1978 in some sets; this car had a red and yellow body in a "half-and-half" paint configuration. In 1980 a black and yellow 9379 Santa Fe Gondola of the same design was made for the Cross Country Express Set. The black and yellow one is harder to find, although neither is really scarce. To add to the confusion, Republic Steel models have been made in different numbers in yellow, blue, and green cars, all with the same Republic Steel logos and markings. All these are fairly common, though the yellow 9055 model is less frequently seen.

Since the Quaker City Limited Collector Set of 1978, most of the collector sets have included a gondola in colorful markings with Standard O trucks. Many of these gondolas, and some more common ones, have included round canisters like those of the postwar era. These canisters can be found in varying shades of orange, white, silver-gray, and red. A few cars have the square radioactive waste canisters without the lighting apparatus.

There have been other gondolas in the modern era Lionel lineup from time to time, some of them quite remarkable. Scale Standard O gondolas were produced for the Standard O Series beginning in 1973. These cars were scale-length with the sprung trucks typical of the series, and they also included a highly realistic coal load. They came in Wabash, Southern Pacific, Grand Trunk, and New York Central markings. In the case of the Wabash, two examples of the car have been reported in gray rather than in black. Needless to say, these are probably factory prototypes and are extremely rare. Another Standard O gondola, again in New York Central markings, was produced in 1985. A colorful Railgon version was made in 1986

Top shelf: 6201 Union Pacific, 6205 Canadian Pacific. Second shelf: 6206 C & I M, 6208 B & O. Third shelf: 9131 Rio Grande, 9136 Republic Steel. Bottom shelf: 9141 Burlington Northern, 9142 Republic Steel.

as part of a special direct-mail offer, and for 1987 there is a Standard O Conrail Gondola as part of the Conrail Limited Set.

Some gondolas were made to operate, using as models two highly successful operating cars from the postwar era. The 9307 Erie animated Gondola is a direct reissue of the 3444 model of the postwar era. In this amusing and colorful car, the pull of a lever sets off a vibrator motor which turns a length of 16 mm film around two spools. Attached to the film by little metal clips are figures of a policeman and a hobo. The film and spools are cleverly concealed by a load of crates, making it appear that the policeman is chasing the hobo around and around the crates. A less expensive version of this car came in Union Pacific markings. This car used a rubber band drive rather than a vibrator motor, and it would only work when the car was in motion. The other operating gondola, the 9290 Union Pacific model issued in 1983 as part of the Gold Coast Limited collector set, is a revival of the popular operating barrel car. A vibrator mechanism sends six wooden barrels up a chute built into the car; at the top of the chute, a workman kicks them off the car into a bin (or onto the postwar barrel ramp, which has not been reissued). This car was made in black and yellow Union Pacific markings. A tuscan Conrail barrel car was scheduled for 1984 production, but it was delayed until September 1985. Both of these barrel cars have the old postwar bar-end metal trucks because these are the only trucks which

can be equipped with the sliding shoe contacts needed for the car's operation. Unfortunately, the Union Pacific version is quite scarce. The handsome Conrail barrel car, however, is readily available. Both barrel cars had a strange and unanticipated problem. Lionel equipped them with varnished barrels instead of the postwar plain wooden barrels. The varnished barrels are so slippery that the vibration of the car cannot send them up the ramp very easily. Unvarnished postwar barrels correct the problem handily, of course, even though the varnished barrels look much better.

The modern era Lionel production of the gondola has added some much-needed color and attractiveness to this usually humdrum piece of rolling stock. The special collector series cars and some of the scarce variations in the earlier production are well worth a search by the Lionel collector.

Gd VG Exc Mt

1987 MOPAR EXPRESS: 1987, tuscan body, white lettering, Symington-Wayne trucks. C. O'Dell Collection.   -- -- -- **20**

6200 F. E. C.: 1981, orange long yellow numbers and letters, three silver-finished plastic canisters, part of 1154 Reading Yard King Set.
-- -- **8 10**

6201 UNION PACIFIC: 1983, yellow long body, tan crates, red lettering, animated car with rubber-band belt drive from axle, railroad cop chases hobo around crates only when car is moving. See 9307 for vibrator motor version.
-- -- **15 20**

Top shelf: 9315 Southern Pacific, 9143 Canadian National. Second shelf: 9290 Union Pacific, 9336 CP Rail. Bottom shelf: 9385 Alaska, 9379 Santa Fe.

6202 WESTERN MARYLAND: 1982, long black body, with white lettering, black plastic coal load, Standard O trucks, part of 1260 Continental Limited Set. To date, this and the 19401 Great Northern model are the only gondolas outside of the large Standard O series which are equipped with a coal load. C. Lang comments.   -- -- 25 30

6205 CANADIAN PACIFIC: 1983, long tuscan body with white lettering, CP electrocal, Standard O trucks, two gray canisters, available as separate sale item.   -- -- 25 30

6206 C & I M (Chicago & Illinois Midland): 1983, red long body with white lettering, two gray atomic energy-type canisters without lights and lettering, Symington-Wayne trucks, part of 1354 Northern Freight Flyer Set.   -- 8 10 15

6207 SOUTHERN: 1983, black short body with white lettering, two red canisters, Symington-Wayne trucks, part of 1353 Southern Streak Set.   -- -- 6 8

6208 B & O: 1983, dark blue long body, yellow "B & O" and "6208" at left of car, yellow Chessie cat at center, and yellow "Chessie System" at right. Reporting marks along lower girders, Standard O trucks, two gray canisters. Designed to be added to the 1980 Royal Limited Set. R. LaVoie comment.   -- -- 25 30

6209 NEW YORK CENTRAL: 1985, Standard O gondola, black body, white lettering, Standard O trucks, simulated coal load.   -- -- 30 45

6210 ERIE-LACKAWANNA: 1984-85, black long body, white lettering and Erie logo, Standard O trucks, two gray unlettered atomic energy containers. From Erie-Lackawanna Limited Set.   -- -- 25 30

6211 CHESAPEAKE & OHIO: 1984-85, unpainted black short body, yellow lettering and logo, two yellow canisters, Symington-Wayne trucks. From Set 1402.   -- -- -- 10
See also Special Production chapter.

6214 LIONEL LINES: 1983-84, orange long body and interior, last four outer panels on right painted dark blue, "LIONEL / LINES" in dark blue across orange panels, red, white, and blue "L" circular herald on blue area, car number underscored and overscored, Symington-Wayne trucks.   -- -- 25 35

6231 RAILGON: 1986, Standard O gondola, black body, yellow lower edge and ends, yellow logo and lettering, Standard O trucks. Available only through special direct-mail offer from Lionel.   -- -- 75 100

6254 NICKEL PLATE ROAD: 1986, long gondola, black body, yellow lettering, two silver canisters, Symington-Wayne trucks. Part of Nickel Plate Special Set 1602.   -- -- 10 12

6258 A T S F: 1985, short gondola, dark blue body, yellow lettering and logo, Symington-Wayne trucks, dummy couplers. C. Rohlfing Collection. Part of Midland Freight Set.   -- -- -- 6

X6260 NEW YORK CENTRAL: 1985, gray long body, black lettering and oval NYC logo, two black canisters, Symington-Wayne trucks. Part of Yard Chief Switcher Set.   -- -- 15 18

6272 A T S F: 1986, long gondola, red body, yellow lettering and cross logo, two black cable reels, Standard O trucks, also included three gray canisters — unusual, since both loads will not fit at the same time. When sold separately, the car is expected to have either load, but not both. Part of Santa Fe Work Train Service Station Special Set. J. Kouba and J. Arman Collections.   -- -- 20 25

9017 WABASH: 1978, 1980-81, short body, red with white lettering, Symington-Wayne trucks, three canisters.   -- -- 8 12

9030 KICKAPOO VALLEY AND NORTHERN: 1972, black base, small tilting dump bin.

(A) Green top.	2	3	5	7
(B) Red top.	1	2	3	4
(C) Yellow top.	2	3	4	6

9031 NICKEL PLATE: 1974, 1979, 1983, brown short body, white lettering, Symington-Wayne trucks, fixed couplers 1974, 1979, operating couplers, 1983. We do not know if the 1983 version has small or large brakewheel. The 1983 version came as part of 1253 Heavy Iron Set.

(A) Large brakewheel.	2	3	5	7
(B) Small brakewheel.	2	3	5	7

9032 SOUTHERN PACIFIC: 1975, 1978, red short body, white lettering, Symington-Wayne trucks, fixed couplers.

(A) Light red body, small brakewheel.	1	2	3	4
(B) Dark red body, small brakewheel.	1	2	3	4

9031 Nickel Plate .

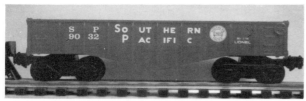

9032 Southern Pacific.

(C) Medium red body, large brakewheel. 1 2 3 4

9033 PENN CENTRAL: 1977, 1979, 1981, 1982, light green short body, white lettering, Symington-Wayne trucks, fixed couplers, small brakewheel.

1 2 3 4

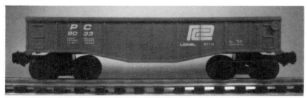

9033 Penn Central.

9055 REPUBLIC STEEL: 1977-81, yellow long body, dark blue lettering, one fixed coupler, one manumatic coupler, Symington-Wayne trucks, three silver canisters, plastic wheels.

4 6 10 12

9131 RIO GRANDE: 1974, orange long body, black lettering, Symington-Wayne trucks, one disc coupler, one fixed coupler, no MPC logo.
(A) Light orange body. 1 2 5 8
(B) Medium orange body. 1 2 5 8
(C) Darker orange body. 1 2 5 8

9136 REPUBLIC STEEL: 1972-79, blue long body, white lettering, Symington-Wayne trucks, one manumatic coupler, one fixed coupler, plastic wheels, MPC logo.
(A) Lighter blue. 2 4 8 10
(B) Medium blue. 2 4 8 10
(C) Darker blue. 2 4 8 10
(D) Darker blue, MPC logo dropped, post-1972 production. C. Rohlfing comment. 2 4 8 10

9140 Burlington.

9140 BURLINGTON: 1970-71, 1976, 1980-81, green long body, white lettering, one manumatic coupler, one fixed coupler, plastic wheels.
(A) 1970, light green body, AAR trucks, flat surface brakewheel, MPC logo.

4 6 10 12

(B) 1971, medium light green body, Symington-Wayne trucks, no MPC logo. Part of 1662 Black River Freight Set of 1976. C. Rohlfing comment.
4 6 8 10
(C) 1971, medium dark green body, Symington-Wayne trucks, no MPC logo.
4 6 8 10
(D) 1971, dark green body, Symington-Wayne trucks, no MPC logo.
4 6 8 10

See also Factory Errors and Prototypes.

9141 BURLINGTON NORTHERN: 1971, green long body, white lettering, Symington-Wayne trucks (except C), one manumatic coupler, one fixed coupler, metal wheels, MPC logo, flat surface brakewheel.
(A) Light green body. 2 4 6 8
(B) Medium green body. 2 4 6 8
(C) Dark green body, AAR trucks. C. Rohlfing comment. 4 6 8 10
(D) Tuscan body, white lettering and BN logo, "BLT 1-70", Symington-Wayne trucks, Canadian production only. Very hard to find. When sold separately, came in Parker Brothers Type I box with small cellophane window and black Parker Brothers logo. G. Halverson, R. LaVoie, "Triple T", and R. Bryan Collections.
50 100 150 200

See also Factory Errors and Prototypes.

9142 REPUBLIC STEEL: 1971: green long body, white lettering, Symington-Wayne trucks, one manumatic coupler, one fixed coupler, plastic wheels, MPC logo.
(A) Dark green body. 2 4 6 8
(B) Medium green body, recessed brakewheel. C. Rohlfing Collection.
2 4 6 8
(C) Same as (B), but metal wheel sets. H. Edmunds Collection.
2 4 6 8

See also Special Production and Factory Errors and Prototypes chapters.

9143 CANADIAN NATIONAL: 1973, maroon long body, white lettering, Symington-Wayne trucks, one manumatic coupler, one fixed coupler, metal wheels, MPC logo, sold primarily in Canada. Somewhat hard to find.
20 30 40 50

9144 Rio Grande.

9144 RIO GRANDE: 1974, black long body, yellow lettering, Symington-Wayne trucks, two disc couplers, metal wheels, no MPC logo.
2 4 6 8

See also Factory Errors and Prototypes.

9225 CONRAIL: 1984-85, operating barrel car, tuscan body, black chute, white lettering and Conrail "wheel" logo, blue man with flesh-colored hands and face, six varnished barrels, postwar bar-end trucks, includes black dump tray.
-- 30 40 50

9283 UNION PACIFIC: 1977, yellow long body, red lettering, Symington-Wayne trucks, metal wheels, no MPC logo. Part of 1760 Heartland Express Set. C. Lang comment. 2 5 8 10

9283 Union Pacific.

9284 Santa Fe.

9821 Southern Pacific.

9284 SANTA FE: 1977-78, red and yellow long body, yellow and red lettering, Symington-Wayne trucks, metal wheels, no MPC logo. Part of 1762 Wabash Cannonball Set. C. Lang comment.   10   12   15   20

9290 UNION PACIFIC: 1983, operating barrel car, man "unloads" barrel, vibrator mechanism, six varnished wooden barrels, plastic unloading bin, black body, yellow lettering. Postwar bar-end trucks used because Standard O trucks were not adaptable to sliding shoe mechanism. Reissue of 3562-type car from 1954-58 although with new road name. Only available as part of 1361 Gold Coast Limited Set. C. Lang comments.   --   50   70   85

9307 ERIE: 1979-80, red with white lettering and Erie logo, O27-style die-cast passenger trucks, tan crate load with black lettering, animated car with vibrator motor, railroad cop chases hobo around crates when lever is pulled.
(A) Partially painted hobo.   --   30   40   50
(B) Completely painted hobo. Mellan, M. Kowalski, C. O'Dell, and J. Glockley Collections. Other observations show differences in the cop and hobo figures, such as elaborate hand-painting on either or both figures which may be factory production. The Glockley version has crates with both sides lettered and the Kowalski version has a fully painted cop figure as well. Further reader comments are invited.   --   --   60   80
See also Factory Errors and Prototypes.

9315 SOUTHERN PACIFIC: 1979, brown plastic long body painted brown, white lettering, "BLT 1-79", Southern Pacific decal with white letters on black background, built-in small brakewheel, part of Southern Pacific Special Set, Standard O trucks.   12   15   25   35

9336 C P RAIL: 1979, red plastic long body, white lettering, brakewheels embossed in car ends, black and white logo appears at end opposite brakewheel, Standard O trucks, came in Type IV box, 6462 mold designation on underside, from 1971 Quaker City Limited Set. Miller and J. Breslin observations.   --   15   20   25

9340 ILLINOIS CENTRAL GULF: 1979-81.
(A) Orange short body with black lettering, yellow canisters, plastic wheels, Symington-Wayne trucks.   --   --   6   10
(B) Red short body with white lettering, no canisters, Symington-Wayne trucks. Part of 1159 Midnight Flyer Set made for Toys 'R Us. G. Kline Collection.   --   --   15   20

9370 SEABOARD: 1980, tuscan long body with yellow lettering, three silver-finished plastic canisters, Standard O trucks, from 1071 Mid Atlantic Limited Set.   --   15   20   25

9379 ATSF: 1980, black and yellow, long body two gray plastic canisters, Symington-Wayne trucks, came with 1072 Cross Country Express.   --   15   25   35

9385 ALASKA: 1981, yellow long body with black lettering, four white canisters, Standard O trucks. Part of 1160 Great Lakes Limited Set.   --   20   25   30

9820 WABASH: 1973-74, simulated coal load, Standard O series with Standard O trucks.
(A) Black body, white lettering.   20   25   30   40
(B) Brown body, coal load, not produced with trucks or truck mounting holes. Produced by Lionel on special order for O Scale modelers to mount own trucks; originally sold by dealer Andrew Kriswalus. C. Lang Collection.   NRS
(C) Same as (B), but black body and coal load. C. Lang Collection.   NRS
See also Factory Errors and Prototypes.

9821 SOUTHERN PACIFIC: 1973-74, brown or black body, white lettering, simulated coal load, Standard O series with Standard O trucks.
(A) Brown body.   20   25   30   40
(B) Black body. Hard to find.   --   --   275   350
See also Factory Errors and Prototypes.

9822 Grand Trunk.

9822 GRAND TRUNK: 1974, blue body, white lettering, simulated coal load, Standard O series with Standard O trucks.   20   25   30   40

9824 New York Central.

9824 NEW YORK CENTRAL: 1975, black body, white lettering, simulated coal load, Standard O series with Standard O trucks.   20   40   60   75

16304 RAIL BLAZER: 1987, short gondola, red body (shown as orange in catalogue, but produced in red to match rest of set), white number and lettering, two black cable reels, arch bar trucks. Part of 11701 Rail Blazer Set.   --   --   --   6

16309 WABASH: Scheduled for 1988, short gondola, medium brown body, white lettering and numbers, two unlettered white canisters, Symington-Wayne trucks, operating couplers. Part of 11703 Iron Horse Freight Set.   --   --   --   8

17401 CONRAIL: 1987, standard O gondola, brown-painted body, white lettering and "wheel" logo, coal load, Standard O trucks. Part of 11700 Conrail Limited Set.   --   --   35   50

19400 MILWAUKEE ROAD: 1987, long gondola, brown body, white lettering, red and white rectangular Milwaukee logo, Standard O trucks, two black cable reels. Part of Milwaukee Fallen Flags Set 2.   --   --   --   25

19401 GREAT NORTHERN: 1988, long gondola; black body, white slanted lettering, red and white "Goat" circular logo, coal load. Part of Fallen Flags Set No. 3.   --   --   --   30

NO NUMBER: 1984, short gondola, orange body, small molded brakewheel, luminous individual letters "DANGER", dummy couplers. Part of Black Cave Flyer Set.   --   --   6   8

Chapter VIII
HOPPER CARS

Top shelf: 6104 Southern Quad Hopper. Middle shelf: 6105 Reading and 6109 C & O Operating Hopper Cars. Bottom shelf: 6113 Illinois Central. G. and D. Halverson and A. Conto Collections, G. Stern photograph.

With all the variety shown in its freight car lines, it is somewhat odd that Lionel has only used two basic types of hopper cars in the modern era until quite recently. Perhaps this is because the company has been able to make good use of the two existing types without resorting to new dies. Some collectors, however, have expressed a desire to see new versions of this car, especially the ultra-modern cylindrical bodied center-flow hoppers such as those recently issued in O scale by the Weaver concern in Northumberland, Pennsylvania. In 1986 Lionel did respond to collector requests by issuing the first of several fine models of the A C F center-flow hoppers. Just prior to that, Lionel came out with a nice model of the little iron ore cars so common on America's bulk ore carriers today. In our first edition, William Meyer and Pastor Philip Smith explained the background of these cars.

The first hopper issued by Fundimensions was the 9010 Great Northern short Hopper Car of 1970, essentially a revised version of the very common postwar 6456 Lehigh Valley Hopper Cars.

The only difference between the Fundimensions car and the postwar car (aside from the usual change of trucks) is the presence of a molded brakewheel on one end of most of the Fundimensions cars. The Fundimensions short hopper has been used almost universally in inexpensive production since the beginning. It has been issued in Chessie, Rio Grande, D. T. & I., Canadian National, and many other railroad markings. Some of the earlier cars have color variations which are quite scarce. For example, there is a very rare 9011 Great Northern in a dark royal blue color and two 9012 T. A. & G. color variations which are hard to find. Some cars have lettering variations, too, which mark them as scarce variations, notably another T. A. & G. Hopper with yellow lettering instead of white.

In 1981 the short hopper was modified to reproduce the operating hopper car of postwar years. It is somewhat curious that six versions of this car have been produced, but the coal ramp to make these cars work has not been reissued to date! (The postwar version is, however, readily available. The only

Top shelf: 6100 Ontario Northland and 6101 BN. Second shelf: 6102 GN and 6103 CN. Third shelf: 6107 Shell and 6114 CNW. Bottom shelf: 6124 Delaware & Hudson and 6446-25 N & W. G. and D. Halverson and A. Conto Collections, G. Stern photograph.

trouble is that the coupler release at the top of the ramp will not work with a disc-operating coupler; perhaps that is what has held up the production of this accessory.) A metal plate is attached to the bottom of the car, and the square bin ports are punched out of the car. A plunger is attached to the plate which, when pulled down by an electromagnet, opens the bins and releases the coal. Lionel has put this car out in Great Northern, Reading, Chesapeake & Ohio, Erie, New York Central, and Wabash markings thus far.

The second type of hopper car issued in the modern era has been the big and handsome "quad" hopper which was first issued in the postwar years in Lehigh Valley markings. This car has come at various times with and without hatched covers, with and (mostly) without a metal center spreader bar, and with metal or plastic plates holding the trucks to the car. The latest versions of this car have come with coal loads instead of hatched covers. Some versions have been produced with rectangular builders' plates on the car sides; others have lacked them. Some cars come both ways. Many, many versions of this car have been produced in both railroad and corporate markings, beginning with the blue uncovered 9130 B & O Hopper of 1970.

Tom Rollo, the author of our 2156 Passenger Station article in the first edition of this book, has pointed out a curious construction feature of this car. If you look at the car's interior, you will see a large drum-shaped projection at the bottom center of the car where the mold mark is. From underneath, there is a deep recess with two bracket slots on each side; just adjacent to the outer edge, there are two holes which look like receptacles for screws. Mr. Rollo's conjecture is that at one time an operating mechanism was considered for this car, but it was never produced. The same construction feature shows up on the postwar cars right from the beginning. (Other collectors have arrived at this conclusion independently.) Even more fascinating is the conjecture that this opening was meant to accommodate a radio receiver such as those designed for the Electronic Radio Control sets produced from 1946 to 1949. It should be noted that the first quad hoppers were not produced in the postwar era until 1954. We would like to hear from our readers about this bit of speculation, for which there is strong circumstantial evidence. It is even more interesting that the Fundimensions, Kenner-Parker, and Lionel, Inc. versions of these hopper cars retain this odd feature so many years later.

Another oddity about these modern era hoppers is that there are frequently differences between the cars offered as part of

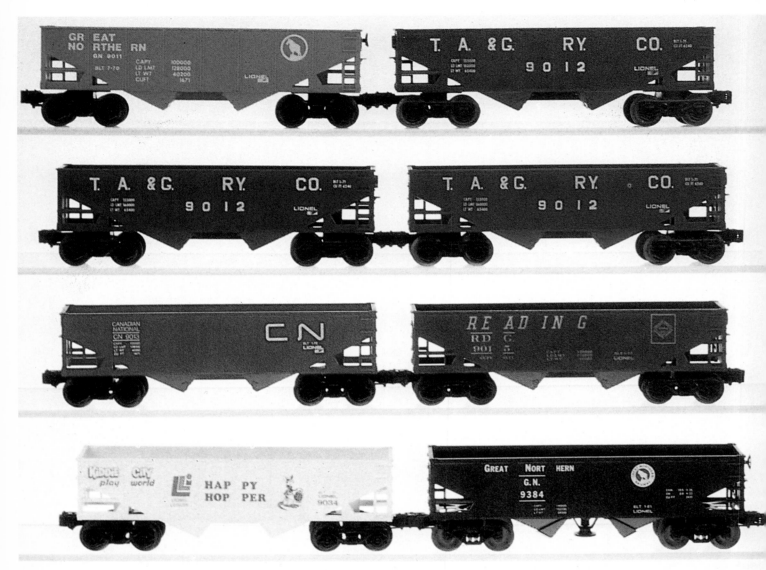

Top shelf: Light blue 9011 Great Northern and dark blue 9012 T. A. & G. Second shelf: Medium blue 9012 T. A. & G. and royal blue 9012
A. & G. Third shelf: 9013 C N and 9015 Reading. Bottom shelf: 9034 Lionel Leisure and 9384 G N. G. and D. Halverson and A. Conto Cc
lections, G. Stern photograph.

sets and the same cars offered for separate sale. For example, the 9111 Norfolk and Western Hopper in sets is an unpainted medium brown color. The same car in separate sale boxes is frequently, though not always, tuscan-painted brown plastic. The normal 9135 Norfolk and Western Hopper is navy or royal blue with white lettering. In the late example included with the 1975 Spirit of America Set, the lettering on the car is gray instead of white. The separate sale 9117 Alaska Hopper has a black cover; reportedly, some versions included in a service station set had orange covers. (A. J. Conto Collection.) There are several other examples of this phenomenon, especially in the early production of these hopper cars.

There seem to be three levels of value attached to the quad hoppers. The most common of these hoppers seem to be the ones with corporate logos, such as the Domino Sugar, Planters Peanut, and Sun-Maid Raisins examples. (A noteworthy exception is the Ralston-Purina car, which is very hard to find.)

Most of the cars with railroad names are a little more desirable and scarce, such as the Pennsylvania, Virginian, Illinois Central, and some of the early B&O and Norfolk and Western cars. The scarcest cars are those available as club convention cars, those available only in special sets, and some variations of the earliest cars. Examples of these are the gray-lettered 9110 B & O, the LCCA Corning car, the Alcoa, and the Southern cars. Most of the hopper cars are relatively easy to find, and the beginning collector can amass quite a few of them readily at reasonable prices. None of these cars can be considered as truly rare, but they add a nice look to an operating layout, especially the cars with railroad markings and full covers.

Another hopper recently introduced is worth mention because it shows that Lionel, Inc. is indeed moving into new areas with these cars. In 1984 Lionel introduced two versions of a stubby little iron ore hopper car similar to those used in western sections of this country. One car came in black with

Top shelf: 9110 B & O and 9111 N & W. Second shelf: 9113 N & W and 9115 Planters. Third shelf: 9117 Alaska and 9119 Detroit & Mackinac. Bottom shelf: 9130 B & O and 9134 Virginian. G. and D. Halverson and A. Conto Collections, G. Stern photograph.

white Penn Central markings, and the other was a tuscan Soo car with white lettering. Since then other road names have been produced, including Canadian National, Northern Pacific, Pennsylvania, Milwaukee, and Lehigh Valley versions.

This little car is an excellent model of the real cars and looks similar to the Atlas scale O cars which have been made for a long time. The only complaint collectors have expressed about these cars is that they sit too high on their Symington-Wayne trucks.

Nonetheless, these cars have been brisk sellers for the very good reason that collectors have bought whole fleets for their unit trains. As a result, the value of some of these cars has doubled in less than a year's time. Lionel, Inc. will probably market many more versions of this car in the years to come.

In 1986 a new and extremely attractive hopper car emerged from Lionel in the form of a scale model of the A C F center-flow hopper car. This car has the wide, chunky appearance of the real thing, and collector reaction to it has been very favorable. Unfortunately, the ones produced so far have been severely limited in production because they have been part of limited edition sets. In 1986 two of them, a Burlington Northern and a Chicago and North Western, were issued as part of a special, direct-from-Lionel mail order promotion. Currently, a gray Conrail A C F hopper is part of the Conrail Limited Set of 1987.

In early 1988 Lionel produced a Chessie unit train with beautifully detailed "stretched" three-bay A C F center-flow hopper. No doubt more of these cars will be produced eventually, but it does seem a shame that so far they are severely limited in availability. With their highly detailed tops and rails, their great bellied sides, and their Standard O trucks, these cars look wonderful on anyone's layout.

It is interesting to guess whether Lionel has other new designs of hopper cars in the works. Whatever the case, the Fundimensions hoppers once more illustrate the ability of the firm to make the most of its existing resources.

        Gd VG Exc Mt

0784: See Special Production chapter.

6076 LEHIGH VALLEY: 1970, short hopper, black body with white lettering, equipped with Symington-Wayne trucks, one operating and one dummy coupler. Possible postwar carry-over equipped with Fundimensions trucks and included in an early set. Reader comments invited. C. Lang Collection.   **NRS**

6100 ONTARIO NORTHLAND: 1981-82, blue sides and cover, yellow trim, yellow "triple lightning" logo; Symington-Wayne trucks.   -- -- **25** **30**

6101 BURLINGTON: 1981, 1983, green sides and cover, white lettering, Symington-Wayne trucks.   -- -- **15** **25**

6102 GREAT NORTHERN: 1981, tuscan body and cover, white lettering, FARR Series 3 logo, Symington-Wayne trucks, from Famous American Railroad Series 3, available only as separate sale item.   -- -- **35** **50**

Top shelf: Purple 9135 N & W, blue 9135 N & W. Second shelf: Two 9213 M St L cars. Third shelf: 9260 Reynolds and 9262 Ralston-Purina. Bottom shelf: 9263 Pennsylvania and 9265 WM. G. and D. Halverson and A. Conto Collections, G. Stern photograph.

6103 CANADIAN NATIONAL: 1981, gray with dark red lettering, maroon cover, die-cast sprung trucks; part of 1158 Maple Leaf Limited Set. C. Rohlfing Collection.   -- -- **25 35**

6104 SOUTHERN: 1983, dark green body with coal load, gold lettering and FARR 4 logo. Available for separate sale. L. Caponi comment.
                                           -- -- **45 55**

6105 READING: 1982, tuscan body, white lettering and logo, operating hopper.   -- -- **30 40**

6106 N W: 1982, gray with black lettering, black cover, die-cast sprung Standard O trucks, disc-operating couplers; part of 1260 Continental Limited Set.
                                           -- -- **35 45**

6107 SHELL: 1982, covered hopper, yellow body and cover, black and red lettering; Symington-Wayne trucks.   -- -- **15 25**

6109 C & O: 1983, operating car with opening bins, black body; white lettering.
                                           -- -- **25 40**

6110 MISSOURI PACIFIC: 1983, covered hopper, black body, black cover, white lettering; Symington-Wayne trucks.   -- -- **15 25**

6111 L & N: 1983, covered hopper, gray body and cover with red lettering, Symington-Wayne trucks.   -- -- **15 25**

6112 COMMONWEALTH EDISON: See Special Production chapter.

6113 ILLINOIS CENTRAL: 1983, short hopper, black with white lettering; sold as part of 1354 Northern Freight Flyer Set.   -- -- **10 15**

6114 C N W: 1983, covered hopper, dark green body and cover, yellow lettering and logo; available only as part of 1361 Gold Coast Limited Set.
                                           -- -- **45 65**

6115 SOUTHERN: 1983, short hopper, gray with red lettering; sold as part of 1353 Southern Streak Set.   -- -- -- **15**

6116 SOO LINE: 1984-85, iron ore car, tuscan body, white lettering; Symington-Wayne trucks, open framework on car ends. Somewhat erratic availability because many operators have bought whole fleets of these cars for unit trains.   -- -- **25 35**

6117 ERIE: 1984-85, operating hopper, black body, white lettering, gold Erie diamond logo, Standard O trucks. Plunger opens bins when activated by remote track. Operating coal ramp has still not been reissued; possible reason is that Standard O trucks will not uncouple by remote control from top of postwar ramp. R. LaVoie comment.   -- -- **25 35**

6118 ERIE: 1984-85, covered hopper, gray body and cover, black lettering, black and white diamond Erie logo; Standard O trucks. From Erie-Lackawanna Limited Set.   -- -- **35 40**

6122 PENN CENTRAL: 1984-85, iron ore car, black ore car body, white "PC" lettering and logo; Symington-Wayne trucks, open framework on car ends. Same comments as those for 6116 above.   -- -- **25 35**

6123 PENNSYLVANIA: 1984-85, covered hopper, gray body and cover, black lettering, white and black PRR Keystone, gold FARR 5 diamond-shaped logo,

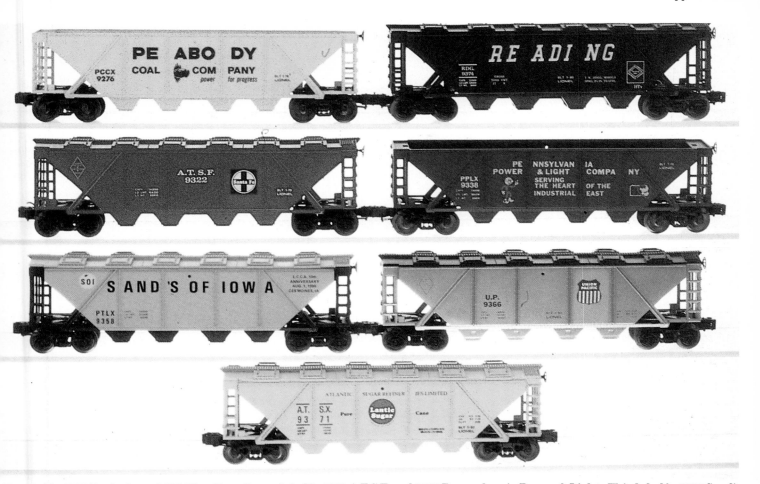

Top shelf: 9276 Peabody and 9374 Reading. Second shelf: 9322 A.T.S.F. and 9288 Pennsylvania Power & Light. Third shelf: 9358 Sand's and 9366 U.P. Bottom shelf: 9371 Lantic Sugar. G. and D. Halverson and A. Conto Collections.

Standard O trucks. From Famous American Railroad Set 5. Reportedly, fewer of these hoppers were produced than the other cars, but the maroon tank car and the N5C caboose are regarded as the most desirable cars from this particular set.
-- -- 30 40

6124 DELAWARE & HUDSON: 1984-85, covered hopper, bright red body and cover, yellow lettering and logo; Symington-Wayne trucks.
-- -- 15 25

6126 CANADIAN NATIONAL: 1986, iron ore car, tuscan body, white lettering, Symington-Wayne trucks.
-- -- 17 25

6127 NORTHERN PACIFIC: 1986, iron ore car, black body, white lettering and logo, Symington-Wayne trucks.
-- -- 17 25

6131 ILLINOIS TERMINAL: 1985, covered hopper, yellow body and cover, red lettering, Symington-Wayne trucks. Erroneously listed as Illinois Central by some dealer lists.
-- -- 17 25

6134 BURLINGTON NORTHERN: 1986, A C F two-bay center-flow hopper, Cascade green body, white lettering and logo, Standard O trucks. Available only as part of a direct-mail campaign from Lionel.
-- -- 75 150

6135 CHICAGO & NORTH WESTERN: 1986, A C F two-bay center-flow hopper, medium gray body, black and yellow North Western logo, yellow lettering, Standard O trucks. Available only as part of a direct-mail campaign from Lionel. R. LaVoie Collection.
-- -- 75 150

6137 NICKEL PLATE ROAD: 1986-87, short hopper, gray body, black lettering, Symington-Wayne trucks, part of Set 1602, the Nickel Plate Special.
-- -- 10 15

6138 B & O: 1986, quad hopper, gray body, black lettering and logo, no cover or center spreader bar, Symington-Wayne trucks. Part of Set 1652, the B & O Freight.
-- -- 20 30

6150 A T S F: 1985-86, short hopper, dark blue body, yellow lettering and logo, Symington-Wayne trucks, dummy couplers. Part of Midland Freight Set. C. Rohlfing Collection.
-- -- 10 15

6177 READING: 1986-87, short hopper, tuscan body, yellow lettering and logo, Symington-Wayne trucks. Part of Set 1605, the Cannonball Express. Appears to be identical to earlier 9015 except for new number.
-- -- 10 15

6446-25 N & W: 1970, covered hopper, special production by Fundimensions with postwar number for Glen Uhl, an Ohio Lionel dealer. Royal blue body and cover, Type I unlabeled box, AAR trucks. This car has many more plastic lap lines than usual; these are formed as the styrene plastic cools in the mold. Reportedly, only 450 were made. M. Schoenberg, T. Rollo, and G. Halverson Collections.
-- -- 150 175

7504 Lionel 75th Anniversary.

7504 LIONEL 75th ANNIVERSARY: 1975, covered hopper, blue body, red cover, no builder's plate.
-- 10 20 25

9010 GREAT NORTHERN: 1971, blue body, white lettering, plastic brakewheels, metal wheels, one manumatic coupler, one fixed coupler, MPC logo.

(A) Medium blue body, AAR trucks, "1-70".   3   4   6   8

(B) Light blue body, AAR trucks, "1-70".   3   4   6   8

(C) Medium light blue body, AAR trucks, "7-70".   3   4   6   8

(D) Light blue body, Symington-Wayne trucks, "1-70".   3   4   6   8

See also Factory Errors and Prototypes.

9011 GREAT NORTHERN: 1971, 1979, medium blue body, white lettering, "7-70", Symington-Wayne trucks, plastic wheels, one manumatic coupler, one fixed coupler.

(A) Externally-mounted brakewheel, MPC logo.   3   4   6   8

(B) Built-in brakewheel, MPC logo.   3   4   6   8

(C) Built-in brakewheel, no MPC logo.   3   4   6   8

(D) Same as (A), but AAR trucks. C. Rohlfing Collection.   3   4   6   8

(E) Deep royal blue mold. Very rare.   --   --   120   165

9012 T A & G: 1971-72, 1979, blue body, white lettering, built-in brakewheel, "1-70," Symington-Wayne trucks, plastic wheels, one manumatic coupler, one fixed coupler, MPC logo.

(A) Dark blue body (navy).   2   3   5   7

(B) Medium blue.   2   3   5   7

(C) Bright blue body (royal blue). This model reportedly came only in Canadian sets. Found in 1972 Cross Country Express Set.   --   --   --   65

(D) Same as (C), but yellow lettering. Confirmation requested.   **NRS**

9013 CANADIAN NATIONAL: 1972-74, 1979, red body, white lettering, built-in brakewheel, "1-72", Symington-Wayne trucks, plastic wheels, one manumatic coupler, one fixed coupler, MPC logo.

(A) Dark red body.   2   3   4   5

(B) Medium red body.   2   3   4   5

(C) Light red body.   2   3   4   5

9015 READING: 1973-74, 1979, brown body, yellow lettering, built-in brakewheel, "1-73", Symington-Wayne trucks, metal wheels, one disc coupler, one fixed coupler, no MPC logo. Has been sought after in Middle Atlantic states for use in unit trains by operators. R. LaVoie comment.   7   12   20   25

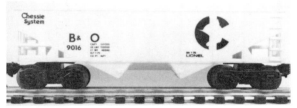

9016 Chessie.

9016 CHESSIE: 1975-79, yellow body, blue lettering, built-in brakewheel, "1-75", Symington-Wayne trucks, metal wheels, one operating coupler, one fixed coupler, no MPC logo.

(A) Yellow body.   2   3   4   6

(B) Light yellow body.   2   3   4   6

See also Special Production chapter.

9017 CANADIAN PACIFIC: 1971, short hopper, tuscan body, gold lettering, Symington-Wayne trucks.   4   5   6   8

9018 DT & I.

9018 D T & I: 1978, 1981, yellow body, black heat-stamped lettering, plastic brakewheel, "BLT 1-78", Symington-Wayne trucks, one manumatic coupler, one fixed coupler.   2   3   5   8

9025 D T & I: 1978, short hopper, came with Santa Fe Double Diesel Set as an optional insert.

(A) Yellow body with black lettering. Forst Collection.   --   --   5   7

(B) Orange body with black lettering. Forst Collection.   --   --   5   7

9028 B & O: 1978, dark blue body, yellow lettering, Chessie emblem, plastic brakewheel, "BLT 1-78", Symington-Wayne trucks, metal wheels, one manumatic coupler, one fixed coupler. The existence of this car has been questioned. Confirmation requested. T. Ladny comment.   **NRS**

9034 LIONEL LEISURE: Made for Kiddie City retail outlet as part of special 1790 Set in 1977; white short hopper body, red, blue, and orange lettering, brown, blue, and orange Casey Kangaroo logo. Hard to find. G. Halverson comment and Collection.   --   --   35   50

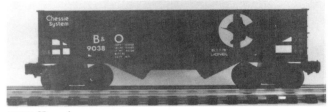

9038 Chessie.

9038 CHESSIE: 1978, 1980-81, plastic trucks and wheels, blue body with yellow lettering, one operating coupler, one fixed coupler.   2   3   5   8

9079 Grand Trunk.

9079 GRAND TRUNK: 1977, deep blue body, white lettering, built-in brakewheel, "1-77", Symington-Wayne trucks, metal wheels, one disc coupler, one fixed coupler, no MPC logo.   5   7   9   12

9110 B & O: 1971, black body, "2-71", builder's plate, not covered, metal truck plate holders.

(A) Gray lettering, reportedly only 1,000 made.   --   --   40   70

(B) White lettering.   10   20   25   35

9111 N & W: 1972, not covered, builder's plate, metal plate holding trucks. Symington-Wayne trucks. Versions found with an unpainted brown body came in sets; those with painted tuscan bodies also came with sets such as 1388 and were sold separately. C. Rohlfing, R. LaVoie, and G. Halverson comments.

(A) Unpainted brown body, white lettering, center spreader bar. R. LaVoie Collection.   5   7   10   20

(B) Painted tuscan body, white lettering, center spreader bar, came with Set 1388, the Golden State Arrow. G. Halverson Collection.   7   10   15   30

(C) Same as (B), but unpainted tuscan body. C. Rohlfing Collection.   7   10   15   30

(D) Same as (A), but lighter unpainted brown body. C. Rohlfing Collection.   5   7   10   20

See also Factory Errors and Prototypes.

9112 Rio Grande.

9112 D & R G W: Orange body, black lettering, orange cover, builder's plate, metal plate holding trucks, Symington-Wayne trucks

(A) Light orange body, deep heat-stamped lettering.	7	10	12	20
(B) Light orange body, flatter heat-stamped lettering.	7	10	12	20
(C) Darker orange body, flatter heat-stamped lettering.	7	10	12	20

9113 N & W: 1973, uncatalogued, gray body, black lettering, from 1973 Canadian Pacific Service Station Set, not covered, center spreader bar, Symington-Wayne trucks, builder's plate, metal plate holding trucks.

10	20	25	30

9114 Morton Salt.

9114 MORTON SALT: 1975-76, navy blue body, white and yellow lettering, yellow cover, builder's plate, metal plate holding trucks.   6   8   12   20

9115 PLANTER'S PEANUTS: 1974-76, dark blue body, yellow lettering, yellow cover, builder's plate, metal plate holding trucks.   6   8   12   20

9116 Domino Sugar.

9116 DOMINO SUGAR: 1974-76, gray body, blue lettering, navy blue cover, builder's plate, metal plate holding trucks.   6   8   12   20

9117 ALASKA: 1974-76, black body, black cover, from 1974 Service Station Set. Also sold separately.

(A) Orange-yellow lettering, builder's plate.	10	12	15	25
(B) Light yellow lettering, builder's plate.	10	12	15	25
(C) Light yellow lettering, no builder's plate.	10	12	15	25

(D) Orange unpainted cover instead of black; came with some of the Service Station Set production. Hard to place a value upon since covers are easily switched. Sample observed came from mint set. G. Halverson observation, A. J. Conto Collection.   **NRS**

9118 CORNING: 1974, see Special Production chapter.

9119 DETROIT & MACKINAC: 1975, red body, white lettering, shiny red cover, "1-76", 1975 Service Station Set, no builder's plate; metal plate holding trucks. Also sold separately.   8   10   15   25
See also Special Production chapter.

9130 B & O: 1970-71, medium royal blue paint on gray plastic, white lettering, "1-70", not covered, center spreader bar; AAR trucks. Some examples came in Type I long boxes with a 9110 label which had the 9110 number crossed out in blue marker ink and the number 9130 reprinted on the label. Incredibly, the picture of the car is numbered 9130! It is also curious to note that this car was produced before the 9110, not afterward. R. LaVoie Collection.

(A) Plastic plate holding trucks.	8	10	15	20
(B) Metal plate holding trucks.	10	12	15	25

(C) Large "B & O" letters, no Capitol dome logo, as shown in 1970 poster catalogue. Confirmation requested.   **NRS**

9134 VIRGINIAN: 1976-77, silver body, blue lettering, blue cover, plastic plate holding trucks, Symington-Wayne trucks.

(A) No builder's plate.	12	15	20	25
(B) Builder's plate.	12	15	20	25

See also Factory Errors and Prototypes.

9135 N & W: 1971, blue or purple body, white lettering, royal blue cover; "9-70", usually Symington-Wayne trucks, metal plate holding trucks, from N & W Set and sold separately.

(A) Royal blue body, no builder's plate.	8	10	15	20
(B) Royal blue body, builder's plate.	8	10	15	20
(C) Purple body, builder's plate; 3,000 manufactured.	15	20	30	40
(D) Light blue body, builder's plate, AAR trucks.	8	10	12	15

(E) Same as (D), but covers glued on by factory. Reader comments requested; this would be a most unusual manufacturing technique.   8   10   12   15

(F) Flat navy blue-painted blue plastic body, glossy unpainted dark blue cover, light gray lettering instead of white, builder's plate, MPC logo, "9-70", Symington-Wayne trucks. It is possible that this particular version was issued in 1974 as part of the "Spirit of America" Diesel Set. Reader comments invited. G. Halverson comment, R. LaVoie and G. Halverson Collections.   --   --   35   50

9213 M & St L: 1978, red, white lettering, cover, sprung die-cast Standard O trucks; part of Service Station Set from 1978.   --   --   20   35

9240 NEW YORK CENTRAL: 1986.

(A) Operating version, tuscan body, white lettering and oval New York Central logo, black metal operating mechanism, Standard O trucks.   --   --   30   40

(B) Non-operating version, light brown body, Symington-Wayne trucks, black plastic plate glued over bin holes, Type VI box. Found in many toy stores as part of 9195 Rolling Stock Assortment. Unusual practice for Lionel, Inc. R. LaVoie, M. Sabatelle, and L. Caponi Collections.   --   --   25   30

9260 REYNOLDS ALUMINUM: 1975-78, "NAHX 9260", blue body, silver lettering, "1-75", metal plate holding trucks, silver cover with blue hatches; Symington-Wayne trucks.

(A) No builder's plate.	8	10	12	20
(B) Builder's plate.	8	10	12	20

9261 Sun-Maid.

9261 SUN-MAID: 1975-76, "GACX 9261", red body, yellow and white lettering, yellow cover, Raisin Lady, and "1-75", no builder's plate; metal plate holding trucks, Symington-Wayne trucks.   10   12   15   20

9262 RALSTON-PURINA RPFX 9262: 1975-76, white body, red and white checks, red and black lettering, "1-75", red and black covers, no builder's plates, metal plate holding trucks, Symington-Wayne trucks. Somewhat hard to find.   20   50   60   90

9263 PENNSYLVANIA: 1975-77, tuscan body, white lettering, black cover, no builder's plate; Symington-Wayne trucks.

(A) Metal plate holding trucks.	10	25	30	40
(B) Plastic plate holding trucks.	10	20	20	30

Note: A few boxes were mislabeled Penn Central, but the cars inside were labeled properly.

9264 Illinois Central.

9264 ILLINOIS CENTRAL: 1975-77, bright orange body, black lettering, black IC circular logo with white "IC", black cover; Symington-Wayne trucks

(A) Metal plate holding trucks, no builder's plate.	15	20	25	30
(B) Same as (A), but plastic plate holding trucks.	15	20	25	30
(C) Same as (A), but builder's plate.	15	20	25	30
(D) Plastic plate holding trucks, builder's plate.	15	20	25	30

See also Special Production chapter.

9265 W M: 1975-77, "Chessie System", yellow body, blue lettering, blue cover, "1-75", no builder's plate; Symington-Wayne trucks.

(A) Metal plate holding trucks.	10	20	25	30
(B) Plastic plate holding trucks.	10	20	25	30

9266 Southern.

9266 SOUTHERN: 1976, gray plastic painted silver, black lettering, red cover, plastic plate holding trucks, red "BIG JOHN" script logo; Symington-Wayne trucks.

(A) Builder's plate.	--	40	50	85
(B) No builder's plate.	--	40	50	75

9267 Alcoa.

9267 ALCOA: 1976, silver-painted gray body, blue lettering, silver cover, no builder's plate, Standard O trucks; from Northern Pacific Service Station Set.

	15	20	30	40

9276 PEABODY: 1978, yellow body, dark green lettering, "BLT 1-78", Standard O trucks, hole for center bar but no bar, part of Milwaukee Limited Set.

	--	15	20	35

9286 B & L E.

9286 B & L E: Orange body, black lettering, black and white decal logo (one of the few instances where Lionel has used decals), black cover, builder's plate, plastic plate holding trucks.

	8	12	15	25

9304 C & O: See Operating Car chapter.

9306 C & O: See Operating Car chapter.

9311 U. P.: See Operating Car chapter.

9322 A. T. S. F.: 1979, red plastic body painted red, white lettering, black and white Santa Fe logo, diamond-shaped herald "Famous American Railroad Series 1" in gold, plastic brakewheel, hole for center brace, no center brace, covers, Symington-Wayne trucks.

	--	40	60	75

9330 KICKAPOO VALLEY: 1972, four wheels.

(A) Green.	1	2	3	8
(B) Red.	1	2	3	8
(C) Yellow.	1	2	3	8

9330 Kickapoo Valley.

9338 PENNSYLVANIA POWER & LIGHT: 1979, tuscan body, yellow lettering, no cover, Standard O trucks, no spreader bar; from 1971 Quaker City Limited Set, an excellent copy of the Bethlehem Steel Corporation prototype. Hard to find because operators have used large numbers of them for unit trains. C. Rohlfing and R. LaVoie comments.

	--	--	55	70

9358 SAND'S OF IOWA: 1980, see Special Production chapter.

9366 U. P.: 1980, silver-painted gray body, black cover, red, white, and blue UNION PACIFIC logo, gold FARR 2 diamond-shaped logo, Symington-Wayne trucks, from Famous American Railroad Series 2, only available as separate sale item.

	--	--	20	30

9371 LANTIC SUGAR (Seaboard): 1980, yellow sides and cover, Standard O trucks, red logo with white "Lantic Sugar" lettering, black lettering. Type IV box is labeled "SEABOARD COAST LINE COVERED HOPPER", but that lettering does not appear on the car; from 1071 Mid-Atlantic Limited Set.

	--	--	25	30

9374 READING: 1980-81, black sides, white lettering, red and black Reading diamond logo, Symington-Wayne trucks; from 1072 Cross Country Express.

	--	--	40	50

9384 GREAT NORTHERN: 1981, operating hopper, dark green body, white lettering, red, black, and white mountain goat logo, bins open by remote control, Standard O trucks; from 1160 Great Lakes Limited Set.

	--	--	55	75

16305 LEHIGH VALLEY: 1987, iron ore car, gray body, black lettering and diamond logo, Symington-Wayne trucks. Part of Set 11702, the Black Diamond.

	--	--	40	50

16402 SOUTHERN: 1987, quad hopper, gray body, black lettering and number, coal load, Standard O trucks. Part of Set 11704, Southern Freight Runner Service Station Special.

	--	--	--	35

16800 See Special Production chapter.

17002 CONRAIL: 1987, A C F center-flow hopper, gray body, black lettering and logo, Standard O trucks. Part of Set 11700, the Conrail Limited.

	--	--	75	90

17100 CHESSIE SYSTEM: 1988, three-bay A C F center-flow hopper, new "stretched" design based on two-bay models introduced in 1986. Bright yellow body, dark blue lettering and Chessie Cat logo, Standard O trucks; part of 11705 Chessie System Unit Train.

	--	--	--	50

17101 CHESSIE SYSTEM: 1988, matches 17100 above.

	--	--	--	50

17102 CHESSIE SYSTEM: 1988, matches 17100 above.

	--	--	--	50

17103 CHESSIE SYSTEM: 1988, matches 17100 above.

	--	--	--	50

17104 CHESSIE SYSTEM: 1988, matches 17100 above.

	--	--	--	50

19300 PENNSYLVANIA: 1987, iron ore car, tuscan body, white lettering, tuscan and white PRR Keystone logo, Symington-Wayne trucks.

	--	--	--	20

19301 MILWAUKEE ROAD: 1987, iron ore car, red oxide body, white lettering, Symington-Wayne trucks. Separate sale item, but may increase in value because it matches the Milwaukee Fallen Flags Set No. 2.

	--	--	--	20

19302 MILWAUKEE ROAD: 1987, quad hopper, yellow body, black lettering, coal load, Standard O trucks. Part of Milwaukee Fallen Flags Set No. 2.

	--	--	--	30

19303 LIONEL LINES: 1987, quad hopper, bright orange sides, blue ends and upper quarter panels, red, white, and blue Lionel logo, dark blue lettering, coal load, Symington-Wayne trucks. Part of year-end package for 1987. Two shades of blue have been observed on the "L" decal. The first run had darker blue; the second had light blue. We do not know which version is scarcer. Reader comments requested.   --   --   **50   70**

19304 GREAT NORTHERN: 1988, quad hopper, light gray body and cover, black lettering, red and white circular "goat" logo, Standard O trucks; part of Fallen Flags Set No. 3.   --   --   --   **30**

19305 CHESSIE: Announced for 1988, ore car, dark blue ore car body, yellow lettering, number, and Chessie cat logo, Symington-Wayne trucks, operating couplers.   --   --   --   **18**

19804 WABASH: 1987, operating hopper, black body, white lettering and Wabash flag logo, black operating mechanism, Standard O trucks.   --   --   --   **35**

19806 PENNSYLVANIA: 1988, operating hopper car, light gray body, black operating mechanism, black lettering and Keystone logo, Standard O trucks, operating couplers.   --   --   --   **35**

Chapter IX

OPERATING CARS:
Cranes, Searchlights, Derricks, Log, and Coal Dump Cars

Many of the operating cars produced by Lionel in the modern era have been mentioned in the various introductions to other chapters in this book because they are best categorized within a larger area of production. Examples of these are the operating boxcars, gondolas, and cars. However, some of the operating cars in the Lionel line do not fit too readily into those categories. These are the log and coal dump cars, the crane cars, the searchlight cars, and the derrick cars.

The Lionel modern era log dump car is modeled after the late postwar Lionel Corporation examples. It is an all plastic car with an open flatcar body and a central log cradle released by a spring-loaded plunger. When the magnet in an operating track pulls down the plunger, the cradle tilts and dumps three wooden dowels serving as logs. The mechanism works well, but the logs sometimes flip off the cradle on sharp curves during operation.

Over the years, Lionel has produced its log cars in several railroad markings. The first one catalogued was a tuscan Louisville and Nashville car in 1970, but that car was never produced. The first of the log cars was a green 9300 Penn Central, which ran from 1970 through 1974 and again in 1977. In 1974 the car was changed to yellow Union Pacific markings as the 9303 — or 9305. The car was designated as a 9305 if the customer purchased it with a remote track included, though the number was always 9303 on the car. This car ran from 1974 through 1978 and again in 1980. The car changed to a red Santa Fe model in 1979 through 1983, and for 1984 a Northern Pacific model in dark green was made. A Pennsylvania log dump car in tuscan was produced in 1985, followed by a B & O version for 1986, a New York Central version in 1987, and another Santa Fe version in 1988 — this time with real logs made of tree sticks.

The modern era Lionel coal dump car is essentially a modified log dump car with a tilting coal bin attached to the cradle. It is a bit ungainly and does not interest collectors very much. In operation, some people had complaints about the coal supplied with the car; it was made of PVC plastic pellets which would pick up static electricity and stick to everything on the layout, including the operator when he/she tried to put the coal back in the car.

The first of the newly designed coal dump cars came out in 1974 with a dark blue color scheme and yellow Chesapeake and Ohio lettering. As with the log car, the number of the car was different in 1974 if the buyer purchased a package with a remote track. The car carried the number 9304 without the track; the package with the track was designated 9306, but 9304 was the car's marking. This car ran from 1974 through 1978, after which it was replaced by a yellow Union Pacific model running from 1979 through 1982. In 1983 a coal dump car was included as part of the Northern Freight Flyer; this car had a black flatcar body with a gray bin and white Chicago and Northwestern lettering and was not offered for separate sale. The separate sale car for 1983 and 1984 was a tuscan Pennsylvania car with gold lettering and a red Keystone. A New York Central coal dump car was produced for 1985; though it was an obvious match for the Yard Chief switcher set of that year, it was not part of the set and was sold separately. The New York Central car continued into 1986, and for 1987 a new Erie-Lackawanna version was scheduled. One 1987 coal dump car, the Southern, was part of the Service Station Special for that year; unlike the others, it had Standard O trucks. An Illinois Central Gulf version appeared in 1988.

The modern Lionel searchlight car is modeled after the 6822 "Night Crew" postwar searchlight car, except that the rubber man of the postwar model is missing from the more recent car. It uses a 6511-2 Flatcar base and the same parts and assembly methods as its postwar predecessor. The first Fundimensions searchlight car was a car of long duration, the tuscan 9302 Louisville and Nashville Car with a gray superstructure and black light hood. This car ran from 1973 through 1978, a long run of six years. The earliest models had an MPC logo on the car side; they are less common than the car without the logo. There is another scarce version of the car with white lettering instead of yellow.

In 1979 the 9302 was replaced by an attractive 9312 Conrail car with a blue flatcar base. The car was pictured with an orange superstructure in the 1979 advance catalogue, but the pictures in all the regular catalogues showed the superstructure as gray. As it turns out, the car was made both ways. Some collectors believe that the example with the orange superstructure is scarcer than the gray example, but this is not so. Apparently, there are significant regional differences which account for the scarcity of one example or another of this car. In the Philadelphia area, for example, nobody had any trouble locating Conrail searchlight cars with orange superstructures; in fact, the gray examples were a little harder to find. In other areas, the reverse is true. We believe that the car was made in about equal quantities of orange and gray superstructures. However, reader comments are still invited about this car. The Conrail searchlight car was produced through 1983.

After producing only two versions of the car over its first thirteen years, Fundimensions decided to diversify its production a bit. In 1983 a Chicago and Northwestern searchlight car with a black base and a gray superstructure was made for the Northern Freight Flyer set but was not available for separate sale. The 1984 and 1985 catalogues showed two new searchlight cars; one is an attractive Reading model in green and yellow colors, and the other is a U. S. Marines model in olive drab camouflage painting. In addition to these cars, the 1985 catalogue showed a New York Central model, which was part of the Yard Chief work train set with the 8615 New York Central Steam Switch Engine. After standing pat through 1986, Lionel, Inc. issued two new searchlight cars as parts of sets in Lehigh Valley and Southern markings. A tuscan and gray Canadian National version has been produced for 1988.

In addition to the controversial and confusing 6560 Crane Car revival of 1971, Fundimensions and its successors have made several different crane cars. However, the first of them did not emerge until 1979, when two of them were produced, both with Standard O trucks. The first one was a Reading crane in green and yellow included with the Quaker City Limited Set; the other was designated (apparently at the last minute) as the sixth car of the Famous American Railroads Set One. It carries the diamond-shaped F. A. R. R. logo (not many collectors seem to be aware of this) and was a separate sale item. This was the attractive blue and yellow 9348 Santa Fe Crane car.

The next crane cars had a significant innovation: the six-wheel die-cast passenger trucks which had been introduced on the Blue Comet passenger cars in 1978. The 9329 Chessie Crane came in the usual bright yellow and blue Chessie "cat" paint scheme and was part of the Royal Limited collector set of 1980. From this point on, most of the crane cars were made for special Collector Sets. The next one came in the maroon and gray colors of the Canadian Pacific as part of the Maple Leaf Limited Set of 1981. A 6510 Union Pacific Crane was made in 1983; it was a separate sale item, but it was also a great match for the Gold Coast Limited Set. An attractive Erie-Lackawanna model came out in 1984 for the Erie-Lackawanna Limited Set. For 1985 a New York Central crane in black with white lettering was issued as part of the New York Central Steam Switcher Set; unlike the others, this crane had Symington-Wayne plastic trucks. A special Illinois Central Gulf crane was made for the Lionel Collectors' Club of America in 1985; and in 1986, a red and black Santa Fe model was made as part of the Santa Fe Service Station Special; it had Standard O trucks instead of the six-wheel versions. The latest crane car is a Great Northern model produced for the Fallen Flags Set No. 3 in 1988. It indicates a return to the six-wheel trucks.

The Fundimensions derrick car is a sort of baby crane car without the cab; it is modeled after a postwar Lionel car. This car has a 6511-2 Flatcar as its base, and the derrick assembly is riveted to the car. The derrick is collapsible and snaps into position when raised; it operates with a hand crank and swivels. In the modern era versions, the outrigger mechanism of the postwar versions has been omitted.

In 1980 a version just like the postwar derrick in Lionel markings with a red flatcar was scheduled for a Texas and Pacific Set headed by an Alco diesel, but that Set was never made. Instead the Lionel car came out the next year as part of the Reading Yard King set. The next derricks both came out in

1983. One was a Chicago and Northwestern derrick, which was part of the Northern Freight Flyer set; the other was a yellow 9235 Union Pacific Derrick, which was available for separate sale in that year and in 1984. The most recent derrick car would have been a black and orange Illinois Central version for 1985, but its production was canceled after its picturing in the catalogue; apparently advance orders did not justify its production. No further derrick cars have emerged since that time except for the 16603 Lehigh Valley model of 1987.

Obviously, the most desirable of these operating cars are the crane cars, which can sometimes be found for separate sale because the set they came in has been split up by dealers. The separate-sale blue and yellow Santa Fe crane is a nice car, which can still be found. Aside from the extremely scarce 6560 revival of 1971, it is a little too soon to tell which of these crane cars will be the scarcest, but preliminary indications show the Canadian Pacific is a big favorite, thanks to its color scheme. However, the other crane cars are bright and colorful, too. The derrick cars are very good for the beginning collector; they make good operating cars and they are very reasonably priced, even the ones in the sets. The searchlight cars make an interesting group when they are all together; the Louisville and Nashville car is very common, while the Reading car shows signs of being in some demand by collectors. The log and coal dump cars do not as a rule interest collectors too much, but there is a Chesapeake and Ohio blue coal dump car without lettering, a little-known factory error which is probably very scarce.

Like all the other operating cars produced by Lionel, these cars add action and animation to an operating layout. As with other freight cars in the modern era Lionel lineup, the variety of these cars adds to the attractiveness of their collection.

LOG AND COAL DUMP CARS

Gd VG Exc Mt

6251 NEW YORK CENTRAL: 1985-86, coal dump, black body, grating pieces added to car ends (earlier varieties did not have these pieces), black bin, white lettering, white NYC oval logo, Symington-Wayne trucks. Comes with simulated coal and dumping bin. Sold separately, but considered by many collectors as a good sixth car for the 1985 New York Central Yard Chief Set. R. LaVoie Collection.   -- -- 15 20

9300 Penn Central.

9238 NORTHERN PACIFIC: 1983-84, log dump car, dark green body and log cradle, white lettering, three stained wooden logs, Symington-Wayne trucks.

-- -- **15 20**

See also Factory Errors and Prototypes.

9241 PENNSYLVANIA: 1983-84, log dump car, tuscan body, grating pieces added to ends of car, gold lettering, Symington-Wayne trucks. Comes with three stained large logs and tuscan dumping bin. -- -- **15 20**

9300 PENN CENTRAL: 1970-73, log dump mechanism, green body, white lettering, MPC logo, two disc couplers.

(A) 1970, Type I box without cellophane, no dumping bin enclosed, MPC logo, AAR trucks, Type I armature (magnet cemented to disc), two operating couplers, three unstained dowels. R. LaVoie Collection. **8 10 12 15**

(B) Same as (A), but with silver-painted wooden helium tanks instead of logs.

8 10 12 15

(C) Type II larger box with dumping bin, Symington-Wayne trucks, three unstained wooden dowels. **5 7 10 12**

9303 Union Pacific.

9303 UNION PACIFIC: 1974, 1979, log dump, yellow body, red lettering, Symington-Wayne trucks, one disc coupler, one fixed coupler.

4 6 10 12

9304 Chesapeake & Ohio.

9304 CHESAPEAKE & OHIO: 1974, coal dump, dark blue body and coal bin, yellow lettering, Symington-Wayne trucks, one disc coupler, one fixed coupler.

(A) White "coal" from raw plastic pellets. **4 5 10 12**

(B) Black "coal." **4 5 10 12**

See also Factory Errors and Prototypes.

9305 UNION PACIFIC: 1974, 1979 log dump car. This number was used to refer to the package, which included a remote-control track, although the car number remained 9303. Add $4 to values of 9303 for presence of track in original package.

9306 C & O: 1974-76, coal dump car. This number was used to refer to the package, which included a remote-control track, although the number on the car remained 9304. Add $4 to values of 9304 for presence of track in original package.

9310 A T & S F.

9310 A T & S F: 1978-79, 1981-82, log dump, red body, yellow lettering, "BLT 1-78", Symington-Wayne trucks, one operating coupler, one fixed coupler, operat-

9311 U P.

ing disc on underside; when plunger is pulled down load dumps three dowels about six inches long, 5/8 inch diameter. **5 7 10 13**

9311 U P: 1978-82, yellow coal dump with black coal, Symington-Wayne trucks, one operating coupler, one fixed coupler; when operating disc pulled down, load dumps. **5 7 10 13**

9325 N & W: See 9363.

9335 B & O: 1986, log dump, tuscan body, white lettering, three stained wooden dowel logs, Symington-Wayne trucks. Part of B & O Freight Set 1652.

-- -- **15 20**

9363 N & W: 1978, dumping car, black base, four plastic wheels, blue snap-on body, part of 1978 "Logging Empire" Set; numbered "9325" on base, but came in box marked "9363". J. Sawruk Collection. -- -- **3 4**

9398 PENNSYLVANIA: 1983, coal dump, tuscan frame and bin, gold lettering, red and gold rubber-stamped Keystone, mechanism activated by special track, Symington-Wayne trucks, one operating and one dummy coupler, with dumping bin and simulated coal; separate sale item. -- -- **12 15**

9399 CHICAGO & NORTHWESTERN: 1983-84, coal dump, black frame, gray bin, plunger mechanism activated by special track, Symington-Wayne trucks, one operating and one dummy coupler; sold as part of 1354 Northern Freight Flyer Set. -- -- **15 20**

16600 ILLINOIS CENTRAL GULF: 1988, operating coal dump car, tuscan flatcar base with white lettering, orange dump bin and bulkheads, Symington-Wayne trucks, includes dumping bin and simulated plastic coal.

-- -- -- **20**

16602 ERIE: 1987, coal dump, gray flatcar and bin, gray end bulkhead pieces, maroon lettering and logo, Symington-Wayne trucks, comes with coal and 2160 Dumping Bin. -- -- -- **18**

16604 NEW YORK CENTRAL: 1987, log dump, black flatcar, cradle, and bulkhead pieces, white "N Y C" lettering, logo, and number, three large stained dowels, includes 2160 Dumping Bin. Separate sale item, but matches rolling stock in 1985 Yard Chief Set. -- -- -- **18**

16607 SOUTHERN: 1987, coal dump, black flatcar and bulkhead pieces, dark green dump bin, gold lettering on car body and gold Southern herald on bin, Standard O trucks (a first for this car). Part of Southern Freight Runner Service Station Special Set 11704. -- -- -- **25**

16611 SANTA FE: 1988, log dump car, black flatcar body with white lettering, yellow log cradle, dumping bin, three real logs (this treatment has not been seen on a Lionel car since the 6361 Log Carrier Car of 1962), Symington-Wayne trucks. The logs are available separately; see the Accessory chapter under entry 12740.

-- -- -- **20**

CRANES, DERRICKS, AND SEARCHLIGHT CARS

6325 NEW YORK CENTRAL: Crane, see 6579 entry.

6508 CANADIAN PACIFIC: 1981, crane car, maroon base and boom with white letters, gray cab with maroon lettering, die-cast six-wheel passenger trucks; part of 1158 Maple Leaf Limited Set. -- -- **45 60**

6510 UNION PACIFIC: 1982, crane car, yellow cab with silver roof, gray plastic base, red "UNION PACIFIC" lettering, tall stack, notched boom at high end, die-cast six-wheel passenger trucks. Separate sale item, but matches Gold Coast Limited Set. Weisblum, R. Sigurdson, N. Banis, and T. Ladny Collections.

-- -- **50 65**

Top shelf: 6560 Lionel Lines, 6560 Lionel Lines. Second shelf: 9332 Reading, 9329 Chessie System. Bottom shelf: 6508 Canadian Pacific, 6510 Union Pacific. G. and D. Halverson and A. Conto Collections, G. Stern photograph.

6522 CHICAGO & NORTHWESTERN: 1984-85, searchlight car, black body, gray superstructure, white lettering, Symington-Wayne trucks; sold as part of 1354 Northern Freight Flyer Set.   -- -- **20 25**

6524 ERIE-LACKAWANNA: 1984-85, crane car, yellow base with maroon logo and lettering, maroon cab with white lettering, gray cab roof and boom, die-cast six-wheel passenger trucks; from Erie-Lackawanna Limited Set.   -- -- **45 60**

6526 U. S. MARINES: 1984-85, searchlight car, camouflage-painted olive and yellow flatcar, superstructure and searchlight hood, Symington-Wayne trucks. Matches 5726 U. S. Marines Bunk Car in paint scheme as well as 8485 U. S. Marines Diesel Switcher. Came with sheet of decals to be applied to car by purchaser, although some examples have been found in sealed sets with decals already applied by the factory. C. Rohlfing comment.   -- -- **15 20**

6529 NEW YORK CENTRAL: 1985, searchlight car, black 6511-2 Flatcar body, white lettering, gray superstructure, black lens hood, Symington-Wayne trucks; part of Yard Chief Switcher Set.   -- -- **15 20**

THE 6560 FUNDIMENSIONS CRANE CAR: AN UPDATE

In our last edition, we analyzed the distinguishing factors between the 1971 Fundimensions reissue of the 6560 Bucyrus-Erie Crane and its 1968-1969 Hagerstown predecessor. We described the different boxes. We examined the critical variables and noted that the attaching rivet at the top of the boom is chromed on the Hagerstown version and blackened or bronzed on the Fundimensions version. We also said that the translucent red cab of the Fundimensions version is slightly darker. So far, so good.

Then along came a letter from a frequent contributor, Harold Powell of North Carolina. Mr. Powell is well known to us as a keen observer of trains, and his descriptions are to be trusted

implicitly. He recently acquired a crane in a Fundimensions box. Unlike our crane, his had a black boom and base and a chromed rivet. In other words, it is indistinguishable from late Hillside and Hagerstown production!

To compound matters further, we had a conversation with Dan Johns, the Director of Product Integrity and Customer Services of Lionel, Inc., a man who has been with the modern era producers of these trains from the beginning. He told us that a lot of scrambling was going on in that year, and trains were being assembled from many different parts bins. He acknowledged that 6560 Cranes as we had described them were indeed Fundimensions issues, but so were a great many strange hybrids of parts — and they, too, went out in the Type I Fundimensions boxes! Apparently, whatever chance we may have had to sort out data about these cranes has been irretrievably lost. That is a shame, because any black frame version or dark blue frame version matching the Hagerstown production would depend solely on the box for its identification. The box being worth more than the product is not an acceptable state of affairs, to say the least.

Does this mean that we have to go back to Square One in our hunt for the history of this elusive crane car? Not quite. We have, at least, identified one variety which is clearly a Fundimensions product with distinctive markings. The fact that other varieties have been found in the same boxes does not diminish our findings. What these reports do tell us is a double truth: The history of this crane car is a great deal more complicated than we had supposed, and we had better collect all the descriptive data about modern era trains now, before it is irretrievably lost to dealer and collector shuffling. We quote a price for the Fundimensions 6560 below on the condition that it matches the one we have identified clearly. Readers are asked to write to us and to describe their boxed cranes precisely. Then, in future editions, we may be able to reconstruct the history of this thoroughly frustrating car! Just before press time, another Fundimensions 6560 Crane turned up, and it just throws a little more gasoline on the fire. This one (see entry (D) in listings) had the dark blue base and translucent red cab, but it also had a black boom and a chromed rivet half the size of the Hagerstown model. No box came with it, but it was unmistakably a Fundimensions crane because it had factory-installed Symington-Wayne trucks! Heaven only knows what other versions are out there in Lionel Land.

	Gd	VG	Exc	Mt

6560 BUCYRUS ERIE: 1971, crane car, very dark blue base and boom (best seen from underside), translucent red plastic cab (darker than Hagerstown postwar examples), solid operating wheels, white lettering on base sides, blackened, unplated, or bronzed rivet holds wire assembly at top of boom, blackened or bronzed U-shaped rivet holds boom crank at base of boom, open AAR trucks, postwar wheels which turn on axles, two operating couplers.

(A) Came in Fundimensions Type I box with red lettering on box end label and picture of car. Mint value must include this box. P. Catalano, C. Rohlfing, and R. LaVoie comments, G. Halverson Collection.　75　100　125　150

(B) Canadian distribution; came in Type I box with smaller cellophane window and Parker Brothers black-printed logo. One example observed in Montreal. We would like to know if there are any differences between this version and the one assembled for American production. G. Halverson comment. One recently observed version had a black base. C. O'Dell Collection.　**NRS**

(C) Black boom and base, chromed rivet; identical to Hagerstown postwar production, but authenticated as original in Fundimensions Type I box. H. Powell Collection.　75　100　150　175

(D) Same as (A), but black boom which does not match blue base, small chromed boom rivet, and factory-installed (metal rivet) Symington-Wayne trucks. R. LaVoie Collection.　75　100　150　175

6567 ILLINOIS CENTRAL GULF: 1986, crane, see Special Production chapter.

6574 REDWOOD VALLEY EXPRESS: 1984, short crane car, 1877-style yellow flatcar base with dark brown lettering, tuscan plastic cab with yellow logo, gray boom, arch bar trucks; part of 1403 Redwood Valley Express Set.

--　--　--　12

6576 A T & S F: 1985, short crane car, dark blue scribed 1877-style flatcar body, dark blue cab, gray boom, gray log cradle and cab attachment piece, yellow lettering and Santa Fe cross logo, Symington-Wayne trucks, dummy couplers. From Midland Freight Set.

--　--　--　12

6579 NEW YORK CENTRAL: 1985, crane car, black base, cab, and boom; white lettering and white New York Central oval logo, Symington-Wayne trucks. Part of Yard Chief Switcher Set.

--　--　25　30

6593 A T & S F: 1986, crane car, red cab, black base with white lettering, yellow lettering and cross logo on cab, black boom, Standard O trucks. Part of Santa Fe Work Train Service Station Special Set.

--　--　--　45

6670: See entry 9378.

9235 UNION PACIFIC: 1983, yellow base with black derrick, Symington-Wayne trucks; separate sale item.

--　--　10　12

9236 CHICAGO & NORTHWESTERN: 1983, black base with yellow derrick, Symington-Wayne trucks; sold as part of 1354 Northern Freight Flyer Set.

--　--　15　20

9245 ILLINOIS CENTRAL: Announced for 1985, derrick car, black 6511-2 Flatcar base with white lettering and logo, bright orange swiveling boom riveted to flatcar, Symington-Wayne trucks. Canceled from dealer order sheets in September 1985.　**Not Manufactured**

9247 NEW YORK CENTRAL: 1985, searchlight car, see 6529 entry.

9302 LOUISVILLE & NASHVILLE: 1973-74, searchlight, brown body, mold 6511-2, Symington-Wayne trucks with disc couplers, gray superstructure with mold 6812-5. Yellow lettering on flatcar base. Superstructure embossed "TRACK

9302 Louisville & Nashville.

MAINTENANCE" and has two shovels, wire, control panel, and oxygen tanks molded in as part of mold 6812-5. The searchlight is not a part of the superstructure as such, but it is fastened to the superstructure by a circular metal fastener and is not intended to be removed. D. Griggs Collection.

(A) MPC logo.　8　10　12　15
(B) No MPC logo.　6　8　10　12
(C) All white lettering. Beware of chemically altered fakes.

--　--　50　65

9312 Conrail.

9312 CONRAIL: 1979-82, searchlight, blue body, white lettering, mold "No. 6511-2", gray or orange plastic superstructure, mold "No. 3520-12", with box embossed "Track Maintenance" and tools, wire, control panel, oxygen tanks, and searchlight unit.

(A) Unpainted gray superstructure, plastic rivet holding trucks. Nordby observation.　--　10　15　20

(B) Unpainted orange superstructure, metal rivet holding trucks. C. Rohlfing and Nordby observations. This version was shown only in the 1979 advance catalogue. Apparently, both versions were produced in about the same numbers, but there were distinct regional differences in distribution which led collectors to believe that the orange superstructure version was scarce. It carries only a small premium over the gray superstructure version. R. LaVoie and Bryan Smith observations.　--　12　20　25

9329 CHESSIE SYSTEM: 1980, crane car, blue base, yellow cab with silver roof, die-cast six-wheel passenger trucks; came with 1070, The Royal Limited.

--　--　45　60

9332 READING: 1979, crane car, green base, yellow cab, green roof, yellow boom, yellow and green lettering and logo, Standard O trucks; from Quaker City Limited Set.　--　--　40　50

9345 READING: 1984-85, searchlight car, dark green 6511-2 Flatcar body with yellow lettering, cream superstructure with black and white Reading diamond-shaped pressure-sensitive decal on both sides, black searchlight hood, Symington-Wayne trucks.　--　--　20　25

9348 SANTA FE: 1979, crane car, blue base with yellow lettering, blue cab with yellow lettering and Santa Fe cross logo, gold diamond-shaped FARR 1 logo on cab, yellow boom, Standard O trucks, came in special Type III box. This crane was issued as the extra car for the first Famous American Railroads Set of 1979. R. LaVoie Collection.　--　45　55　65

9364 N & W: 1978, small crane car, black base, four plastic wheels, yellow snap-on cab and boom pieces, part of 1978 "Logging Empire" set. Base of car has "9325" number, but came in box marked "9364", which distinguishes this car from its dumping car companion listed under 9363 above. J. Sawruk Collection.

--　--　8　10

9378 LIONEL: 1981, red flatcar with yellow derrick, pictured as 6670 in catalogue, but produced as 9378. Symington-Wayne trucks; from 1154 Reading Yard King Set. R. DuBeau and W. Barnes comments.   -- -- **15 20**

16302 LEHIGH VALLEY: 1987, flatcar with derrick, green flatcar body, white lettering and diamond logo, yellow derrick, Symington-Wayne trucks. Part of Black Diamond Set 11702.   -- -- -- **15**

16601 CANADIAN NATIONAL: 1988, maroon flatcar body and searchlight hood, light gray superstructure, Symington-Wayne trucks.   -- -- -- **20**

16603 LEHIGH VALLEY: 1987, searchlight car, black flatcar body, white lettering, light gray superstructure and searchlight hood, Symington-Wayne trucks. Part of Black Diamond Set 11702.   -- -- -- **20**

16606 SOUTHERN: 1987, searchlight car, green flatcar base, yellow lettering, light gray superstructure, black searchlight hood, Symington-Wayne trucks. Sold separately, except for trucks matches rolling stock in Southern Freight Runner Service Station Special Set.   -- -- -- **20**

19402 GREAT NORTHERN: 1988, black frame, black boom, bright orange cab, dark green lettering, red, white, and green circular "goat" logo, die-cast six-wheel passenger trucks. Part of Fallen Flags Set 3.   -- -- -- **50**

Chapter X

PASSENGER CARS

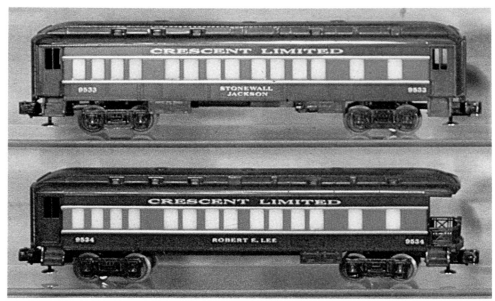

Top: 9533 Stonewall Jackson. Bottom: 9534 Robert E. Lee. W. Eddins Collection, R. Bartelt photograph.

One of the real pleasures of tinplate railroading has always been to start up a train layout, turn off all the lights, and watch the lighted layout by "night." If the layout were well-equipped, street and signal lights would shine, searchlights would beam onto the platform, and the locomotive would come flying around a curve, its headlight reflecting off the tracks. If the operator looked at the train coming at him at eye level, he could watch the locomotive speed past him, followed by a long string of lighted passenger cars, possibly with little human silhouettes in the windows.

Obviously, tinplate doth not live by freight cars alone. That is why Fundimensions tried to respond as quickly as possible to repeated requests for a new passenger car series. In 1973 Fundimensions began the production of its 9500-series Passenger Cars with the Milwaukee Special Set. In this set, an 8304 4-4-2 Locomotive in Milwaukee Road markings pulled three dull orange Milwaukee passenger cars with maroon lettering and roofs. These cars were excellent models of the heavyweight cars used during the 1920s on almost every American railroad. They were lighted and highly detailed, with little vents in the clerestories, detailed closed vestibules, and translucent window inserts. The only sore points about the cars were their length (it did not quite match the length of the classic Irvington cars) and their couplers. These were non-operating and mounted directly onto the car bodies; if the track was not level or had rough spots, the cars could easily uncouple accidentally. Some operators went so far as to put twist-ties around the coupler knuckles to keep them together! In addi-

tion, if for any reason the coupler broke off and took the screw hole in the car with it, the operator was out of luck.

The Milwaukee Special was followed during the next two years by a Broadway Limited Set with Pennsylvania Cars in tuscan and black with gold lettering and a Capitol Limited with Baltimore and Ohio cars in blue and gray with gold lettering. (Unfortunately the color of the B & O cars did not match the 8363 B & O F-3 Diesels.) The three set cars soon had several stablemates. In 1975 separate sale Pullman cars were produced to match all three sets. In the next year full baggage cars came out, and the end of 1976 saw many observation cars made into the Campaign Special series with Presidential posters, bunting, and an American flag decorating the cars in all three series. One Milwaukee car, the 9511 Minneapolis, was offered as part of a coupon deal. In all, there were ten Milwaukee cars, nine Pennsylvania cars, and eight Baltimore and Ohio cars when production was complete. Predictably, diner cars have just been announced for the Pennsylvania and Milwaukee sets in late 1988 — twelve years after the original production. Can a Baltimore and Ohio diner be far behind?

As problems arose with these cars, attempts were made to solve them. It was found that the lights in the cars shone through the car roofs. At first, Fundimensions tried silver paint on the tops of the light bulbs in the cars, but that cut down the illumination too much. Eventually, cardboard inserts were placed into the roofs, and that solved the problem handily. Getting at the light bulbs to change them was a horrendous problem never fully solved. The roof and translucent window

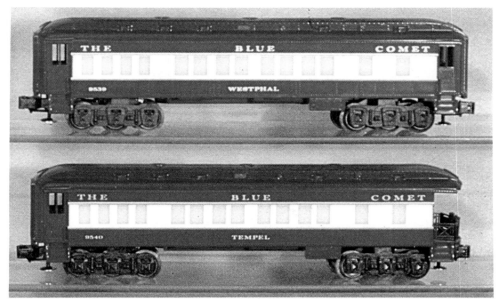

The 1978 Blue Comet Set reused the names of Lionel's 1930s Standard Gauge Blue Comet Set. Top: 9539 Westphal. Bottom: 9540 Tempel. W. Eddins Collection, R. Bartelt photograph.

pieces were made of one casting which snapped into the car bodies. At first, there were tabs on the car bottoms, but these actually had to be cut off to remove the roof! Later, the tabs were eliminated in favor of projections in the translucent window inserts which snapped into the window frames. Even with this arrangement, getting the roofs off these cars has always been a job to tax the most patient of people.

In 1977 the cars were issued in a different railroad scheme, this time with operating couplers. A baggage car, a combine, two Pullman coaches, and an observation car were made in green and gold Southern markings to match the 8702 Southern 4-6-4 Hudson. These made up the Southern Crescent Set (though the items were always sold separately, not as a complete set). Amazingly, it took ten years until Lionel, Inc. produced a diner car to match these cars. Coincidentally, these cars also matched the Southern F-3 diesel pair produced in 1975. The next year, the cars were produced in the Blue Comet Set with a significant improvement — the die-cast six-wheel passenger trucks. Several changes were made to the casting of the car underside to accommodate these trucks, and unfortunately earlier cars cannot be retrofitted with them. The same five-car scheme was used for the Chessie Steam Special Set in 1980 and the Chicago and Alton Set of 1981. In 1986 and 1987 Lionel, Inc. made diner cars to match all four of these sets; so far, the Chessie and Alton diners have become very scarce and — unfortunately — expensive items.

Over the years, several of these cars were also made as T C A special cars in dark Brunswick green. Another similar set in yellow was made for the Toy Train Operating Society. In 1986 Lionel, Inc. issued a set of six 9500-style Wabash cars in handsome dark blue and gray "Bluebird" colors pulled by a matching 4-6-2 Pacific steam engine. These cars were the first entries in the new "Fallen Flags" Series of special collector sets.

In 1976 Fundimensions reissued the short O27 streamlined passenger cars of the postwar period as the Lake Shore Limited

Set. These cars, modeled on the old 2400 Series of postwar years but without some detailing in the originals, were pulled by an Alco in Amtrak markings with four matching cars. Later on, three more cars were added as separate sale items to expand the set. They had the same plastic wooden beam-style trucks as the earlier 9500 cars (odd, since these were archaic trucks for cars of a modern design) and were illuminated. These cars were produced in coach, Vista Dome, and observation configurations. They have also been used for the T C A Bicentennial Set and the Quicksilver Express Set of 1982. In 1987 Lionel, Inc. produced a handsome set of Pennsylvania 2400-series cars in authentic tuscan and black with gold lettering. To make sure that the lettering was bright and crisp, Lionel's factory workers stamped each side of every car three times, using the Tampo process — six operations per car! New Amtrak cars have been made for 1988 as part of a "Silver Spike" set, and combines are in the works for both the Amtrak and Pennsylvania cars.

In 1978 Fundimensions revived the "General" style baggage and coach cars to accompany their reissue of the "General" engine the year before. This old-time car has also been used in Rock Island and Peoria three-car sets, Baltimore and Ohio cars, and in one unlighted version as part of the James Gang Set. In 1986 two more cars identical to the 1978 versions except for their numbers were produced as part of a special set available only through American Express. These cars were faithful reproductions of the postwar issues. The 1988 Service Station Set, the "Dry Gulch," features three of these cars in Virginia and Trucker markings.

Nice as these cars were, they were not the passenger cars everyone was waiting for. Those emerged in 1979 with the reissue of the big extruded aluminum cars from the fabled Congressional Limited in beautiful Pennsylvania markings. Instead of the flat finish of the postwar issues, the new Lionel cars had a polished aluminum finish which looked great behind the Penn-

Top: 9572 Molly Pitcher Pennsylvania. Bottom: 9574 Alexander Hamilton Pennsylvania. W. Eddins Collection, R. Bartelt photograph.

sylvania F-3 twin-motored diesels also produced in that year. A baggage car, two passenger coaches, a Vista Dome car and an observation car formed the original set, but later Fundimensions added a diner car, a combine, and an extra passenger car to the set. These cars were an outstanding success for Fundimensions, and it was inevitable that more would follow.

That is exactly what happened in 1980. A startling Burlington Zephyr Set was produced with chrome-plated twin F-3 diesels and the same five basic cars with authentic Zephyr-style lettering. As with the Pennsylvania cars, the extra cars were soon produced. Perhaps the most breathtaking set of all came the next year, when Fundimensions issued the J class Norfolk and Western steam engine and six stunning aluminum Powhatan Arrow passenger cars painted deep maroon with black roofs and gold lettering and striping. Many collectors believe this set to be the most beautiful passenger set ever produced in tinplate; unfortunately, the quality was reflected in the stiff price exacted for the cars, especially the diner, which was produced later in extremely limited quantities.

The follow-up to the Powhatan Arrow Set was impressive, too. In 1982 Fundimensions produced the long-awaited Southern Pacific Daylight Set. This set was originally pulled by an F-3 pair of diesels, but in 1983 the J class die was used to produce a terrific model of the GS-4 Daylight steam engine. The passenger cars were done in bright red, orange, and black colors made famous by the elite West Coast train of the 1940s. As before, separate sale cars came out later. Unfortunately, Southern Pacific fans noted deviations in the color schemes from the original. Like the Norfolk and Western Set, the Daylight Set has attracted a big following because of its beautiful color scheme.

By this time Fundimensions was really "on a roll", producing set after beautiful set of these passenger cars in colors and styles no postwar aluminum set could hope to match. In 1983, however, Fundimensions changed the style of the cars. All of the previous aluminum cars had been made with stylish fluted sides and roofs, just as their postwar predecessors were. With the New York Central cars of 1983, Fundimensions eliminated the scribed sides and roofs and produced the cars with smooth sides and roofs. To be sure, the cars were still very attractive, but collectors soon voiced complaints about them. For one thing, the smooth-sided cars would fingerprint very easily, and the fingerprints were difficult to remove. Worse than that, the paint on the cars would chip all too easily, leaving unsightly aluminum marks through the paint. This was, of course, one way Fundimensions could keep the cost of these very expensive cars down, but for many collectors the New York Central Set represented a distinct decline in quality. As before, the cars were accompanied by New York Central F-3 diesels, and separate sale cars were added to the set.

The 1984 set, in Union Pacific Overland Limited colors, sparked vehement complaints. Two distinctly different shades of yellow were used for the locomotives, and more often than not they did not match. Collectors would thus have to hunt through many boxes to find locomotive units with the colors matching properly. Worse, the plastic doors used on the passenger cars did not match the color of the paint used on the cars, and there were even two shades of yellow paint. The observation cars did not match the rest of the set. In addition, collectors complained that the red striping on the cars was very poorly applied, giving the smooth-sided cars a rather cheap look. Lionel was in fact having production problems at the time, and it is unfortunate that such a fine set fell victim to the difficulties the factory was experiencing. These sets have sold very poorly as a result.

For 1985 Lionel rectified the error somewhat, but at the cost of repeating a successful formula until it wore out its welcome. This year saw the production of a smooth-sided set in brown and orange Illinois Central "City of New Orleans" colors. This time, at least, the quality was right; the colors looked very good and the set, pulled by a great-looking Illinois Central ABA trio, was very impressive. So was the price! This was the sixth set issued as aluminum passenger cars pulled by F-3 premium diesels. The tremendous expense of these sets raises the question of how extensive the resources of modern era collectors really are. Regardless of the problems, one must admit that these aluminum cars have formed the consist of some truly magnificent sets which illustrate the apex of tinplate achievement.

Overall, modern era Lionel has met the challenge of producing passenger cars extremely well. The beginning collector can secure quite a few passenger cars (aside from the aluminum ones) without severe damage to the wallet. The earliest Pennsylvania, Milwaukee, and Baltimore and Ohio cars are readily available, except for the full baggage cars, which are very scarce items. The 1987 Pennsylvania 2400-type cars are quite inexpensive, and Lionel, Inc. has even produced a good-looking little 4-4-2 Atlantic steamer to pull them. This engine and the Pennsylvania cars make a very handsome train at a modest (for Lionel) cost.

Indeed, with the right locomotive, the beginner can make up a very nice passenger train. For example, a Pennsylvania S-2 steam turbine, an old postwar 675 or 2025 K-4 Steam Locomotive, or the 8551 Pennsylvania EP-5 Electric all look great pulling a string of the Pennsylvania cars — and so does the 8753 GG-1 Electric. The 8558 Milwaukee EP-5 looks fine at the head of the Milwaukee cars, and the Baltimore and Ohio F-3 diesels are a great match for the Baltimore and Ohio cars, color disparity notwithstanding. The Chessie Steam Special cars can be pulled by an 8603 Chesapeake and Ohio Hudson or a Chessie U36B, U36C, or GP-20. They even have the extremely nice six-wheel die-cast passenger trucks. It is possible to get a decent passenger set on a modest budget, comparatively speaking, unless you must have the aluminum cars. With such sets, you too can return to an apparently much more innocent day than ours, when miniature passenger trains ran without a care or a schedule on a tinplate layout. The power to enthrall is still there!

6403 Amtrak.

	Gd	VG	Exc	Mt
6404 AMTRAK: Matches 6403, Pullman.	15	20	30	50
6405 AMTRAK: Matches 6403, Pullman.	15	20	30	50
6406 AMTRAK: Matches 6403, observation.	15	20	30	50
6410 AMTRAK: Matches 6403, Pullman. This and the 6411 and 6412 cars were offered as separate sale items to expand the Lake Shore Limited Set. C. Lang comment.	10	15	30	50
6411 AMTRAK: Matches 6403, Pullman.	10	15	30	50
6412 AMTRAK: Matches 6403, Vista Dome.	10	15	30	50
7200 QUICKSILVER: 1982-83, Pullman, blue and silver, lighted; part of 1253 Quicksilver Express.	--	--	20	40
7201 QUICKSILVER: 1982-83, Vista Dome, matches 7200.	--	--	20	40
7202 QUICKSILVER: 1982-83, observation, matches 7200.	--	--	20	40
7203 NORFOLK AND WESTERN: 1983, dining car, matches 9562, 9563, etc.	--	--	275	400
7204 SOUTHERN PACIFIC: 1983, dining car, matches 9589. See 9589 for background. T. Ladny comment.	--	--	275	400
7205 DENVER: 1982, see Special Production chapter.				
7206 LOUISVILLE: 1983, see Special Production chapter.				
7207 NEW YORK CENTRAL: 1983, extruded aluminum dining car, "TWENTIETH CENTURY LIMITED"; matches 9594 and other New York Central passenger cars.	--	--	150	250
7208 PENNSYLVANIA: 1983, dining car, "JOHN HANCOCK"; matches Pennsylvania "Congressional Limited" passenger cars 9569 to 9575.	--	--	125	225
7210 UNION PACIFIC: 1984, smooth-sided dining car, see 9546 for description.	--	--	65	100
7211 SOUTHERN PACIFIC: 1983, Vista Dome car, "Daylight"; matches Southern Pacific Daylight passenger cars 9589 through 9593.	--	--	300	400
7212 PITTSBURGH: 1984, see Special Production chapter.				
7215 BALTIMORE AND OHIO: 1983, blue sides, gray roof, white window striping and lettering, General-style coach; part of 1351 Baltimore & Ohio Set with 7216 and 7217.	--	--	30	40
7216 BALTIMORE AND OHIO: 1983, matches 7215. C. Rohlfing comment.	--	--	30	40
See also Factory Errors and Prototypes.				
7217 BALTIMORE AND OHIO: 1983, baggage, large eagle electrocal on side; matches 7215 and 7216.	--	--	30	40
7220 ILLINOIS CENTRAL: 1985, "City Of New Orleans" baggage car, smooth-sided medium brown body (although pictured in dark brown in catalogue, production pieces are lighter in shade); orange and gold striping, gold "ILLINOIS CENTRAL", brown "RAILWAY EXPRESS AGENCY" and "BAGGAGE" lettering, smooth black roof, (the other cars in the set are illuminated), black ends, brown doors, die-cast O Gauge four-wheel passenger trucks with operating couplers.	--	--	75	100
7221 ILLINOIS CENTRAL: 1985, "Lake Ponchartrain" combine; matches 7220, illuminated, silhouettes in windows.	--	--	75	100
7222 ILLINOIS CENTRAL: 1985, "King Coal" passenger coach; matches 7221.	--	--	75	100
7223 ILLINOIS CENTRAL: 1985, "Banana Road" passenger coach; matches 7221.	--	--	75	100

491 NORFOLK & WESTERN: See 7203

577 NORFOLK & WESTERN: See 9562.

578 NORFOLK & WESTERN: See 9563.

579 NORFOLK & WESTERN: See 9564.

580 NORFOLK & WESTERN: See 9565.

581 NORFOLK & WESTERN: See 9566.

582 NORFOLK & WESTERN: See 9567.

0511 ST. LOUIS: 1981, see Special Production chapter.

1973, 1974, 1975 TCA: Specials, see Special Production chapter.

6403 AMTRAK: 1976-77, Vista Dome, aluminum with red and blue window stripes. This car and 6404, 6405, and 6406 were part of the 1663 Lake Shore Limited Set. C. Lang comment.   15   20   30   50

7224 ILLINOIS CENTRAL: 1985, "General Beauregard" dining car; matches 7221. -- -- 75 100

7225 ILLINOIS CENTRAL: 1985, "Memphis" observation car, red rear lights, lighted rear "City of New Orleans" drumhead; otherwise matches 7221. -- -- 75 100

7227 WABASH: 1986-87, dining car, dark blue 9500 Series body, gold lettering, gold stripes, die-cast six-wheel trucks, lights, passenger silhouettes, three short stacks atop roof. Separate sale item as part of Fallen Flags Series No. 1. -- -- 35 75

7228 WABASH: 1986-87, baggage car, matches 7227 Diner. -- -- 35 75

7229 WABASH: 1986-87, combine, matches 7227 Diner. -- -- 35 75

7230 WABASH: 1986-87, "City of Peru" Pullman coach, matches 7227 Diner. -- -- 35 75

7231 WABASH: 1986-87, "City of Danville" Pullman coach, matches 7227 Diner. -- -- 35 75

7232 WABASH: 1986-87, "City of Wabash" observation, matches 7227 Diner. -- -- 35 60

7241 W & A: 1986, (Western & Atlantic) passenger coach, pale translucent yellow General-style passenger car body, tuscan roof and lettering, illuminated, operating couplers, arch bar trucks. Part of uncatalogued American Express Set 1608. T. Taylor Collection. -- -- 30 50

7242 W & A: 1986, (Western & Atlantic) baggage car, matches 7241, also part of uncatalogued American Express General Set 1608. T. Taylor Collection. -- -- 30 50

8868 AMTRAK: See Diesels chapter.

8869 AMTRAK: See Diesels chapter.

8870 AMTRAK: See Diesels chapter.

8871 AMTRAK: See Diesels chapter.

A NOTE ON THE LIGHTING PROBLEMS OF THE 9500 SERIES PASSENGER CARS

By Henry Edmunds

When Lionel first made the 9500-series passenger cars in 1973, the firm found that it had a problem with translucence of the plastic when the cars were lighted. If the cars were left unlined, the light would "glow" through the roofs and sides, creating an unsightly "blob" of light instead of the lighted window effect Lionel wanted. One early attempt to fix the problem involved painting the tops of the light bulbs with heat-resistant silver paint. That did not work because it cut the light down too much.

To solve this problem as inexpensively as possible, Lionel designed a cardboard roof liner which would come down a little way over the sides inside the car and completely shade the roof. Overall, this "fix" worked well, except when the liner slid down to cover the windows, in which case the purchaser would have to laboriously pry open the roof pieces to push the liner back up to the roof.

Overall, Lionel's 9500 passenger cars show four different schemes for shading the light in these cars, as follows:

1. No cardboard roof liner present.
2. Unfinished plain cardboard liner.
3. White finished cardboard liner.
4. Unfinished yellow cardboard liner extending down the sides of the car with holes for the windows.

9500 MILWAUKEE ROAD: 1973, Pullman, "CITY OF MILWAUKEE", flat orange, flat maroon roof, lights, roof fastened with tabs through floor. 10 15 25 35

9501 MILWAUKEE ROAD: Pullman, "CITY OF ABERDEEN".
(A) Flat orange, flat maroon paint. 10 15 22 30
(B) Shiny orange and shiny maroon paint. 10 15 25 35

9502 Milwaukee Road.

9502 MILWAUKEE ROAD: Observation, "PRESIDENT WASHINGTON"; matches 9500. 12 18 25 35

9503 MILWAUKEE ROAD: Pullman, "CITY OF CHICAGO"; matches 9500. 12 15 25 30

9504 MILWAUKEE ROAD: 1974, Pullman, "CITY OF TACOMA", flat orange, flat maroon roof, illuminated.
(A) Roof fastened with tabs through floor. 12 15 20 30
(B) Roof fastened through windows. 12 15 20 30

9505 MILWAUKEE ROAD: 1974, Pullman "CITY OF SEATTLE", flat orange, flat maroon roof, illuminated.
(A) Tabs through floor hold roof. 12 15 20 30
(B) Tabs through windows. 12 15 20 30

9506 MILWAUKEE ROAD: 1974, baggage combine, "U. S. MAIL", flat orange sides, flat maroon roof. 12 15 30 40

9507 Pennsylvania.

9507 PENNSYLVANIA: 1974, Pullman, "CITY OF MANHATTAN", tuscan with black roof, gold lettering, illuminated; one center-rail pickup roller, ground pickup contacts on other truck, fully detailed undercarriage. 15 20 30 50

9508 PENNSYLVANIA: Pullman, "CITY OF PHILADELPHIA"; matches 9507. 15 20 30 50

9509 PENNSYLVANIA: Observation, "PRESIDENT ADAMS"; matches 9507. 15 20 30 60

9510 PENNSYLVANIA: 1974, baggage-mail-coach combine; matches 9507, illuminated, "UNITED STATES MAIL RAILWAY POST OFFICE" in gold heat-stamped letters. 10 15 30 50

9511 MILWAUKEE ROAD: 1973, Pullman, "CITY OF MINNEAPOLIS", special coupon car, illuminated. 15 25 30 35

9512 SUMMERDALE JUNCTION: 1974, see Special Production chapter.

9513 PENNSYLVANIA: 1975, Pullman, "PENN SQUARE", illuminated; matches 9507. 10 15 30 50

9514 PENNSYLVANIA: 1975, Pullman, "TIMES SQUARE", illuminated; matches 9507. 10 15 30 50

9515 PENNSYLVANIA: 1975, Pullman, "WASHINGTON CIRCLE"; matches 9507, illuminated. 10 15 30 50

9516 BALTIMORE & OHIO: 1976, Pullman, "MOUNTAIN TOP", matches 9517. 10 15 25 35

9517 Baltimore & Ohio.

9517 BALTIMORE & OHIO: 1975, coach, "CAPITAL CITY", blue, gray windows, yellow stripes, gray roof, illuminated.   20   25   30   40

9518 BALTIMORE & OHIO: 1975, observation, "NATIONAL VIEW"; illuminated, matches 9517.   20   25   30   40

9519 BALTIMORE & OHIO: 1975, baggage combine, "UNITED STATES MAIL", illuminated, matches 9517.   15   20   25   40

9520 TOY TRAIN OPERATING SOCIETY: 1975, see Special Production chapter.

9521 PENNSYLVANIA: 1975, double-door baggage, tuscan with black roof, illuminated. Hard to find.   40   50   75   90

9522 MILWAUKEE ROAD: 1975, double-door baggage, flat orange, flat maroon roof, illuminated. Hard to find.   40   50   60   70

9523 BALTIMORE & OHIO: 1975, double-door baggage, "AMERICAN RAILWAY EXPRESS", illuminated; matches 9517. Hard to find.
    40   50   60   70

9524 BALTIMORE & OHIO: 1976, Pullman, "MARGRET CORBIN", illuminated; matches 9517.   10   15   30   50

9525 BALTIMORE & OHIO: 1976, Pullman, "EMERALD BROOK"; matches 9517.   10   15   30   50

9526 TOY TRAIN OPERATING SOCIETY: 1976, see Special Production chapter.

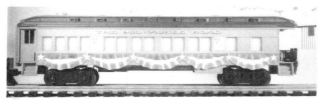

9527 Milwaukee.

9527 MILWAUKEE: 1976, "ROOSEVELT", campaign observation, red, white, and blue bunting on car sides, small flag on rear platform.   10   20   25   30

9528 PENNSYLVANIA: 1976, "TRUMAN", campaign observation, illuminated; matches 9507.   10   20   25   40

9529 BALTIMORE & OHIO: 1976, "EISENHOWER", campaign observation; matches 9517.   10   20   25   40

9530 SOUTHERN: 1978, baggage, "JOEL CHANDLER HARRIS", dark green body and roof; light apple green window stripe, gold edge striping and gold lettering, four-wheel wood-beam plastic trucks with operating truck-mounted couplers. (Previous cars in the 9500 heavyweight series had non-operating body-mounted couplers.)   15   20   30   50

9531 SOUTHERN: 1978, combination, "ANDREW PICKENS"; matches 9530.
    15   20   30   50

9532 SOUTHERN: 1978, Pullman, "P. G. T. BEAUREGARD"; matches 9530.
    15   20   30   50

9533 SOUTHERN: 1978, Pullman, "STONEWALL JACKSON"; matches 9530.   15   20   30   50

9534 SOUTHERN: 1978, observation, "ROBERT E. LEE"; matches 9530.
    15   20   30   50

9535 TOY TRAIN OPERATING SOCIETY: 1977, see Special Production chapter.

9536 THE BLUE COMET: 1978, baggage, "BARNARD", blue unpainted plastic sides, dark blue roof; cream stripe through windows, gold lettering, gold stripes above and below windows, illuminated, die-cast six-wheel trucks, full detailed undercarriage, two disc couplers, glazed windows.   10   15   30   50

9537 THE BLUE COMET: 1978, combination, "HALLEY"; matches 9536.
    10   15   30   50

9538 THE BLUE COMET: 1978, Pullman, "FAYE"; matches 9536.
    15   20   45   60

9539 THE BLUE COMET: 1978, Pullman, "WESTPHAL"; matches 9536.
    15   20   45   60

9540 THE BLUE COMET: 1978, observation, "TEMPEL", matches 9536.
    10   15   30   50

9541 SANTA FE: 1980, 1982, baggage, "RAILWAY EXPRESS AGENCY", light tan body, cherry red roof, black lettering and Santa Fe cross logo, arch bar trucks, plastic wheels; part of 1053 The James Gang Set.   --   --   15   30

9544 CHICAGO: 1980, see Special Production chapter.

9545 UNION PACIFIC: 1984, smooth-sided baggage car, yellow body; red striping and lettering, gray roof and ends. (The rest of the cars in the set are illuminated). Part of the "Overland Limited" Passenger Set.   --   --   75   100

9546 UNION PACIFIC: 1984, combine, illuminated, silhouettes in windows; otherwise matches 9545.   --   --   75   100

9547 UNION PACIFIC: 1984, observation car, red taillights on rear, illuminated "Overland Limited" drumhead; otherwise matches 9546. There have been vehement complaints from collectors that the yellow color on this car is much darker than the other cars in the set, and the doors do not match the body color. Numerous examples observed validate these complaints.   --   --   75   100

9548 UNION PACIFIC: 1984, "Placid Bay" passenger coach; matches 9546.
    --   --   75   100

9549 UNION PACIFIC: 1984, "Ocean Sunset" passenger coach, matches 9546.   --   --   75   100

9551 WESTERN & ATLANTIC: 1977-79, 1860-type baggage car for General set, yellow body, tuscan platforms and roof; tuscan lettering, black stacks and ventilators, arch bar trucks.   --   15   25   45

9552 WESTERN & ATLANTIC: 1860-type coach for General set; matches 9551.   --   15   25   45

9554 ALTON LIMITED: 1981, baggage, "ARMSTRONG", 9500-series heavyweight-style, dark maroon body, silver roof; dark red window striping, gold lettering, die-cast six-wheel passenger trucks.   --   --   35   60

9555 ALTON LIMITED: 1981, combine, "MISSOURI"; matches 9554.
    --   --   35   60

9556 ALTON LIMITED: 1981, coach, "WILSON"; matches 9554.
    --   --   35   60

9557 ALTON LIMITED: 1981, coach "WEBSTER GROVES"; matches 9554.
    --   --   35   60

9558 ALTON LIMITED: 1981, observation, "CHICAGO"; matches 9554.
    --   --   35   50

9559 ROCK ISLAND & PEORIA: 1981, combine, 1860s General-style car, light gold-painted body, tuscan roof and platforms, tuscan lettering, black stacks and ventilators, illuminated, arch bar trucks; matches 9560 and 9561 and goes with 8004 Locomotive; all only available as separate sale. C. Rohlfing comments.
    --   --   30   40

9560 ROCK ISLAND & PEORIA: 1981, coach; matches 9559.
    --   --   30   40

9561 ROCK ISLAND & PEORIA: 1981, coach; matches 9559.
    --   --   30   40

(9562) NORFOLK AND WESTERN: 1981, baggage, "577" and in script "The Powhatan Arrow", first painted extruded aluminum passenger car made by Lionel, with black roof, maroon sides, gold striping and lettering; catalogue number is stamped on the boxes, not the cars.   --   --   75   100

(9563) NORFOLK AND WESTERN: 1981, combine, "578"; matches 9562.
    --   --   75   100

(9564) NORFOLK AND WESTERN: 1981, coach, "579"; matches 9562.
    --   --   75   125

(9565) NORFOLK AND WESTERN: 1981, coach, "580"; matches 9562.
    --   --   75   125

(9566) NORFOLK AND WESTERN: 1981, observation, "581"; matches 9562. -- -- 75 100

(9567) NORFOLK AND WESTERN: 1981, Vista Dome, matches 9562. -- -- 300 375

9569 PENNSYLVANIA: 1981, combination, "PAUL REVERE"; matches 9571. -- -- 75 150

9570 PENNSYLVANIA: 1979, "RAILWAY EXPRESS AGENCY", small door baggage, mirror polished aluminum, plastic ends, same trucks as original Lionel baggage cars but with fast angle wheels. -- 100 150 175

9571 PENNSYLVANIA: 1979, "WILLIAM PENN", Pullman, mirror polished aluminum, iridescent maroon stripes; spring-loaded lamp receptacle, rerun of 1950s 2543, but 2543 had flat finished aluminum, brown flatter stripes, 252 Crossing Gate light unit with sliding shoe or rivet end contact. -- 75 100 150

9572 PENNSYLVANIA: 1979, "MOLLY PITCHER", Pullman; matches 9571. -- 50 100 125

9573 PENNSYLVANIA: 1979, "BETSY ROSS", Vista Dome; matches 9571. -- 50 100 125

9574 PENNSYLVANIA: 1979, "ALEXANDER HAMILTON", observation, matches 9571, "Lionel Limited" on back door inside of protective gate. -- 50 100 125

9575 PENNSYLVANIA: 1979, Pullman, "THOMAS A. EDISON", aluminum passenger car; matches 9571. -- -- 125 175

9576 BURLINGTON: 1980, extruded aluminum baggage, "SILVER POUCH", four-wheel O Gauge die-cast passenger trucks, 16" long, for O Gauge track; only available for separate sale. -- -- 60 90

9577 BURLINGTON: 1980, coach, "SILVER HALTER"; matches 9576. -- -- 60 90

9578 BURLINGTON: 1980, coach, "SILVER GLADIOLA"; matches 9576. -- -- 60 90

9579 BURLINGTON: 1980, Vista Dome, "SILVER KETTLE"; matches 9576. -- -- 60 90

9580 BURLINGTON: 1980, observation, "SILVER VERANDA"; matches 9576. -- -- 60 90

Two of the new series of diner cars made in severely limited quantities to match existing 9500 Series passenger sets. Top: 9586 Chessie Steam Special version. Bottom: 9599 Chicago and Alton version (note that the number does not appear on the car). Other diners have been produced for the Blue Comet and Southern Crescent sets, and Pennsylvania and Milwaukee versions are scheduled for year-end 1988 production. Can a Baltimore and Ohio version be far behind? Each diner was produced with the correctly matched trucks, although Lionel, Inc. wisely avoided duplicating the body-mounted dummy couplers in the Pennsylvania and Milwaukee versions.

9581 CHESSIE: 1980, baggage, yellow sides, gray roof, blue ends and lettering, vermilion stripe on sides. -- -- 40 80

9582 CHESSIE: 1980, combine; matches 9581. -- -- 40 80

9583 CHESSIE: 1980, coach; matches 9581. -- -- 40 80

9584 CHESSIE: 1980, coach; matches 9581. -- -- 40 80

9585 CHESSIE: 1980, observation; matches 9581. -- -- 40 80

9586 CHESSIE: 1986, diner car, matches 9581-9585, above. Sold as part of year-end "Stocking Stuffer" package; already hard to find. -- -- -- 95

9588 BURLINGTON: 1980, Vista Dome, "SILVER DOME"; matches 9576. -- -- 100 150

9589 SOUTHERN PACIFIC: 1982, extruded aluminum baggage with distinctive red, orange, white, and black "Daylight" colors; includes four matching cars and a matching pair of F-3 diesels (8260 and 8262), all sold separately. Part of Spring Collector Series for 1982. In the 1983 Collector Series Catalogue the set was offered again. Then in the 1983 Fall Collector Series, the 7211 Vista Dome was added. Also in 1983 a 7204 Dining Car and an 8261 Diesel B unit were offered. The three later cars were apparently intentionally made in quantities lower than market demand, causing a dramatic short term price appreciation. It will be most interesting to see if the price differentials hold. Five years after the original issue, they have indeed done so. -- -- 100 125

9590 SOUTHERN PACIFIC: 1982-83, combo; matches 9589. -- -- 100 125

9591 SOUTHERN PACIFIC: 1982-83, Pullman; matches 9589. -- -- 100 125

9592 SOUTHERN PACIFIC: 1982-83, Pullman; matches 9589. -- -- 100 125

9593 SOUTHERN PACIFIC: 1982-83, observation; matches 9589. -- -- 100 125

9594 NEW YORK CENTRAL: 1983, double-door, extruded aluminum baggage, painted gray with white lettering and black roof, gray ends; sold as a separate item, with matching diesels 8370, 8371, 8372 and matching cars 9595, 9596, 9597, 9598, and 7207; four-wheel O Gauge die-cast passenger trucks, operating couplers. We have had reports that the smooth-sided cars in this and subsequent series have paint which can chip easily if mishandled. In addition, the dark gray color of the paint on these cars shows fingerprints easily, and these prints, once present, are hard to remove. -- -- 100 125

9595 NEW YORK CENTRAL: 1983, extruded aluminum combine, illuminated; matches 9594. -- -- 100 125

9596 NEW YORK CENTRAL: 1983, extruded aluminum coach, "WAYNE COUNTY" Pullman, illuminated; matches 9594. -- -- 100 125

9596 NEW YORK CENTRAL: 1983, extruded aluminum coach, illuminated, "HUDSON RIVER" Pullman; matches 9594. -- -- 100 125

9598 NEW YORK CENTRAL: 1983, extruded aluminum, observation, "MANHATTAN ISLAND", illuminated; matches 9594. -- -- 100 125

9599 ALTON LIMITED: 1987, dining car, matches 9554- 9558. Sold as part of year-end "Stocking Stuffer" package; already hard to find. -- -- -- 85

16000 PENNSYLVANIA: 1987, 2400-style VistaDome, revival of 2400-style cars not seen since Quicksilver Express cars of 1982. Tuscan-painted body, gold lettering and number, black unpainted roof, illuminated, wood-beam four-wheel passenger trucks, operating couplers. -- -- 20 25

16001 PENNSYLVANIA: 1987, 2400-style passenger coach, matches 16000. -- -- 20 25

16002 PENNSYLVANIA: 1987, 2400-style passenger coach, matches 16000. -- -- 20 25

16003 PENNSYLVANIA: 1987, 2400-style observation, matches 16000. Does not have red marker lights on end. -- -- 20 25

16009 PENNSYLVANIA: Scheduled for 1988, 2400-style combine, tuscan body, black roof, gold lettering and number, plastic O27-style passenger trucks, silhouettes in windows. Made as a match for 16000-series Pennsylvania passenger cars introduced in 1987. -- -- -- 25

16013 AMTRAK: Scheduled for 1988, 2400-style combine, silver-painted body, red, white, and blue Amtrak striping and logo, plastic O27 passenger trucks, operating couplers, passenger silhouettes in windows, illuminated. Part of 11707 Silver Spike Passenger Set. -- -- -- 25

16014 AMTRAK: 2400-style Vista-Dome; matches 16013. -- -- -- 25

16015 AMTRAK: 2400-style observation; matches 16013. -- -- -- 25

19000 THE BLUE COMET: 1987, "Giacobini" diner car, made as a match for the 9536-40 Blue Comet Passenger Cars of 1978-79. Part of "Happy Lionel Holidays" year-end package for 1987. -- -- -- 85

19001 SOUTHERN CRESCENT: 1987, "Crescent Limited" diner car, made as a match for 9530-9534 Southern Crescent Passenger Cars from 1977-78, including the older four-wheel trucks. Same comments as for 19000 above.

-- -- -- 85

19002 PENNSYLVANIA: Announced for late 1988, diner car, matches 9500-series Pennsylvania cars produced from 1947-76, including body-mounted couplers and wood-beam trucks. Expected introductory price.

-- -- -- 50

19003 MILWAUKEE ROAD: Announced for late 1988, diner car, matches 9500-series Milwaukee cars produced from 1973-76, including body-mounted couplers and wood-beam trucks. Since the original production cars featured both flat and glossy maroon-painted roofs it will be interesting to see which version will be found on this car. Expected introductory price. -- -- -- 50

Chapter XI
REFRIGERATOR CARS

THE 9800 REFRIGERATOR CAR SERIES

It is hard to imagine why the 9800 Series of refrigerator cars has not commanded more attention among collectors than it has. These cars represent the creativity of Fundimensions at its best. Longer than their boxcar counterparts, these cars are made entirely of stout plastic pieces which are extremely well detailed with wood-sided scribing on the sides and interior floors. The bottoms of the cars have realistic air tank details, and the plug doors open and close (though with peril to the plastic door guides of the later cars).

Most importantly, the 9800 Series gave Fundimensions a chance to show off its capabilities with graphics. Colorful electrocals grace the sides of these cars, advertising just about every conceivable product in food and drink. These include some strange choices for refrigeration: Bazooka bubble gum, Cheerios, and Old Dutch cleanser among them! Meat packing plants, juice companies, and breweries have advertised their wares on these cars. The situation is reminiscent of the late 19th Century on American railroads, where for quite some time American companies would hire out space on railroad boxcars to advertise their wares. It was not unusual for a boxcar on a New York Central train of those years to advertise Lydia Pinkham's Patented Vegetable Elixir while carrying machine tools!

The numbering system of these cars has been a little odd, too. The 9800 refrigerator cars were introduced in 1973 at the same time the 9800 Standard O Series was produced. Since the Standard O Series began with the 9801 Baltimore and Ohio, the refrigerator cars started with the 9850 Budweiser. In recent years, the 9800 refrigerator cars have begun to use numbers in the lower half of the numbering system, most recently with the Favorite Spirits cars, which are numbered in the 9840s and complete the series. About 70 cars have been produced altogether.

Collectors have been attracted to many sub-series within the 9800 Series. Most prominent are the collectors of the beer cars and the Favorite Spirit whiskey cars. There are about ten beer cars and sixteen spirits cars to collect, and some of these cars command slightly higher prices than other issues. Some collectors, on the other hand, like the soda pop and juices cars, such as the 9861 Tropicana Orange Juice Car and the 9831 Pepsi-Cola Car. For the real high-brow collectors, there is the 9814 Perrier Spring Water Car. Still others like the candy cars, such as the 9816 Brach's, the 9854 Baby Ruth, and the 9858 Butterfinger Cars. Finally, railroad realists like to stick to cars modeled after real prototypes, such as the 9863 Railway Express Car, the 9819 Great Northern Fruit Express Car, and the 9869 Santa Fe. There is something for everybody in this series!

There is a terrific collector story behind the production of the 9853 Cracker Jack Car in 1973 and 1974. The first cars produced were a dark caramel color, as portrayed in the 1973 catalogue. However, a few cars came out at the end of the production run with white sides, and collectors scrambled to acquire them. In 1974 these collectors were surprised to see the car pictured in white in the catalogue, and soon a flood of white 9853 cars hit the market! The expected situation became completely reversed; the caramel car is now regarded as the scarce car, while the white car is readily available. This is a graphic example of the unpredictability of the collector marketplace, though with current marketing policies it does not appear that such a reversal will ever happen again.

These colorful cars represent a fine opportunity for the beginning collector because most of them are readily available, some at real bargain prices. Only a few of the 9800-series refrigerator cars are scarce, mostly those in collector sets. These cars look great when they are placed in a long string behind a modern set of diesels. They add color to a collection and offer many chances for specialization.

CRITICAL VARIABLES

Body Types: The 9800-series refrigerator car is an all-plastic car with the roof and ends made of one piece and the bottom and sides made of another. The two pieces attach at the ends by screws. The oldest body type is more of a carry-over from postwar production than its successors, which had more and more detail eliminated in an attempt to simplify construction. The Type I body features two metal door guides and a

---

9800-SERIES REEFER BODY TYPES
By Donald J. Mitarotonda

Type I

Two metal door guides.

Two metal bars running underneath frame, secured in center by one Phillips-head screw.

Trucks secured to metal.

Doors, underneath the ladders on each side of the body, are wider than the ladders.

Roof has three ice hatches, third ice hatch in one corner.

Type II

Same as Type I, but doors underneath the ladders are the same width as the ladders, roof has two ice hatches in opposing corners.

Type III

Two plastic door guides.

No metal bars underneath frame.

Trucks secured to the frame with a plastic pin.

Doors underneath the ladders are the same width as the ladders.

Roof has two ice hatches in opposing corners.

Top shelf: 5700 Oppenheimer Sausage Casings, 5701 Dairymen's League. Second shelf: 5702 National Dairy Despatch, 5703 North American Despatch. Third shelf: 5704 Budweiser, 5705 Ball Glass Jars. Fourth shelf: 5706 Lindsay Bros. Binder & Twine, 5707 American Refrigerator Transit. Fifth shelf: 5708 Armour, 5709 Railway Express Agency. Bottom shelf: 5710 Canadian Pacific, 5711 Commercial Express. G. and D. Halverson and A. Conto Collections.

metal channel which runs the length of the car bottom and is attached by a single screw to the car body. In turn, the trucks are attached to the channel. The little metal control door and lithographed control gauge panel of postwar production are missing, but three ice hatches are molded into the roof, and machinery doors underneath the ladders on each side of the body are wider than the ladders. The Type II body is similar, but there are only two ice hatches at diagonal corners of the roof. Machinery doors are the same width as the ladders on the sides. The Type III body, the most recent and the most common, retains the two ice hatches and the Type II machinery doors, but the door guides become snap-in plastic pieces and

A selection of Favorite Food cars. Top shelf: 7509 Kentucky Fried Chicken, 7510 Red Lobster. Second shelf: 7511 Pizza Hut, 7512 Arthur Treacher's Seafood. Bottom shelf: 7513 Bonanza, 7514 Taco Bell. G. and D. Halverson and A. Conto Collections.

the metal channel under the car is eliminated. Instead of the channel, the trucks are secured directly to the car body by a plastic or metal rivet. It should be noted that the 7600 Bicentennial cars and the 7700 Tobacco Road cars are constructed quite similarly, except that the doors are sliding boxcar-style instead of refrigerator plug-door style.

THE STANDARD O SERIES

In 1973 Fundimensions introduced a line of full-scale box and refrigerator cars known as the Standard O Series. These cars, reportedly based upon Pola designs made by the firm of Rivarossi in Europe, were also the cars first equipped with the excellent Standard O sprung trucks. Although the cars were extremely well made, they did not meet the sales expectations of Fundimensions and did not persist for very long. Recently, the genre has been revived for rolling stock to match the 8406 Scale Hudson and as part of an interesting Burlington Northern unit train. During the past two years, many more of these handsome box and refrigerator cars have been produced, along with scale flatcars, ACF center-flow hoppers, scale wood-sided cabooses, and gondolas. This would seem to indicate that the reason the cars did not sell well in the 1973-1975 period was that Fundimensions had not produced true scale locomotives and cabooses to match them in an operating train. With the reissue of the Hudson and the creation of the scale SD-40 diesel and the extended vision scale cabooses, that situation has changed. It is possible that these cars will undergo a rebirth of popularity and the original issues will increase in value.

The availability of the Standard O cars varies considerably. Common cars such as the 9803 Johnson's Wax and the 9809

Clark are easy to acquire at good prices. On the other hand, some cars such as the 9807 Stroh's and the 9806 Rock Island are very hard to find. The New York Central box and refrigerator cars command some attention, as do the box and refrigerator cars made available in a direct-mail campaign from Lionel in 1986. Behind the right engine, these cars make a very impressive train on a large layout. Their construction details are excellent as well. The beginning collector may have a difficult time acquiring some of these cars, but a few representative samples of these cars would be good additions to anyone's collection.

THE 5700 TURN OF THE CENTURY REEFERS

In 1980 Fundimensions tried something it had never tried before — a realistic "weathered" paint job. The firm issued eight cars which it called its "Turn of the Century" refrigerator cars. These cars were modeled after wood-sided prototypes which were common on American railroads around 1910. The cars used 9800-series roof and end pieces, but the pieces which formed the sides and bottoms were new; they used horizontal wood scribing, extremely realistic riveting, and a scribed undercarriage. The cars also had true-to-life markings and a special weatherbeaten treatment for the paint which is readily visible when the doors are opened to reveal the real color of the paint and plastic. These cars were also equipped with Standard O trucks; they represented Fundimensions construction practices at their best.

Probably because the weathered look was so dramatically non-Lionel, the cars did not sell very well, and after only eight

Top shelf: 9813 Ruffles, 9814 Perrier. Second shelf: 9818 Western Maryland, 9833 Vlasic. Third shelf: 9834 Southern Comfort, 9835 Jim Beam. Fourth shelf: 9836 Old Granddad, 9837 Wild Turkey. Bottom shelf: 9854 Baby Ruth, 9875 A & P. G. and D. Halverson and A. Conto Collections.

cars were produced, the series was discontinued in favor of the wood-sided reefer series, which sold much better. These cars are still readily available, making them highly desirable items if the collector favors their realistic look. The Oppenheimer, Budweiser, and Lindsay Brothers cars command a slight premium over the other five cars, but none are really scarce. These eight cars look great in a train pulled by a postwar 675 or 2025 Pennsylvania K-4 Steam Locomotive and followed by an all-metal postwar 2457 Pennsylvania N5 Caboose. They make a fine, high-quality set for the beginner's collection, and in later years they may appreciate in value because of their realistic appearance.

THE 5700 WOOD-SIDED REEFER SERIES

In 1982 Fundimensions tried again to introduce a new series of refrigerator cars based upon an old-time theme, and this time the firm was much more successful with sales. The wood-sided reefers began with the 5708 Armour car and, in the first three years, four new cars in the series were produced each year. Three were made for 1985, but they were very dull in appearance and did not sell well, so they were carried over into the next year. Lionel, Inc. closed out the series in 1987 with three new cars using a five-digit number. These cars used the same highly detailed side and bottom pieces used on the Turn

Top shelf: 9876 Central Vermont, 9877 Gerber. Second shelf: 9879 Hills Bros., 9881 Rath Packing. Third shelf: 9882 N Y R B, 9883 Oreo. Bottom shelf: 9884 Fritos, 9885 Lipton 100 Tea Bags. G. and D. Halverson and A. Conto Collections.

of the Century reefers, but without the weathering process. The roof and end pieces are entirely new. The ends are scribed vertically and the roof is scribed across its width. Four ice hatches are present in the corners of the roof, and the wood scribing has been given a skillfully grained look. The brakewheel is atop the roof end rather than on the end itself. Although true to the prototype, this feature can be annoying when the collector puts the car back in its box because the brakewheel always catches on the box divider. In recent production, the brakewheel has been attached to the car bottom with tape to prevent shipping and packaging damage. The cars are equipped with the less expensive but realistic plastic arch bar trucks.

The wood-sided reefers have sold very well as a class, and most are readily available to the beginning collector. The 5709 Railway Express is a little harder to find than most of the others, but only one of these reefers is truly rare: the 5712 Lionel Lines Wood-sided Reefer of 1983. This car ballooned in value almost overnight and is nearly impossible to acquire. The 5720 Great Northern, a very attractive dark green car, was not made in very great numbers and is also quite scarce.

Operationally, the Wood-sided Reefers can look very good when pulled behind any old-style steam engine, even the "General" engines. The new center-cab transfer cabooses have just the right old-fashioned look for a set of these cars. Most have been produced in prototypical orange, yellow, and tuscan colors, so a train of these cars provides a realistic look lacking in the 9800 Series and matched only by the Turn of the Century Reefers.

Gd VG Exc Mt

0104 WHEAT THINS: 1984, Type III reefer body, yellow sides, white roof, ends, and doors, black "Whole Wheat Goodness" and "Wheat Thins" box to left of door, black "Wheat Thins" lettering to right of door. Part of special promotional set for Nabisco, some of which may have been produced outside the factory. Reader comments requested. S. Lindsey, Jr. Collection. **NRS**

0124 OREO: 1984, Type III reefer body, white sides, dark gray roof and ends, black doors, two different illustrations of Oreo Double Stuf cookie packages on either side of door. Same comments as those for 0104 above. S. Lindsey, Jr. Collection. **NRS**

3764 KAHN'S: Reefer, Lionel Operating Train Society, see Special Production chapter.

5700 OPPENHEIMER SAUSAGE CASINGS: 1981, dark blue-green "weathered" paint; black lettering, red and black logo, Standard O sprung trucks,

Top shelf: 9886 Mounds, 9888 Green Bay & Western. Second shelf: 7712 A T S F boxcar, 9811 Pacific Fruit Expresss. Third shelf: 9819 Western Fruit Express, 9887 Fruit Growers Express. Bottom shelf: 9880 A T S F. G. and D. Halverson and A. Conto Collections.

the first in the "Turn of the Century" series. C. Lang and C. Rohlfing comments.
-- -- 20 25

5701 DAIRYMEN'S LEAGUE: 1981, milk reefer, off-white "weathered" paint, black roof and ends; blue lettering and logo, Standard O sprung trucks. C. Rohlfing comment. -- -- 15 20

5702 NATIONAL DAIRY DESPATCH: 1981, Universal Carloading & Distributing Co., silver-gray body, red and silver "weathered" paint, dark red roof and ends; black lettering, Standard O sprung trucks. C. Lang and C. Rohlfing comments. -- -- 15 20

5703 NORTH AMERICAN DESPATCH: 1981, "FRIGICAR", weathered light yellow and dark brown roof and ends; black lettering, Standard O sprung trucks. C. Rohlfing comment. -- -- 15 20

5704 BUDWEISER: 1981, dark green "weathered" paint; white lettering, Standard O sprung trucks. This car is a little scarcer than the others in this group because of interest from beer car collectors. C. Rohlfing comment.
-- -- 20 30

5705 BALL GLASS JARS: 1981, yellow "weathered" paint, brown roof and ends; blue lettering, Standard O sprung trucks. C. Rohlfing comment.
-- -- 15 20

5706 LINDSAY BROS. BINDER & TWINE: 1981, tuscan-maroon "weathered" paint; yellow lettering, Standard O sprung trucks. C. Rohlfing comment. -- -- 20 25

5707 AMERICAN REFRIGERATOR TRANSIT CO.: 1981, yellow "weathered" paint, brown roof and ends; black lettering, Standard O sprung trucks. C. Rohlfing comment. -- -- 15 20

5708 ARMOUR: 1982-83, wood-sided reefer, yellow sides, tuscan roof and ends, blue lettering, arch bar trucks. C. Rohlfing comment. -- -- 12 15

5709 R E A (Railway Express Agency): 1982-83, wood-sided reefer, medium green-painted body; light green and white lettering, red and white diamond REA electrocal, arch bar trucks. Somewhat scarcer than the other early wood-sided reefers. C. Lang, C. Rohlfing, and R. LaVoie comments.
-- -- 30 35

5710 CANADIAN PACIFIC: 1982-83, wood-sided reefer, tuscan body; white lettering, arch bar trucks. C. Rohlfing comment. -- -- 12 15

5711 COMMERCIAL EXPRESS: 1982-83, wood-sided reefer, light caramel body, brown roof and ends; black lettering, arch bar trucks. C. Rohlfing comment.
-- -- 12 15

5712 LIONEL ELECTRIC TRAINS: 1983, wood-sided reefer, bright orange body, bright blue roof and ends; blue and white "LIONEL" electrocal, blue lettering, arch bar trucks. Very hard to find; the price of this car has increased dramatically since it was first introduced. C. Lang, C. Rohlfing, and R. LaVoie comments.
-- 175 200 300

5713 COTTON BELT: 1983, St. Louis Southwestern, wood-sided reefer, yellow sides, brown roof and ends; black "COTTON BELT" logo to right of door, arch bar trucks. C. Lang and C. Rohlfing comments. -- -- 15 20

5714 MICHIGAN CENTRAL: 1983, wood-sided reefer, white sides, brown roof and ends; black lettering, arch bar trucks. C. Lang and C. Rohlfing comments. -- -- 15 20

5715 SANTA FE: 1983, wood-sided reefer, orange sides, tuscan roof and ends (shown as dark blue in catalogue, but not produced that way); black lettering, black and white Santa Fe cross logo to left of door, arch bar trucks. C. Rohlfing comment, R. LaVoie Collection. -- -- 15 20

5716 VERMONT CENTRAL: 1983, wood-sided reefer, silver-gray sides, black roof and ends, black and green lettering, arch bar trucks. C. Rohlfing comment. -- -- 15 20

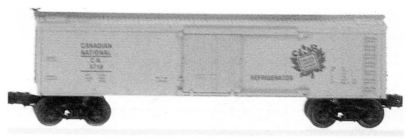

5719 Canadian National.

5719 CANADIAN NATIONAL: 1984, wood-sided reefer, gray body; dark red lettering and maple leaf logo, arch bar trucks. -- -- 15 20

5720 GREAT NORTHERN: 1984, wood-sided reefer, dark green body; gold lettering, red, white, and black Great Northern logo, arch bar trucks. For some unknown reason, far fewer of these cars were produced than the others in its series. As a result, this car has become very hard to find. -- -- 75 90

5721 SOO LINE: 1984, wood-sided reefer, orange sides, brown roof and ends; black lettering, black and white Soo Line logo, arch bar trucks. -- -- 15 20

5722 NICKEL PLATE ROAD: 1984, wood-sided reefer, yellow sides, brown roof and ends, black lettering, arch bar trucks. -- -- 15 20

5730 STRASBURG RAIL ROAD: 1985-86, wood-sided reefer, tuscan body, roof, and ends; yellow-gold lettering and numbering, arch bar trucks. Popular in the Pennsylvania area because of association with Strasburg tourist railroad. -- -- 15 20

5731 LOUISVILLE & NASHVILLE: 1985-86, wood-sided reefer, tuscan body, roof, and ends; white lettering and numbering, arch bar trucks. -- -- 12 15

5732 CENTRAL RAILROAD OF NEW JERSEY: 1985-86, wood-sided reefer, tuscan body, roof, and ends; white lettering, red and white bull's eye logo, arch bar trucks. -- -- 12 15

5734 LIONEL RAILROADER CLUB: See Special Production chapter.

6230 ERIE-LACKAWANNA: 1986, Standard O reefer, orange sides, black ends, silver-painted roof, black lettering and logo, Standard O trucks. Part of special direct-mail Lionel offer. -- -- 85 100

6700 PACIFIC FRUIT EXPRESS: 1982, refrigerator car, modified 6464 boxcar body; orange body, dark brown doors, metal door guides, UP and SP logos, Standard O trucks, operating hatch and bin cut into roof. Made for 2306 Icing Station; price for car only; seldom sold separately. -- -- 50 65

7501 LIONEL 75th ANNIVERSARY: See Boxcar chapter.

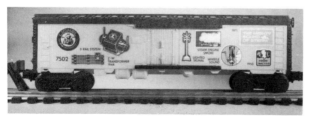

7502 Lionel 75th Anniversary.

7502 LIONEL 75th ANNIVERSARY: 1975, reefer, innovations, yellow body, blue roof and ends. -- 10 15 20

7503 Lionel 75th Anniversary.

7503 LIONEL 75th ANNIVERSARY: 1975, reefer, famous engines, orange body, brown roof and ends. -- 10 15 20

7506 LIONEL 75th ANNIVERSARY: See Boxcar chapter.

7507 Lionel 75th Anniversary.

7507 LIONEL 75th ANNIVERSARY: 1975, reefer logos, white body, blue roof and ends. -- 10 15 20

7509 KENTUCKY FRIED CHICKEN: 1981-82, reefer, dark brown-red sides, tuscan roof and ends, white lettering, Colonel Sanders electrocal, Symington-Wayne trucks; from Favorite Food Freight, available only as separate sale. C. Rohlfing comment. -- -- 15 20

7510 RED LOBSTER: 1981-82, reefer with white sides, black roof and ends; red lettering, lobster electrocal, Symington-Wayne trucks; from Favorite Food Freight, available only as separate sale. -- -- 20 25

7511 PIZZA HUT: 1981-82, reefer with white sides, red roof and ends; red lettering, hut electrocal, Symington-Wayne trucks; from Favorite Food Freight, available only as separate sale. -- -- 20 25

7512 ARTHUR TREACHER'S SEAFOOD: 1982, 9800-type reefer, yellow sides, green roof and ends; green lettering, Symington-Wayne trucks; part of Favorite Food series, sold separately. C. Lang comment. -- -- 15 20

7513 BONANZA: 1982, 9800-type reefer, white sides, red roof and ends; red and black lettering, Bonanza electrocal to right of door, Symington-Wayne trucks; part of Favorite Food series, sold separately. C. Lang comment. -- -- 15 20

7514 TACO BELL: 1982, 9800-type reefer, white sides, brown roof and ends, brown lettering, multicolor Taco Bell electrocal to right of door; part of Favorite Food series, sold separately. C. Lang comment. -- -- 15 20

9220 BORDEN: 1983, operating refrigerated milk car, white body, brown roof and ends; black lettering, yellow and black "ELSIE" cow logo to right of door. Came with gray and white milk can platform and plastic milk cans. Car has postwar bar-end metal trucks because sliding shoe is needed to operate car. C. Lang comment. -- -- 70 85

9802 MILLER HIGH LIFE: 1975, Standard O reefer, white mold, red lettering and logo. 15 20 25 30
See also Factory Errors and Prototypes chapter.

9805 GRAND TRUNK: 1975, Standard O reefer, gray mold, silver paint; black lettering. 15 20 30 40

9807 STROH'S BEER: 1975-76, Standard O reefer, red mold, red paint; gold and white lettering. 40 50 70 90

9809 CLARK: 1975-76, Standard O reefer, red mold, blue lettering.
(A) Medium red paint. 15 20 25 40
(B) Dark red paint. 15 20 25 40

9811 PACIFIC FRUIT EXPRESS: 1980, yellow-painted yellow plastic body and doors; tuscan-painted tuscan plastic roof, gold diamond FARR Series 2 logo, red, white, and blue UP shield, blue SP logo, part of Famous American Railroad Series 2; available as separate sale only. -- -- **25** **35**

9812 ARM & HAMMER: 1980, billboard reefer, yellow sides, red roof and ends, Symington-Wayne trucks, yellow and red electrocal. -- -- **10** **20**

9813 RUFFLES: 1980, billboard reefer, blue roof and ends, Symington-Wayne trucks, red and blue electrocal.
(A) White sides. Existence confirmed; very difficult to find. G. Halverson comment. **NRS**
(B) Light blue sides. Samson and G. Rogers Collections. -- -- **10** **20**

9814 PERRIER: 1980, water billboard reefer, dark Brunswick green sides, light yellow ends and roof, Symington-Wayne trucks. "PERRIER" electrocal to right of door, mountain spring electrocal to left of door shows a Perrier stick-on bottle bubbling from beneath the earth. -- -- **20** **25**
See also Factory Errors and Prototypes.

9815 NEW YORK CENTRAL: 1985, Standard O refrigerator car, orange body, tuscan roof and catwalk; blue N Y R B lettering, "Early Bird" logo, Standard O trucks. F. Cieri and C. Rohlfing Collections. -- -- **50** **80**

9816 BRACHS: 1980, billboard reefer, white sides, tuscan roof and ends, magenta doors, magenta, tuscan, and white lettering and logo, Symington-Wayne trucks. C. Rohlfing comments. -- -- **9** **20**

9817 BAZOOKA: 1980, billboard reefer, white sides, red and blue Bazooka electrocal, Symington-Wayne trucks.
(A) Orange-red roof and ends. -- -- **10** **20**
(B) Orange roof and ends. C. Rohlfing Collection. -- -- **12** **18**

9818 WESTERN MARYLAND: 1980, reefer, orange-red sides, Standard O sprung die-cast trucks; part of 1070 Royal Limited set.
(A) Black roof, ends, and lettering. -- -- **25** **35**
(B) Brown roof, ends, and lettering. D. Griggs Collection. **NRS**

9819 WESTERN FRUIT EXPRESS: 1981, reefer, yellow sides and ends, Great Northern goat logo, FARR Series 3 logo, part of Famous American Railroad Series 3, available as separate sale only. -- -- **20** **35**

9825 SCHAEFER: 1976-77, reefer, white body, red lettering and roof, Standard O Series. **20** **30** **40** **55**

9827 CUTTY SARK: 1984-85, Favorite Spirits reefer, yellow sides and doors, black roof and ends; black lettering, black and white sailing ship electrocal, Symington-Wayne trucks. -- -- **15** **18**

9828 J & B: 1984-85, Favorite Spirits reefer, yellow-green sides and doors, white roof and ends; red and black lettering, red, black, and white herald electrocal, Symington-Wayne trucks. -- -- **15** **18**

9829 DEWARS WHITE LABEL: 1984-85, Favorite Spirits reefer, white sides and doors, red roof and ends; red and black lettering, orange and gold bagpiper electrocal, Symington-Wayne trucks. -- -- **15** **18**

9830 JOHNNIE WALKER RED: 1984-85, Favorite Spirits reefer, yellow-gold sides and doors, maroon roof and ends, maroon lettering, maroon rectangular logo with gold lettering, red, blue, and yellow Johnnie Walker electrocal, Symington-Wayne trucks. -- -- **15** **18**

9831 PEPSI COLA: 1982, reefer, white sides, light blue ends and roof; red, white, and blue Pepsi electrocal, Symington-Wayne trucks. -- -- **20** **30**

9832 CHEERIOS: 1982, reefer, yellow body; black lettering, black Cheerios electrocal, Symington-Wayne trucks. -- -- **15** **20**

9833 VLASIC: 1982, reefer, white sides, yellow roof and ends; black lettering, Symington-Wayne trucks. -- -- **15** **18**

9834 SOUTHERN COMFORT: 1983, Favorite Spirits reefer, white body, gold roof and ends; black lettering, black oval Southern mansion electrocal, Symington-Wayne trucks. C. Lang and C. Rohlfing comments. -- -- **15** **20**

9835 JIM BEAM: 1983, Favorite Spirits reefer, white sides, red roof and ends; white and black lettering, red, white, and black logo to right of door, Symington-Wayne trucks. C. Lang and C. Rohlfing comments. -- -- **15** **20**

9836 OLD GRANDDAD: 1983, Favorite Spirits reefer, orange body, gold roof and ends, black-edged gold and brown lettering, orange, white, and black electrocal to right of door, Symington-Wayne trucks. C. Lang and C. Rohlfing comments. -- -- **15** **20**

9837 WILD TURKEY: 1983, Favorite Spirits reefer, light yellow body, dark brown roof and ends; red, dark brown, and white lettering, dark brown lettering and turkey electrocal to right of door, Symington-Wayne trucks. C. Rohlfing comment. -- -- **15** **20**

9840 FLEISCHMANN'S GIN: 1985, Favorite Spirits reefer, light yellow sides and doors, maroon roof and ends, dark blue and dark orange lettering, blue and gold eagle electrocal, Symington-Wayne trucks. -- -- **15** **20**

9841 CALVERT GIN: 1985, Favorite Spirits reefer, dark blue body, silver roof and ends; silver lettering, red and silver herald electrocal, Symington-Wayne trucks. -- -- **15** **20**

9842 SEAGRAM'S GIN: 1985, Favorite Spirits reefer, cream sides, dark blue roof and ends; dark blue and red lettering, dark blue and cream shield electrocal, Symington-Wayne trucks. -- -- **15** **20**

9843 TANQUERAY GIN: 1985, Favorite Spirits reefer, white sides, dark green roof and ends; red and black lettering, red and black circular electrocal, Symington-Wayne trucks. -- -- **15** **20**

9844 SAMBUCA ROMANA: 1986, Favorite Spirits reefer, very dark blue sides, silver-gray roof and ends, silver and black logo, gray, silver, and white lettering, Symington-Wayne trucks. -- -- **15** **20**

9845 BAILEY'S IRISH CREAM: 1986, Favorite Spirits reefer, dark pea green sides, tuscan roof and ends, orange, brown, and gold electrocal, orange, black, and white lettering, Symington-Wayne trucks. -- -- **20** **25**

9846 SEAGRAM'S VODKA: 1986, Favorite Spirits reefer, dark gray sides, black roof and ends, red and silver logo, silver lettering, Symington-Wayne trucks. -- -- **15** **20**

9847 WOLFSCHMIDT'S VODKA: 1986, Favorite Spirits reefer, dark green sides, gold roof and ends, red, gold, and white logo, white and gold lettering, Symington-Wayne trucks. -- -- **15** **20**

9849 LIONEL: 1983, bright orange refrigerator car with orange doors and blue roof; very large circular old-fashioned "LIONEL" logo in red, white, and blue to the right of the door. Lionel "lion" electrocal to the left of the door. The number to the immediate right of the lion is portrayed as 5718 in the 1983 Collector Center brochure, but 9849 is the number of the production models. This car and others in this series may have been prompted by the unauthorized repainting and sale of Lionel rolling stock in similar fashion by a small New England firm. Symington-Wayne trucks. R. LaVoie and C. Lang comments. -- -- **50** **65**

9850 Budweiser.

9850 BUDWEISER: 1973-76.
(A) Type I body, light red roof, white body and door, red and black lettering. **7** **9** **12** **18**
(B) Same as (A), but with medium red roof. **7** **9** **12** **18**
(C) Same as (A), but dark red roof. **7** **9** **12** **18**
(D) Same as (A), but large period after "BEER CAR" at lower right. **12** **15** **20** **25**

9851 Schlitz.

(E) Same as (A), but Type II body.　　　　　7　9　12　18

9851 SCHLITZ: 1973-76.
(A) Type I body, shiny brown roof, white body and door, brown lettering.
　　　　　　　　　　　　　　　　　　　　6　8　10　14
(B) Same as (A), but with Type II body with dull brown roof.
　　　　　　　　　　　　　　　　　　　　6　8　10　14

9852 Miller.

9852 MILLER: 1973-76.
(A) Type I body, shiny brown roof, white body and door, black lettering.
　　　　　　　　　　　　　　　　　　　　4　5　10　14
(B) Same as (A), but with Type II body with dull brown roof.
　　　　　　　　　　　　　　　　　　　　4　5　10　14
(C) Same as (B), but Type III body. Confirmation requested.　　NRS

9853 Cracker Jack.

9853 CRACKER JACK: Varietal classifications by J. Breslin.
(A) Type I body, brown roof, light caramel body, dark caramel door; red and blue lettering, with white border around "Cracker Jack". C. Rohlfing, F. Salvatore, R. LaVoie, and L. Stever Collections.　15　20　25　35
(B) Same as (A), but with medium caramel body and door.
　　　　　　　　　　　　　　　　　　　　15　20　25　35
(C) Same as (B), but with no border. Reportedly, fewer than 50 made.
　　　　　　　　　　　　　　　　　　　　80　100　125　150
(D) Type I body, brown roof, white body and door, red and blue lettering, with black border around "Cracker Jack", rare. F. Salvatore, L. Stever, and C. J. Grass Collections.　　--　--　100　125
(E) Same as (D), but circled "R" registration mark and without border. D. Coletta and R. LaVoie Collections.　5　7　15　20
(F) Same as (E), but red roof and ends. D. Coletta Collection.
　　　　　　　　　　　　　　　　　　　　5　7　10　14
(G) Same as (E), but no registration mark.　5　7　10　14
(H) Same as (E), but Type II body. Confirmed as existing. G. Halverson comment.　　　　　　　　　　　　　　　　NRS
(I) Same as (D), but "Cracker" in blue, "Jack" in red, without white border, circled red "R" registration mark, slight blue spot under word "Jack". R. P. Bryan Collection.　　　　　　　　--　--　100　125

9854 BABY RUTH: 1973-76.
(A) Type I body, red roof, white body and door, red and blue lettering.
　　　　　　　　　　　　　　　　　　　　6　8　10　14
(B) Same as (A), but with no "R" registration mark.　--　--　60　75
(C) Same as (B), but with Type II body.　6　8　10　14
(D) Same as (A), but Type II body. C. Rohlfing Collection.　6　8　10　14
(E) Same as (A), but darker red roof and lettering.　6　8　10　14

9855 Swift.

9855 SWIFT: 1974-76.
(A) Type I body, black roof, silver body and door, black lettering, "BLT 1-73".
　　　　　　　　　　　　　　　　　　　　10　15　20　25
(B) Same as (A), but Type II body.　10　15　20　25
(C) Same as (A), but Type III body. Confirmed as existing. G. Halverson comment.　　　　　　　　　　　　　　　　NRS
See also Factory Errors and Prototypes.

9856 Old Milwaukee.

9856 OLD MILWAUKEE: 1974-76.
(A) Type II body, gold roof, red body and door; white and black lettering.
　　　　　　　　　　　　　　　　　　　　8　10　15　20
(B) Same as (A), but Type III body. Confirmed as existing. G. Halverson comment.　　　　　　　　　　　　　　　　NRS
(C) Same as (A), but lettering (measured by placement of gold scroll) shifted to right on one side of car and left on other side, borders on electrocals mis-stamped. W. Dyson Collection.　　　　　　　　NRS

9858 Butterfinger.

9858 BUTTERFINGER: 1973-76.
(A) Type I body, flat blue roof, orange body and door; white and blue lettering. F. Salvatore and C. Rohlfing Collections.　6　8　12　14
(B) Same as (A), but with blue gloss roof.　6　8　12　14
(C) Same as (B), but Type II body.　6　8　12　14
(D) Same as (B), but Type III body. Confirmed as existing. G. Halverson comment.　　　　　　　　　　　　　　　　NRS

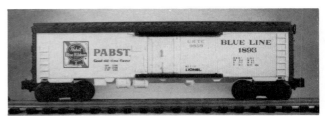

9859 Pabst.

A regular production 9860 Gold Metal reefer was given to General Mills' salesman for special sales efforts. The award car was shipped from General Mills and was accompanied by a letter and a special base with a section and a half of late 027 track with wood-grained ties.

The following is excerpted from the letter which accompanied the car.

Dear Gold Metal Man:

Gold Metal has been sold in volume ever since it won the Miller's International Exposition in 1880. And 1973-74 was no exception to volume selling...

Gold Metal wants you to have this Lionel railroad car to serve as a rewarding reminder of the volume selling job you did in 1973-74...

W. Smith III Collection and comments. M. Feinstein photograph.

(E) Same as (B), but Type I body, postwar trucks. Further sightings requested. C. O'Dell Collection. **NRS**

9859 PABST: 1974-75

(A) Type I body, medium blue roof, white body and door; blue and red lettering.

6	8	12	14

(B) Same as (A), but with Type II body.

6	8	12	14

9860 GOLD MEDAL: 1973-76

(A) Type I body, three openings, bright orange roof, white body and door, black lettering. This is reportedly the version found in separate sale boxes.

6	8	10	14

(B) Same as (A), but dull dark orange, two openings. This version was probably produced for the 1974 Grand National Set. It may also have been sold separately; reader comments requested.

6	8	10	14

(C) Same as (A), but Type II body.

6	8	10	14

(D) Same as (A), but Type III body. Confirmed as existing. G. Halverson comment. **NRS**

(E) Type II body, dull orange roof, postwar trucks. Further sighting requested. C. O'Dell Collection. **NRS**

9861 Tropicana.

9861 TROPICANA: 1975-77.

(A) Type II body, flat green roof, white body and door; green and orange lettering. Only available in Set 1560, the North American Set. C. Lang comment.

12	15	25	35

(B) Same as (A), but with Type III body, shiny green roof, opaque white body and door.

10	12	20	25

(C) Type III body, translucent white body and roof; green and orange lettering.

10	12	20	25

9862 Hamm's.

9862 HAMM'S: White roof, blue body and door; red and white lettering.

(A) Type II body.

10	12	20	25

(B) Type III body. Confirmed as existing. G. Halverson comment. **NRS**

9863 Railway Express Agency.

9863 RAILWAY EXPRESS AGENCY:

(A) Type II body, green roof, green body and door, gold lettering, no electrocals (rubber-stamped).

15	20	30	35

(B) Same as (A), but with electrocals.

10	15	25	30

(C) Same as (B), light green roof, with electrocals (gray mold).

10	15	25	30

(D) Same as (C), but with Type III body and green roof.

10	15	25	30

9864 T C A SEATTLE: See Special Production chapter.

9866 Coors.

9866 COORS:

(A) Type III body, brown roof, white body and doors; black and dark yellow lettering, no "R" registration mark.

10	12	15	20

(B) Same as (A), but has low "R" registration mark.

12	15	20	25

(C) Same as (A), but with high "R" registration mark.

10	12	15	25

(D) Same as (B), low "R" registration mark touching the "S" in "COORS" logo. Hard to find.

40	50	60	75

9867 HERSHEY'S: Type III body, silver roof and ends, maroon body, silver doors, maroon and silver lettering, Symington-Wayne trucks. C. Rohlfing Collection.

10	12	20	25

9868 T T O S: See Special Production chapter.

9869 SANTA FE: Type III body, brown roof, white body, brown door, black lettering, Standard O trucks. Part of 1672 Northern Pacific Service Station Special Set in 1976. C. Lang comment.

15	25	35	45

9867 Hershey's.

9870 Old Dutch Cleanser.

9870 OLD DUTCH CLEANSER: Type III body, red roof, yellow body, red door; white and black lettering, red, black, yellow, and white Old Dutch cleaning lady electrocal.   6   8 12 14

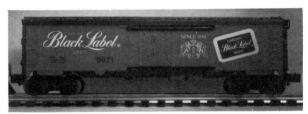

9871 Carling Black Label.

9871 CARLING BLACK LABEL: Type III body, black roof, dark red body and door; white, gold, and black lettering and electrocal.   10 12 15 20

9872 Pacific Fruit Express.

9872 PACIFIC FRUIT EXPRESS: 1978-79: Type III body, silver roof, orange body and door, black and white lettering.   10 12 15 20
See also Special Production chapter.

9873 Ralston Purina.

9873 RALSTON PURINA: 1978-79, Type III reefer, blue plastic ends and roof painted blue, white plastic sides painted white; elaborate Ralston-Purina electrocal in red, white, and blue on car side states "Car used 1945-64", Symington-Wayne trucks.   10 12 15 20

9874 LITE: 1978-79, (Miller Lite), Type III reefer, blue plastic roof painted blue, white plastic sides painted white, white doors painted gold; gold and blue electrocal, dark blue "LITE", Symington-Wayne trucks.   10 12 15 20

9875 A & P: 1979, Type III reefer, brown-painted roof, mustard-painted sides; red and black A & P electrocal, Symington-Wayne trucks.   6 8 12 20

9876 CENTRAL VERMONT: 1978, Type III reefer, black plastic roof painted black, gray sides painted silver; green lettering, silver door, Standard O trucks, part of 1867 Milwaukee Special Freight Set. C. Lang comment.   -- -- 35 40

9877 GERBER: 1979, Type III reefer, dark blue-painted roof and ends, medium blue-painted sides; famous baby shown on black and white electrocal, white lettering. C. Rohlfing comment.   6 8 12 20

9878 GOOD AND PLENTY: 1979, Type III reefer, magenta-painted roof, white-painted sides, Good and Plenty box electrocal.   6 8 12 20

9879 KRAFT PHILADELPHIA CREAM CHEESE: Originally shown in 1979 advance catalogue with gray sides, dark blue roof and ends; blue and white Kraft Philadelphia Cream Cheese electrocal. After the prototype, now in the Lionel archives, was made up, the Kraft Company withdrew its permission to use the name and logo, and the number was reassigned to the next entry.

Not Manufactured

9879 HILLS BROS: 1979, Type III reefer, yellow-painted roof and ends, red-painted sides, coffee can electrocal.   6 8 12 20

9880 SANTA FE: 1979, Type III reefer, tuscan-painted roof and ends, orange-painted sides; black cross logo and "SHIP AND TRAVEL SANTA FE ALL THE WAY", gold diamond-shaped FARR 1 logo, from Famous American Railroad Series 1.   20 25 30 40

9881 RATH PACKING: 1979, billboard reefer, yellow sides, tuscan roof and ends, black, yellow, and white Rath electrocal, Standard O trucks; available only as part of 1970 Southern Pacific Limited Set.   -- -- 25 35

9882 N Y R B: 1979, (New York Central reefer), Type III reefer, tuscan-painted roof and ends, orange-painted sides; Early Bird Service electrocal, black lettering, Standard O trucks; from Quaker City Limited Set.   -- 20 30 40

9883 NABISCO: 1979, Type III reefer, blue-painted roof, gray-painted sides; Oreo cookie package electrocal.   10 12 15 20

9884 FRITOS: 1982, Type III reefer, yellow-orange sides, red roof and ends, dark red doors; Fritos logo electrocal, Symington-Wayne trucks. C. Rohlfing comment.   -- 8 10 14

9885 LIPTON 100 TEA BAGS: 1981, Type III reefer, deep red and yellow sides, dark brown roof and ends, Symington-Wayne trucks. C. Rohlfing comment.   -- 8 10 14

9886 MOUNDS: 1981, Type III reefer, white sides, red roof and ends, brown-maroon doors, Mounds package electrocal. C. Rohlfing comment.   -- 8 10 14

9887 FRUIT GROWERS EXPRESS: 1983, Type III reefer, yellow sides, dark green roof and ends, Standard O trucks, F A R R 4 gold diamond logo, F A R R Series 4, car sold separately. L. Caponi comment.   -- -- 30 35

9888 GREEN BAY & WESTERN: 1983, Type III reefer, gray sides, red roof and ends; black lettering, Standard O trucks, only sold as part of 1361 Gold Coast Limited Set. Catalogue showed car with white sides. L. Caponi comment.   -- -- 40 50

17301 CONRAIL: 1987, Standard O reefer, medium blue body, white lettering and Conrail "wheel" logo, black catwalk, Standard O trucks, part of Conrail Limited Set 11700.   -- -- 40 50

19500 MILWAUKEE ROAD: 1987, reefer, 9800-series reefer body, yellow sides, brown roof and ends, black lettering, red and white rectangular Milwaukee logo, Standard O trucks, part of Milwaukee Fallen Flags Set 2.   -- -- -- 35

19502 NORTH WESTERN: 1987, wood-sided reefer, Brunswick green lower sides, doors and roof, yellow upper sides, dark green lettering, red, yellow, and green North Western decal logo, arch bar trucks.   -- -- -- 25

19503 BANGOR AND AROOSTOOK: 1987, wood-sided reefer, blue lower sides, white upper sides, red roof, ends, and doors, contrasting blue and white lettering and logos, brown potato logo, arch bar trucks.   -- -- -- 25

19504 NORTHERN PACIFIC: 1987, wood-sided reefer, yellow sides and doors, bright red roof and ends, black lettering, red and white Monad logo decal, archbar trucks.   -- -- -- 25

19505 GREAT NORTHERN: 1988, reefer, green and orange Great Northern paint and striping scheme, 9800-style Type III body, Standard O trucks. Part of Fallen Flags Set No. 3. This car expected to be in great demand; price may escalate.   -- -- -- 40

19506 THOMAS NEWCOMEN: 1988, wood-sided reefer. First in a series to be known as the Famous Inventor Series. White sides and doors, bright red roof and ends, black lettering and steam engine electrocal, arch bar trucks.
   -- -- -- 25

19507 THOMAS EDISON: 1988, Famous Inventor Series wood-sided reefer. Light tan sides and doors, dark brown roof and ends, black and white phonograph electrocal, black-, white-, and flesh-colored Edison figure electrocal, black, white, and gold electric lamp electrocal, arch bar trucks.   -- -- -- 25

19802 CARNATION: 1987, operating O Gauge milk car, yellow sides, brown roof, ends, and doors; red, yellow, and black Carnation can logo and lettering; black ornate Union Refrigerated Transit Co. lettering, white man pushes weighted plastic cans out door onto platform with gray base and steps and white railings. Special sheet of decals included to decorate cans. Similar to Bosco operating milk car of postwar years, this car has been a "hot" seller. Its price may rise quickly. However, see 19810 entry below.   -- -- -- 85

19803 READING: 1987, icing station reefer, white sides, black roof and ends, white doors, blue lettering and Reading diamond logo, Standard O trucks; same construction as modern era 6700 and meant to accompany 2306 and postwar operating icing stations.   -- -- -- 37

19808 N Y R B: Announced for 1988, (New York Central) icing station refrigerator car, bright orange sides, maroon roof and ends, black and white "Early Bird" logo, Standard O trucks.   -- -- -- 40

19810 BOSCO: 1988, operating milk car and platform, bright yellow sides, silver-painted roof, ends, and doors, brown, white, red, and black Bosco electrocal, dark brown "Corn Products Co." lettering, postwar bar-end trucks, gray and white platform, seven gray plastic milk cans with self-stick Bosco labels.

   -- -- -- 85

Chapter XII

SPECIAL PRODUCTION

INTRODUCTION

During the last twenty years or so, Lionel has made special products at the request of the major train collecting associations in the United States. Lionel has also made special products for its own railroad club and for special events such as the annual Toy Fairs in New York. By far, the greatest quantity of these items have been made since 1970. We feel that the quantity of these products is sufficient to warrant a separate chapter rather than an individual entry in the main listings.

The following railroad collecting organizations are represented in this chapter:

1. The Train Collectors' Association (T C A)
2. The Lionel Collectors' Club of America (L C C A)
3. The Toy Train Operating Society (T T O S)
4. The Lionel Operating Train Society (L O T S)

In addition, the Lionel Railroader Club special cars will be found in this chapter, as well as the Toy Fair cars. Lionel's Season's Greetings holiday cars do not commemorate a specific train collecting or merchandising event; therefore, they are included in the main listings.

The Train Collectors' Association is divided nationally into the national organization, divisions and chapters. Many times, individual divisions or chapters have had cars stamped for their own events. Usually, these cars are stamped outside the Lionel factory and are not, therefore, part of these listings. However, an occasional division or chapter car elicits considerable collector interest and thus will be included here. *We do not include T C A Division or Chapter cars unless they are factory-produced.* However, upon request we will include some division or chapter cars if they are unusual pieces in demand by collectors. Reader comments will be appreciated.

THE 1973 T C A
SPECIAL CONVENTION CARS

By Norman Fuhrmann

Data supplied by Edward Barbret

I was the Convention Chairman for the 1973 T C A National Convention. In that capacity, I visited Richard Branstner at the Lionel Factory in Mount Clemens to request donations of special cars for the convention. We wanted these cars so that we could use them as door prizes and special awards.

In the course of our conversation, Mr. Branstner stated that he had brought back some cars which had been shown at the 1973 Toy Fair in New York. He asked me if I would be interested in these cars, and I said that I would like to see them. We went out to a small storage room at the factory where he showed me three small cardboard boxes containing between 30 and 40

cars. The Standard O Series cars already had trucks mounted to them, but the other cars did not. Mr. Branstner stated that he would furnish the trucks and, if time could be found in the production schedule, have an employee mount them to the cars.

As the time for the convention drew near, I contacted Mr. Branstner again; he said that he had not found time to mount the trucks onto the cars and asked if I could put them on. This posed a problem for me, since in the meantime I had found that I would be in Florida during the time of the convention and thus could not attend. Since I could not be at the convention, I turned over the chairmanship to my friend Ed Barbret, who picked up the cars and their wheelsets and trucks from Mr. Branstner and mounted the trucks onto the cars at his home just prior to the convention.

During my visit to the factory, I toured the complete plant and the archives with Mr. Branstner. In the course of that tour, Mr. Branstner and I operated the hot press, a new piece of machinery at the time. He put a boxcar shell into the machine and put one road name on one side and another road name on the other. I also made one of these boxcars myself. I asked for one of these cars, but Mr. Branstner explained that the factory was having a problem with oddly-made cars escaping the premises, and he certainly did not want any questions raised about his activities. Consequently, the two boxcar shells went into the crusher immediately and were destroyed.

The following is a complete list of the cars supplied by Fundimensions for the 1973 T C A National Convention. One complete set of these cars, including the unique gray 9820 Wabash gondola, is in the collection of Edward Barbret.

Qty.	Car Number	Road Name	Body Color	Lettering Color	Door Color	Remarks
10	9123	C & O	Yellow	Blue	—	3-tier auto car
6	9123	—	Blue	White	—	2-tier auto car
12	9701	B & O	Blue	Yellow	Black	Boxcar
5	9703	C P Rail	Green	Black	Green	Boxcar
10	9705	D & R G W	Silver	Orange	Silver	Boxcar
11	9705	D & R G W	Silver	Red	Red	Box car
4	9706	C & O	Black	Yellow	Black	Boxcar
5	9802	Miller	Gray	Red	—	Reefer
1	9820	Wabash	Gray	White	—	Gondola
3	9821	S P	Black	White	—	Gondola

THE TOWN HOUSE AND
TAPPAN TRAIN SETS:

A Case Study Of Two Department Store Specials

(Author's Note: The following is a summary of a telephone conversation between Bruce Greenberg and Mike Moore, the proprietor of Town House Appliances, Inc., Niles, Illinois, on November 28, 1986. We are grateful to Mr. Moore for sharing his experiences with us, since they shed considerable light upon the making and the promotion of Lionel's special production sets.)

A selection of special production club cars. Top shelf: 9212 Seaboard T O F C Flatcar (1976 L C C A Convention) made from bottom of auto carrier and two oversized trailers. Second shelf: 9118 Corning (1974 L C C A Convention) and 9358 Sand's of Iowa (1980 L C C A Convention) Covered Quad Hoppers; for some reason the Corning Hopper is much scarcer than the Sand's. Bottom shelf: X9259 Southern Bay Window Caboose (1977 L C C A Convention), 9155 Monsanto Tank Car (1975 L C C A Convention).

Mike Moore's company, Town House Appliances, has for some time contracted with Lionel to make the Town House Superstore Train Sets, which are used as a promotional device by Town House. This practice started 15 years ago, when Lionel made a train set for Town House at a very low price, $9.95, with the purchase of a major appliance. These special Town House sets have become a tradition which has grown to the point where it is very heavily advertised in television, radio, and newspaper ads throughout metropolitan Chicago.

In 1986 Town House offered its Lionel set for $19.95 with the purchase of a major appliance. Over the counter, Town House sold the 1986 set for $89.95. The set includes an 8902 Atlantic Coast Line DC-powered Switcher and Tender, a matching caboose, track, a DC transformer, and, above all, a special 7931 Town House Short Boxcar with a logo designed by Town House. (See the Uncatalogued Set chapter for the full details of this set.) Until three or four years ago, Town House sold leftover regular production Lionel sets. However, Mr. Moore decided that he needed a special set for his Christmas promotions. He found that he could not purchase the number he required from Lionel, so he contacted the Tappan Range Company and was successful in convincing the firm to order a special set to be sold by him; this was the Tappan Special. It is essentially similar to the 1986 Town House Special, but it came with an additional gondola and a red short Tappan Boxcar with white lettering.

Unlike the usual Lionel Department Store Specials, the 1982 Tappan set did not carry a Lionel set number. Instead, it was identified by a Tappan part number used for Tappan's accessories line; the set's formal name is "Tappan Lionel Train Set Kit, 88-1036-10." This set included the 8902 Atlantic Coast Line Locomotive (which has had more lives than the proverbial cat since its initial production in 1979!), its matching Atlantic Coast Line Caboose, a 9340 Illinois Central Gulf Gondola, and the 7908 Tappan Short Boxcar with a built date of "Built 9-82."

Lionel's production of this set has been estimated at 6,000. Mr. Moore bought 4,000 of the 6,000 sets for his company's promotion. Another 1,000 of these sets went to train dealers in Chicago and the final 1,000 to train dealers in Detroit. Mr. Moore opened 100 sets and substituted other regular-production boxcars for the special Tappan Boxcar. These modified sets were given away, and the 100 special boxcars were given to friends.

Mr. Moore also owns the prototype for the 7908 Tappan Boxcar, which differs from the production model in several ways. The prototype has a built date of "Built 1-82", and it is numbered "9040" rather than "7908". Lionel put the "9040" number on the car for its mockup and assigned the number "7908" to the car after Tappan had approved production of the set.

Town House has tried to get other companies to purchase special sets from Lionel, and one such effort has yielded one of the most fascinating toy train stories of the modern era. This is the tale of a set that almost made it into production, and some lucky (or larcenous, as it may be) collector has its prototype. In 1978, Mr. Moore persuaded the Frigidaire Company to purchase a special set from Lionel, and Lionel went so far as to make up the prototype for the set. It included a snow-white

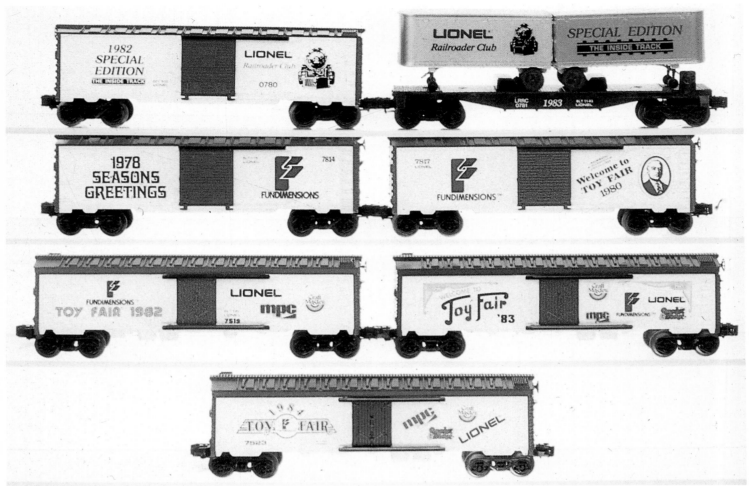

Top shelf: 0780 Lionel Railroader Club Boxcar, 0781 Lionel Railroader Club T O F C Flatcar. Second shelf: 7814 Seasons Greetings Boxcar, 7817 Toy Fair Boxcar. Third shelf: 7519 Toy Fair Refrigerator, 7521 Toy Fair Refrigerator. Bottom shelf: 7523 Toy Fair Refrigerator.

short boxcar with the Frigidaire-GM logo advertising in medium blue lettering. This interesting prototype set was based on one of the Trains 'N Trucking sets made that year; it included an Electromotive Division NW-2 diesel switcher, the white Frigidaire boxcar, a tank car, a gondola, and a caboose. Lionel gave the prototype set to Mr. Moore to deliver to Frigidaire in Dayton, Ohio. One of the Frigidaire executives, a Mr. Carvelli, was to authorize its use as a premium for Christmas of 1978.

So far, so good. Lionel and Frigidaire came to an agreement; Lionel said that the set would be produced, and Frigidaire said that the sets would be purchased by the firm. Then Frigidaire had a dealer convention, and Lionel said that it would provide samples of the special boxcar for the convention. These sample cars had decals applied to white boxcars with no other markings. Lionel had planned to deliver the sets with the special Frigidaire decals to be applied by the consumer; several low-priced regular production sets of the time featured this concept. Apparently reaction to the decaled version of the special boxcar was less than enthusiastic at the dealer convention. Since the use of decals would not insure that Frigidaire's promotional messages would get through to the consumer, Frigidaire

wanted the boxcar to be heat-stamped. For some reason, Lionel replied that the cars could not be heat-stamped. Upon hearing that response, Frigidaire canceled the order.

The ironic part of this story came a short time later. Lionel contacted Frigidaire and said that it could heat-stamp the boxcars after all. However, by the time that message was received, it was too late for Frigidaire to use the set as a Christmas promotion, as that firm had intended. Later on, Mike Moore paid a visit to the Frigidaire office of Mr. Carvelli to pick up the prototype set. That precious set was no longer to be found; someone had appropriated it! The specifications and drawings were last seen in the possession of Frigidaire, so it is possible that the prototype for the Frigidaire set is still somewhere in Dayton, Ohio.

By the time the 1986 Christmas season had come, eight years after the unfortunate Frigidaire incident, procedures had changed — a lot! The prototype for the 1986 Town House set was shipped by Lionel to Town House for that firm's approval. However, this time — undoubtedly in no uncertain terms — Lionel required its safe return to the factory. The hand-lettered prototype for the 1986 Town House set now resides safely within Lionel's archives!

Special production and convention cars. Top shelf: 6926 T C A New Orleans Caboose of 1986, 9611 Boston & Maine "Flying Yankee" T C A 1978 Convention. Second shelf: 7812 Houston Stock Car, 1977 T C A Convention, 9319 25th Anniversary Mint Car, T C A 1979 Convention. (Attendees also received a special coin for this car's bank slot.) Third shelf: 0780 Lionel Railroader Club Boxcar of 1982, 16800 Lionel Railroader Club Ore Car. Bottom shelf: 0782 Lionel Railroader Club Tank Car of 1985, 0784 Lionel Railroader Club Covered Quad Hopper of 1984.

Gd VG Exc Mt

303 STAUFFER CHEMICAL: 1985, single-dome, special production for Lionel Operating Train Society. Unpainted dark gray tank with wide painted black band at center; design similar to original postwar 6315 Gulf model. Black dome top, orange Stauffer Chemicals logo, black "Stauffer Chemical Co." script, "SCHX 303 / CAPY." on tank ends, black-painted metal railings instead of usual chrome, Symington-Wayne trucks, Type III box. T. Herner and "Triple T" Collections.   -- -- 40 45

0511 T C A ST. LOUIS: 1981, convention baggage car, 9500-series type heavyweight car, Brunswick green body with black roof, "THE GATEWAY TO THE WEST / ST. LOUIS" in rubber-stamped gold lettering, gold stripes above and below windows run the length of the car, "0511" on box only, "1981" at both ends of car, white T C A logo, six-wheel die-cast passenger trucks. J. Bratspis Collection.   -- -- -- 75

0512 TOY FAIR: 1981, reefer. Details needed.   -- -- 125 175

665E JOHNNY CASH BLUE TRAIN: 1971, dark gloss blue-painted Baldwin-boiler Pacific steam engine with white stripe and blue "665E" below cab window, matching 2046W Tender with white "JOHNNY CASH BLUE TRAIN" lettering. Came with display case and plaque reading "PRESENTED TO JOHNNY CASH / BY THE MPC LIONEL PEOPLE NOVEMBER 1971". Photo

appears in August-September 1972 issue of O Scale Railroading Magazine. Obviously, one-of-a-kind. I. D. Smith comment.   NRS

0780 LIONEL RAILROADER CLUB: 1982, boxcar, white body, red roof, doors, and ends; black lettering, Symington-Wayne trucks. C. O'Dell collection.   -- -- 35 45

0781 LIONEL RAILROADER CLUB T O F C: 1983, flatcar, maroon body, "LRRC / 0781 / 1983 BLT 1-83 / LIONEL" in white, silver-painted vans with red and black lettering; "LIONEL RAILROADER CLUB" and black train logo on one van and "SPECIAL EDITION / THE INSIDE TRACK" on the other, mold 6424-11 flatcar body. F. Stem, G. Rogers, T. Ladny, and J. Sawruk Collections.   -- -- 40 45

0782 LIONEL RAILROADER CLUB: 1985, single-dome tank car, maroon tank car body, white lettering, black dome, Symington-Wayne trucks. F. Stem and T. Ladny Collections.   -- -- 40 45

0784 LIONEL RAILROADER CLUB: 1984, covered hopper, white body, black lettering and cover, Symington-Wayne trucks. Special issue only available to members of Lionel Railroader Club. This and all other quad hoppers have a cavity in the mold on the bottom center which may have been suitable for mounting a coil or solenoid, as was stated in the introduction. Reader comments are invited. T. Ladny Collection, T. Rollo, Bonney, and G. Cole comments.   -- -- 50 60

More special production club cars. Top: 17870 East Camden & Highland Standard O Boxcar (1987 L C C A Convention), 6567 Illinois Central Gulf Crane Car (1985 L C C A Convention). Second shelf: 6112 Commonwealth Edison Quad Hopper (1983 L C C A Convention), 6323 Virginia Chemicals Tank Car (1986 L C C A Convention). Bottom shelf: 7403 L N A C Boxcar (1984 L C C A Convention), 9460 Detroit, Toledo & Shore Line (1982 L C C A Convention).

1018-1979 TCA MORTGAGE BURNING CEREMONY CAR: 1979, light tan- painted gray plastic body, light yellow-painted white door, hi-cube boxcar; orange, black, and red rectangular mortgage burning logo at left, orange Toy Train Museum logo and black lettering at right. There is an intriguing story behind the making of this car. In 1978 the T C A held its convention in Boston. The 9611 "Flying Yankee" Hi-Cube Boxcar was produced for this convention in official Boston and Maine sky blue and black (see 9611-1978 entry). Large anticipated sales of the Flying Yankee Car never materialized, and at convention's end the TCA found itself in possession of a considerable backlog of unsold cars. In the next year, the organization was to finish paying the mortgage on its museum in Strasburg, Pennsylvania. Rather than order a special car, the T C A shipped its entire backlog of 9611 Flying Yankee Cars to the Pleasant Valley Process Company of Cogan Station, Pennsylvania. There, the Flying Yankee Cars were repainted into the Mortgage Burning Ceremony Car. Faint traces of the original black paint show through the light tan paint on the ends and roof. J. Bratspis observation. -- -- -- **95**

1203 Boston & Maine NW-2 switcher.

1203 BOSTON & MAINE: 1972, NW-2 switcher, cab only, no chassis, made for N E T C A (New England Division, Train Collectors' Association) for 1972 convention; light blue cab, white lettering and logo, no trim pieces supplied. C. Lang comments. -- -- -- **80**

1973 TCA Bicentennial Special.

1973 T C A BICENTENNIAL SPECIAL: 1973, 1974, 1975; red, white, and blue; set of three passenger cars. Price for set. -- -- **125 150**

1973 T C A: 1973, convention automobile carrier, black body, Symington-Wayne trucks. T C A logo in gold on one letterboard, "NATIONAL CONVENTION / DEARBORN, MICH. / 1973" in gold on second letter board, same side, all lettering deep heat-stamped; came in 9123 Lionel Type II automobile carrier box, but 9123 does not appear on car side; gold "TRAILER TRAIN" reporting marks on flatcar side. C. Lang Collection. -- -- **45 55**

1974 T C A BICENTENNIAL SPECIAL: Matches 1973. -- -- **40 50**

1975 T C A BICENTENNIAL SPECIAL: Matches 1973. -- -- **40 50**

Some recent special production cars. Top shelf: 6582 T T O S Flatcar with lumber load for T T O S Convention of 1986, 19417 New York Central TOFC Flatcar with Kodak / Xerox trailers for 1987 T T O S Convention in Rochester, New York (home city of these firms). Second shelf: Two prized Toy Fair cars, 7704 Boxcar from 1976, 7525 Boxcar from 1986 (the only Toy Fair Car issued under Kenner-Parker management). Bottom shelf: 19900 Toy Fair Car of 1987 with its special Type V collector box.

1976 SEABOARD COAST LINE U36B: 1976, diesel, special for T C A with T C A logo and three T C A passenger cars. Stamped metal railings, red, white, and blue body with blue numbers, blue underframe, lighted, nose decal, Type II motor; four white stars and white "TRAIN COLLECTORS ASSOCIATION SEABOARD COAST LINE SPIRIT OF 76" on edge of frame. Price for locomotive only. C. Rohlfing Collection. -- -- **100 150**

1980: 1980, see entry 8068 in this chapter.

2671 T C A CLEVELAND: 1975, tender shell. -- -- **75 125**

3764 KAHN: 1981, refrigerator car, convention car of the Lionel Operating Train Society. Dark tan sides, Symington-Wayne trucks.
(A) Red roof and ends. C. Lang and "Triple T" Collections. -- -- **25 50**
(B) Brown roof and ends. "Triple T" Collection. -- -- **25 50**

5484 T C A HUDSON: 1985, dark green, die-cast boiler, white trim and number; smoke, Magnetraction, Sound of Steam; 224W die-cast Tender, six-wheel die-cast passenger truck, large circular white T C A emblem on tender side.
-- -- **400 450**

5734-85 R E A: 1985, wood-sided reefer, T C A 1985 Seattle Convention Car. Dark green body, black roof and ends, gold lettering, red R E A diamond with white lettering, Seattle convention logo, "TRAIN COLLECTORS ASSOCIATION" above and below diamond logo. Standard O trucks; car actually numbered "5734 / 1985". Available to match previously issued locomotive and passenger cars. C. Rohlfing, W. Berresford, C. Wallace and E. F. Monck comments.
-- -- -- **150**

6014-900 FRISCO: 1975, O27-style short boxcar, uncatalogued; white Type III body, black lettering, numbered "6014" on side as were postwar examples, AAR trucks, came in a Type I Fundimensions box labeled "6014-900 / L C C A 75-76" on its side. This car was previously reported as version 6014(I) in the postwar volume by C. Rohlfing. Apparently, some older stock had been stamped for L C C A by postwar Lionel, and when these cars were found in the warehouse, Fundimensions sold them off. D. Doyle Collection. -- -- **50 75**

6112 COMMONWEALTH EDISON: 1983, covered hopper, produced for L C C A convention in Rockford, Illinois; tuscan body, left third of car side painted black with Reddy Kilowatt logo, black and white lettering, black coal pile; Symington-Wayne trucks; 2,500 made. Somewhat hard to find. C. Lang and C. Rohlfing comments. -- -- **75 95**

6211 CHESAPEAKE & OHIO: 1986, gondola, black body, yellow lettering and logo, two yellow canisters, Symington-Wayne trucks, made for L O T S (Lionel Operating Train Society). Further details requested. J. Kouba comment.
NRS

6315 T C A PITTSBURGH: 1972, single-dome, made for T C A Annual Convention at Pittsburgh. Orange tank body, black dome; black "7-11" lettering, postwar bar-end trucks. -- -- **75 95**

6323 VIRGINIA CHEMICALS: 1986, single-dome tank car, black body, 1986 L C C A Norfolk Convention Car. Further description needed.
-- -- **35 45**

6446-25 See Hopper Cars chapter.

6464-1970 T C A SPECIAL: 1970, uncatalogued T C A Chicago Convention car for 1970; Type V yellow-painted lighter yellow body, red door, no decals, white heat-stamped lettering; about 1,100 made.
(A) Unpainted red door. -- -- **125 160**
(B) Red-painted red door. -- -- **125 160**

6464-1971 T C A SPECIAL: 1971, uncatalogued T C A Disneyland National Convention Boxcar. Type VI white-painted white body, roof, and ends; dark orange-yellow-painted yellow doors; metal door guides, postwar bar-end metal trucks; red, white, and blue heat-stamped Disneyland logos. Note: Color samples and test shells of this car have been seen with gold heat-stamped markings. We are collecting additional information about these for the next edition.
-- -- **200 250**

See also Factory Errors and Prototypes.

6483 NEW JERSEY CENTRAL: 1982, SP-type caboose, heat-stamped for L C C A meets in 1981-82. Unpainted red Type VII plastic body, Type II ends, white lettering, "1982 L C C A MEET SPECIAL" and "BLT. 9-82", one operating and one dummy coupler attached by metal rivets, Symington-Wayne trucks. Repor-

Mr. James P. MacFarland, the former Chairman of the Board of General Mills, retired in 1974 after a forty-year career with the firm. General Mills honored Mr. MacFarland with a special, one-of-a-kind train set. Except for the Johnny Cash Blue Train, which has not been fully described or authenticated, this set is believed to be the first factory-produced train set made to honor an individual. J. A. Fisher Collection.

tedly only 503 examples made. Last issue of the L C C A Meet Car program; sold on a subscription basis only. J. R. Hunt and C. Lang comments, C. Darasko and C. Rohlfing Collections. Hard to find.   -- -- -- **40**

6567 ILLINOIS CENTRAL GULF: 1986, crane car, L C C A National Convention car. Gray cab and base, orange trim and boom, orange and white lettering, die-cast six-wheel passenger trucks.   -- -- **60 875**

6582 T T O S PORTLAND: 1986, flatcar with lumber load, brown body, yellow lettering, black lettering on load.   **NRS**

6926 T C A NEW ORLEANS: 1986, extended vision caboose, white body, dark blue-painted main and cupola roofs, black lettering "32nd National Convention / JUNE 1986 / Lone Star Div."; large red heart with picture of Superdome centered under cupola with black lettering "You'll Love New Orleans / And New Orleans / Will Love You Back!"; T C A logo in dark blue at lower right side corner, Symington-Wayne trucks. H. Lotstein Collection.   -- -- -- **60**

7205 T C A DENVER: 1982 Convention, combine car, matches 0511; "7205" on box only, gold-lettered "THE ROCKY MOUNTAIN ROUTE / UNITED STATES MAIL / RAILWAY POST OFFICE / DENVER". J. Bratspis Collection.   -- -- -- **75**

7206 T C A LOUISVILLE: 1983 Convention, Pullman car, matches 0511; "7206" on box only, gold-lettered "GREAT LAKES LIMITED / LOUISVILLE".   -- -- -- **75**

7212 T C A PITTSBURGH: 1984 Convention, matches 0511. F. Stem and J. Bratspis Collections.   -- -- -- **75**

7403 L N A C: 1984, Louisville, New Albany & Corydon boxcar, dark blue-gray body and doors, red and white lettering, Symington-Wayne trucks. L C C A 1984 Convention Car. D. Daugherty Collection.   -- -- **35 45**

7519 TOY FAIR: 1982, reefer, 9800-series reefer body, white sides, red roof and ends, red doors, red, white, and blue logos, gold "TOY FAIR 1982" lettering.   -- -- **150 175**

7521 TOY FAIR: 1983, reefer, 9800-series reefer body, white sides, dark blue roof and ends, red doors, old-fashioned "TOY FAIR" script and gold edging to left of door, Fundimensions and MPC logos to right of door.   -- -- **150 175**

7523 TOY FAIR: 1984, 9800-series refrigerator car, white sides, dark red roof and ends, dark blue doors, "1984" and "TOY FAIR" logos to left of door, General Mills toy division logos to right of door.   -- -- **150 175**

7524 TOY FAIR: 1985, 9800-series refrigerator car, light brown sides, dark brown roof and ends; brown lettering, varied red and blue Fundimensions logos. This was the last Fundimensions-produced Toy Fair car. L. Caponi comment and Collection.   -- -- **175 200**

7525 TOY FAIR: 1986, 9700-series boxcar body, white sides, dark blue roof, ends, and doors, Lionel logo and red "A / NEW / TRADITION" and number to right of door, "WELCOME TO / TOY FAIR / 1986" to left of door, Symington-Wayne trucks. "Triple T" Collection.   -- -- **150 175**

7600 FRISCO: N5C caboose, Type II, red, white and blue sides: stamped "MIDWEST DIVISION, T C A". H. Azzinaro Collection.   -- -- -- **50**

7704 WELCOME TOY FAIR: 1976 (U. S. Toy Fair), boxcar, opaque-white plastic body painted white, red roof and ends, translucent white doors painted

Eight more cars from the set made to honor James P. MacFarland at his retirement from General Mills. While this set is not, strictly speaking, a collectible because it is one-of-a-kind, it is an interesting set which deserves mention. J. A. Fisher Collection.

red; blue and red lettering, plastic top door guides with molded hook on bottom, American flag logo to right of door. C. Lang comment. -- -- 175 200

7705 TOY FAIR: 1976 (Canadian Toy Fair), 7700-style opaque white plastic boxcar body painted white, red roof and ends, translucent white door painted red; red lettering in English and French to left of door, red Maple Leaf logo and numbers to right of door, plastic top on door guides with molded hook on bottom, Symington-Wayne trucks. "Triple T" Collection. -- -- 300 400

7807 TOY FAIR: 1977, green body, gold-painted doors, roof and ends; red and green lettering, "TRAINS 'N TRUCKIN' " on right side of door in capitals with apostrophes, white locomotive and truck logos, Type IX body. C. Lang comment. -- -- 150 175

7812-1977 T C A: 1977, Convention Stock Car, brown cattle car body, brown-yellow plastic plaque inserted in place of double doors, center metal door guide removed; yellow lettering on car body, "23rd NATIONAL CONVENTION / HOUSTON / TEXAS / JUNE 1977", brown lettering and logos on plaque, Symington-Wayne trucks. -- -- 35 45

7813 SEASONS GREETINGS FROM LIONEL: 1977, 9700-type boxcar, white body, gold roof and ends, unpainted red doors; red and dark green lettering to left of door, red and dark green toy logos to right of door. C. Lang comment. -- -- 175 200

7814 SEASONS GREETINGS: 1978, 9700-style boxcar, white body, dark blue roof and ends, royal blue doors; red "1978 SEASON'S GREETINGS" to left of door, Fundimensions "F" logo in red and blue to right of door. C. Lang comment. -- -- 175 200

7815 TOY FAIR: 1978, 9700-style boxcar, silver body, white doors, red roof and ends; black lettering, "BIG TRAINS / FOR SMALL / HANDS" and boy with locomotive electrocals to right of door in black. C. Lang comment. -- -- 150 175

7816 TOY FAIR: 1979, 9700-type boxcar, white body, gold roof and ends, dull gold doors; red and blue lettering and train electrocal to right of door, blue and red Fundimensions "F" to left of door. C. Lang comment. -- -- 150 175

7817 TOY FAIR: 1980, boxcar, white body, red roof and ends; red and blue lettering, blue and red Fundimensions "F" to the left of door. -- -- 150 175

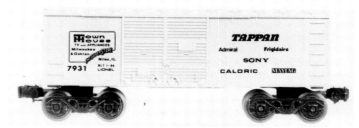

7931 Town House TV & Appliances Boxcar.

7931 TOWN HOUSE TV & APPLIANCES: 1986, short boxcar, medium gray body, black Town House logo and number to left of door, six appliance brand names in black to right of door (brand names differ on each side). Symington-Wayne trucks, one operating and one dummy coupler. Part of uncatalogued Set 1658. R. LaVoie Collection. -- -- -- 50

8068 THE ROCK: 1980 Annual L C C A Convention issue; "1980" on locomotive cab, powered GP-20, 2,700 made. -- -- 100 150

181

A truly special T C A train set! Top shelf: 5484 Hudson Steam Engine and Tender of 1985. Second shelf: 0511 St. Louis baggage car of 1981, 5734-85 Railway Express Wood-sided Reefer of 1985. Third shelf: 7206 Louisville Passenger Coach of 1983, 7205 Denver Combine of 1982. Bottom shelf: 9544 Chicago Observation Car of 1980, 7212 Pittsburgh Passenger Coach of 1984.

9016 CHESSIE: 1980-81, short hopper, yellow body, blue lettering, Symington-Wayne trucks, has "L C C A 1979-80 MEET SPECIAL" overstamp. C. Rohlfing and C. O'Dell comments.   -- -- 25

9036 MOBILGAS: 1978-79, small single-dome tank car, white tank, red lettering, L C C A meet car overstamp, 1978-79. C. Rohlfing comment.

-- -- -- 35

9118 Corning Covered Hopper.

9118 CORNING: 1974, white and mist green body, covered hopper, L C C A 1974 Convention Car; 2,000 made.   -- -- 75 90

9119 DETROIT & MACKINAC: 1975, quad hopper, stamped "SEASON'S GREETINGS" for the Detroit-Toledo Chapter of the T C A: green Christmas ball with gold lettering over-stamped in middle of car side. H. Azzinaro Collection.

-- -- 35 45

9142 REPUBLIC STEEL: 1971, long gondola, medium green body, flat brakewheel, metal wheelsets, stamped "1977-1978 MEET SPECIAL". C. Rohlfing Collection.   -- -- -- 25

9155 MONSANTO: 1975, single-dome tank car, L C C A Convention Car, white tank body; black lettering, red "M" logo on left of tank, Symington-Wayne trucks. C. Rohlfing comment.   -- 50 65 75

9160 I C: 1975, I T T Cable Hydrospace; I T T sticker obscures all but IC emblem on side, one coupler. N5C Type II body, see 8030 entry in this chapter; valued with set.

9212 L C C A: 1976, Atlanta, flatcar with vans, originally stamped only on one side, L C C A offered to restamp them for members and many were restamped, 3500 made.
(A) One side stamped.   -- -- 35 40
(B) Two sides stamped.   -- -- 40 70

X9259 SOUTHERN: 1977, bay window caboose, L C C A Convention Car, red body, 4,500 made.
(A) White lettering. Kruelle Collection.   -- -- 35 40
(B) Gold lettering. C. Lang Collection.   -- -- 35 40

9264 ILLINOIS CENTRAL: 1975-77, quad hopper, metal plate holding trucks, no builder's plate, stamped "T C A MUSEUM EXPRESS", only 108 made. C. Rohlfing Collection.   -- -- -- 100

9289 CHICAGO & NORTH WESTERN: 1980, N5C, two operating couplers, overstamped "T C A MUSEUM EXPRESS, MARCH 8, 1980". Only 144 examples made. C. Rohlfing comment.   -- -- -- 85

9301 U. S. MAIL: 1975-83, operating boxcar, overprinted "SACRAMENTO SIERRA" for T C A regional meet of 1976 in Sacramento, California. C. Lang Collection.   **NRS**

9319 T C A SILVER JUBILEE: 1979, gloss dark blue body, silver bullion car for T C A's 25th anniversary, silver bullion, white lettering on clear sides, special coin available only at T C A's National Convention, coin sits in car slot but does not fall into car, coin lettered "T C A 25 Years", coin about size of half dollar; 6,000 made.
(A) Car only.   -- -- 250 325
(B) Car with coin.   -- -- 300 375

9347 NIAGARA FALLS: 1979, T T O S National Convention car, powder blue tank, black lettering, black frame, ends, and dome caps; Standard O Trucks, "NIAGARA FALLS FOR T T O S / NEW YORK 1979 / NORTHEASTERN DIVISION".
-- -- 40 50

9355 DELAWARE & HUDSON: 1982, bay window caboose, dark blue and gray body, yellow stripe, T T O S decal added. C. Rohlfing comment.
NRS

9358 SAND'S OF IOWA: 1980, L C C A 1980 National Convention car; hopper car, bright powder blue and black body, powder blue cover, black lettering, Symington-Wayne trucks; 4,500 made. R. LaVoie Collection.
-- -- 30 40

9400 CONRAIL: 1978, tuscan-painted tuscan body and doors, N E T C A (New England Division, Train Collectors Association) overprint in gold. C. Lang Collection.
NRS

9415 PROVIDENCE & WORCESTER: 1979, boxcar, red-painted body, white and black lettering, New England Division, Train Collectors Association (N E T C A) overprint for regional convention. C. Lang Collection.
-- -- 20 25

9420 B & O SENTINEL: 1980, overprinted as Guinness Book of World Records Special in red: "World's Longest / Model Electric Train / June 29, 1980 / Columbus, Ohio". One of 200 cars in train. G. Halverson and H. Holden Collections.
-- -- 75 --

9423 NEW YORK, NEW HAVEN & HARTFORD: 1980, boxcar, tuscan-painted tuscan body and doors, black roof, overprinted with N E T C A (New England Division, Train Collectors Association) overprint for regional convention. C. Lang Collection.
-- -- 20 25

9435 CENTRAL OF GEORGIA: 1981, boxcar, made for L C C A Chattanooga, Tennessee convention. Black Type IX body with large silver-painted oval on sides, silver-painted gray doors; black and white lettering, Type III frame, Symington-Wayne trucks. J. Vega Collection, C. Lang and C. Rohlfing comments.
-- -- 40 50

9460 DETROIT, TOLEDO & SHORE LINE: 1982, double-door boxcar, made for L C C A National Convention in Dearborn, Michigan. Blue body and doors, white lettering, metal door guides, bright maroon and white logo to right of door, "EXPRESSWAY FOR INDUSTRY" underscored in white to left of door with built date, Symington-Wayne trucks. C. Rohlfing comment, J. Vega and C. Lang Collections.
-- -- 35 60

9467 WORLD'S FAIR: 1982, boxcar, white-painted white body, tuscan-painted roof and ends; black lettering, white doors, red, black, and white World's Fair logo to left of door, Symington-Wayne trucks. Reportedly only 2,500 made for Ak-Sar-Ben Hobby Company of Nashville. C. Darasko and J. Vega Collections.
-- -- 35 45

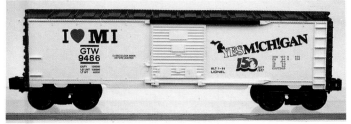

9486 I Love Michigan.

9486 I LOVE MICHIGAN: 1986, boxcar, white sides, violet-painted roof and ends, overstamped with large red and black "150" beside "1837 / 1987". See also Boxcars and Stock Cars chapter.
-- -- -- 150

9512 Summerdale Junction coach.

9512 SUMMERDALE JUNCTION: 1974, passenger car, special for T T O S, yellow with maroon roof, lights.
-- -- 40 50

9520 T T O S combine.

9520 TOY TRAIN OPERATING SOCIETY: 1975, combine, special for National Convention; matches 9512.
(A) No decal. -- -- 40 50
(B) With Phoenix decal for convention attendees. -- -- 55 70

9526 T T O S Observation.

9526 TOY TRAIN OPERATING SOCIETY: 1976, observation, special for National Convention; matches 9512.
(A) No Utah decal. -- -- 40 50
(B) With Utah decal for convention attendees. -- -- 55 75

9535 TOY TRAIN OPERATING SOCIETY: 1977, passenger car, special for National Convention; matches 9512.
(A) No Ohio decal. -- -- 40 50
(B) With Ohio decal for convention attendees. -- -- 55 75

9544 T C A CHICAGO: 1980, Convention Pullman Car; matches 0511, "9544" on box only, gold-lettered "LAND OF LINCOLN / CHICAGO".
-- -- -- 75

9611 T C A: 1978, boxcar, "TWENTY FOURTH NATIONAL CONVENTION BOSTON MA", "Home of the Flying Yankee", light blue sides, black roof and ends, one brakewheel, white doors, white clearance boards on car ends, Symington-Wayne trucks, disc couplers with tabs. Some of these cars were repainted into the 1018-1979 Mortgage Burning Ceremony Car. See entry 1018-1979 for details of this interesting story.
-- -- 35 45

9678 T T O S: 1978, hi-cube boxcar, convention car, white plastic body painted white, red ends and roofs, red doors, lettered "Hooray for Hollywood", Symington-Wayne trucks, two disc couplers with tabs, cars come with T T O S decal; convention attendees received a special decal showing Chaplin with "78" on his derby.
(A) Regular car. -- -- 40 50
(B) With Chaplin decal. -- -- 50 60

9701 BALTIMORE & OHIO: 1972, boxcar, shiny black-painted black body, flat black-painted black doors, white lettering, white decaled "L. C .C. of A. /K. C. Mo. 1972" appears over "Baltimore and Ohio" and word "Convention" is decaled in smaller letters vertically to side. Underside stamped with L C C A membership numbers and "2nd Annual / L. C. C. A. / Convention / Kansas City, Mo." 124 of these cars were lettered and stamped before L C C A ran out of decals, leading to much confusion and disappointment. Further decals were not sent to members. One car was made up with large-lettered decals and hand-stamped in the normal manner. J. R. Hunt Collection and comments. Many of these cars were faked later by rubber-stamping. R. Vagner comment.
(A) As described above. -- -- 125 175
(B) Flat black-painted black body and doors, Symington-Wayne trucks, no stamping on frame or separate decals. It is not certian whether this version was part of the L C C A run or the earliest version of the regular production run. Reader comments requested. Type II box has paper sticker with "B AND O / 9701-B" in black ink on one end only. R. LaVoie Collection. -- -- 100 125

These are the undersides of an all-black 9701 Baltimore & Ohio Double-door Boxcar (top) and a 9727 T. A. & G. Boxcar (bottom). Note that they are serially numbered; no two cars have the same number. To avoid frauds, collectors should make sure that they acquire cars that are stamped in the manner depicted. L. Caponi Collection.

9708 U. S. MAIL: 1972-73, boxcar, gold overstamped "Toy Fair '73" in small oblong box at lower left end of each side. C. Lang Collection.

-- -- 150 200

9723 WESTERN PACIFIC: 1974, boxcar, gold overstamped "Toy Fair '74". C. Lang Collection.

-- -- 150 200

9725 M K T: 1974-75, stock car, yellow-painted yellow body, black doors, green and silver Midwestern Division T C A plate added; 200 made. C. Rohlfing Collection.

NRS

9727 T. A. G.: 1973, uncatalogued, Type IX body, white-lettered "TENNESSEE ALABAMA & GEORGIA" and "1973 LCC of A". Convention car, maroon-painted body, Symington-Wayne trucks, Type II frame.

-- -- 200 250

9728 UNION PACIFIC: 1978, uncatalogued, stock car, yellow-painted yellow body, silver-painted roof and ends, unpainted yellow doors; red lettering, L C C of A 1978 Convention car, "L C C A" stamped on yellow rectangular plate in red which is glued to slats on right side of door, Type III box ends read "L C C A CONVENTION CAR", 6,000 made. C. Lang and R. LaVoie Collections.

-- -- 35 45

9733 AIRCO: 1979, LCC of A National Convention boxcar, a unique Lionel car in that inside there is a full-sized white molded unpainted tank with an orange-painted base. Blue tank lettering cannot be seen unless boxcar shell is removed from frame, leaving only the tank. The tank is secured to the boxcar frame by a screw through a crudely punched hole. This is essentially two cars in one. Tank car is numbered "97330". White boxcar and tank car bodies, light blue lettering, orange striping; 6,000 made. Reportedly, many collectors have fitted the tank car body with a frame, trucks, and trim pieces to make up a second Airco car. Reports state that a few of these cars are still available from the L C C A for its members. Price is for original configuration; add $10 if tank car has been fitted with trim, but be aware that these cars should not be purchased separately, though they are sometimes seen apart. C. Lang and R. LaVoie comments.

-- -- 40 55

9739 RIO GRANDE: 1978, boxcar, dark yellow and silver-painted yellow body, silver painted gray doors. Special edition made for 1978 L. C. C. A. Convention, long stripe, "L. C. C. A. / THE LION ROARS" and heat-stamped lion logo in black to right of door. About one hunderd of these cars were made; sixty of them were distributed to L C C A officers and related parties, and the balance was auctioned off by L C C A at various times. H. Argue, J. Breslin, and L. Bohn comments; J. Breslin Collection.

NRS

9753 MAINE CENTRAL: 1975-76, boxcar, yellow-painted yellow body, green lettering: N E T C A (New England Division, Train Collectors Association) imprint.

-- -- 25 35

9754 NEW YORK CENTRAL: 1976-77, boxcar, Pacemaker Freight color scheme, M E T C A (Metropolitan Division, Train Collectors Association) imprint.

-- -- 25 35

9762 WELCOME TOY FAIR: 1975, boxcar, uncatalogued, Type IX body, red and silver painted white plastic body, red-painted red plastic door; metallic silver lettering, "9762" does not appear on car.

-- 125 150 200

9771 NORFOLK AND WESTERN: 1976-77, boxcar, stamped "T C A Museum & National Headquarters" in silver at upper right of doors, "Dedication, April 14, 1977" in blue lettering under and to right of silver lettering. C. Weber Collection.

-- -- 30 40

9774 THE SOUTHERN BELLE: 1975, boxcar, uncatalogued, Type IX body, orange sides and silver roof and ends painted on orange body, green-painted white doors; green and black lettering, Symington-Wayne trucks, Type II frame, 1975 T C A National Convention car.

-- -- 30 50

9779 T C A BICENTENNIAL CONVENTION CAR: 1976, boxcar, unpainted white body, unpainted blue doors, red-painted roof and ends, Symington-Wayne trucks. Brown, black, white, and gold eagle electrocal and T C A logo to left of door, T C A Philadelphia convention data to right of door. The word Philadelphia is misspelled "Philadephia" on all examples. C. Lang comment.

-- 25 35 50

9785 CONRAIL: 1977-79, medium blue-painted body and doors, overprinted "T C A MUSEUM EXPRESS", only 108 examples made. Pinta and C. Rohlfing observations.

NRS

9786 CHICAGO & NORTHWESTERN: 1977-79, boxcar, tuscan-painted tuscan body, stamped "T C A MUSEUM EXPRESS"; only 144 examples made. C. Rohlfing comment.

NRS

9864 T C A: 1974, Convention Car, 9800-series reefer construction, Type II body with metal door guides and channel, Symington-Wayne trucks. White body with medium royal blue roof, ends, and doors, black, red, and blue Seattle World's Fair Space Needle Tower logo at left of door; "1954-1974" in red and T C A logo in black above large blue "20" at right of door.

-- -- 35 45

9868 T T O S: 1980, national convention car, 9800-style reefer, yellow body, dark blue roof and ends, dark blue lettering; lettered "SOONER DIVISION", and sign hanging down with "1980" on left side; lettered "T T O S 1980 / National Convention / OKLAHOMA CITY, OK." on right side along with two oil derricks. A. Passman and C. Rohlfing comments.

-- -- 40 50

9872 PACIFIC FRUIT EXPRESS: 1978-79, reefer, Type III body, silver roof and ends, orange body and doors, overstamped "MIDWEST DIV. T C A 1979"; only 300 examples made. C. Rohlfing comment.

NRS

16800 LIONEL RAILROADER CLUB: 1986, ore car, yellow body, black lettering, Symington-Wayne trucks. C. O'Dell comment.

-- -- 50 60

16801 LIONEL RAILROADER CLUB: 1988, bunk car, blue sides, blue roof and ends, yellow lettering, illuminated, Symington-Wayne trucks. C. O'Dell comment.

-- -- 50 60

17870 EAST CAMDEN & HIGHLAND: 1987, Standard O boxcar, L C C A Convention Car. Orange body, cream stripe across sides and door, black lettering and logo, silver-painted roof and catwalk, Standard O trucks, Type V box. J. Bratspis Collection.

-- -- 60 75

17873 ASHLAND OIL: 1988, L C C A National Convention, three-dome tank car, black body, white lettering, Symington-Wayne trucks. Came with special token only available at convention. Somewhat hard to find. C. O'Dell comment. Add $30 to value for presence of token.

(A) Shiny black. -- -- 75 90
(B) Dull black, 300 made. C. O'Dell comment. -- -- -- 50

19417 NEW YORK CENTRAL: 1987, T T O S Convention in Rochester, New York; flatcar with Kodak and Xerox trailers, car numbered "81487".

-- -- -- 70

19900 TOY FAIR: 1987, boxcar, red body, silver roof and ends, silver lettering, red, white, and blue "LIONEL" at right of door.

-- -- -- 150

19902 TOY FAIR: 1988, boxcar. NRS

59629 MILWAUKEE ROAD: 1988, L O T S, log carrier. -- -- -- 36

81487: See 19417.
97330: See 9733.

Chapter XIII
TANK CARS AND VAT CARS

As of a few years ago, Lionel has revived all the major tank car styles used in the postwar years. The last such style to be revived was the 6465-type two-dome tank car which emerged in Shell markings in 1983. It is not too surprising that Lionel has paid a great deal of attention to tank cars, even though in the real railroad world these cars are far more common in refinery areas than they are in other parts of the country. After all, one of the largest sales markets for toy trains is on the East Coast, where tankers are rather common.

What is surprising is that Lionel has not produced its own original versions of tank cars. On the real railroads tank cars exist in astonishing variety, and many scale model firms have issued much more modern tank car varieties than has Lionel. Perhaps it is a simple matter of projected sales versus tooling costs. Now that the firm is producing scale-length locomotives such as the Hudsons and the SD-40s and scale cabooses like the extended vision and wood-sided models, perhaps we will see more scale cars in tinplate in the future. It is a promising direction for modern era Lionel to take; new types of rolling stock tend to revitalize a toy train maker's line.

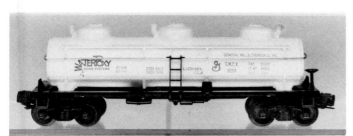

9250 Waterpoxy Tank Car with bar-end trucks. This car is known to have been made in Hillside, New Jersey in early 1971 before the final factory move to Mount Clemens, Michigan. The trucks are later tab-end types attached to the frame with "exploded" rivets, typical of late postwar practice. Note also that the brakewheel is on a raised stalk, like postwar tank cars. The later version has a brakewheel placed flat on the frame. This is an excellent example of efficient use of parts on hand. R. LaVoie Collection, G. Stern photograph.

The modern era Lionel tank cars begin in early 1970 with the interesting 9150 Gulf Single-dome Tank Car, the first versions of which used leftover plastic postwar AAR trucks. These trucks had open axle ends, an uncoupling disc attached to a spring steel strip, and a black plastic knuckle rivet — all characteristics of late postwar production of the AAR truck, which was modified heavily by Fundimensions. This particular tank car illustrated another problem, perhaps one which reflected inexperience. Before the advent of the Tampo decorating process about early 1973, the tank cars had to be decorated by a silk-screening process, in which ink is forced through a nylon screen made from a photograph. This process

had been used on postwar tank cars such as the two-dome 6465 Sunoco and Cities Service models and the three-dome 6315 Gulf and Lionel Lines Tankers. Many early examples of the 9150 have lettering and logos which are badly blurred. Fundimensions soon corrected the problem and applied silk-screening to the 9250 Waterpoxy Three-dome Tank Car as well.

The construction differences between the modern era Lionel cars and those made in the postwar era are more or less minor. The postwar cars had their brakewheels on a raised shaft; most of these are mounted directly on the frame without the shaft in Fundimensions production. The 9250 Waterpoxy Three-dome Tank Car had several interesting varieties. The earliest version of the 9250 came with leftover bar-end metal postwar trucks; it was made in Hillside, not Mount Clemens. (Other collectors dispute this theory, citing the fact that the 9250 was not catalogued until 1971. We invite your opinion.) Soon, the car came with regular issue Symington-Wayne trucks. The latest production of the 9250 featured lettering and coloring which was much brighter than its predecessors; in addition, where these had come in a large Type I box, this last version was shoehorned into a small Type I box.

The three-dome tank car has had many successors since the 9250. It has come in Sunoco, DuPont, Bakelite, Gulf, Magnolia, B & O, Southern, and many other real railroad and corporate names. Strangely, there are not too many variations of these cars, and none of the three-dome tank cars are especially rare. The hardest ones to acquire are the ones in limited sets, such as the black 9138 Sunoco and the 9313 Gulf.

There are two different tank ends found on the single-dome tank cars. The first type was used up to the 9153 Chevron Tank Car in 1974; this tank car end had "Lionel" lettering just above the wire railing, as did all the postwar single-dome tank cars. The second type omits this lettering; and the Chevron Car is the only one which has both types of ends.

97330 Airco Tank and Boxcar with broken truck. See Special Production chapter.

Top shelf: 9050 Sunoco, 9051 Firestone. Second shelf: 6301 Gulf, 6302 Quaker State. Third shelf: 6304 Great Northern, 6305 British Columbia. Bottom shelf: 6306 Southern, 6315-1972 T C A Convention.

There is another curious tank car body available; it is found inside a boxcar! This car-within-a-car was issued for the Lionel Collectors' Club of America as the 97330 Airco. Many collectors have taken the tank out of the boxcar body and added a frame, railings, and a platform to create a 97330 Airco Tank Car to match the boxcar. This curious arrangement has not been duplicated since.

Another unusual situation occurred with two nearly identical yellow Shell single-dome tank cars. Fundimensions issued the 9151 Shell Tank Car in 1972 with a yellow body, red lettering, and yellow ends. Apparently, somebody thought the car looked a little too plain, because in the next production year the car's number was changed to 9152, the lettering became a little more bold, and the ends were made black instead of yellow. As a result, the all-yellow 9151 is a great deal more difficult to find than many collectors believe.

Some innovative decorating schemes have made their debuts with the single-dome tank car. In 1975 Fundimensions surprised collectors with its Borden Tank Car which featured a shiny, simulated chrome-plated body. Black lettering and black ends gave it an extremely formal look which was popular with many collectors. This example was soon followed by others in Gulf, Sunoco, Texaco, and Mobilgas markings. In 1978 Fundimensions hit a jackpot with an unusual and fanciful car which won a great following for its bright decoration. This was the 9278 Lifesavers Tank Car; the body of the car was covered by an incredibly bright pressure-sensitive decal to make the car look like a large roll of multicolored Lifesavers candy rolling down the tracks. This car sold so well that Fundimensions next issued a single-dome tank car which looked like a Tootsie Roll candy package.

Another candy tanker was scheduled for production but was deleted before the advance catalogue came out in early 1979. This was the Stick-O-Pep tank car, which would have been similar to the Lifesavers tank car except for stripes in pink, black, and white. Although the car was never produced, the decals were in fact printed, and some have gotten into circulation. The collector should know that any such car is a product of decal

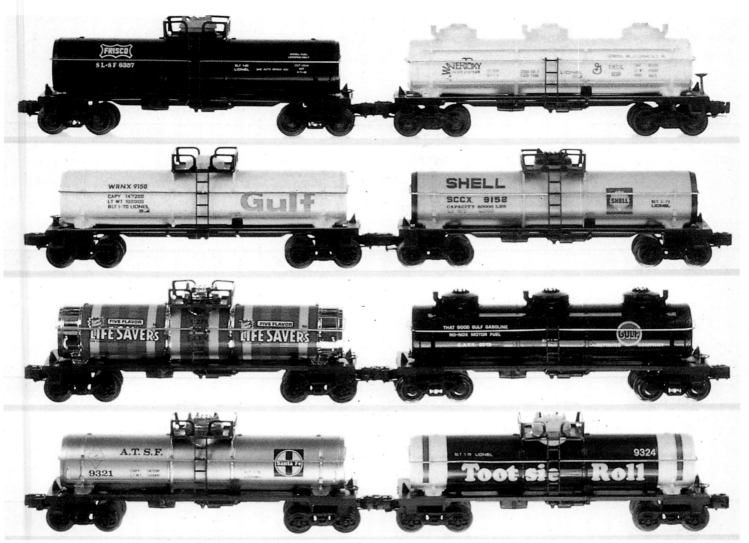

Top shelf: 6357 Frisco, 9250 Waterpoxy. Second shelf: 9150 Gulf, 9152 Shell. Third shelf: 9278 Lifesavers, 9313 Gulf. Bottom shelf: 9321 A T S F, 9324 Tootsie Roll.

application outside of the factory rather than actual production. It is not clear why the car was withdrawn, especially in view of the huge success of the Lifesavers car. Perhaps the candy company withdrew its permission to use its trademark very late in the production cycle. That did, in fact, happen with the 9879 Kraft Philadelphia Cream Cheese Refrigerator Car, for which a few prototypes exist in the Mount Clemens archives. The 9879 number was hurriedly reassigned to the Hills Brothers Car.

A small, all-plastic single-dome tank car similar to postwar models has also been made for inexpensive sets by Lionel. This car has been made in Mobilgas (two colors), Firestone, Alaska, and Sunoco markings on a plastic frame rather than the postwar metal frame. The yellow 9050 Sunoco is a little harder to find than all the others, probably because it was the first and an exact remake of the postwar yellow 6015 car, right down to the old metal frame. These small tank cars do not attract too much collector attention (except perhaps for the 9050 Sunoco Tank Car) and are usually easy to find at inexpensive prices.

The two-dome tank car modeled upon the omnipresent postwar 6465 Sunoco Tank Car was a recent addition to the modern era Lionel line in Shell and Gulf markings. It illustrates a curious phenomenon reported by many dealers in its Shell configuration — yellow cars and locomotives do not, as a rule, sell very well. Nobody seems to know why this is so, unless it is because the public does not perceive yellow as a prototypical color and therefore judges the rolling stock as unrealistic. No more of these two-dome cars have been made in recent years, so perhaps sales were disappointing.

The Lionel vat car is a curious but attractive creation. A metal frame is the foundation for a low-slung open framework car with a roof supported by girder work on the sides and ends. Within this open framework are four round vats anchored to the car base. The roof has simulated hatches atop each of the vats. The first Fundimensions vat car to emerge was the Heinz pickle car in 1974. Like its postwar predecessor, this car has several variations, including unmarked vats as an interesting factory error. This car was followed by a Libby pineapple vat car in 1975 and a Mogen-David wine car in 1977.

Three other vat cars have been produced since the first three, but these may indicate a new direction for the vat cars. In 1983 an extremely handsome Budweiser beer vat car was

Top shelf: 9277 Cities Service, 9331 Union 76. Second shelf: 9334 Humble, 9344 Citgo. Third shelf: 9353 Crystal, 9354 Pennzoil. Fourth shelf: 9367 Union Pacific, 9369 Sinclair. Bottom shelf: 9373 Getty, 9386 Pure Oil.

produced in red, white, and silver markings. It was such a good seller that it was followed by a blue and white Miller Lite beer vat car and a dark maroon Dr. Pepper version. These three cars may mean that Lionel plans on marketing its future vat cars in beer and soda pop markings; this strategy would create an interesting series of cars for collectors.

Although very few of the modern era Lionel tank cars are true rarities, they are certainly colorful, and a good collection can be built by the beginning collector at relatively modest prices. The tank cars from the collector sets, such as the 9277

Cities Service, the 9331 Union 76, and the 6305 British Columbia, show excellent potential for appreciation in value because of their limited production.

Fundimensions adopted the 6315 Chemical Tank Car (the platform, single tank car) as its preferred style. It modified the 6315 Tank by replacing the brakewheel on a standing post with a low brakewheel on the frame. Fundimensions created two types of platform, single-dome cars:

Type 1: Lettering on the ends above the railing.
Type 2: No lettering on the car ends.

The 9153 Chevron comes with both Type 1 and 2 ends. Starting with the 9154 Borden, circa 1975, only Type 2 ends are found.

	Gd	VG	Exc	Mt

303 STAUFFER CHEMICAL: 1985, see Special Production chapter.

0782 LIONEL RAILROADER CLUB: 1985, see Special Production chapter.

6300 CORN PRODUCTS: 1981, dark yellow body, three-dome, black lettering, Symington-Wayne trucks; from 1154 Reading Yard King Set.

	12	15	20	25

6301 GULF: 1981-82, single-dome, white with orange "Gulf", Symington-Wayne trucks.

	--	--	20	25

6302 QUAKER STATE: 1981-82, dark green body; white lettering, black frame, Symington-Wayne trucks, three-dome. C. Rohlfing comment.

	--	20	30	40

6304 GREAT NORTHERN: 1981, dark green tank, black platform, single-dome, white lettering, black and white Great Northern logo, gold FARR Series 3 logo, Symington-Wayne trucks, from Famous American Railroads Series 3, only available as separate sale. R. Sigurdson, T. Ladny, and C. Rohlfing comments.

	--	--	40	55

6305 BRITISH COLUMBIA: 1981, light green tank, black platform, single-dome; white lettering, Standard O trucks; from 1158 Maple Leaf Limited Set.

	--	35	45	55

6306 SOUTHERN: 1983, single-dome, silver tank, black lettering, gold FARR 4 series emblem, Standard O trucks; separate sale item.

	--	--	40	45

6307 PENNSYLVANIA: 1984-85, single-dome, deep maroon tank, black frame, black ladders, catwalk, and dome top; white lettering, gold FARR 5 logo, die-cast sprung trucks. Has become a big favorite with collectors because of its attractive color scheme and logos.

	--	--	40	50

6308 ALASKA: 1982, short single-dome, dark blue tank, black plastic frame; yellow lettering and Eskimo logo, one operating and one fixed coupler, Symington-Wayne trucks.

	--	--	10	15

6310 SHELL: 1983, 6465-style two-dome, yellow tank body; red lettering and logo, black stamped-steel frame, Symington-Wayne trucks; separate sale item. L. Caponi comment.

	--	--	12	15

6312 CHESAPEAKE & OHIO: 1984-85, 6465-style two-dome, dark blue tank body; yellow lettering, stamped metal frame, Symington-Wayne trucks; part of Set 1402.

	--	--	12	15

6313 LIONEL LINES: 1983-84, single-dome, bright orange tank body, blue tank ends; red, white, and blue circular Lionel logo at left and "LIONEL / LINES" in dark blue at right, Symington-Wayne trucks. Limited production.

	--	--	35	45

6314 BALTIMORE & OHIO: 1986, three-dome, dark blue tank body, yellow lettering and logo, Symington-Wayne trucks. Part of 1652 B & O Freight Set.

	--	--	20	30

6315 T C A PITTSBURGH: See Special Production chapter.

6317 GULF: 1984-85, 6465-style two-dome, white tank body; orange lettering, orange and white Gulf logo, stamped-metal frame, Symington-Wayne trucks.

	--	--	12	15

6323 VIRGINIA CHEMICALS: 1986, see Special Production chapter.

6357 FRISCO: 1983, single-dome, black tank; white lettering, yellow tank cover, Standard O trucks. Only available as part of 1361 Gold Coast Limited Set.

	--	--	40	50

9036 MOBILGAS: 1978-80, single-dome, small frame, 7-7/16 inches long, white plastic tank painted white with red lettering, black ends, one brakewheel; Symington-Wayne trucks, one disc coupler with tab, one fixed coupler, metal wheels.

	2	4	6	12

See also Special Production chapter.

9039 MOBILGAS: 1978, 1980, red single-dome plastic tank painted red, black ends; white lettering, black frame, one brakewheel, Symington-Wayne trucks, metal wheels, one disc coupler with tab, one fixed coupler.

	2	4	6	12

9050 SUNOCO: 1970-71, small one-dome tank car, metal frame.
(A) Yellow-orange body, blue lettering, AAR trucks, one operating coupler, one fixed coupler, MPC logo, medium orange-yellow background in Sunoco logo.

	7	10	15	20

(B) Medium yellow body, blue lettering, Symington-Wayne trucks, one operating coupler, one fixed coupler, MPC logo, medium orange-yellow background in Sunoco logo.

	4	5	10	15

(C) Same as (B), but dark yellow body.

	4	5	10	15

(D) Same as (B), but light yellow body, light orange-yellow background in Sunoco logo.

	4	5	10	15

(E) Same as (B), but with green lettering. G. Halverson Collection.

	--	--	30	60

9051 FIRESTONE: 1974-75, short one-dome tank car, Symington-Wayne trucks, one operating coupler, one fixed coupler, no MPC logo.
(A) Unpainted shiny white body, light blue lettering.

	4	6	8	10

(B) Painted flat white body, blue lettering.

	4	6	8	10

Note: There are two vat cars which use the number 9106.

9106 MILLER BEER: 1984-85, vat car, dark blue body and roof; white lettering, metal chassis, four white vats with red, gold, and blue Miller logo, Symington-Wayne trucks.

	--	--	15	20

9106 EASY CHEESE: 1984-85, vat car, dark blue body and roof, white lettering, four vats with red lettering "EASY CHEESE" on all; one vat has yellow "American" on blue band, one has yellow "Chive and Onion" on green band, one has "Cheese & Bacon" on red band, and one has "Cheddar" on yellow band. This car was part of a special promotional set distributed by Nabisco; part of the set may not be factory production. In particular, this car may have used regular production 9106 Miller Vat frames and bodies with redecorated vats. Reader comments requested. S. Lindsey, Jr. Collection. **NRS**

9107 DR. PEPPER: 1986, vat car, dark maroon body, roof, and vats, metal chassis, white lettering on car, white "DR. PEPPER" logo on vats, Symington-Wayne trucks.

	--	--	15	20

9128(A) Heinz Vat Car with lettered vats.

9128 HEINZ: 1974-76, red roof, gray sides, red lettering on frame, Symington-Wayne trucks.

	Gd	VG	Exc	Mt
(A) Medium yellow vats, green lettering.	6	8	15	20
(B) Light yellow vats, green lettering.	6	8	15	20
(C) Light yellow vats, light turquoise lettering.	12	15	20	25
(D) Medium yellow vats, turquoise lettering.	12	15	20	25

See also Factory Errors and Prototypes.

9128(C) Heinz Vat Car with unlettered vats.

9132 LIBBY'S CRUSHED PINEAPPLE: 1975-77, green roof, gray sides, yellow vats; red and brown lettering on vats, green lettering on frame, Symington-Wayne trucks.

	6	10	15	20

9138 SUNOCO: 1978, three-dome, black tank body; white lettering, Sunoco decal, "BLT 1-78", black plastic frame, black brakewheel, Standard O trucks, disc couplers with tabs; part of 1868 Minneapolis and St. Louis Service Station Set.

	15	20	30	40

9132 Libby's Crushed Pineapple.

9146 Mogen David Wine Car.

9146 MOGEN DAVID: 1977-79, silver roof, blue sides, tan vats; blue vat lettering, white frame lettering, Symington-Wayne trucks.   8   10   15   20

9147 TEXACO: 1977, single-dome, chrome and black body; red and black lettering, Symington-Wayne trucks, two operating couplers, no MPC logo.

   10   15   20   40

9148 DUPONT: 1977-79, 1981, three-dome, cream-yellow and green body; green lettering, red logo, Symington-Wayne trucks, no MPC logo, operating couplers.   6   8   12   20

9150 GULF: 1970-71, single-dome, white body; black and orange lettering and logo, Symington-Wayne trucks except (A), operating couplers, MPC logo. Typically, many examples of this car have fuzzy, ill-defined markings. Slight premium for well-marked example.

(A) 1970, early, black silk-screened lettering, orange silk-screened Gulf logo, plastic frame with low brakewheel, leftover late postwar AAR trucks. R. LaVoie Collection.   15   20   25   30

(B) Same as (A), but Symington-Wayne trucks.   10   15   20   25

(C) Same as (B), but black and dark orange lettering. P. Piker Collection.   10   15   20   25

9151 SHELL: 1972, single-dome, yellow body, yellow ends, yellow tank top; red lettering, Symington-Wayne trucks, operating couplers, MPC logo. This car most likely came only in sets.   10   15   20   25

9152 SHELL: 1973-74, single-dome, yellow body, black ends, black tank top; red lettering (bolder and darker than on 9151), Symington-Wayne trucks, operating couplers, no MPC logo. This car came in sets and was offered for separate sale. Early production had postwar-style tank ends with "L" in a circle, as on the postwar 6315. Later production did not have this circle. G. Halverson comment. Same comment applies to next entry.

(A) Light yellow body.   6   10   15   20

(B) Medium yellow body.   6   10   15   20

9153 CHEVRON: 1974-76, single-dome, silver and blue body; blue lettering, Symington-Wayne trucks, operating couplers, no MPC logo.

(A) Light blue and red decals.   6   8   15   30

(B) Dark blue and orange decals.   6   8   15   30

9154 BORDEN: 1975-76, single-dome, chrome and black body, black lettering, Symington-Wayne trucks, operating couplers, no MPC logo. This was the first Fundimensions tank car to feature a chromed finish.   10   15   20   30

9155 MONSANTO: 1975, single-dome, see Special Production chapter.

9156 MOBILGAS: 1976-77, single-dome, chromed tank body; red and blue lettering and logo, Symington-Wayne trucks, operating couplers.

   10   15   20   30

9159 SUNOCO: Single-dome, chrome and blue body; blue lettering, Symington-Wayne trucks, operating couplers, no MPC logo; available only in sets.

   20   25   35   50

9189 GULF: Single-dome, chrome and black body; blue lettering, Symington-Wayne trucks, operating coupler, no MPC logo; available only in sets.

   20   25   35   45

9193 BUDWEISER: 1983, silver roof, red sides, red and white vats, red vat lettering, Symington-Wayne trucks; separate sale item that has sold well. C. Rohlfing and L. Caponi comments.   --   10   15   20

9250 WATERPOXY: 1971, three-dome, white body, blue and green lettering, MPC logo. One sample observed came in Type I box dated July 1971. T. Rollo comment.

(A) Postwar bar-end trucks with tabs, two old-type raised brakewheel stands. This car was manufactured at the old Lionel Hillside, New Jersey plant before the firm moved to Mount Clemens, Michigan. (See Introduction.) R. LaVoie Collection.   7   15   25   50

(B) Symington-Wayne trucks, two operating couplers, one plastic brakewheel.

   6   8   15   25

(C) Same as (B), but white-painted translucent tank and ends, much brighter green and blue lettering than (A) or (B), Symington-Wayne trucks, came in smaller Type I box with black "9250 / G.M.C.X. / TANK CAR" stamped in black on ends. Probably very late production. R. LaVoie Collection.

   8   10   15   25

(D) Same as (B), but dark blue frame instead of black. Similar to frame color variations of 6560 Crane Car. Further sightings requested. M. Sabatelle comment.   NRS

9277 CITIES SERVICE: 1977, single-dome, green body and dome, metal ladder and platform around dome, black plastic frame, one brakewheel, handrails run nearly completely around tank, Standard O trucks. Part of Milwaukee Special Set of 1977.   15   20   30   40

9278 LIFESAVERS: 1978-79, platform, single-dome; extraordinarily bright pressure-sensitive decal showing five flavors, tank and dome are chrome-plated, metal walk and ladders, metal handrails run nearly completely around car, one brakewheel, Symington-Wayne trucks.   10   20   30   40

9279 MAGNOLIA: 1978-79, three-dome, white plastic body painted white, black ends, black lower third of tank, shiny metal handrails, black metal ladders, black plastic frame, Symington-Wayne trucks.   8   10   12   15

9313 GULF: 1979, three-dome, black plastic painted shiny black; white lettering, orange and black Gulf logo, shiny metal handrail, black metal ladders, one brakewheel, Standard O trucks; part of Southern Pacific Limited Set.

   --   25   35   45

9321 A.T.S.F.: 1979, single-dome, silver-painted body, metal walkway, black metal ladders, dull metal handrail almost all the way around, black plastic frame, Symington-Wayne trucks, black and white Santa Fe decal, FARR Series 1 logo.

   15   20   30   40

9324 TOOTSIE ROLL: 1979, 1981-82, single-dome, white ends, brown center tank section; white lettering, Symington-Wayne trucks.

   10   15   25   30

9327 BAKELITE: 1980, three-dome, white upper body, red lower tank body; red lettering, red and white "UNION CARBIDE" logo, Symington-Wayne trucks.

   --   --   15   20

9331 UNION 76: 1979, single-dome, dark blue tank body; orange lettering and "UNION 76" logo, Standard O trucks; from 1071 Quaker City Limited Set. C. Rohlfing comment.   15   20   30   40

9334 HUMBLE: 1979, single-dome, silver-painted tank; red and blue lettering, Symington-Wayne trucks.   6   10   15   25

9344 CITGO: 1980, white, three-dome, blue lettering, red and blue "CITGO" logo, Standard O trucks; from 1070 The Royal Limited.   --   15   25   35

9347 NIAGARA FALLS: 1979, see Special Production chapter.

9353 CRYSTAL: 1980, red, three-dome, white lettering, Symington-Wayne trucks.   --   --   15   20

9354 PENNZOIL: 1981, chrome-finished, single-dome, Symington-Wayne trucks; yellow and black logo.   --   15   20   30

9356 LIFE SAVERS STIK-O-PEP: 1980, single-dome tank car; planned for 1980 release and shown in the Toy Fair catalogue of that year, this car was pulled from production at the last minute for unknown reasons; our guess is withdrawal of corporate permission or the demand of a royalty. The pressure-sensitive decals for the car had been contracted and already made; presumably, all such decals would have been stored or destroyed after production was canceled. However, one surviving set of decals has been found and applied to a chrome-plated tank car after the original decorations had been removed, leaving just the chromed tank body. It is not known how many of these decals have survived, but any 9356 Tank Car in existence was definitely produced outside the factory. F. Fisher Collection. Reader comments invited.   **Not Manufactured**

9367 UNION PACIFIC: 1980, single-dome, silver-painted tank body; black lettering, gold FARR Series 2 logo; available only as separate sale. C. Rohlfing comment.

(A) Red, white, and blue Union Pacific shield decal.   -- **15   20   30**

(B) Same as (A), but Union Pacific shield is smaller and darker colored and is an electrocal rather than a decal. This was probably a running change implemented because the decals had a tendency to peel. L. Lefebvre Collection.

-- **20   30   40**

9369 SINCLAIR: 1980, single-dome, medium green tank; white lettering and logo, Standard O trucks; from 1071 Mid-Atlantic Set.   -- **30   35   40**

9373 GETTY: 1980-81, white single-dome, red dome cap, red and orange logo, Symington-Wayne trucks; from 1072 Cross Country Express Set. C. Rohlfing comments.   -- **15   20   30**

9386 PURE OIL: 1981, single-dome, cream tank body; dark blue lettering and logo, Standard O trucks; from 1160 Great Lakes Limited Set. C. Rohlfing comment.   -- **25   30   40**

16102 SOUTHERN: 1987, three-dome, dark green tank body, black frame, chromed rail around tank, gold lettering and Southern herald, Standard O trucks. Part of Southern Freight Runner Service Station Special Set 11704.

-- **--   --   35**

16103 LEHIGH VALLEY: 1988, two-dome, stamped steel frame, unpainted gray body, black lettering and number, red flag logo, Symington-Wayne trucks. Separate sale item, but will also match 1987 Black Diamond Set.

-- **--   15   20**

19600 MILWAUKEE ROAD: 1987, single-dome, dull orange-painted tank body with black lower edge, black tank cap and ends with white lettering, black lettering on tank body, red and white rectangular Milwaukee logo, Standard O trucks. Part of Fallen Flags Set 2.   -- **--   --   35**

97330: See Special Production chapter.

Chapter XIV
ACCESSORIES

By Roland E. LaVoie and Glenn Halverson

In 1958, amid the placid years of Eisenhower, the "Silent Generation," and the rude awakening posed by "Sputnik," author and social critic Vance Packard published a book called *The Waste Makers*, which climbed rapidly to the top of the best-seller lists. In this book, Packard castigated the hitherto sacred cow of business by detailing the operational concept of planned obsolescence. He accused businessmen of forcing American consumers to buy manufactured goods by making them stylistically unacceptable or, worse, by designing them to wear out just as they were paid for. Given the stylistic excesses of the American automobiles of the period and the notorious tendency of the good old washing machine to self-destruct, Packard made a good case for his thesis.

For one company, the Lionel Corporation, that thesis did not hold true. Even when the business climate for toy trains took a sharp downturn, the legacy of Joshua Lionel Cowen was too strong for the company to ignore until the end of the decade, when Cowen sold his shares and finally retired. Nowhere was the commitment to quality better demonstrated than with Lionel's operating accessories, those little animated joys which seemed destined to last forever. One of the main reasons for this durability was the dependence of these accessories upon solenoid relays and rugged vibrator motors for their operation. Take an old Lionel accessory out of its box after it has been unearthed from a 30-year stay in a dusty attic and, likely as not, the mechanism will operate perfectly. It is not unusual to see even prewar accessories in active use on layouts, day after day.

Building something to last is commendable indeed, but Lionel's commitment to durability in its accessories posed a very unusual marketing problem for the fledgling Fundimensions firm in 1970. The firm found itself in competition with its own past! How could Fundimensions expect people to buy its accessories when so many of the old ones were still out there working perfectly?

The obvious answer to that question was to build new kinds of accessories. Even here, the engineering excellence of the old Lionel Corporation seemed to haunt Fundimensions at every turn. For every reissue of the old accessories which was improved, such as the 2494 Rotating Beacon which worked much better than its 394 and 494 predecessors, other reissues emphasized the inexperience of the firm at making these toys. In our first edition, we told you about the 2125 Whistle Shack and the 2156 Station Platform, two of the more painfully obvious engineering goof-ups. In an article written for this edition, you will read the comments about these early years from Dan Johns, the current Director of Product Integrity and Customer Service for Lionel, Inc. His comments are illuminating and interesting. There is another surprise, too — Lionel tried to correct its error with the 2125 Whistle Shack! Details about that adventure can be found in an update at the 2125 listing.

Thus, it took quite a while for Fundimensions to find its own niche for its accessory line, and even longer to get out of the shadow of its illustrious past. Many of the earliest accessories were direct copies of the older line with subtle differences. These were produced in very limited quantities and are well worth seeking today; they include the three accessories mentioned above, the 2199 Microwave Relay Tower, and a few others. In fact, Fundimensions had a copious supply of leftover production which it re-packaged into its own boxes! Thus, it is quite possible to find a 2154 Blinking Crossing Signal which is absolutely identical to the postwar version but is packed in a Type I Fundimensions box. Only when these supplies were exhausted, around the beginning of 1972, did Fundimensions market its own lines — and even then these were no different from their predecessors except cosmetically. How many collectors know that the postwar 252 Crossing Gate and its Fundimensions 2152 successor can only be told apart by the gate prop at the end of the gate? It is metal in postwar production and black plastic in Fundimensions production. The bases of the 2152 Gates even carry 252 Lionel Corporation markings!

The first stirrings of Fundimensions' individuality came in 1973, when the firm began selling scale O Gauge building kits. This is quite understandable, given the long background of model building possessed by the Craft Master and Model Products Corporation people who ran Lionel at that time. These attractive kits have been a staple of the Lionel line ever since that year. However, it was not until 1976 that Fundimensions introduced accessories which could truly be called its own — and it did so with a vengeance! One accessory, partly derivative from older forms, was the 2127 Diesel Horn Shed, which worked from a 9-volt battery through a speaker hidden in a shack shaped like the one used for the 2126 Whistling Freight Shed, also introduced (or re-introduced, if you prefer) that year. The others were original in every way. One was an ingenious 2175 Sandy Andy Ore Tower Kit which used a system of weights to dump coal into a little ore car which traveled down a rack and dumped its contents into a waiting coal car. It was a devil to keep in adjustment, but it was amusing when it worked. Another was a coaling station kit which dumped coal into a car underneath the building.

The most spectacular of the accessories, however, was a fully-operating 2317 Automatic Drawbridge. This terrific accessory used the same operating principles as the fabled 313 Bascule Bridge of the early postwar years, but it added the dimension of an over-and-under layout. If a train on the upper track approached an open drawbridge, it would stop until the bridge was lowered, a bell ringing all the while. If the train were on the lower level and encountered a closed drawbridge, it would stop until the bridge was raised. The accessory could

2122

2125

2127

2133

2140

2145

be wired for continuous operation using insulated tracks or contactors. Though difficult to hook up, this was a fine accessory which brought great action to a layout and looked handsome.

But the lure of nostalgia proved too strong for Fundimensions to resist. In 1980 the fine 454 Sawmill was revived by the firm, using the number 2301. This was the first revival of the truly magnificent and complex accessories from the glory days of the Lionel Corporation, and it sold very well. Also revived in that year was a manual version of the old 282 Gantry Crane, and operators realized that a remote-control version could not be far behind. The meticulously detailed O Gauge switches were once again made in 1980, and in the next year the popular oil derrick made its appearance.

The year 1982 was accessory heaven as a steady parade of resurrections began apace. In that year, the colorful animated newsstand and the imposing icing station appeared. A nice revival of the old 256 Freight Station appeared as the 2129 in 1983, as well as the American Flyer oil drum loader, the 2316 Remote Control Gantry Crane, the 2315 Overhead Coaling Station, and the 2318 Operating Control Tower. Most of these accessories were delayed in production, but that only whetted the collector and operator appetite for more. In 1984 more did indeed follow. The good die-cast bumpers reappeared in two colors, the dwarf signal made an appearance, and the old 356 Operating Freight Station and 445 Operating Control Towers came out as the 2323 and 2324, respectively. No new accessories of this type were announced for 1985 or 1986, perhaps to give Lionel time to produce those already announced and to catch its collective breath after the production delays the firm experienced in 1983 and 1984.

Then came the new 1987 catalogue and a whole raft of revivals and new accessories. This has been the first year during which the management of the modern era has revived accessories produced in the modern era itself! In an attempt

to show that old wine can indeed be sold in new bottles, Lionel, Inc. has reintroduced many accessories in new and much brighter colors. This makes sense in the marketing arena, because color sells toy trains more than anything else. The 2318 Operating Control Tower has been reintroduced as the 12702 with new colors. The black 2140 Banjo Signal has found new life as the 12709 in tuscan coloring, the attractive and scarce 2285 Engine House kit has been revived as the 12710, the good old 2175 Sandy Andy Ore Loader Tower has been resurrected in new colors, the 2152 Crossing Gate has become the 12714 with a new gray base, the lighted and unlighted plastic bumpers have changed color from black to tuscan, and the 2314 Twin Searchlight Tower has reappeared in gray and bright orange.

Nor have new offerings been shunted aside for 1987. First of all, there is a brand new solid state transformer, the MW, which promises to give Lionel's trains the most power available since the days of the now-outlawed KW and ZW models. To the delight of operators and collectors alike, a new magnetic gantry crane like the old 282R made an appearance in attractive Erie-Lackawanna colors. The operating diesel fueling station of the postwar years also returned, and a brand new set of billboards and frames was developed.

Perhaps it is easy to chastise the current Lionel management for relying on the old tried and true Lionel accessories so much, but when the company has had a good thing going for it, one cannot blame anybody for sticking to a successful formula. With few exceptions, the operating accessories have been very brisk sellers. In addition, there have been some technical innovations worthy of praise. In the modern operating gantry cranes and overhead coal loaders, the rugged but ponderous and noisy Lionel AC electric motors have been replaced by quiet, efficient AC/DC can motors which work more smoothly, never need lubrication (though the gears do), and use fewer

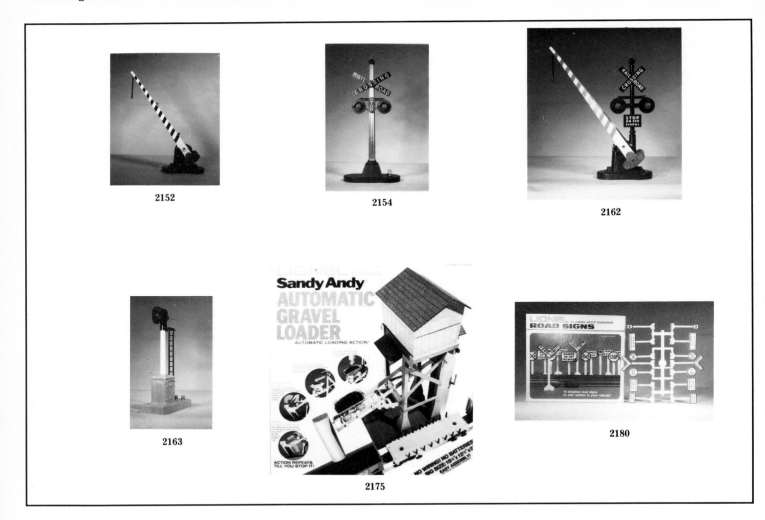

2152

2154

2162

2163

2175

2180

volts than their predecessors. This means that more accessories can be activated on less power, not to mention the maintenance-free features. The good old solenoids and vibrator motors produced by Lionel, Inc. work just as well as their elder Lionel cousins.

In 1988 Lionel, Inc. hit the accessory jackpot again. Several attractive building kits have been reviewed, among them the scarce grain elevator and coaling station. An ingenious roadside diner with a smoke unit has been introduced, new designs for the whistle and diesel horn sheds are being produced, and revivals of the mail pickup set and microwave relay tower are in production. A clever redesign of the animated newsstand and the animated refreshment stand have also been made. Several other revivals are also in evidence.

Will there be further revivals of older Lionel operating accessories? If you need convincing that this will indeed be so, just look through the Lionel catalogues of the middle to late 1950s. There you may view the big water tower, the culvert loader and unloader, the overhead gantry signal, the barrel and coal ramps, the helicopter launching station, and many, many other candidates for revival. Will there be entirely new accessories added to the Fundimensions line? The answer to this is less certain, but eventually the supply of subjects for revival will run low. Then, perhaps, Fundimensions will make accessories found in the old Lionel archives but never produced. Possibly, we could see some accessories with a modern twist, such as a dockside container ship unloading gantry (which would really be a spectacular accessory!).

Yet, the tradition lives on. Only in 1985 did one accessory finally disappear from the catalogue after a continuous 50-year run in one form or another. This was the Operating Gateman, a little fellow who rushed out of his shack as the train went by, swinging his lantern mightily. From 1935 to 1984, this accessory was produced in 45, 045, 45N, 145, and 2145 configurations. It was truly the toy train equivalent of the Ford Model "T"! Despite the gateman's disappearance, this accessory has been too much a part of Lionel tradition to remain unproduced for long — and, in 1987, the gateman returned from his brief vacation sporting bright new colors — a light tan base, a butternut yellow shack, and a bright red roof. Once more, this long-lived and popular little fellow has returned to uphold one of the great truths about Lionel Toy Trains: "Not just a toy... A tradition!"

A LOOK AT LIONEL'S
EARLY MODERN ACCESSORIES:

THE "SCARCE SIX" OF 1971-1975

For the scholar of toy trains, documentation has always been a special and sometimes frustrating problem. Normally, scholarship involves the careful and selective use of written or

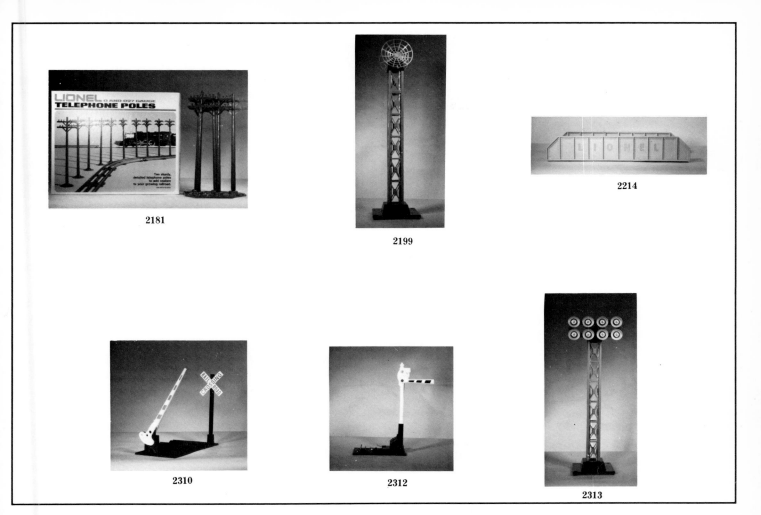

2181

2199

2214

2310

2312

2313

other documentation to confirm or refute a hypothesis. That is the method of good scholars everywhere, and it has its place in toy train scholarship. However, with toy trains documentation is not enough in many instances. If one wishes to make a careful study of some toy trains, he has to be more of an archeologist than a researcher. In other words, the toy train scholar has to work from a careful comparative study of the "artifacts" themselves.

This poses a special problem for toy train aficionados. In many cases, there simply is no documentation available to date a particular piece or set, and the longer the elapsed time between the manufacturing of the piece and its study, the more difficult the study can be. One especially frustrating case in point is the uncatalogued sets made in the postwar years, which have been very difficult to categorize and authenticate. How do we know the set was made in just this way? Were there any substitutions made over the thirty-year time span between the set's manufacture and its study?

These difficulties carry an important message for students of toy trains of the modern era: categorize and document these trains *now,* before the supporting data is lost! In a few cases, such as the 1971 Fundimensions 6560 Crane Car, it is already too late to prove which crane variety was truly a modern era piece rather than a postwar era piece; the data could have been gathered in the early 1970s, but it was not — and there is no

way to know which varieties really came in the Fundimensions boxes.

For another area, that of the accessories produced during the early modern era, we still have a chance to study and record the proper data. Therefore, in this article we will attempt to list the most significant candidates for scarcity among these early accessories, all of which were made in much smaller quantities than those made in later years. In general, there are six candidates which stand out from the rest; these we will call the "Scarce Six." Following their discussion, we will list briefly some other early accessories worth the collector's consideration.

The story of the Scarce Six really begins in the time period of late 1969 to 1971, when the management change from the old Lionel Corporation to General Mills was taking place. A significant number of Lionel's old employees did not move with the trains when the factory was moved from Hillside, New Jersey to Mount Clemens, Michigan; their absence led to people in supervisory positions who were not as much "in tune" with Lionel's manufacturing as the older supervisors. They had to learn the manufacturing processes while simultaneously rebuilding the toy train market — a daunting task which they eventually performed splendidly, but not without some errors and some unique blends of new and old parts. The new managers had inherited a staggering variety of toy train parts, some of which were 25 years old at that time. They did what any efficient company would have done — used up as much of the old stock as possible before going to the expense of producing new parts.

In a recent interview with us, Dan Johns, Lionel's current Director of Product Integrity and Customer Service, told us: "We were really doing a lot of scrambling around in those first years. After organizing the tons and tons of parts, we had to decide on what we were going to produce out of them in a given year. Sometimes we would actually begin production of an item, and we would be missing a vital part or the parts we had didn't fit. By the time we had solved those problems, people would literally be standing outside the factory doors waiting for their consignment of toy trains. It wasn't unusual for one of us supervisors to rush down to, say, a local K-Mart and personally deliver a batch of train sets in time for Christmas. That's why you see some examples of cars and engines which are cobbled together from leftover and new parts. It sure was adventurous in those first years, but we gradually got ourselves together!"

The legacy of those times is a truly fascinating group of accessories. Here, in no particular order, are the "Scarce Six" nominations from those first years:

1. THE 2125 WHISTLE SHACK OF 1971

The story of the 2125 Whistle Shack of 1971 was documented in our last edition, but we have some new information about this fascinating engineering error. Lionel's management had discovered quite a few leftover houses and a supply of the excellent postwar whistle motors and housings. To issue this shack, Lionel made up a supply of dark brown bases, pea green roofs, and translucent red window and door inserts from the old dies. In an attempt to improve on the design, Lionel connected a 12-volt automotive light bulb (the same one used in the diesel locomotives of the period) between the two wiring clips. However, for constant illumination a third clip was needed, and as produced the shack would only light when the whistle was blown!

Recently, a variation of this shack has come to light (you will excuse the pun) which shows that in the last stages of the 2125's production, Lionel realized the error and tried to fix it. In this variation, the top clips controlled only the light. In the bottom of the base, two small holes were drilled, and two metal posts with thumbscrews were inserted into these holes and connected to the motor itself. The whistle button had to be connected to these base posts. We would like to see the instruction sheet which came with this modification! It is, we think, an extremely scarce variation.

2. THE 2156 STATION PLATFORM OF 1970-1971

In our last edition, Tom Rollo told the story of this amazing amalgamation of old and new parts which span at least twenty years! For this accessory, Lionel had a supply of roofs and bases made from the tooling of the old postwar 157 Station Platform; the markings on the base were modified to supply the new firm's data. However, the metal roof stanchions were puzzling pieces; they were either brand new tooling or heavily reworked tooling from the old 156 Platform last made all the

way back in 1949! The electrical connection for the two light bulbs was supplied by a cross rod which was apparently left over from the 156 model made in the 1940s.

The light bulbs were the biggest surprise of the accessory. Either acorn-shaped or round white globes, they had been made no later than 1951, twenty years before the piece's actual production! Apparently Lionel had inherited a large supply of these old light bulbs and decided to use them in this accessory. However, the firm had forgotten that the bulbs were wired in series rather than in parallel. Series wiring meant that twice the voltage of the bulbs was needed to light them fully. This was fine as long as the bulbs were 6-volt screw-base bulbs, as they were in the old 156. However, the bulbs in the 2156 were 14 volts (acorn) and 18 volts (round). That meant a staggering voltage of 28 or 36 volts to light them fully! Actually, at 14 volts from the transformer, the bulbs emit a soft, warm glow which is rather attractive — and they certainly will last a long, long time before burning out!

After 1971 the unlighted 2256 Freight Station supplanted the 2156, and it is somewhat hard to find today, especially with its original light bulbs. Some leftover bases produced for the 2156 found their way onto 2256 Stations, thus creating another variation. This station represented some rather clever thinking, even allowing for the mistake in voltage.

3. THE 2195 FLOODLIGHT TOWER OF 1970-1972

The eight-light 195 Floodlight Tower was a very popular accessory during the postwar years. It was powerful enough to supply ample illumination for night scenes in freight yards, and it could be adapted to use a second light unit sold separately. It is not too surprising that the new Lionel managers decided to reissue it, since plenty of spare parts were left over. In fact, all the parts used for this piece were leftover parts. The light piece retained the construction techniques of the old one; it took eight 6-volt L-12 clear pin-base lamps, and there was a metal piece riveted to the plastic frame which ran around the back and supplied the electrical connections for the bulbs through metal projections with holes which fit onto the posts leading from the clips at the base. The tan base even has postwar markings, and the top tower piece is tan as well.

There are only two somewhat subtle differences which distinguish the 2195 from its predecessor. The 195's tower structure was painted dull silver, and the "LIONEL" tabs near the top of the tower were painted red. On the 2195 revival, the tower structure is an unpainted light gray and the "LIONEL" tabs are unpainted. The tan top part of the tower on the 195 was flat with two half-moon holes. On the 2195, this piece is the type with two crescent-shaped projections found on the 199 and 2199 Microwave Relay Towers. Of course, it came in a Type I Fundimensions box. Without that box, it is difficult to tell from its postwar predecessor without a second look.

Later on, this piece was renumbered 2313 and its construction changed considerably. The light piece became a one-piece gray molded plastic unit without the metal framing. Two wires lead from the bottom of the light bar through the slots attaching the piece to the poles. The base and top piece became black with Mt. Clemens markings, and the tower structure was bright red; the reflectors changed from metal to chromed plastic and the 2313 took the small white-based subminiature plug-in lamps peculiar only to the modern era. One curious variation of the 2313, probably an early production piece, retains the metal reflectors but has the smaller light bulbs!

Possibly because of its close resemblance to its common 195 predecessor, the 2195 is a very hard piece to find. When all the leftover parts were used up, the accessory was retooled extensively.

4. THE 2199 MICROWAVE RELAY TOWER OF 1972-1975

The postwar 199 Microwave Relay Tower represented Lionel's admission of the presence of new technologies, specifically television. It was an attractive piece, but it was quite labor-intensive due to its method of illumination. The general construction of the 199 followed that of the 195 Searchlight Tower, but a pigtail bulb without a base was inserted into a rubber grommet which in turn was mounted onto the poles leading from the base clips. Two very fine and fragile wires leading from the light bulb's base were bent through and over the holes of the rubber grommet to supply the contact. The bulb was a thermostatic unit which blinked on and off very realistically through two white and one red translucent plastic rods — a bit of fiber optics, as it were. The piece with the antenna dishes snapped over the bulb and was held by two projections in the tower top piece.

The reissued 2199 Microwave Relay Tower followed the postwar construction techniques precisely. The black base of the 2199 retains its postwar markings; therefore, we can conclude that these are leftover pieces. However, there are two new pieces which enable the observer to distinguish the 2199 from the postwar 199. First of all, the tower structure itself is a much darker unpainted gray than its 199 predecessor; both pieces had the "LIONEL" tab markings but were unpainted. Secondly, the postwar 199's antenna dishes were made from a somewhat brittle white plastic; they are often found broken today. The 2199, however, used very soft translucent nylon antenna pieces which are a little more durable than the older white plastic. They also reflect light because of their clear color. The 2199 accessory came in a Type II red and white box, and apparently not too many were made because the accessory does not show up very often. This accessory has been reissued in 1988 as 12723 with a gray base and top and an orange tower.

5. THE 2314 TWIN SEARCHLIGHT TOWER: 1975 PRODUCTION

The 2314 Twin-Hood Searchlight Tower, a design particular to the modern era, is generally regarded as a common piece, and rightly so in its most common color configuration of black base and searchlight platform with red tower structure and black searchlight hoods. However, it is generally unrecognized that there are two earlier versions of this tower which are very difficult to find. The base and tower are familiar material; they are made the same way as those found on the 2195 Floodlight Tower and the 2199 Microwave Tower. For the 2314, the bases all have Mt. Clemens markings, and the searchlight platform is a completely new piece. The black lamp hoods have a 3520 part number, showing their early 1950s origin, but in this case they are attached to plastic arms which swivel on the poles. The wires are soldered onto brass rivets in the platform; they

enter the searchlight hoods through the bottom. The reflectors inside the hoods are chromed plastic; the accessory takes a subminiature foreign-made screw-base lamp identical to those used in the 2710 Lamp Posts. Unfortunately, the design is very fragile, and many examples are broken when found today.

Two early color variations of this accessory are very hard to find. The first of them, in fact, may be the scarcest of all the modern era accessories. It has an unpainted medium gray tower structure, a darker gray base, and a darker gray searchlight platform with black hoods. This color variation is extremely difficult to find. Not quite as scarce but still hard to find is an all-black version: black tower structure, base, tower top, and searchlight hoods. Neither variety turns up often; due to the flimsy design of the accessory, it is quite possible that many were broken and discarded.

6. THE 2494 ROTATING BEACON OF 1972-1974

The postwar 494 Rotating Beacon was a bright and cleverly engineered illuminated accessory which warned off any low-flying balsa wood airplanes from many a layout of the 1950s. It featured a little vibrator motor which turned a beacon top mounted on a rubber washer with "fingers." It worked much better than did its 394 predecessor, which relied upon heat from a dimpled light bulb to turn its beacon top through heat convection. In its most common version, the 494 Rotating Beacon featured a red metal tower structure with a top-mounted vibrator connected to the power post by means of a soldered resistor wire and grounded through the metal framework. At its base, the postwar 494 had a metal identification plate attached through tabs.

The modern era 2494 tower is identical in structure to its 494 predecessor, even to the hole punchings in the tower structure. These towers may well have been leftover pieces; the new management had them painted in a slightly glossier shade of red. Instead of a metal identification tag, the 2494 used an aluminized paper sticker, even though the slots for the metal tab were still there.

The first of the 2494 Rotating Beacons were issued with leftover postwar metal beacon tops. However, when these were apparently exhausted, an entirely new top was designed. This piece used the same red and green lenses, but it was black plastic instead of metal, and it did not have a projecting metal collar integral to the beacon top. Instead, the 2494 used a separate metal collar to cover the vibrator motor windings. This metal collar is frequently missing when the accessory is found today, and the newer plastic top is not often found with the 2494. The version with the redesigned plastic beacon and separate metal collar is somewhat difficult to find in intact condition today. This accessory has been reissued for 1988 as the limited-production No. 12720. It has a black top tower piece instead of a red one.

The "Scarce Six" are not the only accessories from the early modern era which demand attention from the collector. Briefly, here are some other accessories which should be noted:

The **2260 Bumper** was only made through 1972; it is the same black plastic design as a postwar version meant to accommodate Super O track and included with sets made in Hagerstown, Maryland during the last years of the Lionel Corporation. It is difficult to say whether or not the 2260

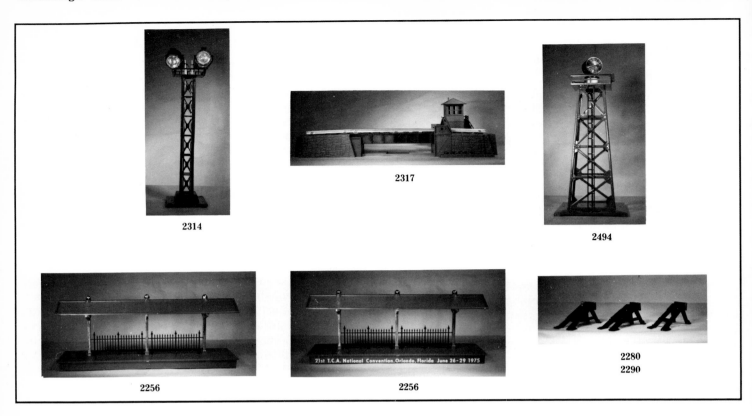

2314

2317

2494

2256

2256

2280
2290

specimens issued in the MPC years are newly minted pieces or leftover production. Supposedly, the postwar versions had solid red lens caps, while the MPC pieces had translucent caps — but these are easily switched. Some pieces found in MPC boxes have postwar markings on the bases; others have no markings at all. Some of these bumpers are also found in shrink-wrap Type II packaging. We may never be able to tell for sure which pieces are postwar and which are MPC.

Some versions of the **2170 Street Lamps** are noteworthy because they are combinations of postwar and MPC features. One variety comes in the darker green of the postwar years and takes the L19 pin-based bulb, but it has MPC markings on the base. Another version has light green poles but mismatched dark green top pole pieces while taking the newer subminiature screw-base bulb. Yet another variety is light green but uses the L-19 pin-based lamp.

While most of the billboards which come with the **2710 Billboard Sets** are quite common, there are a few rare varieties to look for. The yellow, orange, and green Myco Foam Village Packing billboard is very hard to find, as are some special issues such as the Nibco Plumbing billboards of 1980, the T C A special billboards, and the Tappan billboards of 1986. Some of the earlier billboard frames are dark green postwar leftover pieces packed in Type I MPC boxes, but this is not unusual.

Two building kits from the mid-1970s are very difficult to find in mint or any condition. These are the **2785 Engine House** and the **2796 Grain Elevator**. The engine house has been reissued by Lionel, Inc. in 1987, with slightly different colors as No. 12710. The grain elevator is a real prize, but it too has been reissued for 1988 as No. 12726 in different colors.

Finally, there is a version of the humble **2214 Girder Bridge** which has been almost totally neglected despite its scarcity. The first packaging of this accessory in 1970 used a larger Type I MPC box to contain black-girdered leftover postwar 214 Bridges, complete with postwar markings. When these were exhausted, a new knocked-down version was issued in a much smaller Type I box. The metal base of this version had Mt. Clemens markings, and the bridge girders were dark gray plastic with the MPC logo. No fastening screws were supplied with this version; instead, the base fit into slots in the girders themselves. This little bridge is extremely difficult to find because in 1972 Lionel issued a new version which came in a Type II box and had light gray girders without the MPC logo.

It is a shame that these accessories have been so neglected in the past because they are just as interesting as their postwar counterparts, if not more so. Tom Rollo, in his article on the 2156 Station Platform in our first edition, summarized the importance of these accessories well when he said that these accessories were "...eloquent testimony for the thought and research which went into Fundimensions' early product line... Clearly, the early team of Fundimensions executives exhausted every effort to succeed when every decision was a risk."

	Gd	VG	Exc	Mt
1355 Train Display Case: 1983, Set 1355.	--	--	--	40
2110 GRADUATED TRESTLE SET: 1971-87, twenty-two pieces graduated from 3/16" to 4-3/4" high.				
(A) Gray trestles.	5	7	10	12
(B) Dark brown trestles.	5	7	10	12
2111 ELEVATED TRESTLE SET: 1971-87, ten 4-3/4" piers.				
(A) Gray plastic.	5	7	10	12
(B) Brown plastic.	5	7	10	12

THE 2125 WHISTLE SHACK: AN UPDATE

In our last edition, we told you the story of one of Lionel's early attempts at using up spare parts left over from the old Hillside factory, the saga of the 2125 Whistle Shack with a light inside its housing. We told our readers that Lionel simply clipped a light to the two wire clips, forgetting all about the third grounding clip necessary to keep an accessory constantly illuminated. In this way, the 2125 only lighted when the whistle button was pressed — surely not the best way to work the accessory!

Recently, we have discovered an example of this accessory which seems to indicate that the early management of Lionel recognized the error and tried to fix it in the last part of the production run. When this author tried recently to activate a 2125 he had just acquired, only the light went on — the whistle would not blow. An examination of the shack showed something very curious indeed — two small metal knobs had been fitted into the base of the accessory just below the identification lettering (*bottom photograph*). It was a neat, professional job, and the parts were authentic early modern era knobs. These connected to posts which ran inside the accessory (visible through door, *top photograph*). When power was applied to these posts, the whistle blew! The posts were connected directly to the motor.

We would like to hear from other owners of these modified 2125 Shacks to see if this was a sample converted by a Service Station or, as we suspect, a factory quick-fix just before production was halted. As modified, the shack would need four connections — two for the light and two for the whistle motor. This would seem to be a lot of wiring for just a simple whistle! If a Service Station Bulletin was issued, we would like to see it. Stay tuned to this space in subsequent editions as this fascinating little story unfolds some more!

2113 TUNNEL PORTALS: 1984-87, gray plastic stonework, "LIONEL" and circular "L" logo molded into portal.   -- -- 5 6

2115 DWARF SIGNAL: 1984-87, gray body, black twin-light lens hood; uses pin-type bulbs; Type III box. Note that this accessory is operated by a 153C Contactor, while the postwar version was manually operated by a special switch.   -- -- 11 13

2117 BLOCK TARGET SIGNAL: 1985-87, black base, gray pole, red ladder, black two-light lens hood. C. Rohlfing Collection.   -- -- 17 21

2122 EXTENSION BRIDGE: 1977-87, two gray plastic piers, plastic bridge, requires assembly; 24" long by 5" wide, piers 7" high, overall height with piers is 11-3/4".
(A) Brown sides and top.   -- 20 30 40
(B) Brown sides and maroon top. P. Piker Collection.   -- 20 30 40

2125 WHISTLING FREIGHT STATION: 1971, white shed body, translucent red door, window inserts, and toolshed lid, green roof (slight variations of the green shade exist), dark brown base, postwar-type motor. Type I box; mint condition requires presence of box. Roof, window and door inserts, and base are Fundimensions products; shed parts and motor are postwar carry-overs. Has 12-volt automotive-type light connected to clips; light only works when whistle is blown! Very hard to find.
(A) Green roof, as described above. G. Halverson and R. LaVoie Collections.   20 25 40 50
(B) Same as (A), but extra wiring posts added to base to control whistle motor; main clips activate light only. Reader comments invited; appears to be a factory modification, but could also be a Service Station post-factory alteration. R. LaVoie Collection.   20 25 45 50

(C) Same as (A), but maroon roof, same as postwar 125 model. Authenticated from original box; probable use of leftover roof. C. Rohlfing Collection.   20 25 45 50

2126 WHISTLING FREIGHT SHED: 1976-87, dark brown plastic base, off-white yellow shed, green door and windows, opaque window in non-opening door, green toolshed lid, lighter brown plastic roof, diode-activated whistle motor. Found with two types of doors: one type has two large windows; the other has twelve smaller windows.
(A) Brown plastic roof. C. Rohlfing Collection.   10 15 20 25
(B) Same as (A), but green plastic roof; possibly leftover roof from 2125 production. J. Cusumano Collection.   10 15 20 25

2127 DIESEL HORN SHED: 1976-87, height 4-7/8", base 6" x 6", battery-operated by nine-volt transistor battery, not included. Diesel horn remote-controlled, light tan plastic base, red building, white toolshed lid, white door, frosted window, gray roof. Same door variation as 2126 above.   10 15 20 25

2128 AUTOMATIC SWITCHMAN: 1983-85, animated blue switchman waves flag as train approaches. Gray metal painted base with green cardboard bottom, red tanks. Reissue of 1047 from 1959-61. C. Rohlfing Collection.   -- -- 25 30

2129 FREIGHT STATION: 1983, brick red platform, tan building with brown windows and door, green roof, black picket fence with billboards reading "Cheerios", "Wheaties", and "Gold Medal". Also several wall posters, illuminated by one interior bulb. The catalogue shows the station with white walls. 15" long, 5" wide, and 5-1/2" high. This is a reissue of 256 from 1950-53, except for colors and stickers instead of metal signs. Foster observation. Reader comments appreciated on the differences between 2129 and 256.   -- -- 20 30

2285

2787

2788

2791

2133 FREIGHT STATION: 1972-83, maroon plastic base, white plastic sides; box at one time made by Stone Container Corporation, Detroit, Michigan, white corrugated box with colored picture of station on lid. Reissue of 133 from 1957-66. Earliest versions use metal clip-on bayonet-base light socket, rather than the postwar version, in which the light socket is riveted to the bracket. Later Fundimensions stations have plastic clip-on socket using a 12-volt automotive-type bulb. T. Rollo comment.

(A) Earliest production, 1972; Stone Container box with black and white picture of accessory, medium green roof, door, and window inserts, quarter-sized hole in base, green chimney secured by circular speed nut, black metal interior crossbar, bayonet-base metal light socket clips to bar. R. LaVoie Collection.

| | 15 | 20 | 25 | 30 |

(B) Same as (A), but has red chimney instead of green. Probable use of leftover postwar part. G. Halverson Collection. 15 20 25 30

(C) Later production, 1973-75; Stone Container box has color picture of accessory, pea green roof, chimney, doors, and window inserts, maroon base, previous hole in base is filled, chimney secured by rectangular speed nut, black metal interior crossbar, plastic light socket taking automotive-type bulb clips onto crossbar. T. Rollo and G. Halverson Collections. 12 15 20 25

(D) Latest production 1976-83, same as (C), but dull Penn Central green roof, chimney, doors, and window inserts, red-brown base, gray metal crossbar inside station. R. LaVoie Collection. 12 15 20 25

2140 AUTOMATIC BANJO SIGNAL: 1970-83, as train approaches, red light turns on, "stop" arm swings, die-cast construction; 7-1/2" high.

(A) "LIONEL CORPORATION" stamped on underside of base; postwar carry-over. Came in Type I Fundimensions box. G. Halverson Collection.

8 10 15 25

(B) Same as (A), but Type II box; accessory with postwar markings. C. Rohlfing Collection. 8 10 15 20

(C) MPC logo on base, Type II Fundimensions box. G. Halverson Collection.

8 10 15 20

2145 AUTOMATIC GATEMAN: 1970-84; 1985 marked the 50th anniversary of the most famous and long-lived of all Lionel accessories. This little shed was first offered in 1935 as the 45 for Standard Gauge and the 045 for O Gauge (dif-

fering only in the type of special insulated track or contactor included with the accessory). In 1946 its number changed to 45N, and in 1950 it was substantially revised and changed to the 145. Its spectacular market success reflects its great play value. The gateman, who is really a watchman, rushes from his lighted shed as the train approaches. He warns pedestrians and vehicles with his swinging lantern and returns to the shed after the train passes. The accessory came with a pressure contactor and a lockon. Refer to Prewar and Postwar Guides for further history of this accessory.

(A) 1970-71, green metal base, white shed with brown door and window, frosted plastic window inserts, maroon roof and toolshed lid. Mint value must have the Fundimensions Type I box; this accessory was actually a postwar 145 piece in the new Fundimensions packaging. G. Halverson Collection. 10 15 20 30

(B) 1972, same as (A), but brown roof and toolshed lid, darker green base, Type II rectangular box with window; accessory packed horizontally. G. Halverson and R. LaVoie Collections. 15 25 30 35

(C) 1973-75, same as (B), but packed in squared Type II box without window.

10 20 25 30

(D) 1976-84, medium light green base, white shack, maroon doors, windows, toolbox lid, and roof, Type III box. C. Rohlfing Collection. 10 20 25 30

2146 CROSSING GATE: 1970-1971. -- -- 12 15

2151 SEMAPHORE 1978-83, light brown plastic base, black pole, yellow- and black-striped semaphore arm, red ladder, red and green jewel lights; raises as train approaches. Different design from postwar 151, which had die-cast construction and which lowered semaphore arm instead of raising it. C. Rohlfing Collection. 8 10 20 25

2152 AUTOMATIC CROSSING GATE: 1972-86, black plastic base, white plastic gate with gray weights, on bottom "#252 Crossing Gate", with pressure contactor. The Fundimensions version can be distinguished from its postwar 252 counterpart by the presence of a black plastic gate rest at the end of the gate arm rather than the metal one used in the postwar version. Many postwar examples were repacked into Fundimensions Type I and Type II boxes. Some examples were sold in Type III rolling stock boxes with black print; "6-2152 / AUTOMATIC CROSSING GATE" on the ends. R. LaVoie comment, G. Halverson Collection.

7 10 20 25

2792

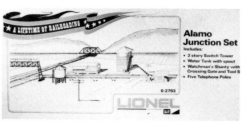

2793

2789

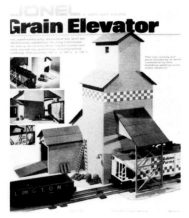

2796

29005

2154 AUTOMATIC HIGHWAY FLASHER: 1970-87, red light blinks alternately as train passes; 8-3/4" high with special track clip, the 154C Contactor. This device clamps over the track and has two thin metal plates which are insulated from the rail. The device is wired so that the train wheels run across the metal flanges, completing the circuit to each of the two bulbs in turn. Thus the left light goes on and off as the wheels pass over the left plate, and the right light goes on and off with the right plate, giving the flashing appearance of the accessory. This clever contactor first appeared in 1940 with the first versions of the 154. Modern era production has been observed in several colors. Reader comments are needed with the specific examples.

(A) White plastic crossbuck with raised black lettering, gray unpainted post with chrome finial cap. This is a postwar 154 packaged in a Type I Fundimensions box. G. Halverson Collection.   **8   10   15   20**

(B) Black crossbuck with raised white lettering, black finial cap, MPC logo stamped on underside of base. G. Halverson Collection.   **8   10   15   20**

(C) Black finial cap, white crossbuck, MPC logo on base, pink "STOP", Type II box. Unusual combination of postwar and MPC parts. C. Rohlfing Collection.   **8   10   15   20**

2156 STATION PLATFORM: 1971, rerun of 156 with 157 roof, new metal roof supports, pea green plastic base modeled after 156, medium red roof, lighted with two large prewar acorn light bulbs, underside of base reads, "CAT. NO. 2156 STATION PLATFORM" and "LIONEL MT. CLEMENS MICH. MADE IN USA". Mint value must have original light bulbs and Type I box. Hard to find with original light bulbs. See first edition for Tom Rollo's article on this accessory. Grossano, G. Halverson, R. LaVoie, and T. Rollo Collections.

   --   25   35   50

2162 AUTOMATIC CROSSING GATE AND SIGNAL: 1970-87, black plastic base, black crossbuck with white lettering and simulated bell at top, white gate, red bulbs with pins, pressure contactor, lockon.

(A) Red-painted diagonal stripes, metal support rod on gate, Type I box, postwar markings on base. Postwar carry-over in Fundimensions box. G. Halverson Collection.   **10   12   20   25**

(B) Same as (A), but black-painted diagonal stripes, black plastic support rod on gate, Type II box, postwar markings on base blanked out. G. Halverson Collection.   **10   12   20   25**

(C) Same as (B), but later production; diagonal stripes are red.

   10   12   20   25

2163 AUTO BLOCK TARGET SIGNAL: 1970-78, green light switches to red as train approaches; 7-1/2" high, contactor, L-19R red bulb, L-19G green bulb, both with pins. Some early examples may have come in leftover plain white boxes with black printing on only one end; reader comments requested.

(A) Light tan base, Type I or Type II box.   **8   10   20   25**

(B) Medium tan base, Type II box. R. LaVoie Collection.   **8   10   20   25**

(C) Dark tan base, brass-colored wire thumbscrews instead of nickel. Box type not known. G. Halverson Collection.   **8   10   20   25**

2170 STREET LAMPS: 1970-87, three per package. Earliest versions carry postwar stamping on underside of base but are packaged in Type I shrink-wrap. Later versions have Lionel MPC markings.

(A) 1970, dark green pole, dark green pole top, cream globe, pin-type bulbs; same bulb was used for postwar 76 Lamp Post. G. Halverson and T. Rollo Collections.   **7   10   20   25**

(B) 1971, early; light green pole, mismatched dark green pole top, white globe, small foreign-made midget bulb with screw base (note that a "midget lamp" is any lamp 1/4" or less in diameter). G. Cole comment, G. Halverson Collection.   **10   15   20   25**

(C) 1971, later; Type I box dated 1971, lamps with light green base, pole and cap base, translucent white globes, embossed on bottom "MADE IN U.S.A. / LIONEL MPC / MT. CLEMENS / MICH.", MPC logo on top part of base, hand-etched "76-

3" part number on bottom, foreign-made 8010-24 subminiature screw-base bulb. G. Cole and R. LaVoie Collections.   **10 15 20 25**

(D) 1972-87, light green pole and pole top, white globe, midget screw-base bulb, Type II shrink-wrap packaging (earlier) or Type II box (later). G. Halverson Collection.   **7 10 12 15**

2171 GOOSE NECK LAMPS: 1980-83, set of two lamps in Type III box, black plastic base and lamp structure mounted to metal pole, frosted pin-base bulbs, reissue of postwar versions from 1961-63.   **8 10 20 25**

2175 SANDY ANDY: 1976-79, mechanically-operated gravel loader, light brown structure, dark brown roof and base, gray plastic girders, light brown ore car. Top of silo is loaded with coal. Car is attached to string with weight. When lever holding weight is released, weight brings car to top of incline, where it pushes against lever which uncovers hole releasing coal into car. When weight of coal overcomes brass weight on line attached to car, car travels down girders and is tripped into chute which unloads coal into waiting car. Cycle then begins again. Difficult to adjust properly, but action is delightful when accessory works properly. Plastic kit. Reissued in 1987 with new colors. Hard to find in intact, working condition. R. LaVoie comments.   **10 20 20 40**

2180 ROAD SIGN SET: 1977-87, plastic signs, attached as shown.
                                              -- -- 2 3

2181 TELEPHONE POLES: 1977-87, ten light brown poles, each 7" high.
                                              -- -- 2 4

2195 FLOODLIGHT TOWER: 1970-72, eight lights, unpainted gray tower, light bracket, and reflectors, takes older two-pin clear bulbs, tan base, "LIONEL" on two tabs near top of tower, transitional hybrid; unpainted gray plastic tower structure with unpainted gray "LIONEL" signs (postwar version has silver-painted tower structure, red-painted "LIONEL"), postwar microwave relay top on tower, postwar markings on base, Type I box. Very hard to find. B. Thomas, R. LaVoie, and G. Halverson Collections.   **-- -- 40 50**

2199 MICROWAVE TOWER: 1972-75, black plastic base, unpainted dark gray plastic tower, black plastic top with three operating blinking light tips, postwar markings on base, Type II box. The gray color of the tower structure is significantly darker than that of the postwar version, and the "LIONEL" plates on the side of the tower are not painted red. The radar dishes are different as well; the postwar 199 has somewhat brittle white plastic dishes, while this version has more flexible translucent plastic radar dishes. Somewhat hard to find. R. LaVoie Collection.   **10 20 30 50**

2214 GIRDER BRIDGE: 1970-87, metal base, black- or brown-painted or brown-anodized, dark or light gray plastic side embossed "LIONEL", comes knocked down or assembled. If knocked down plastic sides must be screwed on with eight Phillips-head screws (but see earlier version below); 10" long, 4-1/2" wide.

(A) 1970-early 1971, flat black girder sides, white-outlined Lionel lettering, black-anodized base, comes assembled in larger Type I box. This is a leftover 214 with postwar markings repackaged into a Type I Fundimensions box. C. Rohlfing and R. LaVoie Collections.   **-- 3 5 8**

(B) 1971-72, smaller Type I box, knocked down assembly, dark gray plastic sides, outlined "LIONEL" with MPC logo to left, black-anodized metal base faintly embossed "No. 2214 BRIDGE / BY LIONEL MPC / Mt. CLEMENS, MICH. / MADE IN U.S.A." Method of attaching base differs from later versions; girders fit into base by means of slots molded into girder sides and has no screws for assembly, snap-together. Hard to find. G. Halverson and R. LaVoie Collections.
                                              -- 8 12 15

(C) 1973-87, Type II box, light gray girders. Earliest production pieces still retain MPC logo; later ones omit it. Screws provided for assembly; girders revert to postwar construction.   **-- 3 5 8**

2256 STATION PLATFORM: 1973-81, green plastic base, metal posts, black plastic center fence, red unpainted plastic roof, not lighted.

(A) As described above.   **3 5 6 10**

(B) T C A special issue: Penn Central green base, lighter red roof than regular issue, overprint heat-stamped in white; "21 T C A National Convention, Orlando, Florida, June 19- 26, 1975". G. Halverson and R. LaVoie Collections.
                                              -- 15 20 30

(C) Same as (A), but has leftover 2156 light green base. Fairly common variation. R. LaVoie Collection.   **5 7 12 15**

(D) Same as (A), but came in unusual Stone Container Corp. corrugated box with red and black wraparound label on one side and both ends. R. LaVoie Collection.
                                              10 15 20 25

2260 BUMPER: 1970-73, same mold used as for postwar 26 and 260 die-cast Bumpers, but black plastic body, four screws at corners, translucent red cap, takes 14-volt bayonet base bulb. Came in Type I box or Type II shrink-wrap packaging. This bumper was originally designed as a less expensive replacement for the metal 260 which had been issued to fit Super O track in the late 1950s. Somewhat hard to find.

(A) Bottom fiber plate marked "NO. 260 / THE LIONEL CORPORATION" in white, hex nut holds plate to chassis. This is identical to late postwar Hagerstown production except for the translucent lens cap; some Hagerstown versions also had translucent caps and cannot be distinguished from this version. G. Halverson Collection.   **10 15 25 40**

These are the two earliest versions of the 2214 Plate Girder Bridge. The box on the right is large enough to hold a pre-assembled bridge; it contained a postwar leftover 214 black model with postwar embossing on the base. The box and bridge on the left are quite different. The box is flat and it contains a dark gray pair of plastic girders which snap into the sides of a metal base with Fundimensions embossing. Note the different construction of the bases of the plastic girder pieces. No screws were used in this version. Soon after this version was produced, Fundimensions changed it production to a dark gray version which was sold in a flat box and used screws for assembly. Both of these versions are very hard to find. R. La-Voie Collection.

The black die-cast 2282 lighted Bumpers are much more difficult to find than their tuscan 2283 equivalents. These black versions came as a limited production item in a Type V box, while the more common 2283 models came in a Type III box. Except for the color, the bumpers are identically constructed. R. LaVoie Collection.

(B) Same as (A), but later production, no lettering on bottom fiber plate. R. La-Voie Collection.   **10   15   25   40**

2280 BUMPERS: 1973-80, 1983.

(A) 1973-75, three to a package, early version with open area, Type I box.

                                         --   1   3   5

(B) 1974-80, 1983, later version with closed area.   **--   --   3   5**

2281 BUMPERS: 1983, black, set of three.   **--   --   15   18**

2282 BUMPER: 1983, black die-cast body which attaches to the track with screws; black plastic shock absorber, red illuminated jewel atop body. Reissue of 260 Bumper from the 1950s with a color change. Illustrated in the 1983 Fall Collector's Brochure. Type V box. R. LaVoie comment. Price per pair.

                                         --   --   20   25

2283 BUMPER: 1984-85, tuscan-painted die-cast body identical in construction to 2282 above. Made in Hong Kong and sold as part of Traditional Series in pairs in Type III boxes. Price per pair.   **--   --   10   12**

2290 LIGHTED BUMPERS: 1974-85, similar in construction to 2280, but with copper contact and small screw-base red bulbs. Type III box. Price per pair.

                                         3   4   6   8

2292 STATION PLATFORM: 1985-87, dark red base, black plastic roof supports, black fencing, dark green roof, chromed acorn nut roof fasteners; unlighted.

                                         --   --   4   6

2300 OIL DRUM LOADER: 1983, reissue of 779 American Flyer accessory from 1955-56. Reader comments and differences between 779 and 2300 appreciated. This reissue is more sensitive to voltage changes than its predecessor and takes more careful operation, although it works well. Listed here as well as in our American Flyer book because it appeared in a Fundimensions catalogue and will be found with Lionel trains.   **--   --   75   90**

2301 OPERATING SAWMILL: 1981-83, maroon plastic base, white mill building, red door, gray shed, red lettering on window facing track, white crane; simulates the transformation of logs into dressed lumber, vibrator mechanism moves lumber; length 10-1/2", width 6", height 6". Reissue of 464 from 1956-60.

                                         --   --   55   75

2302 U. P. GANTRY CRANE: 1981-82, maroon crane housing and boom, black platform spans track and runs on its own wheels, manually-operated, reproduction of 282 from 1954 but without motor and remote control.

                                         --   --   15   25

2303 SANTA FE: 1980-81, manual-operating gantry crane, dark blue plastic cab, yellow boom and lettering, gray superstructure. Came as kit in 1072 Cross Country Express Set.   **--   --   20   430**

2305 OIL DERRICK: 1981-83, walking beam rocks up and down, bubbling pipe simulates oil flow, hand-operated winch; ladder, barrels, red-painted sheet metal base; reissue of 455 from 1950-54.   **--   --   75   100**

2306 OPERATING ICE STATION: 1982-83, red roof, white shoot, sold with 6700 reefer, reissue of 352 from 1955-57. Lately, this accessory has become hard to find. Price includes car. C. O'Dell comments.   **--   120 145 195**

2307 BILLBOARD LIGHT: 1983-84, black die-cast post, hooded black light casting; attaches to base of billboard and blinks by thermostatic control. Reissue of 410 model of 1956-58. I. D. Smith comment.   **--   10   15   20**

2308 ANIMATED NEWSSTAND: 1982-83, reissue of 128 from 1957-60. Newsboy hands paper to dealer, dog circles fire hydrant.   **--   --   90   120**

2309 MECHANICAL CROSSING GATE: 1982-83, operated by weight of train.   **--   --   2   4**

2310 MECHANICAL CROSSING GATE AND SIGNAL: 1973-75, activated by weight of train; black and white plastic, requires assembly.

                                         --   2   3   5

2311 MECHANICAL SEMAPHORE: 1982-83, operated by weight of train.

                                         --   --   2   4

2312 MECHANICAL SEMAPHORE: 1973-75, activated by weight of train, flag raises and green signal illuminates as train approaches, flag lowers and red signal illuminates after train passes contact track.   **--   3   5   6**

2313 OPERATING FLOODLIGHT TOWER: 1975-83, black plastic base, red plastic tower, black plastic top, gray light bar, eight miniature lights, two binding posts on bottom.

A somewhat unusual hybrid 2313 Floodlight Tower. This version had the normal black base, red tower, and newer light standard, but note the use of leftover metal lamp reflectors instead of the usual chromed plastic pieces. The lamps are also the later models with white nylon bases. Note the misspelling of the word "gauge" on the Type II box. R. LaVoie Collection.

(A) Early hybrid, takes miniature plastic-base lamps, but reflectors remain metal. The postwar light bar has a metal frame running around its rear which provides contact for the lights; beginning with this version, the metal frame is absent and two wires come down from the mounting holes of the light bar to make electrical contact and carry power internally to the bulbs. This hybrid version has the later light bar; came in Type II box with the word "GAUGE" misspelled as "GUAGE" on front label. R. LaVoie Collection.   **10   15   25   35**

(B) Same as (A), but regular production, light reflectors are chromed plastic instead of metal. C. Rohlfing Collection.   **7   10   20   25**

2314 OPERATING SEARCHLIGHT TOWER: 1975-83.

(A) Unpainted light gray plastic tower and dark gray base, two black searchlight hoods; rare. G. Halverson Collection.   **--   --   125 160**

(B) Black plastic tower, base, and tower top, two black searchlight hoods. Somewhat hard to find. C. Rohlfing, R. LaVoie, J. Kovach, and G. Halverson Collections.   **15   20   30   40**

(C) Same as (A), but red tower, black base, red tower top. W. Eddins Collection.

                                         7   10   20   30

(D) Same as (C), but black tower top. R. Sage Collection.   **10   15   25   35**

2315 COALING STATION: 1984-85, reissue of 497 from 1953-58. Originally scheduled for number 2324, but that number was used later for the revival of the postwar 445 Operating Switch Tower. Dark red metal structure, gray support base, black pillars, red coal tray, gray roof. (Postwar version had maroon coal tray and green roof, and color of paint was lighter red.) This version uses the new Fundimensions can motor instead of the postwar motor, so it runs more quietly at lower voltage.   **--   --   90   120**

2316 NORFOLK & WESTERN: 1983-84, remote-control gantry crane, essentially similar to the postwar 282R, but with several important construction changes. Dark maroon cab, gold lettering and cab base, maroon boom, gray superstructure. Does not have electromagnet found on the 282R. The single motor and gearing of the 282R has been replaced by two Fundimensions can motors mounted under the superstructure, one for each operation of the crane (swiveling of body and hook operation). Compared to the 282R, this crane is not as strong a lifting device, but it operates much more quietly than the 282R on much lower voltage. The line for the lifting hook has a tendency to tangle and stall the lifting action; crane must be disassembled for rewinding of line. R. LaVoie Collection.   **--   --   90   110**

2317 DRAWBRIDGE: 1975-81, tan base, dark brown plastic piers, dark gray span, gray supports, five pressure binding posts visible on right side of illustration, olive green tender house with light brown roof, dark brown door and steps, with one full length of O27 track and two half sections. Very complex to wire, but excellent operating action. C. Rohlfling Collection.   -- 25 40 60

2318 CONTROL TOWER: 1983-84, yellow building, black superstructure, gray base (postwar 192 predecessor had orange and green colors). Two men move in circles around the building interior; powered by vibrator motor. Caution: many examples of both the postwar accessory and this version have damaged roofs caused by heat from the light bulb. The socket cannot be bent down, since the men pass under it. To prevent roof damage, replace the 14-volt light bulb supplied with the accessory with an 18-volt bayonet bulb. Fasten aluminum foil, shiny side out, to the underside of the roof just above the light bulb. Reissued in new colors and new number in 1987. R. LaVoie comments.

(A) Red tower roof, Mexican production. Possibly scarcer than (B), but more reader observations needed. R. LaVoie Collection.   -- -- 55 65
(B) Maroon tower roof, Mount Clemens production.   -- -- 55 65

2319 WATCHTOWER: 1975-80, lighted non-operating version of postwar 445 Switch Tower. White body, maroon base and staircase, Penn Central green roof, red chimney, green door and window inserts.   -- 15 20 30

2320 FLAG POLE KIT: 1983-87, reissue of 89 from 1956-58. Reader comments on the similarities and differences between 89 and 2320 would be appreciated.   -- -- 3 5

2321 SAWMILL: 1984-85, reissue of American Flyer accessory of late 1950s. Dark red base, light tan house structures, dark green roofs, black metal lumber pickup mechanism, light tan fake sawdust pile, gray circular saw blade, yellow lumber cart. When accessory is activated, lumber cart goes by saw blade, simulating cutting of log. Finished lumber plank emerges from compartment in house, where it is picked up by mechanism and lifted into waiting trackside gondola or flatcar.   -- -- 60 100

2323 OPERATING FREIGHT STATION: 1984-85, essentially similar to postwar 356. Dark red base, black baggage cart pathway, light tan housing, dark green roof, two green luggage carts, stick-on billboards, black fence with poster ads. Baggage carts move around station in alternation. Earliest production suffered from warped bases.   -- -- 50 65

2324 OPERATING SWITCH TOWER: 1984-85, essentially similar to postwar 445. Dark red base, steps, and upper doorway, tan building with dark brown door and window inserts, brown balcony, dark green roof with red chimney. One man runs into station house; other man comes down stairs; illuminated. Postwar man on stairs carries lantern in left hand; this version has a right-handed man. Some examples observed with left-handed man; probable use of postwar leftover figure, even this late after postwar years. R. Sigurdson observation.

                -- -- 55 65

Here is a close-up of the beacon unit used on the 2494 Rotating Beacon. Note the all-plastic black lens holder, as opposed to the metal unit of the postwar 494 model. Just below the plastic lens holder is a round separate metal collar which covered the vibrator motor. The postwar unit was all metal and all in one piece. This unit works a little better than its postwar predecessor.

2494 ROTARY BEACON: 1972-74, red sheet metal tower with revolving beacon powered by vibrator motor, beacon projects red and green illumination, over 11-1/2" high, red-stamped metal base 5" x 5"; black ladder, black-lettered aluminized foil nameplate on base, two clips on underside of base for wires. Construction of light hood differs from postwar 494; black plastic light hood rotates on circular metal collar which is frequently missing from used examples. Box at one time made by Stone Container Corporation; some have glue-on paper overlay with black and white picture of accessory, while other boxes lack this picture. This is one of the scarcest of all the Fundimensions accessories. Some versions are known to have been issued with leftover postwar beacon tops instead of new assemblies. G. Cole, G. Halverson, and R. LaVoie comments; G. Halverson, Kruelle, and R. LaVoie Collections.

(A) Silver beacon heads.   20 30 40 50
(B) Black beacon heads.   20 30 50 75

2709 RICO STATION: 1981-83, large plastic kit; 22" long by 9" wide, different versions were reportedly made. The 2797 from 1976 was made in different colors. Reader comments about specific colors appreciated.   -- 10 15 25

2710 BILLBOARDS: 1970-84, five plastic frames in box with strip of five billboards. Earliest cardstock billboards have lavender bordering instead of dark green used on postwar examples; green frames have "STANDARD" in oval on ribbed bottom. Inside of frames stamped "2710 BILL BOARD MT. CLEMENS, MICH. / MADE IN U.S.A." and Lionel logo.

(A) Type I box dated 8-70, five dark green leftover postwar frames with 310 markings, strip of five public service and other billboards: U. S. Bonds (2), Education (2), and "Get A Dodge." (1). J. R. Hunt and R. LaVoie Collections.
                3 4 5 6
(B) Same as (A), but billboards differ: Sheraton, MPC, Kenner, Parker Brothers, and Lionel. R. LaVoie Collection.   3 4 5 6
(C) 1970-72, same as (A), but light green frames, MPC logo on inside of frame, Type I box. One sample observed had one dark green postwar and four Fundimensions frames. J. R. Hunt, R. LaVoie, and G. Halverson Collections.
                3 4 5 6
(D) 1973-84, slightly darker green frames, Type II or Type III box, Lionel logo on inside of frame.   1 2 3 4

FUNDIMENSIONS BILLBOARD LISTINGS

The following is our second listing of billboards produced by Lionel since 1970. Unless otherwise stated, dates reflect catalogue period for a particular billboard. We welcome additions to this list, especially since we suspect that there are many more uncatalogued billboards in existence. In addition, descriptions of the color and lettering schemes are needed with some of the billboards. The examples listed are from the collections of I. D. Smith, G. Halverson, S. Hutchings, J. Sawruk, and R. LaVoie.

1. "BUY U. S. SAVINGS BONDS", 1970-71, stack of $50 bonds wrapped in red, white, and blue flag wrapper on white background.
2. "EDUCATION IS FOR THE BIRDS (The Birds Who Want To Get Ahead)", 1970-71, uncatalogued; blue and red lettering on plain white background.
3. "GET A DODGE.", 1970-71, uncatalogued; cartoon figure of mule in brown tones, blue lettering on white background.
4. SHERATON HOTELS, 1970-71, blue and red rectangles; black lettering and black Sheraton logo.
5. BETTY CROCKER, 1970, blue script lettering on white background.
6. CHEERIOS, 1970, blue General Mills "G" and red lettering on white background.
7. LIONEL MPC, 1970-71, red "LIONEL" in modern typeface; red and blue lettering; red and blue MPC logo on white background.
8. AUTOLITE, 1970-71, uncatalogued; "Autolite Small Engine Spark Plugs For Work Or Play," red, black, and maroon lettering, green and blue rectangles with lawn mower and motorcycle.
9. PLAY-DOH, 1970-71, uncatalogued; "America's Favorite" in blue; child pulls can of Play-Doh on red wagon.
10. FOAM VILLAGE FOR LIONEL BY MYCO, 1971, uncatalogued; conveyor belt carries housing structures out of factory, black "Imagineering for Packaging & Material Handling Systems", yellow background with black conveyor and green building with black "My-T-Veyor" lettering and logo; very hard to find.
11. LIONEL, 1972-84, picture of Santa Fe F-3 locomotive in red, silver, black, and yellow; "LIONEL" in modern red typeface.

12. FAMOUS PARKER GAMES, 1971-76, dark orange background, black lettering and black Parker Brothers "swirl" logo.

13. CRAFT MASTER, 1971-84, blue square at left with black and white Craft Master logo and white lettering, light brown portrait of mountain range at right.

14. MPC MODEL KITS, 1971-84, dark blue and white MPC logo, red lettering, cars, rocket, and train on yellow and white background.

15. KENNER TOYS, 1972-76, yellow and red cartoon bird at right, white lettering on blue background.

16. SCHLITZ BEER, 1977-84, beer can and white lettering on red background.

17. BABY RUTH, 1977-84, picture of candy bar wrapper, red lettering on white background.

18. NIBCO WASHERLESS FAUCETS, 1982, uncatalogued; black Nibco logo, red lettering, and picture of faucet on white background.

19. RIDE THE NIBCO EXPRESS, 1982, uncatalogued; black and white lettering and script on dark red background.

20. "TAPPAN IS COOKING"; white lettering on black background, "LIONEL" with red, silver, and yellow Santa Fe set, came with 7908 Tappan car as part of special promotional set; hard to find. S. Hutchings and J. Sawruk Collections.

21. T C A CONVENTION billboard; description needed.

22. T C A CONVENTION billboard; description needed.

23A-23B. New double-sided 12707 Billboard. Side A: "Buy U. S. Savings Bonds" in black to left of American flag on white background. Side B: red "Adopt-A-Pet" and white "Support Your Local Humane Society" on blue background with picture of puppy and kitten.

24A-24B. New double-sided billboard with 12707 frames. Side A: large white "BUCKLE UP!" and black "For Safety's Sake" above black seat belt on medium green background. Side B: red "Keep America Beautiful" atop dark, medium, and light blue and gray stylized mountain pass with white background.

25A-25B. New double-sided billboard with 12707 frames. Side A: black "READ...AND KNOW THE WORLD!" with multicolored balloon, airplane, Oriental child, locomotive, windmill, etc. on white background. Side B: black "Take The Train" below large red, white, and blue "AMERICAN FLYER LINES" shield logo on white background.

2714 TUNNEL: 1975-77, 15-1/2" x 13-1/2" x 10", two-piece construction.

2	3	5	7

2717 SHORT EXTENSION BRIDGE: 1977-83, 10" x 6-1/2" x 4-1/2"; plastic kit.

--	2	3	5

2718 BARREL PLATFORM: 1977-83, plastic kit includes figure, barrels, tools, lamp, ladder, and building, 4" x 4" x 3-1/2".

--	1	2	4

2719 SIGNAL TOWER: 1977-83, described as "Watchman Shanty" in catalogue; 7" high, 4" x 4-1/2", plastic kit.

--	1	2	4

2720 LUMBER SHED: 1977-83, plastic kit includes workman, shed, table, lumber, tools, ladder; 4" high, 6" long, 3-1/2" wide .

--	1	2	4

2721 LOG LOADING MILL: 1979, red plastic kit, manual operation, pressing a lever causes plastic log to be released and roll down ramp; part of inexpensive "Workin' On The Railroad" Sets. **NRS**

2722 BARREL LOADER: 1979, green plastic kit, manual operation, workman pushes barrel down a chute; part of inexpensive "Workin' On The Railroad" Sets.

--	--	3	5

2723 BARREL LOADER: 1984, brown plastic kit, manual operation, workman pushes barrel down chute; part of Set 1403.

--	--	3	5

2729 WATER TOWER BUILDING KIT: 1985, orange-brown pump house with gray door and window insert, light tan base, gray ladder, green tower support frame, light tan tank, gray spout, green tank roof. Pictured in the 1985 Traditional Catalogue, but canceled from dealer order sheets in September 1985. Water tower kit in same colors released in 1987 as 12711. **Not Manufactured**

2783 MANUAL FREIGHT STATION KIT: 1981-83.

--	--	7	10

2784 FREIGHT PLATFORM: 1981-87, snap-together realistic O scale plastic kit with opening door.

2	3	6	9

2785 ENGINE HOUSE: 1974-77, plastic kit. Very similar kits have been produced in the past few years by Pola and others. This kit is very hard to find. Reissued in 1987 as 12710.

--	20	30	40

2786 FREIGHT PLATFORM: 1974-77, freight shed with platform, plastic kit.

--	3	4	7

2787 FREIGHT STATION: 1974-77, 1983, highly detailed O scale plastic kit.

3	5	7	10

2788 COALING STATION: 1975-77, plastic kit, coal may be mechanically dumped. Hard to find. Reissued in 1988 as 12736 in different colors.

5	10	20	40

2789 WATER TOWER: 1975-80, water tower on brick structure, plastic kit.

--	3	7	10

2790 BUILDING KIT ASSORTMENT: 1983, details needed. **NRS**

2791 CROSS COUNTRY SET: 1970-71, Type I box, five telephone poles, twelve railroad signs, watchman's shanty with crossing gate; 17-1/4" black trestle bridge; contents wrapped in brown paper inside box. Hard to find in unused condition. G. Halverson Collection.

--	5	10	25

2792 LAYOUT STARTER PAK: 1980-83, snap-together extension bridge kit, barrel platform kit, lumber shed kit, 10 telephone poles, 14 road signs, five billboards, and a Track Layout Book.

--	--	10	25

2792 WHISTLE STOP SET: 1970-71, contains signal bridge, watchman's shanty with crossing gate, freight loading platform with baggage accessories, and five telephone poles. C. Rohlfing Collection.

5	10	15	25

2793 ALAMO JUNCTION SET: 1970-71, contains water tank with gray base, framework, and roof, brown tank; switch tower with brown base, steps, roof, and doors, gray sides; watchman shanty with gray base, roof, and windows, brown building, black and white crossing gate; five light brown telephone poles. R. La-Voie Collection.

--	--	--	25

2796 GRAIN ELEVATOR: 1977, 16" high, 16" long, 13" wide, plastic kit. Very hard to find. Reissued in 1988 as 12726 in different colors.

--	20	60	75

2797 RICO STATION: 1976, large plastic kit 22" x 9" x 9" high, modeled after Rico, Colorado station. See also 2709.

--	20	30	45

2900 LOCKON: 1970-85.

.20	.50	1	1.25

2901 TRACK CLIPS: 1970-85, 12-pack.

--	1	2	5

2905 LOCKON & WIRE: 1972-85, blister pack.

--	.70	.85	1.50

2909 SMOKE FLUID: 1977-85, for locomotives made after 1970.

--	1	1.50	3

2927 MAINTENANCE KIT: 1970-71, 1977-87, consists of lubricant, oiler, track cleaning fluid, track cleaner, rubber eraser, all mounted on a piece of cardboard and shrink-wrapped.

(A) Type I packaging (same scheme as Type I box), oil, lubricant, eraser-type track cleaner, and liquid track cleaner; materials are leftover postwar production with Hillside, New Jersey factory address. G. Halverson and R. LaVoie Collections.

--	--	7	10

(B) Type II or III packaging, Fundimensions-produced materials.

1	2	3	5

2951 TRACK LAYOUT BOOK: 1976-80, 1983, several editions have been issued; see paper listings.

--	.50	.75	2

2952 TRACK ACCESSORY MANUAL: See paper listings.

--	--	.75	1

2953 TRAIN & ACCESSORY MANUAL: 1977-85, several editions have been issued; see paper listings.

--	--	1.25	2

2960 LIONEL 75TH ANNIVERSARY BOOK: 1975, blue cover with 75th Anniversary logo.

--	6	8	10

2980 MAGNETIC CONVERSION COUPLER: 1979 and probably other years as well, kit for replacing other types of couplers with magnetic operating couplers. Consists of plate assembly and coupler. I. D. Smith comment.

--	--	1	2

2985 LIONEL TRAIN BOOK: 1986.

--	--	--	7

8190 DIESEL HORN: 1981, electronic package that can be adapted to engines or rolling stock, operated by whistle button on older transformer. Type V box includes circuit board, speaker, two double-sided adhesive pads, and instructions. Roller pickup assembly must be purchased separately if it is needed; unit can be installed with existing roller pickups. Price for unused unit only.

--	--	--	25

8251-50 HORN/WHISTLE CONTROLLER: 1972-74, rectangular push-button box for early Fundimensions horns and whistles. Easily burned out if contacts stick in closed position, as they often did. Came in black or red case with matching push button. R. LaVoie comment, G. Halverson Collection.

--	--	2	3

9195 ROLLING STOCK ASSORTMENT: 1979. Lionel offered a 12-car assortment of its inexpensive cars for mass market sales (contrasted with collector market sales). Lionel provided two each from the following categories: short box-car, short hopper, long gondola, short tank, work caboose, and flatcar with fences. Each car has Bettendorf plastic trucks with one operating disc coupler and one fixed coupler. However, the specific road names and colors included probably changed during the production period to fit Fundimensions' convenience. We would appreciate reader listings of the contents of their assortments. Some cars needed assembly by purchaser. Bohn comment.

12700 ERIE-LACKAWANNA: 1987, magnetic gantry crane, black gantry frame and platform with white-outlined "LIONEL", gray crane body and boom, yellow cab base and gear, maroon crane cab roof, black magnet picks up loads as did predecessor from postwar years, 282R. -- -- **150 175**

12701 DIESEL FUELING STATION: 1987, dark blue housing on gray base, gray roof, orange sand tower stand and pipe base, black piping, black sand tank with yellow "DIESEL SAND", light gray man with flesh-colored face appears to come from house to fuel hose when button is pressed. Essentially similar to postwar 415 accessory. -- -- **75 90**

12702 OPERATING CONTROL TOWER: 1987, see 2318 entries for earlier versions. This version operates the same but has new colors: red tower house with black roof and platform, black base, red ladders, gray superstructure with red "LIONEL". White arrow and weathervane atop roof. Unlike 2318 version, has aluminum paper shield to prevent roof damage. -- -- **50 65**

12703 ICING STATION: 1988. -- -- -- **64**

12704 DWARF SIGNAL: Scheduled for 1988, maroon signal body, black lens hood, red and green lights operate by means of 153C Contactor (unlike postwar design, which was manually operated). -- -- -- **18**

12705 LUMBER SHED: Scheduled for 1988, black shed structure, black base, dark tan awnings, light tan roof supports, light tan simulated lumber stacks, unpainted gray man. -- -- -- **6**

12706 BARREL LOADER BUILDING: 1987, all-gray platform, barrels, man, barrel chute, and shack; manual turn of lever sends barrel out chute into car. Sold in kit form. -- -- -- **5**

12707 BILLBOARD SET: 1987-88, three large white plastic frames in a new design supplied with three double-sided billboards. Frames fit into white plastic bases, and billboard sheet is folded in half and slid into slot in frame. Includes instruction sheet 71-2707-250. Type VI box. R. LaVoie Collection.
 -- -- **5 6**

12708 STREET LAMPS: 1988, new design, black base and pole, white opaque rounded globe atop pole. Sold in sets of three. -- -- -- **8**

12709 OPERATING BANJO SIGNAL: 1987, same design and operation as 2140, but die-cast frame painted tuscan instead of black. -- -- -- **26**

12710 ENGINE HOUSE: 1987, revival of 2285 from 1975-76; brick red building, black doors and windows, gray roof, measures 20-1/2" x 6-1/8" x 7-1/8".
 -- -- -- **20**

12711 WATER TOWER KIT: 1987, revival of 2789; identical in catalogue appearance to 2729 which appeared in 1985 catalogue but was never produced; colors may differ from catalogue illustration when issued. -- -- -- **11**

12712 AUTOMATIC ORE LOADER: 1987, revival of 2175 "Sandy Andy" Ore Loader in new colors. Bright blue base, roofs, and chute roof, yellow elevator tower and structure, gray tower supports, yellow ore car tracks, gray ore car. Comes with ore and gray dumping bin. -- -- -- **20**

12713 AUTOMATIC GATEMAN: 1987, the longest-lived of all Lionel accessories returns in new colors after a two-year absence. Light tan base, green cardboard base bottom (we would like to know if some earlier 2145 versions also have this base), door stop "bump" designed into metal base, bright yellow shack, red roof and toolbox lid, light gray man with red lantern, white crossbuck with black lettering and metal base. Still illuminated by 431 large-base bayonet bulb present with this accessory since 1950, but cardboard shield added to this version to prevent translucence. -- -- -- **35**

12714 AUTOMATIC CROSSING GATE: 1987, same design as 2152, but new colors: gray base, red safety stripes, brown plastic gate stop rod, Type VI box.
 -- -- -- **22**

12715 ILLUMINATED BUMPERS: 1987, two per package, Type VI box. Same design as 2290, but tuscan in color. -- -- -- **5**

12716 SEARCHLIGHT TOWER: 1987, same design as 2314, but new colors: light gray base and tower platform, bright orange tower structure, black searchlight hoods. -- -- -- **25**

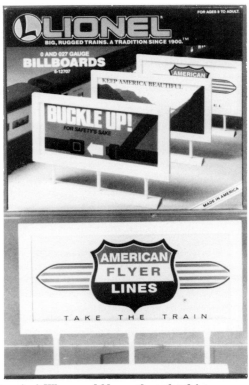

Irony of ironies! Who would have thought thirty years ago that a Lionel billboard set would ever advertise an American Flyer train! This is one of the three two-sided billboards found in the 12707 Billboard Set of 1987-88.

12717 BUMPERS: 1987, non-illuminated. Same design as 2280, but tuscan in color. Three per package. -- -- -- **3**

12718 BARREL SHED KIT: 1987, light tan base and platform, black platform supports, tan man, white barrels, white house with black roof and door. Catalogue illustration may show custom-painted example; most likely will come in all-tan kit. -- -- -- **5**

12719 ANIMATED REFRESHMENT STAND: 1988, redesign of Animated Newsstand. Light gray base, white shed, light green roof, red and white lettering, checkerboard countertop. White-clad attendant moves to front, boy and girl figures rotate, and giant ice cream cone spins. Expected to be in great demand.
 -- -- -- **65**

12720 ROTARY BEACON: 1988. Essentially similar to 2494, but has black tower top piece instead of all-red design. -- -- -- **36**

12722 ROADSIDE DINER WITH SMOKE: 1988, 9500-type passenger car body mounted on dark gray base. Light tan body, red roof, black chimneys, black sign with white "LIONELVILLE DINER" lettering, illuminated, smoke from largest chimney, silhouettes in windows. -- -- -- **40**

12723 MICROWAVE RELAY TOWER: 1988, dark gray base, bright orange tower structure, white radar dish, light blinks thermostatically, remake of scarce 2199 model of 1972, but in new colors. -- -- -- **20**

12724 SIGNAL BRIDGE: 1988, black metal girder structure, light gray plastic bases, two black plastic two-light lens hoods. Essentially similar to postwar 450 model. -- -- -- **40**

12725 LIONEL: Scheduled for 1988, but will not be produced this year. Tractor and trailer. **Not Manufactured**

12726 GRAIN ELEVATOR: 1988, light tan building sides, light gray roof pieces, black platform. Appears to be a remake of the scarce 2796 Grain Elevator kit of 1976-77. -- -- -- **22**

12729 MAIL PICKUP SET: 1988, black base, red pole, semaphore arm, and swinging arm, large red magnetic mailbag. Essentially similar to scarce 161 model of 1961-63. -- -- -- **18**

12730 PLATE GIRDER BRIDGE: 1988, black plastic sides, white-outlined "LIONEL" lettering, chemically blackened metal base. Sold knocked down to be assembled by purchaser. Nearly a direct remake of the postwar 214 model.

-- -- -- 7

12731 STATION PLATFORM: 1988, red roof, dark green base, black tower supports, signs on fence include Coca-Cola, Lionel, Inc., three chromed acorn nuts fasten supports to roof.

-- -- -- 7

12732 COAL BAG: 1988, four ounces of plastic coal pieces packed in white sack with red lettering and logo and string tie. Essentially similar to postwar 206 Coal Sack.

-- -- -- 2.50

12733 WATCHMAN'S SHANTY: 1988, dark red-brown house, black roof, light gray steps and stairway, light gray base.

-- -- -- 6

12735 DIESEL HORN SHED: 1988, uses design of postwar 114 Newsstand with Horn. Light tan house, dark brown roof and window edging, dark brown base, frosted window inserts, illuminated.

-- -- -- 30

12736 COALING STATION: 1988, red-brown lower tower, dark tan housing, light gray roof, dark gray tipple structure and housing.

-- -- -- 22

12737 WHISTLING FREIGHT SHED: 1988, uses design of postwar 118 Newsstand with whistle. Dark maroon building, white window edging, black roof, door, and base, illuminated.

-- -- -- 30

12740 LOG PACKAGE: 1988, set of three real wood logs with bark to retrofit log dump cars and to supply flatcar loads.

-- -- -- 2.50

TRANSFORMERS

4044: 1970-71, 45-watt transformer, black and brown marbled plastic case, metal lever controls speed, two binding posts. H. Edmunds Collection.

-- -- 3 5

4045 SAFETY TRANSFORMER: 1970-71, black case, variable AC output, lever controls speed, automatic circuit breaker, two binding posts with one serving as forward and reverse button, 45-watt output. G. Halverson Collection.

1 2 3 4

4050 SAFETY TRANSFORMER: 1972-79.
(A) Red case. 1 2 3 4
(B) Blue case. 1 2 3 4

4060 POWER MASTER: 1980-87, black case, fixed AC and variable DC output, direction reverse switch, atomatic circuit breaker. 6 9 12 30

4065 DC HOBBY TRANSFORMER: 1981-83; black plastic case, white lettering, red speed control lever, reversing switch, 0-18 VDC, 19VAC. D. Anderson and C. Rohlfing Collections. -- -- 3 4

4090 POWER MASTER: 1970-81, 1983, AC output, right lever controls speed, left lever controls direction; fixed voltage taps, automatic circuit breaker, 90 watts. 10 25 40 55

4125 TRANSFORMER: 1972, 25 watts.
(A) Light blue case. C. Rohlfing Collection. 1 2 3 4
(B) Light maroon case. C. Rohlfing Collection. 1 2 3 4

4150 MULTIVOLT TOY TRANSFORMER: 1976-78, 50-watt AC output, blue plastic case, bright metal or black plastic speed control lever. D. Anderson Collection. -- 3 6 12

4250 TRAIN MASTER TRANSFORMER: -- 3 6 12

4651 TRAIN MASTER: 1978-79, lever controls speed, two posts with button on one post for forward and reverse, automatic circuit breaker.

-- -- 2 3

4690 TYPE MW TRANSFORMER: 1986-87, black metal case, orange knobs and buttons, red, white, and blue Lionel logo, white lettering. Power-off switch (the first in any Lionel transformer, incredibly), 0-17 VAC output, variable accessory voltage knob can also be used to power a second train; solid state construction, variable intensity indicator lights for track and accessory lines, power-on light, horn-whistle, and directional buttons, circuit breaker. This is Lionel's first truly modern transformer; it is somewhat like those which were issued by Model Power and Tech II some years ago. -- -- -- 85

4851 TRANSFORMER: 1987-88, 15 VA, red case, black plastic handle. C. Rohlfing Collection. 1 2 3 4

4870 HOBBY TRANSFORMER AND THROTTLE CONTROL: 1977-78, consists of two pieces: a small black plastic wall-plug AC transformer and a red plastic throttle control. Transformer marked "Made In Taiwan", but throttle control marked "Mt. Clemens, Mich." Similar to arrangements found in racing car sets. D. Anderson Collection. -- -- 3 4

5900 AC/DC CONVERTER: 1979-81, 1983. -- -- 4 6

O27 TRACK

5012 CURVED TRACK: 1980, 1983, four on card. -- -- 2.20 3.50

5013 CURVED TRACK: .10 .30 .50 .55

5014 HALF-CURVED TRACK: 1980-83. .20 .40 .50 .75

5016 3-FOOT STRAIGHT SECTION: 1987. -- -- -- 2.25

5017 STRAIGHT TRACK: 1980-83, four on card. -- -- 3.50 3.50

5018 STRAIGHT TRACK: .20 .40 .50 .75

5019 HALF-STRAIGHT TRACK: .20 .40 .50 .75

5020 90 DEGREE CROSSOVER: 1.50 3 3.50 4.75

5023 45 DEGREE CROSSOVER: 1.50 3 4 6.50

5024 STRAIGHT TRACK: 35-inch. -- -- -- 2.25

5025 MANUMATIC UNCOUPLER: 1971-75, small Type I box with three black plastic uncoupling devices which clamp to track. Pushing a button raises two extensions between the rails; these are supposed to catch the coupler discs and pull them down. As a rule, these uncouplers do not work very well. Packed three to a box; instructions printed on the box. G. Halverson and R. LaVoie Collections. -- -- 1 2

5030 TRACK EXPANDER SET: 1972 Catalogue refers to this as "Switch Layout Expander Set." Type I box. Contains pair of manual switches, two sections of curved O27 track and six sections of straight O27 track. Made for distribution in Canada by Parker Brothers. See next entry for American production. G. Halverson Collection. -- -- -- 25

5030 LAYOUT BUILDER SET: 1978-80, 1983, pair of manual switches, two curved, six straight track. 10 14 17 25

5033 CURVED TRACK: Bulk packed, but sold individually. .10 .20 .30 .75

5038 STRAIGHT TRACK: Bulk packed, but sold individually. .10 .20 .30 .75

5041 O27 INSULATOR PINS: 12 per pack. -- -- .50 1

5042 O27 STEEL PINS: 12 per pack. -- -- .40 .75

5044 O42 CURVED BALLAST: Price per piece. -- -- -- 2.25

5045 O27 WIDE RADIUS BALLAST PIECE: 1987, molded gray flexible rubber ballast. -- -- -- 2.25

5046 O27 CURVED TRACK BALLAST PIECE: 1987. -- -- -- 2.25

5047 O27 STRAIGHT TRACK BALLAST PIECE: 1987. -- -- -- 2.25

5049 O42 CURVED TRACK: Price per piece. -- -- -- 1.10

5113 O27 WIDE RADIUS TRACK: 16 sections make a 54 inch diameter circle per piece. -- -- 1.10 1.50

5149 REMOTE UNCOUPLING TRACK: -- 2.50 3.50 7.25

O27 SWITCHES

5021 MANUAL SWITCH: Left. 4 7 8 13

5022 MANUAL SWITCH: Right. 4 7 8 13

5027 PAIR MANUAL SWITCHES: 8 13 15 26

5090 THREE PAIR MANUAL SWITCHES: 1983. -- -- 60 80

5121 REMOTE SWITCH: Left. 7 11 14 20

5122 REMOTE SWITCH: Right. 7 11 14 20

5125 PAIR REMOTE SWITCHES: 14 20 28 40

5167 O42 REMOTE SWITCH: Right. -- -- -- 25

5168 O42 REMOTE SWITCH: Left. -- -- -- 25

5823 45-DEGREE CROSSOVER: Type I or Type II shrink-wrap packaging, comes in light brown or dark brown base. G. Halverson Collection.

-- -- 4 6

O GAUGE TRACK, SWITCHES, AND UNCOUPLERS

550C CURVED TRACK: 1970, 10-7/8" long.   .25 .30 .75 1.25

550S STRAIGHT TRACK: 1970, 10" long.   .25 .30 .75 1.25

UCS REMOTE CONTROL TRACK: 1970, accessory rails, two-button controller, magnet.   2 3 5 8

5132 REMOTE SWITCH, RIGHT: With controller.   15 20 33 40

5133 REMOTE SWITCH, LEFT: With controller.   15 20 33 40

5165 O72 WIDE RADIUS REMOTE SWITCH: 1987, left-hand, with controller. This and its right-hand version are revivals of the prewar 711 wide-radius Model Builder's switches and are expected to meet with great popularity among Lionel operators.   -- -- -- 50

5166 O72 WIDE RADIUS REMOTE SWITCH: 1987.   -- -- -- 50

5193 THREE PAIR REMOTE SWITCHES: 1983.   -- -- 90 110

5500 STRAIGHT TRACK: 1971, 10" long.   -- .30 .75 1.25

5501 CURVED TRACK: 1971, 10-7/8" long.   -- .30 .75 1.25

5502 REMOTE CONTROL TRACK: 1971, 10" long.   2 3 5 8

5504 HALF CURVED SECTION: -- -- -- 1.05

5505 HALF STRAIGHT SECTION: -- -- -- 1.05

5510 CURVED TRACK: -- .30 .75 1.25

5520 90 DEGREE CROSSOVER: 1971.   2 3 5 7

5522 THREE-FOOT O GAUGE STRAIGHT TRACK SECTION: 1987.   -- -- -- 3.75

5523 STRAIGHT SECTION: 40-inch.   -- -- -- 5

5530 REMOTE UNCOUPLING SECTION: With controller.   6 9 11 13

5540 90 DEGREE CROSSOVER: 3 5 7 8

5543 INSULATOR PINS: 1970, 12 per pack.   .25 .50 .75 1

5545 45 DEGREE CROSSOVER: 1982.   -- -- -- 13

5551 STEEL PINS: 1970, 12 per pack.   .25 .50 .75 1

5560 WIDE RADIUS CURVED TRACK BALLAST PIECE: 1987.   -- -- -- 2.25

5561 CURVED TRACK BALLAST PIECE: 1987.   -- -- -- 2.25

5562 STRAIGHT TRACK BALLAST PIECE: 1987.   -- -- -- 2.25

5572 WIDE RADIUS CURVED TRACK: 16 pieces make a circle with a 72" diameter. Price per piece.   .50 .75 1.25 2

TRUTRACK SYSTEM ITEMS: 1973-74

In 1973 and 1974 Fundimensions attempted a major innovation in its operating system with the introduction of "Trutrack." Trutrack featured a realistic T-shaped rail made from aluminum, wood-grained plastic ties at relatively close intervals, wide-radius curves, and a thin, less conspicuous center rail. The track used a snap-lock assembly with rail joiners. The system featured separate pieces of rubberized ballasted roadbed which snapped onto each track or switch piece. The ballasted roadbed is more plastic than rubber, but it is flexible. The 1973 catalogue listed remote and manual switches, switch roadbed, and lockons, as well as the straight and curved track sections and their roadbed pieces. In 1973 the right manual switches caused derailments because they would not lock tightly, so in 1974 the mechanism was changed and improved for the manual switches. Unfortunately, aluminum track is not compatible with Magnetraction. Although some sources have stated that Fundimensions had problems with the switches, which were supposed to have been made in Italy, we suspect that the incompatibility with Magnetraction is the reason why the track was dropped from production after only small amounts were produced, since Magnetraction was more impor-

tant to Lionel's operating system than an improved track appearance. We have updated our lists of Trutrack which actually reached production since our first edition; more was actually produced than was first believed. F. Vergonet and G. Halverson comments.

5600 CURVED TRACK: 1973. F. Vergonet Collection.   -- -- -- 1.75

5601 CARD OF FOUR CURVED TRACK: 1973. F. Vergonet Collection.   -- -- -- 7

5602 CARD OF FOUR ROADBED BALLAST FOR CURVED TRACK: 1973-74, actually came fastened together with rubber band inside packaging. G. Halverson and F. Vergonet Collections.   -- -- 4 7

5605 STRAIGHT TRACK: 1973. F. Vergonet, R. LaVoie, and G. Halverson Collections.   -- -- 1 2

5606 CARD OF FOUR STRAIGHT TRACK: 1973, actually came fastened with rubber band inside packaging. F. Vergonet and G. Halverson Collections.   -- -- 4 8

5607 CARD OF FOUR ROADBED BALLAST FOR STRAIGHT TRACK: 1973, actually came fastened together with rubber band inside packaging, Type II packaging. F. Vergonet and G. Halverson Collections.   -- -- 4 8

5620 LEFT MANUAL SWITCH: 1973-74, not distributed for sale, but some became available.
(A) First production, 1973. F. Vergonet Collection.   -- -- -- 25
(B) Second production, 1974; redesigned mechanism. F. Vergonet Collection.   -- -- -- 30

5625 LEFT REMOTE SWITCH: 1973. F. Vergonet Collection.   NRS

5630 RIGHT MANUAL SWITCH: 1973.
(A) First production, 1973. F. Vergonet Collection.   -- -- -- 25
(B) Second production, 1974, redesigned mechanism. F. Vergonet Collection.   -- -- -- 35

5635 RIGHT REMOTE SWITCH: 1973. F. Vergonet Collection.   NRS

5640 CARD OF TWO LEFT SWITCH ROADBED PIECES: 1973. F. Vergonet Collection.   -- -- -- 10

5650 CARD OF TWO RIGHT SWITCH ROADBED PIECES: 1973. F. Vergonet Collection.   -- -- -- 8

5655 LOCKON: 1973. F. Vergonet Collection.   -- -- -- 1.50

5660 CARD OF ONE TERMINAL TRACK WITH LOCKON: 1973. F. Vergonet Collection.   -- -- -- 3.50

PERIPHERAL ITEMS

JC-1 LIONEL JOHNNY CASH RECORD ALBUM: 33-1/3 speed.   -- 2 3 6

7-1100 HAPPY HUFF'N PUFF: 1975, train set, Fundimensions pre-school toy push train similar to those made by Fisher-Price and Playskool, whimsical old-fashioned four-wheel steamer and two gondolas embossed with two large squares on their sides. Train is made of plastic simulated to look like wood. Wheels fastened with metal axles. Locomotive has smile-mouth and eye decorations. Came with a circle of two-rail plastic track and a story booklet showing "how Happy Huff'n Puff got his name". Bohn and LaVoie comments.   -- 30 40 60

Note: HUFF 'N PUFF BOOKLET: 1975.   -- -- -- .25

7-1200 GRAVEL GUS: 1975, a three-piece road construction set consisting of a grader with a large squared head seated on the chassis (presumably Gus) and two side dump cars. The grader has four large wheels and swivels in the center with a removable pusher blade. The two cars each have one axle with two large wheels, with the first car resting on the grader and the second car resting on the rear of the first car. The set is made from plastic simulated to resemble wood. It came with a full-color story booklet. Weisblum comment.   -- -- 15 20

7-1300 GRAVEL GUS JUNIOR: 1975, appears to be identical to 7-1200 Gravel Gus, except has only one side dump car. Bohn comment.   -- -- 15 20

7-1400 HAPPY HUFF'N PUFF JUNIOR: 1975, essentially similar to 7-1100 Happy Huff'n Puff, except does not include circle of track, locomotive has much thicker smokestack, and gondolas are not embossed with large squares. These four pre-school toys were apparently offered only in 1975 through large toy outlets. Their success would have been an asset to Fundimensions, but they were launched into the teeth of a highly competitive pre-school market long dominated by giants such as Fisher-Price and Playskool. Bohn and LaVoie comments.

-- -- **40** **65**

2390 LIONEL MIRROR: 1982, old-fashioned mirror with dark walnut wood frame, gold, red, and black decoration showing 1920-era picture of Lawrence Cowen with train set at base of antiqued gold archway. Gold lettering, "LIONEL ELECTRIC TRAINS, THE STANDARD OF THE WORLD SINCE 1900". Also "COPYRIGHT 1981 GPC". Anderson and R. LaVoie Collections.

-- -- **50** **65**

NO NUMBER BELT BUCKLE: 1981, solid antique brass, Lionel logo. A. Passman Collection. -- -- **15** **20**

NO NUMBER LIONEL CLOCK: 1976-77, made by American Sign and Advertising Services, Inc., 7430 Industrial Road, Industrial Park, Lawrence, Kentucky, 41042; white dial with black hand, red second hand, red field on bottom with white "LIONEL", available to Service Stations for $20 to $25.

-- -- **50** **60**

NO NUMBER LIONEL PENNANT: Plastic, white background, black trim on edge, black "LIONEL", left arrow red, right side arrow blue, "A LIFETIME INVESTMENT IN HAPPINESS" in black; 45" wide, 29-1/2" high.

-- -- **2** **4**

NO NUMBER BLACK CAVE VINYL PLAYMAT: 1982, from 1254 Black Cave Flyer Set; 30" x 40"; from Set 1355. -- -- -- **10**

NO NUMBER COMMANDO ASSAULT TRAIN PLAYMAT: 1983, 30" x 40"; from Set 1355. -- -- -- **10**

NO NUMBER ROCKY MOUNTAIN FREIGHT PLAYMAT: 1983, 36" x 54", from Set 1352. -- -- -- **3**

NO NUMBER CANNONBALL FREIGHT VINYL PLAYMAT: 1982, 36" x 54"; two-piece mat, from Set 1155. -- -- -- **5**

NO NUMBER L. A. S. E. R. VINYL PLAYMAT: 1982, 36" x 54"; mat from Set 1150. -- -- -- **5**

NO NUMBER LIONEL PLAYING CARDS: 1975, regulation 52-card poker deck, red and black diagonal "LIONEL" logo, head-on locomotive front against background in black, wrapped in cellophane and packaged in silver and black box. R. LaVoie Collection. -- -- **1** **2**

NO NUMBER STATION PLATFORM: 1983, 23" x 3-1/2" x 5", similar to 2256 Station Platform, details requested; part of Set 1351. -- -- -- **10**

LIONEL 75TH ANNIVERSARY COLLECTION — 1975

Note: As part of this collection, Fundimensions also offered full-color reproductions of the 1937 and 1946 catalogues.

NO NUMBER T-SHIRT IRON-ON: 1975, red, white, and blue cartoon drawing of steam engine, red and blue "Keep On Trackin'!" script. Made by Mach III, Inc., red "LIONEL" on engine cab. R. LaVoie Collection. **NRS**

NO NUMBER RAILROAD LANTERN: Working metal kerosene railroad lantern, red globe, Lionel 75th Anniversary logo stamped on lid. Original mail order price $22.95. **NRS**

NO NUMBER BELT BUCKLE: Round solid pewter buckle with Lionel 75th Anniversary logo. Original mail order price $4.50. **NRS**

NO NUMBER MONEY CLIP AND PEN KNIFE: Brass-plated money clip with fold-out knife; Lionel 75th Anniversary medallion. Original mail order price $3.95. **NRS**

NO NUMBER SEW-ON PATCH: Four-inch diameter circular patch with red, silver, and black Lionel 75th Anniversary logo. Original mail order price .75 cents. **NRS**

NO NUMBER BIB OVERALL T-SHIRT: Crew-neck T-shirt with railroader's blue jean bib pattern on front and back. Original mail order price $2.50. **NRS**

NO NUMBER KEY CHAIN: Stainless steel key chain with Lionel 75th Anniversary medallion. Original mail order price $2.95. **NRS**

NO NUMBER SWITCH LOCK: Solid brass padlock with key on chain; stamped with Lionel 75th Anniversary logo. Original mail order price $11.95. **NRS**

NO NUMBER WRIST WATCH: 1986, special offer to Lionel Railroader Club members. Gold-plated case, gold dial face with circle of "track" around which a small "General"-type steam train revolves as it functions like the second hand; red, white, and blue Lionel logo on dial face, alligator-style leather wrist band. Sold for $99.95, including shipping and handling. -- -- -- **120**

NOTE: The following items numbered in the 5800 Series came as part of a brochure mailed by Lionel, Inc. in 1987. Late in the previous year, Lionel had sent out letters to dealers requesting the cessation of any unauthorized use of Lionel's name and logos. The brochure, known as "Lionel Side Tracks," illustrates that Lionel is using its own name and logos to begin its own peripheral marketing.

5800 BUMPER STICKER: Measures 3" x 14", Lionel logo, black "Made In America" on white background with black locomotive pilot. -- -- -- **1.50**

5801 LIGHTER: Disposable white butane lighter with Lionel logo and black "Lines" lettering. -- -- -- **3.50**

5802 LAPEL PIN: Enameled red, white, and blue Lionel logo.

-- -- -- **4**

5803 LICENSE PLATE: White background, dark blue edges, red and blue lettering and Lionel logo, red and black freight train. -- -- -- **4**

5804 EPOXY KEY CHAIN: Red, white, and blue Lionel logo screened and epoxied onto brass 24k gold-plated medallion attached to brass key ring.

-- -- -- **4.50**

5805 ASH TRAY: Triangular 3-1/2" glass ash tray with red, white, and blue Lionel logo. -- -- -- **6.50**

5806 COFFEE MUG: 12-ounce black ironstone mug with gold rim and gold Lionel logo. -- -- -- **7.50**

5807 SPORT CAP: Red cap with Lionel logo inside white rectangle.

-- -- -- **8**

5808 BRASS KEY CHAIN: Lionel logo and steam engine boiler front stamped into brass-finished medallion. -- -- -- **8**

5809 ENGINEER'S GLOVES: Work gloves with gray cowhide palms, thumb, fingers, and knuckle straps, blue denim collars and backs, black Lionel logo and lettering on glove collars. -- -- -- **8.50**

5810 SLEEPING BOY POSTER: R. Tyrrell poster from 1980 catalogue, 21" x 27". -- -- -- **9**

5811 NICKEL PLATE SPECIAL POSTER: Black border, painting of Nickel Plate freight, "BIG, RUGGED TRAINS SINCE 1900", 20" x 34".

-- -- -- **9**

5812 RAIL BLAZER POSTER: Red border, painting of Rail Blazer tank locomotive and freight train, "No Childhood Should Be Without A Train" lettering, 20" x 34". -- -- -- **9**

5813 (s), 5814 (m), 5815 (l), 5816 (xl) LIONEL T-SHIRT: Blue shirt with rectangular red, white, and blue Lionel logo. -- -- -- **11**

5817 PORTABLE TOOL KIT: 13-in-one ratchet-socket screwdriver folding set, black storage handle, red, blue, and chrome Lionel logo, chromed attachment piece. -- -- -- **11.50**

5818 MINI-MAG-LITE FLASHLIGHT: 5-1/2" long, engraved Lionel logo and steam engine boiler front on black metal flashlight body. -- -- -- **20**

5819 PEN AND PENCIL SET: Black matte barrels, chrome-trimmed, red, white, and blue Lionel logo on cap ends, silver "LIONEL TRAINS" embossed into barrels. -- -- -- **20**

5820 TRAVEL ALARM CLOCK: Red plastic case, quartz movement, dial with circle of track and General train moving around track, red, white, and blue Lionel logo. -- -- -- **20**

5821 BEVERAGE COASTER SET: Polished solid brass coasters with brown leather insert and central Lionel medallion, felt bottoms, oak holding tray. -- -- -- **70**

5822 WRIST WATCH: Gold-plated case and band, black watch hands, dial has circle of track with SP Daylight engine and car moving around track to function as second hand; red, white, and blue Lionel logo on dial face.

-- -- -- **110**

9195 ROLLING STOCK ASSORTMENT: 1988, four pieces of rolling stock including 6430 caboose, 9035 boxcar, 9140 gondola, 9016 hopper. R. Sigurdson comment. **NRS**

Chapter XV
FACTORY ERRORS AND PROTOTYPES

By James Sattler
with the assistance of Clark O'Dell

This is our second listing of modern era factory errors and prototypes. It is substantially expanded from our last listing.

Many collectors and dealers indiscriminately use, fail to use, or misuse the terms "prototype" and "factory error." Along with this there are many types of variations. We hope to explain these terms in the next paragraphs.

PROTOTYPES

A prototype is a one-of-a-kind item, or one of an extremely small number of items, made by Lionel prior to the time when all of the necessary tools, dies, or equipment were available to commence mass-production in order to allow the manufacturer to see what a proposed item would look like, and to study the feasibility of mass producing it.

Prototypes were built for the purpose of making production and marketing decisions. Consequently, a prototype will have one or more of the following characteristics which will readily distinguish it from any similar mass-produced item:

(A) Numbers, lettering, or logos will be hand-applied decals rather than other mass-production methods.

(B) It might not be wired or otherwise assembled for operation. Very few of these prototypes have left the factory, although some of these are legitimate.

A number of prototypes are fakes. Some counterfeit items have made their way into train meets, with the use of decals. Some people have made and sold prototypes manufactured outside of the factory. Therefore, it is always wise to ask someone with knowledge. If the price is much over the regular price, is it worth the risk?

Some prototypes were never put into production, including: 9879 Kraft Reefer, 9237 United Parcel, and 9356 Pep-O-Mint Tank Car.

COLOR VARIATIONS

A color variation will for all intents and purposes be a production run piece. It will not be amateur or crude. It will differ from a prototype in that it will be professionally clean and commercially sellable.

Color variations will fall into one of the following catagories:
(A) One of an extremely small number of items — examples are: 9703 Dark Green (five made), 9706 Black (four made), and 9123 Yellow (ten made).
(B) Color variation of moderate amounts — examples are: 9701 Black (120 made), 9202 Orange (67 made), and 9207 White.
(C) Common color variations — examples are: 9215 Royal Blue (1000 made), 9730, and 9853.

CHEMICALLY-ALTERED CARS

There are many color variations that were produced by Lionel from 1970-1988.

Because of the high prices that legitimate color variations command, certain unscrupulous (or worse) elements of the train collecting hobby have in the past few years attempted to "create" color variations by various techniques to sell at higher prices.

Charles Weber, a chemist and long-time train collector, has concluded that a number of cars which have surfaced in recent years have been chemically-altered after they left the factory and have been sold for much higher prices than "normal" examples would have brought. His observations are explained below.

Recently some cars have been offered for sale at train meets in some very unusual colors. These cars have been subjected to a chemical process which altered the body color and/or the color of the lettering. These cars are not legitimate Lionel color variations.

Some cars are known to have been affected by such chemical processes. Several more may exist, so the collector is advised to exercise great care in the purchase of any car which is significantly different from regular mass-produced examples. Some legitimate color samples and cars with different colors of lettering exist as well, so the introduction of these chemically-altered cars has caused confusion in the marketplace. A good example of this is the 9447 in gold and 9453 in black, not blue.

Cars which were normally produced with yellow heat-stamped lettering have had the original yellow lettering chemically-altered to white or off-white. Examples are: 9427 in white letters, 9439, and 9453.

Chemically-altered cars are nothing but fakes and should be understood and treated as such. In the view of some authorities, these cars have no collectable value, yet others feel that they have modest to moderate value as conversation pieces.

SPECIALLY REQUESTED ITEMS

From time to time, the factory has created special products for large companies, dealers, and train clubs such as LCCA, TCA, and LOTS. Examples are: 6464-500 Timken Boxcars for 1970 Glen Uhl, items made for J. C. Penney, and the Mopar train for Crysler Corp.

FACTORY ERRORS

The most common factory errors would have to be items with printing on one side only. Those excaped detection during production and were shipped out unknowingly by Lionel. The next would be no printing on either side.

These would be items rejected by Lionel for one reason or another and were picked up by employees or collectors (usually without trucks) and sold outside of the factory. The next would be variations in color as previously discussed.

It is important to distinguish a factory error from a variation. A "variation" is the result of an "intended change in the production process." Some variations made by Lionel occurred because of an intentional decision to make it easier or less expensive to manufacture. Examples are: 9861-9863, from metal door guides to plastic. Sometimes a variation exists because of a need to correct a defect in or make a change to an earlier version, example: 9853 Cracker Jack Reefer.

Some variations and errors are highly collectable and add great interest and complexity to the train-collecting hobby.

Some collectors are willing to pay the much higher prices generally asked for Lionel items which differ in some significant way from those which were mass-produced in regular production runs. These collectors are involved in what is the riskiest specialty of all.

Descriptions by Roland LaVoie

Gd VG Exc Mt

1776 NORFOLK & WESTERN: See 8559.

2789 WATER TANK: White unpainted plastic water tank piece. D. Fleming Collection. **NRS**

3100 GREAT NORTHERN: 4-8-4 steam locomotive, same as regular issue, but missing GN logo from cylinder head pieces. R. Sigurdson and G. Romich Collections. **NRS**

5704 BUDWEISER: Turn of the Century reefer, came from factory with one door missing; established by presence of weathering on areas normally covered by door. R. E. Nelson Collection. **NRS**

5717 SANTA FE: Bunk car.
(A) No lettering or numbering on one side. R. Lord Collection. **NRS**
(B) No lettering or numbering on both sides. R. Lord Collection. **NRS**

6177 READING: Hopper, no lettering or numbering on either side. C. O'Dell Collection. **NRS**

6405 AMTRAK: Pullman passenger car, one wood-beam passenger truck and one Symington-Wayne truck with extended coupler shank, like those on bay window cabooses. M. Sabatelle Collection. **NRS**

6425 ERIE-LACKAWANNA: Bay window caboose, one arch bar truck and one Symington-Wayne truck. R. Conrad Collection. **NRS**

6427 BURLINGTON NORTHERN: Transfer caboose, no BN logo on one side of cab. G. Humbert Collection. **NRS**

6464-1 WESTERN PACIFIC: Probably late 1969 or early 1970, boxcar, orange-painted orange body and door, white lettering, Type VII body with 9200 end plates, metal door guides, postwar bar-end metal trucks. Prototype for reissue of 6464-type boxcars by Fundimensions, but this version never produced; believed to be one of a kind. R. M. Caplan Collection. **NRS**

6464-50 MINNEAPOLIS & St. LOUIS: Boxcar, tuscan body with white lettering, MPC logo. Possible prototype; two known to exist. H. Levine Collection. **NRS**

6464-1971 T C A SPECIAL: Disneyland.
(A) Same as regular issue, but Mickey Mouse logo shows half-smile rather than full smile on each side. R. M. Caplan Collection. **-- -- -- 250**

(B) Red body, white, yellow, and green heat-stamping, yellow doors, postwar bar-end trucks. Preproduction color sample. R. M. Caplan Collection. **NRS**

6508 CANADIAN PACIFIC: Crane car, CP herald missing from both sides; only "CP" and "6508" stamped on each side. M. Sabatelle Collection. **NRS**

6905 NICKEL PLATE ROAD: Extended vision caboose, gray stripe and script lettering completely missing from one side. Other types of factory errors may also exist; reader comments invited. **NRS**

6920 B & A: Standard O wood-sided caboose, black-painted roof. C. O'Dell Collection. **NRS**

7216 BALTIMORE AND OHIO: 1983, General-style passenger coach, no white striping along windows. R. LaVoie observation. **NRS**

7303 ERIE: Stock car, lettering completely missing from one side. J. Grzyboski Collection. **NRS**

8006 ATLANTIC COAST LINE: 1980, 4-6-4 Hudson, same as regular issue, but no "LIONEL" cast into inside of boiler front; tender has four-wheel trucks, no Magnetraction. Possible prototype. R. Kuehnemund Collection. **NRS**

8030 ILLINOIS CENTRAL: GP-9, Type II railings.
(A) Lettering and numbering missing from one side. G. Halverson Collection. **NRS**

(B) Gray plastic shell painted Milwaukee Road orange and dull chalk white, unpainted white brake unit, very deeply heat-stamped numbers and letters on side slightly raised, other side stamped normally. R. LaVoie Collection. **NRS**

8042 GRAND TRUNK WESTERN: 2-4-2 steam locomotive, tender printed on one side only. D. Fleming Collection. **NRS**

8050 DELAWARE & HUDSON: U-36C, "Delaware & Hudson" and "8050" missing from one side. G. Halverson Collection. **NRS**

8066 TOLEDO, PEORIA & WESTERN: 1980, GP-20, red body with white lettering. Eddins Collection. Possible prototype. Reader comments invited. **NRS**

8104 UNION PACIFIC: 1981, 4-4-0, General-type locomotive, green cab, pilot, lamp, wheel spokes, and bell, black stack, chrome-finished boiler, "3" appears on side of head lamp and under cab window, green plastic "General"-style tender with one arch bar truck on front of tender and one Symington-Wayne truck on rear and simulated wood pile. This locomotive was sold by J. C. Penney as an uncatalogued special called "The Golden Arrow"; locomotive with wooden base and plastic cover. Moyer Collection. -- -- 195 225

8162 ONTARIO NORTHLAND: SD-18 diesel, stamped with "8162" on body shell, but "8163" on cab below windows. "Triple T" Collection. **NRS**

8252 DELAWARE & HUDSON: Alco powered A Unit. Factory prototype as shown in 1972 catalogue with lighter blue, almost powder blue paint, numberboards read "8022", D & H decal on side but road name and number not printed out. Road name and number shown in 1972 catalogue are printer overlay. Front coupler, side ladder steps do not line up with door, believed to be one of a kind. P. Catalano Collection. -- -- -- 550

8253 DELAWARE & HUDSON: Dummy Alco, light blue, almost powder blue, yellow sticky strip along bottom, ladders do not line up with door. With D & H decal but without number or name on side. 1972 catalogue shows prototype with name and number but these are printer overlay. P. Catalano Collection. -- -- -- 550

8304 ROCK ISLAND: 4-4-2 steam locomotive, tender printed on one side only. D. Fleming Collection. **NRS**

8359 B & O: GM 50th Anniversary GP-7.
(A) Without "B & O" and "GM 50", but with nose decal. **NRS**
(B) No nose decal or numbers on sides, but "B & O" present. G. Halverson Collection. **NRS**

8363/8364 BALTIMORE & OHIO: F-3 AA Units, blue plastic body painted light blue, white and gray top, no lettering or decals. M. Sabatelle Collection. **NRS**

8363/8365: F-3 A unit postwar leftover shell; one side stamped for 8363 Baltimore & Ohio and the other for Canadian Pacific. Believed to be preproduction color sample. G. Halverson Collection. **NRS**

8378 WABASH: Fairbanks-Morse diesel, no flag logos on either side of cab, no Mexico paper sticker on battery box. D. Holst Collection. **NRS**

8404 PENNSYLVANIA: 6-8-6 S-2 turbine steam locomotive, number present on only one side of headlight. J. Sawruk Collection. **NRS**

8460 M K T: NW-2 switcher, deeper red than usual production, lettering missing from one side. G. Halverson Collection. **NRS**

8464/8465:
(A) Shell has Amtrak paint scheme, but stamped with Rio Grande lettering on one side and Amtrak with decal number on the other. Believed to be preproduction color sample; reportedly, ten exist. R. Shanfeld Collection. **NRS**
(B) Same as (A), but Rio Grande side numbered "8465" and Amtrak side numbered "8466". Two identical shells mounted on powered and dummy chassis. M. Sabatelle Collection. **NRS**
(C) Same as (B), but lettering, stripes, and number double-stamped on both units. M. Sabatelle Collection. **NRS**
(D) Same as (B), but lettering, stripes, and numbers missing from one side of both units. M. Sabatelle Collection. **NRS**

8466 AMTRAK: F-3 A unit, lettering, number, and logo double-stamped on one side. M. Sabatelle Collection. **NRS**

8466/8467 AMTRAK: F-3 AA units, no Amtrak logo or number on either unit. M. Sabatelle Collection. **NRS**

8474 RIO GRANDE: F-3 B unit, lettering and stripes missing from one side. M. Sabatelle Collection. **NRS**

8556 CHESSIE SYSTEM: NW-2 Switcher, Chessie System lettering and logo missing from both sides. G. Halverson Collection. **NRS**

8559 NORFOLK & WESTERN: Spirit of America GP-9, missing circle of stars from cab front on both ends. This is a well-known factory error. R. LaVoie Collection. -- -- 120 145

8701 W & A: General 4-4-0 steam locomotive, yellow rectangle and "No. 3" omitted from one side of cab. R. Sage Collection. **NRS**

8702 CRESCENT LIMITED: 1977, tender is missing "Southern" on left side only. J. Bonney Collection. **NRS**

8754 NEW HAVEN: Rectifier electric, engine numbers missing from cab sides. D. Fleming Collection. **NRS**

8759 ERIE-LACKAWANNA: GP-9, has maroon and yellow paint and stripe but no lettering either side. D. Fleming Collection. **NRS**

8763 NORFOLK AND WESTERN: GP-9, black-painted plastic body with white lettering, red overspray inside cab, painted over 8666 Northern Pacific cab, frame riveted instead of spot-welded. Prototype displayed at 1978 Toy Fair. G. Halverson Collection. **NRS**

8764 BALTIMORE AND OHIO: Budd railcar, no lettering or numbering on either side. D. Fleming Collection. **NRS**

8801 THE BLUE COMET: 4-6-4 Hudson steam locomotive.
(A) Painted locomotive and tender, but no lettering. One known example. D. Fleming Collection. **NRS**
(B) Tender is dark and light blue, unpainted blue coal, lettered on only one side. D. Fleming Collection. **NRS**
(C) Tender painted dark blue only, blue coal, lettered only on one side. D. Fleming Collection. **NRS**
(D) Same as (C), but tender lettered on both sides. D. Fleming Collection. **NRS**
(E) Same as (C), but coal on tender three-quarters painted black. D. Fleming Collection. **NRS**

8851 NEW HAVEN: F-3 A unit, number missing from cab. D. Fleming Collection. **NRS**

8852 NEW HAVEN: F-3 unit, NH logo missing from nose of cab. D. Fleming Collection. **NRS**

8855 MILWAUKEE ROAD: F-3 unit, "8855" and Milwaukee logo missing from one side. D. Fleming Collection. **NRS**

8857 NORTHERN PACIFIC: U36B number and Monad logo missing from cab sides; one known example. D. Fleming Collection. **NRS**

8866 MINNEAPOLIS & ST. LOUIS: GP-9, lettered and numbered on one side only. G. Deffeo Collection. **NRS**

8868 AMTRAK: Budd railcar, painted stripe but no lettering. D. Fleming Collection. **NRS**

8869 AMTRAK: Budd railcar, painted stripe but no lettering. D. Fleming Collection. **NRS**

8872 SANTA FE: SD-18.
(A) Numbers missing from cab. D. Fleming Collection. **NRS**
(B) Painted, but no lettering. D. Fleming Collection. **NRS**

8900 A T S F: 4-6-4 Hudson steam locomotive.
(A) Boiler front in silver has feedwater heater; no evidence of removal or alteration. G. Parsons Collection. -- -- -- 320
(B) Tender missing "8900" on right side and gold FARR diamond logo on both sides. One example known. D. Fleming Collection. **NRS**

8951 SOUTHERN PACIFIC: Fairbanks-Morse, same as regular issue, but "SOUTHERN PACIFIC" missing from left side of diesel cab. Six examples reported to exist. N. Hussey observation, R. A. Hicks and J. Grzyboski Collections. **NRS**

8952/8953 PENNSYLVANIA: F-3 AA units, power and dummy units with lettering and striping on one side only. D. Fleming Collection. **NRS**

8960 SOUTHERN PACIFIC: U36C.
(A) Painted but lettered only on one side. D. Fleming Collection. **NRS**
(B) Painted but lettering missing from both sides. D. Fleming Collection. **NRS**

9010 GREAT NORTHERN: 1971, short hopper, lettering missing from one side. G. Halverson Collection. **NRS**

9021 SANTA FE: Work caboose, same as regular issue, but frame is stamped with "9022" number and "ATSF" lettering, not 9021. J. R. Hunt Collection. **NRS**

9035 CONRAIL: Blue short boxcar, number printed on one side only. Two known examples. D. Fleming Collection. **NRS**

9037 CONRAIL: Brown short boxcar, lettering and number on one side only. D. Fleming Collection. **NRS**

9042 AUTOLITE: Short boxcar, number printed on one side only. Three known examples. D. Fleming Collection. **NRS**

9045 TOYS 'R US: Short boxcar, lettered and numbered on one side only. Two known examples. D. Fleming Collection. **NRS**

9058 LIONEL: SP caboose, some examples missing lettering due to improper stamping. D. Fleming comment. **NRS**

9090 MINI MAX: 1971, boxcar, dark blue roof and ends, "G" in fourth panel from left, missing "USLX 9090" lettering on lower left side. -- -- 50 60

9111 NORFOLK & WESTERN: 1971, quad hopper, dark red body, white lettering, less than 40 reportedly produced. Probable trial run. A. Otten Collection. -- -- -- 125

9111 NORFOLK & WESTERN: 1972, quad hopper, tuscan body, white decal lettering, prototype, rare. C. Lang comment. **NRS**

9121 L & N: 1975, flatcar with dozer and scraper, brown flatcar body, white lettering on one side only. J. Breslin Collection. **NRS**

9123 C & O: 1973-76, automobile carrier.
(A) Three-tier black body, C & O markings on both upper and lower boards on each side. This is a legitimate factory error. Any attempt to fake this piece by combining tiers from two different cars can be detected easily by the absence of the "TRAILER TRAIN" lettering on the lower board. G. Halverson comment. -- -- -- 100
(B) Three-tier blue body, yellow lettering, two boards lettered. G. Halverson Collection. -- -- -- 100
(C) Three-tier yellow body, blue lettering, "BLT 1-73", only upper board lettered; only ten in existence. Fuhrmann Collection. -- -- 400 --
(D) Two-tier blue plastic body, no road name, white lettering, "BLT 1- 73" and "9123"; only six made. Fuhrmann Collection. -- -- 600 --

9126 CHESAPEAKE & OHIO: 1973-74, automobile carrier car, light yellow body, two boards lettered. -- -- -- 100

9128 HEINZ: 1974-76, vat car, medium yellow vats, no lettering. Purchaser should beware of switched vats; unlettered replacement vats are easily available. **NRS**

9134 VIRGINIAN: 1976-77, covered hopper, silver roof cover instead of blue. This is a legitimate factory error, not a switched cover, because the silver cover is painted over the normal blue unpainted cover. When the hatches are lifted, the blue shows through, and there are silver paint specks on the inside of the car, which is unpainted gray. Most likely, this car was run through the paint spray booth with the cover installed. R. LaVoie and C. Lang Collections. -- -- -- 100

9136 REPUBLIC STEEL: Long gondola, lettered and numbered on one side only. M. Sabatelle Collection. **NRS**

9140 BURLINGTON: 1971, long gondola, flush-molded brakewheel, lettering on one side only. G. Halverson Collection. **NRS**

9141 BURLINGTON NORTHERN: 1973, long gondola, flush molded brakewheel, lettering on one side only. G. Halverson Collection. **NRS**

9142 REPUBLIC STEEL: 1973, long gondola, lettering on one side only. G. Halverson Collection. **NRS**

9144 RIO GRANDE: Long gondola, recessed brakewheel molding, lettering on one side only. G. Halverson Collection. **NRS**

MX 9145 AUTOLITE: 1972 apparent prototype of 9042 Autolite short 027 boxcar. The lettering on the left side of the car is hand-lettered with a brush and a Rapidograph-type pen. There are guide lines visible for the lettering. The words "AUTOLITE / SPARK PLUGS" are somewhat larger than those on the production 9042. The car does not have "MPC" or "9040" Series embossed on the end plates. The body is embossed "Part No. 100 4-3" on the inside. The technical data on the right is simulated by rough "chicken scratch" writing. There is no

"LIONEL" or "BLT. 1-71". The "MX" lettering may indicate "MOTORCRAFT EXPERIMENTAL". Symington-Wayne trucks, one operating and one dummy coupler. R. DuBeau Collection. **NRS**

9200 ILLINOIS CENTRAL: Boxcar, unpainted orange Type VI body, IC close, open AAR trucks, metal door guides; preproduction sample. G. Halverson Collection. **NRS**

9202 SANTA FE: Boxcar, orange-painted orange body, black-painted black door, black lettering, Type I door guides, AAR trucks; prototype, one of 69. "Triple T" Collection. -- -- 800 900

9207 SOO: Boxcar, Type VII body, Type I frame.
(A) White-painted sides and black-painted roof on white plastic body with red-painted red door, black lettering, metal door guides, Symington-Wayne trucks; preproduction sample, one of twenty-four. -- -- -- 225
(B) Same as (A), but all white-painted car. -- -- -- 225

9238 NORTHERN PACIFIC: 1984-85, log dump car, same as catalogued issue, but mirror imaged lettering on both sides of car; electrocal was applied in reverse. G. Wilson Collection. -- -- -- 75

9239 LIONEL LINES: N5C caboose, one Symington-Wayne truck and one arch bar truck. A.Broderdorf Collection. **NRS**

9271 MINNEAPOLIS & ST. LOUIS: Bay window caboose, no lettering or numbers on either side. D. Fleming Collection. **NRS**

9274 SANTA FE: Bay window caboose, red with black roof.
(A) Completely lettered, but with red unpainted roof; one known example. D. Fleming Collection. **NRS**
(B) Painted black roof but no lettering either side. Two known examples. D. Fleming Collection. **NRS**
(C) Red unpainted roof, no lettering either side. Four known examples. D. Fleming Collection. **NRS**

9276 PEABODY: Quad hopper, "PEABODY" double-stamped on one side. D. Fleming Collection. **NRS**

9279 MAGNOLIA: Three-dome tank car, letters "MA" missing from "MAGNOLIA" on both sides. D. Fleming Collection. **NRS**

9301 U. S. MAIL: Operating boxcar, stamped "9301" on one side and "9708" on the other. Probable color sample. J. Grzyboski Collection. **NRS**

9304 C & O: 1973-76, coal dump car, no lettering on either side. **NRS**

9306 A T S F: Flatcar with two horses; from 1053 James Gang set, one arch bar and one AAR truck. R. Grandison Collection. **NRS**

9307 ERIE: 1979-80, animated gondola.
(A) Lettering and numbering completely absent from one side of car; probable factory error. Moss Collection. **NRS**
(B) Unpainted turquoise gondola body, unpainted tan crate load, no lettering or numbering; possible prototype. A. Otten Collection. **NRS**

9308 AQUARIUM CAR: 1981-83, unpainted and unlettered clear plastic. A. Otten collection. **NRS**

9320 FORT KNOX: Mint car, clear unpainted bullion bar stacks. D. Fleming Collection. **NRS**

9321 ATSF: Single-dome tank car, lettered correctly but unpainted (regular issue painted silver). D. Fleming Collection. **NRS**

9322 ATSF: Quad hopper, lettered and numbered on one side only. D. Fleming Collection. **NRS**

9352 CHICAGO & NORTH WESTERN: TOFC flatcar, no lettering on one trailer. J. Grzyboski Collection. **NRS**

9401 GREAT NORTHERN: Boxcar, misprinted with additional electrocal Monad logos. D. Fleming Collection. **NRS**

9456 PENNSYLVANIA: Boxcar, PRR logo missing from Keystones on both sides. J. Grzyboski Collection. **NRS**

9536-9540 THE BLUE COMET: Passenger cars, about 200 factory production samples were discarded but retrieved by collectors. These were sold in quantity to a dealer who advertised and sold them to the public. Some of these cars were repainted with circus designs. D. Fleming comments.
(A) Unpainted blue plastic. **NRS**
(B) Dark blue painted blue plastic. **NRS**
(C) Dark blue painted blue plastic with white window stripe, no gold stripes on edges. **NRS**

9537 HALLEY BLUE COMET: Combine, painted normally, but gold striping along windows missing from one side. R. LaVoie observation.   **NRS**

9576-9580 BURLINGTON: Aluminum passenger cars, cars have Amtrak markings instead of normal Burlington. Possible set of preproduction samples. J. R. Hunt Collection.   **NRS**

9602 A T S F: 1977, hi-cube boxcar, all markings to right of door on both sides are missing.   --   --   --   **350**

9669 BAMBI: Hi-cube boxcar, missing "Mickey Mouse" and "9669" markings from both sides. D. Fleming Collection.   **NRS**

9700 SERIES: Boxcar, true number unknown, white Type IX body, white doors, no letters, numbers or other markings on either side. M. Sabatelle Collection.   **NRS**

9700 SOUTHERN: Boxcar, tuscan-painted tuscan Type IX body, tuscan-painted tuscan doors, Symington-Wayne trucks, Type II box. Possible pre-production sample for 9711 Southern boxcar, which was produced in this color. Two examples examined and known to exist. J. LaVoie Collection.   **NRS**

9701 BALTIMORE & OHIO: Double-door boxcar.
(A) Black-painted sides, silver roof painted on blue plastic, yellow-painted yellow doors, yellow lettering, Type II frame; 12 made.   --   --   **400**
(B) Black sides and silver roof painted on gray plastic body, light blue-painted light blue doors, light blue lettering, Type II frame, preproduction sample.   **NRS**
(C) Deep blue-painted deep blue plastic body, black-painted black doors, yellow lettering, printed on only one side, Type II frame. R. M. Caplan Collection.   **NRS**
(D) Unpainted blue plastic body, yellow lettering, one side blank. R. M. Caplan collection.   **NRS**

9703 C P RAIL: Boxcar.
(A) Dark green-painted light green body, dark green-painted light green doors, Type II frame; one of five preproduction samples, one side blank.   --   --   **600**
(B) All "C P Rail" lettering stamped twice, once on each side of door. R. M. Caplan Collection.   **NRS**

9705 DENVER & RIO GRANDE: Boxcar.
(A) Silver-painted gray Type IX plastic body, red-painted red doors, Type I frame, red lettering, 16 made. Red doors installed outside factory. R. Vagner comment. Preproduction sample.   --   --   **400**   --
(B) Same as (A), but Type II frame. Red doors installed outside factory. R. Vagner comment. Preproduction sample.   --   --   **400**   --
(C) Silver-painted Type IX gray plastic body, orange lettering, Type II frame; ten made.   --   --   **500**   --

9706 C & O: Boxcar, black-painted gray plastic, black-painted door, Type II frame; four preproduction samples known.   --   --   **700**   --

9708 U.S. MAIL: Boxcar, reversed striping colors; blue on top and red on bottom. J. Grzyboski Collection.   **NRS**

9708-9709 U. S. MAIL/BAR: Boxcar, same color scheme on both sides, but one side is lettered for 9708 U. S. Mail car and one side for 9709 BAR State of Maine car. R. M. Caplan collection.   **NRS**

9709 BAR STATE OF MAINE: Boxcar.
(A) Same as (D) in listings, but no printing on the white areas of either side.   --   --   --   **125**
(B) Blue- and light red-painted gray body, blue- and red-painted gray doors, white- and black-painted lettering, number stamped on angle.   --   --   **100**
(C) Blue- and dark red-painted gray body, blue- and red-painted gray door; white lettering, printed one side only in white areas, factory error.   **35   45   50   60**

9729 CP RAIL: Boxcar, CP Rail logo is black with white only. D. Fleming Collection.   **NRS**

9757 CENTRAL OF GEORGIA: Boxcar, tuscan-painted brown body, silver-painted gray doors, number misprinted.   **NRS**

9758 ALASKA: Boxcar.
(A) Blue-painted white body, blue-painted white doors, white lettering, without "at your service".   --   **150   225   325**
(B) Blue-painted dark blue body and doors, yellow lettering, without "at your service." R. Vagner Collection.   --   --   **325   350**

9768 BOSTON & MAINE: Boxcar, BM logo and weights data missing from one side. R. Lord Collection.   **NRS**

9772 GREAT NORTHERN: Boxcar.
(A) Missing number and "GN" on one side. We wish to learn how many of this variety are in collector hands. Reader comments are invited. J. Grzyboski Collection.   **NRS**
(B) Same as (A), but completely missing GN logo on right. Black lettering and underscoring on left side is present, but has shifted downward so that the underscoring is through the yellow line. J. Breslin Collection. We wish to learn how many of this variety are in collector hands. Reader comments are invited. **NRS**

9776 SOUTHERN PACIFIC: Boxcar, black-painted body and black doors, white and gold lettering, double-stamped lettering and emblems.   --   --   **35   50**

9783 BALTIMORE & OHIO TIMESAVER: Boxcar, no lettering or decal on either side. M. Sabatelle and D. Fleming Collections.   **NRS**

9784 A T S F: 1977-78, boxcar, dark maroon-painted body, flat black roof and ends, white lettering "washed out" with tinge of pinkish-maroon. Meisel comment, R. Vagner Collection.   **NRS**

9801 BALTIMORE AND OHIO: Standard O Boxcar.
(A) Dark blue lower stripe, B & O decal is misplaced on one side only. T. Klaassen Collection.   **NRS**
(B) No lettering in upper left corner of one side. D. Newman Collection.   **NRS**

9802 MILLER HIGH LIFE: Standard O reefer, gray plastic body, red doors and lettering, "BLT 1-73", red plastic snap-on walkway, die-cast sprung trucks, disc-operating couplers, the "2" in 9802 is slightly higher than "980", probable prototypes, five known to exist. Fuhrmann Collection.   --   --   **700**   --

9814 PERRIER: 1980 billboard reefer, Perrier bottle missing from mountain spring electrocal. D. McCabe Collection. We do not know how rare this variety is. Reader comments requested.   **NRS**

9820 WABASH: Gondola, gray body, black lettering, simulated coal load, Standard O series with Standard O trucks, die-cast sprung trucks, disc couplers; only two in existence. E. Barbret Collection.   --   --   **800**   --

9821 SOUTHERN PACIFIC: 1973-74, Standard O gondola, black body, white lettering, "Blt 1-73", Southern Pacific decal, no brakewheel but hole for brakewheel, only three known. Fuhrmann Collection.   --   --   **800**   --

9830 JOHNNIE WALKER: Favorite Spirits reefer, possible preproduction sample; logo is less defined than regular production and differs in the following ways: hat is less black, face is flesh-colored instead of gold, ascot and buttons are white instead of gold, top of cane is a mallet instead of a ball with loops, solid black pocket flap, white trim on boots instead of yellow, blue-shaded white pants, and trademark next to left foot. Reader comments invited. W. Cunningham Collection.   **NRS**

9855 SWIFT: 1974-76, reefer, Type I body, black roof and ends, silver body and doors, built date is "BLT 1-7" instead of "BLT 1-73", factory error.   **15   20   30   40**

9873 RALSTON: Reefer, no checkerboard paint on one side; ten known examples. D. Fleming Collection.   **NRS**

9880 ATSF: Reefer, numbering and lettering missing from one side. D. Fleming Collection.   **NRS**

1-6307 NICKEL PLATE ROAD: Flatcar with trailers; one trailer missing lettering on both sides. C. O'Dell Collection.   **NRS**

1-6801 LIONEL RAILROADER CLUB: Bunk Car, no painting on one side. C. O'Dell Collection.   **NRS**

Chapter XVI

MODERN ERA LIONEL SETS

By Donna Price and Glenn Halverson
With the assistance of Brenda Patterson,
Dan Johns, and Chris Rohlfing

Lionel has produced a remarkable number of sets since 1970. Some of these sets were illustrated and described in either Lionel's consumer catalogues or the collector center brochures. These we refer to as Lionel Catalogue Sets; they are listed below by year.

Just what are the criteria for a catalogue set? With the advent of the Service Station Special sets and the "separate sale" sets, this is not as easy a question to answer as one may suppose. There are three criteria for determining whether a set should be included in this segment: (1) Obviously, the set had to appear in the consumer catalogue or collector brochures and not be a set to include in the Service Station or separate sale categories; (2) the set had to be marketed as a complete set, regardless of what dealers have done with it since it came from the factory; and (3) the set must have included a set box upon its shipment from the factory.

Lionel's catalogue record is moderately accurate. However, since each year's catalogue was prepared considerably before the sets' actual production, some production changes were made that are not reflected in the catalogue. This report is based on the catalogue record and, when deviations are known, we have reported the actual set components. If you note differences in your set(s) from those listed in this chapter, we would appreciate your describing the differences to us.

This chapter includes all known catalogued sets. Sets for Canadian distribution are listed separately later in the chapter. Uncatalogued, Service Station, or "Separate Sale" sets are described in the next chapter. We have arranged Lionel catalogue sets for each year by set number and have dropped the prefix "6" which was used from 1971 on by Fundimensions and its successors.

Editor's Note: Donna Price, a staff editor, and Brenda Patterson, a word processor, prepared the listing of catalogued sets for our first edition. Glenn Halverson, a tele-communications major at Michigan State University and a resident of Clifton Park, New York, has been one of the major researchers for this book. He is responsible for substantial changes in the text, especially in the accessories and steam engines chapters. During his research for this segment, he contacted Fundimensions, where he was ably assisted by Dan Johns, the Director of Product Integrity and Customer Relations for the firm. Mr. Johns has been most helpful in this and other areas. Chris Rohlfing has provided superb editorial assistance to a number of our publications. He carefully reviewed his collection for this chapter. The same people have aided us for our second edition, and several readers have made comments specific to individual sets, where their help has been duly noted.

LIONEL CATALOGUE SETS

1970

1081 WABASH CANNONBALL: 8040 Locomotive and Tender, 9140 or 9141, 9020, 9060, 4045, eight 5013s, two 5018s, new mechanical automatic uncoupler, 2CTC, wires, owner's maintenance and instruction manual.

1082 YARD BOSS: 8010 Diesel, 9140 or 9141, 9010, 9021, 4045, eight 5013s, two 5018s, new automatic uncoupler, 2CTC, wires, owner's maintenance and instruction manual.

1083 PACEMAKER: 8041 Locomotive and Tender, 9010, 9140 or 9141, 9020, 9062, 5020, twelve 5013s, four 5018s, 4045, train crew (three figure set), 2911, mechanical automatic uncoupler, 2CTC, wires, owner's maintenance and instruction manual.

1084 GRAND TRUNK & WESTERN: 8042 Locomotive and Tender, 9010, 9040, 9020, 9063, 5149, eight 5013s, three 5018s, 4045, train crew (three figure set), 2911, 2CTC, wires, owner's maintenance and instruction manual. (9050 Sunoco tank car is pictured but not included in set description.)

1085 SANTA FE EXPRESS DIESEL FREIGHT: 8020 Twin-Diesel, 9050, 9120, 9041, 9010, 9140 or 9141, 9061, 5149, 5020, twelve 5013s, seven 5018s, 4045, train crew (three figure set), 2CTC, wires, owner's instruction and maintenance manual.

1086 THE MOUNTAINEER: 8062 Locomotive and Tender, 9300, 9120, 9130 (catalogue states C & O but picture shows B & O), 9202, Great Northern steel caboose, 5149, eight 5013s, seven 5018s, 4090, train crew (three figure set), 2911, 2CTC, wires, owner's maintenance and instruction manual. Catalogued but not manufactured.

1087 MIDNIGHT EXPRESS: 8030 Diesel, 8031 Dummy, 9300, Penn Central communications satellite car, 9120, 9130, 9203, 9160, ten 5013s, eleven 5018s, 5022L, 5022R, 5149, 4090, train crew (three figure set), 2CTC, wires, owner's maintenance and instruction manual. Catalogued but not manufactured.

1971

1081 WABASH CANNONBALL: 8040 or 8043 Locomotive and Tender, 9142, 9020, 9060, eight 5013s, two 5018s, mechanical uncoupler, 25-watt Trainmaster transformer, 2900, wires, instructions.

1085 SANTA FE TWIN DIESEL: 8020 Twin-Diesel, 9040, 9141, 9050, 9012, 9120, 9061, 4050, push-button electric uncoupling track, twelve 5013s, seven 5018s, 5020, two figures, 2900, wires, instructions, foam model buildings.

1182 THE YARDMASTER: 8111 Diesel, 9090, 9142, 9300, 9021, eight 5013s, four 5018s, mechanical uncoupler, 25-watt Trainmaster transformer, 2900, wires, instructions.

1183 THE SILVER STAR: 8141 Locomotive and Tender, 9010, 9020, 9142, 9062, twelve 5013s, four 5018s, 5020, 4050, two figures, mechanical uncoupler, 2900, wires, instructions. Some sets came with mis-marked 8041 Locomotive. R. LaVoie comment.

1184 THE ALLEGHENY: 8142 Locomotive and Tender, 9022, 9040, 9012, 9141, 9064, eight 5013s, five 5018s, push-button electric uncoupling track, 4050, two figures, 2900, wires, instructions, foam model buildings. This set came in three configurations: (A) Sound of Steam locomotive and Wheaties boxcar for regular dealers; (B) Sound of Steam locomotive and Autolite boxcar for Autolite Car Parts stores; and (C) in 1972, the set came with Sound of Steam locomotive and Autolite boxcar for regular dealers. This meant the collectors who thought they were purchasing a limited edition boxcar in 1971 when they bought the set in Autolite stores were unpleasantly surprised the next year! C. Weber comments.

1186 CROSS COUNTRY EXPRESS: 8030 Diesel, 9135, 9200, 9250, 9121, 9300, 9160, ten 5013s, eleven 5018s, 5149, 5121, 5122, 4090, mechanical uncoupler, two figures, 2900, wires, instructions.

1972

1081 WABASH CANNONBALL: 8040 Locomotive and Tender, 9136, 9020, 9060, eight 5013s, two 5018s, mechanical uncoupler, 4050 25-watt Trainmaster transformer. C. Rohlfing comment. This set was also offered in the 1972 J. C. Penney catalogue unchanged from Lionel's version. L. Bohn comment.

1182 YARDMASTER: 8111 Diesel, 9300, 9136, 9013, 9025 or 9061, eight 5013s, four 5018s, mechanical uncoupler, 4125 25-watt Trainmaster transformer. Distributed in Canada as T-1272.

1183 SILVER STAR: 8203 Locomotive and Tender, 9136, 9013, 9020, 9062, twelve 5013s, four 5018s, 5020, mechanical uncoupler, 4150. Distributed in Canada as T-1273.

1186 CROSS COUNTRY EXPRESS: 8030 Diesel, 9111, 9151, 9121, 9700, 9701, 9160, ten 5013s, eleven 5018s, 5149, remote switches, figures, 4090.

1280 KICKAPOO VALLEY & NORTHERN: 8200 Locomotive, operating dump car, 9020, 9067, eight 5013s, two 5018s, 25-watt Trainmaster transformer. Distributed in Canada as T-1280.

1284 ALLEGHENY: 8204 Locomotive and Tender, 9042, 9141, 9012, 9022, stakes and load, 9064, eight 5013s, five 5018s, 5149, figures, whistle controller, 4150. One original set is known to exist with a 9142 Republic Steel Gondola substituted for the 9141 Burlington Northern Gondola. J. R. Hunt comment. This set was also offered unchanged from the Lionel version in the 1972 J. C. Penney catalogue. L. Bohn comment.

1285 SANTA FE TWIN DIESEL: 8020 Diesel, 8021 Dummy, 9700, 9140 or 9141, 9300, 9012, 9122, 9061, twelve 5013s, seven 5018s, 5149, 5020, figures, 4150.

1287 PIONEER DOCKSIDE SWITCHER: 8209 Locomotive and Tender, 9013, 9136, 9060, nine 5018s, eight 5013s, manual switch, 4150.

1973

1380 U. S. STEEL INDUSTRIAL SWITCHER: 8350 Diesel, 9031, 9024, 9068, eight 5013s, DC power pack.

1381 CANNONBALL: 8300 or 8502 Locomotive and Tender, 9031, 9024, 9061, eight 5013s, two 5018s, 25-watt transformer.

1382 YARDMASTER: 8111 Diesel, 9136, 9013, 9300, 9025, eight 5013s, four 5018s, 25-watt transformer.

1383 SANTA FE FREIGHT: 8020 Diesel, 9300, 9136, 9013, 9021, eight 5013s, six 5018s, 25-watt transformer.

1384 SOUTHERN EXPRESS: 8140 Locomotive and Tender, 9013, 9140, 9020, 9066, twelve 5013s, four 5018s, 5020, 4150.

1385 BLUE STREAK FREIGHT: 8303 Locomotive and Tender, 9013, 9136, 9043, 9140, 9020, 9066, eight 5013s, six 5018s, 4150.

1386 ROCK ISLAND EXPRESS: 8304 Locomotive and Tender, 9125, 9131, 9023, 9015, 9070, eight 5013s, six 5018s, 4150.

1387 MILWAUKEE SPECIAL: 8305 Locomotive and Tender, 9500, 9502, 9503, eight 5013s, six 5018s, 4150.

1388 GOLDEN STATE ARROW: 8352 Diesel, 9135, 9126, 9707, 9152, 9708, 9163, 4150, ten 5013s, eleven 5018s, 5149.

1974

1380 U. S. INDUSTRIAL SWITCHER: 8350 Diesel, 9024, 9031, 9068, eight 5013s, DC power pack.

1381 CANNONBALL: 8300 Locomotive and Tender, 9031, 9024, 9163, eight 5013s, two 5018s, transformer.

1382 YARDMASTER: 8111 Diesel, 9136, 9120, 9013, 9025, eight 5013s, four 5018s, transformer.

1383 SANTA FE FREIGHT: 8351 Diesel, 9013, 9020 or 9300, 9136, 9021, eight 5013s, six 5018s, transformer. Reader reports requested.

1384 SOUTHERN EXPRESS: 8302 Locomotive and Tender, 9013, 9136, 9020, 9066, transformer, twelve 5013s, four 5018s, 5020.

1385 BLUE STREAK FREIGHT: 8303 Locomotive and Tender, 9140, 9020, 9136, 9043, 9013, 9069, transformer, eight 5013s, six 5018s.

1386 ROCK ISLAND EXPRESS: 8304 Locomotive and Tender, 9015, 9131, 9023, 9125, 9070, transformer, eight 5013s, six 5018s.

1388 GOLDEN STATE ARROW: 8352 Diesel, 9135, 9707, 9126, 9301, 9152, 9163, transformer, 5149, ten 5013s, eleven 5018s.

1460 GRAND NATIONAL: 8470 Diesel, 9860, 9303, 9121, 9114, 9126 or 9123, 9740, 9167, two 5121-22 remote-controlled switches, 5149, 5020, transformer, twenty-three 5018s, eighteen 5013s.

1463 COCA-COLA SPECIAL: 8473, 9743, 9744, 9745, 9073, eight 5013s, two 5018s, 4050 50-watt tranformer, CTC, wires. Uncatalogued in 1974, but catalogued in 1975.

1487 BROADWAY LIMITED: 8304 Locomotive and Tender, 9507, 9508, 9509, eight 5013s, six 5018s, transformer.

1489 SANTA FE DOUBLE DIESEL: 8020 Diesel, 8021 Dummy, 9013, 9140, 9042, 9036, 9024, 9061, eight 5013s, six 5018s, transformer.

1975

1380 U. S. STEEL INDUSTRIAL SWITCHER: 8350 Diesel, 9031, 9024, 9067, eight 5013s, DC power pack.

1381 CANNONBALL: 8502 Locomotive and Tender, 9024, 9031, 9061, eight 5013s, two 5018s, transformer.

1384 SOUTHERN EXPRESS: 8302 Locomotive and Tender, 9136, 9013, 9020, 9066, twelve 5013s, four 5018s, 5020, transformer.

1388 GOLDEN STATE ARROW: 8352 Diesel, 9135, 9707, 9126, 9301, 9152, 9163, transformer, 5149, ten 5013s, eleven 5018s.

1461 BLACK DIAMOND: 8203 Locomotive and Tender, 9136, 9020, 9043, 9140, 9013, 9052, eight 5013s, six 5018s, transformer.

1463 COCA-COLA SPECIAL: 8473, 9743, 9744, 9745, 9073, eight 5013s, two 5018s, 4050 50-watt tranformer, CTC, wires. Uncatalogued in 1974, but catalogued in 1975.

1487 BROADWAY LIMITED: 8304 Locomotive and Tender, 9507, 9508, 9509, eight 5013s, six 5018s, transformer.

1489 SANTA FE DOUBLE DIESEL: 8020 Diesel, 8021 Dummy, 9020, 9013, 9140, 9136, 9042, 9061, eight 5013s, six 5018s, transformer.

1560 NORTH AMERICAN EXPRESS: 8564 Diesel, 9121, 9861, 9303, 9129, 9260, 9755, 9168, two-remote control switches, twenty-three 5018s, eighteen 5013s, 5020, 5149.

1581 THUNDERBALL FREIGHT: 8500 Locomotive and Tender, 9011, 9020, 9032, 9052, eight 5013s, two 5018s, transformer.

1582 YARD CHIEF: 8569 Diesel, 9140, 9044, 9011, 9026, 9027, eight 5013s, two 5018s, transformer.

1584 N & W SPIRIT OF AMERICA: 1776 Diesel, 9135, 9153, 9707, 9129, 9708, 1776 Caboose, 5149, ten 5013s, eleven 5018s, 4150 transformer. C. Rohlfing Collection.

1585 75TH ANNIVERSARY SPECIAL: 7500 U36B Diesel, 7507, 7502, 7501, 7504, 7503, 7505, 7506, 7508.

1586 CHESAPEAKE FLYER: 8304 Locomotive and Tender, 9131, 9125, 9016, 9022, 9064, eight 5013s, four 5018s, two canisters, transformer.

1587 CAPITOL LIMITED: 8304 Locomotive and Tender, 9517, 9518, 9519, eight 5013s, four 5018s, transformer.

1976

1384 SOUTHERN EXPRESS: 8302 Locomotive and Tender, 9136, 9013, 9020, 9066, 5020, transformer, eight 5013s, four 5018s.

1489 SANTA FE DOUBLE DIESEL: 8020 Diesel, 8021 Dummy, 9013, 9136, 9042, 9140, 9020, 9061, eight 5013s, six 5018s, transformer.

1581 THUNDERBALL FREIGHT: 8500 Locomotive and Tender, 9011, 9020, 9032, 9172, eight 5013s, two 5018s, transformer.

1582 YARD CHIEF: 8569 Diesel, 9026, 9044, 9140, 9011, 9027, girders, eight 5013s, two 5018s, transformer.

1585 LIONEL 75th ANNIVERSARY SPECIAL: 7500 Diesel, 7507, 7504, 7503, 7506, 7505, 7501, 7502, 7508.

1586 CHESAPEAKE FLYER: 8304 Locomotive and Tender, 9016, 9125, 9131, 9022, 9064, eight 5013s, four 5018s, two canisters, transformer.

1660 YARD BOSS: 8670 Diesel, 9032, 9026, 9179, DC power pack, eight 5013s. One set found with 9031 NKP Gondola substituted for 9032 SP Gondola. T. Ladny Collection.

1661 ROCK ISLAND LINE: 8601 Locomotive and Tender, 9033, 9020, 9078, die-cut cardboard freight station, bridge and tunnel, eight 5013s, two 5018s, transformer.

1662 THE BLACK RIVER FREIGHT: 8602 Locomotive, 9021, 9016, 9140, 9026, 9077, two canisters, twenty-two telephone poles and road signs, die-cut freight station, bridge and tunnel, trestle set, eight 5013s, four 5018s, transformer.

1663 AMTRAK LAKE SHORE LIMITED: 8664 Diesel, 6403, 6404, 6405, 6406, eight 5013s, four 5018s, transformer.

1664 ILLINOIS CENTRAL FREIGHT: 8669 Diesel, 9767, 9139, 9606, 9852, 9121, 9178, 5021, 2280, 2317, 5149, twelve 5013s, nine 5018s, two 5019s, six trestles, transformer. Set is pictured in catalogue with 9852 reefer, but several substitute reefers are known to have come with original sets, e. g. 9854. C. Rohlfing comment.

1665 N Y C EMPIRE STATE EXPRESS: 8600 Locomotive and Tender, 9772, 9773, 9266, 9159, 9174. Set listed in catalogue with eight 5013s, ten 5018s, and transformer, but it was produced without these items. C. Rohlfing comment.

1977

1585 LIONEL 75th ANNIVERSARY SPECIAL: 7500 U36B Diesel, 7507, 7502, 7501, 7504, 7503, 7505, 7506, 7508. Nine-unit train commemorating Lionel's 75th anniversary.

1586 THE CHESAPEAKE FLYER: 8304 Locomotive and Tender, 9016, 9125, 9022, 9131, 9064, eight 5013s, four 5018s, two canisters, transformer.

1661 ROCK ISLAND LINE: 8601 Locomotive and Tender, 9033, 9020, 9078, three canisters, six wood railroad ties, die-cut freight station, bridge and tunnel, eight 5013s, two 5018s, transformer.

1662 THE BLACK RIVER FREIGHT: 8602 Locomotive and Tender, 9140, 9016, 9026, 9077, two canisters, twenty-two telephone poles and road signs, die-cut freight station, bridge and tunnel, trestle set, eight 5013s, four 5018s, transformer.

1663 AMTRAK LAKE SHORE LIMITED: 8664 Diesel, 6403, 6404, 6405, 6406, eight 5013s, four 5018s, transformer.

1664 ILLINOIS CENTRAL FREIGHT: 8669 Diesel, 9767, 9139, 9606, 9852, 9121, 9178, 5021, 2280, 2317, 5149, twelve 5013s, nine 5018s, two 5019s, six trestles, transformer.

1760 STEEL HAULERS: 8769 Diesel, 9016, 9020, 9033, 9071, Peterbilt tractor with die-cast chassis, trailer, operating crane kit, pull cart, eight 5013s, two 5018s, DC power pack, die-cut factories and shed. Plastic loads include pipes, I-beams, engine blocks, culverts, posts, train wheels, crates with loads, warehouse skids.

1761 CARGO KING: 8770 Diesel, 9026, 9032, 9016, (9021, 9025, or 9027), Mack and Peterbilt tractors, two trailers, two operating crane kits, pull cart, eight 5013s, four 5018s, die-cut buildings, transformer. Plastic loads include cement blocks, barrels, wood stacks, I-beams, culverts, pipes, crates, warehouse skids, posts.

1762 THE WABASH CANNONBALL: 8703 Locomotive and Tender, 9851, 9079, 9284, 9771, 9080, canisters, 2110, twelve 5013s, fourteen 5018s, transformer.

1764 THE HEARTLAND EXPRESS: 8772 Diesel, 7808, 9302, 9116, 9283, 9187, 5027, ten 5013s, seven 5018s, transformer.

1765 ROCKY MOUNTAIN SPECIAL: 8771 Diesel, 9789, 9610, 9286, 9189, 9285, 9188, 5125, two 2290s, three-piece trestle, 5149, nine 5013s, twenty-three 5018s, transformer.

1978

1662 BLACK RIVER FREIGHT: 8602 Locomotive and Tender, 9140, 9016, 9026, 9077, 2180, 2181, die-cut girder bridge, tunnel and freight station, eight 5013s, four 5018s, twelve-tier graduated trestle set, 2905, transformer.

1760 TRAINS N' TRUCKIN' STEEL HAULER: 9769 Diesel, 9020, 9011, 9033, 9071, Peterbilt tractor, truck with stakebed trailer, operating 10" crane kit, eight 5013s, two 5018s, DC power pack, two die-cut buildings. Plastic loads include I-beams, train wheels, crates, warehouse skids, barrels.

1761 TRAINS N' TRUCKIN' CARGO KING: 8770 Diesel, 9032, 9026, 9016, 9027, 2905, eight 5013s, six 5018s, transformer. Mack truck with stake bed trailer, Peterbilt truck with a flatbed trailer, two 10" tall operating cranes, three die-cut buildings, cargo and accessories. Plastic cargo includes I-beams, train wheels, crates, warehouse skids, barrels.

1860 WORKIN' ON THE RAILROAD TIMBERLINE: 8501 Locomotive, slope-back tender, operating log dumper car, operating crane car, 9021, plastic operating log loading mill, four figures, throttle, eight 5013s, two 5018s, transformer.

1862 WORKIN' ON THE RAILROAD LOGGING EMPIRE: 8501 Locomotive, slope-back tender, operating dump car with logs, operating crane car, 9019, 9043, flatcar with fences, 9025, 2721, 2722, four plastic workman, throttle, twelve 5013s, six 5018s, 5020, transformer. All the cars in this set use the same frame: two four-wheel trucks are simulated in the sides of the frame, but single axles with two wheels are located at the inboard bearing on each simulated truck frame. All frames have a piece on the top surface to knock out to attach crane cab for crane car. Frames are all black, 8-3/16" long, without couplers. The couplers are non-operating with a snap-in plastic arm. Decals were supplied to be installed by the purchaser. (A) through (D) below were reissued in separate boxes with two four-wheel trucks with lettered frames, as in 9363 N & W Dump Car and 9364 N & W Crane; see Operating Car chapter. The following cars can be made up by assembling this set:

(A) Yellow cab with boom for crane car, IC decals.
(B) Flatcar with tan fence around perimeter.
(C) Blue snap-on dump car body.
(D) Red snap-on work caboose body with Santa Fe decals.
(E) White snap-on double-door short boxcar body (similar, but not identical, to the 9040 body; part no. 9019-T-055A molded into roof). Doors molded open on one side and closed on other side. PC decals fit to right of doors, Penn Central decal fits to left of closed doors only. This car was also used as the basis for a Toys 'R Us car using different decals.

The preceding discussion is from the J. Sawruk Collection and comments. This set was also offered for sale unchanged from the Lionel version in the 1978 J. C. Penney catalogue. L. Bohn comment.

1864 SANTA FE DOUBLE DIESEL: 8861 Diesel, 8862 Dummy, 9035, 9018, 9033, 9014, 9058, eight 5013s, six 5018s, manual uncoupler, 2905, 2717, transformer.

1865 CHESAPEAKE FLYER: 8800 Locomotive, 8800T, 9036, 9017, 9035, 9018, 9058, 2717, 2180, eight 5013s, six 5018s, 2905, manual uncoupler, 2909, transformer.

1866 GREAT PLAINS EXPRESS: 8854 Diesel, 9729, 9036, 9121, 9011, 9140, 9057, 2717, ten 5013s, seven 5018s, 5027, transformer. Pictured in catalogue with 9121 and 9140, but has also been seen with 9124 and 9136 as substitutes. C. Rohlfing comment.

1867 MILWAUKEE LIMITED: 8855 Diesel, 9277, 9276, 9216, 9411, 9876, 9269.

1979

1864 SANTA FE DOUBLE DIESEL: 8861 Diesel, 8862 Dummy, 9035, 9018, 9033, 9014, 9058, 2717, eight 5013s, six 5018s, transformer, 2905.

1865 CHESAPEAKE FLYER: 8800 Locomotive and Tender, 9036, 9017, 9035, 9018, 9058, 2717, 2180, eight 5013s, six 5018s, 2905, transformer.

1866 GREAT PLAINS EXPRESS: 8854 Diesel, 9417, 9036, 9121, 9011, 9140, 9057, 2717, ten 5013s, seven 5018s, 5027, transformer.

1960 MIDNIGHT FLYER: 8902 Locomotive, 8902T, 9339, 9340, 9341, eight 5013s, two 5018s, DC power pack, 2905.

1962 WABASH CANNONBALL: 8904 Locomotive and Tender, 9016, 9035, 9036, 9080, eight 5013s, four 5018s, AC transformer, 2905.

1963 BLACK RIVER FREIGHT: 8903 Locomotive and Tender, 9136, 9016, 9026, 9077, 2717, eight 5013s, six 5018s, DC power pack, 2181, 2180, manumatic uncoupler, 2905.

1964 RADIO CONTROL EXPRESS: 8901 Locomotive and Tender, boxcar, gondola, operating dump car, work caboose, log loading mill, barrel loader, ten 5113s, 5027. Shown in the Toy Fair catalogue but never manufactured.

1965 SMOKEY MOUNTAIN LINE: 8905 Locomotive, operating dump car, gondola, bobber caboose, 2180, eight 5013s, two 5018s, DC power pack.

1970 THE SOUTHERN PACIFIC LIMITED: 8960 Diesel, 8961, 9313, 9881, 9732, 9315, 9320, 9316. This set was shown in the Toy Fair catalogue but deleted from the regular consumer catalogue because it was a rapid sell out.

1971 QUAKER CITY LIMITED: 8962 Diesel, 9882, 9332, 9331, 9338, 9336, 9734, 9231.

1980

1050 NEW ENGLANDER: 8007 Locomotive, 8007T, 9036, 9140, 9035, 9346, eight 5013s, four 5018s, telephone poles, manumatic uncoupler, 2905, 4060, DC power pack.

1052 CHESAPEAKE FLYER: 8008 Locomotive, 8008T, 9037, 9036, 9017, 9038, 9381, 2717, 2180, eight 5013s, six 5018s, 4060, 2905.

1053 THE JAMES GANG: 8005 Locomotive, 8005T, 9306, 9305, 9541, 2784, four plastic figures, six telephone poles, eight 5013s, four 5018s, DC power pack, 2905.

1070 THE ROYAL LIMITED: 8061 Diesel, 9818, 9234, 9329, 9432, 9344, 9328.

1071 MID ATLANTIC LIMITED: 8063 Diesel, 9370, 9369, 9433, 9233, 9371, 9372.

1072 CROSS COUNTRY EXPRESS: 8066 Diesel, 9374, 9232, 9428, 9373, 9379, 9309, 2303, eight 5013s, six 5018s, 4060, 2905.

1960 MIDNIGHT FLYER: 8902 Locomotive, 8902T, 9339, 9340, 9341, DC power pack, eight 5013s, two 5018s, 2905.

1963 BLACK RIVER FREIGHT: 8903 Locomotive, 8903T, 9011, 9140, 9026, 9077, 2717, telephone poles, road signs, manumatic uncoupler, eight 5013s, six 5018s, DC power pack, 2905.

TEXAS & PACIFIC DIESEL: 8067 Diesel, 9379, 9140, boxcar, flatcar with fences, 9039, four 5018s, eight 5013s, telephone poles, road signs 4-4060, 2905. Catalogued but never manufactured.

1981

1050 NEW ENGLANDER: 8007 Locomotive, 8007T, 9036, 9140, 9035, 9346, eight 5013s, four 5018s, telephone poles, manumatic uncoupler, 2905, DC transformer.

1053 THE JAMES GANG: 8005 Locomotive, 8005T, 9306, 9305, 9541, 2784, four plastic figures, six telephone poles, eight 5013s, four 5018s, DC power pack, 2905.

1072 CROSS COUNTRY EXPRESS: 8066 Diesel, 9374, 9232, 9428, 9373, 9379, 9309, 2303, eight 5013s, six 5018s, 2905, DC transformer.

1150 L. A. S. E. R. RAIN: 8161 Diesel, 6504, 6505, 6507, 6506, L. A. S. E. R. train play mat, eight 5013s, four 5018s, 4065 DC power pack. C. Rohlfing comment.

1151 UNION PACIFIC THUNDER FREIGHT: 8102 Locomotive, 8102T, 9017, 9018, 9035, 6432, eight 5013s, six 5018s, 2717, 2180, AC transformer, 2905, manumatic uncoupler.

1154 READING YARD KING: 8153 Diesel, 9448, 6200, 6300, 9378, 6420, eight 5013s, four 5018s, AC transformer, 2905, manumatic uncoupler.

1158 MAPLE LEAF LIMITED: 8152 Diesel, 6103, 9440, 9441, 6305, 6508, 6433.

1160 GREAT LAKES LIMITED: 8151 Diesel, 9384, 9437, 9436, 9386, 9385, 9387.

1960 MIDNIGHT FLYER: 8902 Locomotive, 8902T, 9339, 9340, 9341, DC power pack, eight 5013s, two 5018s, 2905.

1963 BLACK RIVER FREIGHT: 8903 Locomotive, 8903T, 9011, 9140, 9026, 9077, 2717, telephone poles, road signs, manumatic uncoupler, eight 5013s, six 5018s, DC power pack, 2905.

1982

1053 JAMES GANG: 8005 Locomotive, 8005T, 9306, 9305, 9541, 2784, four plastic figures, six telephone poles, eight 5013s, four 5018s, DC power pack, 2905.

1150 L. A. S. E. R. TRAIN: 8161 Diesel, 6504, 6505, 6506, 6509, L.A.S.E.R. train play mat, eight 5013s, four 5018s, DC power pack, 2905.

1151 UNION PACIFIC THUNDER FREIGHT: 8102 Locomotive, 8102T, 9017, 9018, 9035, 6432, eight 5013s, four 5018s, DC power pack, 2905.

1154 READING YARD KING: 8153 Diesel, 9448, 6200, 6300, 6509, 6420, eight 5013s, four 5018s, AC transformer, 2905, manumatic uncoupler.

1155 CANNONBALL FREIGHT: 8902 Locomotive and Tender, 9035, 9033, 9341, play mat, manual barrel loader, two 2710s, 2180, 2181, DC power pack, eight 5013s, four 5018s, 2905.

1252 HEAVY IRON: 8213 Locomotive and Tender, 9031, 9339, 9020, 9077, 2180, 2309, eight 5013s, four 5018s, AC transformer, 2905.

1253 QUICKSILVER EXPRESS: 8268-8269 Alco AA Diesel pair, 7200, 7201, 7202, 2311, eight 5013s, four 5018s, AC transformer, 2905.

1254 BLACK CAVE FLYER: 8212 Locomotive and Tender, short gondola, boxcar, caboose, play mat, die-cut cave scene, DC power pack, 2905, eight 5013s, two 5018s.

1260 THE CONTINENTAL LIMITED: 8266 Diesel, 9461, 9738, 6106, 7301, 6202, 6900.

1983

1252 HEAVY IRON: 8213 Locomotive and Tender, 9031, 9339, 9020, 9077, 2180, 2309, eight 5013s, four 5018s, AC transformer, 2905.

1253 QUICKSILVER EXPRESS: 8268 Diesel, 8269 Diesel, 7200, 7201, 7202, 2311, eight 5013s, four 5018s, AC transformer, 2905.

1351 BALTIMORE & OHIO: 8315 Locomotive and Tender, 7217, 7215, 7216, station platform, five telephone poles, eight 5013s, six 5018s, 4065 DC power pack, 2905. C. Rohlfing comment.

1352 ROCKY MOUNTAIN FREIGHT: 8313 Locomotive and Tender, 9020, 7909, 6430, eight 5013s, four 5018s, play mat, DC power pack, 2905.

1353 SOUTHERN STREAK: 8314 Locomotive and Tender, 6207, 7902, 6104, 6434, five telephone poles, 2180, 2717, eight 5013s, six 5018s, DC power pack, manumatic uncoupler, 2905.

1354 NORTHERN FREIGHT FLYER: 8375 Diesel, 6206, 6522, 9399, 9236, 6428, 2311, 2309, 2181, 2180, twelve 5013s, seven 5018s, 5020, AC transformer, 2905.

1355 COMMANDO ASSAULT TRAIN: 8377 Diesel, 6561, 6562, 6564, 6435, play mat, eight 5013s, two 5018s, figures, operating supply depot kit, 4065 DC power pack, 2905. C. Rohlfing comment.

1361 GOLD COAST LIMITED: 8376 Diesel, 9290, 9468, 6357, 9888, 6114, 6904.

1984

1351 BALTIMORE & OHIO: 8315 Locomotive and Tender, 7217, 7215, 7216, passenger station platform, five telephone poles, eight 5013s, six 5018s, 4065 DC power pack, 2905.

1352 ROCKY MOUNTAIN FREIGHT: 8313 Locomotive and Tender, 9020, 7909, 6430, eight 5013s, four 5018s, play mat, DC power pack, 2905.

1353 SOUTHERN STREAK: 8314 Locomotive and Tender, 6207, 7902, 6115, 6434, five telephone poles, 2180, 2717, eight 5013s, six 5018s, DC power pack, 2905, manumatic uncoupler.

1354 NORTHERN FREIGHT FLYER: 8375 Diesel, 6206, 9236, C & NW coal dump car, C & NW searchlight car, Illinois Central hopper, 2311, 2309, 2181, 2180, twelve 5013s, seven 5018s, 5149, 5020, AC transformer, 2905.

1355 COMMANDO ASSAULT TRAIN: 8377 Diesel, 6561, 6562, 6564, 6435, play mat, eight 5013s, two 5018s, figures, operating supply depot kit, 4065 DC power pack, 2905.

1402 CHESSIE SYSTEM: 8402 Locomotive and Tender, 6312, 7401, 6211, Chessie square window caboose, five telephone poles, 2180, eight 5013s, four 5018s, transformer, 2905, manumatic uncoupler.

1403 REDWOOD VALLEY EXPRESS: 1983 Locomotive and Tender, flatcar with fences, crane car, log dump car, square window caboose, barrel loader kit, five telephone poles, 2180, eight 5013s, four 5018s, DC power pack, 2905, manumatic uncoupler.

1451 ERIE LACKAWANNA LIMITED: 8458 Diesel, 6210, 7303, 9474, 6118, 6524, 6906.

1985

1353 SOUTHERN STREAK: 8314 Locomotive and Tender, 6207, 7902, Southern hopper, 6434, five telephone poles, 2180, 2717, eight 5013s, six 5018s, DC power pack, 2905, manumatic uncoupler.

1354 NORTHERN FREIGHT FLYER: 8375 Diesel, gondola, 6113, 6522, 9236, 9399, maintenance caboose, semaphore, crossing gate, 2180, twelve 5013s, seven 5018s, 5020, AC transformer, 2905.

1402 CHESSIE SYSTEM: 8403 Locomotive and Tender, stock car, tank car, gondola, 6485, five telephone poles, 2180, eight 5013s, four 5018s, transformer, 2905, manumatic uncoupler.

1403 REDWOOD VALLEY EXPRESS: 4-4-0 Locomotive and Tender, flatcar with fences, crane car, log dump car, square window caboose, barrel loader kit, five telephone poles, 2180, eight 5013s, four 5018s, DC power pack, 2905, manumatic uncoupler.

1501 MIDLAND FREIGHT: 8512 Locomotive, 6258, 6576, 6150, A T & S F bobber caboose, eight 5013s, two 5018s, five telephone poles, DC power pack, 2905. Also offered in 1986 J. C. Penney Christmas catalogue unchanged from Lionel version, but with extra materials: two 25" x 50" mats, large cardboard tunnel, trees, people, road signs, and landscaping; these items apparently made by Life-Like O Scale products. L. Bohn comment.

1502 YARD CHIEF: 8516 Locomotive and Tender, 6579, 6529, 5735, X6260, 6916. Set pictured numbers as 6127 Bunk Car, 6325 Crane Car and 9247 Searchlight Car, but actual numbers were 5735, 6579 and 6529, respectively. C. Rohlfing comment.

1552 BURLINGTON NORTHERN LIMITED: 8585 Diesel, 6234, 6235, 6236, 6237, 6238, 6913.

1986

1602 NICKEL PLATE SPECIAL: 8617 4-4-2 Locomotive, 7926, 6137, 6254, 6919, five telephone poles, fourteen road signs, mechanical crossing gate, eight 5013s, four 5018s, CTC, 4045 transformer.

1615 CANNONBALL EXPRESS: 8625 2-4-2 Locomotive, 6177, 7925, 6585, 6921, five telephone poles, fourteen road signs, 2905 bridge, eight 5013s, four 5018s, DC power pack, manumatic uncoupler, CTC.

1652 B & O FREIGHT: 8662 GP-7 Diesel, 5739, 6314, 6138, 9335, 6916. No track or transformer.

1987

11700 CONRAIL LIMITED: 18200 SD-40 Diesel, 17201, 17301, 17401, 17002, 17501, 17602. No track or transformer.

11701 RAIL BLAZER: 18700 Tank Switcher, 16300, 16304, 16200, 19700, trackside snap-together crane, two cable reels, five telephone poles, 20-piece crate load, eight 5013s, two 5018s, manumatic uncoupler, DC power pack, CTC.

11702 BLACK DIAMOND: 18800 GP-9 Diesel, 16608, 19305, 16609, 16509, mechanical semaphore, five telephone poles, fourteen road signs, eight 5013s, six 5018s, manumatic uncoupler, 4050, CTC.

91687 FREIGHT FLYER: 8902, 9035, 9033, 9341, two white canisters, eight 5013s, two 5018s, manumatic uncoupler, DC power pack, CTC. Older rolling stock reissued in set with new number.

1988

11701 RAIL BLAZER: 18700 Locomotive, 16200, 16304, 16300, 19700, trackside snap-together crane, five telephone poles, car loads, eight 5013s, two 5018s, DC power pack, manumatic uncoupler, CTC, wires.

11703 IRON HORSE FREIGHT: 18604 Locomotive, 16201, 16309, 16505, 4045 tranformer, mechanical semaphore, eight 5013s, four 5018s, CTC, manumatic uncoupler, wires.

11705 CHESSIE SYSTEM UNIT TRAIN: 18201 SD-45 Locomotive, 17100, 17101, 17102, 17103, 17104, 19700.

11707 SILVER SPIKE: 8903-8904 Alco AA Locomotive pair, 16013, 16014, 16015, eight 5013s, four 5018s, 4045 tranformer, manumatic uncoupler, CTC, wires.

61602 NICKEL PLATE SPECIAL: 8617 Locomotive, 7926, 6137, 6254, 6919, road signs, telephone poles, mechanical crossing gate, eight 5013s, four 5018s, 4045 tranformer, manumatic uncoupler, CTC wires. This set has frequently been used as a department store special and as a merchandise premium set without change.

61615 CANNONBALL EXPRESS: 8625 Locomotive, 6585, 7925, 6177, 6921, road signs, telephone poles, eight 5013s, two 5018s, short extension bridge, DC power pack, CTC, wires, manumatic uncoupler.

91687 FREIGHT FLYER: 8902 Locomotive, 9001, 9033, 9341, eight 5013s, two 5018s, DC power pack, CTC, manumatic uncoupler, wires.

NORTH OF THE BORDER:
THE PARKER BROTHERS CONNECTION
By Glenn Halverson

When you are a new company just putting your wares out for sale, it is only natural for you to ask where your markets may be. It is even more true that if you have taken over a struggling concern, you seek to expand your horizons a bit. That is just what the new makers of Lionel Trains tried to do as the Fundimensions team first began its struggle to rebuild a market fallen into stagnation.

It is important to remember that the Lionel Corporation, despite its sale of trains the world over, was for most of its tenure a family-held firm. That meant a limitation of marketing to the abilities of the family itself, especially after the untimely death of Arthur Raphael, the Lionel Corporation's most skillful marketer, in the early 1950s. Inevitably, the lack of a firm marketing policy helped to drag the Lionel Corporation into poor decisions, which meant its ultimate demise as a manufacturer of toy trains. Raphael would have gagged at the sight of the ill-advised Girls' Train of 1957 and 1958, just a few years after he had passed on.

For Fundimensions, the question was how to take advantage of the many resources of its parent company, General Mills, which has contacts and divisions all over the world. One place, thought likely for marketing, was Canada; and the Parker Brothers toy firm seemed a natural outlet for the new line of trains in that country. According to Dan Johns, Parker Brothers never produced anything themselves; all the trains, even the cars marketed only in Canada, were made in Mount Clemens.

According to Fran Mauti, the Director of Customer Relations at Parker Brothers in Canada, the firm distributed Fundimensions trains between 1970 and 1974. Fundimensions train products were packaged in bilingual boxes, French as well as English, because the trains were intended only for the Canadian market. These trains were not featured in the regular Parker Brothers toy catalogues; rather, Parker Brothers imported catalogues from the United States and listed the Fundimensions trains on its own price sheets for dealers.

Most of the trains marketed by Parker Brothers were identical to contemporary Fundimensions American products, but a few items were not — and that is where the special interest in the Canadian distribution lies. Some of these trains, such as the 8031 Canadian National GP-9 with large metal or all-plastic railings, the maroon Canadian National gondola, and the tuscan Grand Trunk caboose, were never marketed in the United States and are thus very hard to find here. Most of the Parker Brothers efforts were aimed at large department store accounts, such as Simpson-Sears, Ltd., the Canadian subsidiary of Sears, Roebuck & Co.

The trains distributed by Parker Brothers in Canada for separate sale come in boxes which are similar to the regular Fundimensions Type I boxes. However, as a rule the cellophane window in these boxes is much smaller, the "whirlpool" Parker Brothers logo is present, and the boxes are bilingual. When compared to Fundimensions' success in the United States, the Canadian venture was not nearly as successful. The marketing efforts were not aggressive, so not very many sets and individual sale items were distributed in Canada; and, as a result, these trains are very difficult to find.

In 1971 Fundimensions put out a special train catalogue for the Parker Brothers distribution. This catalogue came in two forms: a regular 8-1/2" x 11" version somewhat similar to the American catalogue and a smaller size catalogue, which represents real production more accurately. The Canadian sets and individual cars are preceded in number by a "T" prefix instead of the universally ignored "6" prefix Fundimensions used for its American distribution.

We have listed the following sets by set number and name. Reader comments, corrections and/or additions are requested.

Most of the individual rolling stock and accessory pieces found in the American catalogue were also sold as separate sale items in Canadian Parker Brothers-marked boxes. Clearly, the original box adds quite a bit of value to the car!

1971

T-1171 CANADIAN NATIONAL STEAM LOCOMOTIVE: 8040 Locomotive, 9143, 9065, eight 5013s, two 5018s, CTC, T-4045, wires, instructions.

T-1172 YARDMASTER: 8010 Diesel, 9141 or 9143, 9010 or 9011, 9061, eight 5013s, four 5018s, mechanical uncoupler, CTC, T-4045, wires, instructions.

T-1173 GRAND TRUNK AND WESTERN: 8041 or 8042 Locomotive and Tender, 9143, 9012, 9020 or 9022, 9062 or 9063, eight 5013s, six 5018s, CTC, T-4045, smoke fluid, wires, instructions.

T-1174 CANADIAN NATIONAL: 8031 Diesel with Type I railing and Hillside roller pickup, 9012 TAG navy blue hopper, 9120 green NP flat car with plain white vans, 9040 Wheaties short boxcar with Type IV body, 9143 Canadian National tuscan gondola, 9065 Canadian National tuscan Type IV body SP caboose, twelve 5018s, eight 5013s, T-5020 90-degree crossover in early Type I shrink-wrap packaging, CTC, manumatic uncoupler, T-4045 transformer with black marbled plastic case, wires, bilingual instructions. Estimated set value: $350. G. Halverson Collection.

1972-1973

T-1173 GRAND TRUNK AND WESTERN: 8041 or 8042 Locomotive and Tender, 9143, 9012, 9020 or 9022, 9062 or 9063, eight 5013s, six 5018s, T-4045, smoke fluid, wires, instructions.

T-1174 CANADIAN NATIONAL: 8031 Diesel, 9013, 9120, 9703, 9143, 9065, twelve 5018s, eight 5013s, T-5020, CTC, T-4045, wires, instructions.

T-1272 YARDMASTER: 8111 Diesel, 9300, 9136, 9013, 9025 or 9061, eight 5013s, four 5018s, mechanical uncoupler, 25-watt Trainmaster transformer.

T-1273 SILVER STAR: 8203 Locomotive and Tender, 9136, 9013, 9020, 9062, twelve 5013s, four 5018s, 5020, mechanical uncoupler, 4150.

T-1280 KICKAPOO VALLEY & NORTHERN: 8200 Locomotive, operating dump car, 9020, 9067, eight 5013s, two 5018s, 25-watt Trainmaster transformer. Colors of freight cars appear to differ from American production.

Chapter XVII
UNCATALOGUED SETS

With the assistance of Al Weaver and Paul Ambrose

This listing is in a category which is growing in importance to the collector: Lionel uncatalogued sets. These sets were sometimes depicted in the yearly Advance Catalogues, but not in the Consumer Catalogues. Moreover, these sets included all those which were made by Lionel for a particular store or chain — Montgomery Ward, Sears, etc. The manufacture of special sets for specific department stores was a long tradition with Lionel, going back at least to 1911 and continuing even today in the modern era.

It is expected this listing will grow considerably in future editions. Much information is still to be learned and more sets continue to be discovered, but the picture becomes clearer with each report from readers. Curiously, the Lionel uncatalogued sets we list seem to gravitate either towards the very low end or the very high end of the price scale. Some of these sets can only be considered as cheap loss-leaders.

For the uncatalogued sets, we have used the following criteria: (1) The set must never have appeared in a Lionel catalogue or brochure; (2) the set must have been marketed as a full set and include a set box; and (3) the set must not fit into the Service Station or Separate Sale categories. The uncatalogued sets consist almost entirely of sets made by Lionel for special sale through department stores such as J. C. Penney or Sears, toy stores such as Toys 'R Us or Kay-Bee, or other stores such as Town House Appliances. These sets have been marketed to an astonishing array of American businesses, from American Express to Montgomery Ward. They have also been made by Lionel for special promotions, such as the I T T Cable Hydrospace set and the Nibco Plumbing set.

Each set has a set number, the name (if any) and the retail outlet for which the set was produced. If no retail outlet is named, the set was available through regular Lionel distributors. Although our listing is extensive, it is not complete and we look forward to reader reports on sets not listed here. As far as we know, every set had an official Lionel number, but some of these sets also have catalogue numbers particular to the company selling them, such as Sears catalogue numbers, and we are missing the Lionel set numbers. We need reader assistance in this area as well.

We have listed these sets by their Lionel-assigned set numbers or their department store catalogue numbers. To place a value upon a set, follow the general guidelines on set box price premiums in an article in this volume. If you can clarify one of these uncatalogued sets for us, be sure to let us know the set number, the date and all the contents — even the lubricant, wires, and instruction leaflets. Photographs of the set boxes are an immense help.

UNCATALOGUED SETS

1970

1091 Sears Special: 8043 Locomotive, 8040T, 9140, 9011, 9060.

49N9707 Sears: 8040 Locomotive and Slope-back Tender, gondola, Boxcar, 9300 Bobber Caboose, 25-watt transformer, eight 5013s, two 5018s.

49N97092 Sears: 8041 Locomotive and Tender, gondola, NYC Bobber Caboose, eight 5013s, 25-watt transformer.

79N97081C Sears: 8042 Locomotive and Tender, gondola, 9010, flatcar, 9063, eight 5013s, four 5018s, three figures, 2909, 4045.

79N97082C Sears: 8040 Locomotive and Tender, 9140, 9010, 9060, two 5018s, eight 5013s, manual, 4045.

1971

1190 Sears Special #1: 8140 Locomotive, 8040T, 9140, 9020, 9060.

1195 J. C. Penney Special: 8022 Diesel, 9140, 9011, 9021.

79C95204C Sears: 8020 Diesel, Boxcar, gondola, 9012, 9050, 9012, 9061, (catalogue shows two hoppers), five 5018s, twelve 5013s, push-button remote track, 5020, two figures, three canisters, 50-watt transformer.

79C97101C Sears: 8040 or 8043 Locomotive and Tender, 9141, 9020, 9060, two 5018s, eight 5013s, 25-watt transformer.

79C97105C Sears: 2-4-2 Locomotive and Tender, 9141, 9142, hopper, 9063, (catalogue shows two gondolas), four 5018s, eight 5013s, uncoupling unit, two figures, two canisters, 50-watt transformer.

79C95265C SPEEDRAIL: (This train set is from the same Sears catalogue pages, which listed the three preceding sets. Although the page heading is "Lionel", it is not known if this set was made by Fundimensions.) Modernistic metal and plastic engine, streamlined boxcar, flatcar, and gondola, 18" x 44" elevated figure-eight layout, see-through tunnel, 39-piece trestle set, 16-watt power pack.

SR-1092 Sears: 8042 Locomotive, 9020, 9141, 9011, 9063, 4150, eight 5013s, two 5018s, CTC. C. Rohlfing Collection.

This generic box is identical to the one used for the 1971 Service Station Set, but its paste-on label tells us that a far different set was enclosed. This box contained uncatalogued set No. 1292, which was offered for sale through Sears. It had an unusual 8042 steam locomotive with a Penn Central tender and common-issue freight cars. R. LaVoie Collection.

1972

1290: 8140 Locomotive, 8040T, 9136, 9020, 9060.

1291: 8042 Locomotive with Pennsylvania 1130T tender, 9022, 9141, 9012, 9062, 4150, twelve 5013s, four 5018s, 90-degree crossover, manumatic uncoupler, CTC, wires. Generic set box with paste-on label. R. LaVoie Collection.

79C95204C Sears: 8020 Diesel, boxcar, gondola, 9012, 9050, 9012, 9061, (catalogue shows two hoppers), five 5018s, twelve 5013s, push-button remote track, 9020, two figures, three canisters, 50-watt transformer.

79C97101C Sears: 8040 or 8043 Locomotive and Tender, 9141, 9020, 9060, two 5018s, eight 5013s, 25-watt transformer.

79C97105C Sears: 2-4-2 Locomotive and Tender, 9141, 9142, hopper, 9063, (catalogue shows two gondolas), four 5018s, eight 5013s, uncoupling unit, two figures, two canisters, 50-watt transformer.

79C95265C SPEEDRAIL: (This set is from the same Sears catalogue pages, which list the three preceding sets. Although the page heading is "Lionel", it is not known if this set was made by Fundimensions.) Modernistic metal and plastic engine, streamlined boxcar, flatcar, and gondola, 18" x 44" elevated figure-eight layout, see-through tunnel, 39-piece trestle set, 16-watt power pack.

79N9552C Sears: 8141 Locomotive and Tender, 9012, 9020, 9140, 9062, 5020, four 5018s, twelve 5013s, canisters, 5025, 4150.

79N9553C Sears: 8020 Diesel, 9300, 9040, 9140 or 9141, 9011, 9141, 9061, 5020, eight 5018s, twelve 5013s, canisters, 5025, 4150.

79N97101C Sears: 8042 Locomotive, slope-back tender, 9136, 9011, 9060, two 5018s, eight 5013s, 25-watt transformer.

1973

1390 Sears Seven-Unit: 8310 Locomotive, 8310T, 9013, 9020, 9136, 9040, 9060.

1392 Sears Eight-Unit: 8308 Locomotive, 8308T, (1130T-type), 9124, 9136, 9013, 9020, 9043, 9069.

1395 J. C. Penney: 8311 Locomotive, 8311T (1130T-type), 9140, 9013, 9024, 9043, 9050, 9066.

49C95225 Sears: Heritage trestle train set, pictured on Lionel O27 page, but not made by Fundimensions.

79C95223C Sears: 8351 Diesel, 9043, hopper, 9136, 9020, A T S F Caboose, eight 5013s, two 5018s, 25-watt transformer.

79C95224C Sears: 8303 Locomotive and Tender, flatcar with stakes, 9043, 9136, hopper, flatcar, 9069, ten 5013s, twelve 5018s, two manual switches, 4150.

1974

1492 Sears Seven-Unit: 8310 Locomotive, 8308T (1130T- type), 9124, 9136, 9013, 9043, 9069.

1493 Sears: Same as 1492, but with mailer.

1499 J. C. Penney Great Express: 8311 Locomotive, 8311T (1130T-type), 9136, 9013, 9020, 9066.

79N95223C Sears: 8351 Diesel, 9020, 9013, 9043, 9142, 9061, eight 5013s, two 5018s, uncoupler, 7-1/2-watt transformer.

79N96178C Sears: 8502 Locomotive and Tender, gondola with canisters, 9071, eight 5013s.

79N96185C Sears: 8310 Locomotive and Tender, flatcar with logs, 9136, 9013, 9043, 9069, eight 5013s, eight 5018s, manual switch, bumper, uncoupler, 25-watt transformer.

1975

1594 Sears: 8563 Diesel. Details needed.

1976

1693 Toys 'R Us Rock Island Special: 8601 Locomotive, 8601T, 9047, 9020, 9078.

1694 Toys 'R Us Black River Special: 8602 Locomotive, 8602T (1130T-type), 9026, 9048, 9140, 9077.

1696 Sears: 8604 Locomotive, 1130T, 9020, 9044, 9140, 9011, 9069.

1698 True-Value: 8601 Locomotive and Tender, 9020, 9046, 9078.

1977

1790 Lionel Leisure Steel Hauler: 8769 Diesel, 9033, 9034, 9020, 9071.

1791 Toys 'R Us Steel Hauler: 8769 Diesel, 9033, 9049, 9020, 9071.

1792 True-Value: Same as 1698, except 9053 True-Value Boxcar replaces 9046 True-Value Boxcar.

1793 Toys 'R Us Black River Freight: 8602 Locomotive, 8602T (1130T-type), 9026, 9052, 9140, 9077.

1796 J. C. Penney Cargo Master: 8770, 9026, 9032, 9054, 9025, 4651.

1978

1860 Timberline: 8803 Locomotive, 8803T-5, 9019-5, 9019-14, 9019-25, 9019-35, 9019-45, 9019-26, 9019-27, 9019-250, 3207-45, 9019-30, 8803-T10.

1862 Logging Empire: Same as 1860, but with additional track and building.

1892 J. C. Penney Logging Empire: Same as 1862.

1893 Toys 'R Us Logging Empire: Same as 1862, but with special decal sheet.

79N98765C: 8601 Locomotive, A T S F slope-back tender, log dump car, crane car, boxcar, Caboose, plastic log loader building, barrel loader building, four plastic figures, four plastic logs, twelve 5013s, six 5018s, 5020.

1979

1960 Midnight Flyer: 8902 Locomotive, 8902T, 9339, 9340, 9341.

1962 Wabash Cannonball: 8904 Locomotive, 8904T (1130T- type), 9036, 9035, 9016, 9346.

1963 Rio Grande: 8903.

1990 Mystery Glow Midnight Flyer: Same as 1960, but with glow decals, road signs, and barrel loader.

1991 Wabash Deluxe Express: 8904 Locomotive, 8906T (1130T-type), 9325, 9035, 9346, barrel loader, short bridge, graduated trestle set, billboards, telephone poles.

1993 Toys 'R Us Midnight Flyer: Same as 1960, except 9365 instead of 9339.

1981

1159 Toys 'R Us: 9388. Further details needed.

1982

1264 Nibco Express: 8182 Diesel, 9033, 9035, 6482, two special billboards. (Set made in 1981, but distributed in 1982.)

(Number Unknown) Toys 'R Us Heavy Iron: 8213 Locomotive, 1130T, 9020, 9013, 7912, 9077.

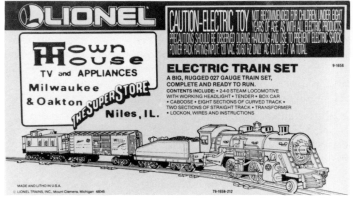

This is the bright orange and black label attached to the Town House Appliances train set box. The picture of the train is accurate, right down to the special boxcar, except that the Atlantic Coast Line emblem is missing from the steam engine's tender and from the caboose. This could be a generic label with the boxcar logos and store information printed as needed by a second run through the presses.

1985

1594: Information requested.

(Number Unknown) Sears Centennial: Identical to 1984-85 Chessie System regular catalogue set, except Chessie short stock car is replaced by special edition Sears Centennial O27-style short boxcar. Sears catalogue number is 95339C.

1986

Town House Set: 8902, 7931, 9341, 4660 DC transformer, eight 5013s, two 5018s, CTC.

1987

11751: 18602 Locomotive, 16000, 16001, 16003, eight curved and two straight track sections, five telephone poles, 4050, lockon, wires. According to our sources, Lionel made this set, which comes in a white box with a brown and white paste-on label, for Sears for Christmas sales in 1987. The sets could not be made ready in time, so Sears canceled the arrangement after the sets were made up. To dispose of the sets, Lionel distributed them to its major wholesale dealers by apportionment. Approximate set value is $225 at this writing. All the rolling stock in the set is also available for separate sale.

95178 Sears: Identical to 1988 Iron Horse catalogued set, except Wabash short boxcar replaced by Sears "Disney Magic" short boxcar. R. Sigurdson comment.

XU671-2970A J. C. Penney ACL Timber Master: 18600 Locomotive, 6585, 9341, eight 5013s, two 5018s, extension bridge, telephone poles, DC power pack. R. Sigurdson comment.

1988

11757 Mopar Express: 8605 Locomotive, 8605T Tender, 6205, 6311, 6310, 6507 Caboose.

SERVICE STATION SETS
By Emil C. Vatter and Emil C. Vatter, Jr.

[**Editor's Note:** The authors have written extensively for the publication of the Lionel Collectors' Club of America, *The Lion Roars*. (This article first appeared in the October 1980 issue of that publication, and the authors have since sent us additional information and corrections to it.) For the Second Edition, we have updated and revised the original material further to accommodate the revival of the Service Station Special Sets for 1986 and beyond.]

From 1971 to 1978, Lionel issued a yearly Service Station Set. The purpose of this set was to give authorized service stations a special set to sell. With the advent of uncatalogued collector sets in 1979, the practice was discontinued. Fundimensions apparently felt dealers were splitting up the sets and the larger dealers, who were not necessarily authorized service stations, were cornering the market on the sets.

Both the 1971 and the 1972 sets have aroused controversy because their existence has been questioned. In fact, service station sets were made in both years. I vaguely remember seeing a 1972 set, and I have a picture of this set and its set box from a fellow collector. All the items from these two sets were subsequently available on the open market, which has created the difficulty. [We have since confirmed both sets.]

Most collectors agree the 1973 Canadian Pacific Set is the most prized, followed by (in my opinion) the 1977 Budd Set and the 1974 Rio Grande Set.

At the end of this article is a list of all Service Station Sets. The reader will notice many cars were catalogued separately in later years. I have heard there are differences between set

cars and those available separately. (This has been confirmed by several collector observations — ed.)

Some interesting observations on Service Station Sets:

(a) Some cars were sold separately but never catalogued. Examples: gray 9113 Norfolk & Western Hopper, 9626 Erie Lackawanna Boxcar and 9138 Sunoco Tank Car. Since none of these are hard to find, Lionel must have produced them in large quantities. An alternative conclusion is that many of the original service station sets were in fact broken up for the individual cars.

(b) Some cars, though catalogued the next year, are hard to find: 9723, 9724, and 9166. Perhaps Lionel never ran them again, and those available came from broken sets. The production run for the separate sale may also have been short.

(c) The 1972 set was the only one with a Steam engine, the 8206, which was catalogued and available for four more years. The 1971 and 1972 sets were the only ones which came with track.

(d) The 1976 set came with a green and yellow caboose, which was true to the prototype. However, it did not match the engine; so, in response to collector demand, Fundimensions later introduced a black and gold caboose to match the locomotive. (This problem occurred again two years later, when the blue and yellow Santa Fe SD-18 locomotive was issued with a red and black 9274 A T S F Caboose. Collector demand forced Fundimensions to issue a blue and yellow 9317 A T S F Caboose. Thus, the 9274 is a scarce item — ed.)

In 1986, Lionel, Inc. revived the service station sets, including the original concept of marketing them through authorized service stations. Just as before, many of the sets found their way into the hands of other dealers or were broken up for separate sale — although the 1986 Santa Fe set has remained intact more than it has been broken up. The usual non-service station dealer's practice is now to keep as many of the sets intact as possible and insist that the sets be sold intact. In that way, the dealer — service station and non-service station alike — gets rid of the less desirable cars in the set as well as the "good" ones. Fortunately for collectors, the sets issued so far have been excellent and desirable items. See John Kouba's article on the 1986 Santa Fe Work Train elsewhere in this edition.

In 1971-72, Lionel used generic boxes to package many of its sets. This set box had a special label attached to it which proclaimed the contents as the 1971 Service Station Special, whose existence has finally been confirmed. All the products in this set were offered for sale later on, unlike later Service Station sets. Contrast this box with the box for set 1291. L. Caponi Collection.

SERVICE STATION SETS BY YEAR

1971

No. 1187: 8030 I. C. GP-9 Diesel, 9200, 9215, 9211, 9214, 9230, 9160, eight O curve, eleven O straight, 5502 remote-control section; estimated production: 1,000. When sold, set will carry a 35 percent premium over the value of the individual items only if the original box for the set is present.

The following example has been located and described: Set came in generic set box with paper label; purchased in November 1971 from Glen Uhl in Ohio. All rolling stock came in Type I boxes except locomotive, which came in postwar-type box with Fundimensions label (the early plain 8030 box with double flaps on the ends and a punch-through display piece on the side). Set included the following: 8030(A) Illinois Central GP-9 (Type I railings), 9200(F) Illinois Central Boxcar, 9211(G) Penn Central Boxcar, 9214(A) Northern Pacific Boxcar, 9215(A) Norfolk and Western Boxcar, 9230(A) Monon Boxcar, and 9160(B) Illinois Central N5C Caboose. Set also included UCS remote track in older Hillside box, 11 straight and 8 curved MPC O Gauge track, and styrofoam "house" packaging material by Myco. G. Mueller Collection.

1972

No. 1250: 8206 N Y C Locomotive, 9111, 9707, 9709, 9151, 9710, 9162; eight O curved, twelve O straight; production not known. When sold, set will carry a 35 percent premium over the value of the individual items only if original box is present.

1973

No. 1350: 8365 and 8366 Diesels, 9113 available separately, 9723, 9724, 9725, 9165; 8469 B unit available separately; estimated production: 2,500. Very hard to find as an intact set.

1974

No. 1450: 8464 (powered) and 8465 (dummy) Rio Grande Diesels, 9144, 9117, 9739, 9863, 9166; set production 3000; also available separately, 8474.

1975

No. 1579: 8555 and 8557 F3-A Diesel, 9119, 9132, 9754, 9758, 9169; 8575 available separately; estimated production: 6,000.

1976

No. 1672: 8666 GP-9 Diesel, 9267, 9775, 9776, 9869, 9177; 8668 available separately, 9268; estimated production: 6,000.

1977

No. 1766: 8766, 8767, and 8768; 8764, 8765 available separately; estimated production 5,000. In considerable demand from collectors.

1978

No. 1868: 8866 Diesel, 9138, 9213, 9408, 9726, 9271; 8867 Diesel available separately; estimated production: 6,000. Readily available both as a complete set and as individual components, even though at least half these sets were broken up.

1986

No. 1632: 8635 Switcher, 5745, 5760, 6272, 6593, 6496. Very strong seller as an intact set.

1987

No. 11704 The Southern Freight Runner: 18802 Southern GP-9, 16607, 16102, 16402, 16701, 16504.

1988

No. 11706 The Virginia & Truckee Dry Gulch Line: 18702 Locomotive, 18702T Tender, 16012, 16010, 16011.

THE 1632 SANTA FE
SERVICE STATION SET OF 1986

By John Kouba

In late November of 1986, Lionel's new management, Lionel, Inc., revived a custom which had been abandoned in 1978 — the Service Station Special. The original purpose of the Service Station Special was to give Lionel's authorized Service Stations a set of their own to sell exclusively. The concept had been abandoned because the larger Lionel dealers had been acquiring these sets and breaking them up for individual sale, but in 1986 the Santa Fe Work Train revived the concept and there is also a 1987 Southern Freight Runner diesel-powered Service Station Set as well as the 1988 Dry Gulch Special Service Station Set.

The Santa Fe Work Train represents an ambitious endeavor for Lionel, Inc. It is based upon the highly successful catalogued New York Central Yard Chief Set of 1985, but it is also a much more highly developed set. It comes in a rather plain white carton, as did the Yard Chief, but that is where the resemblance ends. It is evident from the first examination of the Santa Fe set that Lionel, Inc. wanted to make a highly favorable impression upon collectors.

Lionel chose this set to introduce a colorful version of its new tool car, first seen in an all-gray version in the B & O Freight catalogued in 1986. This tool car is one of only two all-new cars issued to the general public for 1986, the other being the ACF center-flow hopper available only through a direct-mail order from Lionel. Finished in red oxide with yellow lettering, the tool car boasts some interesting design changes from its predecessor, the bunk car, also present in the Santa Fe set. Lionel had its die makers busy changing the side window scheme and adding two door inserts, one in each end panel. In the photograph issued to dealers, the end doors were shown to be the same silver color as the ends and roof. However, in the production model the doors are red oxide — a wise choice, as this makes the doors stand out from the silver ends.

Lionel modified the sides of the bunk car by eliminating the holes for the clear marker lights packed with those cars. Next to go were the bunk car's four square windows. These were replaced by two eight-pane rectangular windows with sills. The ladder on the right side of the bunk car doors was removed, as were the ladders at either end of the sides. These were replaced by cast-on rungs; two of these were on the left corner, five on the left side of the door, and six on the right corner. Gone also were the two reporting boards on the bunk car next to the left side of the door. These were removed because they were in the path of the new rungs placed there instead. Finally, Lionel designed a new two-pane door with a small bottom step and long vertical grab-bars on either side of the door frame. Unlike the bunk car door, which is a solid piece, illuminated versions of the tool car door have frosted window inserts for illumination. In addition, frosted window inserts replace the clear ones of the bunk cars. All these changes make the tool car look distinctively different from its predecessor, though the roof and bottom pieces remained the same. The Santa Fe tool car still has a hole for the smokestack, and this piece and the brakewheel are packed separately to prevent breakage. On the new 19651 Santa Fe illuminated Tool Car, the smokestack hole is eliminated from the roof.

The finishing touch on the tool car — indeed, on all the cars — was the use of Standard O die-cast trucks. The Standard O trucks cannot be adapted to take pickups for light rollers, so their use, of course, negates any interior illumination, and the tool and bunk cars remain dark in this set. All in all, Lionel's designers have come up with a tool car which could have a prototype rolling around on the country's railroads somewhere. [**Editor's Note:** Prototypes for the bunk cars have been photographed in the mid-1960s on the Pennsylvania-Reading Seashore Lines; they resemble Lionel's model quite a bit.] The tool car is certainly a nice, handsome edition to add to one's maintenance train roster. The Santa Fe edition of the tool car will probably appreciate in value rapidly because of its limited availability; time will tell.

Another first in this Santa Fe set was the issuance of the 6496 Work Caboose with Standard O trucks. It is finished in red with a black base; the logo and number are yellow. The crane car, too, has the Standard O trucks. Most of Lionel's recent crane cars use the die-cast six-wheel passenger trucks; the Standard O trucks on this crane pose a problem because they couple too closely with other cars. Lionel should have provided a longer coupler shank for these trucks so that the couplers extended further away from the body. Still, they do add a touch of class to an otherwise standard-fare car.

The 6272 Long Gondola is shown in Lionel's literature carrying two black empty cable reels. These are packed separately in the set box. Inside the box containing the car, however, are three gray canisters identical to previous loads issued with other Lionel gondolas of the Fundimensions years. Apparently Lionel, Inc. found that it had a large supply of these canisters in inventory and decided at the last minute to include these with the car as well. The box description for the car makes no mention of either load.

The 0-4-0 steam switcher engine included with the Santa Fe set is the second edition of the Lionel steam switchers with working smoke units and backup lights in the tenders. However, with this engine Lionel, Inc. made one omission which shows some lack of thought. The Santa Fe Service Station Special is a limited edition set including new Lionel cars with the desirable Standard O trucks on all the cars. After making major improvements to the switch engine, Lionel ironically put the less expensive Symington-Wayne plastic trucks on the tender! There is no logical explanation for this, since the tender does not provide a center-rail pickup for the locomotive. Since the set was obviously designed, executed, and released for sale through Service Stations, strictly for the collector market, it would have been logical and desirable for Lionel to have placed the excellent Standard O trucks onto the tender as well as the rolling stock. If the reason is that such a step would have driven up the cost of the set, it is a poor one. Most collectors would gladly pay an additional $10 or so to have Standard O trucks on the tender.

There may be legitimate construction reasons why Standard O trucks are not found on the tender. First of all, steam engine tenders with metal trucks have always been equipped with six-wheel die-cast passenger trucks, which are far too large for this tender. The Standard O truck was never modified into a version without the coupler. Secondly, the tender has a plastic bottom piece which may not be compatible with the screw-mounted Standard O trucks. Collectors might try to purchase Standard O trucks and mount them to the tender on this set, but some further modification may be necessary. Probably, shim washers would be necessary both inside and outside of the tender frame. The tender might also ride too high on Standard O trucks for the drawbar from the engine, and some way would have to be found to attach a drawbar to the front truck of the tender while eliminating the coupler.

The engine itself, however, is a work of art. It is obvious that Lionel took great pains to make sure that it was the best looking as well as the best running steam switcher produced thus far. Upon first inspection, one notices that considerable hand work went into smoothing off the casting seams from the die-cast boiler shell. The casting detail, rivets, etc. seem to be sharper than previous models, giving the impression that the dies for this engine have been retooled. This attention to detail, combined with a first class paint job, result in one of Lionel's finest steam switchers ever.

Another new feature listed in the dealer brochure is a new type of smoke unit. This unit solves a problem which has plagued Lionel ever since the advent of the modern era with fast-angle wheels for the rolling stock. By making the rolling stock easier to pull, Lionel created a new problem for its smoke units. The effort required to pull the cars of a modern era train is far less than in the postwar era, and this results in the train operating at lower voltage, especially with the quieter and efficient can motors used in the Santa Fe switchers. Generally, Lionel's newer engines can pull three times the number of new cars at far less voltage than required by the older postwar cars. Apparently the Lionel engineers overlooked the fact that the smoke units require a higher operating voltage than do the motors — hence, far less smoke is produced in modern era engines. One cure for this problem is for the operator to add several postwar cars with old-style wheels to the train consist to put more drag on the engine. The engine then needs a higher voltage which will, in turn, produce more smoke. This is hardly the ideal solution! The locomotive motors of modern era engines are good, but over extended periods of operation at high voltage serious motor problems are likely to develop.

The smoke problem seems to be solved by the new smoke units used in the 8516 New York Central Switcher and the new Santa Fe Locomotive. Lionel's engineers lowered the smoke unit resistance in these engines. With as little as eight volts, these engines will send up volcanic, impressive chuffs of smoke from their stacks. Of course, the operator will have to refill the smoke units with liquid smoke fluid more frequently, but that is a small price to pay for the very nice smoking effect produced by these engines. Care has to be taken not to overload the engine's pulling capacity, of course; too much voltage could burn out the smoke unit. In addition, many operators caution against refilling the smoke unit when it is very hot, for the same reason. A load limit of 14 volts seems reasonable and safe for these switcher engines.

The packaging for the Santa Fe Service Station Special is interesting, too. The rolling stock comes in Type III boxes and the engine and tender are packed in a long Type II box; this is the same packaging found on the earlier Yard Chief Set. These boxes all have either Fundimensions logos or the new Lionel Trains, Inc. logos. Lionel is using up the box inventory on hand rather than printing up new packaging for the set. It seems logical that when this stock is used up, all Lionel, Inc. products will come in newly-designed boxes. [**Editor's Note:** We have designated these boxes as Type VI. For a full discussion of box types, see the Trucks and Boxes chapter.] The literature packed with the Santa Fe set bears the new corporate logos.

Nit-picking aside, the 1632 Santa Fe Service Station Special is a "class act." The set has an excellent looking and operating engine with a vastly improved smoke unit, a new tool car, and Standard O trucks on the rolling stock. These add up to a set which should be received by collectors and operators alike with great enthusiasm. It shows continuing concern with improvement on the part of Lionel, Inc. and, hopefully, a sign of even higher quality coming forth from the new leadership at Lionel.

SEPARATE SALE SETS

The above heading may sound like a contradiction, but it really represents a marketing strategy first used in 1974 with the advent of the Spirit of '76 Set and its matching special boxcars. Lionel's catalogues carried the legend, "All items sold separately, not as a set." Perhaps they were meant for separate sale, but in fact these matching items were sold as sets by dealers. The separate-sale device freed Lionel from producing the exact numbers for each item. For example, in both the Southern Crescent and Blue Comet sets, many more sets of cars were made than engines. In addition, the separate sale ploy made it possible for Lionel to add other cars to the sets later, as they indeed did, especially with the extruded aluminum passenger cars. Incredibly, ten years have passed between the introduction of the Southern Crescent and Blue Comet sets and the introduction of dining cars for them!

What are the criteria for separate sale sets? First of all, they must constitute a legitimate set, no matter in what order the items were produced. That means a locomotive, cars, and (for freights) a caboose. Secondly, they must have been marketed as separate sale items. That leaves out such boxed sets as the Royal Limited, even though extra cars were issued for that set. Finally, they must be perceived by both collector and dealer as separate sale items, which combine into sets. That is why the Lionel Lines items constitute a separate sale set, but the Hudson and Standard O New York Central cars do not. Neither do the mint cars despite Lionel's catalogue hints to the contrary. Collectors and dealers just do not think of those items as sets, and they are seldom found for sale together. However, the Lionel Lines items, at least partially, are in fact found together for sale a good part of the time. Of course, the Service Station Sets are covered above.

The following listings show sets which were meant for separate sale but have matching components and, in many cases, additions in later years. We specifically *exclude* any groups which were in fact made by Lionel to be sold as sets. The sets are listed by year with the locomotive and/or original components first. Later additions are then listed along with the year of their issuance. In practice, many dealers sell these matching components as sets, no matter what Lionel may have said or is saying. We have also shown where these matching components are described in the literature.

Note: Recently, some dealers have begun to sell the mint cars and their matching GG-1 locomotive and caboose as a separate sale set. For the information of the interested collector, these items, and the years of production, are as follows: 18300 GG-1 Locomotive (1987), 7515 Denver (1982), 7517 Philadelphia (1982), 7518 Carson City (1983), 7522 New Orleans (1985), 7530 Dahlonega (1986), 9319 T C A (1979), 9320 Fort Knox (1979), 9349 San Francisco (1980), and 19702 N5C Caboose (1987). As a complete set, these items are extremely difficult to assemble.

SEPARATE SALE SETS BY YEAR

1974

THE SPIRIT OF '76: Commemorative series, consumer catalogue: 1776 Seaboard U36B, 7601 Delaware, 7602 Pennsylvania, 7603 New Jersey, 7600 Spirit of '76 N5C. Later additions: 7604 Georgia, 7605 Connecticut, 7606 Massachusetts, 7607 Maryland, 1975, consumer catalogue; 7608 South Carolina, 7609 New Hampshire, 7610 Virginia, 7611 New York, 7612 North Carolina, 7613 Rhode Island, 1976, consumer catalogue.

1977

THE SOUTHERN CRESCENT: Consumer catalogue. 8702 4-6-4 Hudson, 9530 Baggage, 9531 Combine, 9532 Pullman, 9533 Pullman, 9534 Observation. Later addition: 19001 Diner, 1987, year-end brochure.

THE MICKEY MOUSE EXPRESS: Consumer catalogue. 8773 Mickey Mouse U36B, 9660 Mickey Mouse, 9661 Goofy, 9662 Donald Duck, 9183 Mickey Mouse N5C. Later additions: 9663 Dumbo, 9664 Cinderella, 9665 Peter Pan, 9666 Pinocchio, 9667 Snow White, 9668 Pluto, 1978, consumer catalogue; 9669 Bambi, 9670 Alice In Wonderland, 9671 Fantasia, 9672 Mickey Mouse 50th Birthday, 1978, dealer brochures.

THE GENERAL: Consumer catalogue (locomotive only). 8701 General locomotive. Later additions: 9551 Baggage, 9552 Coach, 9553 flatcar with horses, 1977, dealer year-end brochure.

1978

THE BLUE COMET: Consumer catalogue. 8801 4-6-4 Hudson, 9536 Baggage, 9537 Combine, 9538 Pullman, 9539 Pullman, 9540 Observation. Later addition: 19000 Diner, 1987, year-end brochure.

AMTRAK: Budd railcars, consumer catalogue: 8868 Baggage, 8869 passenger, 8870 passenger, 8871 Baggage.

1979

SANTA FE: Famous American Railroad Series No. 1, consumer catalogue: 8900 4-6-4 Hudson, 7712 Boxcar, 9880 Reefer, 9321 Tank Car, 9322 Hopper, 9323 Bay Window Caboose. Later addition: 9348 Santa Fe Crane, Collector's Accessory Center brochure, 1979.

PENNSYLVANIA: Congressional Limited, consumer catalogue: 8952-8953 Pennsylvania F-3 AA units (green), 9570 Baggage, 9571 William Penn Coach, 9572 Molly Pitcher Coach, 9573 Betsy Ross Vista Dome, 9574 Alexander Hamilton Observation. Later additions: 8970-8971 Pennsylvania F-3 AA units (tuscan), 9575 Thomas Edison Coach, 1979, Collector's Accessory Center brochure; 8059 F-3 B unit (green), 8060 F-3 B unit (tuscan), 1980, Fall Collector Center brochure; 8164 F-3 B unit (green, with horn), 9569 Paul Revere Combine, 1981, Fall Collector Center brochure; 7208 John Hancock Diner, 1983, Fall Collector Center brochure.

1980

UNION PACIFIC: Famous American Railroad Series No. 2, consumer catalogue: 8002 Union Pacific Locomotive, 9811 Reefer, 9419 Boxcar, 9367 Tank Car, 9366 Quad Hopper, 9368 Bay Window Caboose. Later addition: 9383 T O F C flat car, 1980, Fall Collector Center brochure.

THE TEXAS ZEPHYR: Burlington passenger set: 8054-8055 F-3 AA units, 9576 Silver Pouch Baggage, 9577 Silver Halter Coach, 9578 Silver Gladiola Coach, 9579 Silver Kettle Vista Dome, 9580 Silver Veranda Observation. Later additions: 8062 F-3 B unit, 9588 Silver Dome Vista Dome, 1980, Fall Collector Center brochure.

JOSHUA LIONEL COWEN: Commemorative, consumer catalogue: 9429 Early Years, 9430 Standard Gauge Years, 9431 Prewar Years, 9432 Postwar Years (sold in Royal Limited set), 9433 Golden Years (sold in Mid-Atlantic set). Later additions: 9434 The Man Boxcar, 1980, Fall Collector Center; 8210 Joshua Lionel Cowen 4-6-4 Hudson Steam Locomotive, 6421 Joshua Lionel Cowen Bay Window Caboose, 1982, Spring Collector Center brochure.

CHESSIE STEAM SPECIAL: Passenger set, consumer catalogue: 8003 2-8-4 Steam Locomotive, 9581 Baggage, 9582 Combine, 9583 Pullman, 9584 Pullman, 9585 Observation. Later addition: 9586 Diner, 1986, year-end brochure.

ROCK ISLAND & PEORIA: General set, consumer catalogue: 8004 4-4-0 General Steam Locomotive. Later additions: 9559 Combine, 9560 Coach, 9561 Coach, 1981, consumer catalogue.

1981

NORFOLK AND WESTERN: Passenger set, "Sneak Preview" brochure and consumer catalogue: 8100 4-8-4 Steam Locomotive, 9562 Baggage, 9563 Combine, 9564 Coach, 9565 Coach, 9566 Observation. Later additions: 9567 Vista Dome, 1981, Fall Collector Center brochure; 7203 Diner, 1982, Fall Collector Center brochure.

ALTON LIMITED: Passenger set, "Sneak Preview" brochure and consumer catalogue: 8101 4-6-4 Hudson Steam Locomotive, 9554 Baggage, 9555 Combine, 9556 Pullman, 9557 Pullman, 9558 Observation. Later addition: 9599 Diner, 1986, year-end brochure.

FAVORITE FOOD FREIGHT: Consumer catalogue: 8160 Burger King GP-20, 7509 Kentucky Fried Chicken, 7510 Red Lobster, 7511 Pizza Hut, 6449 Wendy's N5C Caboose. Later additions: 7512 Arthur Treacher's, 7513 Bonanza, 7514 Taco Bell, 1982, consumer catalogue.

GREAT NORTHERN: Famous American Railroad Series No. 3, consumer catalogue: 3100 4-8-4 Steam Locomotive, 9449 Boxcar, 9819 Reefer, 6304 Tank Car, 6102 Quad Hopper, 6438 Bay Window Caboose. Later addition: 9450 Stock Car, 1981, Fall Collector Center brochure.

1982

NO. 1970 SOUTHERN PACIFIC: "Daylight" passenger set, Spring Collector Center brochure and consumer catalogue: 8260 and 8262 F-3 AA units, 9589 Baggage, 9590 Combine, 9591 Coach, 9592 Coach, 9593 Observation. Later additions: 8261 F-3 B unit, 7204 Diner, 1982, Fall Collector Center brochure; 8307 4-8-4 Steam Locomotive, 1983, Collector Preview brochure; 7211 Vista Dome, 1983, Fall Collector Center brochure.

1983

NEW YORK CENTRAL: Twentieth Century Limited passenger set, 1983 Collector Preview and consumer catalogue: 8370-8372 F-3 AA units, 8371 F-3 B unit, 9594 Baggage, 9595 Combine, 9596 Coach, 9597 Coach, 9598 Observation.

Later additions: 7207 Diner, 1983, Fall Collector Center brochure; 8206 4-6-4 Hudson, 1984 Spring Preview brochure.

SOUTHERN: Famous American Railroad Series No. 4, consumer catalogue: 8309 2-8-4 Steam Locomotive, 9451 Boxcar, 6104 Quad Hopper, 9887 Reefer, 6306 Tank Car, 6431 Bay Window Caboose. Later addition: 7304 stock car, 1983, Fall Collector Center.

LIONEL LINES: Diesel freight set, Fall Collector Center: 8380 SD-28 Diesel, 9849 Reefer, 9239 N5C Caboose. Later additions: 5712 Wood-sided Reefer, 1982; Fall Collector Center brochure (actually predates rest of the items); 6313 Tank Car, 6214 Gondola, 1984, Spring Collector Center; 5733 Bunk Car, 1986, year-end brochure; 19303 Quad Hopper, 1987, year-end brochure;

1984

PENNSYLVANIA: Famous American Railroads Series No. 5, consumer catalogue: 8404 6-8-6 S-2 Steam Locomotive, 6123 Quad Hopper, 9476 Boxcar, 9456 Boxcar, 6307 Tank Car, 6908 N5C Caboose.

UNION PACIFIC: passenger set, consumer catalogue: 8480-8482 F-3 AA units, 8481 F-3 B unit, 9545 Baggage, 9546 Combine, 9548 Coach, 9549 Coach, 7210 Diner, 9547 Observation.

1985

ILLINOIS CENTRAL: "City of New Orleans" passenger set, consumer catalogue: 8580-8581 F-3 AA units, 8582 F-3 B unit, 7220 Baggage, 7221 Combine, 7222 Coach, 7223 Coach, 7224 Diner, 7225 Observation.

1986

JERSEY CENTRAL: "Miss Liberty" commemorative, consumer catalogue: 8687 Fairbanks-Morse Diesel, 7404 Boxcar, 6917 Extended Vision Caboose.

WABASH: Fallen Flags Series No. 1, consumer catalogue: 8610 4-6-2 Steam Locomotive, 7227 Diner, 7228 Baggage, 7229 Combine, 7230 Pullman, 7231 Pullman, 7232 Observation.

1987

PENNSYLVANIA: passenger set, consumer catalogue: 18602 4-4-2 Steam Locomotive, 16000 Vista Dome, 16001 Coach, 16002 Coach, 16003 Observation, 16009 Combine (1988), 18901-18902 Alco AA Diesel pair (1988).

MILWAUKEE ROAD: Fallen Flags Series No. 2, consumer catalogue: 18500 GP-9, 19400 Gondola, 19500 Reefer, 19204 Boxcar, 19600 Tank Car, 19302 Quad Hopper, 19701 N5C Caboose.

1988

GREAT NORTHERN: Fallen Flags Series No. 3: 18302 EP-5 Electric Locomotive, 19205 Double-door Boxcar, 19505 Refrigerator Car, 19402 Crane, 19304 Covered Hopper, 19401 Long Gondola with coal load, 19703 Extended Vision Caboose.

Chapter XVIII
TRUCKS AND BOXES

Modern Era Lionel Construction Practices: Some Variations

Throughout this book, the descriptions of the rolling stock issued by modern era Lionel may include phrases such as "Type IX body" or "Standard O Trucks." In an effort to make clear what is meant by such classifications, we often preface the particular chapter with descriptions of body, railing, or other variations which apply to the cars in those chapters alone. However, it is important to recognize construction variations which affect the whole range of modern era production, even though they may not have a dramatic effect upon value. The beginning collector will soon see that these universal variations have their own stories to tell.

One good example of the intricacies of the manufacturing process occurred rather early in Fundimensions' history. The couplers on rolling stock made by Fundimensions and its successors work by a snap-in plastic armature which, when pulled down by the magnet on a remote track, opens the coupler knuckle and uncouples the car. Postwar Lionel used several different assemblies which would be either ineffective or too costly in today's train world. Therefore, Fundimensions did considerable experimenting with its uncoupling armatures. We think that at first the company tried to glue a flat metal disc onto the plastic surface of the armature shank where it was molded into a rounded end, although we have not been able to confirm this. Then a metal bar was glued into a recess cut into the bottom of the armature shank. A short time later, someone at the factory came up with an idea which has no doubt saved thousands of dollars for the firm. Fundimensions changed the mold of the downward shaft of the armature so that there was a hole running down the shaft tube. Then, the workers placed a simple large, chrome-headed thumb tack into the hole! This solution has worked so well that it is standard practice on even the most expensive trains made by modern era Lionel. Operationally, it is just as good as the reliable metal flap on the old postwar bar-end metal magnetic trucks — and it is a great deal cheaper!

In this introduction, we will try to classify four areas which cut across all of modern era Lionel's production of rolling stock: the types of trucks, the types of coupler armatures, the types of wheelsets, and the types of packing boxes. For areas particular to the type of car, see the introductions to the individual chapters.

TYPES OF TRUCKS

The plastic trucks used by modern era Lionel are made of Delrin, a low-friction plastic patented by the duPont Corporation. These trucks have a gloss and an oily feel to them; furthermore, they are much more flexible and far less brittle than the styrene plastic used in postwar production. These trucks have small holes drilled part way into the frames; these are the bearings for the wheelsets, which have their wheels fixed to the axles. The needle points of the axles fit into the holes and rotate within them as the car rolls. The wear characteristics of the bearings appear to be excellent. Since the rolling surfaces of the wheels are angled to allow for a differential action around curved track, modern era trucks have been far better performers than their postwar equivalents. In addition, the knuckle springs are integral to the knuckle instead of a separate metal spring, which often became dislodged in postwar trucks.

The metal trucks used by modern era Lionel also show advances over their postwar counterparts. In 1973 the firm produced a marvelously well detailed truck for its scale Standard O Series. This die-cast truck features a bolster bar suspended from the truck frame by functional springs, just like the prototype. It has been used on many other cars because of its high quality. Lionel has also produced a well-detailed six-wheel passenger truck in metal; it too has been used on steam locomotive tenders, crane cars, and other pieces of rolling stock. In late 1986 Lionel, Inc. introduced a beautifully detailed die-cast arch bar truck for its revivals of the wood-sided cabooses. Unlike the Standard O truck, this truck can be adapted for illumination.

TYPE 1: AAR TRUCKS WITH TIMKEN BEARINGS. These trucks are carry-over pieces from later postwar production, except that they are made of Delrin plastic rather than styrene. The detail on these trucks tends to be grainy and rather blurred; apparently, the postwar die used to make them was worn badly. For that reason, these trucks are found only on stock issued in 1970 through early 1972, particularly some of the 9200-series boxcars and the earlier large hopper cars. All of these trucks are of the later, open-axle style (the ends of the axles are visible from the bottom).

TYPE II: SYMINGTON-WAYNE TRUCKS (formerly known as Bettendorf). These trucks are by far the most common ones on modern era Lionel rolling stock. For many previous editions, we (along with the entire train fraternity) had been calling these trucks Bettendorf types. That is an error. In November 1964 an advertisement appeared in the trade magazine *Modern Railroads* for the Symington-Wayne Company of Chicago. This ad shows clearly that the truck Fundimensions and its successors have used for their models is the Symington-Wayne high-speed XL-70 truck. The next issue of the magazine contains a feature article on these trucks. We are indebted to Mr. Thomas Hawley of Lansing, Michigan for sending us this information. There are several variations of these trucks. Most variations have to do with the rear projection of the truck as viewed from the underside, but there are other variations in coupler shank height to compensate for the differing fastening points on varying rolling stock. All variations may be found with either a coupler shank which angles downward or a coupler shank which comes straight out from the truck frame.

TYPE II A: The top of the truck frame is smooth when viewed from the side. There is a small, flat, square-shaped tab at the rear of the truck when viewed from the underside.

TYPE II B: Identical to Type II A, except that the top of the truck frame side is not smooth; it has a projection with five rivets.

TYPE II C: Large, round projection on the truck rear with a flat punched hole. Smooth truck frame side.

TYPE II D: Identical to Type II C, except that the truck frame has the five-rivet projection.

TYPE II E: Rounded projection on the truck rear, but much smaller than Types II C or D. The hole at the rear of the projection is raised by a peg-like structure. Smooth-sided truck frame.

Type II B. R. Bartelt photograph.

Type II D. R. Bartelt photograph.

Type II E. R. Bartelt photograph.

TYPE II F: Identical to Type II E, but has the five-rivet projection on the truck frame side.

TYPE II G: Medium-sized block-like square projection on truck rear, much more massive than Types II A and B. Longer, self-centering couplers. Smooth truck sides. This truck can be found most often on bay window cabooses. There may be a version with the five-rivet projection, but confirmation is needed.

TYPE II H: Identical to Types II A, C, or E, but coupler is a nonoperating solid plastic piece. Used on inexpensive production. There may be a version with the

Type II G. R. Bartelt photograph.

Type II H. R. Bartelt photograph.

five-rivet projection, but confirmation is needed. Note that the top surfaces of the nonoperating couplers are hollowed out, while the operating ones are solid.

TYPE III: STANDARD O SPRUNG TRUCKS. Many collectors regard these trucks as the finest ever made by Lionel, postwar or modern era. Except for the Delrin armature, they are entirely die-cast; they fasten to their cars with a small screw and a fiber collar. The bolster bar running across the truck is suspended from the truck side frames by two tiny coil springs on each side; these springs actually are functional. The truck is close in design to the standard freight trucks used by the Association of American Railroads for many years; like the prototypes, the construction is open, with most of the wheel surfaces showing. There are no known variations except perhaps in the gloss of the wheels themselves. Lionel has used this truck on most of its Collector Series freight cars.

TYPE IV: WOOD-BEAM PASSENGER TRUCKS. These plastic trucks have been used on the early 9500-series passenger cars and the short 6400-series Amtrak O27 passenger cars. Their latest use has been on the O27 Pennsylvania passenger cars issued for separate sale in 1987. They are modeled after the old wooden-beam trucks used in the 19th Century. It is curious that Lionel would use such an old-fashioned truck on relatively modern passenger cars, but so it goes.

TYPE V: PLASTIC ARCHBAR TRUCKS. These plastic trucks are a carry-over from the "General" style trucks used by postwar Lionel in the late 1950s for its Civil War locomotive and passenger coaches. They were also used on the Fundimensions revival of those cars, and lately they have been used for the new bunk and tool car series and the Wood-sided Reefer series. They are more sturdy than their forebears, thanks to the Delrin plastic formula, but they are more fragile than other modern era Lionel trucks.

TYPE VI: DIE-CAST O27 PASSENGER TRUCKS. These die-cast trucks are carry-overs from the original metal trucks used on the postwar O27 passenger cars, beginning with the 2400 Series in the late 1940s. Ironically, Fundimensions bypassed these trucks when it revived the O27 passenger cars, but the firm then reissued them for use on certain pieces such as the 9307 Animated Gondola, the four-truck depressed center flatcar and certain bay window cabooses.

TYPE VII: DIE-CAST O GAUGE PASSENGER TRUCKS. When Fundimensions revived the extruded aluminum passenger cars with the Congressional Limited cars in 1979, the firm also revived the original trucks. These four-wheel die-cast trucks feature long coupler shanks which are made self-centering by a hairspring where they meet the truck frame. They have been used in all aluminum O Gauge passenger cars produced since then, but nowhere else.

TYPE VIII: DIE-CAST SIX-WHEEL PASSENGER TRUCKS. Fundimensions introduced an entirely new passenger truck when it issued its Blue Comet Set in 1978. The truck frames are die-cast, as is the coupler and its shank. As with the O Gauge four-wheel trucks, the couplers are made self-centering by means of a hairspring. These trucks have been used on the Blue Comet, Chessie Steam Special, Chicago and Alton, and Wabash passenger cars, as well as the six-wheel tenders on most deluxe steam engines since then and most of the newer crane cars. It has one operating weakness; the axles are fastened to the trucks by slide-in plastic bearings which may come loose if not periodically checked.

TYPE IX: DIE-CAST ARCH BAR TRUCKS. When Lionel put out a brochure for a special direct-mail order Hudson and series of freight cars in late 1986, most of the freight cars had Standard O trucks, but the two wood-sided cabooses, excellent revivals of the prewar New York Central Semi-Scale caboose, had an entirely new truck — a highly realistic die-cast arch bar truck. These trucks have the same good open-style construction as the Standard O trucks, but no operating springs. They have one highly significant advantage; they can be adapted for a roller carriage for illumination. So far, they have been put onto all wood-sided cabooses and the Pennsylvania N5C caboose which matches the bronze GG-1 of 1987. Expect these excellent trucks to be placed on many more cars in the future.

TYPES OF COUPLER ARMATURE

In the beginning, Fundimensions and its successors have used a detachable armature for all their trucks. This has operating advantages over the older postwar arrangement, since the operator can often cure a stubborn coupler which refuses to close properly by simply exchanging armatures. These armatures are made of Delrin plastic; they are made to plug into two holes in the coupler shanks and can be removed by simply prying them out with one's fingernail. They feature a small tab projection for manual uncoupling. Variations involve the uncoupling shaft protruding downward from the armature.

TYPE I: A small, flat metal disc is simply glued onto the flared bottom of the armature shaft. Confirmation of this is requested.

TYPE II: A metal bar is inserted into a recess cut into the flared bottom of the armature shaft. This variety is found most often on cars equipped with the AAR trucks with Timken bearings.

TYPE III: A flat-headed thumb tack with a blackened point is pressed into the armature shaft. This first appears in later 1970 production.

TYPE IV: A chrome-plated, large, round-headed thumb tack is pressed into the armature shaft. First appearing in late 1971 production, this variety is by far the most common.

TYPES OF WHEELSETS

As has been mentioned, Fundimensions designed a new set of wheels for its rolling stock from the outset of its production. Regardless of type, these wheels feature angled rolling surfaces to provide for a differential action around curved track. This cuts drag and rolling resistance to a minimum. The wheels are integral with the axles, which have needlepoint bearings. Since Fundimensions and its successors have subcontracted for the production of these wheelsets (a much more common practice than one may think), there have been several different types of wheelsets used over the years. The differences are found for the most part in the inside of the wheel surfaces. So far, we have identified eight varieties:

TYPE I: Blackened wheels and axles, deeply recessed inner wheel section with thick outer rim on inside surface stamped "LIONEL MPC". Four large round raised metal dots near junction of wheel with axle. This lettering is very hard to see on some examples because the die wore down with use. There is usually a casting mark between and just outside the circumference of two of the dots.

TYPE II: Same as Type I, except no "LIONEL MPC" lettering. These are clearly different from worn-die versions of Type I.

TYPE III: Blackened axles, shiny bronzed inner and outer surfaces, four less distinct (as opposed to Types I and II) flat metal dots near junction of wheel with axle. On some examples, there appears to be a manufacturer's mark which looks like a letter "F" extended to form a letter "C". The mark could also be a large "L" connected to a small "L" inside a slightly open rectangle.

TYPE IV: Blackened wheels and axles, no lettering, three barely visible small flat round dots near junction of wheel and axle.

TYPE V: Same as Type IV, but shiny chromed axles, no dots on inside wheel surfaces. Except for axles, Types IV and V are very difficult to distinguish.

Type I, Type III, Type II, Type IV, and Type V boxes. G. Stern photograph.

TYPE VI: Heavy light gray pressed powdered iron wheel (which can suffer chipped flanges with abuse), solid inner surface with one slight indentation, shiny chromed axles. Cars equipped with these wheels roll better because their center of gravity is lower. These wheels are the most common in current use.

TYPE VII: Black plastic wheel and axle, deep inner recess. Used exclusively for inexpensive production; will not operate track-activated accessories using insulated rails.

TYPE VIII: Same as Type III, except has shiny chromed axles. A. Passman comment.

TYPES OF BOXES USED FOR ROLLING STOCK

Sometimes, especially with early production, it is important to know which type of box Fundimensions used for its rolling stock. A case in point is the rather limited distribution in early 1971 of the 6560 Bucyrus-Erie Crane Car. The Fundimensions box itself commands a substantial premium because it is critical to identifying the car. (For the full story of this mixed-up piece, see the First Edition of this book and our update in the Crane and Searchlight listings.) Sometimes Fundimensions simply packaged postwar leftover stock into the new firm's boxes, as with many accessories. Each type of box has several variations, and of course the boxes differ according to the product. Special boxes have been made for, among other items, the Walt Disney series and the Bicentennial products. However, there are only six basic types of modern era Lionel boxes for rolling stock, as follows:

TYPE I: This box was used from the beginning until some time in early 1972. Its basic color is white; unlike its successors, it has no inner divider. It features a banner done in red and blue with the lettering, "A LIFETIME OF RAILROAD-ING", in white. Larger boxes have a paste-on label across the right edge of the box front extending down the end flap; this label both pictures and describes the product. The product description is usually in red. The smaller boxes have no such label; instead, one or both ends may be rubber-stamped with the product description. One side of the box is blue, the other red. The back of the box has an elaborate banner with a central rectangle containing "LIONEL" in modern red typeface. Recently, we have observed early Fundimensions production in plain white boxes. These are leftover boxes from postwar Hillside production in 1969.

TYPE II: The production of this box began some time in early 1972. Much plainer than its predecessor, it has an inner divider and is thus larger and more rigid. The front of the box is red with "LIONEL" in white modern typeface. The product description on the ends may be rubber-stamped on a glued label or printed in black directly on the box. These descriptions have the prefix "6" in front of the number for the first time. Part of the sides and all of the back portray line drawings of various Lionel accessories and products in black. A variation of this box, notably those labeled "Specialty Cars", has a third place for a product description on the lower right front of the box. The lower left of this particular Type II box has small white letters, "For Ages 8 To Adult". I.D. Smith comment. Some recent steam locomotives have come in large boxes with a Type II decorating scheme.

TYPE III: This box, which was first produced some time in 1975, was still in use for rolling stock in the Traditional Series as late as 1986. Its basic color is white; the front has "LIONEL O AND O27 GAUGE" in red modern typeface. The box ends follow the same pattern. The product description is either printed in black directly onto the box ends or printed onto a white label which is then glued to the box. Some of the front and all of the box sides and ends feature color photos of Lionel rolling stock, accessories, and other equipment.

TYPE IV: This box was first used in 1978 for limited production sets; it was superseded by Type V in 1983. It is the most plain of all the rolling stock boxes. Its basic color is gold; the front has a black scrollwork logo and the wording "LIONEL LIMITED EDITION SERIES" within a black oval. There are no markings on the sides or back at all. The product description is either printed in black directly on the box or printed on a gold label affixed to the box ends.

TYPE V: First produced in 1983, this box is in current use for Collector Series products. It is a recreation of the older postwar box with some modern refinements. The basic color of the box is bright orange, as was postwar Lionel's basic box. Atop the front of the box is "LIONEL ELECTRIC TRAINS" in dark blue Art Deco typeface between two blue stripes on a cream or white background. The sides and ends of the box follow the same design, and the back of the box features a recreation of the old postwar Lionel rectangular logo in blue, orange, and white. Collectors feel that this is an exceptionally handsome box, recalling as it does the glory days of the old Lionel Corporation. The product description is printed in black on a glossy orange sticker which is affixed to the box flap and matches the box color.

TYPE VI: This box was introduced during the brief Kenner-Parker management period in 1986, but its main marketing has been by Lionel, Inc. within the Traditional Series. It represents some important new marketing strategies. The front of the box is white with a large black band running across the top edge. Within the black band is the new red, blue, white, and black Lionel lettering and logo and blue lettering "Big, Rugged Trains. / A Tradition Since 1900." At the lower left of the cellophane window is a diagonal cardboard band overscored by a red stripe and underscored by a blue one with black lettering, "Made In America". Just below the window is red lettering "O And O27 Gauge Rolling Stock". The ends of the box follow the same scheme, and the product within the box is named by a white sticker with black lettering and a Uniform Pricing Code. The sides of the box show black drawings of Lionel accessories and rolling stock much like those on Type II boxes, but the rear of the box has an interesting product pitch. To the right, there is a black line drawing of a large Lionel layout, and to the left a father and son are shown playing with a set of trains (where have we seen this

before?). Within a bold black vertical band is white lettering, "LIONEL TRAINS TO GROW UP/WITH, NOT OUT OF".

A NOTE ON BOX DATES

Mr. Thomas Rollo, a Milwaukee collector who has made many significant contributions to our books of late, has deciphered the dating process used on many modern era Lionel boxes and, indeed, prewar and postwar boxes. This is important because it helps establish the date when a particular piece was issued. Sometimes variations in production occur which can be dated by the box dates. For example, it is quite possible to have two 9200 Illinois Central Boxcars in the same style of box. Suppose one of them has the "I. C." spread apart in the black logo and the other has the "I. C." close together; this is a legitimate variation. Which one was produced first? The box dates may tell you the exact manufacturing sequence!

On many Type I and some Type II Fundimensions boxes, one of the small flaps has a symbol which looks like a clock face numbered from one to twelve. Two digits are inside the circle of numbers. To date these boxes, look at the circle of numbers; one of them will usually be missing. Then read the first of the two numbers inside the clock. The inside number designates the last digit of the year and the missing number of the clock numerals indicates the month. So, if the number "4" is missing from the clock face and the numerals inside the clock are "01," the box was made in April of 1970! The inside numerals of the Type I boxes will usually be "01" or "12". On some boxes, the die apparently broke, and there is only an indeterminate squiggle inside the clock. We believe that this represents 1972 production. The early Type II boxes may show the same type of clock face, usually with "23" or just "3".

Specific examples of this clock face dating from my own collection include a 9110 B & O Hopper in a Type I box from August of 1970, a 9161 Canadian National N5C Caboose in a Type I box with a smashed die, probably made in February, July, or September of that year (three numbers are missing from the clock), and a 9214 Northern Pacific Boxcar in a Type II box dated August 1972. This last example is revealing because the 9214 car was first made the year before; thus, my particular car is a late production model.

Some of the later boxes can be dated in a similar fashion. There are some Type II and Type III boxes which just have two numbers on the flap — a single digit and a double digit. The single digit is the month and the double digit the year. Other boxes feature a variation of the clock face. There is a circle of numbers surrounding a company logo "P" with a dot in its middle. Below the clock face is the word "MENTOR" and a two-digit number corresponding to the year. Thus, I have a 9213 Minneapolis and Saint Louis Hopper Car whose box was made in January or February of 1977. This car was not produced until 1978, so it follows that you cannot always date the car by its box.

Unfortunately, not all boxes can be dated. The Type II, III, and IV boxes marked "STURGIS DIVISION" have no discernible dating method. However, even some of the latest boxes have date marks. My 7522 New Orleans Mint Car shows evidence of an entirely new dating system. On the flap of this box, there is a row of numbers from 2 to 12 to the left of a corporate symbol. Below that are the numbers "85 86 87". This box must be read differently from the clock types. The missing number of the series 1 to 12 gives the month of manufacture, while the number immediately before the listed years gives the year. Thus, the box for the 7522 was made in January 1984, some time before the car came out in June 1985, but corresponding to the date stamp on the car! (All modern era Lionel cars have a built date which shows the time of first production.) This raises an interesting question: Was the car made and then stored away for a year and a half before it was issued to dealers? That is not a likely scenario, given modern era Lionel's distaste for warehousing. More likely, it indicates that a stupendous number of boxes were printed up at one printing and not used until much later. Remember that the product inside the boxes is identified with a pressure-sensitive label, not print on the box itself, in this case. My 5724 Pennsylvania Bunk Car has an entirely different dating system. Below the word "FEDERAL" are two small numbers. One is "83", which should be the year the box was made. Just below it in microscopic print is "10", which should be the month. There is also a part number: "705713200". The presence of "5713" in that part number indicates that this box was first designed for Wood-sided Reefer 5713, a Cotton Belt reefer first made in 1983. It was also designed to accommodate successive cars in that series. Apparently, only the later Type V boxes have been dated in this fashion.

As a point of interest, it should be noted that the brown corrugated boxes used to pack many prewar and postwar Lionel accessories and locomotives can be dated just as precisely. Every one of these boxes has a circular testing seal. Beneath this seal, you may find a single digit, a double digit, or the entire year printed. (In the case of the single digit, it is not too hard to deduce the decade of manufacture!) The month dating can be done in one of two ways. There may be a row of numbers from 1 to 12 printed around the disc. Let us assume that you see the numbers 5 through 12. In that case, the box was made in the month preceding the earliest digit; 4 would correspond to April. The other method uses a series of dots or stars around the circle on either side of the date. Count them up, and you will have the month. Eight dots would mean that the month of manufacture was August. I have seen transformer boxes dated in this way as early as 1921! Thanks to this information, I also know that my 1038 Transformer was made in April 1940, my 2046 Locomotive in August of 1950, and my ZW Transformer in March of 1954.

Perhaps box dating is a relatively small matter for now. However, further research might uncover more information about the manufacturing process used by Lionel and its modern era successors, and even tell us about actual production figures. For that reason, we hope that many of you will add your own observations to this relatively new field for subsequent editions.

A NOTE ON JULIAN DATING OF LIONEL'S BOXES

Data Supplied By
Jim Tomczyk and Tom Rollo

Observers of Lionel's packing boxes may have noticed a five-digit set of numbers rubber-stamped in black on both outer cartons and individual boxes of Lionel's production beginning about late 1979. This is a box industry dating system known as the Julian Dating System, and it will enable Lionel owners

To convert the Julian number to the date of the year, use the following chart. The number represents the cumulative number of days in the year at the end of the month.

JANUARY	FEBRUARY	MARCH	APRIL
31	59	90	120
MAY	**JUNE**	**JULY**	**AUGUST**
151	181	212	243
SEPTEMBER	**OCTOBER**	**NOVEMBER**	**DECEMBER**
273	304	334	365

to date their products more accurately than they have ever been dated before. In fact, by using the Julian System, the collector can determine the exact day the item was packed into its box, let alone the month and the year!

The system works like this: The first number is always a "1"; since every five-digit number begins with it, this number is of no help. The next three digits represent the day of the year, and the last number is the last number of the particular year. As a practical example, we have data about a Jersey Central Fairbanks-Morse locomotive with the number "11346" rubber-stamped in black. This means that the locomotive was packed into its box on the 134th day of 1986, or May 14, 1986.

How do we know that all cars were not packed into the box with the same number, and that this five-digit number does not signify something else? A simple comparison shows that this cannot be true. Jim Tomczyk's 6908 Pennsylvania N5C Caboose has the number "11655" stamped onto its box flap. This means that his caboose was packed into its box on June 14, 1985. The author's 6908 bears the number 11685, which means that it was packed on June 17, 1985, three days later!

The significance of this dating system is not to be underestimated by the collector. The Julian Dating System can tell the collector about the relative scarcity of variations within the production of a particular piece. For example, the author has a 16303 Pennsylvania TOFC Flatcar with dull gold lettering on the trailers; it carries the number "10517". This translates to February 20, 1987. Later production of this flatcar has gold lettering on the trailer which is much brighter. Which version is scarcer? By finding the Julian date which is earliest and the latest Julian date, then determining the latest Julian date of the first version and the earliest Julian date of the second version, the collector can actually estimate the relative percentage of production for each version — and that will determine scarcity, all other factors being equal.

This is one case where seeing is believing. In a visit to the Lionel factory in Mount Clemens, Michigan on July 8, 1987 (for more information, see the Introduction), I observed the new Rail Blazer Sets being assembled and packaged on a production line. At the end of the line, an employee was putting the sets into their packing boxes for shipment. I also saw him rubber-stamping a number on the boxes. Managing a closer look, I saw that the number was "11897" — July 8, 1987!

The Julian Dating System may open up a new area for research by collectors. We would welcome reaction from our readers, and we will report on their conclusions in our next edition. For now, we are grateful to Mr. James Tomczyk for his fine analysis of the system and to Tom Rollo for his explanation of the system's significance to the packaging industry.

Index

"-C" indicates a color photograph.   † indicates that an item appears in the Factory Errors and Prototypes chapter.

"-C" indicates a color photograph. • † indicates that an item appears in the Factory Errors and Prototypes chapter.

"-C" indicates a color photograph.   •   † indicates that an item appears in the Factory Errors and Prototypes chapter.

"-C" indicates a color photograph.   •   † indicates that an item appears in the Factory Errors and Prototypes chapter.

"-C" indicates a color photograph. • † indicates that an item appears in the Factory Errors and Prototypes chapter.

LIONEL 1989 PRODUCTION

The following information is based on preliminary reports from Lionel. The actual production items may differ in number and in other characteristics. We appreciate very much the assistance of Michael Braga of Lionel Trains, Inc.

Please note that carry-overs from the 1988 line have not been included in this supplement.

DIESELS, ELECTRICS & MOTORIZED UNITS

8203: See 18203.

8303: See 18303.

8501: See 18501.

8806: See 18806.

8900: Four-wheel diesel switcher, tuscan body, gold-color grille, gold "8900" on cab side, part of set 11708.

9100: See 18205.

18203 C P RAIL: SD-40, illuminated, red body, black and white pac-man herald, white safety stripes on nose, white lettering, part of 11710 C P Rail Limited Freight Set.

18205 UNION PACIFIC: GE-8 40C locomotive with yellow blinking cab roof light, detailing, engineer in cab, cab interior; cab lettered "9100", yellow and gray body, red stripes, red lettering, red, white and blue herald.

18303 AMTRAK: GG-1, silver, red and blue, black lettering.

18405 SANTA FE: Operating burro crane, black, white lettering.

18406 LIONEL: Operating track maintenance car, black body, red superstructure with white lettering, white platform with red and white "DANGER" sign, man on platform.

18501 WESTERN MARYLAND: NW-2 switcher, die-cast frame, mechanical ringing bell, gray and white body, white lettering with fireball herald, "8501" on cab, part of Fallen Flags Series 4.

18805 UNION PACIFIC: RS-3, yellow body, gray roof, red striping and lettering.

18806 NEW HAVEN: RS-3, black body, orange cab roof and sides, white "8806" on cab side, red and white "NH" on side.

STEAM ENGINES

8004: See 18004.

8606: See 18606.

8607: See 18607.

8612: See 18612.

8977: See 18000.

18000 PENNSYLVANIA: B6 0-6-0 switcher with electronic bell and sound of steam, smoking stack and steam chests, black, white lettering, "8977" on cab side.

18004 READING: Pacific 4-6-2 with smoke, black, yellow lettering, cab marked "8004", twelve-wheel Sound of Steam tender.

18606 NEW YORK CENTRAL: 2-6-4 with smoke, black body, white lettering, "8606" on cab side.

18607 UNION PACIFIC: 2-6-4 with smoke, gray body, yellow stripe on locomotive, "8607" on cab side, black and yellow band with yellow lettering on tender.

18612 CHICAGO & NORTH WESTERN: 2-6-4 with smoke, black body, silver smokebox, white "8612" on cab side, red, white and black herald on tender.

AUTO CARRIERS

16208 PENNSYLVANIA: Multi-level auto rack with cars, brown body, yellow and white lettering.

BOXCARS

16614 READING: Cop and Hobo car, yellow sides, green roof and ends, green letttering.

16617 C & N W: Boxcar with ETD (end of train device), brown body, white lettering, illuminated ETD.

17200 C P RAIL: Silver body, black roof and ends, red lettering, multi-color herald, part of 11710 C P Rail Limited Freight Set.

19210 SOO LINE: White body, red door, large black and white "SOO" logo at left.

19211 VERMONT RAILWAY: Green body, white lettering, mountain logo at right.

19212 PENNSYLVANIA: Brown body, white lettering, "Don't Stand Me Still!" slogan at left, Keystone herald at right.

19213 S P & S: Brown body, white lettering, billboard-style "S. P. & S." at left, oval herald at right.

19214 WESTERN MARYLAND: Brown body, white speed style lettering, part of Fallen Flags Series 4.

19654 AMTRAK: Bunk car, orange body, black lettering.

19906 I LOVE PENNSYLVANIA: Brown body, white lettering, red heart.

CABOOSES

9706: See 19706.

16510: Bay window caboose, red, black roof, white lettering, black and white "NH".

16511: Bobber caboose, brown body, gold-color railings and underframe, gold lettering, part of set 11708.

16513 UNION PACIFIC: SP type caboose, gray, black roof, red lettering.

17605 READING: Low-cupola woodside caboose, illuminated, red body, black roof, white lettering, yellow grab rails at ends and on top of cupola.

19704: WESTERN MARYLAND: Extended-vision caboose with smoke, red body, black roof, white speed style lettering, part of Fallen Flags Series 4.

19705: C P RAIL: Extended-vision caboose with smoke, illuminated, yellow body, black roof, black and white pac- man herald, black lettering, part of 11710 C P Rail Limited Freight Set.

19706: UNION PACIFIC: Extended-vision caboose with smoke, illuminated, yellow body, red roof, red lettering, black and white safety billboard on side.

19709: PENNSYLVANIA: Work caboose, black flat car, tuscan superstructure with black roof, yellow lettering.

LIONEL 1989 PRODUCTION

FLATCARS

16308 BURLINGTON NORTHERN: Flat car with single trailer, green body, white lettering; silver trailer with green lettering.

16314 WABASH: Flat car with two trailers, blue body, white lettering; blue trailers with blue and white lettering.

16315 PENNSYLVANIA: Flat car with fences, brown body, white lettering, part of set 11708.

16317 PENNSYLVANIA: Barrel ramp car, brown body, gold lettering.

16318 LIONEL LINES: Depressed flat car with two wire reels, brown body, white lettering.

17500 C P RAIL: Flat car with log load chained to bed, black body, white lettering, part of 11710 C P Rail Limited Freight Set.

19404 WESTERN MARYLAND: Flat car with two trailers, red body, white lettering, "TRAILER TRAIN" on flat car; silver trailer vans with yellow speed style "WESTERN MARYLAND", part of Fallen Flags Series 4.

GONDOLAS

16313 PENNSYLVANIA: Gondola with cable reels, green body, white lettering, part of set 11708.

17400 C P RAIL: Gondola with coal load, red body, black and white pac-man logo, part of 11710 C P Rail Limited Freight Set.

19403 WESTERN MARYLAND: Gondola with coal load, black, white speed style lettering, part of Fallen Flags Series 4.

HOPPERS

16400 PENNSYLVANIA: Two-bay hopper, gray body, pblack lettering.

17107 SCLAIR: Covered hopper, orange body, broad white band with black stripes, black lettering, yellow box over computer identification panels.

19307 B & L E: Ore car, brown body, white lettering.

19308 GREAT NORTHERN: Ore car, brown body, white lettering.

19309 SEABOARD: Covered hopper, white body, black lettering.

19310 LANCASTER & CHESTER: Covered hopper, blue and white body, blue and white lettering.

OPERATING CARS

16612 SOO LINE: Log dump car, brown, white lettering; bin included.

16613 KATY: Coal dump car, black, white lettering; bin included.

16615 LIONEL LINES: Extension searchlight car, black, white lettering, removable searchlight.

16618 SANTA FE: Track maintenance car, red body, white lettering, gray superstructure with black lettering.

PASSENGER CARS

9100: See 19100.

9101: See 19101.

9102: See 19102.

9103: See 19103.

9104: See 19104.

9106: See 19106.

16016 NEW YORK CENTRAL: Baggage, two-tone gray, black roof, white lettering.

16017 NEW YORK CENTRAL: Combine, two-tone gray, black roof, white lettering.

16018 NEW YORK CENTRAL: Coach, two-tone gray, black roof, white lettering.

16019 NEW YORK CENTRAL: Vista-Dome, two-tone gray, black roof, white lettering.

16020 NEW YORK CENTRAL: Coach, two-tone gray, black roof, white lettering.

16021 NEW YORK CENTRAL: Observation car, two-tone gray, black roof, white lettering.

16022 PENNSYLVANIA: Baggage, brown body, black roof, yellow lettering.

16023 AMTRAK: Passenger car, 027, silver finish, red and blue stripes.

19100 AMTRAK: Baggage car, aluminum body, red, white and blue striping, black "9100".

19101 AMTRAK: Combine, aluminum body, red, white and blue striping, black "9101".

19102 AMTRAK: Passenger car, aluminum body, red, white and blue striping, black "9102".

19103 AMTRAK: Vista-Dome, aluminum body, red, white and blue striping, black "9103".

19104 AMTRAK: Dining car, aluminum body, red, white and blue striping, black "9104".

19106 AMTRAK: Observation car, aluminum body, red, white and blue striping, black "9106".

REFRIGERATOR CARS

17300 C P RAIL: Brown body, white lettering, part of 11710 C P Rail Limited Freight Set.

19511 WESTERN MARYLAND: Orange sides, red ends, brown roof, black speed style lettering, part of Fallen Flags Series 4.

19508 LEONARDO DA VINCI: Woodside reefer, yellow sides, brown roof and ends, black and white Mona Lisa at left.

19509 ALEXANDER GRAHAM BELL: Woodside reefer, gray sides, blue roof and ends, picture of inventor at left, telephone at right.

TANK CARS

16104 SANTA FE: Two-dome tank car, black body, white lettering.

19601 NORTH AMERICAN: Single-dome tank car, silver body, blue and black "NORTH AMERICAN" herald, black lettering, part of Fallen Flags Series 4.

LIONEL 1989 PRODUCTION

ACCESSORIES

12720 ROTARY BEACON: Red base and tower, black platform and searchlight.

12721 ILLUMINATED EXTENSION BRIDGE: With rock piers, brown bridge, gray piers.

12725 TRACTOR AND TRAILER: Die-cast vehicle, orange with multi-color printing.

12727 AUTOMATIC OPERATING SEMAPHORE: Brown base, black shaft, red and green lights.

12728 ILLUMINATED FREIGHT STATION: Yellow structure, brown roof, doors and windows, black platform.

12734 PASSENGER / FREIGHT STATION: Yellow and green sides.

12739 TRACTOR AND TANKER: Die-cast vehicle, blue tractor, gray tanker with white "LIONEL GAS CO.".

12741 INTERMODAL CRANE: Accessory for unloading TOFC cars, orange superstructure, black wheels, red, white and blue herald, black lettering, "MI-JACK".

12742 GOOSE NECK STREET LAMPS: Ornamental lamps, lighted.

12744 ROCK PIERS: Gray, for use with bridges.

12745 BARREL PACK: Six wooden barrels.

12748 ILLUMINATED STATION PLATFORM: Colored base and cover, multi-color signs, two lights.

12749 ROTARY RADAR ANTENNA: Brown form, gray tower, white antenna.

12750 CRANE: Yellow and black construction vehicle.

12751 SHOVEL: Yellow and black construction vehicle.

12753 ORE LOAD: To fit ore car.

12754 GRADUATED TRESTLE SET: Twenty-two sturdy piers.

12755 ELEVATED TRESTLE SET: Ten piers.

O GAUGE LIONEL CLASSICS

51000 MILWAUKEE ROAD HIAWATHA: 1988, set with 350E Locomotive, 350WX Tender, 882 Front Coach, 883 Center Coach, 884 Coach).

51001 LIONEL: "#44 Freight Special", set with 51100, 51500, 51800, 51400, 51700.

51100 LIONEL: Electric engine, orange body, silver name plates with red "LIONEL" and "44E", orginally a No. 4.

51400 LIONEL LINES: Boxcar, yellow, brown roof and door guides, three silver plates, numbered "8814".

51500 LIONEL LINES: Hopper, black, two plates, numbered "8816".

51700 LIONEL LINES: Caboose, red, white end rails, two plates, numbered "8817".

51800 LIONEL LINES: Searchlight car, black, white lettering, numbered "8820".